A Short History of New York State

THIS BOOK HAS BEEN GRANTED A
DIXON RYAN FOX MEMORIAL AWARD
by the New York State Historical Association

Portrait of James Fenimore Cooper by John Wesley Jarvis, now owned by Dr. Henry S. F. Cooper.

A SHORT HISTORY OF
NEW YORK STATE

David M. Ellis
HAMILTON COLLEGE

✣

James A. Frost
STATE UNIVERSITY OF NEW YORK
TEACHERS COLLEGE AT ONEONTA

✣

Harold C. Syrett
QUEENS COLLEGE

✣

Harry J. Carman
COLUMBIA UNIVERSITY

PUBLISHED IN CO-OPERATION WITH THE

New York State Historical Association by

CORNELL UNIVERSITY PRESS

ITHACA, NEW YORK

Dedicated to the memory of

DIXON RYAN FOX

Foreword

HERE in your hands is the story of the Empire State, or as much of it as four able scholars could fit into one volume. The very nature of their task has set limits to their accomplishment: indeed, history can never do more than show the peaks of a people's experience. Ours has been a long road, beginning with narrow Indian trails, coming at last to the Thruway and airways.

From the beginning we in New York were many peoples. After the Leni-Lenape came the Iroquois, a confederation of conquerors and conquered. On the heels of the first Dutch settlers, men sailed in from across the face of Europe; four decades after Hudson's voyage eighteen languages could be heard on the streets of New Amsterdam and more were being spoken all the time. When the English raised their flag and changed the name to New York, the flow of strangers did not stop. From Africa and France, from the little duchies along the Rhine and the cities of the Italian peninsula, from the ghettos of Portugal they came to find a corner for themselves in the New World. The English tongue borrowed from other tongues and British ways absorbed other ways.

These men and women coming on the four winds brought with them the limitless hopes and gnawing fears of all mankind. For some the hopes eroded away on stony farms or in fetid sweatshops, and the fears became realities, but for others and their children the hopes and fears gave strength to action, to protest, to law and change, and their dreams came to life in the land.

If the people were various, so too was the land to which they came: the sandy stretch of Long Island pointed a remembering finger to the sea they had traveled, and the valley of the Hudson, with its proud Highlands, its purple-cloaked Catskills, its gaunt Adirondack crests, formed the first highway. Many other rivers were here waiting: the Mohawk was found early, and later the Genesee with its great falls, and the knotted, moody Susquehanna that married us forever to Pennsylvania, the Salmon and

vii

Black, the Unadilla and Sacandaga, and, on the far border, the Niagara plummeting four inland seas into a fifth, and, finally, the river of the North Country, the St. Lawrence. Rolling hills and lush valleys cried out for a plow that they might give forth corn and apples, wheat and flax; forbidding swamps were found which even in much later times are left to the wild fowl who relish only solitude. Forests abounded—and they still do—millions of acres of evergreens and hemlocks, oaks and elms, and, most gratefully discovered, the maple, the tree that sweetened the pioneer's porridge and gave him his first crop in a resisting wilderness.

If the rivers were roadways, the lakesides were refuges and oases of serenity. The winters were tempered on their shores, and the summer breezes whistled through the young corn. There were fish there and laughter for boys swimming white and glistening in the brightness. There were lakes no bigger than a banker's parlor and lakes ninety and a hundred miles from source to outlet, lakes inland lying like the fingers of a giant's hand, and others bordering Canada and stubborn Vermont.

This is the state with a slow start; it did poorly under kings and royal governors. The bungling rulers in Whitehall and St. James made decisions for New York on foggy days, while here a rich few held the fertile earth and the powerful streams tight in their jeweled hands. Only under the surface did the yeast of freedom work silently, with now and then a bubble bursting the surface calm—Leisler's seizure of the government, Zenger's attacks in his press, the rebellion of the men of Flushing, and black slaves rising in terrible anger. As the second century moved toward its great drama, the yeast worked more actively—Sons of Liberty, Prendergast and his down-rent farmers, the tea party in Manhattan—but by and large the people were docile, touched with lethargy, their fears tugging ever at the coatsleeves of their hopes.

War came and much of it was fought over our fields and in our woods. There were defeats here—Brooklyn Heights, White Plains, the lost battle for the soul of Benedict Arnold, and the burned villages of Springfield, Unadilla, German Flats, and Cherry Valley; there were hard-won victories at Oriskany and, the most far-reaching of the war, at Saratoga.

Following the peace, a new spirit moved across the valleys. The veterans with their brides trod on the heels of speculators who dealt in thousands of acres. The sweet song of the ax and the soft tread of oxen transformed a forest into cornfields, and soon the retted flax, broken and hatcheled through the magic of strong young fingers, grew to thread, then on the loom to homespun for britches and diapers, always diapers for the big young crop that would clear more land and harvest more grain and go still farther west.

Ships by the thousand found the snug harbor at New York, and the tills were full of money from the West Indies, from Spain and London and tortured France. Roads unwound in place of trails, and talk grew of canals —Mr. Washington himself had recommended one. Men quarreled about the constitution and balanced in their hearts the dangers of a federal union against the greater dangers of loose confederation. The spirits of men stood straighter, and the Revolution, which had sometimes seemed so meaningless, became a turning point, a bold release of human spirit.

All the pent energies burst into flower. New Englanders, pouring across the disputed borders, over the Hudson, through the valleys, brought changes and in turn were changed. The freer air of New York released them too, and the towns they built were raised with a difference, subtle but unmistakable. Their daughters chose German names for their children, and their sons found good the blue-eyed Irish girls, and a new nation of born Americans went to schools for which all the people paid, and they read the books and papers cascading from the ever-growing number of hand presses. They had opinions, strongly held. In the ebb and flow of politics, of change and skulduggery and reform, they inched their way forward. More and more men went to the polls, and fifty years after Saratoga the last slave in New York was free.

The women too moved up, noisily sometimes, gently at others, standing ever closer and surer by their men. Here Iroquois women had once ruled their tribes and spoken to be listened to in council—perhaps something of this clung to our earth and infected our air. We have come to fancy this breed of women with their blunt truths and their speaking out in meeting; confident men are not abashed by confident women.

In that half century after the Revolution the Empire State came into its own, and the capstone of its progress was Clinton's Ditch, dug by hand from Waterford to Buffalo. Where crossroad villages had sprawled lazily, suddenly cities sprang up and then factories and all the good and evil of great towns. Amsterdam, Utica, Syracuse, Rochester, Buffalo— the mules plodding on the towpath brought the wide world to their gates and they flourished. People going west and wheat coming east —the bloodstream of a nation flowing ever faster. Back in the hills, too far to the south or north to benefit, other towns of promise withered on the vine as coal replaced the great mill wheels. Then the railroads once more altered the pattern and still another growth set in, with wide-funneled puffers speeding up life, changing the pace, adding new towns, new ways, newcomers. More tongues to be filtered into English, more ways to mold with ours, more young muscles to be party to the building and the growth.

Yesterday, like today, was not all bathed in sunlight. There are shameful passages and dark stains on the wide pages, the cheap crooks, the character assassins, pullers of strings, the calloused in high places and low. But we have been lucky in the long run of years, for we have raised up in every generation leaders who shone through the worst murkiness of their day, the Clintons, the Livingstons, Jedediah Peck, Grover Cleveland, William Seward, the Roosevelts, and Al Smith with his rough speech and his greathearted vision. And there are others, to the end of a long folio, men and women who could not be bought, or tamed, or forced back into their places. Blessed be their names, including all those long forgotten or never known beyond the village caucus.

The latter portions of this book come down to our day, and once again we sense how difficult it is to see ourselves in any true perspective, indeed to see the last half century, when life has so altered and so accelerated with each year. It is when we read of our own stage that we become aware of how little any history book can tell, how many chapters shyly slip away from capture and will not be secured.

History forgets much that happens to men, but the scholars who wrote this book have recorded as much as could be told in this space, selecting, paring, trimming, but giving finally a comprehensive picture of the Empire State and the Empire people. Nearly a quarter of a century has passed since Alexander Flick's ten-volume history appeared, and historians have learned much and reassessed more since that day. That set, like this volume, was sponsored by the New York State Historical Association, and we are proud to place this new telling of the story of our people in your hands.

In a book which has more authors than one the reader has a right to know how the work was distributed. Book I was written by Professor Ellis and Dean Frost, Professor Ellis being responsible for Chapters 1–8, 13–17, and 20–26. Dean Frost was responsible for Chapters 9–12 and Chapters 18 and 19. In Book II Professor Syrett wrote Chapters 27–33 and Chapter 41, while Dean Carman wrote Chapters 34–39. Dean Carman and Professor Syrett wrote Chapter 40 together, and Dean Carman and Robert Martin Adams collaborated on Chapter 42. Mr. Frank Devecis drew most of the maps and charts.

This is also an appropriate place to point out that during the decade while this book has been in the making Miss Mary E. Cunningham, Associate Director of the New York State Historical Association, has acted as editorial adviser, guide, consultant, and friend to the authors. I think that they will all agree with me that without her devoted and tireless service the volume could not have come to fruition.

Louis C. Jones, Director
New York State Historical Association

Cooperstown, New York
March 31, 1957

Contents

BOOK II.   1865-1956

Maps, Charts, and Tables

Tables

BOOK I

1609-1865

✤

Introduction

THE history of New York is the story of millions of people from all parts of the world who have tried to live together with good will. In fact, one may justly claim that New York and Pennsylvania anticipated other parts of the nation in developing those traits loosely labeled the "American way of life": a heterogeneous population; a diversified economy marked by a strong business spirit; a high degree of urbanism; the creation of a pluralistic culture tolerating significant differences in social institutions, national backgrounds, and economic status; and a dynamic society cherishing traditional values but responsive to popular will.

Colonial New York was slow in developing. At the outbreak of the Revolutionary War in 1775 it was in many ways the most backward of all the thirteen colonies, for only a fringe of land along the Hudson River and the coast of Long Island was settled. Two factors were largely responsible for this tardy development: the French and Indian attacks on the frontier settlements and the land system, which was encumbered by speculation, monopoly, and the tenancy system of landholding. New Yorkers made some progress toward offsetting these handicaps by the beginning of the Revolution. Members of the New York Assembly, after decades of skirmishing with the British authorities in London and the royal governors, had secured effective control over finance and administration and responsible parliamentary government.

The new culture growing up in New York was a curious mixture of various European traditions modified by the harsh features of the American environment. Immigrants from England, France, the German Palatinate, Ireland, and Africa soon outnumbered the original Dutch stock and created a variegated cultural and religious pattern.

No state suffered more severely or benefited more handsomely from the Revolutionary War than New York. The exodus of from thirty to forty thousand Loyalists, roughly more than one-tenth of the pre-Revolutionary population, transformed the social structure, disorganized the economy,

3

and embittered political life. Fully one-fourth of the dwellings on Manhattan Island went up in flames in the great fires of 1776 and 1778, and over half of the population, including a high percentage of the professional and business leaders, had left the metropolis. Upstate, conditions were hardly better. In 1784, when George Washington journeyed to Fort Ticonderoga and Fort Stanwix, he saw many farms and villages in blackened ruins. But his sharp eyes also saw the commercial possibilities as well as the strategic importance of the magnificent network of inland waterways. His descriptive phrase "seat of Empire" may have inspired the unknown enthusiast who happily called New York "the Empire State."

Map 1. Rivers, mountains, and lakes of New York State. (By Harold K. Faye from *Exploring New York* by Wainger, Furman, and Oagley, © 1956 by Harcourt, Brace and Company, Inc.)

His optimism was fully warranted, for by 1825 New York had earned first place in population, commerce, transportation, and agriculture. The Continental armies had destroyed the power of the Iroquois, and the peace treaty of 1783 gave upstate farmers a feeling of peace and security. Fertile land by the millions of acres and at reasonable prices awaited settlement. Most important of all, Yankees by the tens of thousands were ready to stream across the border and make their fortunes behind the plow, the work bench, and the store counter. Paralleling the growth in population and wealth were the strides made toward political democracy, culminating in the Constitution of 1822, which established manhood suffrage for white males. In this period, the state government under the dynamic leadership of De Witt Clinton constructed the Erie Canal, the most successful venture by any state during the early part of the nineteenth century.

The era between 1825 and 1865 was the heyday of the merchants, who developed new trade, amassed great fortunes, and helped promote pioneer industrialization. Perhaps the most startling development was the achievement of the Manhattan merchants in capturing control of well over half of the nation's imports and over one-third of its exports. To express it another way, the businessmen of New York City acted as middlemen for the wheat and cotton growers of the United States and for the textile and steel manufacturers of Great Britain.

The introduction of power turbines, the construction of railroads (especially those to the coal fields of Pennsylvania), and the immigration of skilled workers were some of the factors spurring industrial and factory growth. New York benefited immensely from the construction of canals and railroads, which not only encouraged foreign and domestic trade but also stimulated manufacturing and commercial agriculture. Dairy farming developed into a major industry and set the pace in the production of milk, cheese, and butter.

Urban development paralleled the expansion of the transportation system and the rise of industry. By 1865 over a third of the citizens of New York lived in cities of ten thousand or more. Immigration became a torrent in the 1840's, bearing on its crest hundreds of thousands of Irish, Germans, and English, who formed almost one-half of the population of Buffalo, Rochester, and New York City in 1860. The cosmopolitan population accentuated the religious and cultural diversity so noticeable in colonial New York. Roman Catholicism rose to first place among the various Christian branches, a development which alarmed many New Yorkers. Evangelical Protestantism also made impressive gains, and the seeds of excitement stemming from the Finney revivals of 1825 sometimes flowered into exotic cults. Far more important as an offshoot of the religious ardor of the period were the humanitarian movements for temperance, abolition of slavery, and the extension of women's rights. Equally important was the progress made toward giving each child free schooling on the elementary level.

New Yorkers led the nation in journalism, music, drama, and the creative arts. Even in belles lettres they were keen rivals of the giants of Boston-Cambridge. But the cultural arbiters of New York continued, though less slavishly, to look to England and the continent for literary models and intellectual fashions.

The diversity in economic interests and population elements expressed itself in politics. Factionalism riddled the major parties and led to the creation of new ones. Such issues as state aid for internal improvements, the granting of bank charters, and the extension of slavery split both the Democratic and Whig parties. Some New Yorkers held political beliefs so intensely that they created several new parties, such as the Anti-Mason, Know-Nothing, Working Men's, Free Soil, Antirent, and Republican. Politics attracted an unusually large group of able leaders. Certainly the Whig party in no other state could match the triumvirate of Thurlow Weed, Horace Greeley, and William Seward, who later joined the Republican camp. The list of Democratic statesmen was equally distinguished: Silas Wright, Martin Van Buren, Horatio Seymour, and William Marcy.

The Civil War left many scars on the political, economic, and social life of New York. The Empire State provided the greatest number of soldiers and the largest amount of supplies and money. New chapters were written in the annals of valor and sacrifice.

New York set the pace for the nation in practically all phases of the economy, in cultural activities, and in urban living. Like most pioneers, the citizens of New York experienced the heartaches and disappointments of pathfinders, but they also reaped the rich harvest of those who plant in virgin soil.

PART ONE

Colonial New York

✤✤✤✤✤✤✤✤✤✤✤✤

amt

Algonkians and Iroquois

Were they savages who had fixed habitations; who cultivated rich fields; who built castles, (for so they called their not incommodious wooden houses, surrounded with palisadoes;) who planted maize and beans, and showed considerable ingenuity in constructing and adorning their canoes, arms, and clothing?—Mrs. ANNE GRANT, c. 1770

LESS than two centuries ago "the fire that never dies" burned brightly near Syracuse. This fire was the symbol of unity for the Iroquois confederation, which held the balance of power between Britain and France for over a century. Certainly no other group of New Yorkers has swung so much weight, man for man, as the two-thousand-odd warriors of the League of the Five Nations. Tribes living as far south as the Carolinas, as far west as the Illinois region and the Lake Superior country, and as far north as the mouth of the St. Lawrence taught their children to dread the tomahawks of the Senecas, Cayugas, Onondagas, Oneidas, and the Mohawks of central and western New York. Dutch, French, and British emissaries, respectful of Iroquois power and anxious to curry favor at the great Council of the Five Nations, learned well every turn in the Ambassador's Road, the name given to the trail extending from the lower Mohawk River to the Genesee country.

Men have lived in New York for well over five thousand years. Legends, confirmed and supplemented by excavations, tell of waves of migrating people pushing their way across mountains, plains, and forests in a southeasterly direction from the Bering Sea over which their ancestors had made their way between ten to twenty thousand years ago. The first bands to settle in New York usually selected sites along the banks of rivers. All around them was the dense forest which shaped their customs and way of life.

The first major group of Indians to occupy the North Atlantic region spoke the Algonkian language. The last wave of Algonkians flowed into

9

New York shortly before the year 1000, and these Indians dominated the New York region for over three hundred years, despite the presence of some mound builders in the southwestern corner of the state. A branch of the Algonkians, known sometimes as Leni-Lenape or later as the Delawares, had their main center in eastern Pennsylvania, but related tribes occupied Long Island and the Hudson Valley. The strongest of these tribes in New York was that of the Mohicans, celebrated in James Fenimore Cooper's novel, *The Last of the Mohicans.* Another Algonkian tribe was the Wappinger, which lived on both sides of Long Island Sound.

The Iroquois, composed of several tribes, invaded upstate New York

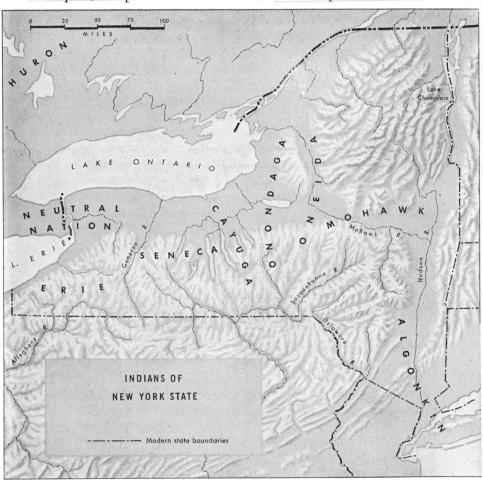

Map 2. Indians of New York State. (By Harold K. Faye from *Exploring New York* by Wainger, Furman, and Oagley, © 1956 by Harcourt, Brace and Company, Inc.)

about the year 1300. Apparently famines, wars, and internal strife forced some of the Indians living in the mid-Mississippi Valley to seek new hunting grounds. Small bands paddled up the Ohio and Allegheny Rivers and settled in western New York. This group became known as the Senecas, and it shared the land between the Genesee River and Skaneateles Lake with its easterly offshoot, the Cayugas. Other bands following the watercourses south of Lake Erie became known as the Eries and the Susquehannocks, or Andastes. The Eries occupied the southwestern corner of New York, but the Susquehannocks moved into the Susquehanna Valley in the area south from the Chemung Branch to Chesapeake Bay.

Other Iroquoian bands swarmed into the region north of Lake Erie. The Hurons, the most numerous subgroup, established two score villages in the Georgian Bay–Lake Simcoe district of Ontario. A fighting vanguard driving onward toward the mouth of the St. Lawrence met increasing resistance from the Algonkian inhabitants. Some of the Iroquois retreated to the Watertown region and still further south as Algonkian attacks increased in intensity. One group of the Iroquois emerged as the Onondagas and occupied hilltop sites west of Cazenovia Lake. In the late sixteenth century another band fled southward to the Mohawk Valley, named for them. The Oneidas, a branch of the Mohawks, set up their villages between the parent stem and the Onondaga tribe. Finally the resident Algonkians were killed, expelled, or absorbed by the new tribes.

The basic social unit was matriarchal. The large family, made up of children, parents, grandparents, cousins, uncles, and aunts, paid deference to the oldest woman in the family, who settled most disputes and exerted most authority. An Indian child took the name of his mother, a practical procedure in a society where the chase and the warpath often brought death to the males. Childbearing women of the privileged families nominated the civil sachems, and they also had a voice in deciding matters of supreme importance to the tribe. All real property, both land and huts, belonged to the women. Compensation for a woman's life required twice the amount of wampum as that for a male's, convincing evidence of the high regard with which females were held.

Tribal organization was complex and varied. Each tribe was made up of several families or of several distinct groups of families known as clans. For example, the Mohawks were divided into three clans— the Turtle, Bear, and Wolf. The Turtle was the most eminent clan, since it claimed descent from the first woman on earth. Custom ruled that young people had to marry outside the clan. This meant in effect that the village of a clan included males from other clans. A common language and tradition cemented the feeling of kinship within the tribe.

Each clan and village had a governing council. The tribal council of civilian leaders was formed of representatives from the clan councils, who were nominated by the matrons of privileged clans, probably those of the original stock. After the council of women had made their selections, the council of men generally approved their choice. The warriors, however, picked the chiefs who led them into battle. The chiefs kept their positions only as long as they retained the favor of the people.

The Iroquois tribes of central and western New York were unusual in that they formed a confederation noted for its strength. According to legend, Hiawatha, a member of the Onondaga tribe, was converted by the saintly Deganawidah, a Huron, who brought a message of peace and power from the Great Spirit. Hiawatha, giving up his cannibalistic practices, agreed to spread the message among the Iroquois, who were wearied by dissension and warfare. After winning the assent of the Oneidas, Cayugas, Senecas, and Mohawks, Hiawatha "combed the snakes out of the hair" of Atotarho, the tyrannical chief of the Onondagas, and succeeded in establishing the League of the Five Nations. This organization, founded about 1570, preserved a delicate balance between central authority and tribal autonomy. Each tribe ran its internal affairs and could make war only against nonmembers of the league. The main restriction was that no tribe in the confederation might make an offensive or defensive alliance against a brother nation. A joint council of fifty sachems met each year to discuss matters of common concern. The Mohawks and Oneidas had nine representatives each; the Onondagas, fourteen; the Cayugas, ten; and the Senecas, eight. Each tribe, however, voted as a unit and had its own special obligations and privileges within the confederacy. The Onondagas, for example, kept the central council fires, while the Senecas nominated the two war chiefs of the league.

Any tribe or individual had the right to join the confederation or, to use the Indian phrase, come under the Tree of the Great Peace planted in the heart of the Onondaga territory. In 1715 the Tuscaroras, fleeing from the Carolinas, were admitted to limited privileges, and the confederation became known as the Six Nations.

The confederation did not enjoy great success during its first century of existence. Professor George Hunt noted:

The supposed unity of the League . . . may be dismissed, for such unity never existed. In no war down to 1684 were all the tribes engaged, and intra-League war threatened again and again, actually coming to pass several times between the Mohawks and the upper Iroquois. Each tribe made war solely in its own interest, and the conspicuous feature of their League is its lack, not its possession, of political unity.

Such a conclusion, however, discounts the intangible feeling of common purpose which united the Iroquois in the hope of universal peace. Admittedly the Five Nations often broke their pledge of peace within the league, but Hiawatha's concept of an ideal society in which all nations would eventually sit down under the Tree of Peace was a deeply cherished belief. The constitution of the Five Nations reads:

When the proposition to establish the Great Peace is made to a foreign nation, it shall be done in mutual council. The nation is to be persuaded by reason and urged to come into the Great Peace. If the Five Nations fail . . . after a third council . . . then shall the Five Nations seek to establish the Great Peace by a conquest of the rebellious nation.

Most neighboring tribes, including many of Iroquoian stock such as the Hurons, Eries, and Susquehannocks, saw no advantage in joining the confederation and in fact regarded it with distrust. Ironically enough, the league of the Great Peace thereby became a cause of war.

The Indians of New York cultivated the arts of peace as well as war. They spent much of their time making earthen pottery, carving and chipping implements from stone and bone, weaving baskets and nets, tanning and curing skins, quarrying flint, and manufacturing bows and arrows. Since they moved their villages almost every decade, they became skilled in the construction of huts, lodges, and stockades.

The forest greatly influenced the life and customs of the Indians. Their clothing, food habits, methods of warfare, concepts of property, government, and even their religion reflected the forest setting. Village life in the forest was safer and more pleasant than the life of the isolated family. The men of the village could band together to protect their families from enemies and from hunger. The villages numbered from ten to fifty families, or from fifty to 250 people. Each contained a long house in the center where councils and ceremonies were held, and around the long house was a rough circle of huts, usually one for each family. An Indian family cooked food and heated its hut with a small fire. They usually slept on hemlock boughs or skins on the dirt floors, although sometimes they had bunks made from bark. A palisade made of pointed logs enclosed the Iroquoian village; outside this barrier lay the cornfields which merged into the encircling forest.

The Indian men engaged in the more dangerous tasks of hunting and fighting, while the women cultivated their primitive crops and prepared food. After a new village had been founded, game gradually became more scarce, and as a result the men had to set out on long trips to secure meat. They hunted in groups because they needed protection against human and animal enemies and because several men were needed to carry the kill back to the village.

After the braves had made a clearing in the forest by girdling the trees, the "matriarchs" of each family were allotted plots of ground. The women worked in groups, planting, weeding, or harvesting each plot in its turn. In the spring they planted a few kernels of corn in tiny mounds, using pointed sticks to break the soil. Later in the season they planted pumpkins, squash, and beans among the sprouting corn. The Iroquois of New York, in common with most North American aborigines, grew tobacco, which was smoked in the pipe of peace at the council fires. To supplement these cultivated crops, they gathered berries, grapes, nuts, wild fruit, and even the bark of the sassafras root. The Indians near the seacoast added oysters and clams to their diet. The Green Corn Festival and other feasts noted by the Jesuits and explorers indicate that gluttony weighed lightly on the Indian conscience. Perhaps it foreshadowed the marked appetite for rum and whisky which rivaled disease and bullets as the destroyer of Indian civilization.

Although each village tried to be self-sufficient, the tribes welcomed traders offering flints, dried fish, birch canoes, tobacco, furs, and skins. The Indians carried on considerable trade with each other along well-established routes long before the white trader arrived. The trails usually followed ridges above the valleys. Modern engineers have often laid out highways along the same routes because the Indians were skilled in selecting the best and shortest paths. In general, the east-west paths were called paths of peace, whereas the north-south trails, which brought rival tribes into contact, became known as warpaths.

The religious beliefs of the Iroquois and the Algonkians were a curious mixture of pantheism, folklore, and witchcraft. As with most forest dwellers, their religion was largely a worship of nature. Birth, death, the blossoming of plant life, thunder, lightning—all inspired feelings of wonder, fear, and awe. To explain these mysteries, the Indians developed a hierarchy of unseen spirits, headed by the Great Spirit. These spirits filled all the creatures of this world, who were thus bound together in brotherhood by a common creator. Good spirits, especially the Great Spirit, caused the corn to grow bountifully and the enemy warriors to lose heart. When the Great Spirit was displeased, the cutworm ruined the corn and the plague descended upon the village. Two of their most important beliefs were that the virtuous would win favor in the eyes of the gods and that the soul would live on after death. The Indians tried diligently to keep the favor of the Great Spirit and held seasonal festivals of thanksgiving. The more important were the Maple Festival in the spring, the Strawberry Festival in the summer, and the Green Corn Festival in the autumn. Around the campfires they handed down their religious beliefs by song, legend, and ritual.

Education was informal and almost exclusively utilitarian. The older men taught the boys manual skills and hunting. The girls learned house-hold duties from the matrons. Oratory was highly prized as an art because it was useful not only in negotiating treaties but also in perpetuating traditions and religious myths.

The advance of European civilization created a social revolution among the American Indians, and its effect was greater than the oft-noted in-fluence of the forest and Indian upon the white man. Among the skills and practices brought by the whites were the ability to read and write, the organization of business, the use of the wheel (unknown to the Indian) and more complex machinery, and the development of urban living patterns. Inevitably Indian civilization and power broke down under the superior techniques and greater numbers of the white men. What is more remarkable was the ingenuity of such tribes as the Iroquois in adopting the techniques of their foes and in maintaining their dominant position in upstate New York for well over a century after the voyage of Hudson. In fact, the Iroquois reached the summit of their power after the Dutch, French, and British came to New York in the seventeenth century.

The demand by French, Dutch and British traders for beaver skins intensified the struggle for power among the Indians. The tribes of the Five Nations at first hunted the beaver within their own territory and exchanged pelts for goods with the Dutch at Fort Orange (Albany), established in 1624. These hunting grounds gave out by 1640, and the tribes were forced to look westward for supplies. But the more numerous Hurons north of Lake Erie not only controlled the finest beaver country but also had established contacts with the Indians farther west in Illinois and Wisconsin. In addition, the Hurons commanded the western approaches to the seacoast via either the Ottawa–St. Lawrence or the Mohawk-Hudson gateways. Behind them stood the power of French arms.

To maintain their new standard of living, including firearms and whisky, the Iroquois tried to persuade the French and the Hurons to divert some of the fur trade to the Mohawk Valley. Meeting no success, they raided the brigades carrying furs down the Ottawa and St. Lawrence Rivers to Montreal. In 1645 the French agreed to several concessions in order to buy off the Iroquois bands, but the next year the Five Nations were dismayed to see the great trading fleet float past their territory and go directly to Montreal. This violation of the agree-ment opened up a period of warfare and conquest between the Iroquois and the French that continued for over forty years.

The Mohawks and the Senecas decided in the 1640's to supplant the Hurons as middlemen in the fur trade with the western Indians. In the spring of 1649 a thousand braves struck the villages of Huronia. Fleeing in panic, thousands of Hurons took refuge on a small island and starved to death during the following winter. Having annihilated the Hurons, the Senecas and the Mohawks fell upon the Neutrals, a small tribe living west of Niagara Falls and potentially a rival in the fur trade. In 1654, after this victory, the Iroquois sent eighteen hundred warriors to storm the palisades of the Eries, who had incurred their anger by sheltering some Huron fugitives. During all these conquests the Iroquois took hundreds of captives, whom they treated with considerable kindness. In fact, a key factor in their success was the adoption of large numbers of prisoners who filled their ranks thinned by disease and warfare. Despite these impressive victories, the Mohawks and Senecas did not win complete control of the fur trade. In the north the Ottawas continued to collect furs from the western Indians and to run canoes to Montreal. Iroquoian bands in retaliation cut the Ottawa route and even besieged Montreal.

Meanwhile, fresh troubles beset the Five Nations. A plague swept through their villages in 1662, bringing death to hundreds. Scarcely had they recovered from this calamity when a French expedition destroyed the largest Mohawk village. In western New York the Senecas had to fight a rearguard action against the Susquehannocks, who were emulating the Iroquois by seeking to divert the western furs, in their case to Philadelphia. The Senecas also had to weigh the maneuvers of the French, who sought to establish a post on the Niagara River. In 1687 the Senecas suffered a severe defeat when a French expedition attacked their villages. In the meantime the unity of the confederacy was being undermined by French missionaries, who made many converts among the Onondagas and Oneidas. To counter these moves, Governor Thomas Dongan of New York offered protection to the Iroquois and sent English traders into the Michigan and Wisconsin region.

As the Anglo-French rivalry for control of the interior of North America grew more intense and broke out into open warfare after 1689, the Iroquois swung toward a policy of neutrality. Chapter V, on imperial relations, will explore some of these maneuvers during the eighteenth century. With the skill and finesse of Old World diplomats, the chiefs threw their weight to the side granting them the most concessions.

Although after the Revolution the influence of the Indian became less evident, the early settlers learned a great deal from the Indians: how to clear the forests, how to hunt and trap game, and how to live in the wilderness. Farmers were quick to realize the value of corn, which has probably been the most valuable crop of New York farms since 1650. Traders and hunters in the colonial period, as well as turnpike, canal, and railroad builders in the nineteenth century, discovered that Indian paths were usually the shortest and best routes. New York colonists were stimulated to take the first steps toward co-operation with other colonies, as in the Albany Congress of 1754, largely because of the dangerous attitude of the Iroquois.

Perhaps the citizens of the new republican states learned something of the value of a confederation of equal states from the Iroquoian example. The governments established by both the Articles of Confederation and the Constitution exhibit certain similarities to the League of the Five Nations. New Yorkers of the twentieth century remember their Indian heritage largely because of some five hundred place names of Indian origin between Montauk Point and Chautauqua Lake, including the names of twenty counties and twelve of the state's sixty-odd cities.

The Dutch in New York, 1609-1664

We derive our authority from God and the West India Company, not from the pleasure of a few ignorant subjects.
—PETER STUYVESANT, *1653*

NEW YORKERS, especially those living in the Hudson Valley, remember with affection their Dutch predecessors, although only a small percentage can claim Dutch blood. The story of Peter Minuit's purchase of Manhattan from Chief Manhasset with goods valued at twenty-four dollars and the legend of Peter Stuyvesant's storming about on his wooden leg have become part of a common tradition cherished even beyond the borders of New York. No doubt the warm-blooded nature and zest for living exhibited by the Dutch settlers inspires in us a warmer affection than does the dour rectitude of the Puritans of Massachusetts. The Calvinists of New Netherland were inclined—more so than those of New England —to regard the pleasures of this world as more substantial than the uncertain delights of the next. At Christmas they made merry with Santa Claus and chimney stockings a century before their fellow Calvinists to the east were ready to worship joyfully at the manger of the Christ child. They treated religious nonconformists with toleration long before the Puritans ceased their efforts to expel "heretics."

In 1664 Governor Peter Stuyvesant surrendered to the British about eight thousand subjects in the tiny settlements fringing New York Bay and dotting the banks of the Hudson River. After forty years of sporadic effort the Dutch West India Company had succeeded in planting there only a handful of traders and farmers, who were barely able to resist the raids of the Indians and the encroachments of Connecticut men.

The failure of the Dutch to supply many colonists was probably the most important reason for New Netherland's slow development. Why should men and women leave Holland with its stable republican govern-

18

ment, its religious toleration, its thriving economy, for a life of danger in the rude settlements along the Hudson? As historian Dixon Ryan Fox puts it: "The failure of New Netherland is a testimony to the successful organization of life in old Netherlands."

The long Dutch revolt against Spanish religious persecution and political domination in the Netherlands ended when the Calvinist United Provinces achieved virtual independence in the truce of 1609. During the struggle Dutch captains had raided Spanish treasure ships carrying the gold, silver, and spices of Mexico, Peru, and the Philippines to Seville. The Dutch chartered companies to send ships around the Cape of Good Hope and established footholds in Ceylon, Java, the Moluccas, and other islands despite Spanish and Portuguese opposition. The directors of the Dutch East India Company sought a shorter route to India and in 1609 directed the English mariner, Henry Hudson, to search for a northeast passage. It was on this voyage that Hudson guided the high-pooped *Half Moon* upstream to a point near Albany. Other ships followed during the next decade, but their captains made no permanent settlement. The Indians along the Hudson had only furs to offer, and the enterprising merchants anticipated greater profits in the trade of the West Indies and South America. In 1621 they organized the Dutch West India Company and received a monopoly of trade for twenty-four years along the shores of the Americas and in the Atlantic south of the Tropic of Cancer. The company founded New Netherland and made the first permanent settlement, at Fort Orange, in 1624. Although the company ruled the colony for forty years, its directors always regarded New Netherland as an incidental outpost among their far-flung activities. They spent most of their resources and manpower trying to capture Brazil from the Portuguese and in establishing colonies in Guiana and in the West Indies.

New Netherland—in fact New York throughout the colonial period— was largely a salt-water civilization, with its two most important settlements, Fort Orange and New Amsterdam, lying about 150 miles apart on the banks of the ocean-flooded Hudson, or North, River. The maritime origins and character of the colony had a great influence in molding the economy, determining the type of settler, and deciding upon the functions of government.

The skins of the beaver played a large role in the growth of New Netherland. A report to the States-General of Holland in 1638 stated, "Nothing comes from New Netherland but beaver skins, mincks, and other furs," showing that the Dutch had little other interest in the colony, and the Dutch West India Company always regarded the fur trade as its primary concern and took steps to ensure a steady supply of pelts. The company had not only to compete with the English traders in the

Connecticut Valley and the Swedes in the Delaware but also to guard against unlicensed Dutch traders who bought furs illicitly and smuggled them out of the province without paying the proper duty to the company.

The Dutch were usually on excellent terms with the Iroquois, although they had many quarrels with the Algonkian tribes in the Hudson Valley. At first the company refused to permit the sale of guns to the Indians, but they relaxed this prohibition during the 1650's because the Indians were able to secure guns and powder from the French, the Swedes, and even from unlicensed Dutch traders. Furthermore, the Dutch recognized that the Iroquois needed arms in order to defeat the Hurons and that if the Iroquois could not secure control of the furs of the Great Lakes region, the Dutch merchants would lose their business at Fort Orange.

New Amsterdam, at the lower tip of Manhattan Island, became the heart of New Netherland. In 1625 the company erected a fort and within its walls built the governor's house, a double-gabled church with a squat tower, a prison, barracks, gallows, and the office of the company. Outside, the company engineer laid out "bouweries," or farms, along the water front. The town had only one thousand people in 1650, but its population more than doubled during the following decade. When the English captured the city in 1664, they found several hundred houses south of present-day Wall Street, where Stuyvesant had erected a palisade in 1653 to ward off attacks by Indians and English. There were several other small settlements on Manhattan Island and around the bay. Brooklyn, for example, was a tiny village dating from 1646.

New Amsterdam soon outgrew its status as a fur post. By the end of the Dutch period the settlement with its water front, curving streets, and gabled skyline had become a miniature Amsterdam. The important merchants formed a burgher aristocracy similar to that which dominated the cities of Holland. They asserted political leadership by sending strong protests to the Dutch West India Company and to the Estates-General of Holland when the governor ignored their wishes. They imported artisans to construct large brick houses with roofs of red and black pantiles and with the quaint stepped or straight-line gable ends. Spacious fruit orchards and tulip gardens lay behind the houses of the wealthier merchants.

More numerous than these merchants were the middle class: tavern-keepers, who seldom lacked customers; petty traders, who evaded the regulations against buying furs from the Indians and exporting them untaxed; doctors, who were kept busy patching up the victims of tavern brawls and Indian raids; surveyors, who catered to the land hunger among merchants and officials; accountants, who tallied the beaver pelts and inventoried the warehouses; shopkeepers, who haggled with customers in open stalls. Artisans of every description drifted to Manhattan

Island—smiths, carpenters, sailmakers, cabinet makers, shoemakers. Below these groups in income and status were common laborers and those (Negro and white) who attended to the personal wants of their masters.

New Netherland from the outset had a heterogeneous population. Curiously enough, the first shipload of settlers sent out by the Dutch West India Company was composed chiefly of French-speaking Protestants. In 1664 the Dutch formed about two-thirds of the population. The British, the second largest group, were active as traders and even officials under the Dutch governors. Hundreds of Connecticut citizens had crossed the Long Island Sound since 1640 and settled on Long Island. Germans, French, Finns, and Jews were also present in small numbers. A few hundred Swedes lived along the Delaware River, a region claimed and taken over by New Netherland. The Dutch also brought in slaves from Angola and Brazil who formed the nucleus for the largest Negro population in 1750 north of the future Mason and Dixon line. Governor William Kieft told Father Jogues in 1644 that eighteen languages were spoken at or near Fort Amsterdam. The worthy Jesuit observed that Manhattan had already acquired the "arrogance of Babel," a judgment in which the Puritans of New Haven joined.

Farming developed slowly despite the urging of some company directors, who sent out cattle, horses, and seeds. Profits in the fur trade lured many farmers from their acres, and Indian wars frightened settlers from going far from the forts. Heavy import and export taxes stifled agricultural development until their relaxation in the early 1650's stimulated production.

The Charter of Freedoms and Exemptions, adopted in 1629 by the Dutch West India Company and the Estates-General, included several significant clauses in regard to land policy. It authorized private persons with the permission of the governor and his Council to "choose and take possession of as much land as they can properly cultivate and hold the same in full ownership." Another act in 1640 held out hope that local self-government would be granted to groups of free persons. Throughout the Dutch period the majority of farmers were independent proprietors owning their own property.

Far less important although much better known was the provision for the grant of patroonships. Kiliaen Van Rensselaer, a diamond merchant of Amsterdam, led a faction in the company which advocated vigorous colonization. At his urging the directors authorized members of the company to acquire large estates provided they colonized their land with fifty settlers within four years. A patroon might claim land for twenty-four miles along one bank of the Hudson or the seacoast or for twelve miles along each bank of the river. Of the five patroonships created, only Rensselaerswyck was a success and lasted for any length of time. Lack of co-operation by the company, scarcity of skilled managers and able tenants, Indian raids, and distance from Holland, were the most important reasons for the failure of the patroon system.

Rensselaerswyck succeeded partly because of its fine location near Fort Orange and partly because of the able direction of Van Rensselaer. Settlers on the patroonship could sell produce to the traders and rely upon the fort for protection. Van Rensselaer gave his colony careful supervision and invested large sums in it. He shipped out cattle, horses, tools, brewing vats, millstones, and brick. He sent out indentured servants to construct barns, houses, sawmills, and gristmills, and he offered liberal terms to settlers. Van Rensselaer began the practice of leasing and not selling farms. The establishment of the vexing tenancy system and the growth of a landed aristocracy will receive detailed treatment in the chapters on land policy during colonial and post-Revolutionary days.

The Dutch West India Company was governed by a board of directors called the College of Nineteen. The eight members from Amsterdam on their board had charge of New Netherland and appointed as their chief officer a governor, called the "director-general," to serve in New Netherland. To assist him they created a Council of four men empowered to give advice, vote on local regulations, and serve as a court in both civil and criminal cases. The company also appointed lesser officials, such as the schout-fiscal who acted as sheriff and prosecuting officer, the secretary who carried on administrative work, the clergymen, and the schoolteachers. The directors of the company were seldom concerned with long-range policies of government in New Netherland, since they were primarily interested in framing regulations to bring in the greatest amount of profit. They did reserve the power to approve all laws for the colony, which were subject always to the higher authority of Holland. At first, the new laws simply followed the regulations in regard to shipping and the rights and duties of seamen on shipboard. In fact, the government of New Netherland seemed an extension of quarter-deck rule with ship captains in port often serving as members of the Council.

The governors had a formidable task—to make money for the company and to fight off foreign enemies and domestic troublemakers. Indian attacks, border aggression from Connecticut, and the presence of the Swedes within the region claimed by New Netherland gave much trouble. In addition, the governor had to administer the elaborate trading regulations of the company and to review every administrative decision. Although he possessed broad powers, the governor could not ignore local opinion. The dominies (pastors of the Dutch Reformed church), the merchants, the agents of the patroon at Rensselaerswyck, and especially the republican-minded Yankee immigrants, undermined his authority whenever they found their interests jeopardized. The directors in

Holland sometimes overrode the decisions of their governors after weighing the protests of colonists. The position of governor called for a man of great ability, tact, and force of character, but the company appointed a succession of governors distinguished for their incompetence and perversity.

Peter Minuit took charge of New Netherland in 1626 and held office for six years. The purchase of Manhattan Island and the strengthening of New Amsterdam were his most important achievements. Minuit was a shrewd and determined leader, but his coarse behavior affronted at least one clergyman. The directors recalled Minuit in 1631 because they felt he was more interested in aiding the large landholders than in guarding the company's monopoly of the fur trade.

Wouter Van Twiller, the next governor (1633–1638), took some important actions despite his taste for whisky, his failure to make reports, and his quarrels with other officials and a prominent pastor. He tried to increase trade by constructing a fort on the Connecticut River near present-day Hartford. He placed a garrison on the Delaware River in order to safeguard the trade and land of that region from interlopers from Virginia and Sweden. Van Twiller also helped to settle Long Island by granting several land patents.

The administration of William Kieft (1638–1646) was a succession of crises and controversies. He mismanaged Indian relations so badly that a four-year war resulted. The Algonkins (a tribe of the Algonkians) and several related tribes speaking Algonkian languages revolted in 1641 because Governor Kieft favored the Iroquois and because he tried to tax them for the repairs of Fort Amsterdam. The hard-pressed governor called an unofficial council of twelve local men, but when this group demanded some control over taxes and policy, he dismissed it. This was the first attempt of the colonists to obtain some measure of self-government.

In February 1643 Governor Kieft and his men set out to attack two camps of Algonkins fleeing from the relentless Mohawks. He massacred over a hundred natives, but the remainder retaliated by burning farms and killing settlers. In desperation Kieft called a group of eight men to organize resistance and to authorize an excise tax. This group quarreled with Kieft and appealed to the officials of the Dutch West India Company for Kieft's removal. After suffering many losses, the Dutch, in February 1644, sallied forth into the region later known as Westchester County and killed over five hundred Indians. The next year Kieft negotiated a peace treaty ending the war, which had cost both sides over one thousand lives. Kieft was lost at sea as he sailed home in 1647 to defend himself against charges of blundering and cowardice.

An old soldier but new bridegroom entered the governor's mansion in 1647 and kept office until the English conquest, despite the constant stream of complaints against his autocratic rule. From the outset Peter Stuyvesant (1647–1664) exhibited a hot temper, vitriolic language, and autocratic habits. One of his first actions was to try to convict two men who had dared to challenge the authority of Governor Kieft and his inner Council. Stuyvesant felt obliged to secure the co-operation of the settlers, and in 1647 he established a board of nine men, the first formally constituted and permanent board of local officials in New Amsterdam. Although this unofficial advisory council agreed to new taxes, its members soon quarreled with the governor. Van der Donck, secretary of the board, drew up a long indictment of misrule by Kieft and Stuyvesant. This remonstrance of 1649 called for more settlers, freer trade, and better protection from the Indians. Its criticism of Stuyvesant as domineering and tyrannical did not persuade the Amsterdam directors to withdraw their support of the governor.

New Amsterdam received a "burgher government" in 1653, thus becoming the oldest municipal corporation in the United States. At first Stuyvesant appointed the burgomasters and schepens (or aldermen), who formed a municipal court of justice. These magistrates by the end of five years won the right to nominate their successors. They followed the medieval practice of setting up a system of "burgher rights," by which only those newcomers who paid a fee could buy or sell goods or practice their craft within the city of New Amsterdam. Governor Stuyvesant carefully reserved the right to enact ordinances, since he was suspicious of every step toward representative government.

The grant of municipal rights to New Amsterdam set off a demand for more self-government among the settlements on Long Island. Settlers from Connecticut were especially eager to secure all the rights of self-government to which they had become accustomed. In December 1653 representatives from both Dutch and English towns joined with delegates from the unofficial board of nine men and from the city of New Amsterdam in petitioning for the end of arbitrary rule by governor's decree. They criticized the appointment of officials and magistrates without the consent of the people, the enactment of laws without the knowledge of the people, and favoritism to insiders. Governor Stuyvesant declared their resolutions illegal and dismissed the delegates.

Stuyvesant showed more skill in handling external affairs than in governing his unruly subjects. New Netherland, like Holland, was resisting Spanish efforts to regain control of world trade and was attempting to thwart British ambitions to displace Holland as the leading mercantile power. In addition, New Netherland had its own problems, such as bickerings over the indefinite boundaries with Connecticut, the intrusion of the Swedes on the Delaware, and bad relations with the Indians. Technically the Estates-General and the Dutch West India Company directed the foreign policies of New Netherland, but the governor had some discretionary power, especially in making treaties with the Indians and other European colonies in the New World.

Stuyvesant achieved his greatest success in taking over New Sweden on the Delaware. During the first half of the seventeenth century Sweden was a great power, and her leaders sought to enter the race for foreign trade and colonies by chartering trading companies. In 1637 the New Sweden Company, with considerable Dutch money behind it, sent out an expedition to the Delaware River. The Dutch refused to recognize the legality of the Swedish settlement; but because they feared even more the various attempts by New Englanders to establish colonies in the Delaware Valley, they did little to stop it until Stuyvesant in 1651 invaded the region and erected Fort Casimir. Three years later the Swedes demolished the fort, whereupon the Dutch governor sent an armada of seven ships and 650 men to the Delaware. Confronted with this large force, the Swedish governor surrendered.

The claims of Massachusetts and Connecticut for land westward to the Pacific conflicted with the rights of the Dutch West India Company, which had founded posts in the region from the Connecticut Valley to the Delaware River. The dispute broke out in the 1630's, when hundreds of Englishmen settled along the Connecticut River and surrounded the tiny Dutch fort at present-day Hartford. During the next decade more English towns were established along both the northern and southern shores of Long Island Sound despite the protests of the Dutch governors. Southampton, East Hampton, and Southold were settlements by New Englanders in the eastern part of Long Island which denied Dutch authority.

The Amsterdam directors authorized Stuyvesant to make a "provisional settlement" with New England in order to prevent open conflict. In 1650 Governor Stuyvesant, in the humiliating Treaty of Hartford, gave up all effective claim to the Connecticut Valley. This agreement set the border at a line running northward from the west side of Greenwich Bay. This line, however, was never to be less than ten miles from the Hudson River, a provision which Massachusetts and Connecticut officials were later to ignore. Long Island was divided, with New Netherland retaining only the small portion west of a line dropped from Oyster Bay to the ocean. The treaty in which Dutch weakness was officially recognized opened Stuyvesant to much criticism. Significantly, the treaty was first repudiated by Massachusetts and Connecticut, both of which revived their claims to land west of the line of 1650. The Connecticut settlements secured a charter in 1662 which claimed a broad belt of land across New Netherland. In fact, the governor of Connecticut ordered people in Greenwich and Westchester to send deputies to the General Court of his colony.

Other issues embittered relations between New Netherland and its neighbors to the east. The close ties between the Dutch and the Mohawks irritated settlers in the Connecticut Valley, who suffered from occasional Indian raids. Merchants in New England, eager to buy and sell from the Iroquois, resented the trading monopoly claimed by the Dutch company. Traders, both English and Dutch, complained against the heavy imposts levied on all imports and exports at New Amsterdam. The Anglo-Dutch competition for trade, colonies, and bases in the Indian Ocean and the Caribbean led to a series of wars during the third quarter of the seventeenth century. Neither New Netherland nor the New England colonies could avoid involvement in these wars.

Immigrants from Connecticut living west of the borders drawn in 1650 proved even more disagreeable as citizens than as neighbors. The small palisaded towns of Hempstead, Flushing, Newton, Gravesend, and Jamaica copied the characteristic institutions of New England—the town meeting, the autonomous church congregation, and the co-operative land system. These towns and their sister settlements along the Sound in what is today western Connecticut were centers of unrest against the rule of Stuyvesant. In 1653 rebels in Flushing raised the cry of "English Union," which was echoed in other townships. During the next decade these towns usurped more political rights; finally in 1663 Stuyvesant granted them the right to elect their own magistrates in town meeting. The following year Governor John Winthrop of Connecticut asserted his colony's rights to all of Long Island, but he surrendered the island to Colonel Richard Nicolls when the latter captured New Netherland for the Duke of York.

Religion played a less important role in both the public and private lives of the citizens of New Netherland than in either Roman Catholic Quebec or Puritan New England. The Dutch were concerned with neither the conversion of the Indians to the "true faith" nor the establishment of a wilderness Zion ruled by God's elect. The company directors were unabashedly seeking profits. The settlers, reflecting the same secular spirit, were often rough and unruly characters who became notorious for their addiction to strong drink.

In the United Provinces, however, Calvinism had sunk deep into the Dutch consciousness. Few doubted that Jehovah had chosen the Dutch to smite the Spanish overlord and, incidentally, to capture the carrying trade of the world. The directors of the West India Company gave their blessing to the Dutch Reformed church (a form of Calvinism) in New Netherland and sent out clergymen to serve the people, but some of the dominies seemed more interested in denouncing the governors than in advancing the spiritual welfare of their communicants. Dominie Bogardus (1633–1647) had a sharp tongue and delighted in castigating Governors Van Twiller and Kieft. The former is reported to have pursued the young divine with drawn sword; the latter, to have ordered cannon shot off and drums beaten during church services. Such antics certainly gainsay Washington Irving's description, in his *Knickerbocker's History of New York,* of phlegmatic officials seldom aroused from their alcoholic torpor.

The Protestant Netherlands was the haven of persecuted religious groups during the seventeenth century. For example, the Pilgrims left England for Holland before they took voyage on the *Mayflower.* Reflecting this tolerant spirit, the Dutch company urged their officials to welcome newcomers and to minimize religious persecution. Gradually members of many creeds drifted to New Amsterdam despite the opposition of the clergymen of the Dutch Reformed church. Governor Stuyvesant regarded nonconformists as potential rebels against his rule. Certainly his unhappy experiences with the Connecticut Yankees on Long Island confirmed his fears. The governor therefore expelled Quakers, discouraged the immigration of Jews, and even blocked the formal organization of a Lutheran church. The more tolerant directors censured him for his attitude and laid down the rule that the "consciences of men should be free and unshackled."

A landmark in the fight for freedom of religion is the Flushing Remonstrance of 1657. In 1645 Flushing, Long Island, had received a charter guaranteeing settlers "liberty of Conscience, according to the custome and manner of Holland, without molestation or disturbance." When Stuyvesant forbade Quakers to hold meetings, twenty-six freeholders representing various religious viewpoints issued a remonstrance. This bold assertion of the right of freedom of conscience foreshadows New York's great tradition of religious freedom and toleration.

Cultural activities were extremely limited in sparsely settled New Netherland. The Dutch, however, were one of the most literate people in Europe and recognized the value of basic schooling. The famous petition of 1649 complained that there was no school, although a schoolmaster had arrived in New Amsterdam before 1640. Stuyvesant showed considerable interest in education and helped establish primary schools in several localities, including Brooklyn, Flatbush, and Harlem. The Catechism was the basic textbook, supplemented by the *ABC* book, the Gospels and Epistles, and arithmetic books. Stuyvesant lent his support to a secondary school in which Latin was taught.

Charles II of England and his advisers decided to take over New Netherland because traders at New Amsterdam made the enforcement of the British acts of trade and navigation difficult. In 1664 he awarded to his brother James, the Duke of York and Albany, "all the land from the west side of Connecticutte River to the East Side of De la Ware Bay" with "power and Authority of Governement and Commaund in or over the Inhabitants of the said Territories or Islands."

Charles II dispatched four warships to seize New Netherland, after securing the assistance of the New England colonies. News of the expedition leaked out and reached the ears of Governor Stuyvesant, already troubled by threats of rebellion on Long Island. The British fleet dropped anchor in New York Bay on August 18, 1664, and Colonel Richard Nicolls, the future English governor of New York, and Governor John Winthrop of Connecticut sent letters to Stuyvesant inviting him to surrender. At first Stuyvesant refused to yield, and he tore the Winthrop letter to pieces when the burgomasters asked for a copy. But when the merchants and populace refused to take up arms and the British increased their pressure, Stuyvesant on August 26 (or September 5 according to the new-style calendar), agreed to surrender.

The terms of surrender were generous, guaranteeing liberty of conscience and granting the Dutch full property and inheritance rights. All judgments previously given in courts were to remain unquestioned. Minor civil officials continued in their offices until the next election. The terms granted to the city of New Amsterdam (renamed New York) a choice of deputies with "free Voyces in all publique affaires."

The Dutch remained after 1664 a piquant strain in the New York melting pot. Dutch enclaves in Ulster County, northern New Jersey, and western Long Island clung to the language until the early years of the nineteenth century. Place names such as Harlem, Brooklyn, Kinderhook; common words such as boss, stoop, cruller; political figures with names such as Van Buren and Roosevelt, all kept alive the heritage from New Netherland. A recent historian of the Dutch colony makes the suggestive comment that they "developed a culture resembling more nearly the American way of today than did any other group of colonists in their part of the world." Certainly New Yorkers can find in these early settlers some of our most cherished characteristics—a commercial spirit, a keen interest in material things, a zest for life, and a tolerant attitude toward people of varying religious and racial backgrounds.

Revolt against Autocracy,

1664-1708

The people here have no claim of right to General Assemblys. . . . It is purely the grace and favour of the Crown that allows them to have Assemblys.—EDWARD CORNBURY, *c. 1705*

THE charter for New York which King Charles II gave to his brother James in 1664 continued the pattern of arbitrary government established by the Dutch West India Company. The Duke of York, unrestricted by any popular assembly, enjoyed the sole power to make laws and to govern as he saw fit. He appointed all officials and determined judicial matters, and these actions were subject only to the right of appeal to the Privy Council in England. As proprietor, he controlled the trade of his colony, fixed the imposts, granted land, and directed the defense, but he delegated many of these powers to his governors.

Several factors, however, curtailed these sweeping powers. The terms of surrender guaranteed certain rights, such as liberty of conscience and possession of private property. In addition, the charter of 1664 provided that all laws had to harmonize with those of England. Apparently James had little desire to rule autocratically, and he instructed his governors to treat the people "with humanity and gentleness." He consulted local opinion by selecting a few influential citizens to serve on the governor's Council.

James ruled New York for twenty-one years as duke, and for three years as king. His primary concern in New York was financial, and he took particular interest in the duties laid on imports and exports. But because the cost of maintaining the defenses more than offset the revenues, New York proved a disappointing investment. The governors found it impossible to enforce trading regulations and to collect imposts in the teeth of colonial resistance. The governors were no more able to satisfy provincial demands than to fill the duke's treasury. They failed to solve several recurring problems: the question of boundaries; defense against the Indians and the French; the demand for representative government and home rule for localities; and the regulation of economic activities. Failure to meet these problems created social unrest which erupted in rebellion in 1689.

Colonel Richard Nicolls proved an enlightened governor (1664–1668) not only in conciliating the Dutch but also in establishing proprietary rule without stirring to revolt the autonomous English towns on Long Island. The governor, with the advice of a Council and secretary, collected the revenue, granted land patents, regulated Indian affairs, erected forts, and created a court system. He reconstituted the municipal government of New York, appointing a mayor, aldermen, and sheriff but leaving the powerful Dutch merchants in substantial control of city affairs.

The English towns on Long Island continued their campaign for a representative assembly. These transplanted New Englanders were not only accustomed to self-government but they also disliked the customs and trade regulations. In 1665 Nicolls established the shire of Yorkshire, consisting of Long Island, Westchester, and Staten Island, and he called a general meeting at Hempstead to which seventeen towns from these areas were asked to send delegates. The governor turned down their request for an assembly but he granted them considerable local self-government. He compiled a code of laws derived from the statutes of Massachusetts and New Haven and known as the "Duke's Laws." In addition to criminal and civil clauses, there were clauses outlining a system of local government. Freeholders elected a constable and a board of overseers. These officials were responsible to the governor, who also maintained some control over localities by appointing the justices of the peace. The laws worked well on the whole and were gradually extended to the entire province, but the fact that the initiative came from James and that he retained the power to appoint magistrates left the Long Islanders dissatisfied.

The jurisdiction of courts and the principles of law were of special importance in New York. Perhaps the transfer of sovereignty made citizens more sensitive to their rights under English and Dutch law. Perhaps the precarious validity of land titles made landholders and their challengers—tenants, governors, neighboring provinces, and rival landholders—more aware of the need for a sympathetic judiciary. Perhaps the unusually large number of lawyers in the province stimulated as well as accommodated the litigious spirit of the inhabitants.

The British contended that the law of conquered territories was what the King willed. Thus the charter of 1664 granted the Duke of York plenary power to make laws provided they did not contravene the common law of England. At first glance the charter might seem to open the way to dictatorial control of the colony. Actually, the difficulty of enforcing unpopular laws so far from the seat of British power made this eventuality very unlikely.

The inhabitants of New York gradually developed their own theories as to what the law of their province should be. In general, the Dutch recognized the transfer of sovereignty, and Dutch legal precedents died away. The Yankees on Long Island were more tenacious in their conception of law—a curious blend of Biblicism, Puritanism, and the institutions of local jurisdiction functioning in seventeenth-century England. Among the latter were the borough courts in the cities, the county courts, and the quarter sessions held by the justices of the peace in the county. On the manors were introduced the court baron, which handled questions of tenancy and the petty litigation of tenants. Few manor lords felt it worth while to exercise their right to establish a police court (court leet).

At the top of the court system in New York was the Court of Assizes, consisting of the governor, his Council, and the several justices of the peace. This court handled criminal justice, civil suits exceeding twenty pounds, matters of equity, and appeals from lower courts. In 1684 this court was abolished and most of its cases turned over to a court of chancery run by the governor and his Council. The majority of civil and criminal cases were tried and received adjudication in the courts of session, three of which were set up in 1665. All cases in sessions were taken to a jury. Appeals were permitted only in cases where the law was in question or the amount of money exceeded twenty pounds. Township courts were erected, and justices of the peace presided over them. Local courts gradually absorbed the functions and jurisdiction of the manorial courts of New York.

Important territorial changes took place under Nicolls. In 1664 the Duke of York gave New Jersey to his friends John Lord Berkeley and Sir George Carteret. At first only the land was assigned to the Jersey proprietors, but in 1665 they issued their Concessions and Agreements which assumed government powers as well. To the east, New York was also whittled down in size. Although New York regained title to all of Long Island, it lost its claim to the Connecticut River. In 1667 Nicolls agreed to hand back to Connecticut the lands east of a line drawn north from Mamaroneck.

Colonel Francis Lovelace (1668–1674) followed Nicolls' policy of conciliation and immersed himself in an ocean of administrative details. The restive towns on Long Island renewed their complaints against arbitrary power. In fact, Southold, East Hampton, and Southampton on the eastern part of Long Island petitioned the King in 1672 to restore them to the jurisdiction of Connecticut, but the petition was refused.

The outbreak of the Third Anglo-Dutch War led to the recapture of New York by a Dutch fleet in 1673. The peace settlement of February 19, 1674, restored New York to England. The Dutch reoccupation had little effect upon New York, although it caused Lovelace to lose his position and his property.

Major Edmund Andros (1674–1681) was an honest and devoted servant of the Duke of York, who overrode Andros' recommendation for an elected assembly. Although Andros threatened the rebellious towns on Long Island and warned Governor John Winthrop of Connecticut to stop supporting them, unrest spread to Manhattan Island. Many merchants in 1681 refused to pay import duties, claiming that Andros had failed to provide for the continuation of the duties after his return to England in 1680. When Anthony Brockholls, the local commander in chief who temporarily took over the functions of the governor, ordered the collection of imposts, he met general resistance. The sharp reduction in revenue and the virtual collapse of the duke's authority forced James to agree to the formation of a provincial assembly. He realized that the co-operation of New York citizens was needed if his government was to continue.

To quiet the uproar, James sent out a new governor, Colonel Thomas Dongan (1683–1688), with instructions to call a general assembly. This body was to pass laws subject to the approval or disapproval of both the governor and the proprietor. Although it had power to raise money, the governor was to retain control over all expenditures.

The delegates, called by Dongan to sit with him and the five members of his Council, met at Fort James, near the present Battery, in the city of New York in October 1683. The first session of this assembly adopted the so-called "Charter of Liberties and Privileges," largely the work of the speaker, Matthias Nicolls. It provided for an assembly composed of delegates elected by freeholders and freemen. This body, sharing with the governor and Council the supreme legislative power, was to meet at least once in three years. Other sections of the charter provided for freedom of worship and trial by jury. The charter also set up a system of local and county courts. Both Dongan and the Duke of York approved the charter, but the document was later disallowed by James after he became King of England in 1685.

Why did James reverse himself? Apparently the answer is wrapped up in his assumption of royal powers. James, acting on the advice of the Lords of Trade, hoped to strengthen royal control over all the northern colonies, partly for purposes of defense, partly for purposes of enforcing the Navigation Acts. To accomplish these ends, he determined to establish a Dominion of New England which would include New York, New Jersey, and the New England colonies in a single governmental entity. Furthermore, James II disliked the principle of representative government either in England or the colonies. In any case, the charter was disallowed on the basis that it asserted too strongly the legislative supremacy of the governor, Council, and Assembly—an action which created much alarm in New York.

Meanwhile Governor Dongan was showing a firm hand and political skill in developing New York. He was the first governor to recognize fully the key position of the Iroquois in holding back the French and in guaranteeing to Albany a steady supply of furs from the western tribes. Dongan was also a skillful politician who shrewdly built a loyal group of henchmen. He strengthened the aristocracy by erecting several manors, and he aided the merchants of New York City and Albany by granting more privileges to those cities. Albany received exclusive right to the fur trade and shared with New York the monopoly of bolting flour for export. New York was designated the port where all foreign goods had to be loaded or unloaded. This order annoyed the residents of Long Island, who often found a better market for their products in Boston than in New York City. Hudson River trade was reserved for the freemen of New York City. The officials of that city alone could determine who should have freeman rights. These privileges irritated citizens in other parts of the province who complained of high prices and discriminatory practices.

Governor Dongan granted liberal charters to New York City and to Albany. The charter for New York City provided that there were to be six wards; each ward was to elect an assistant and an alderman. The six assistants, meeting with the mayor, recorder, and aldermen, were to form a Common Council. The Council had full power to make laws, orders, and ordinances not contrary to the laws of England and the province. To check excessive popular control, the governor appointed the mayor and also named the other city officials.

In spite of these concessions to some groups, New York citizens were ready for revolt by 1688. The abolition of the Assembly in 1686 had enraged many citizens, particularly those on Long Island. Farmers and country millers resented the monopoly granted to flour bolters in New York City and Albany. Seaports on eastern Long Island complained that regulations requiring them to funnel all their trade through New York City were ruining their business with Boston and the West Indies. Merchants outside the inner clique complained of high taxes laid without popular consent. The deteriorating economic situation caused by the founding of Pennsylvania in 1681 intensified these grievances. Philadelphia merchants captured much of the trade of New Jersey, gained control of the fur trade along the Delaware, and diverted much of the tobacco trade from New York shippers. Rumors spread through New

York in 1688 that Governor Dongan and James II, both Roman Catholics, were hatching a plot to restore Catholic power in New York.

New Yorkers were incensed with the King's grandiose project by which they became subjects of the Dominion of New England under Governor Edmund Andros. Andros clashed with the citizens of Massachusetts and Connecticut, who opposed his efforts to foster Anglicanism, to collect quitrents, to impose higher taxes, and to enforce the Navigation Acts. In New York his deputy, Captain Francis Nicholson, earned the distrust of the populace by his autocratic ways. Tension with the French over the Iroquois and the western fur trade convinced many citizens that the French might invade New York as part of a Catholic conspiracy to destroy Protestantism in New York. Memories of the religious troubles that took place a century earlier made Protestants fearful of persecution. And the recent revocation of the Edict of Nantes in France (1685) made them particularly wary of the French. New Yorkers of Dutch descent recalled the suffering their ancestors endured under the rule of the Spanish Duke of Alva and the Council of Blood.

When James II was dethroned in the Glorious Revolution of 1688 and Governor Andros was imprisoned in Boston by the colonials, rebellion in New York became open. Nicholson's delay in recognizing the new Protestant monarchs, William and Mary, lent color to the charge that the royal officials in New York were up to some mischief. A group of citizens formed a Committee of Safety to defend the province against French invasion and the alleged Catholic conspiracy. It selected Jacob Leisler, one of the wealthiest merchants, as commander in chief.

Leisler was a figure of controversy to his own generation and remains a puzzle to historians. In the eyes of royal officials, the Anglican clergy, and the aristocrats, Leisler was a firebrand inciting the rabble to rebellion. To the populace and especially to the Dutch artisans, he was the champion of freedom against autocracy, Protestantism against Catholicism, and the lower classes against the ruling oligarchy. That Leisler was hot-tempered and domineering is well established. That his administration represented a popular protest against corrupt rule by a clique of merchant-landlords is also evident. Under Leisler artisans served as officials, a representative assembly was reconstituted, and the people of New York City had their one chance in colonial times to vote for a mayor. Leisler also broke the monopoly of bolting flour for export held by the merchants of New York City.

The fiery governor ruled with some claim to legality. In December of 1689 letters arrived from England instructing Nicholson or "in his absence to such as for the time being take care of preserving the Peace and administering the Lawes." Leisler claimed his authority under these letters and always affirmed his complete loyalty to William and

Mary. The merchants of Albany at first refused to recognize his right
to rule, but the French raid on Schenectady in 1690 caused them to
welcome the protection of his troops.

Meanwhile envoys denouncing and upholding Leisler besieged William III to win his support. The new king selected Colonel Henry
Sloughter, a weak person who was easily swayed by the aristocrats, to
replace Leisler. Leisler played into the hands of his enemies by refusing
to surrender the fort on Manhattan Island to an advance guard of
Sloughter's troops. After Sloughter arrived on March 29, 1691, he picked
enemies of Leisler as members of his Council. At once the aristocrats
demanded revenge for Leisler's treatment of them while he was governor. Treason was the charge brought against Leisler and nine of his
men. A special commission of *oyer* and *terminer* condemned Leisler and
his son-in-law to death. Leisler appealed to King William for redress,
but Sloughter denied the request and yielded to the clamor of the aristocrats for immediate hanging. Tradition has it that Sloughter signed
the death warrants while intoxicated.

The revolutionary troubles in England and America had three important effects upon the government of New York. First of all, King
William abandoned James's plans for a Dominion of New England.
Secondly, New York secured a permanent elected Assembly. Although
only a minority of the inhabitants had the right to vote, the farmers
had the opportunity to defend their interests. For example, in 1695
their representatives in the Assembly secured the right for all farmers to
bolt, bake, and pack flour for export by refusing to pass any other
measures. The establishment of the Assembly was thus an important
step in the history of representative government in New York. Finally,
the Council became the upper house of a legislature. Originally part of
the executive branch, the Council after 1691 exercised both a legislative
and a judicial function.

Leisler dead was almost as troublesome as Leisler alive. His memory
split the tiny colony and bedeviled politics until well into the first decade
of the eighteenth century. His followers tried to vindicate his name,
while his foes, including most of the English, French, and Long Island
Yankees as well as the largest landholders, tried to keep political control.
For a time this feud obscured and complicated economic issues.

In 1691, at the death of Sloughter, the province of fewer than twenty
thousand people was in confusion and the treasury was empty. The
northern frontier was unprotected from French attack, as evidenced by
the burning of Schenectady in 1690. The Council had chosen Robert
Ingolsby, the commander of the troops, to hold the powers of the governor
until the arrival of Governor Benjamin Fletcher. It re-established the
courts and institutions of local government and, in effect, re-enacted the

charter of liberties of 1683. The aristocrats in the Council and Assembly passed vindictive acts against Leislerians, insisting upon punishment and the payment of damages to those who had lost property during the revolt.

In 1691 the Assembly reconstructed the judiciary. In place of township courts, justices of the peace tried minor cases of debt or trespass. A court of sessions of the peace met in every city or county to handle criminal matters. Courts of common pleas, held in the various cities and counties, considered civil cases. The Assembly created a Supreme Court of Judicature which had cognizance in all cases, civil, criminal, and mixed. The judges of this court sat once every three months in New York City, and each judge made an annual circuit through each county of the province.

Two others features of the act of 1691 deserve attention because they were often the source of controversy between the governor and the Assembly. The governor and his Council constituted a court of appeals from which was authorized limited appeal to the British Crown in privy council. To handle cases in equity, provision was made for a court of chancery. The governor had the right to sit as chancellor of the court of chancery. This court was always the target of colonial suspicion. To most colonists it smacked of royal prerogative since neither Parliament nor the Assembly had clearly established this court. Furthermore, it seemed to bypass the regular courts and the common law. The governors upheld their rights in chancery and charged that the enemies of chancery were afraid to have their defective land titles examined. The right of the governor to create courts and define their jurisdiction became a burning issue and set the stage for the famous Zenger case discussed in Chapter 4.

Governor Fletcher (1692–1698) brought comfort and aid to the aristocrats, since he realized the value of their support in carrying through his defense program and in lining his own pockets. Members of the Council received extensive grants of land. Fletcher also encouraged the illegal activities of some merchants who were financing and supplying pirates in the Indian Ocean. In fact the governor received bribes from pirate captains who used New York harbor to refit their vessels. Shopkeepers, tavernkeepers, and shipwrights welcomed the free-spending buccaneers.

Fletcher's successes, however, were not to go unchallenged. In 1695, the Leislerian faction won control of the Assembly, and it repealed the bolting monopoly and the penalties imposed on followers of Leisler. In fact, Parliament also agreed to restore the estates of Leisler and his family. Reports of Fletcher's venality reaching London resulted in his dismissal in 1697.

Richard Coote, the Earl of Bellomont, Fletcher's successor, who was also named governor of Massachusetts and New Hampshire, received instructions requiring him to annul exorbitant land grants, to check illegal trade, and to stop piracy; and these measures antagonized the aristocracy. He allied himself with the Leislerians, who won a splendid victory in 1699 when he agreed to acts exonerating and indemnifying "rebels" in return for a bill granting him certain revenues for six years. His attempt to nullify the large land grants alarmed not only the Fletcher clique but also landholders in general. Very few landholders wanted any governor to scrutinize and vacate land titles. When Bellomont died in 1701, Lieutenant Governor John Nanfan took charge and continued a pro-Leislerian policy. The Assembly outlawed certain magnates and tried others for treason. Ironically enough, Nicholas Bayard, who had brought Leisler to the gallows, narrowly escaped the same fate.

The appointment of Lord Edward Cornbury as governor (1702–1708) brought the Leislerian domination to an end. Governor Cornbury swept out all the Leisler officials from the Council at the top to the justices of the peace at the local level. This frivolous and grafting nephew of Queen Anne so debauched his office that even his aristocratic friends could not stomach his greed or tolerate his buffoonery. His greatest contribution to New York was to create such a scandal that the citizens of all camps were united in opposition and demanded some curb to his power.

Cornbury's mismanagement of public money combined with the deepening depression during the first decade of the century forced the Assembly to consider remedial action. Leadership in this body was passing into the hands of younger anti-Leislerians from the counties of Suffolk and Queens who also rallied the rich importers and exporters of New York City, Albany, and Suffolk by advancing a program of economy and free trade. In the hope of building up this trade of New York City, they urged the abolition of tariffs and port charges. They also opposed the regulation and protection of local industry demanded by the artisans.

The Assembly in 1704 asked for the appointment of a treasurer to receive and pay out funds. It also denied the right of the governor's Council to amend money bills. The British government strongly supported Governor Cornbury's position that his Council could amend money bills. On the other hand, it granted permission to the Assembly to appoint its own treasurer when it needed to raise "extraordinary supplies" outside the regular standing revenue. Thereafter all expenditures became "extraordinary" except for provision of officials' salaries, which Cornbury had secured for five years. As a result of his outrageous extravagances, public credit sank to a low point. The leaders of the Assembly, reflecting their Connecticut background, began to advance the extreme position that the Assembly alone had legislative power.

The gradual transfer of effective power from the governor to the Assembly is clearly discernible prior to 1710. The leaders of the Assembly worked through parties with a disciplined membership. The basic division was between the artisans, shopkeepers, and yeomen farmers, on the one hand, and the rich merchants and land barons on the other. Geographically speaking, this cleavage was a clash between the rich merchants of Albany and New York City and the small farmers in the Hudson Valley and the "Yankee" towns on Long Island. Of course, many exceptions obscured and contradicted this pattern. The jealousy between Presbyterians and Anglicans and the latent hostility between Dutch and English, not to mention factional feuds, complicated political developments. The next chapter will show in detail later steps taken by the assemblymen of New York to perpetuate their gains over Cornbury and to enlarge their powers over the governors.

The Rise of the Assembly,

1708-1763

*The New York Assembly had seized from the governor the
nomination of all officers of Government . . . and in short almost every other executive part of Government, by which un-
warrantable Encroachments and Invasions of your Majesty's
just and undoubted authority, Order and good Government
were subverted, Your Majesty's Service obstructed, and the
Security of the Province endangered.*—PRIVY COUNCIL, 1753

THE basic constitutional principles of provincial New York were ham-
mered out in the period 1708–1739. Gradually, constitutional procedures
developed that were similar to but not identical with those of Great
Britain. An assumption common to both governments was that executive
officials were responsible to the majority party of the lower house. The
Assembly of New York, following the practice of the House of Commons,
secured more control over the executive by providing for an accounting
procedure and by controlling appointments either directly or indirectly.
The leaders of the Assembly by 1739 were advancing the right to act as
a court of appeals which might judge the misdemeanors of executive
officers. Two parties emerged, each subscribing to a given theory of
government, each advocating a reasoned economic program, each following recognized leaders, and most important of all, each responsible
to the public. Lieutenant Governor George Clarke in the 1740's worked
with majorities held by two different parties. He was the first governor
to accept his function as a constitutional executive rather than a partisan
leader.

Lewis Morris, Sr., skillfully built up a party dominating the legislature
much of the time between 1708 and 1739. Morris was a remarkable
figure who maintained party leadership despite his brusque manners,
incurable tardiness, and frequent drunkenness. Distributing patronage

and contracts with great skill, he rallied to him able young men, notably Cadwallader Colden. The Morris party attracted support from the members of the middle class, such as the small traders of New York and Albany, the artisans of New York City, and the yeomen farmers of the Hudson Valley. Morris also managed to win over the bulk of the Dutch, the remnants of the Leislerians, and the Quakers in Westchester and Queens counties. He offered a complicated program to attract and to keep the support of these diverse elements. He gave the shopkeepers protection against the auctioneer and peddler, and he offered the artisans protection against imports and subsidies for native industries. He courted the farmers by better roads, cheaper money, and favorable land laws. The middle class were relieved of direct taxes when the main burden of taxation was shifted to the imposts paid by the large merchants. The Dutch were favored with patronage and indemnities for the losses incurred by the followers of Leisler.

Prior to 1728 the Morris party did not press constitutional issues largely because it normally enjoyed cordial relations with the governors. Thereafter, Morris swung more clearly to the side of constitutional reform and claimed that his party members were the servants of the people. For example, Lewis Morris, Jr., in 1733 told the citizens of Westchester that he would follow their instructions to the letter.

The wealthy merchants of New York City and Albany disliked the Morris program and rallied behind Adolphus Philipse, a merchant with much land in Westchester County. The large landholders—the De Lanceys, Beekmans, Van Cortlandts, and the like—generally supported the merchant princes. This was partly because of family alliances and partly because many of them had retained or acquired an interest in trade. This party of big businessmen wanted free trade, a stable currency, economy in government, and the end of subsidies to artisans. Philipse claimed that protectionist measures diverted trade to Perth Amboy and to Connecticut ports. He and his followers favored direct taxes instead of high customs and excises. The Philipses tried to win the votes of poorer freemen by pledging the repeal of the imposts on rum, salt, and molasses.

The first strong bid by the Assembly for control of government finance and policy came in the years 1708–1710, when the executive branch was weakened by the death of Governor John Lovelace (1709) and was preoccupied with preparations for an expedition against Canada (see Chapter 5). Appropriation bills placed the money in the hands of an elected treasurer accountable to the Assembly. The Assembly nominated the military officers, fixed the wages and number of men to be paid, and specified the purposes of each appropriation. The Assembly even dared to cut the regular civil list. Salaries for the customhouse officers, those of the admiralty court, and the attorney general were omitted because all these officials had been tarred with corruption under Cornbury and were entrusted with the enforcement of the unpopular Navigation Acts. The Assembly insisted that henceforth it would make money grants for only one year at a time. This amounted to holding a club over the head of recalcitrant governors.

Robert Hunter (1710–1720) was probably the ablest governor of colonial New York. Hardly had this former associate of the literary Whigs of London reached New York when he ran into the revenue problem. The Assembly hit the Scot in a sensitive spot by reducing his salary and by denying him the power to spend money without legislative check, so that Hunter was forced to turn to Lewis Morris for assistance. In 1714 a settlement of the important debt problem was reached. The proceeds of the excise for twenty years were to pay all claims owed by the government, but an equivalent amount of bills of credit was to be issued. This currency would satisfy the farmers, who feared that contraction would mean deflation. The bill also stated that the consent of the Assembly was needed before the money would be issued.

Hunter made a bargain in 1715 whereby he received a five-year support bill, in exchange for which he signed a naturalization bill sought by the citizens of Dutch descent. Furthermore, he agreed informally to spend funds according to a schedule drawn up by the Assembly leaders. In short, Hunter realized the necessity of establishing responsible parliamentary government, and he was willing to use Morris as his prime minister.

Politicians of every stripe surrounded William Burnet (1720–1728) upon his arrival in New York. Burnet had consulted Hunter in England and decided to co-operate with the Morris faction. Morris received patronage, land grants, and contracts for his henchmen. In return, Morris saw to it that Burnet received a five-year support bill. The outstanding achievement of Burnet's administration was his Indian policy. His aim was to attract the fur trade of the western Indians by erecting a post at Oswego and by prohibiting the trade in Indian goods between Albany and the French in Montreal. The latter action stirred up the Albany merchants, who enlisted the aid of James de Lancey and Manhattan importers, who in turn persuaded their London associates to attack Burnet's measures before the Board of Trade. His policy was a success measured in terms of peltry reaching Albany directly from the west. Nevertheless, the ban on trade with Montreal was difficult to enforce, and in 1726 Burnet secured an act charging duties on goods going to the north at twice the rates as on those passing to the Indians to the west.

Burnet's foes, led by Adolphus Philipse, won control of the Assembly by 1725. Burnet dissolved the body when Philipse offered a support bill

Chancery — equity
quitrent — rent paid by a freeholder in
lieu of services

for only two years. The result of the election was a strengthening of the Philipse faction in the next Assembly, which reduced customs and challenged the governor's right to set up a court of chancery. Landholders were afraid that such a court would enforce the collection of quitrents and question land titles.

Burnet's successor, Colonel John Montgomerie (1728–1731), was a mild figure who tried with some success to avoid controversy. The Assembly granted him a revenue in support of the government for five years, and Montgomerie took care to issue his warrants in conformity with the schedule set down by the Assembly. He also was careful not to exercise his right to sit in chancery. Upon his death, Rip Van Dam, head of the Council, assumed the governor's duties and collected the governor's salary.

When Governor William Cosby arrived in 1732, he asked Rip Van Dam to refund half of his salary. The latter refused, whereupon Cosby looked about for some way of recovering the money. Fearing a rebuff from a jury, Cosby asserted his disputed prerogative of creating new courts of equity. He might have set up a chancery court with himself as presiding judge but he could hardly hand down a ruling in favor of himself. Therefore he chose to have the Supreme Court double as a court of exchequer. The British Crown was interested in enlarging the equity jurisdiction of the Supreme Court because it hoped to collect unpaid quitrents through its operation. Presumably Chief Justice Lewis Morris, who relied on the governor for his appointment and tenure, would hand down a favorable ruling. To Cosby's chagrin, Morris made a sweeping attack on the constitutionality of the new court. Critics of Morris pointed out that he feared a demand on his salary as acting governor of New Jersey before the arrival of Cosby. The enraged governor fired Morris without ceremony, but the powerful political leader and his son won sweeping victories in the by-election of 1733.

Morris' followers gave much publicity to their program of political and economic reform through the New York *Weekly Journal* published by Peter Zenger. Articles, thinly disguised in the form of fables and foreign dispatches, attacked Cosby and his prerogative. The governor ordered the paper burned and Zenger arrested for libel. Cosby's new chief justice, James de Lancey, gave willing support to the governor. He disbarred practically all the lawyers who might have aided Zenger, but the powerful faction of landowners behind Zenger imported Andrew Hamilton, the most distinguished barrister of Philadelphia. Hamilton insisted that the jury and not the chief justice should decide whether the statements in question were false and seditious. He convinced the jury that what Zenger had printed was true, hence he could not be found guilty. The jury agreed with Hamilton, and Zenger went free. Zenger's acquittal was a landmark in the fight for a free press in America.

Cosby on his death bed in 1736 suspended Van Dam from the Council so that his favorite, George Clarke, might inherit the governor's powers. Although Lieutenant Governor Clarke was an experienced official who tried to "render himself Agreeable to the People in General to bury all Resentment," the Assembly was suspicious of him. When the Morris faction won important electoral victories in 1736 and 1737, Clarke felt it necessary to compromise. He agreed to give the Assembly control of appropriations and expenditures. He also accepted a one-year support bill and a triennial act, the latter requiring that new elections be held every three years. Obviously the Assembly was seeking for itself most of the privileges exercised by the House of Commons in England.

In the period 1740–1760 significant developments took place in political, constitutional, and economic history of New York. The Assembly retained, in fact, enlarged, the powers which it had won over finances and administration despite sporadic efforts by the British government and its governors to reassert their full authority over New York. The need for more money to fight the two wars with France forced the governors to make concessions to the Assembly. Political parties and struggles also reflected the economic changes attending the general prosperity of the period. New York City grew rapidly as a trading center, and manufacturing also showed a great increase. During the 1740's an alliance of land barons and merchant princes co-operated closely and outmaneuvered the disintegrating Morris faction. In the 1750's, however, the landlords and the merchants split into two camps and a new party alignment emerged.

The yeomen, shopkeepers, and artisans, the backbone of the Morris party, broke into small groups after 1740; some even accepted the leadership of the Philipses, who claimed that they were responsible for the prosperous times. The Philipses put through a program of free trade and economy and established harmonious relations with the governor. In 1745 James de Lancey, the chief justice, took over the leadership of the party. De Lancey modified the program by permitting the expansion of the currency and some regulation of the export trade.

Opposition to the Philipse–De Lancey faction soon developed from several quarters. David Jones of Queens led a small group of assemblymen from Long Island who opposed favors to the merchants of New York City, and he made further attacks on the governor's authority. The greatest threat to the Philipse–De Lancey regime came from Cadwallader Colden, a former Morris backer who was selected by Governor Clinton to combat the Assembly. Colden attracted a strange assortment of groups, who either opposed the Philipse program or who hoped to get patronage from Clinton and Colden.

George Clinton (1743–1753) had one of the longest and stormiest terms of any provincial governor. At the beginning, the money-mad governor sought the co-operation of James de Lancey. The judge, a fine speaker and excellent leader, received most of the patronage and secured for Clinton a one-year support bill specifically appropriating funds to certain officeholders. Clinton had plans for building forts along the northern frontier and nourished great ambitions for sending an expedition to Canada. De Lancey secured considerable funds for defense, but not enough to satisfy Clinton. The governor denounced the merchants of Albany for their trade with the French, and the magistrates of Albany for their dilatory tactics in providing ample supplies for the troops. The magistrates or commissaries of Albany since the days of the Dutch regime had exercised a great deal of control over the details of the Indian administration and trade. Clinton's attack on the Albany commissaries caused the De Lanceys to break with the governor.

From 1746 to 1750 the bitterest and most significant political battle in the history of colonial New York was fought. The important question was one of sovereignty. The De Lanceys stated that the Assembly possessed all powers of government, whereas Clinton and his main spokesman, Colden, insisted that the governor shared sovereignty with the legislature. The battle raged from year to year, each side circulating pamphlets. When the Assembly tried to supervise military policy, Clinton asserted:

I will not give my assent to any bill in which the issuing or disposition of the public money is directed otherwise than as his Majesty's commission or instructions to me direct, or which shall lay any limitations or clogs on his Majesty's authority with respect to the disposition or command of the forces.

The battle between Clinton and the Assembly over the power of initiation, administration, and review ended in an uneasy compromise in 1750. The De Lanceys, fearful of disclosure of their extensive embezzlement of public funds, were in an accommodating mood. Clinton was also willing to make concessions. He accepted a one-year support bill which named the officers and fixed the salaries. Furthermore, he permitted the Albany commissaries to reassert their old authority over Indian affairs. Clinton insisted, however, that salaries of civil officers be paid on his warrant, that past salaries have prior claim on the funds, and that debts not paid in six months be carried at interest. The Assembly gave up its more ambitious claims, such as the right to exclusive control of finance. It admitted that the governor had the power of initiating money bills and the power to examine the authenticity of all claims passed by the Assembly. In brief, the Assembly receded from its extreme position of monopoly and sovereignty. After 1750 no important changes in the structure of provincial government took place.

The Board of Trade in London watched with alarm the battle between Clinton and the Assembly and in 1753 severely scolded the Assembly. It instructed Sir Danvers Osborne, the new governor, to demand a perpetual support and revenue for the officers and regular services of the government. After two days of instruction in New York politics, Osborne hanged himself as a result of family troubles. Strangely enough James de Lancey, the foe of the prerogative, inherited the governor's powers, serving as lieutenant governor for the next two years. He proved quite adept in enlarging the governor's formal powers without cutting down the Assembly's actual powers.

The rise of the Livingston party was the most important development in the political life of New York in the 1750's. The Livingston family had belonged to the Philipse–De Lancey party and one of its members usually had sat on the governor's Council. Angered by the De Lancey decision to raise war funds by a tax on land and disturbed by the rise of antirentism among their tenants, the great landlords of the upper Hudson Valley organized a party of their own. They accused James de Lancey of favoring the merchants and of corruption in office. They also charged the governor with seeking to fasten Anglican control over King's College. In 1755 James de Lancey quarreled with Governor William Shirley of Massachusetts over the direction of the war. He found an ally in William Johnson, the famous Indian trader and agent, who was made commander of the New England and New York forces against Crown Point and later Niagara. Johnson wanted to enlist the active support of the Iroquois and to abolish Albany's trade with Montreal. To secure Johnson's support, De Lancey had to abandon his former friends among the Albany commissaries and merchants. In reprisal, the Dutch merchants swung over to the Livingston opposition.

The new governor, Sir Charles Hardy (1755–1757), gave his support to James de Lancey, since he needed Assembly support for a vigorous war program. The death of Hardy in 1757 gave De Lancey another chance to serve as lieutenant governor, a position he held until his death in 1760. He also continued to hold his office of chief justice.

The death of James de Lancey in 1760 raised the question of the tenure of judges. Cadwallader Colden, then president of the New York Council, assumed the duties of governor during the interim period before the appointment of General Robert Monckton as governor in 1761. Colden asserted that judges held office during the King's pleasure instead of during good behavior as claimed by the New York Assembly. The Livingston party, which was now in control of the Assembly, and the judges on the bench were incensed at this attempt to make justices more dependent upon the royal prerogative. Interestingly enough, the Assembly had not hesitated to exert control over the judges by making them dependent for their salaries on annual appropriations from the legislature. Colden stirred up a tempest but won the backing of the British authorities.

The charter granted by Governor Montgomerie to New York City in 1731 laid down the basic principles of municipal administration for over a century. The city fathers wanted concessions not authorized by the Dongan charter. They secured the extension of the city's borders to 400 feet beyond low-water mark on the Hudson and East Rivers and received the right to create another ward. They failed, however, to persuade the governor to give up his power to appoint the mayor, recorder, sheriff, coroner, and town clerk. Mayors were ordinarily men of wealth and standing drawn from the ranks of the aldermen. They did not receive an annual retainer until the 1760's, although for decades they had kept the revenues from liquor licenses despite the protests of the Common Council.

"Freeholders" and "freemen" could vote in the city and province. To qualify as a freeholder, a citizen had to possess estates in fee or for life of the value of forty pounds or more. Freemen were those who had bought the privilege of engaging in certain occupations—wholesalers, retailers, and independent handicraftsmen. The corporation of New York granted "freedoms" sparingly until mid-century, when it lowered the fees.

Although the aristocratic families among the landlords and merchants provided most of the political leaders of colonial New York, they had to pay considerable attention to the wishes of a large fraction of the people. How large was this fraction it is difficult to estimate with any precision. It is known that the percentage of voters among the white population rose from 7 per cent in 1731 to over 10 per cent by 1761. Of course, women did not vote. Furthermore, well over half of the male population was under twenty-one years of age. No doubt, many eligible voters then as now failed to exercise their right. Taking all these factors into consideration, we can safely generalize that at least one-half of the white male population over twenty-one was eligible to vote. A much smaller percentage of Englishmen voted in British elections in that period.

Municipal elections were spirited affairs although the merchant aristocracy generally had its way. On Michaelmas Day (September 29) the freemen and freeholders of each ward assembled and voted for their candidate. If a "show of hands" did not clearly indicate the result, each voter registered and declared for his choice. Elections in the wards were placed under the management of the aldermen and in the counties under the sheriffs. Complaints were frequent that aldermen and sheriffs manipulated the elections in order to help their friends. Candidates often sought votes by offering free drinks and bribes or by coercing their employees and tenants. In 1771 the Assembly took heed of the complaints and deprived the aldermen of their right of election supervision. In their place, the Common Council was directed to appoint a freeman or freeholder of each ward as returning officer. Each voter was required to swear that he had not voted before in that election.

Merchant control was challenged after 1750 by the rising power of the lawyers. Cadwallader Colden was fearful of their dangerous power "greatly strengthened by inlarging the powers of the popular side of the government." Of course, most lawyers had close family and business connections with the merchants, but a few of the more liberal became spokesmen for the mechanics and clerks, who were demanding more control in the decade before the Revolution.

The Common Council faced many complicated problems. It spent most of its sessions enacting "police legislation," broadly defined. It laid down the rules of fire protection, regulated the behavior of slaves, and banned peddlers. The regulation of business functions such as markets, docks, and slaughterhouses was another important area of activity. The Council took a hand in administration by setting up committees to perform such functions as superintending public improvements and auditing the accounts of the treasurer.

It could not lay taxes on real or personal property, however, without the permission of the provincial legislature. Over their protests the citizens of New York City were forced to pay one-third of the provincial taxes although they never numbered one-fifth of the total population. The representatives of the rural counties, particularly those surrounding New York City, often proposed legislation hostile to the city's interests, but the governor's Council, including many merchants resident in Manhattan, was able to check most of these proposals.

Care of paupers, the ill, and prisoners fell upon individuals and the city, since the province placed the responsibility for these unfortunates upon the localities. After 1697 New York City put the poor under the care of a board of vestrymen and wardens who were elected annually by the voters. The city's paupers were boarded at public expense in private families. Dependent children were usually bound out as apprentices or servants. In 1734 New York City erected a two-story brick structure which served as a house of correction for unruly servants, a workhouse for beggars, tramps, and loafers, and an almshouse for paupers. The greater share of charitable work, however, fell to private individuals and church societies.

In order to protect the city from contagion, the Common Council enacted a sanitation and quarantine code, built a pesthouse, and took steps to build a hospital. New York's care of criminals mirrored the harsh practices common during the eighteenth century. The city used the basement of the City Hall as a jail until the erection of a jail in 1759. Prisoners suffered a great deal from cold, poor food, and callous supervision. Only the help of private societies alleviated some of the suffering.

The presence of soldiers, sailors, slaves, and transported felons complicated the problem of keeping the peace. Soldiers often got into brawls, and the populace sometimes resisted the press-gangs seeking sailors for the Royal Navy. The large Negro population presented a special problem because of the fear of conspiracies. New York City had its share of ordinary crime and misdemeanors. Gambling, prostitution, and heavy drinking were common social evils, and robbery, assault, and murder were commonplace.

The municipality maintained a watch, and theoretically all inhabitants listed by the aldermen were required to serve a turn on night duty. Two men were elected annually in each ward to the unpopular post of constable to supervise the watch. For eight years, beginning in 1734, the city created a paid, standing guard of two squads, but in 1742 the corporation returned to a citizens' watch. Every able-bodied man took his turn at standing watch about once a month. The system worked badly, partly because the wealthier inhabitants hired substitutes who were too often of dubious character themselves. In 1762 the Common Council restored the system of a paid standing force. The previous year it established a system of street lighting by oil lamps.

Fire hazards forced the city government to draw up many regulations, but enforcement was sporadic and halfhearted. A serious danger was the storing of highly inflammable materials—hay, straw, naval stores, gunpowder—in the congested area south of Duane Street. Regulations governing the storage of combustibles and the inspection of chimneys were poorly observed. In 1731 the city purchased its first fire engine from London and gradually acquired engines, buckets, firehouses, hose, and ladders for each ward. In 1737 the Common Council authorized an organized force of firemen consisting of five men from each of six wards. Their duties foreshadowed those of the volunteer firemen of today. Closely tied to fire fighting was the question of water supply. At first the city supplemented private wells and springs with public wells paid for by assessments upon residents in the neighborhood. Beginning in 1741 the city ordered pumps for these wells which were under the general supervision of the alderman and assistant of each ward. The Common Council recognized the need for a better water supply and in the years immediately preceding the Revolution authorized an elaborate system of waterworks with a storage reservoir and wooden conduits. The war put a stop to the construction of this system.

Ferry franchises were important not only because of Manhattan's insular position but also because they brought in more revenue than any other source. The charter of 1731 gave New York City complete control of ferries across the lower East River. The city fought off attempts by citizens of Brooklyn to break into this monopoly, but the Supreme Court in 1775 ruled that any resident of Brooklyn had the right to maintain a boat on the East River and to land at any point on the Long Island shore. The corporation of New York City leased the ferry rights to individuals, but the operators often failed to pay the rent or to provide good service.

Our survey of provincial and municipal government demonstrates that by 1760 citizens of colonial New York had reached a fair degree of political maturity and acquired much experience in public affairs. In fact, responsible parliamentary government emerged, facilitating compromise between provincial opinion and royal command. By 1761 New York was a political democracy, cast in the form of a parliamentary monarchy.

Of course, this conclusion as to the democracy of New York requires some qualification. Obviously the large Negro population had few rights, democratic or otherwise. Moreover, the propertyless workers and farm laborers had little influence. Leadership throughout the colonial period came almost entirely from the small group of landlord-merchant aristocracy and the legal fraternity. A few score families—the De Lanceys, Livingstons, Schuylers, Philipses, Beekmans, Morrises, Joneses, Scotts, to mention the most prominent—dominated New York as long, if not longer, than any similar group in the history of any other province.

Virtually every power of government—initiation, administration, review—was officially or unofficially divided between the governor and the Assembly. But the governors were seldom a match for the shrewd and vigilant leaders of the provincial parties. Able administrators such as Hunter and Hardy could not offset the damage done by scoundrels such as Cornbury and timeservers such as Cosby.

The rise of colonial autonomy paralleled the development of parliamentarianism. Gradually the feeling hardened into conviction that both King and Parliament were limited not only by the constitution of England but also by that of New York. By the end of the French and Indian War the government of New York was "almost completely responsible to the expressed will of the electorate."

Outpost of Empire

*[New York] ought to be looked upon as the Capital Province
or the Citadel to all the others; for secure but this and you secure all the English colonies, not only against the French but
also against any insurrections or rebellions against the Crown
of England.*—RICHARD COOTE, *Earl of Bellomont, 1699*

NEW YORK was perhaps the most important outpost of the British
Empire between 1664 and 1775. Its position athwart the Mohawk and
Champlain gateways had made it a key point in the century-long struggle
between France and Britain for control of North America. New Yorkers
realized their dependence upon the redcoats for the defense of the frontier
and also upon the Royal Navy for the protection of commerce. Furthermore, the social pattern of New York, with its aristocracy of landlord-
merchants and its strong emphasis on trade, created a society more
similar to that of England than either the New England or the southern
colonies.

The British colonial system exhibited in striking fashion the British
genius (or weakness) for improvisation and "muddling through." Neither
King nor Parliament, which was dominant after the Revolution of 1688,
developed a consistent and systematic plan of colonial administration.
Rather, Parliament attacked the problem in piecemeal fashion through
using executive offices such as army, navy, and Privy Council. To consult
and to placate local opinion, it authorized assemblies, which gradually
demanded control over the purse strings and local affairs. By 1763 the
colonies on the American mainland enjoyed a great deal of home rule,
but London retained the general powers later exercised by the President,
the Congress, and the federal judiciary over the states—the powers to
conduct foreign relations, to regulate commerce, to manage the currency,
public lands, and post office, to hear appeals from local courts, and to
pass on the constitutionality of laws.

The Board of Trade created in 1696 had the general task of supervising the imperial administration and of regulating colonial affairs for the bene-fit of the mother country. The members of the board drafted instructions for the royal governors, heard complaints, gave advice to various execu-tive officers, to Parliament, and the Privy Council, and maintained a correspondence with the governors. Several executive departments car-ried out duties in the colonies: the Secretary of State for the Southern Department chose the royal governors; the Admiralty defended the coast and enforced the Navigation Acts; the Treasury tried to collect customs and to check on the expenditures of each colony. The Privy Council some-times set aside the colonial laws that were contrary to the laws of Eng-land, the charter, or the governor's instructions.

Many imperial symbols—temporal and spiritual, military and com-mercial—dotted the New York skyline in 1760. Old Fort George, symbol-izing New York's role as military capital of the British Empire in North America, hugged the lower tip of Manhattan. Throughout the period 1664–1775 children could watch troops on parade in New York. The War Office treated the garrison of four companies with scandalous neglect. The governor remained master of foreign relations and defense and the symbol of imperial authority no matter how successfully the Assembly sought control of the purse strings. A cadre of officials surrounded him, and the social life of the aristocracy circled around the governor.

The squat chapel tower in Fort George, like the spire of Trinity Church farther uptown, was a symbol of empire as well as religion. The governors interpreted the law in such a way as to make the Church of England the established church in the lower countries. The aristocracy gravitated to Trinity Church, where the clergy preached sermons upholding the King and Empire before and during the Revolution. Close by Trinity Church stood the new building of King's College, whose architecture, curriculum, and Anglicanism were patterned after those of Oxford and Cambridge.

The customhouse was a less imposing structure, but it was no less an important sign of imperial power. Here were located the collector, comp-troller, surveyor, and subordinate officials who enforced the Navigation Acts. The objects were fourfold: to force the colonists to buy manufac-tured goods in England; to keep foreign shipping, especially the Dutch, from the colonial sea lanes; to secure valuable raw materials such as tobacco; to prevent colonists from manufacturing goods for export which England produced. The main post office for the northern colonies was established in New York in 1764. This became the western destina-tion for government packets carrying mail to America. Even the City Hall was indirectly an agency for the Crown since the main officials were appointed by the governor.

Albany and the frontier settlements were very much aware of their dependence upon the British Empire. The first intercolonial Congress called by the Privy Council met at Albany in 1754. The next year Sir William Johnson was appointed superintendent of Indian affairs for the northern colonies, an imperial post of great influence. From Albany supplies went forth to provision the garrisons in the forts guarding the Lake Champlain and the Mohawk gateways.

The desire for control of North American trade and territory was a major cause behind the five wars fought by England and France between 1689 and 1783. No colony was more directly affected than was New York, whose nearness to Canada exposed it to attack. The French realized that British armies operating from Albany could menace their line of communications with the posts in the interior and might also launch an overland attack upon the key centers of Montreal and Quebec. The French therefore erected forts on Lakes Champlain, Ontario, and Erie and carried on intrigues with the Indians in order to hem in the English. A struggle for control of the fur trade and of the Iroquois intensified the rivalry between British and French.

The Iroquois, who were becoming more and more the middlemen in the fur business, clashed with the French in the 1680's for the trade of the Illinois tribes. When Governor A. J. L. de La Barre in 1684 seized fifty Indian negotiators and attacked the Senecas, Governor Thomas Dongan offered them aid. In 1687 he formally placed the Iroquois under English protection.

The expulsion of pro-French James II from England in 1688 intensified the bitter feeling between New York and Canada. The next year, the new monarch, William of Orange, formally declared war upon France. The opening of war found both New York and Quebec in confusion. In New York, Jacob Leisler had seized power during the collapse of the Dominion of New England to which New York had been temporarily attached in 1688. His coup paralyzed effective action for a time, since certain groups such as the great landlords and the magistrates refused to recognize his authority.

An Iroquois raid on Montreal in 1689 disrupted Governor Louis Frontenac's plan to attack New York, but the resourceful Frenchman soon reorganized his forces, which ravaged the New York and New England frontier. In February 1690 about 150 Frenchmen, paced by two hundred Algonkins and Christian Iroquois, marched through waist-deep snow to Schenectady, whose only sentinels were snowmen. Screams filled the night as the howling invaders broke down doors, scalped their victims, and applied the torch. Three years later the French burned the Mohawk castles south of the Mohawk River, and in 1696 Governor Frontenac led an expedition against the Onondagas. These raids cowed the Iroquois, who never again were a serious threat to Canada.

The region around Albany suffered so severely that by 1698 fewer than fifteen hundred settlers remained in the county of Albany. Frontiersmen under Peter Schuyler's able leadership had to rely largely upon their own forces, since the assemblymen from the southern counties disapproved taxes for frontier defense and the British government maintained only four companies of soldiers in the colony. As mayor of Albany, Schuyler rallied the militia and led raiding parties against the French forces.

The Treaty of Ryswick (1697) which concluded King William's War was actually a mere truce, broken by Queen Anne's War (1701–1713). Some leaders of the Five Nations, who felt that the English had not given them enough protection during the war, listened to French agents who promised peace and trade. The pro-French faction got the upper hand by 1701 and asked the French governor for a treaty of friendship. In return for a French promise not to attack them and to permit them to trade freely with Albany, the Iroquois agreed to recognize the French King as their overlord. The founding of Detroit annoyed the Iroquois since it threatened to cut off furs coming down the Great Lakes. Quick to see the advantage of keeping a balance of power between France and England, they ceded to the King of England in 1701 all the beaver grounds of the Confederacy northwest of Lake Ontario and between Lake Huron and Lake Erie.

New York's ruling class split deeply over Indian policy. Governor Bellomont urged the construction of forts and the promotion of settlements in the Mohawk country and farther west. Many fur traders in Albany opposed this policy because western posts might intercept the shipments of pelts before they reached their stores. Also, some merchants had built up a thriving trade in Indian supplies with the French traders of Montreal who could buy goods cheaper in Albany than import them from France. In 1701 several Albany traders visited Montreal and pledged a policy of neutrality in the event of war. By this agreement they expected to escape Indian raids, avoid high taxes, and keep open the trade route to Montreal.

During the early years of Queen Anne's War a strange but welcome peace existed on the New York frontier. The Albany traders had little trouble in persuading the Manhattan merchants and large landholders to endorse the policy of neutrality, especially since none of these groups wanted to grant Governor Cornbury additional funds or power. Furthermore, the badly mauled Iroquois heeded French warnings against breaking the peace treaty of 1701. Indeed, they had recognized the advantages of playing off the British against the French.

Meanwhile the French centered their military efforts on the New England frontier. In 1704 a raiding party struck at Deerfield, killing 53 people and taking 111 captives. New Englanders criticized the Albany merchants for selling arms to the French and the Indians. In 1708 they asked Great Britain to invade Canada and to destroy French power in America. The British government, flushed with successes on the Continent, promised aid for a colonial attack on Canada. This promise caused New Yorkers to raise forces for an expedition in 1709, but the project collapsed when the British failed to send needed support. New York then disbanded its forces. Two years later another expedition got under way from Albany but gave up when the British fleet met defeat in the St. Lawrence River.

The Treaty of Utrecht (1713) awarded to Britain much American territory, such as Newfoundland, Acadia, and Hudson's Bay, and won French recognition of British suzerainty over the Iroquois, which the British had claimed since the 1680's. During the next three decades of peace, officials in Montreal and New York maneuvered to secure strategic posts and to line up Indian allies. The French cemented their hold on the upper lakes and Illinois country and even won over a part of the Senecas through their agent Louis Joncaire. They built a post at Niagara in 1726 and five years later one at Crown Point on Lake Champlain.

Divided counsels prevented New Yorkers from taking decisive countersteps. Merchants trading with Montreal opposed the erection of posts west of Albany, but other traders and the royal governors argued that a post at Oswego would recapture for New York the trade of the western tribes. Moreover, New York could best pry loose the French hold on these tribes by curbing the flow of cheap British manufactures from Albany to Montreal.

Governor Burnet adopted a vigorous western policy by banning trade with Montreal and by founding Fort Oswego in 1727. His enemies in the Assembly forced him to relax the trade ban, but the fort remained an important outpost. As a result, the quantity of furs reaching Albany mounted rapidly, until by 1750 New York rivaled Pennsylvania as the leading exporter of furs to England.

The War of Austrian Succession, known in America as King George's War (1744–1748), found many New York leaders anxious to avoid open conflict. The Six Nations or Iroquois Confederacy were eager to maintain their neutrality, but former naval officer George Clinton favored a vigorous policy toward the French. He used his authority as governor to send cannon and provisions for the successful assault on Louisbourg, Nova Scotia. He tried to stir up the Six Nations against the French by calling a conference with the Indians at Albany in 1745. Clinton's efforts, however, had little chance of success because of his bad relations with the Assembly. James de Lancey and his political allies, including the Indian commissaries at Albany, refused to grant the governor funds to carry on the war. As a result, Clinton broke with the Indian commissaries and transferred the control of Indian affairs to William Johnson. The Assembly retaliated by refusing to grant funds to Johnson, who had to make advances to the Indians out of his own pocket.

Johnson had come from Ireland in 1738 to administer the lands of his uncle, Admiral Peter Warren, near the modern town of Amsterdam. This energetic Irishman, one of the most fascinating figures in colonial history, became a farmer, trader, soldier, Indian agent, land speculator, statesman, and churchman. After building a house at Warrensbush, Johnson added a store so that he might trade with Mohawk neighbors and with the white traders operating out of Oswego. He earned the respect of both groups by his fair dealing, and he won the affection of the Mohawks by his willingness to treat them as equals. Johnson learned the Mohawk dialect, joined the braves in their sports and dances, and made an Indian girl, Molly Brant, mistress of his household. Johnson became the greatest trader with the western Indians, sending tons of goods to Oswego.

Johnson favored a strong imperial policy, partly because of his interest in the fur trade and partly because of his friendship with Governor Clinton, who appointed him colonel of the Albany County militia. In 1746 Johnson's eloquence persuaded the Mohawks to take up arms, although this action affronted the Great Council of the Iroquois at Onondaga which was striving to maintain unity of action. After much haggling, the Iroquois agreed to assist the English in an attack on Canada, but the failure of the British fleet to arrive in the St. Lawrence forced Clinton to abandon the expedition. During the last two years of the war the Mohawks actively protected the frontier, but the rest of the Iroquois gave only token aid to the English cause.

The settlement arranged in 1748 at Aix la Chapelle did not drive away the French threat on the New York and Virginia frontiers. French engineers built forts on strategic waterways, especially along the upper Ohio River, and French agents tried to win the Iroquois from the British. Conrad Weiser, the Indian agent for Pennsylvania, on his visit to Onondaga in 1750 found that the Onondagas, the Cayugas, and the Senecas had "turned Frenchmen." The Iroquois were angry about the land speculators of Albany who had cheated them of many tracts, and they resented the insolent attitude of Governor Clinton. Their grievances reached a peak when William Johnson gave up in 1751 his post as Indian agent for New York. Johnson could no longer afford to advance the funds for this position for which the enemies of Governor Clinton would make no provision.

In 1753 the British Board of Trade recognized the critical situation and directed the governor of New York to call a colonial congress at Albany in 1754 in order to re-establish friendly relations with the Iroquois Confederacy. James de Lancey of New York promised the chiefs of the Six

Nations that New York would not take away any Indian lands without just payment. The Iroquois returned home half satisfied but rejoicing in their thirty wagonloads of presents.

Benjamin Franklin proposed to the Congress at Albany a plan for colonial union, calling for a grand council chosen triennially by the colonial assemblies and for a president-general appointed by the Crown. The council and president would have charge over Indian relations, would regulate new settlements, and levy necessary taxes. Although the delegates approved the plan, the assemblies in the various colonies refused to transfer their power to a new agency. The Board of Trade was fearful that the proposed intercolonial government would take power away from the Crown. Thus the beginnings of a colonial union had to wait for over twenty years, until the Continental Congress met to protest against Parliament's encroachments upon the rights of the colonial legislatures.

When the French routed George Washington and his Virginia militia from the forks of the Ohio (the site of Pittsburgh) in July of 1754, the colonies and the British government realized that they must take effective countermeasures or lose control of the trans-Appalachian region. Fortunately, the tactless Clinton had returned to England, and James de Lancey, acting governor, was able to end the paralyzing feud between the executive and the New York Assembly, and the Assembly voted in August 1754 to aid the hard-pressed Virginians. Also, noting the aggressive attitude of the Indians, it decided to strengthen the palisades of Albany.

The British government late in 1754 determined to oust the French from Acadia, Niagara, Crown Point, and the Ohio Valley. They authorized three campaigns: General Edward Braddock, commander in chief of the British forces in America, was to seize Fort Duquesne (Pittsburgh); Colonel Robert Monckton was to sail from Boston and take Acadia; and William Johnson was to lead an expedition against Crown Point. Braddock delegated to Governor William Shirley of Massachusetts the task of capturing Fort Niagara.

The defeat of Braddock in July 1755 foreshadowed and contributed to the failure of Shirley's expedition against Niagara and Johnson's attack on Crown Point. Shirley discovered that James de Lancey was jealous of his authority and was quietly obstructing his efforts to raise troops and to collect supplies. Furthermore, a violent feud broke open between Shirley and Johnson. Shirley, who succeeded Braddock as commander-in-chief of British forces, ordered Johnson to divert some of his Indians to Shirley's expedition against Niagara. Johnson, however, felt he needed all his Indian guides and warriors for his own expedition to Crown Point. When Shirley appealed directly to the Iroquois chiefs for recruits, he enraged Johnson, who claimed exclusive control over Indian relations because of his office of Superintendent of Indian Affairs north of the Ohio River.

Neither Shirley nor Johnson captured their objectives in 1755 or 1756. Shirley led his men up the watercourses to Oswego, but the stormy waters of Lake Ontario, controlled by the strong French garrisons at Forts Niagara and Frontenac (Kingston, Ontario), made an attack on Niagara too hazardous for the small British force. In October 1755 Shirley pulled back part of his expedition to Albany. Meanwhile, Johnson, driving himself to exhaustion, took his forces up the Hudson on bateaux and over a wilderness road to the southern tip of Lake George. There he constructed an earth fort which he named William Henry. The French under Baron Ludwig August Dieskau advanced southward from Crown Point and established a strong fort at Ticonderoga. Hoping to surprise Johnson's forces, Dieskau with a picked force attacked Johnson's encampment. The French broke off after heavy fighting and retreated northward to their strong positions at Ticonderoga and Crown Point. Johnson was unable or unwilling to pursue the French and resigned his command in the fall of 1755.

During 1756 and 1757 the French seized the initiative and inflicted several serious defeats upon the British. In August of 1756 General Louis Joseph de Montcalm, recognizing the importance of Oswego in influencing the Six Nations, captured the fort. He also wished to prevent the British from cutting the French line of communication to the Ohio country. At this time, the British were suffering from the confusion caused by a change of command. De Lancey, Johnson, and others had intrigued against Shirley in London, and the Board of Trade dismissed the able governor in 1756. The new commander, the Earl of Loudoun, was a master of procrastination and permitted Montcalm to select his targets at will. Loudoun wasted the summer of 1757 in a fruitless expedition against Louisburg. Meanwhile, Montcalm and white-uniformed French regulars, equipped with siege guns and accompanied by thousands of habitants and befeathered Indians, rowed down Lake George. Their cannon blasted to pieces the bastions of Fort William Henry. Despite Montcalm's orders his Indians butchered scores of prisoners.

In 1758 the British government reorganized its armed services and rushed reinforcements to America. The great war leader, William Pitt, selected Louisburg as the main goal, with Ticonderoga and Fort Duquesne as secondary objectives. The British fleet recovered control of the seas in a series of engagements and prevented the French from sending supplies to their garrisons in North America.

In contrast with the brilliant assault on Louisburg, the campaign against Ticonderoga was a fiasco. Pitt removed Loudoun just at the time when he was beginning to show enough spirit to carry through his sound strategy. The new commander, James Abercromby, committed many errors in both strategy and tactics. Most disastrous of all was his order to storm the breastworks of Ticonderoga before he had softened up the defenses with his artillery.

Colonel John Bradstreet redeemed British prestige by sweeping up the Mohawk Valley and by making a lightning raid on Fort Frontenac, the key point to French control of the interior. The French lost their command of Lake Ontario and their communications with the interior. The raid destroyed vast stores needed for the defense of Fort Duquesne, which fell to the British soon after. The Iroquois, impressed by these victories, veered to the British side. The western Indians also began to waver in their allegiance to the French.

The British won a succession of great victories in 1759. General James Wolfe made a brilliant and decisive assault on Quebec, and Lord Jeffery Amherst, who had taken over the New York command, methodically moved his forces northward toward his ultimate target, Montreal. His siege of Ticonderoga, which forced the French to blow up their fortress, was followed by his capture of Crown Point. There he set his carpenters to construct lake craft, and his new navy captured the French boats and gave him command of Lake Champlain. Winter set in before he could push north to Montreal and forced him to withdraw most of his forces to Albany.

In the summer of 1759, Amherst sent out General John Prideaux to attack Niagara. After Prideaux lost his life in the siege of Fort Niagara, Johnson took over the command and received the surrender.

The settlers of German Flats were overjoyed in 1760 to see General Amherst's army of ten thousand men passing up the Mohawk River in their bateaux. The army was traveling up the Mohawk and down the Oswego River to Lake Ontario, where hundreds of boats awaited to carry it down the St. Lawrence to Montreal. Arriving at the outskirts of the great French stronghold, Amherst met General William Haviland, who had pried the French out of their last strongholds on Lake Champlain. The capital of New France surrendered on September 8, 1760.

The victories of Amherst marked the end of French rule in North America. For New Yorkers they promised peace and security. Not only was French power eliminated, but the Iroquois were also cowed and weakened. Within a few years the various tribes ceded large tracts to the province. The New York frontier expanded rapidly after 1763 as thousands of settlers poured into the territory north of Albany and west of Schenectady.

Paradoxically, the war deepened the colonists' loyalty to the Cross of St. George at the same time it stimulated their spirit of self-confidence. No citizens of the British Empire toasted Lord Amherst more sincerely than those of New York in 1760. Both frontier farmers and the Manhattan merchants regarded the redcoats and the royal fleet as their defenders. Thousands identified their self-interest with that of the Empire which protected their property and permitted a good measure of self-government. How deep this loyalty ran was amply demonstrated during the Revolution, when New York furnished more Loyalists than any other colony.

The colonial wars hastened the growth of political maturity. The members of the Assembly took advantage of war-harassed governors and browbeat them into surrendering control over the purse. Moreover, New Yorkers became increasingly proud and confident of their own military abilities as they joined the British regulars in various campaigns. After all, it was Sir William Johnson, a Mohawk Valley man, who had won two resounding victories over the lilies of France.

One ironical result of the war was the diversion of the fur trade to Montreal. Merchants in Albany and New York protested that the furs of the western tribes were no longer reaching their stores, but in 1774 the British government encouraged the shift by granting the Ohio country to the province of Quebec.

Victory forced Britain to reorganize her imperial policies because the war had revealed serious weaknesses. New York merchants, like those of New England, had carried on trade with the French during the war. The colonial legislatures failed to vote adequate funds for defense, and they tried to escape debts by issuing paper money. In addition to these problems were those created by victory itself. Would the Board of Trade or would the colonial legislatures determine Indian policy, regulate the fur trade, and distribute land? Would colonies such as New York have to support the imperial army defending the frontier? Would British merchants and planters in the West Indies cripple the northern colonies by securing a strict enforcement of the Navigation Acts? Throughout the next decade the changing British ministries were to seek answers to these problems, and their policies antagonized many New Yorkers of almost every class and region.

Colonial Society and Culture

The City is so conveniently Situated for Trade and the Genius
of the people are so inclined to merchandise that they gener-
ally seek no other Education for their children than writing
and Arithmetick.
　　　　—JOHN SHARPE, *chaplain of the King's forces, 1713*

PERHAPS the most remarkable features of New York province were its
slow growth and the cosmopolitan character of its population. In 1775,
after over a century and a half of colonization, New York had fewer than
200,000 inhabitants. Massachusetts, Virginia, Maryland, Pennsylvania,
and Connecticut all had larger populations. The English had acquired
fewer than ten thousand subjects in their conquest of 1664. This population doubled by the turn of the century and rose to approximately
seventy-five thousand by the middle of the eighteenth century. Thereafter, population increased rapidly until the losses of the Revolution
caused a temporary interruption in New York's growth.

Most New Yorkers lived in the southeast corner of the province, and
practically all lived within a few miles of the Hudson River, Long Island
Sound, or the Atlantic Ocean. The counties along the lower Hudson were
becoming well-settled communities by 1763, as was the western tip of
Long Island, where many Dutch farmers had settled in the neighborhood
of Brooklyn. Beyond Hempstead on Long Island the distance between
farms and villages lengthened and large portions of the island were
uninhabited. The population of New York City ranged from 10 to 20 per
cent of the province's total, a higher urban proportion than in any other
colony except Rhode Island. The rest of the population was dispersed
along the Hudson River and its tributaries. During the decade after 1700,
a few hundred Palatine Germans moved beyond the tiny Dutch settlement at Schenectady and settled along the Schoharie and later the
Mohawk. William Corry in the late 1730's and George Clarke in the
following decade "seated" some Scotch-Irish families in the Cherry Valley

region, but in general the hill country—Catskill, Adirondack, or Taconic —remained unbroken wilderness at the time of the Revolution.

The potpourri of nationalities which has always characterized New York was established in 1624 with the first shipload of settlers. On board were many French-speaking Walloons as well as Dutch. The latter eventually assimilated the Walloons and most of the Huguenots in settlements such as New Paltz. But the Dutch in turn were gradually absorbed by the English stock, especially in the eighteenth century. Nevertheless, although they were outnumbered by at least four to one in 1775, the Dutch still dominated Albany and were numerous among the farming population of the Hudson Valley.

About one-half of the white population in 1775 was of English origin, although no great waves of immigrants had come from the mother country. Rather, a steady trickle of soldiers, officials, craftsmen, and servants flowed to New York. As important as England itself as a source of Anglo-Saxon blood were the big families of New England. Connecticut men brought the hallmarks of their civilization to Long Island and to a few towns on the eastern bank of the Hudson.

Representatives of practically every nationality settled in New York, although the Dutch and English were dominant in numbers and influence. The French came in small numbers, but the Huguenot contingent contributed several outstanding families, notably the De Lanceys, De Peysters, and the Jays. The Scotch-Irish were another minor element, but they were strong in Ulster and Orange counties. In addition, there were a considerable number of Germans, a good-sized Negro group, and a few Swedes and Jews.

The vanguard of the Palatine Germans, who formed the largest mass migration during the colonial period, reached London in 1708, seeking refuge from the armies of Louis XIV and the exactions of petty princes. The British government welcomed the Protestant refugees and made plans to disperse them through the empire. It sent a small band to New York and gave it land to lay out the town of Newburgh.

Governor Robert Hunter tried to colonize some twenty-five hundred Palatine Germans in New York. The Germans were to reimburse the government for the cost of passage and their maintenance by producing naval stores—tar, pitch, and tall masts—needed by Queen Anne's navy.

Robert Livingston willingly sold a part of his manor to the province for the site of this experiment and secured the contracts to supply the Palatines with flour, beer, salt pork, and tools. The undertaking ran into severe difficulties from the outset, partly because the supervising officials knew nothing about extracting pitch from virgin pine, partly because they tried to run the camps under military discipline. In 1712 Governor Hunter abandoned the project in disgust.

The disillusioned Germans scattered along the Hudson, but the largest number, in 1713, trekked through the snows to the Schoharie Valley, which they believed had been promised to them by the English. The settlers laid out seven villages, fashioned their crude farm tools, and began to plant wheat. But Albany speculators holding title to land in that region demanded that the Palatines sign leases. After seven years of controversy, the Palatine settlers gave up their resistance. Some remained in the Schoharie Valley; others took advantage of Hunter's offer of free land in the Mohawk Valley near the towns of Stone Arabia and Palatine Bridge; a group founded Herkimer (near Utica) in 1723. A considerable number, including the famous Indian agent, Conrad Weiser, migrated to Pennsylvania, which subsequently attracted most of the Germans arriving in America during the eighteenth century.

The Negro minority was large for a northern colony, fluctuating from 12 to 24 per cent of the total population at various times. Negroes were found in every county, although most of them lived in or around New York City. Most of the slaves came from the West Indies, although both the Dutch and English traders sometimes brought back slaves from the African coast.

Slavery was primarily a labor system, but it was also a method of race control. Citizens lived in fear and sometimes panic of their enslaved neighbors or servants, who were often sullen and defiant. The Negroes created a subterranean society of their own, securing rum in unlicensed taverns in trade for stolen goods. In the 1680's the Common Council of New York began to pass ordinances prohibiting the sale of liquor to slaves and forbidding any transaction of business with them. In 1702 the Assembly passed a comprehensive slave code which forbade trading with slaves and prohibited them from carrying weapons and assembling without authorization. Harsh treatment caused a group of slaves to revolt in 1712, but soldiers quickly hunted them down. After the uprising the city and provincial codes were made more severe. In 1741 white citizens became terrified at the rumor that slaves were planning to take over the city and kill the whites. Carried away by hysteria, the judges sentenced eighteen Negroes to hanging, thirteen to burning, and seventy to exile.

During the second half of the century, relations between whites and blacks improved, largely because of the arrival of many new white immigrants. Proportionately reduced in number, the blacks seemed less menacing. Furthermore, the slaves became less defiant as they adjusted to white customs through their contacts as house servants and farm laborers. Humanitarian impulses generated by the Quakers resulted in better treatment and education for the slave. A few bold spirits began to advocate emancipation, and by 1777 one-third of the legislators were willing to free the slaves. Opposition was strong, however, among conservatives, property holders, and white laborers, and local emancipation was not to come for another half century.

The English conquest deprived the Dutch Reformed church of its privileged status, but the terms of surrender guaranteed that "the Dutch here shall enjoy the liberty of their consciences in divine worship and church discipline." The Duke's Laws of 1665 (extended in 1674 to the whole province) allowed certain communities to select a Protestant clergyman and to pay his salary from taxes. Since the Dutch were the majority in most settlements, this meant a limited re-establishment of the Dutch Reformed church. As the governors were loath to press non-Dutch to pay taxes for the Dutch Reformed church, each congregation had to rely more and more upon free will offerings.

The Reformed church grew in numbers but declined in importance. Several factors more than offset its head start. The shift to English rule not only deprived the Reformed church of financial support from the Dutch West India Company but also cut off immigration from the Netherlands. The Dutch congregations therefore had to rely upon natural increase for membership except in a few communities where the Dutch absorbed smaller pockets of Walloons, Huguenots, and Germans. Scarcely had the adjustment been made to English rule when Leisler's rebellion in 1689 disrupted church congregations. The dominies (as the Dutch Reformed clergy were called), by aligning themselves with their wealthy parishioners (Van Cortlandts, Bayards, and the like), caused many people from the lower classes to drop out of the Dutch churches. Most damaging of all was the stubbornness of the clergy and the elders in clinging to the Dutch language in the church services, thus losing many of the young people. Peter Kalm noted in 1749 that the youths

begin however by degrees to change their manners and opinions chiefly indeed in the town and in its neighborhood; for the most of the young people now speak principally English, and go only to the English church; and would even take it amiss if they were called Dutchmen and not English.

The more enlightened members recognized the necessity of using English in the services and of training ministers fluent in English as well as Dutch. In 1747 the younger element demanded a provincial church assembly (coetus) in order to free themselves from the Classis (governing body) of the Reformed church at Amsterdam. Seven years later this organization assumed the powers of a classis. Meanwhile the conservatives drew together in another group protesting that God could be properly worshiped in the Dutch tongue alone. The younger leaders won an important victory in 1764, when the Dutch Church on Nassau Street in New York adopted English for its services. For a time the other

Dutch congregations held out, but by 1805 all the Dutch churches in New York City had given up the use of the old tongue. The progressive group in New York and New Jersey also demanded a college in America to train young men for the ministry. In 1770 they secured the charter for Queens (Rutgers College). The old guard agreed in 1771 to a plan of union with their rivals which John H. Livingston had worked out with the tacit approval of the Classis in Amsterdam. The long struggle over the language question and bickering over theological issues diverted the attention of the Dutch Reformed leaders from the many opportunities to convert the heathens (Indian and white) on the frontier and to win adherents among the immigrants.

Anglicanism followed in the train of English officials sent out to govern the colony. As late as 1687 Governor Dongan (himself a Roman Catholic) noted that the Church of England had only one chaplain in the province. After New York became a royal colony, the British government took steps to set up an establishment of the Church of England. The Dutch in control of the new Assembly resisted the move but reluctantly agreed in 1693 to an act "to settle and to maintain" a ministry in the city of New York and in the counties of Richmond, Westchester, and Queens. This law made no mention of either the Church of England or the Book of Common Prayer, but the governors interpreted it as establishing the Church of England in the four lower counties. In 1697 Trinity Parish, the mother church for the Episcopal communion in New York, received its charter. On its board of vestrymen was Colonel Caleb Heathcote, a merchant, member of the governor's Council, and first lord of Scarsdale Manor. Heathcote was a vigorous leader and helped to set up congregations at Westchester, Rye, New Rochelle, Eastchester, and Yonkers. The Society for the Propagation of the Gospel in Foreign Parts, which was founded in 1701 in England, assisted the expansion of the Church of England in New York and other colonies. Between 1702 and 1783 the Society sent fifty-eight men to labor in New York. Sir William Johnson, who sought to Christianize the Mohawks, was an ardent supporter of this society.

Despite official favor and social prestige, the Anglican church remained largely a "class church" of officials, rich merchants, and large landholders. At no time did it enroll as much as a tenth of the population. The Church of England began to display more life and activity after 1750. In 1754 its leaders sponsored the establishment of King's College (later Columbia University) and agitated for an American episcopate so that their young men would not have to go to England for ordination. These proposals, however, stirred up much opposition among the other denominations. The turmoil of the Revolutionary War struck a body blow at the Church of England, which naturally suffered from its close connections with the British Crown. During the Revolutionary period, in fact, the Loyalists were sometimes referred to as the Episcopal party.

The Presbyterians were the most vigorous rivals of the Anglicans and outnumbered them throughout the colonial period. The Puritans of Connecticut brought their Calvinist traditions with them when they settled on Long Island after 1640 and established towns in Westchester and Dutchess counties in the late seventeenth century. These Yankees were drifting toward a more centralized form of church government and usually organized Presbyterian churches in the new communities. Presbyterianism was strengthened not only by the steady influx of New Englanders but also by the immigration of Scots and Ulster Irish. Dutch, and later English, officials looked askance at the newcomers because of their dissenting opinions and rebellious history both in America and England.

Formalism and bickering stultified much religious activity. In addition, the shortage of clergymen made it difficult for the various denominations to reach either the artisan on Manhattan or the pioneer on the Mohawk. During the second quarter of the eighteenth century the tremendous religious movement known in Germany as "Pietism" and in England as the "Methodist Revival" erupted in America as the "Great Awakening." New York was not the center for this phenomenon, but its Calvinist churches could not help but be stirred by the exhortations of the Tennents and Theodore Freylinghuysen of New Jersey and the revivals begun by Jonathan Edwards in western Massachusetts. George Whitefield also made hundreds of converts in New York on his triumphal visits in 1740 and 1763.

These evangelists pitched the appeal of their message to the humble folk and stressed an individualistic and emotional religion. Although the revival created some divisions, it had many beneficial results for both individuals and the colonies as a whole. Some of the effects of the Great Awakening were far reaching. It deepened the spiritual life of thousands, stimulated the growth of intercolonial feeling and humanitarianism, broke down some of the barriers separating nationality groups, united the dissenting groups in opposition to the privileges of the Church of England, and encouraged a more democratic spirit.

The religious revivals attending the evangelistic Great Awakening in the middle of the eighteenth century stimulated but disrupted the Presbyterian church as well as the Dutch Reformed and other denominations. The "New Lights," as the evangelistic wing was called, were more interested in saving souls than in observing the niceties of Presbyterian polity. In 1743 they organized the Synod of New York and three years later set up the College of New Jersey (now Princeton). The conservative clergy opposed the emotional evangelism of the New Lights as leading to heresy and as destructive to church discipline. After a decade and a half of bickering the two wings of the Presbyterian church were reunited.

Relations between Anglicans and Presbyterians were often strained during the colonial period. The governors often used their powers to obstruct the activities of Presbyterians. In 1706 Governor Cornbury arrested Presbyterian minister Francis Makemie on the ground that he had failed to secure a license to preach in the province. Makemie's lawyers claimed that the instructions to the governor allowed liberty of conscience to all except Roman Catholics. Makemie's acquittal by a jury was a notable victory in the fight for religious liberty in the colonies. Several governors turned down Presbyterian requests for a church charter in New York City. Presbyterian congregations in turn refused to accept Anglican priests imposed on them by the governors. This sectarian bickering spilled over into political life. The Anglicans, along with most of the Dutch, lined up in the governor's party, especially during the period when the De Lancey family was in power. The Presbyterians rallied to their side many of the middle class, the farmers on Long Island, and the Scotch-Irish of Orange and Ulster counties. They followed the banner of the Livingston clan.

During the third quarter of the eighteenth century these factions fought a politico-religious battle of great bitterness. The sharpest skirmishing came over the chartering of King's College in 1754. Trinity Church, which was already famous for its holdings of Manhattan real estate, offered a tract to the college provided that the president would be an Anglican and that the college services follow the Book of Common Prayer. The triumvirate of famous lawyers, William Livingston, John Morin Scott, and William Smith, attacked the charter and the proposed grant of public aid, but Lieutenant Governor James de Lancey forced through the charter although the amount of public aid was cut. King's College remained firmly under Anglican direction until after the Revolution. In 1784 it became Columbia College.

The establishment of an American bishopric was another issue which stirred the Presbyterians to violent protest. In general, the Presbyterians were most active in the movement against British taxes and regulations, whereas the Anglicans tended to uphold the concept of imperial control.

The Lutherans were fourth in church membership, following the Dutch Reformed, Presbyterians, and Episcopalians. During Governor Stuyvesant's regime German settlers had called for a minister, but the Lutheran denomination did not spread upstate until the Palatine immigration after 1708. Quaker and Baptist missionaries invaded the province before 1700 and met some persecution from the authorities. Nevertheless, the Quakers established several meetinghouses on Long

Island and in the Westchester area near Quaker Hill. The Friends gave up some of their more distinctive customs with the passage of time. Only a handful of Methodists, Roman Catholics, and Jews settled in New York prior to the Revolution.

Estimates of church membership in most periods are notoriously guesswork, but Augustus Shearer's reckoning of the number of congregations is probably a good guide to the relative strength of the various denominations in 1776: Dutch Reformed, 81; Presbyterian, 61; Episcopalian, 30; Quaker, 26; Lutheran, 22; Baptist, 16; Congregationalist, 5; Associate Presbyterian, 2; Covenanter, 1; Moravian, 3; Methodist, 1; Jewish, 1.

Probably a majority of the children of colonial New York never saw the inside of a schoolhouse, and the favored minority received little more than an introduction to reading, writing, and arithmetic. Night schools remedied some of the neglect, especially for apprentices whose indentures called for basic instruction in reading and writing. In general, parents had to rely upon private agencies for the education of their children. A few towns on Long Island with Yankee traditions set up elementary schools. Other towns and the provincial government also granted some support to private schools.

The elementary school run by the Dutch Reformed church in New York City continued to instruct boys and girls in the Dutch language until 1772, when the conservative group finally permitted the use of English. Other Dutch centers, such as Albany and Kingston, also had schools run in connection with the Reformed church. The Society for the Propagation of the Gospel promoted several schools which instructed some charity scholars. A few wealthy families hired tutors, but the middle class and gentry usually sent their children to masters who set up private schools.

The handful of lads preparing for college studied with tutors or attended the few grammar schools. A scattering of young men prepared for the Dutch Reformed ministry at the University of Utrecht, and a few sons of the aristocracy attended Oxford and Cambridge. In the New World Yale was the favorite, or for many years the most convenient, college for New Yorkers. Its orthodox Calvinism irked "New Light" Presbyterians, who sent their sons to the College of New Jersey after 1746. The Anglicans also distrusted Yale. They, accordingly, pressed for the establishment of King's College. Samuel Johnson, the first president of King's College, and his successor, Dr. Myles Cooper, made this institution a center of Anglican and Loyalist sentiment.

Culturally, New York City lagged behind Boston and Philadelphia throughout the colonial period. The *American Gazetteer* of 1762 complained about New York:

Through a long shameful neglect of all the arts and sciences, the common speech is extremely corrupt, and the evidences of a bad taste, both as to thought and language, are visible in their proceedings public and private. There is nothing the ladies so generally neglect as reading and indeed all the arts for the improvement of the mind—a neglect in which the men have set the example.

In 1725 William Bradford founded the New York *Gazette,* the fifth colonial newspaper, and the first in New York. Bradford not only trained scores of printers but also published books and ran a bookshop. He sold Bibles, prayer books, textbooks, and classical works. A few printers settled in New York City and published books on various topics. Probably the first important book was Cadwallader Colden's *History of the Five Indian Nations* (1727). Almanacs were a staple item published by printers of this period.

Music, painting, and architecture followed the trends in England. In the 1750's William Tuckey, organist and concert master, gave many concerts with his choir at Trinity Church. The merchants and landlords sought out portrait painters. Probably the ablest artist before John Copley was Robert Feke of Long Island, who tried to go beyond a mere photographic reproduction of his subject. Benjamin West painted in New York City for over a decade after setting up his studio in 1758. Copley after 1771 found himself besieged by merchants eager to have their portraits painted.

The Dutch after 1664 continued to build houses characterized by gables turned toward the street and handsome roofs that curved outward, forming an overhang beyond the wall. With increasing prosperity the Dutch built larger houses, adopting such features as the two-pitched gambrel from New England and introducing Renaissance notes of décor, especially in the interior trim.

Georgian architecture, to use a loose term, gradually spread through the province, finding its fullest expression in the houses of the merchants and landlords. The merchants built square brick houses with stone trimmings and triangular, semicircular, or broken pediments above windows and doors. Other typical features were pillars framing the doorways, fanlights, and balustraded roofs or simple gables with dormer windows. Schuyler Mansion (1762) in Albany is interesting for its hipped gambrel roof and Chippendale railing. Landlords in the country frequently built their houses of wood and added small porches.

The élite followed the fashions of London in their house furnishings, clothing, and amusements. The influx of hundreds of British officers during the French and Indian War gave a stimulus to social life. The gentry consulted *The Gentleman and Cabinetmaker's Directory* put out by Thomas Chippendale to select their house furnishings. They usually imported their furniture from England, although local cabinetmakers had begun to copy the elegant rococo chairs, with their Chinese frets and friezes. The walls of drawing rooms were paneled or covered with hangings.

The style of living was luxurious enough to evoke favorable comment by visitors from England and other colonies. Householders had Negro slaves to serve as butlers, footmen, cooks, coachmen, and maids. The ladies entertained their friends on Staffordshire or Wedgwood china and brought out their collection of silver teapots and cutlery. In their clothing and personal adornment they mirrored London drawing rooms. Their gowns were made of alamode or paduasoy, and their hair was drawn up on frames. The men were equally desirous of keeping up with London fashions and they ordered their suits and wigs from agents in England.

The rich diverted themselves by riding, hunting, and boating. During the 1730's public balls and the theater became fashionable. In 1750 Thomas Kean presented *Richard III*, and three years later the Hallam Company of London gave New Yorkers their first real season of drama. David Douglas, the founder of America's first permanent theater in Philadelphia in 1766, brought his company to New York a short time later.

The life of the aristocratic minority was quite different from that of the farmers and middle class, not to mention the servants, workers, and slaves. Farm families were largely self-sufficient, the men building houses, barns, and some furniture, the women making homespun and "putting down" much meat for the winter. Servants had virtually no home life of their own and wore the castoffs of their masters. Altogether life for most New Yorkers was grim. Nevertheless gaiety and laughter burst through. Men of all classes found relaxation in groghouses and flocked to the horseraces and cockfights. The lower-class women enjoyed their pipes and gossiped on their front stoops.

Social life centered around the taverns, of which there was one for every fifty-five inhabitants of New York City in 1772. The best inns had long rooms useful for musical parties, balls, political and fraternal meetings, and dinners. The larger taverns were information centers supplying papers from other cities and entertaining travelers from other colonies. Persons engaged in various trades or activities had their favorite taverns. The aristocracy and the cliques around the governors patronized Todd's Sign of the Black Horse, while the opponents of Cosby in the 1740's met at D'Honneurs' Tavern. The lower classes found dozens of groghouses ready to serve them.

Science and experimental knowledge made widespread advances during the eighteenth century, in colonial America as well as in the Old

World. No scientists stood forth as prominently in New York as Benjamin Franklin in Philadelphia or John Winthrop at Harvard. Cadwallader Colden, amateur philosopher and historian, dabbled in Linnaean botany and medicine and corresponded regularly with Franklin and scientists in other colonies. Colden, who had studied medicine at Edinburgh, wrote many articles on medical topics and urged the establishment of a medical society in New York. Progress in medicine, however, was slow, and the only important gain was the growing practice of inoculation for the prevention of smallpox.

New York remained a cultural fief of Great Britain and western Europe throughout the colonial period. The intellectual currents flowing from Europe reached New York through various channels: newspapers, books, traders, clergymen, and amateur scholars. The rationalism of the Enlightenment won converts among the educated class, who in turn influenced the thinking of the populace through their speeches and writings. The scientific mentality and secularism, in all branches of knowledge and the arts, made their influence felt in New York as they did in all parts of Europe and America during the Enlightenment of the eighteenth century.

Landlords and Farmers in Colonial New York

And every year the Young people go from this Province and Purchase Land in the Neighboring Colonies, while much better and every way more convenient Lands lie useless to the King and Country. The reason for this is that the Grantees themselves are not, nor never were in a Capacity to improve such large Tracts and other People will not become their Vassals or Tenants for one great reason . . . leaving their native Country, was to avoid dependence on landlords, and to enjoy in fee to descend to their posterity that their children may reap the benefit of their labor and Industry.
—CADWALLADER COLDEN, 1732

NEW YORK had probably the most aristocratic social structure of all the British American colonies. Landlords in alliance with Manhattan merchants dominated the political scene, overawing royal governors and the common folk alike. In their manor houses they aped the genteel manners of their English compeers. In order to understand the political and social structure of colonial New York, one must therefore examine the land system.

The Duke of York as proprietor took title to all unclaimed lands in 1664 after recognizing the validity of titles granted by the Dutch company. His governors made a few relatively small land grants such as Fordham Manor in 1671. After James rose to the throne in 1685, Governor Dongan granted lands more liberally. In that year he confirmed the landed rights of the Van Rensselaer family, although he limited their political privileges and denied to them control over Albany. The next year he authorized Livingston Manor, which eventually included 160,000 acres in Columbia County.

The squandering of the royal domain on a prodigal scale really began

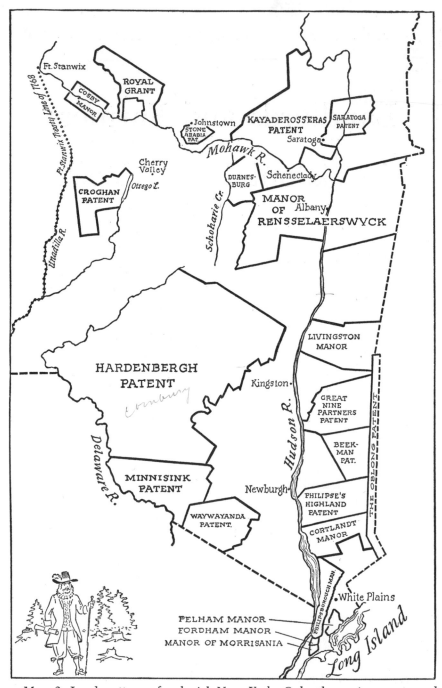

Map 3. Land pattern of colonial New York. Only the major grants and patents are shown.

with Governor Fletcher (1692–1698), who, in return for bribes, awarded huge tracts. His successor, Governor Bellomont (1698–1702), temporarily stopped this practice. He was determined to end the lavish policy which had placed three-fourths of the province in the hands of ten or eleven men. He annulled Fletcher's grants west of the Hudson, persuaded the Board of Trade to limit any one individual holding in the future to two thousand acres, and urged that all tracts pay quitrents and be improved within three years. His reforms alarmed the landlords, who blocked all moves to vacate their grants east of the Hudson River.

Governor Cornbury (1702–1708) worked hand in glove with the land jobbers, distributing as much land as all his predecessors combined. His most flagrant grant was the Hardenbergh Patent (over a million acres) which covered most of present-day Ulster, Delaware, Sullivan, and Greene counties. Furthermore, the Cornbury patents were vaguely defined, encouraging landlords to "stretch" their claims. This resulted in decades of litigation. After Cornbury's extravagance there was a comparative lull for twenty years, partly because most of the choice lands in eastern New York had passed into the hands of speculators.

During the 1730's royal officials and land jobbers turned their eyes to the Mohawk country. Governor Cosby (1732–1736) irritated speculators in New York City, Albany, and along the Hudson River by using his office to secure choice tracts for himself. Because of his highhanded tactics, his rivals supported Peter Zenger's attacks on the governor. Lieutenant Governor George Clarke (1736–1743) acquired over 100,000 acres through the use of dummy partners. Governor George Clinton (1743–1753) and Sir William Johnson, arriving in America in 1738, also built up large estates through their contacts with the Mohawks and through the use of dummy partners. Sir William owned upward of half a million acres of land in modern Herkimer, Oneida, Fulton, and Otsego counties.

Between 1763 and 1775 speculators sought tracts in the upper Susquehanna Valley and especially in the region between Lake Champlain and the Connecticut River which the charter of 1664 and the rulings of the Privy Council had assigned to New York. But fee-hungry Benning Wentworth, governor of New Hampshire, had already sold scores of townships in that region to Yankee speculators. The endless controversy over these claims will be discussed in the chapter on the American Revolution. Suffice it to say that the four governors of New York in the decade preceding the Revolution handed out over two million acres, upon which they collected a fortune in fees.

The greed of officials and the rapacity of speculators thus broke down the policy of the British government against the creation of speculative landholdings. Although competing at times for certain tracts, these two groups co-operated to circumvent troublesome provisions in the land laws: the limit of acreage to any one individual, the requirement for "seating" settlers on tracts, and the payment of quitrents. It should be noted, however, that the tendency of the colonial officials to build up their private fortunes at public expense was in keeping with the accepted practices of the time. They did not regard themselves as dishonest nor were they so regarded by the public.

The rather complicated procedure by which patents were granted favored speculators, who had access to high officials and had funds to pay the necessary fees. The grants were made by the governors, acting with the advice of their Council. To obtain a grant a speculator needed permission to buy the land from the Indians. He also needed a warrant to survey the land and a second warrant from the governor directing the attorney general to prepare a patent. Fees and fraud attended every step. Legal fees included those to the surveyor general, attorney general, the secretary, and the governor. Speculators got around the restriction of two thousand acres by using indentured servants, tenants, and soldiers as "dummy partners." After the patent was granted, the "partners" released their shares. The purchase of Indian claims was also the occasion for fraud and chicanery. In 1755 an Oneida sachem said to William Johnson as he pointed to a land shark from Albany:

Brother. You promised that you would keep this fire place clean from all filth and that no snake should come into this Council Room. That man sitting there . . . is a Devil and has stole our Lands, he takes Indians slyly by the Blanket one at a time, and when they are drunk, puts some money in their Bosoms, and perswades them to sign deeds.

The landlords with the help of lawyers and judges (themselves knee deep in land deals) also framed the real property law in such a way as to guard their interests. The most unusual development was the erection of manors. In the county of Westchester a mere six manors controlled more than half the acreage. Pelham, Fordham, and Morrisania were comparatively small manors in the southern part of the county, but Scarsdale, Cortlandt Manor, and Philipsborough Manor farther north included approximately four hundred square miles. In Albany County were Van Rensselaer and Livingston manors. Historians and lawyers are in disagreement as to whether these manors possessed genuine feudal powers. It can be argued that as a conquered country New York was not subject to parliamentary acts of 1290 and 1660 which limited the Crown's powers to grant feudal rights in England. Certainly the legal and political aspects of the manors were suspiciously similar to the traditional feudal practices. Manorial privileges included the right to hold courts leet and baron and representation in the assembly in the case of Rensselaer, Livingston, and Cortlandt manors. In actual practice the court privileges were seldom exercised, largely because town and county administrations supplanted them. The payment of a quitrent tended to confirm the feudal nature of the grants, although nonmanorial landholders also paid quitrents. The landed proprietors resisted every effort to make them pay quitrents, not only because they wished to avoid payment but also because the revenue might make the governor more independent of the financial grants of the Assembly.

Whether they enjoyed manorial rights or not, the landed proprietors exercised great economic and political power. In general, the landed class believed that the best way to develop an estate was to lease, rather than to sell, the land. Conditions for the tenants on the patents were hardly preferable to those endured by manorial tenants, although tenants on the patents usually paid cash rents, avoided clauses providing for quarter sales, services, and water reservations, and escaped the direct supervision of the landlord. Leases varied from patent to patent and even on the same estate, but in general there were two main types: the perpetual lease and the lease for life (the lifetime of the two or three persons named in the leases).

Perhaps a brief description of the manor of Rensselaerswyck will illustrate some of the features of the land system. From the days of the first patroon, the Van Rensselaer family ordinarily did not sell their lands. At first, they offered short-term leases, but in the eighteenth century they adopted "durable" leases. These "durable" leases were in reality freehold estates in perpetuity to which were attached certain restraints on alienation and the payment of perpetual rent. In the lowland townships of Albany County the leases usually called for an annual payment of ten bushels of winter wheat per hundred acres, four fat hens, and three days' service with a team of horses or oxen. Other obligations were more burdensome. When a tenant sold his farm, he had to pay one-fourth of the money to the patroon, or, in some leases, an extra year's rent. In addition, the patroon reserved the right to seize property for nonpayment of rent, the right to cut timber, and all milling and mining rights. The tenants were also responsible for all taxes.

The real property law protected and perpetuated the privileges of landlords. Acts intended to ensure security of tenure to landlords with weak titles received speedy approval by the Assembly. The law of inheritance prohibited the division of real property and required that the estate pass to the eldest son.

The land pattern and land policy of New York was a deterrent to settlement, since neither Yankees accustomed to outright ownership nor Europeans fleeing from landlord exactions wanted to become tenants in the New World. Governor Bellomont in 1700 was only anticipating the conclusions of later officials when he noted, "What man will be such a fool as to become a base tenant to Mr. Delius, Colonel Schuyler, Mr. Livingston . . . when, for crossing Hudson's River that man can for a song purchase a good freehold in the Jersey's [sic]."

Political power and social prestige awaited those who acquired large holdings. The New York aristocracy, using the English nobility for their models, reproduced a genteel society along the banks of the Hudson in which family pride, Anglicanism, and conservative principles were judiciously fused. Generations of intermarriage created a tightly knit clique with an intense class loyalty. The Schuylers, to take but one family, were related to the Van Cortlandts, Van Rensselaers, Livingstons, Verplancks, Bayards, De Peysters, De Lanceys, Beekmans—all landholding as well as commercial families. The provincial aristocracy also had ties with prominent families in other colonies and in Britain. For example, William Johnson's uncle, Sir Peter Warren, married Susan de Lancey, who was the sister of Lieutenant Governor James de Lancey. William Johnson's son, John, married a daughter of Councilor John Watts, himself married to a De Lancey.

Although landlords were admittedly unscrupulous both in acquiring tracts and protecting their holdings, a sense of public responsibility accompanied their drive for power, and a spirit of paternalism softened their relations with the lower classes. The landed families provided the bulk of local and provincial officials, and their sons served as officers in the militia. They supported charitable organizations and gave their aid to the Anglican church and King's College. Probably no group of Negro household servants in America was treated more kindly than those serving the landed families of New York.

The aristocracy's hearty dislike of New England contrasted with its emulation of the English nobility. Since most of them belonged to the Church of England, they hated "dissenters" not only because of Cromwell and the Civil War in England but also because the Calvinists in both New England and New York were fighting an American episcopate. As officials they disliked the Yankee's challenges of New York's claims along its eastern border and especially in the Vermont area. As landholders they feared the spread of "leveling" ideas by Yankee farmers who contested land titles and led antirent wars. As true monarchists they looked askance at the republican principles which had made great strides in New England. As a proud caste they resented the cultural arrogance of New Englanders such as John Adams, who claimed there was not a cultured man in New York. No one has better expressed this fear and contempt for New England than Lewis Morris, Jr., did in his will, dated 1760. Morris directed that his son Gouverneur never be sent to Connecticut for his education, lest he should imbibe in his youth that low craft and cunning so incident to the People of that Colony which is so interwoven in their Constitutions that all their art cannot disguise it from the World, though many of them under the sanctified garb of Religion, have endeavored to impose themselves on the World for honest men.

The tenant farmers, who numbered more than five thousand by the beginning of the Revolution, resented their inferior status, and in the years between 1751 and 1766 they revolted against their wealthy landlords. First to rebel were the tenants on Livingston Manor, who made use of Indian claims and enlisted the help of Massachusetts speculators. A miniature war broke out as posses from Massachusetts raided the Livingston ironworks at Ancram and captured several workmen. In reprisal Robert Livingston armed scores of men to evict squatters. The "infection" of revolt spread to Van Rensselaer Manor and southward to the great estates in Dutchess and Westchester counties.

The issue was soon brought to court. The judiciary, dominated by wealthy landowners and their friends, made short shrift of the Indian land claims. Defeated in the courts, the tenants in November 1765 rose up in open rebellion to win greater security of tenure and to restore dispossessed tenants. For a short time in April 1766 citizens of New York City feared an invasion of "Westchestermen" under the banner of William Prendergast. General Thomas Gage called forth the militia to strengthen his regular troops, and Governor Henry Moore sent out the redcoats to hunt down Prendergast. The antirent leader was cornered near Quaker Hill and tried for treason. He was convicted, which meant death by hanging. The judges, however, recommended clemency, partly because of the devotion of Mehitabel Prendergast, who begged that her husband be saved from the gallows.

Although active resistance died away, the tenants remained bitter and restless. They defeated candidates put forward by the Livingston family. Ironically enough, some of the main instigators of the riots against the Stamp Act, such as John Morin Scott and William Smith, Jr., were active in suppressing the antirenters in 1766 because of the attack on property rights. As a result, many tenants during the Revolution swung over to the Tory side because the Van Rensselaer and Livingston families joined the Patriots. Other disgruntled tenants left their homes to take up land in the New Hampshire grants (now Vermont). Antirentism was to be a political issue for many years.

Scarcely had the great rebellion of 1766 been put down than the Yankee speculators and farmers in the New Hampshire grants began their famous campaign against the land claims of New York's citizens. Since 1741 Benning Wentworth, governor of New Hampshire, had been insisting that the western boundary of New Hampshire extended to within twenty miles of the Hudson River. Proceeding on this assumption, he began to grant titles to lands lying west of the Connecticut River. By 1764 there were 131 townships in what later became the Vermont region, in which Wentworth and his friends set aside millions of acres for themselves.

The controversy over Vermont was not only a contest between rival land speculators and a clash between Yankees and Yorkers but it was also a fascinating chapter in the struggle between the colonies and Great Britain. The Allen brothers, who defied the authority of New York and its courts, organized their followers into a militia, which in 1775 seized Fort Ticonderoga in one of the first actions of the Revolutionary War. (Additional details in this story will be found on page 122.)

Agriculture was the mainstay of the colonial economy. It directly supported 80 per cent of the population. Furthermore, the merchants in the cities and their employees made most of their livelihood handling the products of farm and forest and supplying farmers with imports. The small farm was the basic unit even on the large tracts owned by the aristocracy. Tenant-operated farms were quite similar in size to those owned by the independent farmers, who were by far the most numerous element of the agricultural population.

The condition of agriculture was very low. The principles of rotation and the use of fertilizers were universally ignored. The abundance of land and the scarcity of labor made intensive cultivation pointless. An almost inevitable corollary was the custom of cropping the land until it was exhausted. Unfortunately, farm implements were so primitive that they did not permit farmers to make sufficient economies in the amount of labor to compensate them for their extensive cultivation. As a result they benefited but slightly from the low cost of land. The detailed description of crops, implements, and farm practices given in the chapter on agriculture between 1783 and 1825 will serve as well for the colonial period, since few changes took place in agricultural methods before 1800.

New York and Pennsylvania were known as "bread colonies" because of their important exports of wheat and flour. As early as 1678 Governor Andros noted wheat exports of sixty thousand bushels, as well as considerable amounts of peas, beef, pork, furs, horses, and lumber. The sharp contest between the New York City and the upstate millers over the right to bolt export flour illustrates the importance that wheat culture had attained by the last decade of the seventeenth century. Throughout the eighteenth century wheat continued to be the most important export of New York.

Lumbering was also an important activity of the countryside. Most farmers were perforce lumbermen. Clearing the land was one of their first tasks. Furthermore, each farmer needed wood for his home, barns, fences, and tools. From an early date some mills began to supply lumber for the West Indian trade. Anne Grant, who as a girl lived near Still-water a few years before the Revolution, recorded her memories of her early years. She recalled, "The settlers . . . set up saw-mills on every stream, for the purpose of turning to account the fine timber which they cleared in great quantities off the new lands. The planks they drew in sledges to the side of the great river."

In 1775, after more than 150 years of colonization, most of the New York countryside remained wilderness. Only a handful of settlers had moved more than a few miles from the seashore or the Hudson-Mohawk Rivers. During the next fifty years the borders of the state were fixed, the land transferred to private hands, and millions of acres brought under cultivation.

O mit

Traders and Artisans

*The Markets for your Flour (the present staple of the Province)
are already so much overdone, by the great Importations that
are made to them, from this and other Northern Colonies,
that unless some Manufactures be set on Foot, that are wanted
in Great-Britain, or do not interfere with theirs, there will be
no Way to imploy the People to any Advantage.*
—GEORGE CLARKE, *1736*

COMMERCE was the outstanding feature of the provincial economy apart from agriculture, which occupied the energies of the great majority of inhabitants. The English reinforced the emphasis on trading begun by the Dutch. Businessmen were quick to see and to exploit the advantages of New York port: its fine harbor, central location, and magnificent approaches. Moreover, the agricultural development of the Hudson Valley provided a good deal of produce for traders. The colonial historian, William Smith, noted the exceptional position of the farmers along the Hudson:

There is scarce a farmer in the province that cannot transport the fruits of a year's labour from the best farms in three days, at a proper season, to some convenient landing, where the market will be to his satisfaction, and all the wants from the market cheaply supplied.

A rapid survey of shifts in the price level and an analysis of the major trends in economic development will provide a frame of reference for analyzing the mercantile and labor conditions of colonial New York.

The upsurge in wheat exports during the 1680's slowed down after 1694, when the legislature repealed the monopoly on bolting flour for export given New York City and Albany during the previous decade. The rapid deterioration of New York flour when it was no longer subject to inspection caused buyers in the West Indies to prefer other sources. Governor Fletcher offset this loss to some extent by winking at the illegal trade with the pirates of Madagascar, but Governor Bellomont sternly forbade this traffic. Commodity prices, which fell from 1700 to 1708, remained depressed until an upward movement began in 1713. Shipowners suffered from the attacks of French privateers and the closing of the Spanish West Indian ports during the War of the Spanish Succession. In addition, their Boston rivals undercut them by accepting a lower profit margin and by manipulating the currency.

Better times returned after 1713. The provincial government protected artisans by imposing duties on imports, and it encouraged shipbuilding by requiring that goods indirectly imported from England should bear customs higher than if directly imported by New York merchants. This action was a slap at New England shipowners.

During the 1720's a moderate decline in the price of export commodities and breadstuffs took place. An even sharper drop in the next decade brought distress to the farmers. The continuation of imports from Europe, when receipts from exports to the West Indies and New England were dwindling, created a heavy indebtedness. To add to their difficulties, merchants and shipowners faced stiff competition from foreign carriers, especially those operating out of Bermuda. Conditions were so bad in 1733 that Cornelius Van Horne queried:

> Pray tell me the cause of trade being so dead,
> Why shops are shut up, goods and owners all fled,
> And industrious families cannot get bread?

The turn came in 1740, and for the next two decades New York enjoyed boom times. Farm prices rose and exports expanded, largely because the French and Spanish West Indies were demanding more foodstuffs. Imports showed a comparable rise, particularly in the war years between 1756 and 1761. The outbreak of the French and Indian War did not ruin provincial trade, since New York ships continued to trade with the French through neutral islands and under flags of truce. Furthermore, privateering became an important occupation and brought in much ready cash.

From a high point in 1759 business gradually declined and fell off more sharply after the signing of the peace in 1763. The British government intensified the depression by tightening the Navigation Acts and imposing new taxes such as the Stamp Tax. Prosperity returned in 1770, but business fluctuated wildly as relations with England worsened.

The commerce of New York during the colonial period consisted chiefly of the exchange of commodities (mainly foodstuffs) for manufactures and semitropical products. Furs remained an important export throughout the period, although wheat soon surpassed furs in value. (Some of the details of the fur trade are discussed in Chapter 5.) The export of breadstuffs became so important by 1686 that New York added the flour barrel to the official seal of the province. During the next century New York ranked second only to Pennsylvania as an exporter of cereals. The province also packed beef and pork for export and shipped out flax, hemp, and forest products. Boards, staves, and shingles were carried mainly to the West Indies, but potash and pearlashes (purified potash) flowed to England in substantial amounts after 1763.

Aside from potash, Great Britain did not take many of New York's products except for some furs, flaxseed, and iron. These exports, however, earned but a fraction of the exchange needed to pay for the manufactured goods bought in England. So the merchants of Manhattan turned to the West Indies for customers who could pay gold or provide products acceptable in England. The islands between the Bahamas and Dutch Guiana produced sugar, cotton, spices, and logwood, which were purchased by New York shippers and re-exported to Britain. Jamaica furnished the main market, with Curaçao and Honduras next in importance. The Latin countries of Europe also took much flour, salt fish, and rice from America. Fish from New England and rice from South Carolina were acquired by New Yorkers in the extensive coastal trade. A few venturesome traders sought profits in the African ivory and slave trade.

New York's imports covered the whole range of manufactured goods as well as some raw materials and semitropical foods. Among the principal items were clothing, furniture, hardware, tea, spices, gunpowder, paints, drugs, and coal. As the aristocracy gained affluence, luxury items became an important addition to the list of imports.

The conduct of business in the provincial town of New York, with some twenty thousand people, was quite different, of course, from that of the modern city. In 1775 the Chamber of Commerce, which enrolled practically all the merchants, had only one hundred members. All the mercantile houses of Manhattan in 1750 could not have stocked either Macy's or Gimbels. The larger houses had several clerks and were usually directed by two or more partners. Two of the wealthiest and most important merchants, Philip Livingston and Robert Murray, however, had no partners. Businessmen often took shares in large undertakings, but before 1765 they did not use the corporate form. Shopkeepers ran their establishments with the help of the family and one or two servants.

Most merchants in New York sold goods at both wholesale and retail, although a specialized group of retailers was emerging. Certain houses were beginning to stress a particular line of goods, but most houses carried a little of everything on their shelves. Gerardus Duyckinck, for example, called his establishment "The Universal Store or the Medley of Goods." Handlers of manufactured imports—such as ironmongers, tobacconists, and apothecaries—and artisan shopkeepers—such as silversmiths, cutlers, and cabinetmakers—made the greatest strides toward specialization.

Merchants performed a wide variety of functions: importing, shipping, exporting, insuring, banking, and serving as agents. Since they could not use cable, telegraph, and radio, they had to rely upon shipmasters or resident agents in foreign ports to sell their goods and to buy return cargoes. The agent watched the local markets and advised the American merchant what goods could be sold at a profit. After he had made a sale, the agent remitted specie or bills of exchange or sent back cargo according to instructions. He also arranged for proper shipment, including provision for insurance. Since transactions took months and even years to complete, merchants selected their agents with care in order to avoid misunderstandings and to forestall dishonesty. Quite often they dispatched their sons or relatives to foreign stations. Agents served as bankers, honoring bills of exchange and collecting debts. For their troubles, they received commissions varying according to the service performed. The usual commission for selling goods overseas was 5 per cent.

Businessmen suffered from a lack of commercial banks and from an unstable currency. Barter took the place of money in the countryside, and Manhattan merchants sometimes advertised they would receive "country pay." Unfortunately the situation was further complicated by the adverse balance of trade with Great Britain, which drained off the gold and silver earned in the West Indies. Foreign coins circulated freely in New York but they were often debased and clipped. The province of New York was forced to issue paper money in 1709 to finance the expedition against Canada. A half century later more bills of credit were used to pay for military supplies during the French and Indian War. The Assembly was reasonably successful in maintaining the value of paper currency by providing for early redemption. When the British government banned the issue of paper money by the colonies in 1764, New York merchants were angered and alarmed, feeling there was not enough specie available for the needs of business.

Mercantilism permeated the thinking of British statesmen and provincial officials throughout the colonial period. That colonies existed for the benefit of the mother country and that government should regulate commerce and industry were principles seldom challenged before Adam Smith published his *Wealth of Nations* in 1776. The businessmen of New York conducted their affairs in a framework of imperial, provincial, and municipal regulations.

The system of regulations and duties known as the Acts of Trade and Navigation were more of a threat than a burden to New York before 1763. Shipmasters boldly evaded the Molasses Act of 1733, which prohibited the colonies from trading with the foreign West Indies. They naturally preferred to sell their flour, meat, and lumber to the Spanish and French planters who paid higher prices than the British planters on Jamaica and at the same time provided sugar, molasses, and coffee at lower prices. In fact, many officials in New York and in London winked at this illegal trade, since New Yorkers were thus able to earn gold and acquire semitropical products helpful in paying for English manufactures.

The undercover trade with Holland in tea, canvas, gunpowder, and arms was more damaging to imperial interests. In 1756 Governor Hardy charged that the smuggling of Dutch goods had made it unprofitable to import certain British manufactures. During the Seven Years' War royal officials complained that citizens of New York were trading with the enemy. Merchants would send ships to Spanish Hispaniola, where they exchanged goods with the French. False clearance papers, flags of truce, and outright bribery were some of the devices used to disguise illegal activities. The illicit trade with Holland continued despite the efforts at enforcement.

To enforce the Navigation Acts was not easy. The hundreds of inlets and bays up and down the coast were ideal havens for small ships smuggling contraband. The handful of officials were unable to watch the approaches to New York, especially since they had no boats to patrol Long Island Sound or to watch the ships off Sandy Hook. These poorly paid officials were open to bribes. Furthermore, juries composed of merchants refused to convict smugglers, and judges, linked by marriage and friendship to the mercantile class, tended to interpret cases in favor of natives.

The New York Assembly as well as the British government regulated trade in many ways. It sought to encourage home industry and to stimulate local shipping. For example, it laid a double duty on goods imported from colonies when such goods were not produced in those colonies. At times it supervised the packing of flour and meat for local and overseas consumption in order to protect consumers and to preserve the reputation of New York's products in the West Indies. In 1679 Governor Andros and his Council decreed that no flour be bolted or packed for export except in New York City, where mills could be inspected. Millers in the countryside ignored this prohibition and pushed through its repeal in 1694. Subsequently the quality of flour declined so much that it brought less money than Pennsylvania flour. Merchants between 1725 and 1750 kept urging the government to inspect flour sold for export. As a result, the Assembly finally required the branding of all flour casks and the registration of brand marks of bakers with the clerk of the municipal court. It insisted upon inspection of flour and imposed a system of penalties for false branding. A similar act provided for the inspection of meat. These laws were only moderately successful, and the reputation of New York flour remained low in the West Indies.

The cities of New York and Albany supervised the sale of foodstuffs for local consumption. The Common Council of New York continued the medieval practice of an assize of victuals fixing the quality, size, and price of bread in accordance with the price of flour. Inspectors fined bakers who violated the law. The sharp rise in prices after 1750 squeezed the citizenry, who accused the butchers of unfair prices. This agitation caused the Common Council to fix the price of meat and other provisions. Enraged at this action, some farmers set up a storehouse at Tarrytown and proposed to tax every vessel carrying supplies to the city. The city officials yielded and raised the price set for beef and made other concessions.

The Common Council also regulated the public markets. The first market in New York City was set up in 1677 and was held every Saturday. In 1731 city officials designated every day, except Sunday, as a market day from sunrise to sunset. It established markets on the water front, where goods could be easily landed. In order to give housewives the advantage, hucksters and retailers were not permitted to attend the market before noon. The regulations prohibited such practices as trying to secure a monopoly of the goods offered for sale. Sellers of rotten meat and "stale victuall" were subjected to penalties.

The charters of New York City and Albany did not allow anyone to keep shop or to sell goods at retail, or to pursue any handicraft or trade within the town unless he were granted the "freedom of the city." In the decade before the Revolution this grant cost five pounds for a merchant and twenty shillings for a craftsman. Peddlers were not permitted to sell their goods in Albany or New York City. Both the provincial and municipal authorities required vendors of liquor to take out licenses.

Many private groups and public authorities held the free market in low esteem and did their best to circumvent it. Unquestionably some businessmen managed to fix prices to their own advantage and to restrict competition. The frequent outcry against monopoly was a sign of the success of their activities.

While merchants invested their surplus capital in a variety of enterprises, real estate was the favorite outlet. Most merchants owned their own homes and stores. The more successful went on to buy wharfs, country homes, and backcountry lands. The merchant princes were often tied to the landed aristocracy by marriage and by interest.

Personal loans in the form of "bonds" or notes were the most common investments for the merchants. Those eager to gamble underwrote marine insurance and bought lottery tickets.

Manufacturing developed slowly in New York because of the scarcity of skilled labor, the lack of banking facilities, mercantile regulations imposed by Britain, and the availability of cheap English goods. Moreover, merchants preferred to invest their capital in raw lands and shipping ventures rather than to finance manufacturing.

Such manufacturing as existed was closely associated with the processing of foodstuffs and lumber. Sawmills and gristmills accompanied the northward and westward push of settlers. Sugar refining, beginning as early as 1689, centered in New York City. Brewing and distilling used up local grain products and furnished easily transported products. Shipbuilding was important, although New York's industry lagged behind that of Massachusetts. The earliest and the most advanced ironworks was operated by the Livingston family at Ancram. During the 1760's entrepreneurs set up several furnaces in New York and New Jersey.

Craftsmen supplied most of the needs of their neighbors. Perhaps the best way to see the range of their activities is to list the men admitted to the freedom of New York City between 1694 and 1706, when the city had about 5,000 inhabitants. There were 63 merchants, 51 cordwainers (shoemakers), 50 mariners, 46 carpenters, 33 bakers, 25 victualers, 24 bricklayers, 23 blacksmiths, 19 carters, 16 yeomen, 15 tailors, 14 butchers, 12 coopers, 12 surgeons, 11 joiners, 10 bolters of flour, 9 weavers, 9 silversmiths, 9 shipwrights, 8 feltmakers, 7 ship carpenters, 7 turners, 7 schoolmasters, 7 masons, 6 tallow chandlers, 5 wigmakers, 4 shopkeepers, 4 brewers, 3 vintners, 3 porters, 3 pot makers, 3 boatmen, 3 sailmakers, 3 saddlers, 3 barbers, 2 gunners, 2 carriers, 2 confectioners, 2 hatters, 2 laborers (*freeman* laborers), 2 pewterers, 2 limners, 2 ropemakers, 2 wheelwrights, 2 wool combers, 2 blockmakers, and one each of a host of trades from cutler to seamstress. The majority of nonfarm workers were artisans and lived in the two chartered cities of New York and Albany.

The English labor system of the sixteenth and seventeenth centuries was carried to New York. But the labor institutions and practices which had developed in the fixed economy and settled community of medieval England were necessarily modified in the sparsely settled and rapidly expanding settlement on the Hudson River. One must therefore look behind the forms and names in order to discern the changes taking place. The presence of slavery and the absence of guilds were two circumstances in New York contrasting most sharply with those in Britain.

There were four categories of labor: free labor, apprenticeship, indentured servitude, and slavery. In general, the trend was toward free labor. Apprenticeship, indentured servitude, and slavery gradually lost ground because New Yorkers found free labor more efficient, reliable, and flexible.

Free labor included most of those who were skilled in some trade or handicraft. These artisans usually worked by themselves for outsiders. Unlike their European counterparts, they had to observe few regulations since there were no guilds to fix hours and wages, to set standards, or to prescribe the training for apprentices. In the countryside handicraftsmen were less common. Some, however, set up their shops at the crossroads, and others traveled from farm to farm. The farmers themselves tried to do most of their own work, but from time to time they had to hire cobblers and tailors, and they patronized blacksmiths and sawmill and gristmill operators.

An apprenticeship required a boy or girl to serve a master or mistress for a term of years (usually seven). The master was required to teach the apprentice a trade and to provide food and shelter. He assumed the role of parent, but his power to punish was limited by law. The system of apprenticeship retained some popularity in the countryside, but it gradually declined in New York City, where the influx of trained craftsmen made it unnecessary to train apprentices.

Indentured servants were less numerous and less important in New York than in Pennsylvania and the Southern colonies. An indentured servant was usually a destitute person who agreed to work for a term of years in exchange for passage to America. Sometimes the British government "transported" minor criminals to America as indentured servants, but few of this type came to New York. Employers preferred slaves to indentured servants, who often ran away and proved recalcitrant. Those needing temporary workers preferred to hire free laborers or the slaves of neighbors.

Negro slaves performed most unskilled and menial tasks. Many substantial farmers had one or two slaves, and the aristocracy used Negroes as household servants. Owners preferred docile and "broken" slaves from the West Indies to the "wild" slaves from Africa. As the number of Negroes increased, a slave code evolved which defined the limits of slavery as a labor system. Other parts of the code dealt with the Negroes as a potentially dangerous racial minority. The laws protected the owner's property and gave him the power to punish unruly slaves. Slavery, however, was losing ground during the last half of the eighteenth century. People found it generally cheaper to hire free laborers than to maintain slaves during periods of idleness as well as usefulness.

The traders and workers of colonial New York, though few in number, were influential in establishing the foundations of the commercial and manufacturing supremacy of the Empire State. The merchants were particularly important in creating a seaport of international significance and in providing much of the leadership for the home-rule movement. The contributions of artisans were less impressive, but who will deny their achievement in demonstrating the greater efficiency and dignity of free labor over bound and slave labor? Not until the next century were the merchants and craftsmen ready to supply the capital, leadership, skill, and brawn which created the industrial might of New York.

Severing the Ties of Empire,

1763-1776

Pro Patria
The first Man that either distributes or makes use of Stampt Pa-
per, let him take Care of his House, Person, & Effects.
Vox Populi;
We dare.
—*Warning posted by antistamp faction, 1765*

IF A seer had prophesied in 1763 that in less than a decade and a half New York would declare its independence, establish a state government, and fight a decisive war with Great Britain, he would have been laughed out of the colony. For almost a century the Union Jack had waved over this outpost of empire. New Yorkers were proud to call themselves British subjects; they were proud of their rights as Englishmen; they were proud of the Empire; it was theirs; and they had fought, bled, and died to extend its authority over vast areas of the New World.

Imperial patriotism was strong among all classes, but nowhere was it stronger than among the wealthy landlords and merchants who later were to furnish the leadership in the struggle for independence. These men saw themselves in the role of English gentlemen and identified themselves with their counterparts on the other side of the Atlantic. Indeed, a large portion of the inhabitants of the state could trace their ancestry to the British Isles. Binding the merchants still more closely to England was the fact that the governmental agencies for administering British North America were concentrated in New York, a circumstance which inflated the colonists' pride and fattened their money belts.

Profit was an important factor in imperial relations. The Empire offered excellent trading opportunities, and the British fleet gave protection to colonial shipping on the high seas. Security was an important matter to New Yorkers in the years prior to the 1760's because in those days the Dutch, Spanish, and especially the French were rivals of the British in the establishment of empire. By 1763 the fear of conquest was greatly reduced, however, because New York and her sister colonies had grown strong enough to discourage sea-borne invasion and because the French had been driven from Canada.

The conquest of New France by England and the colonies held great promise for New York. The French had been very active in the Indian trade, and it was anticipated that a large share of this business would be captured by New Yorkers. New Yorkers hoped that since the French had encouraged the Indians to resist white settlement on Indian lands, the elimination of French support would weaken Indian power and allow the frontier to expand westward with greater rapidity.

These hopes soon were dashed. The imperial government, presumably believing that the independent action of the American colonies could never result in a consistent Indian policy, issued the Proclamation of 1763. This fiat provided for strict control of the Indian trade and prohibited the acquisition of Indian lands west of the Allegheny watershed. Several groups were immediately affected by the edict: Indian traders, merchants who supplied them, and frontier settlers. More important in the light of future events was the anger of speculators who had hoped to reap profits from the sale of Indian lands. These wealthy men more often than not were members of the colonial aristocracy, and they were a politically powerful group. Although no serious disturbances grew out of the Proclamation of 1763 and although the Treaty of Fort Stanwix negotiated with the Iroquois five years later extended the area open to settlement, the imperial restrictions on Indian trade and frontier settlement helped to change the temper of the people.

In 1764 the celebrated case of *Forsey* v. *Cunningham* further quickened public feeling. In the summer of the preceding year Waddel Cunningham had assaulted Thomas Forsey on the streets of New York City with a sword hidden under a cloak. In the civil suit which followed, a jury awarded Forsey £1,500. Cunningham appealed this verdict to the governor and Council. When Acting Governor Cadwallader Colden agreed to review the case, Chief Justice Daniel Horsmanden declared that English common law made a jury verdict sacred and that an appeal could not be made. Horsmanden received the support of a great majority of the members of the legal profession, including John Morin Scott and William Livingston, two of the most important lawyers in the province, who were destined to play leading roles in the struggle for independence. The provincial Council ruled against Colden and refused to review the case, a position upheld by the British government. The Assembly reacted to the Forsey case by passing a resolution reaffirming the right of trial by jury and by reprimanding the governor. The Assembly by this time had grown from what amounted to an advisory council to a strong lawmaking body which claimed powers similar to those of the British House of Commons, and in it was lodged much of the opposition to imperial control.

Most of the difficulties between the colony and the mother country had a theoretical basis in their conflicting hypotheses concerning the authority to tax. The colonists held that the British Parliament had no right to levy taxes on Americans except for the purpose of controlling imperial trade. Parliament, on the other hand, claimed the power to tax the colonists for any purpose and after 1763 enacted a group of laws which were frankly designed to raise revenue rather than to control trade. Colonial reaction grew increasingly violent.

In 1764 Parliament passed the Sugar Act to replace the Molasses Act of 1733. The new law reduced the duty on foreign molasses from sixpence to threepence per gallon, prohibited the importation of all rum except that of British distillation, which was admitted without charge, and placed new taxes on other products from the foreign West Indies. On the surface the Sugar Act was more liberal than the Molasses Act, but the British government had never effectively enforced the provisions of the latter. The determined effort to enforce the Sugar Act by giving customs officials more authority and by enlarging the powers of the admiralty courts alarmed the merchants, who feared the new law would hamper the domestic production of rum and seriously curtail trade with West Indian islands which were under French or Spanish rule. These worries were aggravated by the fact that the colony was suffering a depression following the properous times of the French and Indian War.

Reaction to the Sugar Act was rapid. Even before April 6, 1764, when news reached the colony that the act had become a law, New York merchants sent a protest to the Board of Trade. In October the provincial Assembly sent memorials to the King, Lords, and Commons denying the right of Parliament to tax New Yorkers without their consent. Prominent citizens not only suggested that the colony should refuse to import British goods but organized societies to stimulate local manufacturing and thus reduce colonial dependence on Great Britain. Relations were further strained when Lord Grenville, Chancellor of the Exchequer, estimated that it cost about £360,000 per year to maintain troops in America for defense and suggested that the colonies ought to bear one-third of the expense. He calculated that the Sugar Act would net about £45,000, and the American legislatures were invited to suggest a plan which would provide an additional £75,000 to make up the quota. When the colonists took no action, Parliament passed the Stamp Act, which was to become effective November 1, 1765. News that the law had passed reached New York on April 11 and set off a steadily increasing roar of protest.

Businessmen, who were still suffering from the economic depression, became excited at the prospect of new imposts. The law required that tax stamps should be placed on news journals, legal documents, and official papers, thus directly affecting lawyers and printers, the two most vocal groups in the province. Since there could be no question that the purpose of the Stamp Act was not to control trade but solely to obtain revenue, the colonists had excellent technical grounds for resistance on the basis that Parliament had no authority to pass the law. So bitter was the reaction that for the first time there appeared some sentiment for independence. The following quotation taken from an article published June 6, 1765, in *The New-York Gazette; or, The Weekly Post-Boy* illustrates the point. It is believed to have been written by John Morin Scott.

If then the Interest of the Mother Country and her Colonies cannot be made to coincide (which I verily believe they may) if the same Constitution may not take Place in both, (as it certainly ought to do) if the Welfare of the Mother Country, necessarily requires a Sacrifice of the most valuable natural Rights of the Colonies Their Right of making their own Laws and Disposing of their own Property by the Representatives of their own choosing;—if such really is the Case between Great-Britain and her Colonies, then the Connection between them ought to cease.

Between the time New Yorkers learned that the law had been enacted and the date it took effect, they had over six months in which to organize resistance. So well did they organize that the Stamp Act was never enforced within the colony. On July 1 it was learned that James McEvers, a merchant, had been appointed stamp collector for New York City. McEvers resigned his commission on August 30 because he feared bodily harm at the hands of the opponents of the law. In response to a circular letter dispatched by the General Court of Massachusetts, nine colonies sent delegates to the Stamp Act Congress, which sat in New York City October 7 to 25. This assembly denounced the Stamp Act in ringing words, to the delight of the local citizens.

During the hectic month of October 1765, the Sons of Liberty, an ultra-radical organization which advocated the use of force to resist Parliament, made its initial appearance in New York. The active leaders of this organization apparently were John Lamb, Isaac Sears, and Joseph Allicocke, who, unquestionably, were aided and abetted by other men of wealth. The rank and file was made up largely of laborers, artisans, and small shopkeepers. With the advent of the Liberty Boys there appeared a hint of violence to enforce the suggestions and proclamations of radical leaders. On October 23 the first cargo of stamps arrived. Rioting threatened both ship and cargo until the stamps were removed to a warship, from whence they were later taken to a British fortress. On the twenty-eighth the leading merchants, under the goading of the Sons of Liberty, signed an agreement to buy no more European goods until the Stamp Act was repealed. Meanwhile extremists were urging people to carry on their business without the use of stamps.

The events of November 1, the day the law was to become effective, indicated that the antistamp faction had done its work well. The drawn shutters of shops, the flags flying at half-mast, and the tolling church bells registered public mourning at the death of American liberties. Some newspapers carried the gruesome emblem of a skull in the place where the stamp was supposed to be affixed. But New Yorkers did more than lament. They issued fiery pamphlets denouncing the tax, and in the evening they congregated by the thousands before Fort George, in which Acting Governor Colden had stored the stamps. Angry crowds stoned British troops, hung Colden in effigy, and, at Bowling Green, seized and burned his coach.

By November 5 the acting governor realized the gravity of the situation and delivered the stamps to the mayor of New York City with a promise that he would make no effort to enforce the law. Sir Henry Moore, who arrived later in the month to replace Colden, quickly reached the same conclusion. On March 20, 1766, the Stamp Act was repealed, largely because American boycotts injured the business of British merchants. At the same time the threepence duty on foreign molasses was removed and a one-penny tax was placed on all molasses, British and foreign.

New Yorkers celebrated this victory with enthusiasm, even though it had not been achieved without cost. The boycott had curtailed business, which in turn had caused the price of agricultural products to tumble. Governor Moore and Sir William Johnson reported that unrest over the Stamp Act did not seriously affect rural areas until early in 1766. Actually the agricultural areas were not so concerned about the stamp tax as they were with the oppressive leasehold system. Falling farm prices prodded them to rebel, while the riotous activities of the lower classes of city dwellers inspired hope for urban support.

As we have seen, tenant unrest was by no means uncommon during the first half of the eighteenth century. In the 1760's the struggle broke out anew in Philipse Highland Patent, an estate of some 200,000 acres in Dutchess County. The Wappinger Indians led by their chief Daniel Nimham claimed ownership of all but a small section of this patent on the ground that the Indian title had not been extinguished. Many tenants seeing an opportunity to escape semifeudal obligations to the Philipse patentees bought title or accepted leaseholds on much more favorable terms from the natives. The Stockbridge Indians, noting the success of their Wappinger cousins, began to make similar claims against lands held by the Livingstons and Van Rensselaers. This was enough to unite the great landlords to fight the claims of the Wappingers.

The issue was soon brought to court. The judiciary, dominated by wealthy landowners and their friends, did not give the Indians a fair chance to defend their titles. But the unrest was not so easily quieted, and in April 1765 the Mohicans advanced a claim to a large portion of the Van Rensselaer estate. By November of that year the tenants in Dutchess County led by William Prendergast and others were in open rebellion to win greater security of tenure and lower rents. The revolt of the small farmer grew steadily, and by the spring of 1766 many sections of rural New York were affected. The embattled tenants confidently expected support from the Sons of Liberty, but it was not forthcoming because the wealthy citizens who controlled the Liberty Boys had no sympathy for this agrarian attack on the rights of property. Worse still, the colonial government which had dealt cautiously with the Stamp Act rioters did not hesitate to use force to crush the disaffected tenants.

The formidable opposition of the colonial government and the wealthy classes was too much for the rebellious farmers. The revolt was defeated quickly and its principal leaders were imprisoned. Prendergast was sentenced to be tortured and then executed by beheading, following which his body was to be quartered. Fortunately, he was saved from this gruesome fate and granted his freedom by a royal pardon.

The tenant uprising of 1766 left behind it much hatred of the landlords. When most of the great landholders of the upper Hudson, notably the Van Rensselaers and the Livingstons, joined the Patriotic cause, many of their tenants automatically became Loyalists. Some disgruntled tenants left their homes to take up lands in the New Hampshire grants. These men had little love for the colony and generally supported the separatist movement which finally resulted in the establishment of the state of Vermont in territory claimed by New York. The uprising also left a distaste for the British in the minds of the great landlords, who felt that the Crown was unduly lenient with the revolting tenants.

The focal point for discontent in the pre-Revolutionary era was in the realm of economics, as is indicated by the reaction to the stamp tax and by the tenant revolt. But the uneasiness which found focus in economic matters was generated in the social, cultural, and political phases of living as well. Present in the colony were people of Dutch, British, and French descent, together with smaller proportions of other nationality groups. Except for the English segment of the British group, these people had no firm attachment to the culture represented by the Crown. Perhaps it is a tribute to the skill of the British government, which at this time was relatively inexperienced in imperial management, that it succeeded in preventing discontent from appearing openly in areas apart from the economic. Certainly it could have arisen. The Forsey-Cunningham affair threatened to develop into just such a point of dissension. Another nearly came to a head when late in the 1760's there was a movement to create an Episcopal bishopric in New York City. Immediately there was a strong reaction on the part of non-Episcopalians, who feared that the Church of England, which had been established as the state church in the four lower counties by the Ministry Act of 1693, would be granted similar status throughout the entire province. John Morin Scott and William Livingston were among the leaders who opposed the establishment of the bishopric. The British backed down, and no bishop came to New York.

It is important to note that while economic affairs brought on the crises, the colonial demands were always expressed in terms of political philosophy. Thus the Stamp Act brought the cry: "No taxation without representation"—a theory defended in the press and on the rostrum. As a result, during the pre-Revolutionary and Revolutionary eras New Yorkers were bombarded by the liberal theories of democratic political philosophy. In short, the leaders of the revolt educated their countrymen in democratic theory.

The year 1767 brought renewed effort on the part of Parliament to assert its authority over the colonists. The New York legislature was forbidden to transact business until British troops within the colony were furnished barracks and certain supplies under the terms of the Mutiny Act of 1765. Although the province had an unusually heavy military burden because General Thomas Gage made his headquarters within its borders, it complied with the parliamentary law, but only after Governor Moore had suspended the Assembly in 1766 and called for a new legislature. In the next year the Townshend Acts were passed, placing an import tax on paper, glass, painters' colors, and tea.

In New York the new tariffs were collected for over twelve months with only minor objections. On August 27, 1768, however, the merchants agreed to purchase no more British goods after November 1 unless the duties were removed. This delayed reaction probably was set off by a decline in business prosperity, which in turn was at least partially the result of other parliamentary legislation. In 1764 a British law had prohibited the issuance of paper money by the American colonies and had made it illegal to extend the legal tender provisions of bills in circulation after the date set for redemption. Under the terms of this act paper money issued by New York would be valueless after 1768. Since there was not enough gold and silver coin in the colony to transact business, prosperity waned.

The Sons of Liberty reappeared to whip up the inhabitants of New

York City, who were already disturbed by unemployment. "Liberty poles" sprang up as symbols of opposition to imperial authority. British soldiers considered the poles offensive and cut them down almost as quickly as they were raised. On January 18, 1770, the Sons and a group of soldiers clashed in a riot which had been exalted as the Battle of Golden Hill. Actually it was nothing more than a mob fight, and the most serious casualties were cuts and bruises. In April of this year Parliament repealed the import duties except for the tax on tea and in the same session authorized New York to issue £120,000 in paper money. The tension between the colony and the mother country quickly relaxed, and the years 1771 and 1772 were quiet.

Peaceful relations, however, were shaken in 1773, when the British East India Company was authorized to export tea to America subject to a threepenny tax per pound. This arrangement would have provided New Yorkers with cheap tea, cheaper in fact than smuggled tea. Colonial merchants, except those chosen to handle the East India Company's product, would lose customers. Furthermore, the ruling raised the old issue of taxation. The leading radicals prepared a document entitled "The Association of the Sons of Liberty," which called for a boycott of anybody who accepted tea from the East India Company. On the enforcement committee were the old radicals John Morin Scott, Isaac Sears, and John Lamb and, in addition, Alexander McDougall, who had attained important standing in the Sons by his open defiance of Acting Governor Colden three years earlier. The success of the Boston Tea Party, news of which was carried to New York City by Paul Revere, hardened the determination to prevent the landing of tea in Manhattan. The first tea ship to reach the colony returned to England without unloading her cargo. Finally, when the *London*, commanded by Captain Chambers, arrived in April 1774, irate colonists boarded her and dumped eighteen boxes of tea into New York harbor.

The British government retaliated against the Boston Tea Party early in 1774 by passing a series of laws which have come to be known as the Intolerable Acts. Two of these laws greatly disturbed New Yorkers: one provided for the closing of Boston Harbor until the tea was paid for, and the other reconstructed the government of Massachusetts along lines which reduced the power of local citizens to control their own affairs. Even the dullest New Yorker realized that similar steps could be taken against his own province. Colonial sentiment was exemplified by such men as the conservative William Smith, who deplored these measures: "I fear we shall lose all that attachment we once had in so great a degree for the mother country."

New York was by no means inexperienced in the techniques of political self-defense. For many years the province had enjoyed a large measure of home rule, and for over 150 years prior to the Revolution New Yorkers had used committees to win concessions from their rulers. Even Dutch burghers had used them successfully against their governors and the Dutch West India Company, and later, in the time of William and Mary, the committee type of organization had been employed during Leisler's Rebellion. The New York Assembly conducted much of its business through committees in which the leading citizens were trained in the intricacies of committee work. Thus the colonists were familiar with the machinery of political action. Two types of committees were widely used in the struggle against the authority of Parliament. The members of the first were appointed by governmental authorities and enjoyed legal status; the members of the second were selected by the people—by economic groups such as the merchants or by the Sons of Liberty and similar organizations.

As early as 1755 the Assembly had appointed a Committee of Correspondence to communicate with other colonies concerning common problems, with colonial agents in Britain, and even with members of Parliament. In January 1774 the Assembly established a new Committee of Correspondence to exchange views with the sister colonies concerning the acts of the British government. In May of that year word reached New York City that Boston harbor would be closed. Soon thereafter the local citizens created a Committee of Fifty-one to deal with the situation. Wealthy merchants, alarmed by the banning of Boston's seaborne trade, actively supported the resistance movement.

The Bostonians proposed that the colonies should adopt a policy of complete nonintercourse with Great Britain. The Sons of Liberty in New York City endorsed this suggestion, but the Committee of Fifty-one, which was controlled by more moderate elements, looked upon it with disfavor. On May 15, 1774, the New York Committee of Correspondence recommended that a congress of all the colonies should meet in New York City for the purpose of deciding on a common course of action. The movement for a continental congress gained headway when the Virginia House of Burgesses called for a September meeting in Philadelphia. Ultimately the Virginia proposal won out, and the congress was held at the Pennsylvania seaport.

For the most part the New York delegates to the First Continental Congress were elected or appointed by local committees of citizens, but the method of selection varied widely. The delegates were Isaac Low, chairman of the Committee of Fifty-one; John Alsop, vice-chairman of the Committee; and James Duane, John Jay, Philip Livingston, William Floyd, Henry Wisner, John Haring, and Simon Boerum. While it seems likely that an active and radical minority chose the delegation without much opposition from the more conservative elements, who refused to take part in so revolutionary an action, the representatives were generally conservative. Jay and Duane particularly were active in seeking the redress of grievances while trying to hold extreme measures in check. In October 1774 the First Continental Congress adopted the "Continental Association" (often called merely the "Association"), which was an agreement not to import from or export to Britain until American rights were restored. It called on each town, city, and county to have its qualified voters elect a local committee to enforce the Association. In New York City the Committee of Fifty-one had been advocating the creation of local organizations. Under this double-barreled stimulation local committees rapidly came into being. By 1776 every county in the province, with the possible exception of Kings, had a committee and subcommittees. Again the conservative majority hung back, allowing a radical minority to seize control of the committee organization throughout the state.

In New York City the Committee of Fifty-one gave way to the more radical Committee of Sixty in November 1774. When the Assembly refused to appoint delegates to the Second Continental Congress, the Committee of Sixty asked the county committees to send representatives to a provincial convention which would select congressional delegates. This provincial convention (usually called the First Provincial Congress) met on April 20, 1775, and adjourned two days later after having appointed a delegation to the Second Continental Congress. The composition of the new delegation was similar to the original one. All the former members except Low and Haring were retained, and Philip Schuyler, George Clinton, Lewis Morris, Francis Lewis, and Robert R. Livingston were added. It is interesting to note that the Assembly's refusal to select delegates for the Continental Congress resulted in the creation of the First Provincial Congress, which was the first extralegal body in New York to represent the entire province. With the formation of this body, the foundations for the revolutionary government were firmly laid on the local, state, and national level.

On the day after the First Provincial Congress closed, news of the Battle of Lexington reached New York City. The radical leaders were ready for action. The Sons of Liberty, under the able leadership of Isaac Sears, John Lamb, and Marinus Willett, served as a cadre around which the excited citizens rallied. A voluntary corps was formed and armed with about six hundred muskets seized from a government arsenal. The colonials told Acting Governor Colden not to expect aid from the militia. Under the persistent prodding of the Sons of Liberty, on April 28 the Committee of Sixty called for the establishment of a permanent government of the state. While plans were going ahead to select a group to serve this purpose, the Committee of Sixty was replaced by the still more radical Committee of One Hundred, which governed both city and colony until the Second Provincial Congress met on May 22, 1775. By this time many citizens had become more extreme in their thinking, and John Morin Scott, whose viewpoint long had been too radical for most of his contemporaries, was named to both bodies and served each with distinction.

Meanwhile, in the north, Ethan Allen, accompanied by Benedict Arnold, led a group of Green Mountain Boys to capture Fort Ticonderoga in a surprise attack on May 10. Two days later Seth Warner, at the head of a band of New Englanders, took Crown Point. Thus armed action had reached New York soil even before the Second Provincial Congress assembled. When British troops were withdrawn from New York City on June 6 to aid the royal garrison in Boston, the entire province was left under the control of the extralegal Provincial Congress and the local committees. In October, Governor William Tryon fled from New York City to establish headquarters on a British warship.

This Revolutionary committee system, controlled by a radical minority, bridged the gap between the colonial government and the constitutional government of the state. At the apex of the radical organization stood the Continental Congress. Under it was the Provincial Congress which passed down orders to the county, town, city, district, and precinct committees for enforcement. In all, New York probably had about 150 committees.

The most pressing problem facing the Second Provincial Congress was defense. By midsummer local committees under the direction of the Provincial Congress were busily collecting arms and organizing militia companies. This activity provoked a serious incident on August 23, when the royal warship *Asia* opened fire as New York troops began to remove the cannon from Fort George at the tip of Manhattan Island. The colonials returned the fire, killing one British soldier and wounding others. The incident strengthened the resolution of the citizens to defend themselves.

In the latter part of August General Richard Montgomery left Fort Ticonderoga with about twelve hundred men to invade Canada. This small force included one New York regiment under Colonel Alexander McDougall and three regiments from Connecticut. Fort St. Johns was captured after a bitter siege lasting fifty days. On November 12 Montreal was taken without great effort. Montgomery now advanced to Quebec, where he met Benedict Arnold, who had led a band of approximately five hundred Patriots through the Maine wilderness. They launched a joint attack on the city in a violent snowstorm at two o'clock on the morning of December 31. The assault was unsuccessful, and it was also costly, since Montgomery, one of the most promising colonial officers, was killed.

New Yorkers were grateful to Montgomery and afterward named a county after him. Arnold wintered near Quebec, but in the spring British attacks forced him to retreat to Crown Point.

While the soldiers fought, the question of independence from Britain began to occupy the political scene. Ironically, although war reached New York soil at an early date, it was among the last of the colonies to endorse the Declaration of Independence. On December 14, 1775, the Provincial Congress stated that resistance was the result of oppression by Parliament and that independence was not an objective. As late as January 12, 1776, this position was reaffirmed in a letter to the merchants of Quebec. Nevertheless, the sentiment for independence was slowly gaining headway in the latter part of 1775 and in the early months of 1776. The Sons of Liberty, whose most prominent leaders at this time were the ultraradical Isaac Sears, John Morin Scott, John Lamb, and Alexander McDougall, were among the first to advocate it. The continuous growth of this organization reflected the changing temper of the people. In January, Thomas Paine's pamphlet *Common Sense* appeared and converted many New Yorkers to the cause. By July 4, 1775, or shortly thereafter many distinguished citizens, including John Jay, Gouverneur Morris, Robert R. Livingston, Philip Schuyler, Alexander Hamilton, George Clinton, and James Duane, had urged independence, but no action could be taken until the political organization of the colony was structured to do so.

In April the Third Provincial Congress had been chosen, and it met for the first time on May 14. Ten days later a committee was appointed to make recommendations concerning the proposal by the Continental Congress that each of the colonies establish a state government. The report of this committee was presented to the Provincial Congress on May 27 and approved on the same day. Acting Governor Tryon's flight, declared the committee, had been a voluntary abdication, and, coupled with the armed assault on the colonials, it automatically dissolved the old form of government. The report went on to state: "It hath become absolutely necessary for the good people of this Colony to institute a new and regular form of internal government and police." There was some doubt, however, that the Third Provincial Congress had the authority to establish such a government. For this reason the county committees were asked to hold elections for a Fourth Provincial Congress which would meet on July 9 and establish the new government. It can be maintained that this action of the Third Provincial Congress was tantamount to a declaration of independence, although the Fourth Provincial Congress conceivably could have rejected the proposal to establish a state government.

Meanwhile, the issue of independence had been raised in the Second Continental Congress, and the New York delegates asked for instructions.

The Third Provincial Congress replied on June 11 that the delegates were not empowered to commit New York to independence. When the Declaration of Independence was adopted by the Continental Congress on July 4, 1776, the representatives from New York refrained from voting.

The election of members of the Fourth Provincial Congress was controlled by the county committees. The radicals easily triumphed, and the new Provincial Congress was a thoroughly revolutionary body. It met in the courthouse at White Plains on July 9, 1776, and, assured of its power and authority, immediately approved the Declaration of Independence. The next day it changed its name to the Convention of the Representatives of the State of New York. The metamorphosis was now complete. The ties of empire had been severed. A new and independent state was born.

Few New Yorkers were surprised at the outcome. After the French and Indian War had eradicated the fear of conquest from Canada, events had moved with ever-increasing momentum, until the announcement of independence came almost as an anticlimax. The scenes of this drama were played against a background of economic depression. It is evident that resistance to the authority of Parliament was stimulated by the fact that the acts of that body frequently aggravated poor economic conditions. Nearly all New Yorkers, including the great majority of those who opposed independence, felt that Parliament had overstepped its authority. Many men who desired to retain the imperial ties served on the early committees which were organized to regain the rights of the colonists. As the committees became more radical in their actions, persons of moderate inclinations withdrew from them. Thus the committee system which took over the province after the collapse of the colonial government fell into the grasp of the radicals.

It is fruitless to try to estimate how many New Yorkers were Loyalists and opposed to the Declaration of Independence. Certainly there were many thousands of them. In any case, most of these people objected to parliamentary domination and favored resistance short of a struggle for independence. When the ties of empire were severed, they were forced to choose between the empire and the state. It was a hard choice.

PART TWO

Rise of the Empire State,

1775-1825

✹✹✹✹✹✹✹✹✹✹✹✹✹✹

New York in the

Revolutionary War,

1776-1783

Most of the houses are thoroughly and indiscriminately plun-
dered, the beds cut up, the furniture and windows broke to
pieces, the men rob'd of their watches, shoe buckles and
money, whilst their wives and daughters have their pockets
and clothes torn from their bodies, and the father or husband
who does not survey all this with a placid countenance is beat
or branded with the name of traitor and rebel.
—CAPTAIN PATRICK FERGUSON, *British Army, 1779*

THOSE who travel the Hudson and Mohawk valleys and those who
survey the quiet charm of Lake George and Lake Champlain cannot help
but be impressed by the beauty of the scenery and the peaceful industry
of the countryside. Except for a few quaint old forts defended by ancient
and useless cannon, no hint remains of the terror, carnage, and destruction
strewn along these picturesque waterways by the warfare of the eighteenth century. Unfortunately, these streams and lakes, which in years of
peace served splendidly as channels of commerce, were enticing avenues
of invasion in time of war. For ages Indian warriors had advanced and
retreated in battle along the valleys. European gunpowder and military
science increased the savagery of later contests. During the Revolution
the slaughter and wreckage reached their dreadful climax.

The British controlled the Atlantic, and if their forces had seized the
Hudson–Lake Champlain–Richelieu waterway they would have cut off
New England, the citadel of patriotism, from the other colonies. Strangely
enough, the British apparently did not perceive the full implications of

this strategy. They looked upon the Mohawk Valley and the Richelieu–
Lake Champlain watercourse merely as paths of invasion over which
troops could advance from Canada. New York City with its excellent
harbor was regarded simply as an important base for British seapower
and a central location from which offensive forces could be dispatched
in various directions.

New Yorkers recognized the strategic position of their state and saw
that they were seriously threatened in the spring of 1776. The defeat of
the Montgomery-Arnold expedition left the way open for an attack from
Canada. In the interior, Indians and Loyalists led by Sir John Johnson,
Guy Johnson, John Butler, and Walter Butler were raiding the frontier.
A seaborne assault on New York City was expected at any time.

On April 13, George Washington, escorted by the Philadelphia light
horse, arrived in New York City, where he was met by nine militia companies, members of the Provincial Congress, cheering crowds, and ringing
bells. On June 28 Sir William Howe reached Sandy Hook with 130 sail
and 10,000 men. Two days later, while the Declaration of Independence
was debated in the Continental Congress, British forces landed on Staten
Island. During the next few weeks each side prepared for battle. Into the
imperial camp poured reinforcements from the West Indies, Gibraltar,
and the British Isles. By August 15, Howe had over 31,000 troops, including 8,000 seasoned Germans. This force was well trained, well officered,
fully equipped, experienced, and supported by a fleet. Against this formidable array Washington was able to muster 28,000 poorly trained and
inadequately supplied Patriots, many of whom were physically unfit for
duty. The Americans had the advantage of fixed fortifications, but this
was more than offset by the British fleet, which afforded Howe mobility
and easily concentrated fire power. Nor was Washington able to focus his
full attention on Howe, because in the north Sir Guy Carleton was mobi-
lizing an army to march up the Richelieu–Lake Champlain waterway and
seize the upper Hudson Valley.

After a fruitless effort to negotiate a peaceful settlement with Washington, Howe landed 15,000 men on Long Island near the Narrows. The
defenses of the island were entrusted to General Israel Putnam, who was
entrenched at Brooklyn Heights with 7,000 soldiers. Outside this well-
fortified position were advanced lines held by some 5,000 Americans.
The right wing of the outlying force was commanded by Stirling and
Parsons, the center by Sullivan, and on the left was a weak detachment
under Miles. On the night of August 26 the British offensive began.
British troops under Grant and Hessian soldiers under Von Heister feigned
an assault on the American right and center, holding Stirling, Parsons,
and Sullivan in position, while Clinton, Cornwallis, and Percy launched
a surprise attack which penetrated Miles's weak detachment on the left.

So effective was this maneuver that by ten o'clock on the morning of the twenty-seventh the advance lines were overrun and the Patriots were driven back to the entrenchments on Brooklyn Heights. Only valiant action by a small group under Alexander Stirling prevented a rout.

When Washington arrived on the scene in the afternoon, he found that Stirling and Sullivan had been captured along with 1,100 officers and men. The morale of the troops on Brooklyn Heights was at a low ebb. Fortunately, Howe declined to follow up his victory, and on the night of August 29 Washington in a brilliant maneuver screened by rain and fog withdrew his forces and his supplies to Manhattan Island. Howe, in spite

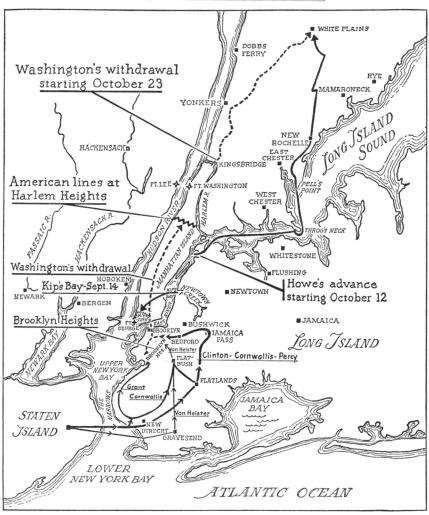

Map 4. George Washington's retreat from the Battle of Long Island, 1776.

of the advantages of superior discipline and a powerful fleet, allowed the American Army to slip through his fingers.

Having used the sword with considerable success, Howe again extended the olive branch. The captured General John Sullivan was dispatched to Philadelphia to invite the Continental Congress to send a delegation to Staten Island for a conference on the peaceful solution of the difficulties between the mother country and the colonies. John Adams, who referred to this proposal as a "decoy duck," attended the meeting with Benjamin Franklin and Edward Rutledge. The colonials proved intractable and, as the conference ended, Admiral Richard Howe (Sir William's brother) stated he regretted being unable to recognize the congressional delegates as public officials. Adams retorted, "Your Lordship may consider me in what light you please . . . except that of a British subject."

Diplomacy having failed, General Howe again took up arms. On September 15 New York City was taken with little effort. The ill-equipped and poorly trained American troops fled in disorder, abandoning a considerable quantity of supplies. Only the skill and steely determination of Washington prevented the disintegration of the Patriot army, which was plagued with large-scale desertion. The new colonial line ran from the junction of the Harlem and East rivers across Manhattan. On September 16 British forces attacked the American center but were driven off in a brisk skirmish which is known today as the Battle of Harlem Heights. This success did much to restore American morale.

A few days later Captain Nathan Hale, who had been sent by Washington to spy on the British, was captured. Hale confessed his espionage and bravely met his death on the gallows near the present corner of Sixty-sixth Street and Third Avenue in New York City.

About the time of Hale's execution a fire broke out in the city, to the south, and burned approximately one-sixth of the houses. The next year a second conflagration destroyed more buildings and added to the discomfort of the inhabitants. Some of the Patriot leaders, including John Jay and General Nathanael Greene, advocated burning the city so that it could not afford shelter for the British troops. It is impossible to say whether Patriots set the fires, but, if they did, it was without official sanction, for the Continental Congress had forbidden the burning of the city.

On October 12, Howe began moving his army up the East River in an obvious effort to cut off the Americans' avenue of retreat. Realizing the danger, the Patriots withdrew northward to the Bronx River and later to White Plains, leaving a garrison of about 3,000 in Fort Washington on the upper end of Manhattan Island. The British attacked White Plains on October 28 and drove the Americans from the field, but they suffered much heavier losses than the defenders. By this time Fort Washington was deep in enemy held territory, and prudence dictated the immediate evacuation of the garrison. Unfortunately orders for a withdrawal were not issued, and on November 16 Colonel Robert Magaw, the commander of the fortress, was compelled to surrender in the face of overwhelming odds. About 2,800 men were captured together with a large quantity of ammunition and stores.

The struggle between Washington and Howe now shifted to New Jersey and Pennsylvania, where the American general was to seize victory from the very jaws of defeat. The battle for New York City had lasted three months. The British sustained about 1,000 casualties and lost a few supplies and prisoners. The Americans were driven from the city, abandoned most of their artillery, and suffered the loss of 4,000 soldiers captured, 600 killed, and a large number of wounded. The bitterness of this defeat was somewhat mitigated by a successful defense in the north.

British strategy in 1776 called for Sir Guy Carleton to advance up the Richelieu–Lake Champlain–Lake George waterway to join forces with Sir William Howe in the upper Hudson Valley. Since British equipment and manpower were superior to his own military resources, General Benedict Arnold wisely decided to employ the strategy of delay. With great effort and untold hardship, Arnold constructed a small flotilla on Lake Champlain. This action forced the British to consume precious summer weeks building vessels with which to oppose the Patriot squadron. On October 11, 1776, the British and American fleets locked in battle near Valcour Island. The superior fire power of the imperial forces resulted in the ultimate destruction of the American squadron, but not until the Patriots had inflicted severe damage on the enemy.

Carleton followed up his advantage by capturing Crown Point. By this time the season was so far advanced that he feared to attempt the siege of Fort Ticonderoga, which was defended by 9,000 Americans under General Gates. Consequently, Sir Guy withdrew to Canada, expecting to renew the assault the next summer.

Only the military skill and steel-hard determination of Washington and Arnold enabled their poorly trained and inadequately supplied forces to prevent the complete conquest of New York in 1776. Washington's victories in New Jersey at Trenton (December 26) and Princeton (January 3) kept Revolutionary hopes alive during the winter of 1776–1777, but as spring approached and the imperial forces prepared to take to the field the fate of New York once again hung in the balance. The British campaign plans for 1777 called for three movements. General John Burgoyne was to move up the Richelieu–Lake Champlain–Lake George waterway and overland to the upper Hudson Valley; Colonel Barry St. Leger was to move along the Mohawk to the Hudson; and Sir William Howe was to move up the Hudson to meet St. Leger and Burgoyne.

By June 15, Burgoyne had 8,000 British and German troops, 150 Canadian militiamen, and about 400 Indians at St. Johns ready for the advance to the south. On May 5 his artillery appeared on Mount Defiance overlooking Fort Ticonderoga. General Schuyler, who had inadequate forces to oppose Burgoyne in open combat, wisely abandoned the fortress and retreated, felling trees to block the road. This scheme was singularly successful, because Burgoyne was overburdened with artillery and equipment. While the British floundered through the backwoods, the local in-

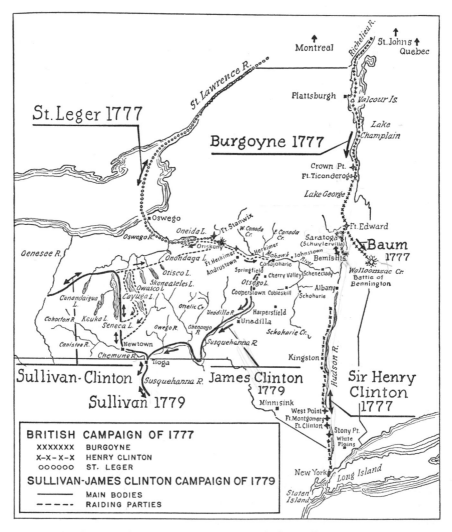

Map 5. The British campaign of 1777 and the Sullivan-Clinton campaign of 1779.

habitants drove off the stock and burned the fields so that they would not furnish food and fodder to the invader. The British forces did not reach Fort Edward at the head of the Hudson River until July 30.

As time wore on, Burgoyne became increasingly concerned over a shortage of food. On August 13, he sent Colonel Baum with about 600 men to attempt a capture of American supplies at Bennington, Vermont. Three days later Baum was cut off by Continental irregulars and defeated at Walloomsac, New York. Lieutenant Colonel Breyman, who went to the rescue with 500 troops, was badly mauled. This success encouraged the Patriots, and volunteers hastened to join the growing army under General Gates, who had taken command of the American forces on August 2. A few days later the Continental forces were further encouraged by good news from the Mohawk Valley.

About mid-July, St. Leger reached Oswego, where he was joined by Loyalists under Sir John Johnson and Colonel John Butler, as well as a force of Indians led by Joseph Brant, the celebrated Iroquois chief. On August 3 the British forces, 1,700 strong, appeared before Fort Stanwix (now Rome) which was defended by about 550 men under Colonel Peter Gansevoort. Three days later Continental reinforcements led by General Nicholas Herkimer were ambushed near Oriskany in the midst of a violent thunderstorm. This was the bloody Battle of Oriskany which pitted neighbor against neighbor, since most of Johnson's and Butler's Loyalists had come from the Mohawk region. Early in the struggle the doughty Herkimer's leg was shattered and his horse killed. The courageous general then sat at the base of a beech tree, where he smoked his pipe and directed the battle, undeterred by the fact that he had suffered a fatal wound. The ferocity of the American resistance discouraged the Indians, and many of them abandoned St. Leger. A few days later when General Benedict Arnold arrived with 1,200 men, the British forces fled, leaving much equipment in American hands. This victory freed Arnold's force and the Mohawk militia to join Gates in the struggle with Burgoyne.

On September 15, Burgoyne crossed the Hudson at old Saratoga (now Schuylerville) and began his advance down the river. Gates entrenched his forces at Bemis Heights about eight miles below the crossing and awaited the invader. Four days later the two forces met in battle and remained facing each other until October 7, when Burgoyne withdrew after a sharp skirmish. By this time the British were in desperate circumstances. Supplies were low, and the number of effective troops had been greatly reduced by sickness and wounds, while the American forces continued to increase. Gates had over 17,000 men, whereas the invading army had well under 5,000 fit for combat. On October 17, Burgoyne surrendered, lamenting that Howe had not arrived with the expected reinforcements. This struggle is known as the Battle of Saratoga. The Patriot victory never will be forgotten by Americans because it was the turning point of the Revolutionary War.

Military men and historians always will ponder why Howe failed to send his main body up the Hudson to join forces with the armies moving south from Canada. It is sufficient for us to note that Sir William elected to attack Philadelphia and left Sir Henry Clinton at New York City with eight or nine thousand men to defend that important post and to aid Burgoyne. Clinton made a gallant effort to comply with impossible orders. With a small force he moved northward. His own great skill and a fair share of luck enabled him to capture Forts Clinton and Montgomery on October 6. Just as it seemed that success might be within his grasp, he learned that Burgoyne had surrendered. Sir Henry now found himself in difficult circumstances. His forces were spread thinly along the Hudson from New York City to a little below Albany. With the surrender of Burgoyne, Gates was free to attack the British in the upper Hudson Valley. Outnumbered and poorly situated for defense, Clinton wisely decided to withdraw to New York City. In his diary Sir Henry Clinton confided that once again Howe's stupidity had cost the British victory. Certainly the charge is well founded, but Burgoyne, who allowed an excess of baggage and artillery to delay his advance through the backwoods while the Patriots rallied to Gates, also merits a share of the blame, and the Patriot defenders deserve credit for courage and for military skill.

It is surprising that New Yorkers found time and energy to frame a constitutional government during the tempestuous years of 1776 and 1777. As we have seen, the Fourth Provincial Congress declared New York independent on July 9, 1776. The Congress then changed its name to Convention of the Representatives of the State of New York and on August 1 established a committee composed of John Jay, John Sloss Hobart, William Smith, William Duer, Gouverneur Morris, Robert R. Livingston, John Broome, John Morin Scott, Abraham Yates, Henry Wisner, Samuel Townsend, Charles De Witt, and Robert Yates to recommend a form of government for the new state. A few weeks later James Duane was added to the committee.

On March 12, 1777, the committee presented a proposed state constitution to the Convention. Probably John Jay played the major role in writing the draft. It is likely, too, that Livingston, Morris, and Abraham Yates made significant contributions. Beyond this little is known concerning the work of the committee members. After much debate, in which Jay took an active part, and after important amendments were made, the Convention adopted the committee's draft on April 20, 1777, as the first Constitution of New York. It went into effect on the authority of the Convention without being submitted to popular referendum.

The Constitution of 1777 established a government which was closely modeled after that of the colony. The courts remained much the same except that a Court of Errors and Impeachment made up of the president of the Senate, the senators, the chancellor, and judges of the Supreme Court was created to exercise final appellate jurisdiction. The legislature was composed of two houses, the Senate and the Assembly. Members of the Senate were elected from four senatorial districts and held office four years. Each county was allotted a quota of assemblymen based on its population. Members of the Assembly served terms of one year.

New York followed the prevailing pattern of curtailing the authority of the governor. This distrust of executive authority reflected the bitter memory of past struggles between royal governors and the Assembly. The chief executive, who was elected every three years, was made commander of the military forces and was given the power to call special sessions of the legislature, to prorogue the legislature for periods of sixty days in any year, and, except in cases of murder and treason, to grant pardons. In other important aspects his power was sharply restricted. Veto power rested in a Council of Revision made up of the governor, the chancellor, the judges of the Supreme Court, and four senators selected by the Assembly. A two-thirds majority in both houses could override a veto. Important nonelective posts were filled by the Council of Appointment composed of the governor and one senator from each district, elected by the Assembly. Both the Council of Appointment and the Council of Revision proved to be cumbersome agencies which permitted political hucksters to thwart the public will.

The Constitution of 1777 contained the entire Declaration of Independence with all its democratic sentiments. It stated, "No authority shall, on any pretence whatever, be exercised over the people or members of this State, but such as shall be derived from and granted by them." It called for the separation of church and state. It guaranteed freedom of religion and trial by jury. Yet it was far from an egalitarian document because it severely limited the elective franchise. Only persons who owned property valued at one hundred pounds or more could vote for the governor and senators. Certain merchants and artisans of Albany and New York City who paid for the right of doing business in those municipalities and men owning property valued at not less than twenty pounds or leasing property on which the annual rental was at least forty shillings were privileged to vote for assemblymen.

In June 1777 George Clinton was elected governor of the new state, an office he was to hold for eighteen years without a break. After much delay the legislature was organized at Kingston in September. A short time later the government officials were forced to flee from the imperial forces under Sir Henry Clinton who was advancing up the Hudson in his fruitless attempt to join Burgoyne. The British captured Kingston and on October 16 put it to the torch.

Seldom has a government been established in the face of more forlorn circumstances. Although Sir Henry was forced to retreat and Burgoyne was captured, New York City, the most wealthy municipality and the only important seaport in the state, remained in enemy hands. Salt, spices, pepper, tea, coffee, and rum were cut off, as were the more important materials of war. This, in addition to the fact that farmers and manufacturers were reluctant to accept the depreciated paper money issued by the state, made it very difficult to obtain the supplies required by the American military forces. Fortunately, the extralegal local committees continued to function, and they aided in the collection of military stores. As time went on, the government gradually became more effective, and local committees, many of which remained active until the end of the Revolution, played a lesser and lesser role.

One of the most difficult questions facing the Patriots was what to do with the large group of Loyalists. Generally speaking, Loyalists were leniently treated prior to July 4, 1776. After that date the treatment became more severe, and many were tarred, feathered, and ridden out of town on a rail. If their property was not destroyed or stolen, it was confiscated by the state. Patriots received similar treatment at the hands of the imperial authorities. Prior to the establishment of a constitutional government, the Provincial Congress established a Committee on Loyalists. Later the state legislature established an agency to detect conspiracies, and its duties included the ferreting out of Loyalists.

It is impossible to estimate the number of New Yorkers who were Loyalists. Unquestionably a large share of the population retained a strong affection for the Crown. Many of these were alienated when imperial soldiers—British and German alike—were permitted to loot and molest civilians. An intelligent leadership might well have won many to the imperial cause. In any case, thousands fled to British-held territory. Many went to New York City.

The great metropolis took on the aspects of a European capital. Here was the principal seat of British power. In the streets, soldiers and citizens conversed in a strange medley of English, Dutch, and German. The higher stratum of society—consisting of military officers, governmental officials, and wealthy civilians—enjoyed the theater, lavish parties, and even horse racing, fox hunting, and cricket. The lesser lights had the usual diversions offered by the local tavern and by public spectacles. The seaport carried on a brisk trade with the West Indies and the Continent. Revenues were increased by privateering, in which at least six thousand men were engaged. During the six and a half months prior to March 1, 1779, New York privateers took 150 prizes. Many Loyalists, who, for the most part, were men who had been established in the city prior to the outbreak of hostilities, made fortunes from trade or in privateering.

The refugee Loyalists who fled to New York City from all over North

America were often in desperate straits, having lost all their property to Americans. These people were supported meagerly by the Crown. Hundreds of them enlisted as royal provincial troops and took an active part in the war against the Patriots. Militarily, probably the most vexatious group of Loyalists were the frontiersmen who fled to Canada to join the imperial forces. Some of these men fought at Oriskany; others took part in later raids along the wilderness frontier.

In 1778 the British unleashed a ferocious attack against the frontier settlements. On May 30, Cobleskill was burned; in June, Springfield was destroyed; during the month of July, Andrustown (near German Flats) was burned and the Pennsylvania settlement at Wyoming was left in ruins. In September, German Flats was laid to waste for ten miles along the Mohawk, and, in October, Unadilla was given to the torch. On November 11 imperial forces sacked the isolated village of Cherry Valley.

These assaults were carried out chiefly by Loyalists, many of whom were frontiersmen, and by Iroquois Indians, the majority of whom actively supported the Crown. The raiders were usually led by able men, notably Colonel John Butler, his son, Captain Walter Butler, and the Indian chief, Captain Joseph Brant. While the attacking forces were small, they were composed of men who were wise in the ways of the wilderness. Bands of such men moved quickly, striking before the Patriots had time to mobilize for defense, and the small battles which resulted were swift and savage. All too often captured Continentals and their defenseless women and children were abused or slaughtered by the infuriated Indians, although Joseph Brant and the British officers made efforts to prevent mistreatment of their conquered foes.

Some writers have characterized these actions against frontier villages as orgies of revenge on the part of the Loyalists or as wanton savagery on the part of British officials. It is more accurate to say that they were carefully calculated military maneuvers designed to weaken the Revolutionary forces. The Continental armies drew food, fodder, and horses from the frontier settlements. The raiders succeeded in destroying large quantities of these much-needed supplies and often prevented the production of more. Furthermore, the Patriots were forced to send troops and supplies to protect the wilderness frontier, reducing thereby their military power in other critical areas.

To counteract British strategy, the American military leaders determined to break the power of the Iroquois. In April 1779 General James Clinton, the brother of Governor George Clinton, sent troops to destroy Indian villages and supplies along the upper reaches of the Mohawk River and in the region of Onondaga Lake. Having successfully accomplished this mission, Clinton moved his army of about 1,500 men overland from Canajoharie on the Mohawk to Lake Otsego. From here he moved

down the Susquehanna River to join forces with General John Sullivan
at Tioga, Pennsylvania. On August 24 the combined force of about 3,500
began to advance under Sullivan's command toward the Genesee country.
Five days later a small and poorly equipped band of Indians and Loyalists under Colonel John Butler attempted to impede the Patriot advance
near the modern city of Elmira, in a skirmish known as the Battle of
Newtown. The casualties were light—twelve of Butler's men and three
Americans were killed. No other concerted effort was made to halt Sullivan, who advanced through the Finger Lake region to the Genesee Valley, destroying the villages of the Indians, slaughtering their livestock,
and burning their fields.

The original plans had called for a force under Colonel Daniel Brodhead to join Sullivan by ascending the Allegheny River from Fort Pitt
(now Pittsburgh). Brodhead probably got north of the New York–
Pennsylvania border, but he failed to make contact with Sullivan. The
American campaign of 1779 was at least partially successful, since, as a
result, the power of the Iroquois was reduced greatly. A further strain
was placed on the imperial supply lines when the British were forced to
feed and shelter their Indian allies.

The Sullivan expedition did not bring an end to the frontier raids.
Even while the Patriot forces were making the first movements of the
campaign against the Iroquois, Joseph Brant destroyed Minisink on July
20, 1779, and two days later he inflicted severe casualties on a group of
militiamen sent to the relief of the settlement. The next year attacks were
made against several towns, and Riemensnyder's Bush, Harpersfield,
Johnstown, Canajoharie, and German Flats were devastated. Raiding continued during 1781 but on a reduced scale.

The Sullivan expedition was not the only Patriot triumph in 1779. On
July 16, when Generals Clinton and Sullivan were still assembling their
armies, General Anthony Wayne captured the British fortress at Stony
Point. This was a daring attack in which a picked body of Patriots
stormed a works believed by the British to be impenetrable. The fort
stood on a promontory which thrusts out more than a half mile into the
Hudson River and rises 150 feet above the water. On the landward side
the point is protected by a marsh. Wayne's force, divided into three de-
tachments, attacked at night. One group was to feint at the center, keeping up a rapid fire; the other two forces were to enter the British lines
on the right and left. At the head of each flanking force were 150 determined men carrying axes to cut through the abatis. Accompanying each
group of axmen was a forlorn hope or, in modern terminology, a suicide
squad.

Washington planned well. The defensive forces were drawn to the center by the firing in that sector. Meanwhile, the axmen cut through two lines of abatis and the Patriot right and left led by the forlorn hope and using only bayonets and knives poured into the fortress shouting their battle cry, "The fort's our own!" In the darkness the attackers identified one another by pieces of white paper worn in their hats. The confused defenders were soon overwhelmed. The British suffered heavily: 63 killed, over 70 wounded and 543 captured, together with the loss of fifteen artillery pieces and a large quantity of military stores. The Patriots had 80 wounded, including General Wayne, and 15 killed. This daring attack raised the morale of Patriots throughout the nation.

Probably the last battle of the Revolution fought on New York soil was an engagement between a band of British raiders and Patriot defenders which took place near Johnstown. On October 25, 1781, about 600 Indians, Loyalists, and British regulars commanded by Major John Ross were attacked by some 400 Americans under Colonel Marinus Willett. Ross was forced to retreat. Five days later Willett again attacked as the British withdrew across Canada Creek. In this final struggle Captain Walter Butler, the well-known Loyalist leader, was shot through the head. An Oneida Indian took his scalp, which was sent to Albany.

While the frontier was kept in flames by incessant attack, other major maneuvers were being conducted. In the summer of 1779 General Benedict Arnold began treasonable correspondence in code with Sir Henry Clinton, who commanded the British Army in New York City. In 1780 the British moved from Canada to occupy Fort Ticonderoga, which had been abandoned by both sides since 1777. At the same time there was considerable activity by British raiders in the Mohawk region. In September of this same year Arnold, who commanded the American garrison at West Point, agreed to surrender that fortress to the British.

It seems likely that the Mohawk raids and the occupation of Ticonderoga were timed to coincide with Arnold's proposed treachery. If West Point had been surrendered, Sir Henry Clinton would have been in a position to move swiftly up the Hudson to join forces with the imperial troops who had seized Ticonderoga. The Patriots defending the Mohawk frontier probably would have been unable to oppose Sir Henry's advance. Fortunately for the Revolutionary cause, Major John André, a British officer who was carrying messages from Arnold to Clinton, was captured by American soldiers and the plot became known. As a result West Point was saved from possible capture, Arnold fled to the British lines, and André was hanged.

This was the last major threat to New York State. On October 19, 1781, Cornwallis, who had been trapped at Yorktown by the Americans and their French allies, surrendered. Thereafter, the fighting was on a reduced scale. Peace negotiations began the following spring, and on September 3, 1783, a treaty was signed in which the British government recognized the independence of the United States.

On November 25, 1783, the British evacuated New York City. When the American troops were drawn up at the Battery on the southern tip of Manhattan Island, it was found that the halyards were missing and that the pole had been greased. After considerable effort a sailor managed to climb the staff and tear down the British colors. As the American flag was run up, the cannon below boomed out a thirteen-gun salute.

It was fitting that a thirteen-gun salute should mark the departure of the British from New York State. The Revolution was a united effort on the part of all thirteen colonies. Soldiers of the Continental Army who came from all states fought and died on New York soil, and the Continental Congress furnished a considerable quantity of money and supplies for the defense of New York. New Yorkers fought outside the boundaries of their native state and gave strong support to the Continental Congress. On February 6, 1778, New York became the second state to approve the Articles of Confederation.

No other state suffered more for the cause of independence than did New York. Its frontiers blazed constantly in guerilla warfare. Armies marched and countermarched through its principal river valleys, strewing death and destruction behind them. Nearly one-third of the engagements of the war were fought on New York soil. New York City, which controlled most of the commerce of the state, was continuously in enemy hands from 1776 until 1783. Two major fires destroyed many buildings in the great seaport. After British evacuation the population of the city fell to ten thousand, half of what it had been on the eve of revolution.

The recitation of these facts cannot bring home to the modern reader the grief of those who saw their loved ones slaughtered and their property destroyed. No real understanding can be conveyed of the suffering of those whose bodies were maimed in the conflict. Nor is it easy to sympathize with the thousands of Loyalists who were driven from their homes by the exigencies of war, often never to return. No history can adequately portray the cost of independence in terms of human suffering. The conclusion of hostilities brought little respite. Roads, factories, farms, and business houses essential to the economy had been destroyed or damaged. Many of the old trade connections enjoyed by New York City had been lost. The currency was unstable and inflation stalked the land. Mistrust and hatred of the Loyalists who remained within the state ran high. New Yorkers who found their courage and resourcefulness heavily taxed during the Revolution faced equally serious problems at the war's end. Small wonder historians have termed the post-Revolutionary era in New York "the critical period."

The Age of George Clinton,

1783-1800

> *Report says that you are very civil to the young and handsome*
> *of the sex that you flattered the old and ugly—and even em-*
> *braced the toothless and decrepit, in order to obtain votes.*
> —Philip Schuyler *to William Cooper, 1792*

SHORTLY after George Clinton won the first gubernatorial election held in the state of New York, Philip Schuyler wrote to John Jay that Clinton's "family and connections do not entitle him to so distinguished a predominance; yet he is virtuous and loves his country, has abilities and is brave." Schuyler accurately reflected the sentiments of the old aristocratic families of New York, who believed that the reins of government ought to be in the hands of wealthy men of established families. Such persons, the argument ran, not only were best qualified by reason of upbringing, but had an enormous personal stake in the welfare of the state and, therefore, could be trusted to fulfill their official duties energetically and effectively.

Although Governor Clinton did not belong to the topmost stratum of society, he was well-to-do and had both social and business contacts with the aristocracy. Among his friends and business partners was George Washington, to whom he loaned a considerable sum of money. Clinton was at ease in most social situations but showed a marked distaste for the ostentatious display of pomp and ceremony so dear to the hearts of the aristocrats.

In all probability the governor's love of simplicity and lack of family eminence were political assets. At any rate the excellent characteristics mentioned by Schuyler were to carry him seven times to the governorship and twice to the vice-presidency. From the time he first took over the governor's office in 1777 until the turn of the century, George Clinton exerted more influence on the politics of New York than any other individual. Circumstances and the astuteness of his opponents sometimes defeated his efforts. Nevertheless, he won and retained a public confidence seldom matched in the history of the state.

A host of problems faced George Clinton in 1783 as he took the oath for his third term as governor. How severely should the Loyalists be treated? How could New York make good its claims to Vermont and settle its dispute with Massachusetts for control of the western half of the state? What policy should New York follow in selling its lands and in attacking the semifeudal land system? Should New York print more paper money, place tariffs on imports, and encourage banks? Did the law codes need revision? How far should New York go in co-operating with the other states? These were only a few of the difficult questions which confronted Clinton and the state legislature.

The Revolution brought striking and far-reaching social changes to New York, well beyond those experienced by most states. The legislature disestablished the Anglican church and put all sects on an equal footing. The pattern of landholding became increasingly democratic as new tracts were opened up in the west and settled by freeholding farmers. The abolition of entail and primogeniture, under which vast estates passed exclusively to the first born, and the confiscation of Tory property helped to break up the aristocratic land system in eastern New York. Because of the property qualifications for the suffrage the spread of land ownership increased the number of voters. It also increased the number of self-employed and independent farmers, who eventually became a potent force for democratization. The revolutionary upheaval stimulated the movement for the abolition of slavery in New York as well as other states. The exodus of the Loyalists and the impoverishment of many old families as a result of war devastation and inflation tended to break up the rigidity of social lines by reducing the economic gulf between rich and poor. It is noteworthy that the two leading political figures, George Clinton and Alexander Hamilton, were "new men," not drawn from the colonial aristocracy.

The upsurge of democratic and humanitarian feeling also brought about reforms in the civil and criminal code. An act of 1784 provided that a jailed debtor could be released if the person or persons holding three-fourths of his debts petitioned for it, but not until the 1830's did the state abolish the practice of placing debtors in prison. Some progress was made in tempering the brutalities in the criminal code, which in 1780 listed no fewer than sixteen capital crimes, including forgery and housebreaking. Governor Clinton denounced the "sanguinary complexion of our criminal code" and called upon the legislature in 1794 to correct the situation. No action was taken until the first administration of John Jay, when the list of capital offenses was reduced to murder, treason, and robbing a church.

While the Revolution set democratic forces in motion, the triumph of
independence brought no radical political changes. True, the guiding
hand of the royal governor was gone, the legislature had more power,
and it was easier to secure title to a small farm; but such changes were
almost inevitable as the result of victory. Actually, New Yorkers had not
fought for the new democratic principles but for the traditional rights of
Englishmen. The idea of expanding these rights grew gradually over a
long period of time. The Constitution of 1777 limited the franchise to
twenty-pound freeholders or the renters of tenements worth forty shillings
a year. It is estimated that fewer than one out of ten of the male inhabitants of New York City were eligible to vote for governor in 1790.

The treatment of the Loyalists became an important issue in state
politics in the 1780's. Governor Clinton urged the passage of severe laws
against the return of Tories and the recovery of their confiscated property. The Trespass Act of 1783 provided that a citizen might sue the oc-
cupant of his property if it had been occupied while that property was
behind British lines. Interestingly enough, the Mayor's Court of New
York City voided the act on the ground that it violated the accepted
principle of the law of nations in regard to the rights of occupation
forces. By 1788 the legislature had lifted many of the restrictions imposed upon the Loyalists and most of them had recovered their rights
as citizens. The Tory element naturally threw its political support to the
conservative faction led by Hamilton and the Schuyler and Livingston
families.

Riotous outbreaks often marred the peace during the years following
the Revolution. Fortunately, George Clinton was a man of action who
moved quickly to maintain law and order. In 1787, when a rebellion of
small farmers led by Daniel Shays, a veteran of Bunker Hill, threatened
to spread from Massachusetts to New York, the governor called up three
regiments and personally led the troops which restored tranquillity.
Clinton had less success in establishing the authority of the New York
government in the northeastern section of the state. The Province of
New York as granted by the King in 1664 to the Duke of York had the
Connecticut River as its eastern boundary. Later Connecticut and Massachusetts by agreement with New York extended their borders to a
line twenty miles east of the Hudson River.

Previous to 1741 New Hampshire had been under the jurisdiction of
the governor of Massachusetts. In that year New Hampshire obtained
a governor of its own in Benning Wentworth, who maintained that the
western boundary of New Hampshire was similar to that of Massachusetts and extended to within twenty miles of the Hudson River.
Proceeding on this assumption, he began to grant titles to lands lying
west of the Connecticut River. By 1764 there were 131 New Hampshire

townships in this region in which Wentworth and his friends laid aside millions of acres for themselves.

New York refused to honor the claims of New Hampshire and issued titles to land in the disputed area. When New Yorkers holding such titles tried to take possession, they met armed opposition. Their homes were burned; their cattle stolen; and their persons manhandled. Into this confused situation moved the Allen brothers—Heman, Ira, and Ethan—who formed a group known as the Onion River Company to buy up New Hampshire titles from discouraged holders at bargain prices. Obviously these landjobbers would reap a fortune if the New Hampshire titles could be made valid. The Allens organized an effective militia known as the "Green Mountain Boys" which successfully repelled the authority of New York. In 1777 a convention at Westminster proclaimed the independent state of Vermont and drew up a constitution.

Governor George Clinton refused to recognize Vermont, although in 1778 he did offer to confirm the titles of all inhabitants who would admit the jurisdiction of New York. This concession came ten years too late. Vermont under its resolute leaders continued its independent way, coining money, setting up post roads, establishing post offices, and, following the Revolution, negotiating treaties with British officials in Canada. Clinton did not try to coerce Vermont with armed force partly because other problems nearer at hand were far more pressing and partly because the New England states strongly supported the Yankee inhabitants of Vermont. Finally, New York wisely decided to accept the inevitable. In 1790 commissioners from the two states agreed that New York would recognize Vermont's independence and boundaries in return for which Vermont would pay New York $30,000 for land claims. On March 4, 1791, Vermont entered the Union as the fourteenth state.

Economic problems also disturbed New York politicians during the "critical period." A postwar boom disguised for a time the devastation and dislocation caused by war, but in 1785 hard times set in. Business was handicapped by lack of a sound and stable currency. Paper money issued by the state and the Continental Congress depreciated, fluctuated in value, and was counterfeited easily. To avoid such difficulties businessmen sought to use coins, usually British, French, or Spanish in origin. Pistareens, doubloons, half joes, and moidores are the picturesque names of only a few of the many coins in daily use. The farmers, troubled by heavy debts and low prices, advocated their traditional solution—cheap paper money. Some shopkeepers who relied upon the trade of the farmers also urged the state to issue more paper money. In opposition, however, were most of the large merchants, the bankers, and large landholders. As creditors, they did not want to be paid back in depreciated currency. As businessmen, they disliked a wildly fluctuating medium of exchange.

As the depression deepened, the clamor for paper money grew more intense. By 1786 the advocates of cheap money won control of the legislature and secured Governor George Clinton's somewhat grudging support. The legislature provided for £200,000 in bills of credit which were to be distributed to county loan offices where farmers could secure loans if they presented their mortgages as collateral. This modest measure helped stimulate business suffering from a scarcity of currency. New York's credit remained good, partly because Clinton's administration was honest, economical, and efficient, but also because ample revenues were secured from import duties and the sale of state lands.

In the 1780's New Yorkers held themselves to be citizens of New York and not citizens of the United States. Most of them regarded a strong centralized government as evil in principle and believed their rights and privileges could best be preserved by the state. After all, they had fought British rule largely because they opposed government from a distant capital. The long quarrel over the proposal to give Congress a 5-per-cent tariff on imports reveals the distrust of the central government. In 1783 Clinton forced the repeal of the impost which the state had granted to Congress during the emergency of war, and Congress' requests for the renewal of the right to collect a duty on goods imported to New York were sidetracked by the governor and the state legislature. In 1786, when Congress asked Clinton to call a special session of the legislature to reconsider its position on the impost, Clinton refused to do so on the ground that special sessions could only be called on "extraordinary occasions." Despite the attacks of Alexander Hamilton, Clinton's stand on this issue was strongly supported by the legislature. As a result Hamilton threw his support behind the effort to strengthen the federal government.

Generally the states followed the practice of trade reciprocity, that is, all American goods were exempt from the payment of state imposts, and in 1784 New York provided that all products grown or manufactured in the United States were free from duty charges. The following year the state legislature placed a tax on all imports from outside the federal union which entered by way of neighboring states, and later it placed clearance fees on ships sailing to or from New Jersey and Connecticut. These imposts were resented by New York's sister states, but a much sharper criticism was directed at the New York tariff on imports from outside the union. Since many imported goods were shipped through New York on their way to other states and since merchants had to add the duty charge to the price of the products, consumers ultimately were forced to pay the New York tariff fee even though they resided in another state. Naturally, retaliatory measures were taken by sister states. Congress under the Articles of Confederation was powerless to put an end to the bickering over interstate trade and was unable to secure favorable commercial treaties with foreign nations.

In the face of these perplexing difficulties, the Virginia legislature called for a convention of states to be held at Annapolis in September 1786. Delegates from New York and four other states attended the convention, which adopted a report written by Alexander Hamilton pointing out the conspicuous defects in the Articles of Confederation and suggesting that a new convention be called which might give the central government greater power. Clinton was not well disposed toward the proposal, and the legislature disapproved the action of the Annapolis Convention. State loyalty was partly responsible for this attitude but other factors were equally important. New York was situated so favorably for trade that the tariff barriers between the states did not prevent its commercial prosperity. Furthermore, an elaborate central government might require heavier taxes. A more serious objection was the belief of many that a strong federal government would be less responsive to democratic control and would place civil liberties in jeopardy.

When Congress issued a call for a new convention to meet at Philadelphia in May 1787, the New York legislature agreed to send delegates "for the sole and expressed purpose of revising the Articles of Confederation." Robert Yates, John Lansing, and Alexander Hamilton were selected, but only Hamilton had a real interest in strengthening the powers of Congress. The Philadelphia Convention exceeded its instructions and drew up a new constitution. In early July, Yates and Lansing withdrew, claiming the Convention had overstepped its power by proposing a strong federal government. Hamilton, who played a minor role at Philadelphia, was the only New York delegate to sign the document.

When the proposed Constitution was submitted to the Continental Congress, Melancton Smith of New York protested against recommending its adoption by the states unless a bill of rights was added. Smith's protest was disregarded, and on September 28, 1787, Congress submitted the Constitution to the states for their approval. Since the New York legislature did not meet until January 1788, there was considerable time for discussion.

The debate over ratification was so intense that, for the first time since the Revolution, two clear-cut political factions emerged. The Federalists, who formed what was first known as the Federal and later as the Federalist party, were championed by Alexander Hamilton and argued for adoption. The Anti-Federalists, led by George Clinton, urged rejection. The campaign over ratification was fought largely in the newspapers, where letters written by men of various viewpoints were published under pseudonyms. The Federalists were at a decided disadvantage because Governor Clinton had a strong personal following among New Yorkers. Hamilton realized the need to win converts—an objective not to be accomplished by the usual invective letters to newspapers. Consequently, he enlisted the aid of James Madison, a Virginian, and John Jay to write a series of scholarly letters explaining the merits of the Constitution. These appeared in the newspapers under the name "Publius." The articles were quickly gathered together and republished in a book called *The Federalist*. Although the letters were written expertly and read widely, they were too scholarly to have much appeal to the average citizen. They remain to this day the most important commentaries on the Constitution.

Although the New York legislature of 1788 was controlled by the Clintonians, the governor adopted a strategy of delay. Perhaps he feared that some of his followers would accept the Constitution under the pressure of debate or perhaps he feared the political consequences of defeating it. In all probability he hoped to avoid the issue entirely. Since the Constitution would not become effective unless ratified by nine of the thirteen states, if Clinton could delay discussion of the proposal until it had been rejected by five states, there would be no need to even consider it. Under such circumstances the onus of defeating the Constitution could not be laid at the door of the Clintonians.

The first delaying tactic was a legislative resolution calling for the election of a convention during the month of April to reject or ratify the Constitution. The enactment provided that all free male citizens of twenty-one years and over could vote for delegates to the convention. No other state allowed such wide suffrage on this issue. Apparently the followers of Clinton desired to place ballots in the hands of the farmers and city workers who, they expected, would oppose the Constitution. The election was a triumph for Clinton's forces, with forty-six Anti-Federalists and nineteen Federalists chosen. The backers of Hamilton won less than 25 per cent of the popular vote despite the overwhelming support of the press. Only the region of metropolitan New York and Westchester County elected Hamiltonian delegates.

An able and distinguished group assembled at Poughkeepsie on June 17, 1788, to argue the issue of ratification. Foremost among the Federalists was Alexander Hamilton, capably supported by John Jay, Robert R. Livingston, James Duane, John Sloss Hobart, and Richard Harison. The Anti-Federalists relied upon Melancton Smith and John Lansing to carry the greater share of the debate. George Clinton, who spoke rarely, worked behind the scenes. The Anti-Federalists elected Clinton president of the convention and, strangely enough, agreed to discuss the Constitution at length instead of putting it to an early vote.

The issue of ratification resulted in the organization of an effective party to oppose the Clintonians, who had controlled the state since 1777 with little opposition. Some generalizations can be drawn as to the composition of both parties. On the whole the same line-up of groups continued for the rest of the century, although individual leaders occasionally crossed over to the opposing camp.

The Federalists could draw upon a tradition of aristocratic rule, which was stronger in New York than in the other northern states. Their leaders believed that one of the primary purposes of government was the protection of property. Men of wealth and family, they insisted, had the chief stake in government, whereas propertyless persons were irresponsible and improvident. The bulk of large landholders endorsed the Federalist position, although a few, such as Pierre Van Cortlandt, John Lansing, and John Williams, were numbered among the Anti-Federalists. The landed families wanted a national government strong enough to protect property rights. The frequent antirent movements in the colonial period, the leveling doctrines of Daniel Shays in 1786, and the violation of land titles by the Vermont insurgents made the landholders keenly aware of the necessity of a strong government. The landed aristocracy and their close associates among the merchants were acquiring huge tracts in western and northern New York and often sent their sons to develop these wilderness lands. The Federalist group thus had outposts in the upstate counties. Probably William Cooper of Cooperstown and the Wadsworths of Genesee are the best examples of back-country Federalist leaders.

Most of the great merchants favored the adoption of the Constitution for the same reasons as the landlords. They hoped a strong central government would eliminate interstate trade barriers and secure favorable commercial treaties with foreign nations. Furthermore, the new Constitution forbade the states to issue bills of credit and to pass stay and tender laws; these provisions would prevent inflation-minded farmers from disturbing the stability of business. The ablest lawyers, especially those who had business ties with merchants and landlords, tended to side with their clients. In brief, the Federalist party represented the rich and well born.

On the other hand, the Anti-Federalists drew their strength from the humble but more numerous lower classes. The yeoman farmers and the tenant farmers were ordinarily staunch supporters of Clinton. These men had no love for the landlords, whom they often regarded as petty tyrants, and they also feared that a strong national government would impose a tax on land—a matter of great concern to tenants because leases usually required the leaseholder to pay such a tax. Perhaps the mocking words of young De Witt Clinton, the nephew of the governor, will illustrate the fears of the Anti-Federalists:

From the insolence of great men—from the tyranny of the rich—from the unfeeling rapacity of the excise-man and Tax-gatherer—from the misery of despotism—from the expense of supporting standing armies, navies, placemen, sinecures, federal cities, Senators, Presidents, and a long train of et ceteras Good Lord deliver us!

The Federalist minority at the Poughkeepsie Convention had the advantage of striving for a definite goal, whereas their opponents were forced to take a purely negative position. Indeed, some of them, apparently including Governor Clinton, were willing to ratify the Constitution if certain amendments were added. On June 21 New Hampshire became the ninth state to ratify, and the future of the new national government was assured. At 2 A.M. on July 2 news reached New York City that Virginia had approved and a jubilant day-long celebration began at dawn. Feelings ran high and there was talk that the southern section of the state would secede if the Constitution were not ratified. On July 4 a riot took place in Albany between Federalists and Anti-Federalists; one person was killed and eighteen wounded. By this time New Yorkers who did not wish to ratify the Constitution realized that their cause was lost. Since all states bordering on New York had accepted the Constitution, New York would have been hemmed in by a powerful and not too friendly union, which certainly would not hesitate to place commercial restrictions against it. The only real issue remaining was whether the Constitution would be approved with or without amendments.

On July 26 the Poughkeepsie Convention voted thirty to twenty-seven for ratification "in full confidence" that the other states would endorse the amendments submitted by New York. All delegates from counties north of Orange and Dutchess voted against ratification, whereas all but one of the delegates from counties south of Orange and Dutchess voted for it. The argument of the Anti-Federalists were not entirely in vain, because a bill of rights which contained most of the provisions called for by Melancton Smith and other Clintonians was later appended to the Constitution. New York cannot claim exclusive credit for its enactment because strong sentiment in favor of it was shown in other states during the debate over ratification.

George Clinton's opposition to the Constitution focused national attention upon him. It also made the Federalists in New York determined to defeat him for governor in 1789. Although Clinton had avoided splintering his party on the question of ratification by refusing to make it a party issue, the Clintonians suffered for their unfriendly attitude toward the Constitution, which was continuing to grow in popularity. The Federalists tried to divide Clintonian forces by nominating Robert Yates for governor. Yates had voted against the Constitution at Poughkeepsie but subsequently urged all men to rally to its support. Despite these maneuvers George Clinton was re-elected by a narrow margin for a fifth term. Control of the Assembly passed into the hands of the Federalists, but the Senate remained under the control of the governor's party.

George Washington was inaugurated as first president on April 30, 1789, at Federal Hall, at the intersection of Wall and Broad Streets in New York City. Under his administration Alexander Hamilton dispensed patronage with an eye to strengthening the Federalist party. Hamilton himself became secretary of the treasury; John Jay, chief justice of the Supreme Court; Richard Harison, United States district attorney; and James Duane, district judge. All were unusual men, New Yorkers, and zealous Federalists. Clinton retaliated by using state patronage for his own party. Strangely enough, Hamilton did not secure an important post for the politically powerful Livingston family, which had been staunchly Federalist. When Robert R. Livingston differed with Hamilton's financial plans, the Livingstons went over to the Clintonians in 1790. Of more lasting significance was the governor's decision in this year to retain his nephew, De Witt Clinton, as his personal secretary, starting De Witt on his own political career.

In an effort to unseat George Clinton, the Federalists put up John Jay for governor in 1792. Jay had a long and honorable record of service in both the state and federal governments. He was the principal author of the New York Constitution of 1777. With John Adams and Benjamin Franklin he had negotiated the Treaty of Paris ending the Revolutionary War. Even in the distinguished company at Paris, Jay was outstanding, for it was he who proposed that the American envoys deal directly with Great Britain and disregard their instructions that no agreements should be made without the knowledge and concurrence of France. This step resulted in a treaty much more favorable to the American states than had been expected. In recognition of his talent, Washington in 1789 selected Jay to be the first chief justice of the United States.

The campaign of 1792 was marred by bitter charges and counter-charges. The Federalists attacked Clinton for favoring his friends with offices and for granting large tracts of state land to speculators at low prices. The backers of Clinton charged that Jay was the captive of the aristocracy and would subvert the principles of republican government. Clinton won the election but only under a cloud of scandal. The Anti-

Federalists on the board of election canvassers invalidated the ballots of Otsego, Tioga, and Clinton counties on tenuous technicalities. In each case it was charged that the ballots were delivered improperly to the secretary of state. Had the votes of these counties been tallied, it is certain that Jay would have been elected. Since there was no question of the regularity of the election, the identity of the ballot boxes, or their contents, it is clear that the will of the voters was ignored. Even Thomas Jefferson was moved to comment that the Clintonians had acted dishonorably.

Fortunately, Jay refused to excite himself over this bad treatment and calmed some of his more ardent backers who were threatening violence. The Clinton forces, stung by charges of fraud, struck back by attempting to impeach Judge William Cooper on the charge that he had used illegal means to obtain votes for Jay in Otsego County. Although a grand jury had already dismissed similar charges, the Assembly undertook an investigation. Unquestionably the judge had campaigned vigorously and, perhaps, overbearingly, for Jay, but the evidence which was presented fell far short of proving him guilty of improper conduct. The Clintonian Assembly failed to take any action against him, and, when the Federalists captured the majority of the legislature in 1794, the charges were dismissed as "frivolous and vexatious."

Meanwhile, the outbreak of the French Revolution intensified political controversies in New York. George Clinton and his followers hailed with enthusiasm the fall of the French monarchy and the establishment of the Republic. The slogan of the French revolutionists, "liberty, equality, fraternity," revived the democratic fervor of 1776. When trouble developed between Great Britain and France, the French sent Edmond Charles Genêt to the United States to recruit American aid. The Federalist-controlled national government showed him little sympathy. Fearing to return home, Genêt settled in New York City. The Clintonians were charmed by the Frenchman—who married the governor's nineteen-year-old daughter, Cornelia. Genêt ultimately became a successful gentleman farmer, whose scientific dabblings included experiments in aerial navigation. His marriage quickened George Clinton's interest in France, and with most other Anti-Federalists, Clinton became a strong supporter of France in her struggle with the British. This point of view was held by many New Yorkers who were irritated by the British policy of seizing seamen from American vessels for impressment into the Royal Navy and by the British refusal to evacuate Niagara and the other western forts in compliance with the Treaty of Paris.

The Federalists favored the cause of Great Britain over France. They looked with suspicion upon the pronouncements of the Rights of Man and were horrified by the Reign of Terror. Furthermore, they realized that if the United States became involved in war with Great Britain foreign trade would suffer severely. Hamilton and his associates insisted on peace with Britain because war would destroy revenues from imports and thus jeopardize Hamilton's national financial program. Eager to relieve the tension between the United States and Great Britain, President Washington in 1794 appointed Jay to negotiate a treaty between the two. Jay knew full well that no man could perform the task "without making himself unpopular and odious." His job was made almost impossible by Hamilton, who confided to the British minister that the United States would not join other nations in strong action against Britain no matter what attitude the British took. As a result, Jay was unable to win trade concessions in the British West Indies, a matter of great importance to New York, nor could he persuade the British to discontinue impressment. He did succeed, however, in getting them to evacuate the fur posts along the western border.

In 1795 Clinton wisely refused to run again for governor. Hamilton and the Federalists nominated Jay while he was still in London negotiating with the British. Jay won handsomely over Robert Yates, who had returned to the Anti-Federalist ranks. The day after his formal installation as governor, the text of the Jay Treaty was printed. A storm of abuse fell upon the governor, who, however, remained calm and confident. Angry mobs denounced Jay and stoned Hamilton, who defended the treaty in a public meeting. Despite this bad beginning John Jay and the Federalists ruled New York competently until 1801. Jay was an able and conscientious governor who made many excellent appointments. His opponents could find little to criticize in his administration, but they could fasten upon him some of the mistakes committed by the Federalists in charge of the national government.

The Republicans—for so the Anti-Federalists came to be called—worked hard to strengthen their party, under the leadership of Aaron Burr and De Witt Clinton. They helped transform the Tammany Society from a social and benevolent organization into an efficient political machine. In 1797, De Witt Clinton ran for the Assembly in New York County, long a Federalist stronghold. His victory marked the beginning of Manhattan's century-long allegiance to the party of Jefferson. The Republicans, however, were not successful in their attempt to defeat Jay in 1798. When President John Adams attempted to reach a friendly understanding with France, the American delegates were asked for a bribe as the price for opening negotiations. This scandalous event, known as the XYZ Affair, turned New Yorkers against the French and against the Republicans who were sympathetic to them. Chancellor Robert Livingston, who ran on the Republican ticket, was roundly beaten by Jay.

The victorious Federalists soon came to grief. Hamilton, eager for an opportunity to win personal military glory in a war with France, was astonished and incensed when President Adams named a commission in 1799 to make an agreement with Talleyrand. The split between Adams and Hamilton practically guaranteed the defeat of their party in the approaching election. In 1798 the Federalists forced the adoption of the Alien and Sedition Acts, which among other things made it a crime to organize for the purpose of opposing the legal acts of the federal government or to direct malicious writing against the President and Congress. The Republicans saw in the laws not only a threat to liberty but an opportunity to embarrass their political rivals. On the national scene, Thomas Jefferson and James Madison effectively denounced the acts in the Kentucky and Virginia Resolutions. In New York, Jay and Hamilton defended the laws without much success against Erastus Root, who was at the beginning of his long and brilliant career as a radical Republican, during which he used the floor of the Assembly as his sounding board. Meanwhile Jedediah Peck, a flaming Republican from Otsego County, was circulating a strongly worded petition calling for the repeal of the Alien and Sedition Acts. At the request of Judge William Cooper, a United States marshall arrested Peck and carried him off to New York City to await trial, on the grounds that the circulation of the petition violated the Sedition Act. This manhandling of a popular leader and Revolutionary War veteran shocked the people and demonstrated the awesome scope of the Sedition Act. The Federalists, realizing their error, released Peck, but public reaction could not be stayed.

The presidential election of 1800 was of unusual interest to New York because the state's electoral votes, as expected, determined the new president. Since, at that time, the state legislature chose presidential electors, both parties knew that it was essential to capture the state government. Aaron Burr persuaded George Clinton to come out of retirement and to run for the Assembly on a slate studded with the names of unusually able men. Upstate, Jedediah Peck, Erastus Root, and other politicians labored equally hard for a Republican legislature. Their activities, combined with the mistakes of the Federalists, nullified Hamilton's strenuous efforts, and the Republicans won.

The election of Thomas Jefferson to the presidency now seemed a certainty. Hamilton, seeking to deprive Jefferson of the honor, urged Governor Jay to call a special session of the old legislature, which was safely in Federalist hands, and have it change the method of choosing presidential electors before the newly elected legislators took office. He advised Jay not to hesitate from "the taking of a legal and constitutional step to prevent an atheist in religion and a fanatic in politics, from getting possession of the helm of state." Although the memory of the "steal of 1792" must have tempted him to seek revenge upon his enemies and although he had a grave distrust of Jefferson, Jay declined to subvert the will of the people.

As a result of the victory of their party in New York, the Republican congressional caucus decided to nominate a citizen of that state for the vice-presidency and sent Commodore James Nicholson to canvass the sentiments of the local party leaders. Nicholson persuaded Clinton to accept the post on condition that he could resign if elected. Burr's friends heard of the mission and succeeded in getting Nicholson to change his mind and recommend Burr. Probably this action irked Clinton but nothing came of it at the time.

When the electoral college voted, it was discovered that the Republican electors had each cast one vote for Jefferson and one for Burr. Since the Constitution provided for no distinction between ballots for president and vice-president, Jefferson and Burr were tied. Therefore, the election went to the Federalist-controlled House of Representatives. Although it was well understood that he was the vice-presidential candidate, Burr attempted to win the presidency by courting the Federalists. He might have succeeded had not Hamilton used his influence to support Jefferson as the lesser of two evils.

The Republican tide was running strong, and in 1801 George Clinton was elected to his seventh term as governor and his party captured the legislature. The Federalists, attacked on the national scene for the Alien and Sedition Acts and on the state scene for the imposition of a tax on land, rapidly lost their political power. John Jay, the only Federalist ever to win the governorship, retired to his estate to study soils, stock breeding, and varieties of melons. President Jefferson took care to cultivate George Clinton and to strengthen Republican unity. Aaron Burr was purged from the party because of his efforts to steal the presidency.

During the eventful years between 1783 and 1801 New York made many gains in the political realm even as its merchants were winning great commercial triumphs and its farmers were conquering the wilderness. Except for Virginia and possibly Massachusetts, no other state produced such an able group of political leaders. Hamilton throughout the period was the outstanding Federalist spokesman in the country. Jay was an honest and capable governor, whose self-restraint and integrity in 1792 and again in 1800 furnished a model of intelligent conservatism.

George Clinton, however, enjoyed the greatest and most devoted following of any political leader in New York. He embodied the radical republicanism and democratic ferment which Hamilton feared and distrusted. The farmers and workmen of New York trusted Clinton for his integrity and his essential democracy. But Clinton's influence did not go very far beyond the borders of New York, largely because he had little skill with the pen. Had he possessed Jefferson's ability to turn a phrase and to express democratic principles in felicitous language, he might have won the presidency. Nevertheless, considering the strength of the conservative tradition and the abilities of his political opponents in New York, his election to seven terms as governor was a remarkable achievement.

Victory in the War of Independence did not automatically result in political democracy. Probably the greatest contribution of the party of Jefferson and Clinton was its education of the citizens in democratic principles. Even before Jefferson took the oath of office, Jedediah Peck was agitating in the state legislature for the direct election of presidential electors, aid to the public schools, the abolition of imprisonment for debt, and the emancipation of slaves. Democracy cannot be achieved unless it is understood by the citizenry. In 1801 New Yorkers were beginning to awaken to its full implications.

The Rise of the Democratic Commonwealth, 1801-1825

*I cannot but think that the considerate men who have studied
the history of republics, or are read in lessons of experience,
must look with concern upon our apparent disposition to vi-
brate from a well balanced government, to the extremes of
democratic doctrines.*—CHANCELLOR JAMES KENT, *1821*

THE period from 1801 to 1825 was one of violent political controversy,
largely between factions of the Jeffersonian Republicans. Since the
campaigns were fought by rival groups all professing to be disciples of
Jefferson, the liberal philosophy of that great leader was brought actively
to the attention of New Yorkers. Slowly his thinking penetrated the
minds of the citizens and influenced their action. In 1822 it resulted
in universal manhood suffrage. In a sense the liberal principles of the
Revolution came to fruition in this era.

The bitter rivalry between the various political factions, whose leadership changed with almost bewildering rapidity, was not without its costs.
In the fierce electioneering, unwarranted assaults on the character of
various leaders not only broke up old friendships but lowered the
effectiveness of many able men as political instruments. Even humble
and faithful servants of the state were removed from minor posts after
years of service for political expediency. The intraparty struggles cost
the state dearly in national leadership and prestige. During this quarter
century New York had four great leaders in George Clinton, Aaron Burr,
De Witt Clinton, and Daniel D. Tompkins, any one of whom might
have become president had it not been for the internecine warfare within
the Republican party in New York.

The Council of Appointment, established under the Constitution of
1777, was responsible for many political quarrels. This agency was composed of one senator from each of the four senatorial districts, elected

each year by the Assembly. The constitution did not define clearly the powers of the governor who presided over the Council. George Clinton, however, acted on the assumption that as governor he had the sole right to make nominations and in the case of a tie to cast the deciding vote. Clinton was a keen judge of men and in general made excellent appointments, frequently from among members of the Federalist group. The Federalists in 1794 got control of the Council and insisted upon making their own nominations, overriding Governor Clinton's vigorous objections. The issue died down in 1795 when the Federalist John Jay became governor. The Federalists frankly endorsed the spoils system and filled public offices with their supporters. The controversy was revived in 1801 when the Republicans regained control of the Council and challenged Jay's power to nominate. Neither party apparently had any qualms about reversing its position on this issue.

The legislature called for a constitutional convention, which, in 1801, met in Albany to decide who should exercise the power to nominate. It was here that Daniel D. Tompkins, who was later to become governor of New York and vice-president of the United States, made his first major appearance in public life. Also present were De Witt Clinton, who currently dominated the Council of Appointment, and Aaron Burr, the vice-president of the United States, who was elected president of the convention. Tompkins held that the governor had the power to nominate. He was opposed by Clinton, who argued that all members of the Council held the power concurrently. De Witt Clinton and his supporters won the day. It was a most unfortunate decision. No longer could the governor be held responsible for appointments. Safely concealed in the anonymity of the Council, political hucksters dispensed government jobs without regard for the qualifications of the appointee. In 1818 particularly outrageous removals were made and some fifteen thousand offices were dispensed without any public check. The Republicans thus greatly enlarged the spoils system begun by the Federalists.

At the turn of the century De Witt Clinton was emerging as a Republican leader, partly because George Clinton was aging but mostly because he used the Council of Appointment to build up a political machine. His main objective in 1801–1802 was to weaken the power of Aaron Burr, who was his chief rival for party leadership. Clinton refused to appoint any of Burr's henchmen to office. Soon the bitterest of charges and countercharges were hurled between the two factions. John Swartwout angrily proclaimed that Clinton desired to destroy Burr merely for the purpose of furthering his own interests. Clinton replied that Swartwout was "a liar, a scoundrel and a villain." The outcome was a duel. Swartwout was shot twice in the leg and Clinton escaped with a ball through his coat.

In 1802 De Witt Clinton was elected to the United States Senate, but he resigned a year later to accept appointment as mayor of New York City. Seemingly, Burr had been routed, but the more the Republicans attacked Burr the more acceptable he appeared to some Federalists. Burr determined to capitalize on Federalist support and secured a nomination for the governorship. The Clintonians selected the amiable Morgan Lewis as their candidate. The campaign descended to depths of scurrility not seen since the time of the Revolution. The Republicans exposed Burr's questionable private life, while the Burrites accused the Livingstons and Clintons of packing state offices with their relatives. Hamilton refused to back Burr, whom he regarded as completely unprincipled. Consequently, Burr failed to obtain the full Federalist support he had expected and lost the election by the wide margin of over nine thousand votes.

Once again Hamilton had blocked the hopes of Aaron Burr. The embittered Burr determined to destroy his old enemy. He charged that Hamilton had maligned him to a Dr. Cooper in Albany, an accusation which Hamilton declined to acknowledge or deny on the ground that he could not be responsible for the remarks of third parties. Burr insisted on forcing the issue and Hamilton felt compelled to accept a challenge to duel. The two met on July 11, 1804, on a field in Weehawken, New Jersey. They faced each other at a distance of ten paces. When the command was given, Burr shot instantly. Hamilton fell forward, firing into the ground. The forty-seven-year-old Hamilton died in agony some thirty-one hours later. Morgan Lewis probably reflected the common sentiment when he referred to Burr as "the damned reptile." So great was the public reaction that Burr's political future was ruined.

Governor Lewis entered office in 1804 with an impressive popular majority and with the Republicans in control of the legislature and the Council of Appointment. Lewis, however, made many unfortunate appointments and affronted De Witt Clinton by approving a charter for the Merchant's Bank in New York City. Since Clinton's family controlled the Manhattan Company his opposition to the establishment of a rival institution is understood easily. The breach widened into active opposition between the Clintonians and the Lewis-Livingston faction, who came to be known as Lewisites or Quids.

Seeking to augment their forces, the Clintonians agreed to unite with the Burrites. To consummate the union a supper was held at Dyde's Hotel in New York City on February 20, 1806. The next day several disgruntled Burrites and friends of the Livingston clan called a protest meeting which was held on February 24 in the Long Room of a tavern owned by Abraham Martling, an officer of the Tammany Society. The group represented at this meeting became known as Martling Men. Actually the Martling Men were almost identical with the Tammany Society, and the two terms grew to be synonymous. In spite of De Witt Clinton's best efforts the Martling Men remained his implacable foes.

The majority of the Republicans elected to the legislature in 1806 were Clintonians. The Quids, however, allied with the Federalists to control the legislature of 1807. De Witt Clinton was removed as mayor of New York City and his friends were turned out of political office. Stung by this action, the Republican caucus by-passed Morgan Lewis and nominated Daniel D. Tompkins for governor. Clinton, who supported Tompkins' nomination, did not dare offer himself because he was the favorite target of the Livingstons, the Federalists, and many Burrites. The Quids named Governor Lewis for re-election, but he was defeated by the Clintonian candidate.

Governor Tompkins soon found himself in disagreement with De Witt Clinton. In his opening address to the legislature Tompkins made an able defense of the embargo imposed by Congress at President Jefferson's request in order to isolate the United States from the conflict raging in Europe. Both Clintons had condemned the embargo. De Witt Clinton now reversed himself and endorsed Tompkins' position. A more serious clash took place in 1808. Four years earlier Jefferson had been re-elected president and George Clinton had been elected vice-president. The Clintonians had confidently anticipated that George Clinton would move up to the president's office in accordance with custom. The Virginian Republicans, however, cleverly called together the congressional caucus which nominated James Madison and renamed George Clinton for vice-president. De Witt Clinton insisted that the New York legislature select electors who would support George Clinton for the presidency. Tompkins opposed the move as futile and provocative. Ultimately, George Clinton was returned to the vice-presidential chair and Madison received the higher office.

In 1810 the Republicans re-elected Tompkins and John Broome as governor and lieutenant governor, respectively, but the death of Broome in August forced the legislature to authorize a special election to determine his successor. De Witt Clinton, who had been returned to the mayor's office in New York City, was eager to fill the vacancy and received the nomination of the Republican legislative caucus. Tammany Hall—the name used more and more to describe the Martling Men—protested Clinton's candidacy and held a huge mass meeting presided over by Mangle Minthorne, the father-in-law of Governor Tompkins, which nominated Colonel Marinus Willett, a Revolutionary officer with a record of meritorious service. The Federalists named Nicholas Fish for the office. Notwithstanding the opposition of President Madison, Governor Tompkins, Tammany Hall, and the Federalist party, De Witt Clinton won a handsome victory.

The fortunes of the Federalists, which had fallen to a low ebb, showed signs of reviving after the imposition of the Jeffersonian embargo. Outraged merchants led by Isaac Sebring, Richard Varick, and Gulian C. Verplanck organized the Washington Benevolent Society. This fraternal order, with its secret ritual, solemn pledges, and public ceremonies, was designed to exploit the name of Washington for the benefit of the Federalist party. It spread rapidly to all sections of the state and reinvigorated the party for a time. The Federalist denunciation of Jefferson's foreign policy as destructive to commerce and subservient to Napoleon won popular support, as did their charge that the fall in farm prices properly lay at the door of the Republicans. Public disapproval of Republican policies enabled the Federalists to win temporary control of the legislature in several elections, notably those of 1809, 1812, 1813, and 1814. These victories represented a protest against the Republican line of action rather than a popular endorsement of the principles of Federalism.

Bank charters were another source of controversy throughout this period. The Republicans, whose background was chiefly agrarian, tended to oppose banks as tools of the rich, whereas the Federalists repeated Hamilton's arguments that banks were needed to facilitate trade. As population and trade increased, the pressure by businessmen for banks grew. Since the Federalist party was declining, promoters tried to win the support of influential Republicans by offering at discounts shares in proposed banking corporations—or even outright bribes. When agents of the Bank of America sought a charter, they tried to overcome Republican resistance by offering to pay the school fund $400,000 at the end of a twenty-year period plus an additional $200,000 to the state treasury, provided no rival institution had been incorporated in the meantime. In a further effort to win support bribes were offered to lawmakers. Governor Tompkins denounced the scheme and even prorogued the legislature to prevent incorporation, but the lobbyists had reached too many legislators and in 1812 the Bank of America secured a New York charter.

Vice-President George Clinton died on April 20, 1812. The next month a Republican convention nominated De Witt Clinton for the presidency in opposition to James Madison, who had been named for re-election by a caucus of the Republican members of Congress. In June, Congress declared war on Great Britain, and the prosecution of the conflict became the major issue in the political campaign. Ostensibly the reason for declaring hostilities was the British violation of neutral rights. Actually the South and West were more interested in terminating British incitement of the Indians and in winning more territory in Canada and Florida. New York and the Northeast were more concerned with the deleterious effect the war would have on commerce. When the British announced their willingness to comply with American demands for respect of neutral rights, their proposal offered a basis for withdrawing from the conflict. The British, however, did not agree to abandon impressment.

Madison demanded that the war be fought. In New York he won the support of Governor Tompkins and Tammany Hall. Clinton vacillated but was regarded generally as the peace candidate. The Federalists, traditionally friendly to Great Britain and strong supporters of commercial interests, swallowed their pride and endorsed Clinton although they had fought his family for more than a generation. Madison won, carrying the southern and western states. Clinton garnered most of the votes of New England, New York, and some of the Middle Atlantic states.

Although New Yorkers were divided on the issue of war, most of them desired peace. The values of goods exported from New York exceeded that of any other state, and this profitable trade was stifled by the British fleet. Even on the frontier there was strong opposition to war, for frontier traders sent potashes, pearlashes, and lumber duty free to Montreal and Quebec, from whence they were shipped to Great Britain as Canadian products under favorable duty charges. New York Federalists severely criticized the conduct of the war and agitated for peace, but they did not flirt with secession as their fellow Federalists were doing in New England.

In the face of divided opinion, Tompkins proved himself to be a great war governor. His problems were formidable: an inefficient militia, a hostile Assembly, insufficient funds, a bureaucracy subservient to the spoilsmen on the Council of Appointment. There were about ninety-five thousand citizens subject to militia duty, but these men were poorly trained and equipped. According to the law, militiamen could be called upon to serve only for a maximum of six months each year. The theory that the militia could not be ordered out of the United States was accepted widely. Few of the officers had reasonable experience or training in military matters, and only two general officers, Jacob Brown and Peter B. Porter, were to attain distinction in combat. Discipline was unbelievably lax. As late as 1814, when the armed forces had been improved greatly, several companies of Rockland County militia left their post at New York City in a body to harvest their crops.

During the summer and fall of 1812 this inadequate militia was scattered along the Canadian frontier, facing superior British forces. The roads were so poor that in many cases neighboring American garrisons could not have supported one another. Fortunately, the British knew that their government had agreed to accept American terms in regard to neutral rights and expected the declaration of war to be withdrawn. For this reason they failed to attack and thereby gave the United States time to organize its defenses.

In 1812 the American government had grandiose plans for the speedy conquest of Canada by three campaigns: William Hull, governor of the Michigan Territory, was to invade Upper Canada from Detroit; Major General Stephen Van Rensselaer of the New York militia was to attack Niagara; and Major General Henry Dearborn was to march northward from Plattsburgh and capture Montreal. In the west Hull was defeated by the able British general, Sir Isaac Brock, who captured Detroit on August 16 and then shifted his forces to the Niagara frontier. On the morning of October 13 Van Rensselaer sent a force under Colonel Solomon Van Rensselaer across the Niagara Gorge. Early in the struggle Brock was killed, and the invaders seized a strong toehold on the heights above Queenston. Victory seemed assured, but the New York militia on the American side of the river refused to leave the territory of the United States. As British reinforcements arrived, the invaders, now commanded by Lieutenant Colonel Winfield Scott, were forced down the escarpment to the river. Here they were surrounded and forced to surrender in sight of armed American militiamen on the other side of the Niagara. Stephen Van Rensselaer, sick at heart after the humiliating débâcle at Queenston, resigned his command. The following month General Dearborn's army, marching northward from Plattsburgh, reached the Canadian border, where the militia refused to advance further. Thus all three campaigns ended in failure.

Twice during the first year of the war the British attacked New York territory. On July 19 several enemy vessels assaulted Sackets Harbor, on Lake Ontario, but were beaten off. On October 4, General Jacob Brown repelled a raid on Ogdensburg. These defensive victories were the only glory salvaged from a year of combat along the northern border. The first blow in 1813 was struck on February 23, when the British crossed the St. Lawrence on the ice and destroyed public property at Ogdensburg. Earlier in the month the ineffectual William Eustis was replaced as secretary of war by John Armstrong, a New Yorker. Armstrong reasoned soundly that if the British base at Kingston were captured the St. Lawrence could be closed and the communications of the enemy armies in the west severed, thus rendering them helpless. However, when Captain Isaac Chauncey, commander of the fleet at Sackets Harbor, and General Dearborn indicated preference for a different plan, Armstrong unwisely consented.

In April an American flotilla crossed Lake Ontario with 1,600 troops and burned the buildings of the provincial parliament at York (Toronto). The fleet under Chauncey and the army under Dearborn then proceeded to the mouth of the Niagara River and captured Fort George on May 27. The next day Sir George Prevost, taking advantage of the absence of the main American force, landed 800 men at Sackets Harbor under the covering fire of his fleet. The defender was General Jacob Brown of the New York militia, who repulsed the attack with heavy losses to the enemy. In July, British raiders who crossed the Niagara near Black Rock were badly mauled and driven back by Peter B. Porter, a New Yorker. During this same month an enemy naval squadron gained control of Lake Champlain, and the barracks at Plattsburgh were burned and the magazines plundered. Early in November General James Wilkinson, who had replaced Dearborn, advanced down the St. Lawrence with an American fleet for an attack on Montreal. As he progressed, Wilkinson was harassed from the flanks and the rear and finally defeated on November 11 at Chrysler's Field.

In December, General McClure of the New York militia evacuated Fort George in the face of the advancing enemy and, after burning the Canadian villages of Newark and Queenston, retired across the Niagara. The destruction of these two villages was an act of cruelty which drew prompt requital. During the night of December 18–19 two enemy forces under Colonel Murray and General Riall invaded New York. Murray captured Fort Niagara, and Riall laid waste the countryside along the Niagara River. A few days later the British defeated a small group of militia under General Amos Hall and burned Black Rock and Buffalo. Although the war did not go well along the New York frontier in 1813, American forces won important victories in the west. On September 10 Captain Oliver Hazard Perry crushed the British naval squadron at Put in Bay, securing Lake Erie to the Americans, and during the month following William Henry Harrison defeated the major enemy army in the west at the Battle of the Thames.

The crisis came in 1814. By spring Napoleon had been defeated and the British began to send veterans of Wellington's army to North America, which now occupied Great Britain's undivided attention. Fortunately, two years of war had tested the American forces and had resulted in the removal of most incompetent officers. By August the American navy had won control of Lake Ontario, and early in July Major General Jacob Brown, formerly of New York militia but now an officer in the regular army, had crossed the Niagara to invade Canada. Brown had about 3,550 troops and some 600 Indians under his command. A large part of this force came from New England and Pennsylvania, but the Twenty-Third Regiment was composed of regulars from New York. In addition there were some New York militia and volunteers. On July 5, Brown's army won a brilliant victory at Chippewa. On the twenty-fifth it fought a bloody battle at Lundy's Lane, driving the enemy from strong positions, capturing its artillery, and withdrawing during the night. In August and September, Brown gave an excellent account of himself around Fort Erie, where he held superior British forces at bay. Among the most able officers in this fighting was Peter B. Porter.

The real danger, however, was in the Lake Champlain region, where the British massed a large body of veteran troops. The British plan was for Sir George Prevost to invade the United States by following Burgoyne's old route up Lake Champlain. Could this be accomplished, New England, which strongly opposed the war, might be cut off from the rest of the nation and perhaps be returned to the Empire. To accomplish his mission Prevost had at his disposal about 11,000 troops plus a naval squadron on Lake Champlain. Facing him was General Alexander Macomb, who was entrenched at Plattsburgh with some 3,300 soldiers, less than half of whom were fit for duty, and Captain Thomas McDonough, who commanded the American flotilla. The two fleets met in battle outside Plattsburgh Bay on September 11. McDonough destroyed the statistically superior British squadron in a notable and crucial engagement. Prevost, fearing to advance without control of Lake Champlain, returned to Canada. This was the last important battle of the war along the northern frontier of New York.

Until the closing months of the struggle New York City was left largely to its own resources, and during the course of the war 120 privateers sailed from its harbor and captured 275 prizes. After 1813, however, the British tightened the naval blockade and forced the city to look to its defenses. When the news of Napoleon's defeat reached the city on June 10, 1814, there was a somber realization that the British now had available enough ships and troops to attack the port. Under the able direction of Mayor De Witt Clinton the defense work was quickened. On August 26 came the news that the British had raided Washington and burned the government buildings. There was panic in the city. By November the defenses were completed and it was estimated that 25,000 troops could be assembled in three hours, but the attack never came. On February 11 the British sloop of war *Favorite* arrived off Sandy Hook with the terms of the Treaty of Ghent, a treaty which settled none of the points over which the United States had gone to war, but which was received with universal joy.

One cannot escape the conclusion that New York never wholeheartedly supported the War of 1812. Not until the summer of 1814 did its soldiers fight with determination. On several occasions the militia refused to advance beyond the national boundary. Throughout the struggle supplies poured from its northern farms into Canada. On June 29, 1814, the Federalists celebrated the defeat of Napoleon with a public dinner in New York City. Such distinguished citizens as Gouverneur Morris and Rufus King took part in the festivities, which were certainly disloyal if not treasonable. Fortunately, it was a relatively inexpensive war. De Witt Clinton calculated its cost to that state at $1,959,477.06. Except for the destruction of a few border towns, New York emerged with its farms, factories, commercial houses, and port facilities intact.

Political activities did not subside during the War of 1812. The Federalists kept sniping at Governor Tompkins, refusing to vote funds for the militia in 1812 and interfering with appointments. Tompkins in 1814 secured a Republican majority in the legislature, which promptly voted for a stronger militia and defenses. Although the Republicans continued to be riddled by factional feuds, Tompkins maintained his control. Meanwhile, De Witt Clinton was falling to one of the lowest points in his career. His party refused to renominate him for the office of lieutenant governor in 1813, and ardent Republicans kept demanding his dismissal as mayor of New York City. To their aid came Gulian C. Verplanck, a young Federalist litterateur, who wrote a series of satirical articles under the pseudonym Abimelech Coody. Clinton, skilled in the art of political invective himself, replied in kind: "He has become the head of a political sect called the Coodies, of hybrid nature, composed of the combined spawn of Federalism and Jacobinism, and generated in the venomous passions of disappointment and revenge." Thereafter Verplanck and his political associates were known as Coodies. In 1815 an alliance of Coodies, Tammany Hall, Ambrose Spencer, and other malcontents secured Clinton's removal from the mayoralty.

Governor Tompkins' great popularity continued, and in 1816 he won re-election. During this same year he was looked upon by many as presidential timber. However, the Virginia dynasty again asserted itself by dictating the nomination of James Monroe. Consequently Tompkins had to be satisfied with second place on the ticket. Both he and Monroe were elected to office.

De Witt Clinton soon rebounded from the collapse of his political fortunes and served as governor for nine years (1817–1822, 1824–1828). His return to public favor resulted from his advocacy of the Erie Canal proposal, with which he became identified in the public mind. In December 1815 he made a remarkable speech calling for the construction of canals to link the Hudson River with Lake Erie and Lake Champlain. This speech revived the latent procanal sentiment which had died down during the War of 1812. Clinton was appointed chairman of a committee to present a memorial to the legislature. To accomplish this purpose he traveled from New York City to Albany. His journey was nothing short of a triumphant tour, no doubt sweet solace to a man whose foes thought they had buried him the previous year. In response to public demand the legislature created a Canal Commission and named Clinton to head it.

Clinton began to rebuild his political alliances. He became reconciled with Ambrose Spencer, who promptly started a movement to elect Clinton governor. When Tompkins departed to assume vice-presidential duties, the governor's chair became vacant and leadership of the anti-Clintonian faction of the party fell to Martin Van Buren. Realizing that any caucus of Republican legislators would be dominated by Van Buren, Spencer demanded the party call a state nominating convention. Van Buren could not prevent this innovation and the subsequent nomination of Clinton. Endorsed by the Republicans and unobstructed by the Federalists, Clinton in 1817 swept aside the opposition of Tammany to win a smashing victory in which he obtained over 95 per cent of the popular vote.

The Tammany Society formed the core of the Republican group which opposed the new governor. Since it was the custom for members of the Tammany Society to wear the tails of deer in their hats at patriotic gatherings, that political faction became known as the Bucktail party. The guiding genius of the Bucktails was Van Buren, but he received able assistance from Benjamin F. Butler, Samuel A. Talcott, Benjamin Knower, and William Learned Marcy.

By this time the Federalist party had crumbled and many of its members had shifted their support to the Clintonians. Apparently Clinton was master of the state, but his love of power and lack of tact, combined with the skill of his enemies, created many difficulties for him. He was charged with arrogance, nepotism, disloyalty, and ingratitude. By 1818 Van Buren had won sufficient support to name the speaker of the Assembly. Van Buren also got control of the Council of Appointment and the Canal Commission, which enabled him to build up a political machine. Two years later he detached a faction of the Federalists from Clinton by supporting Rufus King for the United States Senate.

In 1820 the Bucktails, who enjoyed the support of the Monroe administration, induced Vice-President Tompkins to run for governor, hoping his war record would offset Clinton's appeal to canal partisans. Unfortunately for Tompkins, his opponents publicized the fact that his accounts kept during the hectic war years revealed many shortages. Strangely enough, a group of forty-eight Federalists denounced Clinton as "disgusting to the feelings of all truly high-minded and honorable men." Clinton promptly lampooned the signers as "High-Minded," and still another curious designation for a party faction came into being.

This division among the Federalists between the "High-Minded" who supported Tompkins and the larger group which followed Clinton marked the end of the Federalists as a party organization. Clinton won re-election in a rancorous campaign during which unwarranted vituperation was heaped on the personal integrity of former governor Tompkins.

Clinton promptly became involved in a bitter fight with the Monroe administration, which he accused of interfering in New York politics. After the state Senate had censured him for this attack, Clinton sent a message to the legislature together with a green bag containing some evidence to document his charges. Among the papers was a letter from Van Buren asking the dismissal of certain postmasters, stating, "Unless we can alarm them by two or three prompt removals, there is no limiting the injurious consequences that may result from it." Van Buren later claimed the postmasters were removed for failing to deliver Bucktail newspapers. In 1821 the Bucktails got control of the Council of Appointment and ruthlessly ousted not only their political opponents but also such loyal public servants as Gideon Hawley, the nonpolitical State Superintendent of Common Schools, who was recognized widely as an excellent administrator.

Van Buren, who was at this time a United States senator, frankly endorsed the spoils system as a means of maintaining party discipline. About this time the group of men who controlled the Bucktail party became known as the Albany Regency. The first members of the Regency in addition to Van Buren were William Learned Marcy; Benjamin Knower, father-in-law of Marcy; Samuel A. Talcott; and Roger Skinner. This inner circle was soon joined by Azariah Cutting Flagg, who later distinguished himself in the field of finance, and Edwin Croswell, editor of the Albany *Argus*. Van Buren was the most influential member of this coterie of talented men, but he did not dominate the group. By bestowing political appointments on friends and turning enemies out of office, the Albany Regency welded the Bucktail party into the most powerful political organization the state had yet seen. The Regency has been charged unjustly with originating the spoils system—a charge made easier by Marcy's statement that he could see no evil "in the rule that to the victor belongs the spoils of the enemy." Actually the charge of originating the spoils system could more properly be laid against the Federalists because of their conduct in the 1790's. In any case, De Witt Clinton had practiced political patronage long before the Regency came into being.

By 1821 the rampant use of the spoils system led many to believe that the Council of Appointment should be dissolved. But the Council of Appointment was only one of several features of the Constitution of

1777 which either prevented efficient administration or checked the popular will. Gradually the transplanted Yankees of upstate and the common people in New York City rebelled against restricted suffrage and the Council of Revision, which frequently vetoed popular legislation. The upsurge of democratic feeling in New York State was a part of the tidal wave sweeping the northern and western states.

During a period of some forty years the Council of Revision, which was composed of the five judges of the Supreme Court, the chancellor, and the governor, disallowed 118 laws. Some of these were repassed over its veto by a two-thirds vote of the legislature. The Council was intended to check hasty and foolish laws, but unfortunately it tended at times to reflect Federalist thinking of a purely partisan nature. The Council checked the legislature's attempt to change the charter of Columbia College, a citadel of Federalism, and during the War of 1812 it curbed Tompkins' efforts to enact conscription and drastic property taxes. When the Council in 1820 rejected a popular bill calling for a constitutional convention, the public was aroused and the Republicans demanded the Council be abolished.

On August 28, 1821, a constitutional convention finally assembled at Albany. It was a body of distinguished men and included practically all the outstanding political figures of the time. Among the small group of remaining Federalists were such able men as Chancellor James Kent, the most determined defender of the status quo; Peter Augustus Jay, gifted son of the principal author of the first constitution; Jonas Platt; Abraham Van Vechten; Elisha Williams; and Stephen Van Rensselaer, III, scion of the old and wealthy landholding family. They tried to salvage as much as was possible in face of the Bucktail demand for reform, but their cause was hopeless. Out of 126 seats the Bucktails controlled 110. These Republicans were not men of limited experience and ability. Among their ranks were Daniel D. Tompkins, who presided over the convention, the astute Martin Van Buren, the distinguished Peter R. Livingston, and Erastus Root, a master of sarcasm.

The convention quickly abolished both the Council of Appointment and the Council of Revision, despite the somewhat perfunctory protests of the Federalists. It gave the governor the veto power, but a two-thirds vote in each house could override his veto. The appointing power was distributed in a fashion more democratic but not necessarily wiser from the standpoint of improved administration. The chief officers of the state, such as the secretary of state, the attorney general, and the comptroller, were to be elected by the legislature, whereas lesser officials were to be appointed by the governor with the consent of the Senate. The convention also revised the judiciary system by creating a new Supreme Court consisting of a chief justice and two associate justices and by providing for the establishment of from four to eight judicial districts, in each of which would be a district judge.

The changes in the suffrage, however, aroused much more controversy and proved far more significant. The old constitution prescribed the possession of a twenty-pound freehold or the payment of a yearly rent of forty shillings as qualifications of voters for assemblymen. To vote for senator and governor the citizen had to possess still more property. To the dismay of the Federalists, the Republicans advocated clauses permitting voters to qualify by payment of taxes, by service in the militia, by work on the roads, or by established residence. In short, the Republicans were proposing the equivalent of universal manhood suffrage for white voters.

Abraham Van Vechten stated the Federalist case succinctly. "Life and liberty are common to all, but the possession of property is not. Hence the owners of property have rights which, in relation to those who are destitute, are separate and exclusive." The most eloquent defense of the old order came from Chancellor James Kent, who warned of the dangers in extending the suffrage:

The growth of the city of New-York is enough to startle and awaken those who are pursuing the *ignis fatuus* of universal suffrage. In 1773 it had 21,000 souls, in 1801 it had 60,000 souls, in 1806 it had 76,000 souls, in 1820 it had 123,000 souls.

It is rapidly swelling into the unwieldy population, and with the burdensome pauperism, of an European metropolis. New-York is destined to become the future London of America; and in less than a century, that city, with the operation of universal suffrage, and under skilful direction, will govern this state.

Nor was it safe to adopt universal suffrage as an experimental measure, said the chancellor:

Universal suffrage once granted, is granted forever, and never can be recalled. There is no retrograde step in the rear of democracy. However mischievous the precedent may be in its consequences, or however fatal in its effects, universal suffrage never can be recalled or checked, but by the strength of the bayonet.

The Federalist appeal was dashed aside by Erastus Root, who replied: "We have no different estates, having different interests, necessary to be guarded from encroachments by the watchful eye of jealousy— We are all of the same estate—all commoners; nor, until we have privileged orders, and aristocratic estates to defend, can this argument apply." The Federalists were inundated by the democratic tide. Although property qualifications were retained for Negroes virtual universal suffrage was established for white males. A few other minor changes were made. The governor could no longer prorogue the legislature, and his term was reduced to two years. The date for state elections was shifted from April to November.

On November 10 the constitutional convention closed. Sixteen members, including Abraham Van Vechten and Peter Augustus Jay, refused to sign the finished document. The voters overwhelmingly approved the new constitution, which went into effect December 31, 1822.

During the early 1820's the political situation in New York was confused. The conservative forces were searching for a new party as they hurriedly gave up the Federalist label. Most regarded Clinton as their champion, partly because of his cultural attainments but largely because of his canal policy. Moreover, the conservatives were adding to their natural strength. Not only could they command the support of the old creditor, commercial, and landed classes but they were also beginning to enlist the aid of the growing manufacturing class as well as the substantial farmers along the route of the Erie Canal. The liberal elements, whose strength was augmented by the widened suffrage, followed the leadership of the Albany Regency. The Bucktails preached economy and low taxes while they continued to denounce the old aristocracy. In general, they were lukewarm in their support of internal improvements. In 1822 Clinton did not dare to run for re-election because his political organization had vanished. Robert Yates, the Bucktail candidate for governor, was swept into office by virtually a unanimous vote.

Early in 1823 the Regency threw its support to William H. Crawford, the hand-picked candidate of the Virginia dynasty, in his quest for the presidency, although many important Bucktails preferred John Quincy Adams, Henry Clay, or John C. Calhoun. The Clintonians favored Andrew Jackson. Realizing that party machinery enabled the Regency to control the legislature, the anti-Crawford men used northern opposition to Virginian dictation of presidential candidates to lend force to their demands that nomination by legislative caucus be abandoned for a nominating convention and that presidential electors be chosen directly by the people rather than the legislature. When the Albany Regency refused to accede, the People's party was organized to seek the desired reforms. In this delicate situation the Regency made a fatal blunder by removing De Witt Clinton from the Canal Commission where he had long served with distinction and without pay. The citizenry was enraged, and Van Buren, who was at his post in the United States Senate, professed to be astonished.

When the convention called by the People's party met in Utica during September 1824, it was dominated by De Witt Clinton's friends, who secured his endorsement for the governorship. The Regency obtained the nomination of Samuel Young—the last nomination made by legislative caucus in New York State. When Van Buren appeared at the polls, derisive cries of "Regency! Regency!" greeted him. Clinton was elected by a sizable majority—rising for the second time from political oblivion to the highest office in the state. After witnessing this event, Van Buren remarked to Roger Skinner, a member of the Regency who had been a prime mover in recalling Clinton from the Canal Commission, "I hope, Judge, you are now satisfied that there is such a thing in politics as *killing a man too dead!"*

The replacement of the legislative caucus as the nominating agency by party conventions did not seriously hamper political machines. Party leaders controlled conventions by seeing to it that convention delegates were men of their own choice. A vastly more important change was the modification of the electoral law which followed the decisive Clintonian victory. Henceforth presidential electors were chosen by district and selected by the people. The presidential election of 1824 marked, therefore, the last time presidential electors were picked by the state legislature. Since the legislators elected at the same time as Clinton would not take office until after the first of the year, it was presumed that the Regency would remain in control and would place New York behind Crawford. In a surprising turn of events New York's vote was split: Adams 26, Crawford 5, Clay 4, and Jackson 1. This amazing upset was the result of the backstage work of Thurlow Weed, a twenty-seven-year-old journalist, who made a deal with the backers of Henry Clay whereby they agreed to support Adams in exchange for seven Clay votes under certain conditions. To facilitate voting Weed printed a split ticket including both Clay and Adams supporters. Weed became one of the ablest political managers in the history of the nation. The national election failed to produce a majority, and the issue went to the United States House of Representatives, where Adams needed the vote of New York to win. After some wavering, Congressman Stephen Van Rensselaer, III, cast the deciding vote which swung the state to Adams.

During the first quarter of the nineteenth century, politics in New York were unusually bitter, because personalities rather than issues were dominant. The disintegration of the Federalists accentuated the factionalism so characteristic of the Republicans. At times the government, cursed with the spoils system, the restrictive vetoes of the Council of Revision, outrageous lobbying, and petty squabbles, seemed to work badly. Yet out of this welter of faction emerged a new concept of equality and democracy—well exemplified in the Common School Law of 1812, which greatly widened opportunities for education—and revealed in the Constitution of 1822, which virtually banished property qualifications for white male voters. The last political strongholds of the conservative landholding class which had dominated New York for over 150 years were swept away. A bloodless political revolution had been effected.

Heyday of the Land

Speculator

Could you not introduce a few good inhabitants in each town-
ship by exchanging new lands for old or improved
farms? . . . Twenty good families will by their connections
soon fill up a township, and by still holding on about one-
quarter of your lands you will be able to sell for the price of
cleared land.—JAMES WADSWORTH *to David B. Ogden, 1817*

INDEPENDENCE seemed to sharpen the interest of New Yorkers in
land acquisition. To land-hungry Americans no state offered a more
varied or richer bill of fare than New York: choice lots in Manhattan,
townsites along the Hudson and at inland crossroads, improved lands
confiscated from the Tories, and—greatest prize of all—millions of acres
of wild lands north and west of Fort Stanwix (Rome). As a result, a
saturnalia of speculation took place, with a relatively few master promoters gorging themselves on raw lands. Nevertheless, land monopoly
did not eventuate, for within a generation many of the great land
jobbers had disposed of most of their holdings to tens of thousands of
freehold farmers. This turn of events had important political implications,
for the freeholders joined forces with the yeomen followers of George
Clinton and Martin Van Buren and forced the landed aristocracy to
accept manhood suffrage in the constitutional convention of 1821.

The New York back country attracted the attention of speculators
throughout the eastern seaboard and piqued the curiosity of capitalists in
Europe. Cautious Dutch bankers, titled English gentlemen, and refugee
French noblemen jostled native Americans in the rush for lands. Yankees
plunged heavily in New York lands, as did practically every merchant
in Albany and New York. George Washington and Alexander Hamilton
dabbled in central New York real estate.

During colonial times the British officials had handed out large tracts to men with political influence. The New York state legislature continued the practice of disposing of public land in large lots at nominal prices, and in 1786 it created a board of land commissioners empowered to dispose of unsold land. Within the next five years this board sold over 5,500,000 acres of land in northern and central New York, chiefly in large tracts. It laid out townships of approximately 64,000 acres, set aside one-twentieth of the area for the support of highway building, and gave lots to endow "the gospel and schools." Purchasers received tax exemptions for seven years if they developed their tracts during that time. The homestead idea, that is, the granting of land in small parcels to actual settlers rather than to absentee speculators, won little support in New York until well along in the nineteenth century. The major exception to the policy of sale was the grant of approximately 1,500,000 acres to veterans of the Revolution, who were given the right to select land within the Military Tract of central New York.[1]

Land speculation was no "open sesame" to fortune. Alexander Macomb and Robert Morris, both of whom acquired millions of acres of New York lands, became bankrupts. Other speculators, however, notably the Wadsworth family, William Cooper, and Peter Smith, laid the foundations of family fortunes. But speculation in land was a hazardous business. Sharp setbacks in the long-term upswing of land values often ruined those operating on limited financial resources. The costs of carrying land—taxes, interest on capital, agent's commissions, and capital investments such as roads, schools, and mills—sometimes outstripped the increase in land values. The price of any particular parcel was influenced by many factors, including climate, soil, nearness to market, degree of improvement, density of population, and, perhaps most important of all, expectation of further increase in value.

The land jobber performed a function which the state was not yet prepared to assume. He surveyed and subdivided large tracts. He attracted settlers by advertisements and by agents. He extended credit during the crucial years of pioneering. Sometimes he helped build roads, mills, and schools. In short, he was a sort of middleman between the state and the frontier farmer, with his profits kept in line by the competition of other landholders in New York and surrounding states. The speculator, therefore, shares some of the credit for developing the New York frontier, since he risked his capital and often personally braved the rigors of the wilderness.

After the Revolution, the Iroquois still held title to "new" New York, the territory west of the Property Line of 1768 running from Fort Stanwix to the head of the Unadilla River. But six thousand Indians could not hold back tens of thousands of land-hungry whites. The

---

[1] Veterans showed no interest in the "old" Military Tract, located in modern Clinton and Franklin counties in northern New York.

federal and state governments made peace treaties with the Iroquois, who had been weakened by the war. In the second Treaty of Fort Stanwix, in 1784, the Iroquois surrendered to the United States all their traditional claims to land west of Buffalo Creek. In addition, the Senecas, Cayugas, and Onondagas agreed to cede to New York State large tracts west of the Property Line. This cession was the first of a series negotiated between 1784 and 1790 in which the various tribes of the Six Nations signed away most of their lands east of the Genesee River. Before the century closed, practically all their claims to land in New York State had been surrendered. The members of the once-powerful Iroquois Confederacy had retreated to Canada or to a few small reservations.[2]

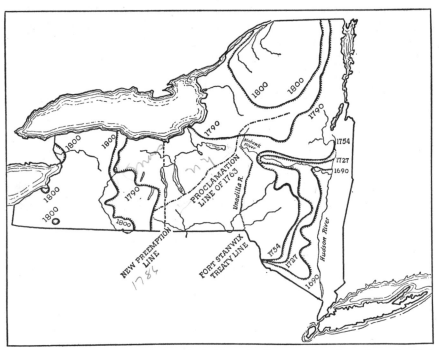

Map 6. Frontier map of New York. Frontier lines are based on dates for first settlement of towns west of the Hudson River. (Adapted from Ruth Higgins, *Expansion in New York.*)

Meanwhile, commissioners for New York and Massachusetts met at Hartford in 1786 to work out a compromise of their rival claims to west-

[2] Today more than six thousand Indians live on eight reservations: Onondaga near Syracuse; Allegheny; Cattaraugus near Gowanda; Tuscarora near Niagara Falls; Tonawanda near Akron; the St. Regis near Hogansburg; and the Poosepatuck and the Shinnecock on Long Island.

ern New York. They drew a Pre-emption Line south from Sodus Bay through Seneca Lake to the Pennsylvania border. Massachusetts received the lands west of Seneca Lake and ten townships lying between the Owego and Chenango Rivers. New York won *title* to all land east of the line and *political* sovereignty over all the area in dispute.

During the Revolutionary War the state government had pledged to many soldiers a bounty of 600 acres. Officers received proportionately larger grants. In 1782 the legislature set aside a tract of over 1,500,000 acres, which was divided into twenty-eight townships six miles square. This tract in the Finger Lakes district, readily identified today by the sprinkling of classical names such as Cato and Sempronius, included the present counties of Onondaga, Cayuga, Seneca, Cortland, and portions of Oswego, Wayne, Schuyler, and Tompkins counties. Soldiers, however, represented only a minority of the settlers since many veterans sold their land warrants to speculators.

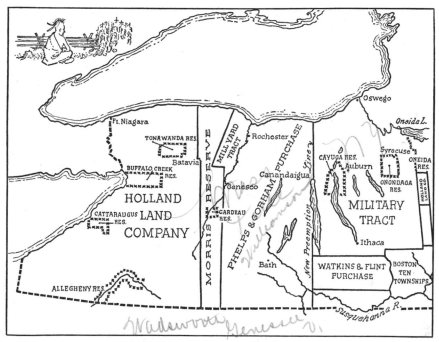

Map 7. Western New York land pattern, 1790–1812.

Speculators also got control of several large tracts between the Property Line and the Military Tract. In 1789 the surveyor-general laid out the Chenango Twenty Townships covering the southern half of present-day Madison and the northern half of Chenango counties. A group of speculators bought the 230,400 acres in the Boston Ten Townships from Massachusetts for twelve and a half cents an acre. Other speculators bought up the Watkins and Flint Purchase and the Chemung Township. William Bingham, a wealthy Philadelphia merchant, acquired the site of Binghamton, which his agents laid out and developed. The Holland Land Company bought 100,000 acres south of Cazenovia. Peter Smith, the father of the reformer Gerrit Smith, acquired from the Oneida tribe several thousand acres south of Oneida Lake. Settlers followed close on the heels of the speculators and soon acquired title to farms.

Massachusetts officials also adopted the policy of selling their huge tract of 6,000,000 acres west of Seneca Lake to land jobbers. Oliver Phelps and Nathaniel Gorham headed a syndicate of capitalists and politicians who agreed to pay the state approximately $175,000 in gold for the land. Phelps hastened west to clear the Indian title and to run surveys. The sachems and chiefs of the Iroquois assembled about the council fire at Buffalo Creek in July 1788 and sold about 2,500,000 acres lying east of the Genesee River for $5,000 and an annuity of $500. Phelps laid off townships six miles square and opened one of the first land offices in the United States at Canandaigua.

Financial troubles soon caught up with Phelps and Gorham. They could get little hard cash out of the settlers, and some of their fellow capitalists backed out of the venture. Most disheartening of all was the upsurge in the price of Massachusetts securities, which they had expected to buy at depreciated levels and to turn over to the state at par. In 1790 they turned back the western two-thirds of the tract in order to retain full title to the eastern section.

Their ill luck did not deter Robert Morris from buying 1,000,000 acres from Phelps and Gorham in the region lying between Seneca Lake and the Genesee River. A few months later Morris paid Massachusetts $333,333 for approximately 4,000,000 acres west of the Genesee River. Morris was basically a wholesaler who expected that his reputation as secretary of finance during the Revolution would enable him to unload his holdings on bankers in Amsterdam, London, and Paris.

At first Morris enjoyed great success. A syndicate of English capitalists headed by Sir William Pulteney, the greatest landed capitalist in Great Britain, paid him £75,000 in 1791 for the tract he had acquired for only £45,000 from Phelps and Gorham. A tract twelve miles wide which embraced most of the lush bottom land in the Genesee Valley was kept by Morris for price appreciation. His greatest coup was the sale for over $1,000,000 of some 2,500,000 acres west of the Genesee River to four Amsterdam banking houses speculating in American securities. Theophile Cazenove, their agent in America, had already purchased for them two townships near Cazenovia and two patents near Rome. The Dutch capitalists organized the Holland Land Company to administer their large holdings in New York and Pennsylvania.

Despite these spectacular deals, Morris found his debts climbing faster than his income. A sheriff's sale stripped him of his special reserve of 500,000 acres, which passed to several creditors. Among the purchasers was Jeremiah Wadsworth, who placed his tracts under the supervision of his nephews, James and William. James Wadsworth secured the agencies for several tracts, including tens of thousands of acres located in the upper Genesee Valley. With the money he made as agent, Wadsworth gradually built up a family estate still famous in western New York.

What effect did the entrance of the European capitalists have upon the development of New York apart from sprinkling the countryside with Old World place names? The permanent effect was negligible, although the immediate result was the acceleration of settlement. The London and Amsterdam bankers had ample capital to improve their holdings by adding buildings, roads, taverns, gristmills, and sawmills. In general, foreign investors found it necessary to abandon preconceived ideas of developing their holdings and found it wise to follow rather closely the practices of native Americans in disposing of their tracts.

Charles Williamson, the agent for the Pulteney estates, was a sanguine Scot who introduced the "hothouse" method of developing the country. Williamson built miles of roads, laid out towns, erected stores, taverns, gristmills, and extended credit to settlers. He selected sites for export centers on the Genesee River (Williamsburg), Lake Erie (Sodus), Cohocton River (Bath), and Seneca River (Lyons). Within ten years Williamson had spent over $1,000,000, against which he had collected only $146,000. Such meager returns alarmed his English sponsors, who replaced him with Robert Troup in 1801. Troup was a cautious Federalist lawyer who cut back on expenditures and stepped up debt collection. Within ten years he recovered the investment of his principals, but the Pulteney interests never got out much more than their original investment. The liquidation of their holdings was a painful process lasting until well after the Civil War.

The Amsterdam bankers also experimented for a few years with the "hothouse" method, pouring over $100,000 into their tract near Cazenovia and an even greater amount into their holdings north of Utica. Comparable expenditures on their 3,300,000 acres west of the Genesee would obviously have plunged them into bankruptcy. Accordingly, the Dutch company appointed an experienced American woodsman, Joseph Ellicott, to run their surveys and to supervise land sales. Ellicott believed that the settlers preferred a policy of low prices and liberal credit with few improvements to the hothouse system, which, naturally, made for higher land prices. He frequently accepted only 5 to 10 per cent of the purchase price in cash, the remainder payable within six to ten years. On the whole, the terms were reasonable, and Ellicott and other agents were responsive to the settlers' needs.

Unrest did flare up during the 1820's when the Holland Land Company demanded payments which had been allowed to lapse after the panic of 1819. Farmers complained that their accumulated debts often exceeded the resale value of their farms. The Holland Land Company made numerous concessions, scaling down the debt of some delinquents and accepting payment in cattle and wheat. Discontent continued, since many debtors were unable or unwilling to meet the new terms. In 1833, when the legislature passed a law taxing the company for debts still owing to it upon land sales, the agents redoubled their efforts to collect arrears. In protest, the farmers called a convention in Buffalo, but their attempts to challenge the title of the company proved fruitless. In 1835 a mob of enraged farmers sacked the office of the company agent in Mayville, and debtors throughout the Holland Purchase refused to pay any more money. The revolt induced the Dutch bankers to sell out their holdings, which had brought them approximately 5 per cent per year for the period of ownership. This action was actually bad news for the debtors, since the purchasers, hard-headed Americans, insisted upon prompt payment of debts. The Farmers' Loan and Trust Company of New York bought out the Holland Land Company's interests in Erie, Orleans, Niagara, and Genesee counties for a sum of over $2,282,382.63.

Northern New York was virtually unbroken wilderness in 1783 except for a few settlements fringing Lake Champlain. In fact, most of the region lying between Lake Champlain on the east, Lake Ontario on the west, the St. Lawrence River on the north, and the southern slopes of the Adirondacks remained wilderness until late in the nineteenth century. The rugged topography, the stony soils, the shortness of the growing season, and the lack of roads discouraged settlers, who preferred central and western New York. Several thousand settlers, largely from Vermont, drifted into the St. Lawrence and Black river valleys between 1783 and 1825.

Land jobbers were the first to take an interest in this region, which the state auctioned off at rock-bottom prices. Their leader was the adventuresome Irish fur trader, Alexander Macomb. In 1787 Macomb, acting for himself and several associates, bought most of the Ten Towns along the St. Lawrence. Four years later he got control of practically all of the unpatented portions of northern New York for eight cents an acre— 4,000,000 acres in all. But Macomb, like Morris, found it easier to acquire tracts than to sell them. His first move was to divide his holdings into six great tracts. Those numbered Tracts Four, Five, and Six fell under the supervision of William Constable, who took over complete control after Macomb became insolvent.

Constable was as important in the development of the Black River and St. Lawrence River country as James Wadsworth in the Genesee and Williamson in the Phelps and Gorham Purchase. He sold about 600,000 acres in Tract Four to the Antwerp Company and another 210,000 acres to Peter Chassanis of Paris. The latter enticed several émigrés fleeing the tumbrels of the Jacobins to establish homes in the New York frontier.

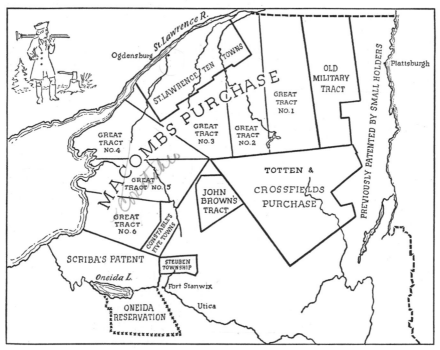

Map 8. Northern New York land pattern, 1790–1815.

Constable sold smaller tracts to William Inman and John Brown of the famous Providence family. Brown divided his tract into townships labeled Frugality, Industry, and Temperance; but such nomenclature, however comforting to Yankee consciences, could not compensate for the cold and thin soils of these mountainous acres.

The northern part of the Macomb Purchase—Great Tracts One, Two, and Three—had a similar history. A notable figure in developing this region was Samuel Ogden, who laid out the town named for him. Equally famous was David Parish, scion of an English and German family that controlled an important business house with branches in various cities of northern Europe. Parish, who made his fortune in the Spanish-American trade, fell victim in 1807 to the blandishments of Gouverneur Morris, who was trying to sell his tracts along the St. Lawrence River. Parish bought 200,000 acres in 1808 and kept adding to his holdings. In 1811 he moved to Ogdensburg to administer his estate. Following the example of Williamson, Parish poured hundreds of thousands of dollars into turnpikes, iron forges, and wharves at Ogdensburg. All in all, the north country proved a disappointment to most land speculators, who could not successfully compete with the holders of the richer lands of western New York and, subsequently, of the Great Lake states.

In "old" New York, the section south and east of Rome which was developed before the Revolution, the pattern of land ownership underwent some important changes after 1775. The confiscation of Loyalist estates struck a sharp blow at the landed aristocracy. Speculators fattened on the spoils taken from the De Lanceys, Philipses, and the heirs of Sir William Johnson. These speculators, however, usually sold the land in small parcels to actual settlers. As a result Westchester and Dutchess counties, once the stronghold of manorial owners, registered a rapid increase in freeholders in the years following the Revolution. Furthermore, the legislature pulled out some of the legal props supporting the aristocratic land system. It forbade entail and primogeniture, thus ensuring the eventual partition of the manors held by Patriots. The legislature abolished all feudal obligations and feudal tenures.

The "Patriot" aristocracy, led by the Van Rensselaer, Livingston, and Schuyler families, developed most of their holdings in the Hudson Valley on a leasehold basis. Leasehold tenure and the landed aristocracy were two colonial legacies that lasted well into the nineteenth century. The leasehold system was transplanted, as well, to the Mohawk and upper Delaware valleys, and as far west as the Genesee Valley. James Duane tried to develop on a lease basis some 30,000 acres southwest of Schenectady, and Philip Schuyler leased lands in Saratoga County and near the site of Utica. In 1812 George Clarke, descendant of a colonial governor, owned land worth over $1,000,000 in Oneida, Otsego, Montgomery, and Dutchess counties. Baron Steuben owned 16,000 acres in Oneida County, half of which he attempted to lease to tenant farmers.

The tenancy system, however, was the exception. The freehold farmer outnumbered the tenant farmer by more than five to one. Even in Albany County, where there were almost 1,400 farmers leasing their farms from Stephen Van Rensselaer, tenants were nevertheless in a minority. The great majority of landowners followed the practice of William Cooper, who urged the sale and not the lease of land. His advice was sound, since few Yankees, who made up the bulk of the settlers, would lease farms when they could secure the title to farms of their own.

The term "lease" as it was used at this period may require some explanation, since it was quite different from the word as used in reference to the modern legal instrument. Referring to the Van Rensselaer lease, Samuel Tilden wrote: "It is, in a word, a warrantee deed. . . . The reservations, condition and convenants are in the nature of a grant by the buyer to the seller, of an annuity secured on the land, or mortgage for the purchase money."

The leases were by no means uniform. The "durable" lease, the most commonly used, was in perpetuity. Farmers on Van Rensselaer Manor had to pay the patroon a perpetual rent of between ten to fourteen bushels of winter wheat per one hundred acres, four fat fowl, and a day's work with a team of horses or oxen. Philip Schuyler and George Clarke usually leased their farms for three lives; upon the death of the third person named as lessee the farm reverted to the landlord. In addition, most leases provided that the lessee had to pay to the landlord one-third, one-fourth, or one-tenth of the sale price when he disposed of his interest. Moreover, the landlord sometimes reserved all rights to mines and mill sites and retained timber and water rights.

How heavy a financial burden did the tenant farmer bear? Many advantages were on his side. He often entered upon his farm without making any down payment and without paying rent for four to seven years. Thereafter he paid an annual rent either in kind or in money, varying according to the location, fertility, and date of leasing. Few leases, however, called for less than ten or more than twenty bushels of wheat per one hundred acres. The average estimated rental for farms in the four western towns of Albany County for the thirty-year period prior to 1846 was about thirty-two dollars a year.

The landed gentry, on the other hand, had many vexatious problems of their own. Good tenants were hard to get and difficult to keep. The average American regarded tenancy as somewhat degrading and often moved away or failed to pay the rent on time. Sometimes the landlord had to offer extensions or accept payment in goods or services. Tenants generally failed to maintain the fertility of the soil. Their houses and barns were "exceedingly dilapidated," and their fields were covered with brush.

In spite of the failure of the great antirent uprising of 1766, the tenant farmers in the Hudson Valley kept alive a hope for the end of landlord control. Did not the "Green Mountain Boys" make good their defiance of New York landlords as well as of the British redcoats? Antirent feeling rose to the surface in Columbia County throughout the decade of the 1790's. Again in 1811–1812 tenant farmers petitioned the legislature to investigate the title of the Livingston family and bedeviled the sheriffs who tried to enforce rent payment.

The death of Stephen Van Rensselaer, the "last of the patroons," on January 26, 1839, symbolized the passing of an era. The spectacle of a landed gentleman living in semifeudal splendor among his three thousand tenants was anachronism to a generation which had become acclimated to Jacksonian democracy. Van Rensselaer's leniency toward his tenants created a serious problem for his heirs, who were instructed by his will to apply the back rents (approximately $400,000) toward the payment of the patroon's debts. As soon as the rent notices went out, the farmers organized committees and held public meetings in protest. Stephen Van Rensselaer, who had inherited the west manor (Albany County), refused to meet with a committee of antirenters and turned down their written request for a reduction of rents. His brusque refusal infuriated the farmers. On July 4, 1839, a mass meeting at Berne called for a declaration of independence from landlord rule but raised the amount the tenants were willing to pay.

The answer to this proposal was soon forthcoming. The executors of the estate secured writs of ejectment in suits against tenants in arrears. Crowds of angry tenants manhandled Sheriff Michael Archer and his assistants and turned back a posse of five hundred men. Sheriff Archer called upon Governor William Seward for military assistance. Seward's proclamation calling on the people not to resist the enforcement of the law and the presence of several hundred militiamen overawed the tenants. The tenants, however, persisted in their refusal to pay rent. Of course the sheriff could and did evict a few, but he could not dispossess an entire township.

By 1844 the antirent movement had grown from a localized struggle against the Van Rensselaer family to a full-fledged revolt against leasehold tenure throughout eastern New York. Virtual guerilla warfare broke out. Riders disguised as Indians and wearing calico gowns ranged through the countryside, terrorizing the agents of the landlords. In late 1844 Governor William Bouck sent three companies of militia to Hudson, where antirenters threatened to storm the jail and release their leader, Big Thunder (Dr. Smith A. Boughton in private life). The following year Governor Silas Wright was forced to proclaim Delaware County in a state of insurrection after an armed rider had killed an undersheriff at an eviction sale.

The antirenters organized town, county, and state committees, published their own newspapers, held conventions, and elected their own spokesmen to the legislature. The success of candidates endorsed by antirenters in 1845 caused politicians in both parties to show a "wonderful anxiety" to "give the Anti-renters all they ask." The legislature abolished the right of the landlord to seize the goods of a defaulting tenant and taxed the income which landlords derived from their rent. Shortly thereafter, the constitutional convention of 1846 prohibited any future lease of agricultural land which claimed rent or service for a period longer than twelve years. Yet neither the convention nor the state legislature was willing to disturb existing leases.

The antirenters played politics with remarkable success in the years between 1846 and 1851. They elected friendly sheriffs and local officials who virtually paralyzed the efforts of the landlords to collect rents. They cleverly threw their weight to the candidates of either major party who would support their cause. The bitter rivalries between and within the Whig and Democratic parties enabled the antirenters to exert more influence than their numbers warranted. As a result they had a small but determined bloc of antirent champions in the Assembly and the Senate who kept landlords uneasy by threatening to pass laws challenging land titles. The antirent endorsement of John Young, Whig candidate for governor in 1846, proved decisive. Governor Young promptly pardoned several antirent prisoners and called for an investigation of titles by the attorney general. The courts eventually ruled the statute of limitations prevented any questioning of the original titles. Declaring that the holders of perpetual leases were in reality freeholders, the Court of Appeals outlawed the "quarter sales," i.e., the requirement in many leases that a tenant who disposed of his farm should pay one-fourth of the money to the landlord.

Assailed by a concerted conspiracy not to pay rent and harassed by taxes and investigations of the attorney general, the landed proprietors gradually sold out their interests. In August 1845 seventeen large landholders announced that they were willing to sell. Later that year Stephen Van Rensselaer, IV, agreed to sell his rights in the Helderberg townships. His brother, William, who had inherited the east manor in Rensselaer County, also sold out his rights in over five hundred farms in 1848. Finally, in the 1850's, two speculators purchased the remaining leases from the Van Rensselaers.

The antirent movement was more than a selfish campaign to escape rent payment. It was a ringing protest by democratic farmers against the aristocratic clique which had dominated New York for so many decades. By dramatizing the evils of land monopoly, the antirenters also helped to arouse the nation to the importance of granting free homesteads to actual settlers on the public domain.

Undoubtedly speculators in urban real estate were making more money in this period than developers of backcountry lands. The rapid growth of cities created fortunes for those lucky or shrewd enough to own property in the pathway of growing population. Gerrit Smith, for example, made a fortune out of his holdings in Oswego, while John Jacob Astor amassed his fabulous wealth largely through purchases of Manhattan real estate.

Property values on Manhattan Island soared upward even in the period prior to 1825. The city held title to 11,000 acres of the total of 14,000 in 1789. Mayor De Witt Clinton appointed a committee to draw up a street plan for the city, and the committee recommended a gridiron pattern in its famous report of 1811. This proposal had the merit of providing for the maximum number of small lots, but encouraged the subsequent erection of high buildings.

Meanwhile the city was practically giving away much of the common land, which was regarded as almost worthless. Astor, however, calculated that growth would drive up land values. Between 1800 and 1819 he invested in Manhattan real estate an average of $35,000 each year from the profits derived from his ships in the China trade. Although he did not neglect to purchase water-front property, Astor invested chiefly in the inaccessible lands lying just outside the built-up portion of New York. A great coup was his acquisition of the farm of Medeef Eden, which ran from Forty-second to Forty-sixth streets and from Broadway to the Hudson. He also bought two-thirds of the country place of Governor George Clinton. When Astor died in 1848, his holdings were worth an estimated $20,000,000 and destined for a further astronomical rise in value.

Other large landholders in New York City were the Wendel, Goelet, and Rhinelander families. Trinity Church, which had acquired the original West India Company farm in 1705, remained a large owner of Manhattan real estate. Another valuable holding deriving from this period is the tract held by the Sailors' Snug Harbor, which Captain Robert Randall had established in 1806.

The most significant development in the land history of New York between 1790 and 1825 was the rapid division and distribution of large speculative holdings into the hands of small individual proprietors. By mid-century there remained only the remnants of the semifeudal estates and portions of the great tracts engrossed by the speculators of the 1790's. The owners of the New York countryside had become a democratic society of freeholding farmers.

Omit

Farm and Forest

The rural management in most parts of this province is miserable; seduced by the fertility of the soil on first settling, the farmer thinks only of exhausting it as soon as possible, without attending to their own interest in a future day.
—American Husbandry, 1775

"THE American axe! It has made more real and lasting conquests than the sword of any warlike people that ever lived," stated Major Littlepage, a frontier landholder created by James Fenimore Cooper. This assertion was certainly apt for the period from 1783 to 1825, when settlers pushed the agricultural frontier to the western and northern boundaries of New York.

Contemporary writers have left us sympathetic and penetrating accounts of farming in New York. Crèvecoeur in his delightful *Letters from an American Farmer* described the practices of farmers along the lower Hudson and analyzed the forces creating the "American character." In western New York, Orsamus Turner collected the stories of early settlers who recounted the pleasures and described the hardships of the heroic age of farming.

The amount of improved farmland rose from about 1,000,000 acres in 1784 to 5,500,000 acres in 1821. These rough and impersonal figures cannot begin to describe the backbreaking task of hewing farms from the wilderness, an accomplishment which "wore out at least one generation." Of course, the New York frontiersmen faced the same problems met by all pioneers, whether in Maine, the Ohio Valley, or the Gulf plains. Nevertheless, their struggle with the forest deserves retelling if only to remind urbanized New Yorkers of a fascinating chapter in the development of the Empire State.

The pioneer looking for a farm carefully considered such elements as climate, soil, location, drainage, transportation, and future land values. Later generations have wondered why he often preferred uplands to lowlands. There were several reasons. Lowlands were avoided because of the dreaded malaria, or "swamp fever." Hill lands were easier to clear than the valleys filled with underbrush, fallen trees, and deep roots. Hill lands also tended to require little draining. Furthermore, the rich vegetable mold created by centuries of rotting leaves and timber made all lands equally fertile until the topsoil on the hillsides washed away.

The broadsides and advertisements of land agents and the reports from relatives and friends about the fertile lands in New York caused many eastern farmers to migrate westward. Quite often the farmer set out on foot or on horseback to see for himself whether the claims were true. After inspecting vacant tracts and noting the distance from road and town, the supply of water, and the nearness of neighbors, he signed a contract or lease if the price was reasonable. In order to prepare the way for his family he often made a small clearing, sowed some winter wheat or rye, and erected a small hut.

Upon his return home, the settler sold his farm, bulky tools, and heavy furniture, since moving his family and belongings was a formidable task. His wagon or sleigh could carry only the essential items of clothing, bedding, and cooking equipment. The men in the family followed along behind the cart or sleigh driving any livestock they might own.

Clearing cost the farmer a great deal of time and energy. Two methods were commonly used—chopping and girdling. The latter method required only the removal of a ring of bark around the trunk to prevent the sap from flowing to the branches. After the leaves withered, the sun dried the land, which could be quickly planted to corn or wheat. Girdling, however, left the clearing full of obstructive trees whose decaying limbs fell off and sometimes injured the farmer, his crop, or his animals. Consequently, the average settler preferred to chop down the trees. With his oxen and his neighbors' helping hands the settler dragged the felled trees into huge piles for burning. After the piles were burned, he collected the ashes for use either as fertilizer or for the manufacture of potash.

A skilled woodsman, it is estimated, could clear an acre in seven to ten days. The average pioneer could hardly hope to clear and sow ten acres the first year even if he did little else. But he also had to erect a small house, fences, and perhaps a barn, as well as hunt and fish for himself and his family. In addition, he had to aid his neighbors in cutting through roads and performing sundry other duties, all of which interfered with the task of clearing. However, unless he had a market for his produce, there was little point in clearing more land than was necessary to raise foodstuffs for his own use. As a result, few settlers cleared more than three or four acres a year, which meant that it took a lifetime to bring a farm of any size under cultivation. In fact, every farm generation until 1880 added to the acreage of improved land in New York State.

The job of fencing cost many days of labor every year. Usually fences of wooden rails or of rough boards were constructed, although occasionally stone fences were erected, especially in those regions where rocks and stone interfered with plowing.

The pioneer's cabin, built from logs selected during the clearing process, was a temporary structure until the farmer could afford to erect a house made from boards, nails, and glass. A historian of Steuben County describes such an early cabin:

The house was about 20 by 60 feet, constructed of round logs chinked with pieces of split logs, and plastered on the outside with clay. The floors were made of split logs with the flat side up; the doors, of thin pieces of the same. The windows were holes, unprotected by glass or sash; the fire place was made of stone and the chimney of sticks and clay. On one side of the fire place was a ladder leading to the chamber. . . . Behind the door was a large spinning wheel and a reel, and overhead on wooden hooks fastened to the beams were a number of things, among which were a nice rifle, powder horn, bullet pouch, tomahawk, and hunting knife,—the complete equipment of the hunter and the frontiersman.

Keeping his family supplied with food was almost a full-time occupation for the pioneer. There was plenty of game and fish, but hunting and fishing took time and skill. Some berries and fruits grew wild in the forests and provided food at certain seasons. During his first years the frontiersman sometimes ran out of food, especially if he became sick. His great standby was corn, which needed little preparation, yielded well, fattened his animals, and provided food for the table. Since the average settler had little money for such expensive imports as molasses or cane sugar, he sweetened his johnny cake with maple sugar of his own making. Tea brewed from herbs, cider pressed from apples, and whisky made from surplus cereals were common beverages.

The wife and daughters of the frontier farmer made clothing for the family out of the raw fibers of wool or flax and the hides of animals. Men and boys went barefoot during the summer and wore crude moccasins during the winter.

In retrospect, we tend to idealize the frontier farmer for his courage, his resourcefulness, and his individual freedom. Certainly these qualities were possessed by the frontiersman, but what we forget are the chains imposed by a life of self-sufficiency. Obviously the pioneer could not function as an efficient husbandman, carpenter, woodsman, lumberman, toolmaker, cobbler, and handy man at one and the same time. Providing food, clothing, and tools for the family meant drudgery and poverty relieved only by the hope that better times were coming after the first hardships of pioneering had passed.

Judged by modern standards all farms in this early period were predominantly self-sufficient. The primary objective of the farmers was to escape self-sufficiency, not to achieve it. Only if they could find a crop worth carrying to market could settlers pay for their land, buy such necessities as ironware and salt, and hope for a rising standard of living. Farmers in the Hudson Valley were favorably situated to export their wheat, but those farther inland found that the cost of dragging a wagon ten to twenty miles over the miserable roads ate up the market value of the grain. During the winter, grains could be carried profitably for much greater distances by sleigh.

The difficulty of reaching external markets forced frontier farmers to make awkward adjustments. They produced potash, maple sugar, wool, and whisky, which were relatively valuable in relation to their bulk. Or they raised cattle, horses, or mules, which furnished their own transportation to the markets along the Hudson River. But the market was often glutted because other frontier farmers from Maine to Georgia were also driving animals to the seaboard. The obvious solution was the construction of turnpikes and improvements in waterways that would cut down the cost of transporting goods to market.

Between 1783 and 1825 an increasing proportion of farmers spent a growing share of their time producing foodstuffs for the markets as a result of the growth in the world demand for wheat and the expansion of the transportation network. War in Europe, raging from 1793 to 1815 with but few interruptions, increased the demand for wheat. New York wheat farmers and shippers rushed to fill the demand. Unfortunately, reliance upon a war boom exposed farmers to the dangers of rapid fluctuations in prices. For example, the Embargo Act of 1807 sent farm prices tumbling, while the reopening of trade in 1809, followed by the War of 1812, stimulated another upsurge of farm prices. Peace in 1815 brought a temporary price drop; but a revival of European demand bolstered prices until late in 1818. The disastrous collapse of prices at that time led James Wadsworth of Geneseo to observe in the following year:

Real estate has fallen in this county, Ontario, or it would be more correct to say improved farms have fallen 33 per cent in the last three years. Such is the scarcity of money that improved farms from Boston to Lake Erie will not sell. The consequence is that we have none of that class of settlers, who used to come among us, with money in their pockets from the sale of improved farms.

Let us examine more closely the sources of cash income for the farmers of New York in this period. Both forest and farm provided products for the growing foreign and domestic markets.

Practically every farmer was also a lumberman. Each farmer built his home, barns, fences, and tools from wood hewn from his land and processed, when necessary, by the small local sawmills. Farmers also discovered that they could sell the ashes from their burned-over clearings. They scraped together the ashes, ran water through them, and boiled the resulting lye in large kettles. The dried "black salts" formed potash, used for fertilizer and soap, which often brought in enough money to pay for the cost of clearing the land. As late as 1822 Governor De Witt Clinton listed ashes as the main rival of wheat in the exports of the state.

The development of the export trade in lumber differentiated the lumberman from the farmer. During the colonial period operators of sawmills on the streams flowing into the lower Hudson erected larger mills in order to cut out planks, boards, staves, and scantlings for their customers in the West Indies and the southern states. Log driving began on the Hudson in 1813 and led to the erection of great mills at Glens Falls, Sandy Hill, and Fort Edward. Lumbermen after 1800 rafted large amounts of lumber down the Delaware River. Pine lumbering became an important activity in New York, although the state did not displace Maine as the first lumbering state until the 1840's.

Other groups besides the farmers and sawmill operators benefited from the fine stands of timber. Hundreds of coopers made wood receptacles for wet and dry goods. In every community lived a cabinetmaker who produced chairs, tables, chests, beds, gunstocks, and other necessary items. Some craftsmen exhibited a superb skill, and examples of their work are still prized for aesthetic as well as antiquarian interest.

Another forest-farm industry was collecting bark from oak and hemlock for the tanneries. The discovery of improved methods of tanning leather started a rush to the Catskills, where the stands of hemlock and oak were extensive. As a result, tanneries sprang up in almost every township, and New York became the leader in leather production. The largest establishments, such as that of Zadock Pratt in Greene County, tanned thousands of sides of sole leather each year.

During the 1790's a good many people dreamed of supplying the world with sweets from maple sugar groves. Among these was William Cooper, who in 1793 insisted that American farmers could fill all the domestic needs for sugar. Even hard-headed Dutch bankers sent out Gerrit Boon to buy up stands of maple in central New York. Boon hired a score of men to tap the trees and to build wooden troughs leading to large vats. Unfortunately, wind, rain, and sun warped and cracked the troughs. Before the season of 1794 was over, Boon had lost $15,000 of his sponsor's money.

Many small farmers supplied their own needs and sold part of their surplus of maple sugar. Practically all members of the family could help tap the trees in April when the sap began to run. Boiling down the sap in huge kettles was an exciting event for the children.

Wheat brought in the greatest cash returns, although corn was more valuable in feeding the farm family and the livestock. Wheat yields were good, ranging from thirty to forty bushels an acre on fresh soils to an average of twelve bushels in the older fields. Wheat was valuable enough in relation to its weight to permit farmers to carry it to Hudson River warehouses from points as far west as Utica. Since wheat stored well, farmers could hold it back until wintertime and take it by sleigh to Albany. The center of wheat production gradually moved westward. The output of central New York increased after turnpikes reached the area, and the Genesee Valley won the nickname of "The Granary of America" soon after the Erie Canal reached Rochester in 1823.

Wheatgrowers in eastern New York were experiencing many troubles during the first decades of the nineteenth century. Constant cropping had reduced the yield, and winterkilling was proving very destructive in the upland regions. During the Revolution, the Hessian fly ravaged the wheatfields of Long Island and gradually spread up the lower Hudson Valley. Smut, rust, and mildew, not to mention grasshoppers and Canadian thistle, blighted and destroyed many fields. John Jay, writing from his estate in Westchester County, complained in 1811, "To sow wheat here is like taking a ticket in a lottery; more blanks than prizes. The fly destroys more than we reap." The quality of New York wheat declined, alarming farm leaders, legislators, and editors. In 1821 they forced through the state legislature a rigorous inspection system to insure more careful grading of wheat and flour. Within a short time New York breadstuffs had regained their reputation for high quality, a reputation which the millers of Rochester and Oswego were to keep alive for several decades.

The development of New York as a grazing and dairy state was firmly established by 1800. Like most frontiers, New York had its cowboys, and its drovers, who purchased the stunted "native cattle" from the farmers. Periodically, the drovers would take them to the slaughterhouses at Troy and Albany. Closely allied with the cattle business was the raising of horses and mules, which enjoyed a ready sale in the southern states and the West Indies.

A few farmers sold butter and cheese. Farmers in Orange County specialized in making fine butter. Yankee immigrants in Herkimer and

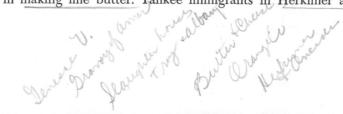

Oneida counties found the hill pastures ideal for grazing and by 1825 had firmly established that region as one of the nation's primary cheese-producing centers.

Chancellor Livingston estimated in 1813 that a farm of 130 acres had eight or nine horses or four horses and four oxen, as well as ten cows and six yearlings. The average farmer had about twenty-five sheep and swine. The wool and beef were primarily for his own use, but his surplus did bring in some cash income. The depredations of wolves and dogs and severe winters had kept down the number of sheep in colonial days. The average farmer paid little attention to the production of wool for the market until 1807, when fine wool from Merino sheep rose to two dollars a pound. The rush to build flocks sent the price of a Merino ram to a thousand dollars and more. The bubble burst in 1810–1811 after some twenty-five thousand sheep were imported from Spain. By 1815 farmers could buy Merinos for one dollar each.

The Merino craze, however, helped establish sheep raising in New York, especially in the hill towns of the eastern part of the state, although many factors continued to threaten the industry's existence. Wolves and winter severities reduced the flocks. After the slump in wool prices which followed 1815, many disgusted farmers killed their flocks for the tallow and the hides. The expansion of wool manufacture in the 1820's helped revive the sheep-raising industry.

How much income did the farmers receive from their various sources? The fragmentary statistics available give little help in answering this question. One estimate is that the average farmer had a cash income of approximately thirty dollars a year. His real income, including the food, clothing, and tools used on the farm, was considerably higher. Furthermore, most farmers were actually creating capital goods in the form of improved fields, fences, barns, and buildings which would eventually produce a greater income, if not for himself, at least for his children. On the other hand, farmers were using up their timber resources and destroying the fertility of the soil by careless agricultural techniques.

Farmers in New York followed roughly the same practices as farmers in neighboring states. The abundance of land and the scarcity of labor operated with telling force in the direction of extensive rather than intensive cultivation. An almost inevitable corollary was the custom of cropping the land until it was exhausted. Unfortunately, farm implements were so primitive and inefficient that they did not permit the economy of labor necessary to compensate for the extensive cultivation. The three-crop system in common use—grain, grass, and fallow—differed little from the agricultural practices of medieval Europe, while the tools—cradle, harrow, wooden plow—stemmed from ancient Rome.

A few voices denounced the husbandry as slovenly and predatory as contrasted with the practices in England. Robert R. Livingston challenged the validity of such comparisons. Should not our agriculture, he argued, be judged in the light of the return it makes for the capital employed? Americans were quite right to take advantage of their greatest assets—timber and cheap land. The true test was output per worker and the standard of living, which, Livingston maintained, were fully as high in New York as they were in rural England.

Perhaps as good a description of New York agriculture as can be found are the comments of George W. Featherstonhaugh, who served as corresponding secretary of the state Board of Agriculture. He noted in 1819:

Until very recently the farming operations which have come under my notice in this state, may be generally described as follows. Indifferent grass made into hay at unseasonable times, and abounding in the worst weeds that can infest the ground. . . . Dung of several years standing, making the cold barnyard a perfect mud hole. Fat sheep weighing eight pounds a quarter; other meat in proportion. Wheat from ten to twenty bushels an acre; corn fifteen to thirty. On the arrival of winter, the sheep, the cows, the lambs, the calves, the oxen, finding their way to a bad shed, or no shed, in a bleak barnyard, and remaining in that situation all winter; having a little hay flung to them two or three times a day; the cows giving a quart or a pint at a milking. I have often seen the emaciated cows, after passing the night in a drizzling rain, freezing as it fell, incapable of rising in the morning . . . On the arrival of spring, the scanty hay being almost exhausted, the whole stock finding nothing more to be had at the barn, again sneaks off to the meadows, through the well-known gaps, poach and tear what had not been quite destroyed in November.

Scientific agriculture made a little headway between 1783 and 1825. However, the experiments of gentlemen farmers, the exhibits at county fairs, and the spread of information in the press helped to popularize the principles of sound husbandry.

The landed aristocrats, following the example of their English compeers, were the first to urge and to adopt improved methods. They organized, in 1791, the Society for the Promotion of Agriculture, Arts, and Manufactures, which became, in 1804, the Society for the Promotion of Useful Arts. The membership included such distinguished figures as Robert R. Livingston, John Jay, Stephen Van Rensselaer, De Witt Clinton, and James Duane. Probably their greatest achievement was persuading the farmers of the lower Hudson Valley to adopt clover crops and to fertilize with gypsum. Artificial grasses, providing better pastures, helped the growth of the dairy industry. The "miraculous" effects of gypsum upon the lime-deficient and worn-out fields won many converts in the region.

Elkanah Watson, however, was the first agricultural leader to reach the great mass of dirt farmers. A native of Plymouth, Massachusetts, he had worked himself up from an apprenticeship to a top position in the firm of the Providence merchant, John Brown. After spending several years in the salons and countinghouses of France and England, Watson settled in Albany, where he promoted banks, canals, schools, and other enterprises. His fortune made, Watson bought a farm in Pittsfield. The craze for Merino sheep captured his interest, and in 1807 he exhibited two sheep in the public square. Three years later he invited his neighbors to exhibit their livestock. The resulting Berkshire County Fair was a huge success and attracted nation-wide attention. New York citizens begged Watson to help them organize county agricultural societies. With his help, fifty-two out of fifty-eight counties in New York formed societies within a few years.

The Schoharie County Fair in 1819 affords a good example of the pageantry which made the county fair an impressive ceremony and a gala occasion for the countryside. Bells and cannon awakened the citizens at dawn. Then a parade, headed by clergymen and agricultural leaders, exhibited agricultural machinery and choice specimens from orchard and field. A band played spirited music and martial airs. On this particular occasion the procession marched to the church, where the service began with the reading of an ode and a prayer. After the president's address, the proud winners of awards marched to the rostrum to receive their prizes. When the service was over, the members retired to the courthouse for dinner. An agricultural ball climaxed the day's festivities.

State financial aid for agriculture rewarded Watson's efforts. In 1819 the legislature created a Board of Agriculture with the duty of publishing an annual report and distributing $10,000 a year to the county societies for prizes. Much good work was done, despite charges of favoritism and waste, but the economy bloc in the legislature cut out the appropriation in 1825.

Such private organizations and public agencies made important beginnings and inspired a small but growing number of farmers to adopt better techniques of farming. More attention was paid to manuring the fields, selecting better seeds, and planting fallow crops. Onlookers at the plowing matches were quick to see the superiority of the cast-iron plow over the inefficient wooden plow. Nevertheless, most farmers continued to mine the soil as their fathers had done before them. Improved agricultural practices were not widely adopted until after 1825, when the decline of wheat culture in eastern New York and the growing demand for butter and cheese speeded up the shift toward a more diversified agriculture.

Founding the Business Empire

But to the York Stater of a hardier time the Grand Western Canal was the pride and glory of the nation, vaunted as the eighth wonder of the world. We had wrought it with our hands and filled it with our sweat. We stood ready to fight and die for it.—Attributed to MYRON ADAMS, *grandfather of Samuel Hopkins Adams*

THE Empire State had won an incontestable claim to that title by 1825. Its population outstripped all contenders. Its farmers had cleared millions of acres and were exporting large amounts of wheat and lumber products. Its merchants were growing wealthy as the wharves of Manhattan Island attracted an increasing share of the western, coastal, and transatlantic trade. Its capitalists had constructed turnpikes and were establishing New York's industrial supremacy. Furthermore, its statesmen had carried to completion the Erie Canal—the most ambitious project of the period.

Table 1 shows an amazing story of growth. Note how New York in a period of forty years increased its total commerce approximately tenfold and also handled a notably increasing share of the nation's exports and imports. The unusually high figure for 1801 reflects the great amount of goods re-exported from New York during the struggle between Great Britain and France.

Several factors helped to lift New York from the post-Revolutionary slump. The opening of the China trade, French purchases of American foodstuffs, the reopening of the British West Indies to American shipping, and the restoration of confidence among businessmen spurred recovery. Business had revived before the ratification of the Constitution in 1787, but businessmen were reassured by the clauses in that

173

Table 1. Exports and imports, 1791–1831.

Year	Combined imports and exports (nearest million)	Percentage of national trade Imports	Exports
1791	$ 8,000,000	21	10
1801	45,000,000	23	20
1811	24,000,000	23	20
1821	36,000,000	37	20
1831	82,000,000	50	27

document prohibiting states from interfering with interstate commerce, issuing paper money, and impairing the obligation of contract.

War in Europe brought good times for merchants in New York because both Britain and France clamored for goods and shipping. New York exports, valued at $2,535,790 in 1792, soared to $26,357,963 in 1807. By the turn of the century New York had outdistanced both Philadelphia and Boston in the export and import trade and in foreign and coastwise shipping. Profits from shipping were high despite the seizures by Britain and France of cargoes bound for the enemy.

The Embargo Act of 1807, followed by the War of 1812, brought the boom in foreign commerce to an end. Idle ships lay at the wharves, and the British fleet off Sandy Hook took many prizes. When news came in 1815 that America and Britain had signed the Treaty of Ghent, the streets of New York were filled with cheering crowds and torchlight parades. During the next decade New York clinched its position as the nation's great port by establishing control of three major trade routes: the transatlantic shuttle, the coastal trade, and the Erie Canal.

The textile trade came to be centered in New York as an incidental result of the city's lively import trade. When British manufacturers selected New York as the place to dump their surplus textiles, swarms of buyers were attracted to the auction rooms of Manhattan. In 1817 the legislature helped along this flood of imports by providing that all goods offered at auction must be sold. Hoping for bargains, thousands of country merchants frequented the auction houses of New York City.

The beginning of regular and frequent packet service between New York and Liverpool also proved helpful in boosting New York's share of the nation's imports from 30 per cent in 1815 to 51 per cent in 1825. The Black Ball Line, chartered in 1817, immediately drew the better class of freight to its packets, although it performed an even more important function by bringing a stream of immigrants to the city.

The little-known coasting trade rivaled the transatlantic trade in tonnage. The number of vessels involved was considerably greater, even when the hundreds of tiny local craft plying Long Island Sound and New

York Bay are omitted. The excellent harbor and central position of New York enabled shippers to capture the major share of the business of distributing imported goods and collecting foodstuffs from many seashore communities.

Most remarkable of all, however, was the success of the Manhattan merchants in getting control of the large export trade in cotton. The "cotton triangle" had three corners: the cotton ports (Charleston, Savannah, Mobile, and New Orleans), the European ports (Liverpool, Le Havre, and others), and New York. A majority of the vessels engaged in the cotton trade sailed directly to Europe from southern ports, returning to New York with many immigrants and such items of trade as cloth from the Lancashire mills. Subsequently they sailed southward with merchandise or in ballast. The alternative route, using only two sides of the triangle, brought even more profits for New Yorkers. Much cotton reached European ports only after being re-exported from New York. The explanation for this rather curious shift from the direct trade is that many packets leaving New York had more than ample room for eastbound cargoes. Furthermore, the South was preoccupied with developing wild lands, acquiring more slaves, and growing more cotton, all of which tended to absorb the relatively small amounts of liquid capital in that region and to attract the energies of its able men, to the neglect of trade and commerce.

Finally, the trade routes to the interior helped to make New York a commercial center. The farmers along the Hudson-Mohawk rivers and later the Erie Canal ordered their goods from the commission houses located on the tip of Manhattan. It should be stressed, however, that New York City had already won commercial primacy *before* De Witt Clinton had lifted the first spadeful of earth for the canal in 1817.

A variety of business concerns—notably wholesaling, retailing, banking, insurance, and manufacturing establishments—grew in New York City in conjunction with the extraordinary rise in foreign commerce. The general course of business tended to follow closely the ebb and flow of foreign trade. Other types of merchandizing carried on in the metropolis will be described in Chapter 21.

On lower Manhattan before 1825 a few hundred men dominated the import and shipping houses on South Street, ran auctions and wholesaled textiles on Pearl Street, and ran the small banking houses on Wall Street. The typical countinghouse was a brick structure of three to five stories. Behind its showrooms on the first floor was the office where the merchant was surrounded by clerks making out manifests and bills of lading and posting ledgers. Most countinghouses were partnerships; only a handful were incorporated. Once a day the partners would sally forth to the

Tontine Coffee House and other meeting places to transact business with neighboring merchants.

Several types of businessmen handled the commerce of the port. Imports usually passed through the hands of an exporter in Liverpool, an importer on Manhattan, then a wholesaler or jobber, and a retailer. The development of the auction system deserves special notice because almost one-half of the total imports were sold in this way between 1815 and 1830. Only a small number of people were granted licenses by the governor and the state Council of Appointment to sell goods at auction. The Hone brothers and John Haggerty made fortunes in this business. (Philip Hone, later mayor, maintained a diary valuable as source material for his times.) They sold the imports to wholesalers from Pearl Street, who distributed the goods to country storekeepers and to jobbing houses in the interior.

Upstate, the storekeeper was an important figure in his community; his neighbors accorded him the prestige of a professional man. He was the first of a long chain of middlemen sending the flour barrel on its way to the ultimate purchaser in England. For example, a farmer would bring in fifty bushels of wheat to Jedediah Barber's Great Western Store at Homer. After the merchant had made an acceptable offer, the farmer would buy such items as salt, potash kettles, rum, hardware, tea, sugar, and perhaps some calico cloth for his wife. Frequently no money passed hands since Barber, like most storekeepers, kept two accounts—one for the farmer's purchases and one for his deliveries. The storekeeper needed a keen knowledge of the affairs of his customers, since he frequently had to wait until the harvest for his pay. When the farmers had brought in enough goods to fill a canvas-covered wagon, Barber would send it north to Fabius and east over the Great Western Turnpike to Albany. The wagon would bring back a varied consignment of goods for the Great Western Store.

Officials appointed by the cities continued, as in colonial days, to supervise the quality of firewood, hay, boards, grain, and other products offered for sale. But the spirit of individualism and free competition was mounting. The bakers of New York, for instance, protested against the assize which fixed the price of bread. Shortly after 1800 this restriction was removed, although the city continued to prescribe the size and weight of the loaf. Similarly, the butchers demanded the right to slaughter animals on their own premises instead of taking them to the public slaughterhouse. Another example of the spread of laissez-faire ideas was the decline of the freemanship, originally the equivalent of a license, required by those who wished to buy or sell at retail. By 1800 practically anyone who had the capital and energy could engage in the business of his choice. The Common Council of New York City continued to prescribe the conditions of sale at public markets. It tried to protect the housewife by prohibiting any purchase for resale before 11 A.M. and by requiring that butchers and handlers of farm produce meet prescribed health and sanitary standards.

The whole structure of trade, both foreign and domestic, rested upon credit. Upstaters lacking sufficient hard money turned to barter, payment in kind, and long-term credit by land agent and storekeeper. Similarly the jobbers, auctioneers, and importers usually bought goods on deferred payments of thirty, sixty, or ninety days. Banks sprang up to expedite and to enlarge these credit arrangements. In 1784 a group of influential citizens sponsored a Bank of New York, which shared the growing boom in business with the New York branch of the Bank of the United States. Unfortunately, bank charters became the plaything of politicians, who could reward friends by granting valuable franchises. For example, in 1799 Aaron Burr spirited through the legislature the charter for the Manhattan Company under the guise of a company to establish a city water-supply works. By 1815 over ten banks competed for the business of the metropolis. A good index of business activity can be seen in the table of banking capital.

Table 2. Banking capital in New York City, 1800–1825.

Year	Capital
1800	$ 3,420,000
1810	7,430,000
1820	21,105,000
1825	25,105,000

The state legislature paid little attention to banking abuses, such as the suspension of specie payment, outright failures, and unstable banknote issues. The requirement of 1804 that all banking corporations have a charter failed to prescribe regulations as to reserves, the amount of loans, or the amount of notes a bank could issue. Not until 1827 did the state begin to exercise strict control of banking practices.

Specialized financial institutions evolved to meet the demand for particular services. A rudimentary stock exchange developed in 1792 when certain merchants found it profitable to devote all their time to buying and selling the securities of the government. Many capitalists were investing in the depreciated securities of the United States and of the various states, hoping that the government would refund these securities at par, a policy Hamilton endorsed. Activity on the exchange tended to decline after 1795 and did not revive until 1813, when the federal government again sought to float loans. By 1817 the brokers decided to set up a formal organization to regulate the conduct of the exchange.

Another specialized need was for marine insurance. When the Revolution ended the quasi-monopoly granted to two British companies, several native concerns sprang up to underwrite shipping losses. In 1820 the companies established a Board of Underwriters which appointed correspondents in the major ports and hired captains to salvage the cargoes of ships that had run aground.

The New York money market during the nineteenth century was only a satellite of the London banking houses, which provided much of the long-term credit to finance the trade in cotton and wheat and, after 1820, to build the canals and railroads. Americans, however, gradually accumulated considerable capital resources, investing largely in land. Between 1800 and 1810 some invested in turnpike companies, and during the War of 1812 others put money into manufacturing.

Transportation remained largely waterborne throughout the period between 1783 and 1825. Probably 90 per cent of New York's trade moved over the waters of the Atlantic Ocean, the Hudson River system, and New York Bay. After 1800 highways became increasingly important as arteries of commerce.

Sail-driven vessels were by far the most important agencies of transportation. Colliers from Philadelphia, sloops coasting lumber from Maine and tobacco from Virginia, brigs loaded with cotton bales destined for the mills of Lancashire, schooners carrying sugar from Jamaica, and slim packets bearing mails and passengers between New York and Liverpool slipped in and out of the Narrows. Most sailing vessels were tramps with no regular schedules. Monthly packet service to Liverpool, which began in 1817, was later extended to Le Havre and London.

Small sailing vessels handled the bulk of freighting on the Hudson River, Long Island Sound, and New York Bay. Coastal shipping took somewhat larger vessels, usually schooners ranging from seventy-five to 150 tons, and still larger ones—brigs and full-rigged ships—handled transatlantic trade. Whalers left each year for the Antarctic from the port of Hudson as well as from Sag Harbor. Most of the four hundred sailing vessels operating on the Hudson River were sloops averaging sixty tons' burden.

Steamboats, whose flimsy paddles could not stand the pounding of high seas, found the approaches to New York harbor an ideal shelter. Eighteen years after the voyage of Robert Fulton's *Clermont* to Albany in 1807, forty-three steamers made New York their home port. The following list indicates the main destinations: 12 ran to Albany and its rival Troy; 2 to Poughkeepsie; 11 to points on Long Island Sound; and 4 to Brunswick, New Jersey. Steamboats likewise appeared on the beautiful upstate lakes:

Lake Champlain in 1809; Lake Ontario in 1817; Lake Erie in 1818; Lake Cayuga in 1819.

The steamboat quickly outclassed the sloop in competition for passengers. The *Clermont* made the trip to Albany three times a week, while a sloop might take anywhere from three to nine days, depending upon the vagaries of the wind. Passenger fares on steamboats were high until the Supreme Court in the famous Gibbons case of 1824 outlawed the monopoly which the legislature had granted to the Fulton-Livingston combination. Thereafter intense competition drove rates downward.

The Mohawk Valley has always been an important gateway to the interior. Unfortunately, the great falls of Cohoes completely sealed the mouth of the Mohawk River, forcing merchandise, produce, and passengers to transship over the sandy plain lying between Schenectady and Albany. At Little Falls, rapids and cascades formed another barrier to navigation. These obstructions, along with shifting sandbars, dangerous rapids, and low water in the upper river, severely limited the size of the boats and made navigation hazardous, uncertain, and costly.

Even before the Revolution royal officials had urged the improvement of the Mohawk River, which was so useful in carrying troops and stores to Fort Oswego. After the Revolution, Elkanah Watson revived public interest by agitating for river improvements. In 1792 the legislature incorporated two companies: the Western Inland Lock Navigation Company to open navigation to Lake Ontario and Seneca Lake, and the Northern Inland Lock Navigation Company to build a waterway from the upper Hudson to Lake Champlain. The Western Company by 1796 had constructed a canal one mile long at Little Falls and had also cleared fallen timbers from the upper Mohawk and Wood Creek leading from Rome to Oneida Lake. The canal permitted boats of ten to eleven tons to pass, in contrast to the former maximum of one to one and a half tons. After 1797 rivermen adopted the Durham boat, which husky men pushed upstream with long poles while the captain used a long sweep oar to steer. Despite all these developments, the Mohawk River could not provide enough safe and cheap transportation to handle the vast increase in traffic and travel accompanying the growth of central and western New York.

The story on the other rivers was much the same. Lumbermen floated arks and rafts loaded with potash, lumber, or wheat down the Genesee, the Susquehanna, and the Delaware. The settlers in western and northern New York floated much of their produce down the St. Lawrence to Montreal.

Frontier farmers were in desperate need of better highways. The roads of 1783 were little more than traces "underbrushed" through the forests.

Stumps and roots tripped man and horse, while spring rains turned the deeply rutted earth into impassable quagmires. Pioneers laid log causeways across swamps and built primitive bridges across streams. Many farmers had to wait until the winter to sleigh their wheat and other bulky products to the storehouses at Albany. A two-horse sleigh could go twice as fast as a wagon, carry a heavier load, and avoid the dangers of swamps and rivers.

Between 1783 and 1825 several significant changes took place in land transportation. The state inaugurated the policy of building a few key roads, but most highways were constructed by private companies. Another unplanned development was the laying out of the permanent road pattern of the state.

Why did private rather than public agencies take the lead in building roads during the turnpike era? It was simply that the government could not move fast enough to meet the pressing need. The legislators representing the older communities along the Hudson River, New York Bay, and Long Island Sound were reluctant to raise taxes to spend on frontier roads. They limited state action to the construction of a few routes, such as the Genesee Road, financed partly by lotteries. Moreover, the townships upon which the entire burden of roadbuilding rested had neither the financial resources nor the experienced overseers to construct adequate roads. Frontier communities obviously lacked both workmen and taxable property, whereas farmers in the older towns, obligated to work several days each year on the roads, felt little desire to keep them in repair for through traffic.

But frontiersmen eager to take their produce to market, large landholders hopeful of increasing the value of their inland tracts, and river towns ambitious to secure the trade of the interior kept demanding more and better roads. The success of the Philadelphia and Lancaster Turnpike aroused keen interest, and New York merchants began petitioning the legislature for charters to build roads in return for the right to charge a traffic toll. Between 1797 and 1807 eighty-eight turnpike and bridge companies, with an authorized capital of $5,556,750, received charters and constructed about nine hundred miles of turnpikes.

Public enthusiasm for toll roads mounted higher during the War of 1812, when the need for supplying the armies at Plattsburgh and Fort Niagara reinforced the demands of the farmers. The legislature handed out charters with a lavish hand, and 278 turnpike companies had constructed four thousand miles of roads by 1821. Thereafter, the movement slackened, and many of the roads, especially those paralleling canals and railroads, fell into disrepair, although a score of turnpikes serving hill towns in the north country and in the southern tier of counties were in use until after the Civil War.

The earliest turnpikes terminated at the Hudson River ports. Albany became and remained the turnpike and staging center of the state. Eight turnpikes thrust outward like spokes in a wheel. To the west were two trunk roads—one going to Schenectady and up the Mohawk Valley, the other following present Route 20. From the east a turnpike approached Albany from Lebanon Springs, and from the south came the New York and Albany Post Road, which was particularly useful in the winter when ice choked the Hudson.

Merchants in Newburgh and Catskill promoted turnpikes to the west. The Newburgh and Cochecton Company and the Susquehanna Turnpike, the latter from Catskill to Unadilla, had western extensions which permitted travelers to reach Ithaca. From Ithaca a traveler could also reach Bath, an important commercial and transportation center. The turnpikes mentioned here are only the more important of the scores covering the state.

Wagons, stagecoaches, herds of cattle and sheep, Yankee peddlers, itinerant artisans, and farm vehicles formed an ever-moving pageant on these roads. Teamsters, as proficient with their tongues as with the long whiplash, walked beside the wagons, which carried wheat, flour, cheese, potash, and whisky. Twenty miles was the daily goal of many drivers. The heavy wagons wore deep ruts even in the few macadam-surfaced roads. The tollhouses often granted special low rates for wagons having wheels more than six inches wide on the theory that they were less wearing on road surfaces.

Taverns for the wagoners and stagecoach passengers dotted the roadside much as gas stations, tourist cabins, and restaurants fringe our modern highways. The innkeeper was often a man of importance, and many were former army officers or judges. One observer noted that to become a lawyer or tavern keeper was the "surest road to public honours and riches."

The stagecoach was the queen of the old turnpike and kept a firm grip on the passenger traffic until the decade of the 1830's, when the railroad stole her customers away. The staging business employed thousands of agents, drivers, hostlers, porters, and division superintendents. Promoters linked together several local companies into larger firms and made traffic arrangements between companies. Stagecoach routes anticipated many of the bus routes of the twentieth century.

But neither the turnpikes nor the Mohawk River could solve the crucial problem of providing cheap transportation for heavy goods. Throughout the frontier region arose the demand for more roads and canals. Leading figures began to point out that the topography of the state was the most favorable in the nation for building a canal from the Atlantic to the waterways of the interior.

Several notables share the credit for promoting the greatest piece of engineering attempted within the United States up to that time. Gouverneur Morris, in 1800, was perhaps the first to advocate building a canal from the Hudson to Lake Erie. James Geddes, a land surveyor of Onondaga County, made a survey in 1809, laid out a practicable route, and in the next year assisted the state survey commission headed by De Witt Clinton. Thence began the drive to secure financial support. A delegation approached Congress but came back empty-handed.

When peace came in 1815, Clinton, then mayor of New York, wrote a famous pamphlet describing the advantages which the canal would bring. Up and down the line of the proposed route citizens echoed his appeal and petitioned the legislature for aid. Many Federalists joined the campaign because they believed the canal would increase trade, raise land values, and promote manufacturing. Representatives from New York City were in general skeptical of the project because taxes would increase and upstate communities would benefit at their expense. De Witt Clinton brushed aside their objections and in 1817 the legislature authorized construction.

The Erie Canal was pushed forward with a vigor and a speed not commonly associated with public enterprise. Most of the contractors were well-to-do farmers who built short sections. The middle portion, running for almost a hundred miles west of Little Falls, was in operation as early as 1820, and three years later boats could pass from the Hudson to Rochester. In October 1825 New York celebrated the completion with a state-wide jubilee, as the first boat prepared to make the journey from Buffalo to New York. Buffalo gave the official party a gala send-off. Its departure was the signal for a grand salute from a battery five hundred miles long, each cannon echoing the report of its neighbor. New York City witnessed another impressive ceremony when Governor Clinton poured a keg of Lake Erie water into the ocean.

The watercourses and topography between Lake Champlain and the upper Hudson made it possible for another canal to be dug, connecting the two waterways by 1823. A channel four feet deep and forty feet wide—the same as that of the Erie—connected Whitehall on Lake Champlain with the Hudson at Fort Edward and later was extended to Waterford. The Champlain Canal gave a great stimulus to the lumbering operations in the eastern Adirondacks.

Although the success of the canal program was evident before 1825, its full effect upon the cities, state, and nation was most marked in the following quarter century and will be examined in a later chapter.

Signs of New York's future supremacy in manufacturing were clearly visible in 1825. In textiles New York's manufacturers trailed those of

Rhode Island and Massachusetts. In iron and steel Pennsylvania took the lead. But in hundreds of manufacturing enterprises New Yorkers were the pacesetters for the nation.

The home remained by far the most important unit of production. The family continued to produce most of its own foodstuffs; it clothed its members; furnished them with handmade tools, and made most of the household equipment. Nevertheless, there was a noticeable drift of many operations to village shops manned by such artisans as millers, shoemakers, blacksmiths, coopers, weavers, and tanners. Furthermore, the tiny gristmills tended to vanish as a few large mills grew up near the major waterfalls. Similarly, local tanneries gave way to the rather large establishments centering in the Catskill region. Gradually operations in the manufacture of clothing moved outside the family. After 1800 small carding mills arose in almost every township where a water-driven wheel could pull the tangled fibers through the combs. Fulling mills often "dressed" and dyed the cloth, which was still usually woven in the home. The growth in the number, size, and complexity of these establishments lying in the twilight zone between the home and the factory was perhaps the most significant development in this period.

Industry in factories, i.e., those equipped with machines and manned by workers performing specialized functions, had scarcely emerged from swaddling clothes at this time. The census of 1820 lists only 6,409 men, 927 women, and 2,423 children as employed in manufacturing. This number was a minute fraction of the total population of 1,372,812. Many factors helped to stunt industrial growth. Few Americans had any money to invest, and those who did usually preferred to buy wild lands, to set up a commission house, or to buy shares in a shipping venture. Besides, the British manufacturers were well established and undersold their American rivals. Few native Americans knew how to operate or repair textile machinery. It is significant that a majority of our early enterprisers and foremen in the textile industry were English immigrants. Many Americans were suspicious if not hostile to the erection of factories. The followers of Jefferson and George Clinton extolled the independent farmer as a much superior citizen to the propertyless urban worker. Even Federalists, with notable exceptions such as Alexander Hamilton, regarded manufacturing as less safe and certainly less genteel than landholding, agriculture, shipping, or merchandising. This uncongenial atmosphere no doubt discouraged many from entering manufacturing.

Despite these handicaps, a small thriving textile industry had become firmly established by 1825. At least three companies got under way in the early 1790's in New York, but they soon failed. The Napoleonic Wars and the conflict with Britain in 1812 reduced imports and brought about an upsurge of American nationalism which enabled the textile industry to gain a permanent foothold. By 1813 forty-three companies were manufacturing cotton or woolen cloth. Most of these factories sought the fine watersites in Oneida, Columbia, and Dutchess counties and below the falls of the Mohawk at Cohoes.

The development of the textile industry in Oneida County deserves special mention because it foreshadowed the future importance of the Mohawk Valley in the manufacture of cotton and woolen cloth and knit goods. Dr. Seth Capron and Benjamin Walcott, both familiar with the cotton manufacture in Rhode Island, organized the Oneida Manufacturing Company in Whitestown in 1809 in association with local and Albany capitalists. In 1811, encouraged by handsome profits, the stockholders established a woolen factory at Oriskany which was among the few to survive the postwar collapse. To underscore the nonindustrial character of the state, one should note that in 1827 fewer than eight hundred people worked in the textile mills of Oneida County—less than 2 per cent of the population of the county.

The government showed some willingness to befriend industry, especially during the period of ill feeling and war with England. In 1815 state legislators, noting the distress of textile manufacturers, urged New York congressmen to place a high tariff on imports. They also exempted textile mills from taxation and relieved textile workers from jury and militia service.

The followers of Jefferson in New York withdrew special favors from industry after the War of 1812 because they preferred to stimulate manufacture in the homes. The protection movement, however, won much support not only among the remnants of the Federalists but also among wool growers and manufacturers of woolens. Naturally enough, these groups supported the tariffs of 1816 and 1828, which protected native products.

The enactment of the first general incorporation law for manufacturers in 1811 was a great boon to industry. It enabled enterprisers to take advantage of the benefits of the corporate form: limited liability, corporate personality before the courts, long or perpetual life, and distribution of shares to an ever-widening group of investors. The legislature extended the act in 1816 for another year, revived it in 1818 for a period of five years, and in 1822 made it permanent.

Scores of firms had incorporated by 1827, including sugar-refining, chemical, textile, iron and steel, brewing, and brick-making establishments. The state government made little effort to regulate the corporations, leaving it more or less to the courts to define their rights and privileges.

The most noteworthy events in the history of labor between 1783 and 1825 were the decline and abandonment of such labor institutions as the apprenticeship system, indentured servitude, and slavery. During the colonial period many occupations had been closed except to those who paid the stiff fees for the freemanship. A state law in 1804 gave the privileges of freemen to all freeholders and to rentpayers eligible to vote in charter elections. After 1815 the New York City Common Council made no further regulations in regard to the freemanship. On the other hand, the Common Council continued to supervise strictly the charges and services of cartmen and hackmen, who were so necessary a part of the mercantile life of the seaport.

The decline of the freemanship deprived the artisans and tradesmen of the advantages resulting from the limitation upon numbers in their trade. The master craftsmen in 1785 attempted to incorporate a Mechanics' Society, but the state Council of Revision vetoed the proposed bills in accents that sounded very much like laissez-faire doctrine. They stated, "No stranger who may choose to reside among us should, therefore, besides the unnecessary and useless expense of taking up his freedom, be compelled to struggle against a combination vested with corporate powers and interested in keeping him unemployed." In 1786, however, a General Society of Mechanics and Tradesmen was formed. It included butchers, hatters, potters, carpenters, masons, tallowchandlers, sailmakers, coachmakers, coopers, ropemakers, stonecutters, tailors, cutlers, tanners, bookbinders, saddlers, bakers, and shipcarpenters—a list which illustrates the growing complexity of the economic life of New York City.

Employee groups also began to form associations to promote their own interests. Skilled journeymen resented the competition of unskilled workers, who no longer passed through the long stage of apprenticeship. Moreover, unemployment was a constant threat and the cost of living kept going up. Printers were among the first to organize, followed closely by the journeymen shoemakers. Other hard-pressed mechanics got together from time to time to strike for higher wages.

Servitude, whether of white immigrants or of Negro slaves, could not withstand the humanitarian and egalitarian currents rising during the last quarter of the eighteenth century. Some shiploads of indentured servants arrived in New York after the Revolution, but the practice of buying the service of immigrants for a certain period of time in exchange for their passage gradually died away. Merchants found it less troublesome and equally cheap to hire day labor.

The withering away of slavery was an important development in the labor history of both the city and rural region. New York had the highest percentage of Negroes of all the northern states. In 1790 over eleven thousand Negroes (some free) lived in rural areas, where the Dutch farmers in particular utilized their labor. Negroes on Manhattan were servants or unskilled laborers and suffered from the severe restrictions imposed upon their liberty as a result of the so-called "plot" of 1741.

The fight for emancipation of the slaves was led by the Quakers and some of the old landed families, whereas white mechanics feared that freedom would swamp the state with cheap labor. The legislature in 1785 prohibited the importation of slaves for sale and provided for the manumission of slaves, either by certificate or by will. The abolition movement gathered strength, and in 1799 the legislature provided that children of slaves born after July 4, 1799, should have the status of bond servants and eventually acquire complete freedom (males at twenty-eight, females at twenty-five). The act of 1817 was another step toward the end of slavery in New York, since it declared that "every negro, mulatto, or mustee within this state, born before the 4th day of July, 1799, shall, from and after the 4th day of July, 1827, be free." In 1841 transients and part-time residents were forbidden to hold slaves within New York.

Labor by 1800 had become free but it remained largely unorganized. The coming of the factory system would test the value of this freedom, especially in the period after 1825.

The creation of the Empire State by 1825 was the combined achievement of millions of New Yorkers in scores of occupations. If two groups deserve special mention, they are the pioneer farmers and the various merchants. The former conquered the wilderness and made New York a leading agricultural state; the latter drew to New York the bulk of the transatlantic, coastal, and interior trade of the nation. After two centuries of growth and development the economic structure of New York rested on the twin underpinnings of agriculture and trade which the Dutch had firmly established.

The Yankee Invasion of
New York

*[The Yankees] faithfully observe all the external forms of de-
cency, and their taciturn, phlegmatic, and calculating disposition, may render them objects of dislike. But their
intelligence, self-esteem, enterprise, and perseverance fit them
for a young country.*—PATRICK SHIRREFF, *1835*

BY 1820 both New York State and New York City had attained leading
positions in population. The 340,120 inhabitants of the state in 1790 had
grown to 1,372,812 three decades later. New York City developed almost
as fast, increasing from 33,131 to 123,706 persons in the same period.
The high birth rate was responsible for part of the increase; the census
for 1800 and that for 1810 shows that over half of the white population
was under sixteen years of age. A majority of families had seven or
more children.

New York remained predominantly rural throughout this period. In
1825 less than 15 per cent of the population lived in centers of more
than three thousand people. Nevertheless, almost all of the large cities
of today had been founded. A string of cities stretched up the Hudson
Valley to Albany, up the Mohawk to Rome, and fringed the newly built
Erie Canal to Buffalo. One hundred years later 84 per cent of the state's
population lived in this narrow belt between New York and Buffalo.

During the 1790's the most striking gains took place in the Hudson
Valley, where new towns such as Hudson, Troy, and Lansingburg and
older settlements such as Albany and Catskill enjoyed a mushroom
growth. At the juncture of every considerable road there grew up a
cluster of houses and stores.

With the exception of Schenectady, which had long served as a transshipment point, the towns along the Mohawk River did not show much
activity until after 1800, when the newly settled farms of central New

York began to pour their wheat and potash into the country stores. Utica was the starting point of the Genesee Road which the state constructed westward toward the fabulous Genesee country. Farther west Cazenovia, Batavia, Canandaigua, Ithaca, Geneva, and Bath came into prominence as centers for turnpikes, land offices, and country stores. Syracuse grew up around its salt deposits and Rochester at the falls of the Genesee.

The Erie Canal not only stimulated the growth of almost all the older urban centers but also proved decisive in determining the location of the most important cities west of Utica. Towns off the canal route, such as Cazenovia, Geneva, and Auburn, did not enjoy the boom in population and trade which Utica, Syracuse, Rochester, and Buffalo experienced. Perhaps Rochester benefited the most from the canal, for between 1820 and 1830 its population quadrupled. It is sometimes called America's first boom town.

The Erie Canal trade had a mixed effect upon the river ports of the Hudson Valley. Hudson was unaffected and continued to send out whaling ships to the Antarctic until the 1830's. Albany and Troy strenuously, even viciously, competed with one another for control of the traffic coming down the canal, and the merchants of both cities reaped a golden harvest as the tonnage mounted. On the other hand, the river ports south of Albany and north of New York City—Hudson, Newburgh, Kingston, Catskill—grew even more slowly after 1820 than in the previous decade. Furthermore, settlers regarded the unimproved lands in that region as inferior to the richer lands of central and western New York opened up by the canal. Most of the farm produce west of the Catskills and in the Finger Lakes region obviously reached tidewater via the Erie Canal rather than over the turnpikes through the Catskills to the old river towns.

Immigration accounted for much of the population increase. Although the flow of migration across the North Atlantic was interrupted by the wars of the French Revolution and of Napoleon between 1793 and 1815, Europe supplied New York with some settlers. Among those who came over during this period were several thousand Frenchmen fleeing the uprising in Santo Domingo and a few score French gentlemen who tried to settle tracts near the Black River. Welsh farmers, after 1796, began to till the hard scrabble lands around Steuben in Oneida County. Germans drifted to the cities and to the lands of Charles Williamson in the Genesee Valley. A few hundred Scots settled in pockets such as Caledonia. A trickle of Catholic Irish reached New York, but only a fraction of the numbers who were to arrive in the 1840's.

After the European wars ended in 1815, foreigners came to New York by the thousands, but they did not markedly change the basic Anglo-

Saxon-Dutch complexion of the population until the decade of the 1840's. Even in New York City, which had always had a much more cosmopolitan population than either urban or rural upstate, a majority of its inhabitants prior to 1830 claimed ancestors in the British Isles or the Netherlands.

After the Revolution, however, the immigration was chiefly from New England, and, to use the phrase of President Timothy Dwight of Yale, by 1820 New York was becoming "a colony from New-England." The "Puritan Pope" estimated that 60 to 67 per cent of the people of New York had originated in New England. The Yankees carried with them the Puritan virtues and vices and made an indelible imprint on the character and institutions of New York State.

As early as 1640 Connecticut men began to invade Long Island. Except for the Dutch settlements near Brooklyn, the population of the island was almost completely Yankee until well in the nineteenth century. Only a trickle in the seventeenth century, this migration became an important stream during the first three-quarters of the following century. By 1775 many Connecticut citizens had filtered into the eastern townships of Westchester and Dutchess counties and across the Hudson into Orange County. After 1783 the influx became a torrent, pouring into the Hudson Valley, sweeping up the Mohawk gateway, and spreading out across the fertile lands of central and western New York. Within a generation the sons of New England had found their way into every town and city of New York.

The Yankees came by land and by sea, in winter and in summer, in groups and as individuals. Sloops sailed up the Hudson while sleighs and oxcarts came overland through the steep hills fringing the border. The citizens of Albany watched a continual parade of restless people. During one three-day period in February 1795 about twelve hundred sleighs passed through that city on the way to the Genesee country. The mania for "turnpiking," reaching its peak between 1800 and 1807, opened up new highways to the migrants. New Englanders drove their wagons westward over the New England network until they met roads leading eastward from Greenbush (opposite Albany), Hudson, and Poughkeepsie. At almost every river landing small boats were ready to ferry them across the river. From Albany settlers struck out for the west over the Cherry Valley turnpike or to Schenectady and thence up the Mohawk Valley. Other settlers used the turnpikes leading from Newburgh and Catskill.

Most Yankees were looking for farms, although thousands headed for the commission houses of New York and the shops of craftsmen. In the first decade following the close of the Revolution newcomers swept into almost every valley except the recesses of the Adirondacks. Of course, the Hudson Valley was the first to feel the onrush, but Yankees were planting corn on the fertile intervales along the Genesee River long before the hill towns of the Catskill region had filled up.

Although land hunger was the compelling drive, other factors swelled the number of migrants. In Massachusetts high taxes levied at a time of falling prices ruined thousands of farmers. Settlers near Lake George told a traveler that the capitation tax in Rhode Island had driven them to New York. Others wished to escape the stern keepers of the New England conscience.

Glowing reports of rich lands piqued Yankee curiosity. Missionaries to the Iroquois sent back accounts of a new Eden, and many Yankee soldiers had carefully noted the fertile lowlands as they followed General Sullivan through the Finger Lakes region in 1779. They realized that the destruction of the Senecas and their allies would open this rich area to white settlers. The first pioneers wrote stirring letters urging their relatives to join them. Hugh White, who claimed to be the first white inhabitant west of the German settlers on the upper Mohawk, sent back to Middletown, Connecticut, his tallest stalks of Indian corn, his largest potatoes and onions. Agents distributed handbills offering new farms at tempting prices and on long-term credit.

The Hudson-Mohawk valleys attracted so many New Englanders that they almost submerged the small Dutch and German settlements. Hundreds of Yankees leased hill farms from Stephen Van Rensselaer in what are now Albany and Rensselaer counties. Others filled up the area north of Albany leading to Lake Champlain. The alluvial soils along the Mohawk and Schoharie valleys also proved attractive. The immigrants bought unoccupied tracts along the sparsely settled river bottoms and struck out into the hill country north and south of the Mohawk. Otsego County, where William Cooper acted as agent for many landholders, was the mecca for thousands.

In the north country the area between the St. Lawrence and the Adirondacks became another Yankee colony. So many Green Mountain residents crossed Lake Champlain to this region in search of land, timber, and millsites that it was designated as New Vermont on some early maps. Vermonters migrated to other parts of New York as well. In 1850 about fifty-two thousand natives of Vermont (equal to one-fifth of its population) had become citizens of the Empire State.

The region drained by the Delaware and the Susquehanna rivers likewise was overrun by New Englanders, although a number of Pennsylvanians, Jersey men, and even Marylanders worked their way up these river systems. Legend has it that the town of Penn Yan on Keuka Lake was so named as a compromise between settlers from the two areas.

Central New York by 1800 had become almost as Yankee in population as Connecticut itself. Timothy Dwight was delighted to find in Oneida County towns such as New Hartford and Clinton, which reproduced in the wilderness the church, the school, and the "sprightliness, thrift, and beauty" of New England.

The story of western New York is much the same. The districts west of the Property Line of 1768, exclusive of Oneida and Oswego counties, received about 60,000 inhabitants between 1790 and 1800. A decade later the population neared 200,000 and by 1820 passed 500,000. By mid-century population in this region exceeded 1,000,000. The great bulk of these people were of New England stock.

The impact of the newcomers on economic, political, professional, and social life was tremendous. Yankee woodsmen cleared most of the forests. Ledgers kept by Yankee clerks for Yankee businessmen recorded most of the expanding trade in New York and upstate cities. Leaders of the textile factories in Oneida County were former residents of Rhode Island. A high proportion of the men who preached the Gospel, pleaded before the bar, bled the patient, and used the birch rod on unruly students were trained in the academies and colleges of New England. Many ingenious craftsmen migrated westward to operate gristmills and forges and to construct homes and buildings.

Yankee brains and initiative stirred the old river ports to feverish activity. The port of New York won top place among the nation's harbors largely under their direction. After 1800 Yankees in large numbers reached Manhattan, concentrating in the shipping and mercantile businesses. By working hard, by seizing every opportunity, by cutting corners, by driving sharp bargains, and by avoiding the pitfalls of wine, women, and song, a considerable number of Yankee farm boys made their fortunes. Several New England families of substance moved their businesses to Manhattan or sent their younger sons to set up branch offices.

A new mercantile group gradually emerged, overshadowing the older aristocracy of New York. The Griswold, Low, Grinnell, Fish and Macy families made their fame in commerce. The old families of colonial days naturally resented this invasion by upstarts who, they felt, had no manners and chased dollars too avidly—and successfully. The newcomers were tireless in extolling the superior virtues of New England and its institutions. How the descendants of the old mercantile families must have writhed to witness the succession of Yankees occupying the presidential chair of the New York Chamber of Commerce almost continually between 1845 and 1875!

The landed aristocracy also disliked the Yankee speculators who got control of the choicest lands of western New York. Opening these lands to settlement reduced the value of older tracts in eastern New York. Furthermore, Yankee settlers brought with them a desire to hold land in fee simple, an idea which threatened the large estates developed under the leasehold system. James Fenimore Cooper bitterly held the Yankee immigrant largely responsible for the antirent trouble of the 1840's.

Albany also felt the invigorating, if unsettling, effect of Yankee enterprise. By 1803 the Yankees there outnumbered the original stock and even succeeded, in their bumptious way, in pushing through an ordinance requiring the enraged Dutch burghers to cut off the long rainspouts on their houses. Troy and Hudson were founded and inhabited by Yankees. Whalers from Nantucket banded together in 1783 to found Hudson. Canny Yankees in Troy made a strong bid for the control of the trade and transportation routes of the upper Hudson Valley. Utica, Syracuse, Rochester, and Buffalo likewise owe much of their early growth to the New England migration. The city of Rochester was noted for its imported Puritan piety. New Englanders dominated the commercial life of these upstate cities in the same way as their compatriots swept to the top in New York City.

Politics in New York felt the Yankee impact. Hardly had the settlers cleared the forests before they began organizing town governments. Soon they were unraveling the twisted skein of state politics. The first generation of New Englanders tended to join the fight for democracy because they disliked the political domination of the landed aristocracy. A majority of the members of the constitutional convention of 1821, which established manhood suffrage, were of New England stock. By the 1830's practically all the most prominent leaders stemmed from New England forebears. The Albany Regency, made up of such Democratic worthies as Silas Wright, William L. Marcy, Azariah C. Flagg, John A. Dix, and Martin Van Buren, could boast of only one member, Van Buren, who traced his roots deeply into colonial New York. The outstanding leaders of the Whig and later the Republican party—William H. Seward, Thurlow Weed, Hamilton Fish, and Horace Greeley—were of New England descent.

The transit of Yankee culture resulted in interesting changes. The new environment modified such typical institutions as the town, the church, and the school. The characteristics of the New England town with its jointly owned and used pasture, mowing, and forest lands seldom appeared except on Long Island. The newcomers often laid out a village green on which the church and homes fronted, but most farmers lived in isolated homesteads. The town was much less important as a unit of local government in New York because the state delegated the more important functions to the county rather than to the town.

The New England tradition influenced many of the churches in New

York. Most of the preachers serving the Presbyterian, Congregational, Baptist, and Unitarian churches were reared in New England and educated in its colleges. Among the most noted religious figures were Charles Finney, Joseph Smith, John Humphrey Noyes, and William Miller, all born in New England.

The New York educational system disappointed the Yankees, who were accustomed to tax-supported schools open to all children. Gideon Hawley, a New Englander, was called to direct the first successful system of state-aided neighborhood schools. Private academies also flourished wherever New Englanders settled. Columbia College was the only institution on the college level not stamped with the Yankee imprint. Hamilton, Colgate, Rochester, Hobart, and St. Lawrence drew most of their faculty members from the east and modeled their curricula after Harvard and Yale. The development of the press was greatly indebted to printers and editors, such as Horace Greeley, hailing from New England.

These cocksure invaders naturally antagonized the early inhabitants. They did not conceal their contempt for the "unenterprising" Germans and Dutch. Citizens of New York struck back by circulating stories about dirty "Yankee tricks," and the upper classes approved James Fenimore Cooper's descriptions of the Yankees as a particularly disagreeable race.

Gradually the passage of time softened these asperities into a feeling of good will. The transplanted Yankees became more mellow and less angular. Moreover, the Dutch and Germans gradually lost their dialects, especially after the public school system was extended. The new aristocracy based on trade and manufacturing began to copy some of the manners and customs of the landed aristocracy. With the influx of the Irish in the 1840's, the older population forgot their differences in their common fear of the new immigrants who were fervently Catholic and disturbingly clannish.

The same distrust of outsiders was to greet each immigrant group in the future: the Poles, Italians, and the Jews after 1900; the Negroes in the 1920's; the Puerto Ricans in the 1940's and 1950's. Fortunately the desire for "Americanization" and the spirit of tolerance among New Yorkers has usually overcome bigotry and prejudice. No group of newcomers, however, left a more permanent imprint upon the racial, cultural, political, and economic life of New York than the resolute sons of New England.

Ed - paper

Social and Cultural Life

I anticipate great advantag in the defusion of useful knolege from them [the school funds], amongst the lower order of the people.—JEDEDIAH PECK, *1810*

THE conquest of the wilderness and the rise of commerce were largely accomplished through the efforts of individuals, working, often, in grim and lonely isolation. But the early New Yorker was not an unsociable or unco-operative person. The citizenry showed a willingness, when it was possible, to work and play together in formal and informal groups. The church, the lodge, and the school were the most important of the organized societies. Bees, clubs, and spontaneous gatherings provided diversion and carried out co-operative neighborhood projects, such as house raisings and quilting parties.

The two decades following the close of the American Revolution constituted the "period of the lowest ebb tide of vitality in the history of American Christianity." Timothy Dwight's observation applies with particular force to New York, and he only one of several travelers who deplored the rough, drunken men poling boats up the Mohawk, thronging the taverns, and attending logging bees and house raisings.

Several factors brought religious activity and moral standards to a low level. Invasion, Indian raids, and inflation had disrupted many communities and closed down many churches. British officials had persecuted the Presbyterian and other "patriotic" sects, while the exodus of thousands of Tories during and after the war left the Episcopal communion in a bad condition. Meanwhile, secular ideals were sweeping into Manhattan, always tolerant of new ideas ever since the days of Dutch rule. Deism from England and Rationalism from France, neatly summarized in Thomas Paine's *The Age of Reason*, made converts, particularly among educated people in New York. Another brake on religious activity was the fact that none of the denominations had enough clergymen to fill the pulpits in the churches already established, much less to follow the pioneer into new country. Unquestionably the hazards, hardships, and poverty of the frontier brutalized many immigrants until they were as wild as the savages they replaced.

The Episcopal church in colonial days enjoyed official status as the Church of England and received some public monies in New York, Queens, Richmond, and Westchester counties. Despite these advantages, it certainly had less than one-tenth of the population in its membership. The Revolution brought on a crisis for the Anglican communion, since its clergy and many of its leading laymen favored the Crown. In 1777 the new state constitution confirmed the disestablishment already carried out and guaranteed the "free exercise and enjoyment of religious profession and worship, without discrimination or preference . . . to all mankind." A series of statutes in 1784 permitted all religious bodies the right to incorporate, and thus to hold property.

The formation of the national Protestant Episcopal church in 1789 was preceded in New York by the elevation of the patriotic Reverend Samuel Provoost to the first bishopric for New York. His selection helped to remove the Tory taint, and during the 1790's the Episcopal church made steady gains in the metropolis and even upstate. Greater progress took place after John Henry Hobart came to Trinity Church in 1801. Hobart was an ardent High-churchman and a born organizer who used the resources of Trinity Church to push missionary activity throughout the state. Whereas there were only two Episcopal missionaries upstate in 1811, there were fifty in 1830. Many persons of social prominence and inherited wealth and many Federalist politicians belonged to the Episcopal church.

The Revolution speeded the drift of the Dutch Reformed church toward complete independence of Amsterdam. Dr. John H. Livingston arranged in 1794 for the convening of a General Synod which marked the church's reorganization along national lines. A major problem was the recruitment of a professionally trained clergy independent of Amsterdam. Although the Reformed church had founded a seminary at New Brunswick (New Jersey) in 1784, it drew many of its clergymen from the other Calvinist churches. The Dutch church showed little initiative either in seeking out souls on the frontier or in winning adherents from among the immigrants; in fact, many congregations lost their young people to other churches by stubbornly clinging to the Dutch language, some as late as 1800.

No sect enjoyed so favorable a position in New York after the Revolution as the Presbyterian. Its unquestioned patriotism, its firm hold on the middle class and particularly the farmer, and its friendly relations with Connecticut Congregationalism permitted this denomination to expand rapidly back in Manhattan and upstate. By 1825 it had twenty-

one churches in the metropolis, but, much more important, it had
gathered in a large number of Yankee frontiersmen.

The Yankee migration to New York would normally have meant the
transplanting of Congregationalism westward. But the delegates of the
Connecticut General Association were co-operating closely in the 1790's
with the General Assembly of the Presbyterian church in carrying on
mission work. In 1801 the two denominations drew up the famous Plan
of Union which permitted churches of the Congregational order to settle
Presbyterian ministers and yet retain the Congregational form of government. Presbyterian churches were accorded the same privilege of
electing Congregational preachers and a Congregational form of government.

The Presbyterian church derived more benefit from this arrangement
because most Congregational associations had united with the Presbyterian synods by 1822. For example, the Association of Ontario dissolved and joined the Presbytery of Geneva. Why did the Yankees adopt
the Presbyterian form? First of all, there was very little difference
theologically between the two groups. Moreover, Congregationalism in
Connecticut was trending toward Presbyterian polity. There was a tradition of co-operation between the two groups. The Presbyterian church
had a more centralized organization, which enabled its leaders to take
more interest in the mission churches of New York. In passing, we
should note that the Presbyterian churches in New York retained some
of the New England tradition of independence and congregational
autonomy. They also tended to dilute the orthodox Calvinism so rigidly
adhered to by the Scotch-Irish in Pennsylvania.

The Methodists made the most spectacular gains during this period.
Whereas they had only one small congregation in New York City in
1776, they had fifteen in 1825 as well as scores of churches upstate.
The Wesley message of free grace was spread by lay preachers, who
were often the first to reach the unchurched common people. These
itinerant preachers sought converts without regard to race or social
status. They had little formal education or training, but they knew
how to reach the hearts of the rank and file. Equally important was the
class leader whose duty was to oversee the spiritual welfare of a small
group of members. Presiding elders and visiting bishops carefully supervised the local congregations.

The Baptists also made important gains, winning some forty thousand
members by 1825. Its loose organization, its flexibly defined creed, and
its reliance upon lay preachers made it easy for the Baptists to adapt
to the needs of the locality. Like the Methodists, the Baptists made
their greatest appeal to the humble folk in city and country.

The German population in New York City and in the Hudson,

Schoharie, and Mohawk valleys had established Lutheran, German Reformed, and Moravian churches in colonial times. A new wave of German immigration after 1815 brought new strength to the older congregations, although the young people tended to drift away from the churches retaining the German language in the service.

The Society of Friends, although it numbered only a few thousand members, was outstanding because of its charitable and humanitarian activities. Quakers Thomas Eddy and John Murray were active in the fight for penal reform, the emancipation of slaves, and the erection of free schools for the common people. During the 1820's Elias Hicks, the Long Island carpenter, preached to thousands the message of the "inner light." The more conservative disliked Hicks' neglect of Christ, and in 1827 the society split. Quaker meetings in rural New York gradually declined throughout the nineteenth century.

The small group of Catholics who had worshiped in secret before the Revolution welcomed the guarantee of religious freedom incorporated in the state Constitution of 1777. The state oath of naturalization, however, required all citizens to renounce allegiance to any foreign ruler in "all matters ecclesiastical as well as civil." This proviso fell into disuse in 1790 with the new federal naturalization law. Sixteen years later the legislature rephrased the oath so as to permit Catholics to hold office.

At first the Catholic church grew slowly. In 1800 it still had only two churches. Several problems troubled its leaders: the unusual assumption of power by lay trustees over local congregations; the lack of sufficient clergymen and churches; the influx of immigrants of various nationalities; the suspicions of many native Americans. Bishop John Connolly (1814–1825) worked hard to take care of the immigrants and to smooth over quarrels within his flock. By 1825 Roman Catholicism had sent down deep roots in the state, but evangelical Protestantism dominated the culture.

"Liberal thought" likewise had its followers. The Universalists sent out itinerants into the rural areas and by 1823 had established nearly ninety congregations in western New York. The orthodox preachers denounced the Universalists as heretics because of their refusal to insist upon the deity of Jesus and upon human depravity. Unitarianism made few converts in New York prior to 1825.

The Jewish population of New York remained small throughout this period. In 1812 there were probably no more than five hundred Jews in New York City, most of them of Spanish-Portuguese background and engaged in foreign commerce. The Jewish congregation was the center of Hebrew life.

The "Second Awakening" which spread southward from Maine to Connecticut during the 1790's reached New York by 1799 and brought showers of "spiritual blessings." The "New Divinity" school of clergy in Connecticut provided leaders for this crusade against infidelity and irreligion. No longer did they regard man as a mere pawn in the hands of an implacable God. Rather they stressed the responsibility of each individual to carry on good works as a means to salvation or at least as a demonstration of his regeneration. The awakening had far-reaching results for the United States and for New York in particular: the beginning of Protestant missionary activity on a large scale; the development of the "activity church," with organizations such as missionary societies and Sunday schools; and the crusade for humanitarian reforms which began in this period but reached its height between 1830 and 1850.

The New York frontier was the favorite field for the Yankee benevolent societies because so many New Englanders were taking up land west of the Hudson. Many residents of New York became converted and joined the missionary crusade. By 1825 the Protestants in the Empire State were outstripping their Connecticut neighbors in revivalism, missionary activity, and reform crusades.

The most notable revivals came in 1799–1800, 1807–1808, and 1815, forerunners of the famous campaigns conducted by Charles Finney between 1825 and 1843. These revivals stimulated almost all denominations. The Presbyterians alone established thirteen new churches in New York City between 1810 and 1830.

Interdenomination co-operation both on the local and state levels made some progress. For example, in 1796 the Presbyterians, the Dutch Reformed, and the Baptists formed the New York Missionary Society to send missionaries to the Indians and the frontier settlements. Most significant of all was the close co-operation between the Congregational Association of Connecticut and the Presbyterian church, which was formalized by the famous Plan of Union in 1801. By 1830 this Calvinist coalition had organized the American Home Mission Society, the American Bible Society, and several other benevolent organizations.

Religious eccentricity emerged before 1825, although its luxuriant growth took place after that date. The Shakers established communities at New Lebanon and at Sodus Bay and won a few converts to the Shaker tenets: celibacy, nonresistance, full equality for women, and perfectionism. Equally fascinating but likewise numerically unimportant was the Community of the Publick Universal Friend which Jemima Wilkinson founded on Seneca Lake in 1787 and moved to Jerusalem, Yates County, a little later. This eccentric woman preached doctrines of celibacy, equality of the sexes, and communal living. These religious phenomena were certainly not typical and cannot be compared with the much more important activities carried on by the clergymen of the major denominations.

Historians have paid little attention to the role of fraternal lodges. By 1826 the Masonic Order had established chapters in many sections of the state. The lodges tended to attract men from the upper classes in the villages and cities—lawyers, land agents, politicians.

Prior to 1825 education was largely supported by private charity and local government. The concept of free, public, secular education had won some converts, especially among the followers of Jefferson. In 1782 Governor George Clinton urged the legislature to establish schools and seminaries, and two years later the lawmakers heeded sufficiently to his request to create the University of the State of New York, an organization supervised by a Board of Regents and authorized to establish secondary schools and colleges. The Regents in 1787 boldly advocated a public school system since the "erecting of public schools for teaching reading, writing and arithmetic is an object of very great importance which ought not to be left to the discretion of private men, but be promoted by public authority."

The legislature acted cautiously, passing an experimental act in 1795 which granted $50,000 annually for the next five years to encourage elementary schools. To receive a state subvention, a county had to raise an amount equal to one-half the state grant. The results were heartening; some 1,352 grammar schools in 1799 were instructing almost 60,000 students. In addition the Regents authorized several academies for secondary education, In 1800, however, the state legislature abandoned the experiment so that the Regents had to resort to lotteries to obtain funds.

Meanwhile, various churches continued charity schools for the poor children, and the middle and upper classes sent their children to private schools or employed tutors. In 1805 Thomas Eddy, a Quaker reformer, organized the Free School Society of New York City to educate those children not provided for by the various religious schools. This organization, under the able leadership of De Witt Clinton, went ahead rapidly, obtaining some support from both state and city treasuries. In 1824 the society had an enrollment of over five thousand students in six schools. Similar nonsectarian charity schools were established in Brooklyn and Albany.

A permanent system of common schools, with school districts for each township, was set up by the legislature in 1812. Jedediah Peck of Otsego County was the moving spirit behind the report favoring the system of common schools. Two years later the revised law added a compulsory

proviso that each town must match state aid. Progress was made under
the brilliant leadership of Gideon Hawley, the first state superintendent
of common schools in the United States. By 1825 New York schools
were probably the best of any state in the Union. The figures for 1828
were encouraging: some 441,856 children were attending school in
8,298 school districts.

The public school movement met opposition from taxpayers and
conservatives. Some poor families in New York and Brooklyn preferred
that their children remain uneducated rather than have them bear the
stigma of "charity scholars." Approximately one-third of the children of
Brooklyn in 1828 did not attend any school. Upstate, the common school
was accepted more widely as part of the democratic organization of
society. In rural communities of freeholding farmers there were few
distinctions between children.

Cold, poorly lighted, and containing only rough benches, the log
schoolhouses of this period had none of the fads and frills which
ornament our modern school buildings. The teacher was usually an
impoverished youth with only a rudimentary education himself. He instructed children of all ages and in all stages of advancement during
the winter term of two or three months. He often got his pay by
"boarding round" with the parents of his charges. Despite his lack of
training and the primitive conditions under which he worked, he succeeded in teaching his students to read the Scriptures and to figure
profits in a business transaction. In addition, he imparted a rough kind
of moral discipline by expounding the lessons contained in Biblical
passages and by applying the birch rod.

Secondary education expanded under private auspices but with some
financial encouragement by the Regents. Every city and many villages
had seminaries or academies where the children of the wealthier classes
could receive instruction in the genteel as well as the "tool" subjects.
Sometimes denominations sponsored academies for boys and seminaries
for girls. There were also mixed schools, but teachers carefully shep-
herded boys and girls into separate classes. Young ladies received instruction in good manners, sewing, music, dancing, and French. Boys
preparing for college studied the classical languages and mathematics.
The academies had a precarious existence because of competition and
lack of financial resources.

Higher education received its first attention in 1784 and 1787 when
the acts providing for the University of the State of New York provided
for the reincorporation of King's College as Columbia College. Dr.
William Samuel Johnson was appointed the first president of the institution, which in 1787 had only thirty students and three professors.
During the next decade Columbia grew rapidly and offered new sub-

jects, such as modern languages, chemistry, and moral philosophy, in addition to the old classical curriculum.

Union College, chartered in 1795, was the first new college begun by the Regents. Its trustees selected the Reverend Eliphalet Nott in 1804 as president, and he held this position until 1866. Hamilton College received its charter in 1812 and became a stronghold of Calvinism and the classical curriculum. In 1824 the Board of Regents awarded a charter to Geneva (Hobart) College after it had met the necessary conditions as to endowment, buildings, and staff.

These colleges suffered the usual troubles of infant institutions: internal quarrels, inadequate income, and boisterous students. Their importance was recognized by the state, which granted generous subsidies. Columbia College received a total of $140,130; Union, $358,111; and Hamilton, $120,000. New York State could also draw upon young men educated in the colleges of New England. Throughout the first half of the nineteenth century a good share of the lawyers, clergymen, teachers, and doctors of New York were graduates of Yankee colleges.

Newspapers provided most of the reading material available to the early New Yorker, although only a small minority of the people could afford the high cost. Papers sprang up first in New York City, which by 1785 had its first daily, the *Daily Advertiser*. Within the next thirty years wandering printers carried presses to practically every village in the state. At first, the printer was also the editor. His job was described in 1830 as follows:

A country editor is one who reads newspapers, selects miscellany, writes articles on all subjects, sets type, reads proof, works at press, folds papers and some times carries them, prints jobs, runs on errands, cuts and saws wood, works in the garden, talks to his patrons who call.

The small number of subscribers were chiefly interested in getting news of political happenings in the state and national capitals and of commercial and military events in Europe. Gossip took care of local matters. The community news was the recording of deaths and marriages. Advertisements contained some information on local events and have become a mine of information to historians, although an advertisement generally indicated only the nature and location of the business. "Personals" calling for the return of indentured apprentices or warnings by irate husbands that they would no longer be responsible for the debts of wives provided a certain amount of local news. The testimonials for patent medicines had already made their appearance prior to 1825.

The printer-editor-publisher usually found it difficult to secure enough paying subscribers and advertisers to finance his newspaper. Most papers, therefore, ardently supported a political party or faction. In this way they secured subscribers, while party leaders awarded them job printing contracts and paid them for publishing legal notices. This arrangement satisfied the politicians, who counted on their papers to belabor their enemies and to spread party viewpoints to the public. The emphasis on partisanship led to vituperation beclouding the real issues and resulted in many suits at law.

The Federalists dominated the first newspapers in New York and established the first journals outside the metropolis. Probably the outstanding Federalist paper of the period was the *Evening Post,* which Alexander Hamilton had supported. The Anti-Federalists and later the Jeffersonian Republicans founded journals in self-defense. Publishers were frequently hot-tempered and strong-willed individuals who jumped party traces. An interesting case is that of Elihu Phinney, who established the Otsego *Herald* at Cooperstown in 1795 with the support of William Cooper and other Federalist leaders. But Phinney broke with Cooper within a few years and, casting his lot with the Jeffersonian Republicans, made his fortune in the publishing business.

The printer was an agent of literacy and occasionally of culture. He included some verse and fiction in his paper, reprinted sermons, and carried articles on agriculture. Some of the more successful printers operated bookstores and reading rooms where their customers examined new books and glanced at newspapers.

James D. Bemis, who settled in Canandaigua in 1804, became known as "Father of the Western New York Press." Bemis made the *Ontario Repository* an outstanding Federalist journal and trained scores of apprentices in his office and bookstore. Perhaps his most famous imprint was James E. Seaver's *Narrative of the Life of Mrs. Mary Jemison* (1824). This account described the life of a white girl captured by the Indians and reared among the natives. Phinney's firm in Cooperstown became famous for its annual *Phinney Calendar* (100,000 copies a year), its quarto Family Bible, and its school texts and children's books. William Williams of Utica published histories, biographies, and novels and specialized in the publication of religious periodicals.

The books stocked in the various bookstores reflect in a rough way the literary tastes of the period. There were books for all tastes: Bibles, Psalms, prayer books, and tracts for the religious; Burns's *Obstetrical Works* for the village doctor; Ostrander's *Arithmetic* and Kirkham's *Grammar* for the teacher; *Scottish Chiefs,* or novels such as *Charlotte Temple* and *Fragments of Miss Smith,* for the ladies; the *American Magazine and Review, Niles' Weekly Register,* and other periodicals for the businessman; legal digests and reports for the lawyers. Schoolbooks were also an important line, both for the printer and the students.

The landlords and merchants were the only persons with sufficient income to make regular book purchases and to build libraries. In 1796 the legislature encouraged the formation of library associations by permitting incorporation on easy terms. As a result, citizens banded together to form hundreds of societies with circulating libraries. For example, the Auburn circulating library had eight hundred volumes in 1816, for which members paid yearly dues of three dollars or a fee for each volume borrowed (six cents for a duodecimo or smaller and twelve and a half cents for an octavo). Students at Hamilton, Union, and Columbia organized literary societies which not only managed debates but also bought and circulated books among their members. Similar steps were taken in New York City by skilled craftsmen. In 1820 the Mercantile Library Association and the Apprentices' Library Association were organized.

New York State wrested literary leadership from Philadelphia during the first quarter of the nineteenth century. James Kirke Paulding and Washington Irving dug deep into the lore of colonial New York, and James Fenimore Cooper won a large audience with his novels of sea and wilderness. These authors, disturbed by the rise of manufacturing and democracy, sought refuge in romantic flight into the past and the realm of nature.

An indulgent family gave Irving plenty of opportunity to experiment with literary forms. In 1807 he and his brother William in collaboration with James Paulding brought out *Salmagundi*, which spoofed New York customs in a genteel fashion. Two years later there appeared Irving's vigorous and genial burlesque, *Diedrich Knickerbocker's History of New York*, a caricature of the early Dutch founders as lethargic and simpleminded folk ruled by the redoubtable Wouter Van Twiller. This, the first important satirical work in this country, was in many respects Irving's best effort. His *Sketch Book* (1819), largely a tribute to English life and manners, included the famous New York stories, "Rip Van Winkle" and the "Legend of Sleepy Hollow." Irving's later works on Spanish history and on the American West lacked the freshness and spontaneity he brought to his New York themes.

James Kirke Paulding, after making his mark in *Salmagundi*, continued to write short stories, novels, poetry, and drama until mid-century. Although never so polished a craftsman as Irving, Paulding wrote more realistically about his native New York. He attacked the literary use of such romantic devices as ghosts, superstitions, and exotic foreign settings when popular acclaim for the Waverley novels of Sir Walter Scott was at its height. His writings also reflect his Anglophobia and his belief in democratic agrarianism. Probably his most interesting novel on a New York theme was *The Dutchman's Fireside,* which gives a realistic portrait of Sir William Johnson. His *Book of St. Nicholas* (1836) includes several stories of Dutch life in colonial New York.

New York City attracted several other literary figures. William Cullen Bryant, who was regarded as America's foremost poet during the 1830's, drew his chief inspiration from his youth in the Massachusetts hill country, but in 1825 he came to New York and won renown as editor of the New York *Evening Post.* His support for the rights of labor, abolition, and other liberal causes will be taken up in the discussion of political developments after 1825. Fitz-Greene Halleck was another poet who wrote in the style of the English romantics.

James Fenimore Cooper (1789–1851) was the most famous American novelist of his day and second only to Sir Walter Scott as a romantic storyteller. The unforgettable characters Natty Bumppo and Uncas were drawn from his memories of Cooperstown during its first settlement. Cooper relied heavily upon New York themes for his novels of sea, forest, and the Revolution. *The Spy* (1821), his first successful novel, described the civil war in Westchester County between Tories and Patriots. In *The Pioneers* (1823) he reproduced the settlement of Otsego County and thinly disguised his own father, Judge William Cooper, as Judge Marmaduke Temple. This novel began the famous series of Leatherstocking Tales devoted to the adventures of the frontier scout, Natty Bumppo.

Cooper regarded his writings primarily as vehicles for his opinions of American life and manners. The irascible novelist managed to affront many of his countrymen with his strong criticisms. Most interesting for students of New York history is the trilogy called *The Littlepage Manuscripts.* Cooper, who had ardently professed democracy and republicanism in Europe, rushed to the defense of the landed aristocracy when the antirent wars threatened their holdings in the 1840's. *Satanstoe* (1845) is a sympathetic portrayal of genteel life in the middle of the eighteenth century. *The Chainbearer* (1846) describes the difficulties of the landholder in developing his frontier tracts, and *The Redskins* (1846) is hardly more than a tirade against the defaulting tenants.

Painters, sculptors, architects, and musicians of the time were either European in origin and training or relied heavily on European models. We shall discuss the beginnings of these arts in the chapter devoted to cultural developments between 1825 and 1860.

The professions, ministry, law, and medicine, were severely disrupted by the Revolution. During the next four decades the numbers in each of these callings grew rapidly, in line with the population growth, but there was a general decline in professional standards. The looser ties with English professional groups and the weakness of theological, law, and medical schools contributed to the lowering of standards.

Lawyers in the 1780's were unpopular with the masses, largely because of their zeal in collecting debts for creditors and land agents. Gradually the legal fraternity won more public acceptance and many young men found the law the best entrée to a political career. The English distinction between attorney and solicitor vanished. The training of young men was casual and unsystematic. Students read law in the office of a lawyer, frequented the courts, and mastered a few texts.

James Kent was the most eminent lawyer in the state. As chancellor of New York, he influenced the course of American law by establishing the written decision as normal court procedure. His opinions in equity cases were widely followed throughout the country. After his retirement from the bench Kent wrote his *Commentaries on American Law,* which called for more safeguards around property rights.

The legislature in 1806 gave the state medical society loose power over the admission of doctors to practice. Most doctors received their training by serving as apprentices to established physicians. The inadequacy of such training led to the founding of the College of Physicians and Surgeons in 1807, and a few years later Fairfield Medical College opened its doors to young men in the Mohawk Valley, but standards in the colleges were as low as the practice outside.

Class lines between 1783 and 1825 lost much of their earlier rigidity with the decline of the landed aristocracy, the influx of Yankees, and the emergence of a free labor system. No other northern state experienced as great a social revolution as New York. It moved rapidly from a highly stratified society to a democratic commonwealth providing a large equality of opportunity to all groups in the population.

The landed aristocracy, whose domination of social and political life has been described in an earlier chapter, found its influence on the wane. The Revolution had split its ranks, a majority remaining loyal to the King. Many of the Loyalists fled to Canada. Most of those who remained found themselves stripped of their property and political power. Egalitarian and democratic ideas were spreading. George Clinton, a supporter of Jefferson, captured the governorship for seven terms; and the demand for manhood suffrage won its place in the Constitution by 1821. As commerce and manufacturing grew, a new aristocracy of wealth appeared, made up largely of immigrants from New England.

The remaining colonial aristocrats, such as the Van Rensselaers and the Livingstons, admitted some recruits to the inner circle. Governor John Jay, James Duane, and Peter Smith of Peterboro married daughters of the Livingston clan. Alexander Hamilton married Elizabeth Schuyler despite his questionable family origin. The landed aristocracy sometimes sent younger sons to administer their frontier tracts, spreading the principles of federalism and the Episcopal church into the wilderness. The old aristocracy found able defenders among property-minded newcomers such as Alexander Hamilton, James Kent, and James Fenimore Cooper. No Livingston ever defended the old regime of landed wealth more vehemently than James Kent at the constitutional convention of 1821 or James Fenimore Cooper in his antirent novels.

By 1825 the merchant-shipping families were competing for social eminence with the landed aristocrats. Their wealth enabled them to live luxuriously and to cultivate genteel manners. Some Manhattan merchants erected suburban homes farther up the island and sent their wives to Saratoga Springs for the summer season. Tutors taught the daughters French and etiquette and prepared the young men for Columbia, Yale, and Harvard.

Lord Chesterfield set the standards of propriety for New York's upper classes, but French ideas in dress prevailed. The influx of hundreds of French refugees from Santo Domingo and France resulted in the spread of French tastes in cooking, ballroom dancing, and music. During the 1790's, when George Washington held "court" at New York, the gentlemen wore smallclothes, silk stockings, and silver buckles. And when the terrorized nobles of France disguised themselves in workingmen's pantaloons, Americans adopted similar attire. By 1825 only a few diehards retained the old style. In the 1790's women in the upper classes also shifted toward simplicity in dress, discarding whalebone and heavy petticoats. By 1820 the trend was reversed and the ladies went back to stays, bustles, and stomach boards.

Keeping house was a full-time occupation for the wives of the aristocracy as it was for all housewives in that period. The problem of securing reliable servants became even more difficult after the decline of slavery and indentured servitude. Few domestics, moreover, could be trusted to supervise the endless round of household duties. Carrying in water, keeping the fireplace supplied, cleaning the iron pots, pans, and kettles, and making candles, soap, and carpets were only a few of the tasks.

Below the aristocracy of birth and of wealth were the members of what we loosely call the middle class. Independent farmers formed the most numerous element in this group, and their manner of life has been indicated in the chapter on pioneer agriculture. The middle class in the villages and the cities included shopkeepers, clerks, tavern keepers, skilled artisans, manufacturers, and most of the professional people. From this group came most of the future leaders of the cultural and business life of the state.

The lower classes included farm laborers, apprentices, slaves, and, later, free Negroes, day laborers, and the most recent immigrants. Life for these people was grim but somewhat relieved by the hope that the way upward was not entirely blocked for the most able and for their children.

Although many social and civic problems, such as the education of the young and the control of fires, faced village and city trustees in this period, only a few tentative steps toward improvement were taken by 1825. The trustees of Rochester, who required that each householder keep a bucket for every two fireplaces, placed chief reliance in the volunteer brigades. Public health measures were virtually nonexistent. Citizens drew water from springs, wells, or cisterns or bought their water from street carriers. Pigs and cows roamed the dirty unpaved streets despite the legal bans. The new cities found it necessary to establish markets in order to get farmers' wagons out of the streets. In 1822 Rochester ordered property holders along the commercial blocks to build a twelve-foot sidewalk to protect pedestrians from the filth.

The problems of antisocial behavior, ill health, and intemperance affected both urban and rural New York. The transient population along the wharves and the canals and the rough men patronizing the grog-houses and taverns provided most of the criminal elements. Municipal authorities strengthened the night watch, but no uniformed police had appeared by 1825. The sheriff maintained order in the countryside, calling out his posse when necessary.

Life expectancy in this period was a fraction of its present figure. Disease ravaged the population almost completely unchecked and little understood. Disorders almost unknown today were commonplace. Smallpox left its ugly scars on thousands, while tuberculosis filled ten times as many graves in proportion to the population as it did in 1952. Malaria, sometimes called the "shakes" or "Genesee fever," riddled the frontier population. Typhoid and many other contagious diseases struck every community, and cholera hit the seaports. Only one-half of the children reached their fifth birthday—a sobering statistic in the light of modern advances.

Medical attention, if available, was practically worthless. The results of the common practice of bleeding the patient were often worse than the diseases themselves. Anesthetics were unknown and gangrene followed many of the operations performed by inexpert surgeons with primitive instruments. Toothaches were universal and dentistry primitive. Travelers noted that few adults had a full set of teeth. The real burden of maintaining health in the family fell upon the overworked housewife, who fed molasses and sulphur to her children and acted as midwife to her neighbors. A community was likely to find it necessary to lay out the cemetery long before it got around to building a school or a church.

Hard drinking was the custom of many New Yorkers, to an extent that might shock even the broad-minded modern. There was little social or religious disgrace attached to heavy consumption of alcohol. Ministers, along with other callers, sampled the householder's best and the ubiquitous barrel of whisky appeared at church raisings as well as at bees for the construction of barns and houses. Parents served ardent spirits and liquors at births, weddings, and funerals. At frolics the dancers and huskers often stopped to take a drink. Taverns along the turnpikes and groghouses or groceries in the cities became centers for carousing.

Intemperance was encouraged by the availability of a wide variety of beverages at low cost. Gentlemen stocked up on port, madeira, claret, and burgundies. Cider was the favorite of all classes, sometimes serving as legal tender in frontier settlements. The poorest farmers had rum and applejack, and whisky was cheap. Almost every township had its distillery and groceries sold "wet goods" as readily as dry goods.

Drinking excesses disturbed many reformers, notably Dr. Billy Clark of Moreau, Saratoga County, who founded the first temperance society in America in 1808. Dr. Clark hoped to cut down the heavy drinking among the lumberjacks in his community. Shortly thereafter, young Lyman Beecher, Presbyterian clergyman of East Hampton, Long Island, began his long crusade against intemperance. These reformers had only local successes and were unable to change in any appreciable measure the drinking customs of the period.

Intemperance was not confined to drinking if the following breakfast fare was typical:

Sausage with boiled fish, eggs, dried beef, dried mutton, slices of ham, tongue, bread, butter, cheese, short cakes, buckwheat cakes, sweetmeats of various sorts, and many other things, make up the breakfast fare of the year, and, a dish of beef steakes is frequently added.

The changes accompanying the Revolution and the rise of New York to first rank in population, agriculture, and commerce broke up the fairly fixed pattern of colonial society. The aristocracy lost its economic and political supremacy. In its place emerged a democratic commonwealth of freeholding farmers and aggressive hard-driving businessmen. In the welter of social change many of our modern problems emerged. The face of New York began to take on its contemporary lineaments.

PART THREE

New York in the National

Period, 1825-1865

Politics, 1825-1846

My God, I knew that my political adversaries thought me a scoundrel, but I never till now supposed that my friends did.—THURLOW WEED, *1839*

THE labyrinthine windings and turnings of New York politics were at no time more in evidence than in the second quarter of the nineteenth century. Personal politics continued as in previous decades, but political groups came more and more to be unified by a common ideology and less by the personal magnetism of one or two great leaders.

The principal issues of the period were the chartering of banks, the construction of canals, and, in the 1840's, the question of prohibiting the extension of slavery into the territories. These issues split the Democratic party, which controlled the state most of the time between 1825 and 1848. The more radical wing led by Martin Van Buren and Silas Wright stood for careful scrutiny of bank charters, a cautious attitude toward spending public money for canals, and for the prohibition of slavery extension. The radical Democrats (later called Barnburners) drew their strength from the farmers and laborers and mechanics. The Hunker, or conservative, wing of the Democrats reflected the wishes of those who favored the promotion of business interests and who wished to keep on good terms with the national leaders of the party. Because they had to rally support from all the states, the national leaders opposed a firm antislavery position, and this opposition embarrassed their supporters in New York.

During this period a host of new parties emerged. Fear of the Masonic Order stirred up a whirlwind of protest in western New York. Solicitude for the rights of property and distrust of Jacksonian democracy promoted the creation and the growth of the Whig party, a strange congeries of differing factions. Under the skillful leadership of Thurlow Weed the Whigs captured control of the state government in 1838, holding power till 1841. Again in 1846 the Whigs took advantage of Democratic feuds to capture the governorship. Like the Democrats, the Whigs suffered from factionalism, one wing favoring the restriction of slavery in the territories. Several minor parties were formed. Enthusiasm for humanitarian reform led to the creation of the Liberty, Prohibition, and Free Soil parties. Loss of status and the desire for free public education led the workingmen to organize a party and to exert some political influence within the Democratic party under the Locofoco banner. Resentment against the leasehold and alarm at the flood of immigrants spawned the Antirenters and the Native Americans.

Two of the most bitter political foes in this era were Van Buren and Weed. In 1824, when Weed's machinations defeated the Albany Regency and placed John Quincy Adams in the presidency, Van Buren determined to support Andrew Jackson for the presidential office in 1828. Consequently, he joined forces with Jackson's faithful ally, De Witt Clinton, and was partially responsible for the latter's re-election as governor in 1826. This political partnership was cut short by Clinton's death on February 11, 1828.

Meanwhile, New Yorkers were shocked at the mysterious disappearance of William Morgan, a resident of the state who had published a tract revealing some of the secrets of the Masonic Order. The tract vanished with Morgan. Feeling ran high against the Masons, although the more responsible members of that organization obviously were baffled and chagrined by the episode. Both Clinton and Jackson were high-ranking members of the Masonic Order. This was an opportunity Weed seized as he helped to fan the flames of resentment into the Anti-Masonic party.

The elections of 1828 were crucial, for both the presidency and the governorship were at stake, together with the political patronage controlled by those high offices. On the national scene the struggle was between the followers of Andrew Jackson and those of John Quincy Adams. The Jacksonians first called their organization the Democratic Republican party, but within a half-dozen years "Republican" was dropped and from that day to the present it has been known as the Democratic party. The Adamsites took the name National Republicans, which was later changed to Whigs. The Bucktail organization within New York remained firmly under the control of the Regency, which, powerfully influenced by Martin Van Buren, swung its support to Jackson. In order to corral the greatest possible number of votes in New York State, Van Buren himself agreed to run for governor, with the understanding that he would resign after election to accept appointment as Jackson's secretary of state if the Democratic plans were successful. For lieutenant governor the Bucktails nominated Enos T. Throop, a circuit judge of excellent reputation.

Thurlow Weed saw clearly that the Anti-Masons would have to combine with the National Republicans if the Jackson–Van Buren alliance were to be defeated, but his frantic efforts to have both parties select identical candidates for state offices failed. Very likely the concealed manipulations of Van Buren prevented the fruition of Weed's plans. The National Republicans selected Smith Thompson, an associate justice of the United States Supreme Court, and Francis Granger, a man highly regarded by the Anti-Masons, for governor and lieutenant governor, respectively. The Anti-Masons named Granger for governor and "Honest John" Crary for lieutenant governor. Both parties supported Adams for president. Van Buren and Throop were elected, although their vote was less than the combined votes of their National Republican and Anti-Masonic opponents. On the national scene Jackson was successful, and in New York he won twenty electoral votes to Adams' sixteen. Nearly a half century later Weed stated that this victory, with its prestige and patronage, enabled the Democrats to control New York for years.

On January 6, 1829, the Fifty-second Legislature assembled in Albany firmly under Regency control and listened to the message of Governor Van Buren. This message contained several interesting recommendations, of which two were enacted. Under the Safety Fund Law all banks were required to contribute to a state fund which was used to liquidate the obligations of banks which failed. The scheme was successful until the fund was exhausted by the Panic of 1837. Perhaps the New York safety fund can be considered a forerunner of the Federal Deposit Insurance Corporation, established over one hundred years later by the federal government under the first administration of Franklin D. Roosevelt. The second enactment required that presidential electors be chosen on a state-wide basis rather than by district. Thereafter the presidential nominee receiving the greatest number of votes throughout the state would get all the electoral ballots to which New York was entitled. Henceforth, because of this all-or-none law and because of the large number of electoral votes allotted to New York, political parties were often willing to make special concessions to win the support of the Empire State.

After serving seventy-one days of his two-year term, Van Buren resigned as governor to become Jackson's secretary of state, and the gubernatorial duties passed into Throop's hands. The acting governor asked for a reform of the criminal code, taking the enlightened position that criminals should be reformed rather than punished. Although the legislature refused this request, Throop did obtain a law abolishing imprisonment for debt after he was elected governor in 1830.

Although William Henry Seward, then twenty-nine years old and already associated with Thurlow Weed, was elected to the state senate in

1830 Anti-Masonism was on the wane. The Working Men's party, led by Fanny Wright and Robert Dale Owen, which had shown surprising strength in New York City the year before, died as a political force about this time. The "Workies" had demanded improved educational opportunities for the poor, laws to protect the rights of labor, and the abolishment of imprisonment for debt. Unquestionably, the anticlerical and agnostic viewpoints of Wright and Owen did much to alienate their followers, but the increasingly liberal attitude of the major parties toward the workingmen's demands was a significant factor in the downfall of the party.

When dissonance within Jackson's cabinet led Van Buren to resign as secretary of state in April 1831, the president nominated him for minister to Great Britain, but the Senate refused confirmation. Most of Van Buren's political enemies thought the incident would end his public career. Said Vice-President John C. Calhoun, "It will kill him, kill him dead; he will never even kick!" The astute Thurlow Weed was of a different opinion and predicted that the public would consider Van Buren to have been martyred for political reasons and that as a result he would "be nominated for Vice-President, and hazzahed into office at the heels of General Jackson." In May of the following year the accuracy of Weed's prediction began to appear, as the Democratic national convention, after naming Jackson for re-election, nominated Van Buren for vice-president on the first ballot. William L. Marcy was the Democratic candidate for governor of New York. The Anti-Masons and National Republicans combined their forces, supporting Francis Granger for governor of New York as Thurlow Weed had wanted them to do in 1828, and divided their electoral ticket equally between the two parties.

During the campaign of 1832 Thurlow Weed made a *cause célèbre* of Marcy's trousers. While Marcy was a state judge, he had sent his pants to a tailor for repair and had entered the charge of fifty cents in his expense account, paid from state funds. Throughout New York anti-Marcy forces displayed pantaloons with a white patch on the seat bearing the numeral "50." The paramount issue, however, was really Jackson's veto of a bill to renew the charter of the Bank of the United States. This action appealed to the labor groups, which regarded the national bank as a monstrous monopoly, and to local bankers, who anticipated federal funds would be deposited in their own institutions if the charter were not reissued. The Democrats won easily, Marcy became governor, and once again a New Yorker, in the person of Martin Van Buren, was vice-president of the United States.

After this campaign it was obvious that the Anti-Masonic movement had run its course, and in the next few years its supporters allied themselves with other anti-Jacksonians. Many Anti-Masons, including such outstanding men as Weed, Seward, Granger, and Millard Fillmore, merged with the National Republicans. The anti-Jacksonian forces adopted the name Whig, during the municipal elections of 1834, when New York City was permitted for the first time in history to elect its own mayor. The Democrats elected their candidate, Cornelius V. R. Lawrence, by the scant margin of some two hundred votes, but the Whigs won control of the Common Council and thus control of the patronage of the city, which amounted to over a million dollars a year. When the National Republicans and other antiadministration forces met in Syracuse during August of that year, they formally adopted the title Whig and nominated Seward for governor. In spite of their vigorous efforts, however, the Democrats re-elected Governor Marcy and retained control of the legislature. The Albany Regency had maintained its hold on the state.

The Democratic tide remained strong in 1836. Martin Van Buren, the heir of Andrew Jackson, was elected president—the first New Yorker to attain that high office. Marcy was re-elected governor and the Democrats held firm control of the state legislature. With two members in high offices—Van Buren and Marcy—the Regency had reached the apex of its power. Strangely enough, this political empire survived only a few months before it was destroyed and the Regency dissolved.

The Jacksonians' refusal to reissue the charter of the Bank of the United States in 1832 had led to a demand for more local banks to handle the financial affairs of the state. The Democratic legislatures of 1834 and 1835 had complied by issuing a number of charters. The state law called for the fair distribution of the stock of new banks, but the party in power selected commissioners who distributed it only among its own followers. This stock was often resold for a profit of 20 to 25 per cent even before the original owner had paid for the shares. In 1836 two Democratic state senators were charged with improper conduct in connection with the chartering of banks. One resigned his seat; the other was allowed to retain his office by the close vote of sixteen to twelve.

Earlier, a faction calling itself the Equal Rights party sought to wrest control of Tammany from the banking interests. When the Equal Righters proved to be in a majority at a meeting in Tammany Hall, the regulars turned off the gas and extinguished the lights. This ruse had been used before and the reformers were prepared. From their pockets they took candles which they kindled from the new friction matches popularly called locofocos. By the following day the members of the new party were known as Locofocos.

Although the activities of the Locofocos and the public scandal in the matter of bank stocks were forces undermining the Regency and the Democratic party, the holocaust which drove the party from power was the Panic of 1837, one of the most devastating economic disasters ever suffered by New Yorkers. The Democrats received the blame, and in 1838 were swept from office as Seward was elected governor and the Whigs seized absolute control of New York. Weed replaced Van Buren and the Regency as the chief political power in the state. William Kent, the son of the famous chancellor, wrote Weed after Seward's election: "Mr. Dictator, the whole State is on your shoulders. I take it, some future chronicler . . . will devote the brightest colours to 'the celebrated Thurlow Weed, who so long filled the office of Governor Seward during his lengthened and prosperous administration.'" The Dictator gloried in his title and unquestionably merited it.

Weed had in Seward a vote-getter and a statesman. In February 1838 he established Horace Greeley as the editor of the *Jeffersonian*, a Whig newspaper, and for many years this able journalist, who later became famous as the editor of the New York *Tribune*, used his facile pen to promote the aspirations of the political firm of Seward, Weed, and Greeley. In 1840 the triumvirate devoted its energy to prevent the re-election of President Van Buren. In this they were aided by the unpopularity of the administration's financial measures. Jackson's policy of placing federal monies in state banks had increased the funds available for the reckless speculative orgy which preceded the Panic of 1837. Van Buren, in an effort to prevent the recurrence of such circumstances, succeeded in getting Congress to pass the Subtreasury bill, which required the placement of United States funds in federal repositories. This scheme, which removed federal deposits from private banks, won the enmity of bankers, who devoted large sums to the Whig campaign. Similarly, the President's opposition to cheap paper money found disfavor among the workers and the debtor class. The Whigs had an easy time of it. Seward was re-elected governor; their candidate, William Henry Harrison, became president; and Van Buren failed to carry his native New York. Elated at this triumph, Weed printed the following statement in the Albany *Evening Journal:* "To all those with whom we have bet—please call one at a time, approaching our office from Washington Street and departing through Congress Street, keeping in line, so as not to block up the highway." The Dictator was not to be so happy about his election wagers for the next few years.

For a time it looked as if war with Great Britain would break out during Seward's administration. The trouble began during Governor Marcy's last term, when, in the fall of 1837, the Canadian insurgent leader, William Lyon Mackenzie, sought to lead an insurrection against the Crown. Mackenzie's revolt brought little response from Canadians but found many sympathizers among Americans. In New York, as elsewhere, it was difficult to enforce neutrality when mobs eagerly sought to furnish the insurgents with munitions and other supplies. The loyalist Canadians easily defeated the rebellion, and Mackenzie fled to Buffalo, where he brazenly set up his headquarters under his own flag at the Eagle Tavern.

With help from American friends, Mackenzie returned to Canadian soil by seizing Navy Island, a small plot of land in the Niagara River. The *Caroline*, a vessel of United States registry, carried supplies to the rebels. Angered by this breach of neutrality, a group of British stealthily crossed into New York on the night of December 29, 1837, and overpowered the men on the *Caroline*, killing one in the process. The raiders destroyed the steamer by fire and retired to Canada. The destruction of an American vessel at anchor in American waters and the killing of one American citizen and the wounding of others was a very serious breach of peace and inflamed the passion of Americans in general and New Yorkers in particular. President Van Buren and Governor Marcy were able to restore tranquillity, but the effort cost them and their party much popular support.

In 1840, during the administration of Governor Seward, Alexander McLeod, a Canadian citizen, while on a visit to New York boasted that he had taken part in the *Caroline* affair. Subsequently he was arrested and charged with murder and arson. The British government, maintaining that McLeod had acted under proper military orders, demanded his release and threatened war if he were executed. Secretary of State Daniel Webster implored Seward to obtain the Canadian's release; the governor refused but confidentially informed Webster he would pardon McLeod if he were convicted. This episode destroyed whatever friendly ties Webster and Seward may have enjoyed previously. Fortunately the trial proved a farce, for McLeod had lied and could not possibly have taken part in the *Caroline* raid. It took a jury of New Yorkers only twenty minutes to acquit him.

Although Governor Seward's actions in the McLeod affair won much popular support, some of his other policies were unpopular and contributed to the downfall of the Whigs. His forthright but gratuitous denunciation of the Virginia slave code resulted in reprisal by that state against New York shipping and drew little applause. His proposal that special schools be constructed for the children of the foreign born and that private schools should receive public support alienated many Protestants. The major factor in the Whig downfall, however, was a reckless program of expanding canals and railroads at state expense. In 1838 Samuel B. Ruggles, a member of the Assembly, made a report on internal improvements, demonstrating the ability of the state to borrow money for the enlargement of the Erie Canal and for other public works. It had been the policy of Governor Marcy and other Democratic leaders to restrict canal expenses to the annual surplus of revenues. When the

Whigs, confident that an improved canal would result in a sufficient increase in tolls to make borrowing worth while, voted to authorize a loan of $4,000,000, they received support from a number of Democrats. The following year Seward recommended the deficit spending of over $12,000,000 for the completion of the Genesee Valley and Black River canals and for the construction of railroads. By 1841 the state debt had reached $18,000,000 and the program of construction was only half completed. Public confidence was shaken and state securities fell 20 per cent under par.

In this same year the Democratic party won the election. The Democrats had divided on the issue of canal expansion at least three years earlier, and when the legislature of 1842 convened the division was still apparent. The Conservative Democrats, led by Edwin Croswell, Daniel S. Dickinson, William C. Bouck, Samuel Beardsley, Henry A. Foster, and Horatio Seymour, favored continued expansion. The Radicals, under the leadership of Azariah C. Flagg, Michael Hoffman, Samuel Young and George P. Barker, opposed any internal improvements which would increase the state debt.

The Radicals won the day and passed the "stop and tax law" of 1842. This popular enactment imposed a direct tax, suspended the completion of public works under construction, and pledged a portion of the canal revenues to the liquidation of the public debt. When the Democratic state convention met at Syracuse in 1842, the Radicals obtained a party pledge to support the work of the last legislature. Having accomplished this, they endorsed the nomination of two Conservatives, Bouck and Dickinson, for governor and lieutenant governor, respectively. Seward, aware of his own unpopularity, refused to run for re-election, and the Whigs nominated Luther Bradish for governor. The election was an overwhelming Democratic victory.

Concord between the two wings of the Democratic party ended soon after the inauguration of Governor Bouck. Horatio Seymour ably stated the views of the Conservatives, calling for a sinking fund to retire the state debt while enlarging the Erie Canal and completing the Genesee Valley and Black River canals out of surplus revenues. Over the bitter protests of the Radicals, who believed state finances could not stand the strain of further construction, Seymour's proposals were enacted into law. The test of time has proven the soundness of the Conservative position on this issue. Although feelings ran high, the Democrats succeeded in maintaining a semblance of unity as the presidential and gubernatorial election of 1844 drew nigh.

It had been anticipated that Martin Van Buren would again be nominated for the presidency by the Democratic party. In March, Congressman William H. Hammet of Mississippi wrote Van Buren asking him to state his position on the annexation of Texas. This placed the former president on difficult political ground. Slavery was legal in Texas, and, consequently, many Northerners were opposed to annexation because it would add another slave state to the Union. Most Southerners favored it for the same reason. Van Buren took a seemingly safe stand by indicating his personal antipathy to annexation while saying he would not oppose the wishes of Congress in the matter. The southern Democrats were not satisfied by this lukewarm position, and by clever parliamentary maneuvering defeated Van Buren's candidacy and nominated James K. Polk, who was pledged to annexation. Although Van Buren had been humiliated by political trickery, he effectively supported Polk in the campaign.

New York was recognized as a critical state. Many Democrats, fearing Governor Bouck would not be a strong candidate for re-election, proposed to strengthen the state ticket by nominating Silas Wright, a friend of Van Buren and a member of the radical wing of the party. Wright was a distinguished statesman, widely recognized for his excellent work in the United States Senate. He enjoyed the advantage of never having taken part in the canal controversy and, consequently, was looked upon as a man who could unite the Radicals and Conservatives behind the state and national tickets. Silas Wright enjoyed his work in the Senate, to which he recently had been elected for a third time, and was very reluctant to accept nomination for governor. In fact, he had repeatedly refused high honors which would remove him from Congress. When it became apparent that Van Buren could not be nominated for president, several persons suggested that Wright be put forward. He refused to permit his name to be used largely because he felt it would be disloyal to Van Buren. He also declined nomination for the vice-presidency and, earlier, had refused appointment to the Supreme Court.

It was not until Van Buren called on him to make the race for governor that Wright agreed to accept the nomination. He had nothing to gain by this decision, which removed him from his place in the national limelight at Washington and which was certain to involve him in the intraparty strife which plagued New York Democrats, thus destroying the broad base of his political support. In this instance, as he often had done before, Wright put the interests of his party above his own ambitions.

In the meantime, the Whigs nominated Henry Clay for the presidency, and Thurlow Weed succeeded in having Millard Fillmore, a former Anti-Mason and a member of the Weed machine, named for the gubernatorial office. This choice of candidates made the task of carrying New York even more difficult for Wright and the Democrats. Clay was one of the best-known men in the nation and much respected for his leadership in Congress. Fillmore, who had distinguished himself as chairman of the

Committee on Ways and Means in the United States House of Representatives, was also a formidable candidate.

During the campaign of 1844 three ugly issues began to come into focus. For several years there had been heavy European immigration. The influx of newcomers into a society almost always results in stress. In this instance matters were complicated by the fact that many of the immigrants were Roman Catholics moving into an essentially Protestant community. On a few occasions riots broke out between the two groups. In 1834 the New York *Observer* printed a dozen letters by Samuel F. B. Morse under the pseudonym "Brutus" which purported that the papacy and the Holy Alliance sought to overthrow American democracy and gain control of the nation. Nativist sentiments were aroused, and within a decade of the Morse letters an esoteric Native American party had come into being and was making itself felt in both Democratic and Whig circles.

A second issue was that of antirentism. Thousands of tenant farmers still occupied land in New York under a semifeudalistic leasehold system. Most of these men were descendants of the original settlers who had cleared the land and established the farms they now occupied. They demanded the right to purchase their lands outright and put an end to the payment of rent, and they were not overly concerned about the legal aspects of the situation. As one of their number put it, if the present tenants' ancestors were "fools enough to enter into any compact with such men, it is preposterous that such should bind or be precedent for them. . . . It is foul, cruel and oppressive to protect and encourage a lazy, worthless, immoral and bastard aristocracy to ride roughshod over the pith and marrow of the country, the laborious husbandman." By 1840 there was sporadic violence as landlords sought to collect their back rents. To accomplish their purpose, the Antirenters agreed to support candidates of either major party who would champion their objectives. In 1844 both Whigs and Democrats covertly sought Antirent support.

The third issue was that of slavery. For years abolitionist strength had been gaining ground in New York. The question of annexing Texas gave new impetus to the movement. In 1844 the Liberty party nominated James G. Birney for president and Alvan Stewart for governor. Supporting Stewart and Birney were Gerrit Smith, William Jay, and many other able zealots, some of whom were wealthy enough to contribute substantial sums to the party coffers. Antislavery sentiment was gaining ground. The major problem faced by both Whigs and Democrats was to lose as few votes as possible to the Liberty party.

Both Fillmore and Wright were on record as opposing the extension of slavery. Consequently, each party devoted the greater share of its energy to attacking the other's presidential nominee on the slave issue. Democrats pointed out that Clay was a slaveholder. Whigs decried Polk for his position on the annexation of Texas, on the ground that it would add another slave state to the Union. The Democrats countered by referring to Polk's demand for the annexation of the Oregon Territory, which presumably would be unattractive to slave owners. Probably the Democrat's policy of national expansion won considerable support, and when Clay reversed his stand in July and declared for the admission of Texas, he cut the feet from under his supporters in New York. Polk carried the state by five thousand votes. Wright, who openly opposed slavery extension, won the governorship by ten thousand ballots. On the Liberty ticket Stewart amassed fifteen thousand votes. Politicians were quick to note that the antislavery ballots could have given victory to either of the major parties.

It is difficult to assess the factors which led to the Democratic victory in New York. Certainly the personal popularity of Wright was influential. The policy of national expansion was popular even though the extension of slaveholding was not. The Democratic demand for a low tariff, in contrast to the high tariff stand of the Whigs, also helped Polk and Wright. A low tariff had natural advantages for a state prominently engaged in foreign trade. It also appealed to farmers, who produced a surplus of foodstuffs and, consequently, could see no benefit in a high tariff even if it did reduce the importation of wool. Silas Wright himself cut the heart out of the Whig argument that high tariffs meant high wages. Farmers could not pay higher wages, he reasoned, because few farm products were imported and therefore subject to tariff protection. While manufacturers might benefit and therefore be able to pay higher wages, Wright doubted that they would do so; he anticipated that instead they would increase their profits at the expense of all other citizens. Apparently this line of reasoning found favor with many.

When the legislature assembled in January 1845, the Democrats again divided into Radical and Conservative factions. The former soon won the sobriquet "Barnburners" because, claimed their opponents, Radical reform measures were similar to those of the farmer who burned down his barn to get rid of the rats. The Conservatives, on the other hand, became known as "Hunkers," apparently by reason of their "hunkering" for office. The sharp cleavage between these two groups made it extremely difficult for Governor Wright, who, like Van Buren, belonged to the Barnburner wing, to maintain party discipline. When President Polk appointed William L. Marcy, a Hunker, secretary of war and allowed him to dominate federal patronage in New York, the governor's position was further weakened. In this situation John Young, a Whig member of the legislature, was able to pass important bills by combining the votes of his own party with those of Barnburners or Hunkers as suited his purpose. Even so, it is possible that Governor Wright could have maintained his hold on the voters had it not been for the renewal of antirentism.

Soon after Silas Wright took office, petitions signed by thousands of tenants were presented to the legislature asking for relief from the lease-hold system. When no action was taken, Antirent Assemblyman Ira Harris berated his colleagues: "Woe to my country when her laws must be sustained with the point of a bayonet." Several sheriffs were threat-ened and beaten, but when, in August 1845, Under-Sheriff Osman Steele was shot to death while attempting to sell some cattle belonging to a delinquent leaseholder in Delaware County, the state was shocked by the murder. Governor Wright, acting with laudatory speed and firmness, declared Delaware County in a state of insurrection and ordered the militia to the scene. Many Antirenters were concerned at the use of military force.

Throughout the whole affair Governor Wright moved with decision and dispatch to bring an end to lawlessness. When the situation was under control, he commuted the death penalties of the men convicted for the killing of Steele to life imprisonment and turned his attention to lessening the evils under which the tenants labored. Early in the follow-ing year he called for laws to mitigate the lot of leaseholders. Several members of the legislature were under Antirent influence, and that body responded to the governor's recommendations by taxing income from long-term leases and by outlawing the forced sale of property for non-payment of rent. The tenants did not, however, obtain titles to the land.

While the antirent issue was still at its height, the United States went to war with Mexico. New York had no vital interests at stake in the Southwest, and many of her citizens viewed the struggle as a southern effort to extend slavery into new territories. Consequently, while nu-merous New Yorkers fought valiantly in the conflict, the state gave only nominal support to the national war effort. Even while battle raged, the local citizenry focused its attention on the constitutional convention which assembled at Albany on June 1, 1846, to modify the supreme law of the state.

The 128 delegates who made up the convention were an able group but hardly as distinguished as the men who had gathered for the same pur-pose in 1821. Only two members of the earlier convention were present —James Tallmadge of Dutchess County and Samuel Nelson, a justice of the United States Supreme Court. Several men who had played im-portant roles in the convention of 1821 were still alive. Martin Van Buren, who had lost his influence with the Democratic party in the election of 1844, lived in retirement, as did Ambrose Spencer. James Kent, now eighty-three, was delivering lectures on law in New York

City. Erastus Root was on his death bed. A new group of leaders had arisen to replace the old; among the more prominent delegates were William C. Bouck, the former governor; Michael Hoffman, noted for his insistence on economy in state expenditures; Charles S. Kirkland and Ezekiel Bacon, gifted lawyers; George W. Patterson, twice speaker of the Assembly; and Churchill C. Cambreling, who had been minister to Russia and served eighteen years in Congress. Present also were two young men at the portal of eminent careers: Charles O'Conor, a southern sympathizer who would win renown at law, and Samuel J. Tilden, later governor of New York.

The Constitution of 1822 had been amended twice—once to remove property qualifications for holding office and once to prohibit the removal of judges without cause. Difficulty in getting additional amendments through the legislature had led to the demand for a new convention. Many citizens desired to place a limit on state debt; others demanded the election of legislators from single districts and the election of many officials who were appointed. The demands of the Antirenters for land reform and for the election of judges may have been the final strokes which forced the calling of the convention.

The Constitution of 1846, which was approved by the voters in November, reaffirmed the continuing trend toward greater democratization and perhaps may be said to mark the division between government delegated to officials by the people and government directly controlled by the people. Senators and assemblymen henceforth were to be elected each from a single district, an arrangement which made legislators more directly responsible to their constituents. The term of senators was set at two years, of assemblymen at one year. All state offices, including judgeships, were made elective. The judiciary system was revised to provide for county courts, a court of appeals, and a supreme court. No longer did the Senate have appellate jurisdiction as a court of errors.

Through the efforts of Michael Hoffman the new constitution placed a limit on the state debt, which in the opinion of Thurlow Weed preserved the credit of New York through periods of financial crisis. The demands of the Antirenters were met by prohibiting feudal tenures and the lease of agricultural land, in the future, for periods of more than twelve years. This, however, did little to alleviate the situation, because the terms of the Constitution did not pertain to leases already in effect. As the fall elections of 1846 approached, it was clearly evident the Antirenters would be a political force.

The balloting in that year marked the climax of a tragic drama with Silas Wright in the central role. Two years before, he had resigned reluctantly from a promising career in the United States Senate to run for governor, thus using his personal popularity to win victory for his party in a difficult campaign which restored the federal administration to Democratic control. His firm handling of the Antirent Rebellion had preserved order but cost him the undying animosity of thousands of tenants who forgot he also had sponsored the laws taxing income from long-term leases and abolishing the forced sale of the property of defaulting tenants. The latter law was not forgotten, however, by the large number of men of moderate means who had invested in tenements and small houses in the cities. These persons, fearful of their ability to collect rent because of the new law, turned their backs on the governor.

In this critical situation Silas Wright was abandoned by the Hunker faction of his own party. For months the conservative group had shown an increasingly reckless attitude. As early as May 1845, they had been far enough estranged to co-operate with the Whigs in passing a bill calling for the resumption of canal construction on a limited scale. Wright had vetoed the bill. It was not until shortly before the election that President Polk, who owed his high office to Wright's sacrifices on the altar of party loyalty, realized that the Hunkers had used national patronage to undercut the governor. The president attempted to swing the support of the federal administration behind Wright, but the effort came too late. John Young, the Whig candidate, made overtures to the Antirenters and won the election. Polk, who had too long denied his fellow Democrat the support he richly deserved, confided to his diary: "The Hunkers seem to have been guilty of disloyalty to Mr. Wright." Less than a year later Silas Wright died at the age of fifty-two.

New York Supports

the Union, 1847-1861

Weed is Seward and Seward is Weed; each approves what the other says and does.—WILLIAM H. SEWARD

PETER AUGUSTUS JAY, the distinguished son of the first chief justice of the United States, speaking on the floor of the constitutional convention of 1821, said, "Some philosophers have held that the intellect of a black man, is naturally inferior to that of a white one; but this idea has been so completely refuted, and is now so universally exploded, that I did not expect to have heard of it in an assembly so enlightened as this, nor do I now think it necessary to disprove it." Jay overestimated his fellow New Yorkers. Although the first steps toward equality had been taken more than twenty years earlier, the Negro had, and for many decades continued to have, inferior status socially, politically, and economically.

Strangely enough, it was the aristocratic Federalist party which had struck the first blows against slavery. John Jay and Alexander Hamilton were active in the Manumission Society. In their battle against human bondage they were aided by many other Federalists, including Gouverneur Morris and Rufus King. Indeed, the latter was chiefly responsible for excluding slavery from the Northwest Territory. In 1799 the Federalists on almost a straight party vote passed a law gradually abolishing slavery in New York, but it was not until 1818 that July 4, 1827, was designated as the date of emancipation for all slaves. Actually an impressive number of Negroes were liberated by 1812, and probably very few had to wait until 1827 for freedom.

After emancipation had been achieved within the state, many New Yorkers, among them nationally known abolitionists like Gerrit Smith and the Tappan brothers, continued to agitate for the elimination of slavery throughout the nation. In March 1833 Arthur Tappan began to publish the *Emancipator,* an antislavery journal, in New York City, and in October the New York City Abolition Society was established. In December a group of abolitionists held a convention in Philadelphia and founded the American Anti-Slavery Society. New Yorkers played an important role: Arthur Tappan was elected president of the new organization, and the *Emancipator* became its official organ. Two years later, under the leadership of Gerrit Smith, Alvan Stewart, and Lewis Tappan, the New York State Anti-Slavery Society was established at Peterboro.

These agitators kept the evil of slavery constantly before New Yorkers. They printed handbills such as one issued in 1841 which proclaimed, "The slave is still clanking his chains on our soil—the captive is still sighing for freedom as he toils the live-long day for naught—tyranny still riots and fattens on human hopes and happiness in our boasted Republic." Ceaseless propaganda, coupled with a succession of crises involving slavery on the national scene, forced the citizenry to take a position on the issue. So important did the question become that party leaders could not ignore it and party loyalty could not withstand it. Consequently, during the decade and a half before 1860 New Yorkers frequently abandoned their political parties for the sake of a principle. The result was political turmoil.

The Democrats were the first to suffer. When President Polk asked Congress to appropriate funds for the purchase of territory from Mexico, David Wilmot, an antislavery congressman from Pennsylvania, introduced his famous proviso that "neither slavery nor involuntary servitude shall ever exist in any part of the said territory." The Democratic state convention which met at Syracuse in September 1847 was firmly under Hunker control. When the majority refused to endorse the Wilmot Proviso, the Barnburners, already stung by the betrayal of Silas Wright in 1846 and of Martin Van Buren in 1844, walked out. Later the seceders met to listen to the excellent oratory of "Prince" John, Martin Van Buren's son, who had won his sobriquet by dancing with Princess Victoria at a court ball in London. The Barnburners refused to accept the actions of the Hunker-dominated convention and called a meeting of their own in February 1848 to select delegates for the national convention of the Democratic party. The Hunkers also sent a delegation. The Barnburners withdrew in a rage when the party managers offered each of the New York factions half of the votes to which their state was entitled.

Although both the presidency and the governorship were at stake in 1848, the Barnburners would not compromise with the Hunkers to keep the Whigs out of office. Soon after the Democratic national convention,

Samuel J. Tilden issued a denunciation of the national platform and called for a convention at Utica on June 22. In response to this call an unusually able group assembled. Present were personal followers of Martin Van Buren: Samuel J. Tilden, John A. Dix, Churchill C. Cambreling, Sanford E. Church, Dean Richmond, Benjamin F. Butler, and "Prince" John. Some leaders were motivated principally by opposition to slavery: Preston King, David Dudley Field, James S. Wadsworth, and William Cullen Bryant—all of whom would later take an active part in the formation of the Republican party. Many others were more interested in getting revenge on Polk and Marcy, who had used federal patronage chiefly for the benefit of the Hunkers. After listening to forceful speeches by Butler, King, and John Van Buren which upheld the Wilmot Proviso and the principle of "free soil," the group brought Van Buren out of retirement and nominated him for president. Dix was nominated for governor. Daniel Webster gibed that the leader of the "Free-Spoil" party was now the leader of the Free Soil party.

In August the Barnburners again met under a monster tent at a national convention in Buffalo. Represented also were "Proviso" Democrats; Conscience Whigs, so-called because they could not tolerate slavery; enemies of Lewis Cass; a few Henry Clay Whigs disgusted at the nomination of Taylor; Land Reformers; Abolitionists; and other minor parties. Van Buren was again endorsed for the presidency. The group took the title Free Soil party. The last plank in their platform had a crusading ring: "Resolved, That we shall inscribe on our banner, 'Free Soil, Free Speech, Free Labour, and Free Men,' and under it we will fight on, and fight ever, until a triumphant victory shall reward our exertions." To the horror of the Hunkers, a new national party, headed by a distinguished Democrat, had sprung into being—a party which demanded the western territories be closed to the slaveholder and opened to the free farmer who dominated the northern voting booth.

The Whig party in this election year was still under the suzerainty of its Dictator, Thurlow Weed, who won the presidential nomination for Zachary Taylor and succeeded in naming Hamilton Fish for governor. Millard Fillmore, a New Yorker, became the Whig nominee for vice-president. Although Weed had supported Fillmore for this very office four years earlier, he did not favor the nomination. The growing coolness between Weed and Fillmore later disrupted party ranks. Interestingly enough, both Weed and Seward were sympathetic to the views of the Free Soilers and were destined to join hands with many leaders of that group to organize the Republican party in New York. In 1848 Whigs elected their candidates on both state and national levels. The Free Soil candidates demonstrated the strength of their party by drawing more votes than their Democratic rivals, but despite its strong showing and its pledge "to fight on, and fight ever" the Free Soil party disintegrated following its failure to win the election.

Hamilton Fish proved to be a good governor. Under his administration the tax laws were overhauled and the criminal code was improved. He initiated the first of a series of reforms in the public schools which continued throughout the decade of the 1850's. During this ten-year period supervision of the schools was taken from the secretary of state and placed in the hands of a superintendent of public instruction, an independent Department of Public Instruction was created, a number of secondary schools came into being, and state financial aid was greatly increased, although it was not until 1867 that all public schools were free of tuition charges.

The political issues of the day, however, did not hinge on state affairs. The burning question was whether slavery should be permitted to expand into the territories. Congress under the leadership of Henry Clay worked out a compromise to admit California as a free state, create the territories of Utah and New Mexico without reference to the Wilmot Proviso, eliminate slave trade in the District of Columbia, and provide a stringent fugitive slave law. During the debate on the compromise, William H. Seward spoke these prophetic words:

It will then appear that the question of dissolving the Union is a complex question; that it embraces the fearful issue whether the Union shall stand and slavery be removed by gradual, voluntary effort, and with compensation, or whether the Union shall be dissolved and civil war ensue, bringing on violent but complete and immediate emancipation. We are now arrived at that stage of our national progress when that crisis can be foreseen—when we must foresee it.

The position of Weed's principal lieutenant was clear. Slavery could not survive. The Compromise of 1850 was no final solution. In July 1850 Zachary Taylor died and Fillmore became president—the second New Yorker to attain that office. Fillmore threw his influence behind the work of Henry Clay, and the Compromise became law. The president was clearly at odds with Weed and Seward, who felt that endorsement of the Compromise would cause the antislavery men to desert the Whigs, thus ruining the party and upsetting its high tariff policy and plans for internal improvements. The growing rancor between Fillmore on one side and Weed and Seward on the other resulted in the president's attempt to get control of the Whig party in New York State. The first trial of strength came at the Whig state convention which met in Utica on September 26. When the delegates endorsed the principles of the Wilmot Proviso and commended Seward for the position he had taken on the Compromise,

Francis Granger, the old Anti-Mason president of the convention, walked out followed by the cohorts of President Fillmore. As Granger left the hall, the attention of the delegates was caught by his silver-gray hair. As a result, the Whig faction which followed him became known as "Silver-Grays."

Although the Silver-Grays and the Sewardites (known as Woolly Heads) disagreed on national policy, they both endorsed Washington Hunt for governor, and he was elected to office. Under Weed's direction, Governor Hunt in 1851 pushed through a $9,000,000 appropriation to enlarge the canal. The act was ruled unconstitutional the following year, and it was not until 1854 that a constitutional amendment made possible the improvements Weed desired. The Whigs could agree on internal improvements, and their policies on them won the party much popular support. On the slavery issue they were divided hopelessly. Weed, Greeley, and Seward kept denouncing the Fugitive Slave Law of 1850, while the "Cotton Whigs," drawn chiefly from among the export merchants of New York City, condemned all agitation of the slavery issue.

The prestige of the presidency and federal patronage were not sufficient to enable the Silver-Grays to wrest control of the Whig party from Weed and Seward. At the national convention in Baltimore in June 1852, the New York delegation refused to endorse the Compromise and supported General Winfield Scott. Unable to control his own state, Fillmore lost his bid for nomination, and Scott became the Whig candidate for president. After this crushing defeat the Silver-Grays ceased to exist as a political force.

The Compromise of 1850 was approved by the Democratic party on both the state and national level. For the most part, the Barnburners who had defected to form the Free Soil party temporarily rejoined the Democrats. Because people were frightened by the latent dangers of the slavery controversy and were willing to bury it under the Compromise, the Democratic canvass was successful—Franklin Pierce was elected to the presidency and Horatio Seymour to the governorship. A hint of the future lay in the election of Gerrit Smith, the ardent New York abolitionist, to Congress from a district which had given Pierce and Seymour a majority of over one thousand votes.

The coalition of Hunkers and Barnburners which enabled the Democrats to regain control of New York was not on firm ground. At this time the party was divided into three main groups: the Barnburners, led by John Van Buren and John A. Dix; the moderate Hunkers or, as they were beginning to be known, Softshells, led by Governor Seymour, William L. Marcy, and the youthful Samuel J. Tilden; and the conservative Hunkers or Hardshells, generaled by Daniel S. Dickinson. When President Pierce appointed Marcy secretary of state, the Hardshells were deeply affronted. During a state convention in September 1853 the quarreling broke into the open. The Whigs had an easy time winning the fall elections. All Democratic factions blamed Pierce for meddling in state politics.

The feuds within the Democratic party hamstrung Seymour's administration and enabled the Whigs to capture the legislature. The governor's suggestion that action be taken to combat intemperance marks the emergence of prohibition as a political issue of importance. Ever since 1851, when Maine had abolished the sale of alcoholic liquors, some reformers in New York, led by Horace Greeley, had urged similar legislation. In 1853 Myron H. Clark won election to the state Senate as an advocate of a "Maine law." Clark skillfully maneuvered a bill through the legislature, but Governor Seymour sent it back with a resounding veto. Seymour pointed out that New York towns had in practice the right to adopt local option, since liquor could only be sold by licensed tavern keepers and grocers. Therefore the friends of prohibition could prevent the sale of liquor by electing supervisors and justices of the peace who would refuse to grant licenses. The governor also claimed that the Clark bill was unconstitutional, a position later affirmed by the courts when they ruled on an antiliquor act passed in 1855.

National events brought the attention of New Yorkers back to the slavery question early in 1854 when the Kansas-Nebraska bill came up for debate in Congress. The proposed legislation would repeal the Missouri Compromise of 1820, which, except for the state of Missouri, limited slavery to the area south of 36° 30′ in the Louisiana Purchase. Once again Seward became the principal spokesman in the cause of antislavery. During the debate in the Senate he said: "You may legislate, and abrogate, and abnegate, as you will, but there is a Superior Power that overrules all; that overrules not only all your actions and all your refusals to act, but all human events, to the distant but inevitable result of the equal and universal liberty of all men." Seward's doctrine of "higher law" caused widespread comment. Many men of conservative leanings feared that the acknowledgment of the nebulous laws of a "Superior Power" which override the Constitution would result in chaos.

Congress enacted the Kansas-Nebraska bill and in so doing set in motion forces that were to result in Civil War. Prior to this time the major political parties had been able to work out platforms and policies which were acceptable to both proslave and antislave factions. By the summer of 1854 the Republican party had come into being. Its major purpose was to prevent the spread of slavery into the territories, and it was in no mood for compromise. Most Democrats of the Barnburner school joined it, and in the North the Whig party crumbled as many Whigs flocked to the Republican banner. New York Whigs, however, did not join the Republicans, for although Seward and Weed were in sympathy with Republican views, Seward's term in the Senate expired in March 1855, and it seemed wise to preserve the Whig party as an instrument for Seward's re-election. Consequently, Weed held the party together and won a Republican endorsement of its candidates. His efforts were rewarded. The Whigs won, placing Myron H. Clark in the governor's chair and returning Seward to the Senate. The Dictator's strategy was sound, but the plan prevented Seward and Weed from seizing undisputed national leadership of the Republican party at the time of its formation.

Few elections have been more confusing or more bitterly contested than that of 1854, when four candidates sought the gubernatorial chair. The controversies aroused by such issues as temperance, free soil, and nativism split both the Whig and Democratic parties and intensified the smoldering quarrels among party leaders. The victor, Myron Clark, was a Whig with temperance and antislavery sentiments. Daniel Ullman, a Fillmore man, was the advocate of nativism. Horatio Seymour, who secured the support of the Softshell and Barnburner factions of the Democratic party, might well have won the prize had not the implacable Hardshells run Greene Bronson. Clark's margin of victory was a mere three hundred votes. In New York City, Fernando Wood, a Democrat, was elected mayor.

Mayor Wood immediately made his presence felt by demanding federal curtailment of the immigration of paupers and felons, the reorganization of the municipal government, and an end to the practice of driving cattle through the streets of the city. Under the existent charter the mayor had no voice in the selection of the heads of executive departments and thus they felt no responsibility to him. Wood believed that department heads should be appointed by the mayor with the consent of the Board of Aldermen. The chaotic condition of the city government underscored the need for reforms. Fernando Wood's aggressive instincts were revealed in his inaugural message to the Common Council: "I shall not hesitate to exercise even doubtful powers when the honor and the interests of the people are abused."

A surprising thing about the election of 1854 was the strong showing made by the Native American party. For a long time it had been a secret society. When its adherents were questioned, they invariably replied, "I know nothing." Naturally enough, the members of the party came to be called "Know-Nothings." This cult was dedicated to the suppression of the foreign born, of whom there were more than 650,000 in New York in 1850—more than one-fifth the total population of the state. Hard times led the native born to fear the competition of the immigrant for jobs, which partially accounted for the rising strength of the American party. Other important factors were the fear that democratic institutions would

Table 3. Major political parties in New York, 1776–1860.

1776 Loyalist (Tories) → died 1783   (Ex-Tories usually became Federalists)

1776 Patriot (Whigs)- - - →1787— { Federalist- - - - - - - - - - - - - - - - - - →
Anti-Federalist (Clintonians) → c. 1800 Republican- - - - - - - - - - →

Federalist- - - - - - - - - →died c. 1821
Republican→c. 1817— { Bucktails (Republican faction: Albany Regency) ↑ → } —1826 Republican→1828— { Democratic Republican— →
Clintonians (Republican faction: De Witt Clinton) ↑ → } National Republican— →
1827 Anti-Masonic- - - - - →
1829 Working Men's - - - - →died c. 1830

Democratic Republican→ c. 1834 Democratic→ c. 1839— { Conservative Democrats→ c. 1845 Hunkers (Democratic faction) - - →
Radical Democrats→ c. 1845 Barnburners (Democratic faction) - - →
National Republican- - - ↑ —1834 Whig - - - - - - →
Anti-Masonic ↑
1839 Liberty - - - - - →
c. 1844 Native American (Know Nothing)- - →
c. 1844 Antirent- - - - →

Whig- → 1850— { Woolly Heads (Whig faction) } —1852 Whig- →
Silver-Grays (Whig faction) } —c. 1853 Hardshell Democrats (Hards) →
Hunkers - - - - - - } —1848 Free Soil 1848— { Barnburner (Democratic faction)- - - → c. 1853 Softshell Democrats (Softs) →
Barnburners - - ↑ Liberty- →
Liberty- - ↑ →died after 1855
Native American- - - - - - - - - - - →Democratic- - - - - →
Antirent- - - - - - - - →died c. 1850

{ Hardshell- - - - - - - →
Softshell ↑ } —1855 Republican - - - - →
Whig ↑
Liberty ↑

Note: The rapidly shifting political alliances in New York during this period do not lend themselves to a schematic diagram. While this illustration seemingly demonstrates the complexity of the political history of the state, the reader is warned that it is really an oversimplification. Sizable groups of voters did not follow the major shifts of alliance which are indicated above. For example, many Softshell Democrats refused to join the Republican party.

be overthrown by the hordes from alien soil and the misgivings of Protestants who saw the number of Roman Catholic communicants increase from about 1,300 in 1800 to approximately 300,000 in 1856.

The Know-Nothings won the state elections in 1855, but although immigration continued on a major scale and over a million foreign born were living in New York by 1860, the issue of nativism was swallowed by the slavery question and the Native American party failed to continue as a significant political force. Following the enactment of the Kansas-Nebraska bill, New Yorkers became increasingly active in their opposition to slavery. The Emigrant Aid Society, dedicated to facilitate the settlement of antislavery men in Kansas, had strong support, and, in spite of the stringent Fugitive Slave Law, the Underground Railroad continued to transport Negroes across the state to freedom in Canada.

The activities of the Emigrant Aid Society and the continuing function of the Underground Railroad were but two of many signs indicating that the chief interest of New Yorkers was retained by the slave question. Weed and Seward, who had long opposed the spread of slavery, read the signs correctly. Having successfully returned his alter ego, Seward, to the Senate, the Dictator devoted his efforts to uniting the Whig and Republican parties in New York into a single organization to which all men who desired to check the spread of slavery could be rallied. By agreement the Whig and Republican state conventions met in Syracuse on September 26, 1855, and both groups nominated the same men for office and adopted the same resolutions. Thereupon the Whigs marched in a body to the hall where the Republicans were meeting. The Republicans rose and cheered them as they entered and took the seats reserved for them, and unification was complete. Although not all who supported the new party were necessarily attracted by its policy on slavery—among others, there were businessmen tired of southern agrarian leadership and its insistence on low tariffs—the issue which called the Republican party into being was slavery, and its major purpose was to prevent the spread of that institution into the western territories of the United States.

Besides Seward and Weed, the Republicans enjoyed the support of other able politicians. John A. King, the son of Rufus King, and who had been in turn Federalist, Anti-Mason, and Whig, cast his lot with the new party. From the Democratic ranks came young Reuben E. Fenton and the venerable Preston King, an experienced hand at politics. Also a member of the inner circle was Edwin D. Morgan, who in later years distinguished himself as governor of the state, as a Union general, and as a United States senator. An eminent group of literary minds supported the party. In New York City no less than three prominent editors—Horace Greeley of the *Tribune*, Henry J. Raymond of the *Times*, and William Cullen Bryant of the *Evening Post*—devoted themselves to the cause, as did George William Curtis, a young author of considerable fame. Not the least of the impressive group of intellectuals endorsing the party was the noted divine, Henry Ward Beecher, pastor of Plymouth Congregational Church in Brooklyn, who was perhaps the most outspoken of all the clergy in his denunciation of slavery.

Late in 1855, while the Republicans worked to improve their party organization, fighting broke out between the slave and antislave factions in Kansas. Henry Ward Beecher, fearing the worst, urged the purchase of Sharps rifles for Kansas settlers. The people responded and many "soldiers" of the Emigrant Aid Society trekked westward equipped with one of "Beecher's Bibles." In the Senate, Seward urged the admission of Kansas as a free state while his southern colleagues demanded Kansas be admitted as a slave state. In the midst of this vehement debate both Republicans and Democrats prepared for the election of 1856 in which the presidency and governorship were at stake.

Historically the Softshell Democrats (including the former Barnburners) had displayed antislavery sentiments. On a nation-wide basis the party was conciliatory to the southern viewpoint. The New York delegation to the national Democratic convention was comprised of both Hards and Softs. The Hardshells looked on with ironic amusement when the convention forced their colleagues from the Empire State to declare that slavery could not be outlawed in any territory of the United States. When James Buchanan was named for president over the protests of the Softs, the Hardshell Democrats seemed to have won a complete victory. Their triumph was short lived, for at the state convention, which nominated Amasa J. Parker for governor, Horatio Seymour, a Softshell, assumed the leadership of the party—a post he was to retain for over a decade. Notwithstanding Seymour's return to power, the New York Democrats endorsed the national party platform. The issue was clear. The Republicans opposed the spread of slavery, the Democrats did not.

The Republican national convention revealed malaise in the political partnership of Seward, Weed, and Greeley. Because of his powerful speeches in the Senate, Seward was the darling of the convention and unquestionably could have had the nomination for the asking. Weed, wise in the ways of politics, knew that the Republican chances for success in 1856 were slight and kept Seward from becoming a candidate, anticipating that Seward's prospect for the presidency would be much better four years later. Although he followed Weed's advice, Seward was vexed, and for a time the relations between the two were strained. Greeley, irritated at the failure of his two partners to help him realize his own ambition to occupy important political office, threw his support to John C. Frémont, who won the nomination.

The Republicans named John A. King for governor at the state convention and conducted a lively campaign. Seward, Beecher, Greeley, and Bryant spoke forcefully for their party. "Bleeding Kansas" furnished an excellent opportunity for emotional appeal. George William Curtis, a gifted young orator and novelist, knew how to capitalize on it:

And yet no victim of those [Revolutionary] days, sleeping under the green sod, is more truly a martyr of Liberty than every murdered man whose bones lie bleaching in this summer sun upon the silent plains of Kansas. And so long as Liberty has one martyr, so long as one drop of blood is poured out for her, so long from that single drop of bloody sweat of the agony of humanity shall spring hosts as countless as the forest leaves and mighty as the sea.

As Weed had predicted, Buchanan won the presidency. New Yorkers, however, responded to the Republican plea. In the Empire State, Frémont ran eighty thousand votes ahead of his Democratic rival, and King easily defeated Parker to become the first Republican governor of the commonwealth. In New York City, Fernando Wood, who had placed the municipal police in uniform for the first time and reorganized the force into a semimilitary body, retained his hold on the local Democratic party despite strong opposition within Tammany Hall and won re-election as mayor. The balloting in the city was marked by riots. Fists, feet, clubs, knives, and revolvers were used with impunity. In the first ward a voter who had his nose shot off was informed he looked better without it. Hoodlums arrested and brought before Mayor Wood were promptly freed. Unquestionably many fraudulent votes were cast during this disgraceful hubbub.

Although the Democrats controlled New York City, the Republicans were well pleased by their success in the contest for state offices. Still, the party's course did not run smoothly following the victory. Many Republicans of Democratic antecedents and some of Whig background resented the control Weed exercised over the party. In 1857 the Dictator sponsored Preston King, a former Democrat, for a vacancy in the United States Senate. King was chosen, but the alienation of James S. Wadsworth and David Dudley Field, who had aspirations for the office, helped to bring about the political disaster suffered by Seward and Weed three years later. The Dred Scott decision, which went against the abolitionists, caused much emotional turmoil favorable to the Republican cause. However, the sharp financial panic of 1857 which offset the natural Republican sentiments of the populace and the quarreling among former Whigs enabled the Democrats to succeed at the polls.

It was in 1857 that the state legislature amended the charter of New York City along the lines suggested by Mayor Wood. The aldermen were reduced from twenty-two in number to seventeen, the number of councilmen was reduced from sixty to twenty-four, and provision was made for the appointment of executive department heads by the mayor with the advice and consent of the Board of Aldermen. These actions were not the result of a desire on the part of the state legislature to withdraw from city affairs. On the contrary, the legislature took over direct control of Central Park and reorganized the city police. These actions increased the political patronage at the disposal of the political leaders controlling the state government. Continued meddling in the affairs of New York City was resented not only by Wood but by many urban dwellers who believed local matters ought to be handled by the city government.

The amended charter called for a new municipal election in December 1857, thus cutting Wood's term in half. Finding himself strongly opposed for re-election by Daniel Tiemann, who had the support of Know-Nothings, Republicans, and Tammany Democrats, Mayor Wood marshaled all his forces. He probably gained three or four thousand ballots by hurriedly naturalizing aliens in time to vote. After promising to support the proper candidate, aliens were given a little red ticket reading:

> Common Pleas:
> Please naturalize the bearer.
> Nicholas Seagrist,
> Chairman

Wood's efforts were unsuccessful, however, and Tiemann won the election by a narrow margin. When Wood's forces were defeated in a Tammany Hall election the following spring, he withdrew and set up his own organization at Mozart Hall on the corner of Bleecker Street and Broadway. Mozart Hall was to exercise powerful political influence in New York City for two decades. Its beginnings were not auspicious, however, for the Democratic state convention in 1858 seated Tammany in preference to Mozart, and in the municipal elections of that year Wood's candidates were defeated overwhelmingly.

When the Republican state convention met in Syracuse in 1858 it was divided into Weed and anti-Weed factions. Edwin D. Morgan, the Dictator's candidate, was nominated for governor, but the opposition mustered considerable strength—even Horace Greeley received three votes for nomination. Weed resolutely refused to permit any alliance with the Know-Nothings.

During the course of the campaign the attention of the citizenry was focused on the issue of slavery. In Illinois Abraham Lincoln, already recognized in his home state as a gifted orator and sagacious politician, accepted Republican support for a seat in the United States Senate saying: " 'A house divided against itself cannot stand.' I believe this govern-

ment cannot endure permanently half slave and half free." His famous
debate with Stephen A. Douglas followed, winning him national recognition. Actually Lincoln said little in the campaign of 1858 that Seward
had not said years earlier. During the debate over the Compromise of
1850 Seward had warned that slavery would be liquidated either by
peaceful or violent means. For a decade he had been recognized as the
most powerful spokesman of the forces resisting the spread of slavery; now
his established position was threatened by Lincoln. Seward rose to the
occasion. Speaking at Rochester on October 25, he warned that the slave-
holding system and the system of free labor were in collision:

Shall I tell you what this collision means? They who think it is accidental, unnecessary, the work of interested or fanatical agitators, and therefore ephem-
eral, mistake the case altogether. It is an irrepressible conflict between opposing and enduring forces, and it means that the United States must and
will, sooner or later, become either entirely a slave-holding nation, or entirely
a free labour nation. Either the cotton and rice fields of South Carolina and
the sugar plantations of Louisiana will ultimately be tilled by free labour, and
Charleston and New Orleans will become marts for legitimate merchandise
alone, or else the rye fields and wheat fields of Massachusetts and New York
must again be surrendered by their farmers to slave culture and to the production of slaves, and Boston and New York become once more markets for
trade in the bodies and souls of men.

The words "irrepressible conflict" caught the public imagination. The
radical elements of the Republican party, including Greeley, claimed
Seward as their own. The more moderate elements thought that he went
too far and by taking so extreme a stand weakened the position of his
party. The Democrats proclaimed him downright dangerous, an arch
agitator, whose purpose was to precipitate a civil war. The Republicans
won a victory, the gubernatorial office passed into the capable hands of
Morgan, and Seward again was recognized as the foremost spokesman
of the party.

On October 17, 1859, John Brown, who had massacred proslavery settlers in Kansas, seized the national arsenal at Harper's Ferry. Colonel
Robert E. Lee and a detachment of United States Marines restored order,
but not until the severely wounded Brown was captured and ten of his
eighteen men were slain. John Brown's plan was to raid plantations and
free slaves, who would be added to his forces. He anticipated that the size
of his band would grow rapidly and that the slave power would crumble
before it. The evidence is clear that Gerrit Smith and other New York
abolitionists aided and encouraged Brown. After the collapse of Brown's
raid, some of these gentlemen found the time propitious for a visit to
Canada. Smith went into an insane asylum in Utica, where he remained

until after Brown rode on his own coffin to the gallows. When the self-appointed liberator was hanged, one hundred guns were fired in Albany to mourn the martyr's death.

Many thinking persons were alarmed at the implications of the attack on Harper's Ferry. The "irrepressible conflict" referred to by Seward weighed uneasily on their minds. The Democrats lost no opportunity to claim that the episode was the natural reaction to the preaching of the Republican party. Fernando Wood, who in 1859 was again elected mayor of New York City in a smashing victory over his Republican and Tammany Hall opponents, denounced the Republican party as a "fiend which stalks within the narrow barrier of its Northern cage." He went on to point out that much northern wealth was invested in the South and that New York trade depended on the prosperity of slave owners.

Seward, Governor Morgan, and other responsible leaders were quick to denounce Brown and his raiders. In February 1860 Abraham Lincoln addressed a large audience in New York City. In his talk, which was received enthusiastically, he set aside Brown as a foolish fanatic and pictured the Republican party as a conservative rather than a radical organization. Two days later Seward, in a major speech in the United States Senate, also called the raid on Harper's Ferry an act of folly. Seward's oration was conciliatory; he did not mention the doctrine of "higher law" or the theory of an "irrepressible conflict," nor did he call for the abolition of slavery. The speech was well received by the moderate elements of the Republican party, but it lacked the emotional fire of his earlier utterances. Radical elements were disappointed, and many questioned whether Seward's moderation was a result of his desire for the presidency rather than of his own conviction.

The New York legislature of 1859–1860 was outrageously corrupt. A corps of self-seeking lobbyists attached itself to the lawmakers with the tenacity of bloodsucking leeches. Among the most vigorously represented groups were the New York City transit interests. Thurlow Weed admittedly agreed to support them in return for their contribution—estimated at $50,000–$1,000,000—to Seward's campaign for the presidency. Whether any part of the contribution was actually paid is unknown, and it is also unknown whether Weed personally profited from the venture. In any case, iniquitous franchises, aided by bribery and the influence of the Dictator, passed the legislature over the veto of Governor Morgan, in spite of forceful opposition from Bryant, Greeley, and Raymond. The New York *Evening Post* broke with Weed and Seward, declaring, "our city has been driven nearly to the point of revolution by the daring and corrupt schemes contemplated at Albany."

The New York delegation to the Republican national convention which met in Chicago on May 16, 1860, was liberally provided with money and talent. Behind the deputation was Thurlow Weed, master political strategist. Aiding him were Governor Morgan and Henry J. Raymond, both men of high repute and both skilled in the art of politics. William M. Evarts served as floor manager, and in George William Curtis the Seward supporters had the most talented orator in the assemblage. When the convention, eager to avoid a radical platform which might weaken the party at the polls, refused to accept a resolution to the effect that "all men are created free and equal," Curtis called upon the delegates "to think well before, upon the free prairies of the West, in the summer of 1860, you dare to shrink from repeating the words of the great men of 1776." The audience was swept away and the motion carried. On May 17, Greeley, who was present as a delegate from Oregon, telegraphed his paper in New York City, "The conviction is that the opposition to Governor Seward cannot be concentrated on any other candidate, and that he will be nominated."

Vigorous and able men were working in opposition to Seward's candidacy, some openly and others beneath the surface. Greeley, who was highly regarded in the West and in New England, actively sought his defeat. Other important New Yorkers, including James S. Wadsworth and David Dudley Field, who remembered that the Dictator had overlooked their own aspirations when Preston King was selected for the Senate three years earlier, and William Cullen Bryant, who resented the intimacy between Seward and "Boss" Weed, strongly supported Lincoln. A well-organized group was active at the convention in behalf of the candidate from Illinois. In their zeal Lincoln's supporters exceeded the authority given to them by their candidate. During the small hours of Friday morning, May 18, cabinet posts were offered in return for support. Deals were made. Some hours later the first vote was taken: Seward, 173½; Lincoln, 102. The next trial failed to produce the swing to the New Yorker his friends had anticipated: Seward 184½; Lincoln, 181. On the third ballot Lincoln received enough votes for nomination, and Evarts moved to make it unanimous. Seated amid the Oregon delegation, Horace Greeley beamed a smile of triumph. Thurlow Weed sat huddled, his face hidden in his hands, tears streaming down his cheeks.

Only by the narrowest of margins was the Civil War president from Illinois rather than from New York. Unquestionably the New York senator deserves much credit for his years of battle against the evil institution of slavery. Probably his active efforts in the struggle weakened him as a candidate. The doctrine of "higher law" offended many men of conservative leanings; others feared the "irrepressible conflict" he saw as inevitable. The stigma many attached to Weed probably was merited and certainly weakened Seward. Yet it was Weed's practical politics which did much to make Seward a statesman of influence and to build the Republican party on both state and national levels into an effective instrument. While the issue of slavery was the clarion call which brought the Republican party into existence, other issues involving tariffs and canals could not be ignored if the party was to endure. Thurlow Weed was one of the master minds who brought the party through the pitfalls of infancy to the strength of maturity in 1860.

In this year of crisis most New York Democrats and their northern colleagues supported Stephen A. Douglas for president. The southern faction of the party could not tolerate the Douglas doctrine of "popular sovereignty," which held that the citizens of a territory had the right to determine whether slavery should or should not be legal within their district. Consequently, the Democrats divided into northern and southern factions, the former nominating Douglas, the latter nominating John C. Breckinridge. Some New York Democrats of Hardshell antecedents and led by Daniel S. Dickinson, Fernando Wood, Charles O'Conor, and John A. Dix also supported Breckinridge, but they had little hope of carrying the state for their candidate. For all practical purposes there was no truly national party in the field. Douglas and Lincoln could expect significant support only in the North, Breckinridge could expect it only in the South. Throughout the nation, and especially in the border states, thoughtful conservatives recognized that sectional parties meant disunion. These men established the Constitutional Union party, hoping to build a new political organization on a truly nation-wide basis. They selected John Bell of Tennessee as their presidential candidate.

It was recognized that the capture of New York's electoral vote would be decisive. In an effort to secure New York against Lincoln, Washington Hunt and Horatio Seymour arranged for a fusion of the Douglas and Bell electoral tickets. This maneuver was known as the "Syracuse juggle." Later the Breckinridge forces were brought into the fold and a Fusion Ticket was established which proposed to divide the electoral votes: Douglas, 18; Bell, 10; Breckinridge, 7. The Fusion Ticket, which Greeley dubbed the "Confusion Ticket," was a real threat to Republican aspirations.

Several groups in New York opposed Lincoln. A sizable number were unwilling to grant the Negro equal status and were not morally opposed to slavery. Others feared that the election of Lincoln would mean civil war or disunion, either of which meant serious economic losses to the industrial and commercial interests of the state. Most of the great merchants of New York City were in the latter group and opposed Lincoln as a threat to business. The gifted group of Republican leaders in New York were equal to the occasion. Pointing to the moral issues involved and picturing the advantages to commerce and industry which would accrue from protective tariffs, free homesteads, and land grants to railroads, the Republicans turned the campaign into a crusade. Lincoln carried New York and won the presidency. Governor Morgan was returned safely to office.

Thurlow Weed had controlled first the Whig party and then the Republican party in New York since their formation. The nomination of Lincoln over Seward at Chicago made it almost inevitable that the Dictator's authority would be challenged following the election campaign. When Seward agreed to become Lincoln's secretary of state—a difficult post which he filled with distinction—the anti-Weed faction headed by William Cullen Bryant, Charles A. Dana, George Opdyke, and David Dudley Field put forth Horace Greeley to succeed him in the United States Senate. Weed's candidate was William M. Evarts, who had labored hard for the cause at Chicago. The Dictator soon discovered that Ira Harris, the old Antirenter, held the balance of power between Greeley and Evarts, and he negotiated with Harris, who placed himself in Weed's hands. As the balloting began in the Republican caucus, Greeley and Evarts were neck and neck, with Harris a poor third. The eighth ballot showed a marked trend to Greeley. When the news reached Weed, he thrust a cigar in his mouth, completely unaware that he already had one between his lips, lighted it, and said excitedly to the messenger, "Tell the Evarts men to go right over to Harris—to Harris—to Harris!" On the tenth ballot Ira Harris was selected and ultimately replaced Seward in the Senate. Once again the Dictator had averted disaster.

While Weed attended to political fence building in New York, Seward was engaged in a more desperate task in Washington, where he was regarded as the principal spokesman for the newly elected administration which would take office on March 4, 1861. Secession was in the air. Southerners plainly were unwilling to accept Republican rule, and President Buchanan made no resolute effort to compromise differences and preserve the Union. The work of congressional committees failed to find solutions acceptable to the Republican party and southern slaveholders. Seward's objective was to preserve as effective a government as possible for Lincoln to take over, but since he could not modify the policies of his party it was impossible for him to reconcile the opposing interests. Consequently, the New York senator made a strong emotional appeal for preservation of the Union, hoping to rally the entire nation around the flag without thought to sectional differences.

Seward's efforts probably won the moderate elements in the northern and middle states to the support of the Republican viewpoint, but he could not prevent secession. By February 1 seven states—South Carolina, Mississippi, Florida, Alabama, Georgia, Louisiana, and Texas—had withdrawn from the Union. On February 8 the Confederate States of America was created. New Yorkers were of two minds—some favored permitting the secession to take place peacefully, while others desired to maintain the Union even at the cost of civil war.

On January 7 Mayor Fernando Wood of New York City proposed that the metropolis withdraw from the Union and establish itself as a free city. This startling proposal was based on Wood's belief that the dissolution of the federal Union was inevitable and that the city ought not to jeopardize its profitable trade relations with the South by taking an anti-southern stand. The mayor believed that such a scheme would free the city from domination by the state legislature, and he proposed a modest tariff to provide the city with revenue. The scheme was cleverly calculated to draw support from the great merchants and from the immigrant groups who feared the competition of free Negro labor.

In reply to Wood's proposal for a free city, Greeley let loose a blast: "Fernando Wood evidently wants to be a traitor; it is lack of courage only that makes him content with being a blackguard." Late in January, John A. Dix, the venerable New York Democrat who was Buchanan's secretary of the treasury, issued his historic dispatch: "If anyone attempts to haul down the American flag, shoot him on the spot." A few days later, at the state Democratic convention, Horatio Seymour and other leaders called for peaceful secession. George W. Clinton, the son of De Witt Clinton, disagreed. Said he, "There is no such thing as legal secession. The Constitution of these United States was intended to form a firm and perpetual Union. If secession be not lawful, then, what is it? I use the term reluctantly but truly—it is rebellion!"

As the days of crisis sped by, more and more New Yorkers came to accept the forthright thinking of Dix and Clinton. The Union was too precious to be abandoned at the demand of a violent minority. In the Union was strength—economic strength resulting from internal trade between sections and from the power to bargain effectively for international trade agreements, physical strength enabling the nation to stand against foreign aggression and to spread into the rich lands of the West. When South Carolina bombarded the federal garrison at Fort Sumter in Charleston Harbor on April 12, New Yorkers were ready to take up the gage of battle. Within a week the Seventh Regiment was on its way to the national capital, and four more states—Arkansas, North Carolina, Tennessee, and Virginia, seceded. On April 20 Major Robert Anderson, who had commanded the forces at Fort Sumter, arrived in New York City, and the occasion was marked by a stupendous demonstration. By July almost forty-seven thousand New Yorkers had enlisted for service in defense of the Union.

Within a short time an army of thirty-six thousand assembled at Washington. Soon Horace Greeley's *Tribune* took up the cry: "Forward to Richmond!" The clamor was joined by other voices. Yielding to public pressure, the federal government ordered the advance. The troops were inadequately trained and the confusion was indescribable. On July 21, 1861, the first major battle of the Civil War was fought at Bull Run. By late afternoon the routed Union forces raced back to the national capital more in the manner of a mob than an army. It was a bitter defeat. New Yorkers now knew that the war would be long and hard. They had reason to know— one-third of the Union casualties in this first battle were citizens of the Empire State.

Building the Transportation Network

Railroads are all the rage of latter years—
They talk of one to go from here to York,
To quell the city people's anxious fears
And carry down the Dutchess County pork.
The cars are wondrous things to load our trash on,
And tho' our boatmen starve, 'twill be in fashion.
                  —Dutchess Intelligencer, *January 1, 1832*

TRANSPORTATION is the key to the development of the political, social, and economic history of New York in the years between 1825 and 1860. The amazing success of the Erie Canal in raising land values, stimulating the growth of cities, and providing easy access to markets converted all but the most skeptical to the importance and desirability of internal improvements. Agitation for canals, railroads, or plank roads filled the newspapers and absorbed the attention of politicians. Every town—indeed every farmer—felt the impact of the changes brought about by the extension of canals, railroads, and highways.

Few undertakings have so completely fulfilled the highest claims and fondest hopes of its sponsors as did the Erie Canal. The slashing of freighting costs (by more than 90 per cent from Buffalo to Albany) released a torrent of produce dammed up by the prohibitive costs of hauling freight overland. Each year after 1825 saw a sharp increase in the number of boats operated and in the amount of tonnage carried. The 218,000 tons carried in 1825 swelled to 4,650,000 tons in 1860 and reached a peak of 6,000,000 tons in 1872.

The Erie Canal was a financial success from the start. The stream of revenues poured into the state treasury so rapidly that it soon paid off the original cost of construction (approximately $7,000,000). The legislators were delighted. They used the revenues not only to build feeder

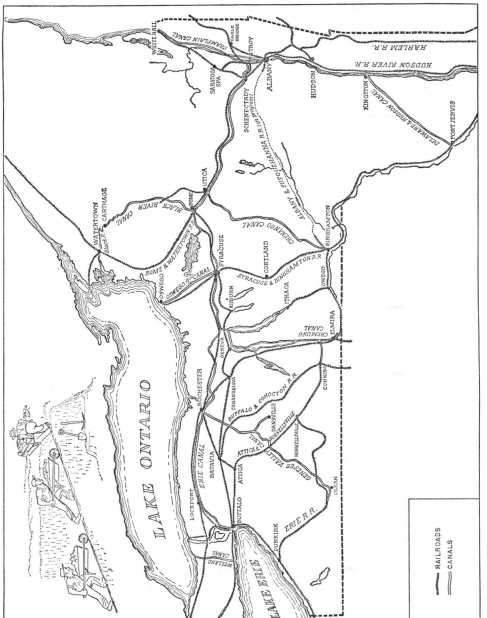

Map 9. Railroads and canals, 1859.

or lateral canals but also to defray the general expenses of the government. They guarded this moneymaker jealously and prohibited railroads along the route of the canal from carrying freight during the season of navigation.

Central and western New York received the greatest benefit from the canal for the first two decades. The wheat grown in the region west of Utica, formerly turned into whisky or fed to pigs, could reach tidewater for a few cents per bushel. Cities along the Erie—Utica, Syracuse, Rochester, and Buffalo—became boom towns. The impact on Rochester was explosive. By 1840 Rochester boasted over twenty thousand inhabitants and produced more flour than any other city in the country. Buffalo grew almost as rapidly because of its strategic position as warehouse for commerce passing down the Lakes. A brisk trade sprang up with Cleveland, the main outlet for the expanding Ohio region. Emigrants by the tens of thousands boarded schooners and steamers at Buffalo harbor and later, as farmers or lumbermen in the Midwest, sent the product of their labor to the harbor for shipment over the canal. The rising volume of traffic also brought prosperity to Albany and Troy.

Some regions of the state received no benefits from the construction of the Erie and Champlain canals. In fact, farmers tilling the worn-out fields of eastern New York found it impossible to compete with those who grew wheat on the rich lands of the Genesee Valley and in the Midwest. Residents in the southern tier of counties complained that it cost them more to get their produce to market than farmers living on the shores of Lake Michigan. Most of the Hudson River ports between New York and Albany which were terminals of the overland road network failed to grow. An exception was Kingston, which grew rapidly because it was the eastern terminus of the Delaware and Hudson Canal.

Canal business gave employment to thousands. The captains usually owned their own boats and picked up cargo wherever they could find it. A few companies maintained regular service between canal ports. Eastbound cargoes were easy to secure because wheat and lumber took up much space. Since westbound cargoes consisted mainly of merchandise, the skippers often filled their boats with emigrants bound for the West. Boatmen were rough and profane, liking nothing better than a chance to fight for the first place in going through a lock. Hundreds of saloons and brothels lined the banks of the Erie Canal, sometimes labeled the "Big Ditch of Iniquity."

Travelers using the packets complained of tedious delays and overcrowded quarters. The ordinary berth was only five and one-half by two feet, and three berths lined each wall of the tiny cabins. During the 1830's packets charged five cents a mile, including food, and managed to cover about one hundred miles a day. The packets lost most of their passenger business after 1842 when the railroads provided through service between Albany and Buffalo.

At first, freight originated largely within the borders of New York. Gradually the amount of freight originating in the western states increased, and by 1847 it equaled that of New York. Four years later it was more than double the New York figure. After 1850 the backbone of canal traffic consisted of grain and lumber from the Lake states, for Erie Canal boatmen were unable to prevent pork, beef, cheese, butter, wool, and hides from slipping to the railroads during the 1850's.

People in other states and in all parts of New York clamored for canals during the early 1830's. Pennsylvania almost bankrupted itself with its elaborate canal system across the Allegheny plateau. The Lake states of Ohio and Indiana constructed canals to connect Lake Erie with the Ohio River ports.

Farmers and businessmen in the "sequestered counties" of New York demanded that the legislature grant as much aid to them as it had to the counties along the routes of the Erie and Champlain canals. Citizens in the Chenango Valley agitated for a canal linking the Erie Canal at Utica with the Susquehanna River at Binghamton, and in 1833 the legislature approved Governor Marcy's recommendation and authorized the ninety-seven-mile-long waterway. The coal brought up from Pennsylvania enabled capitalists, by 1846, to use steam power in the new textile mills of Utica. Important as this coal trade became, the Chenango Canal never paid its operating costs.

In 1836 the legislature ordered work begun on the Black River and the Genesee Valley canals. Neither waterway paid for the cost of maintenance, to say nothing of meeting the interest on the cost of construction.

The Oswego Canal became the most important subsidiary of the Erie because it managed to secure a share of the wheat traffic to the seaboard, despite the hostility of Buffalo. During the early 1850's Buffalo's millers had wrested first place in milling from Rochester, but the millers at the falls of the Oswego River were also grinding millions of bushels of wheat into flour. The merchants and millers of Oswego had the choice of sending their goods directly to Syracuse or up the Oswego River to Oneida Lake where a short branch canal connected with the Erie.

Canals also tied the Finger Lakes into the Erie system. From Montezuma a link ran to Cayuga Lake, which, in turn, was connected with Seneca Lake. Seneca Lake had two other artificial outlets: a short canal to Penn Yan on Keuka Lake, and the Chemung Canal from Watkins Glen to Elmira.

The Delaware and Hudson Canal, running from Kingston to Port Jervis, thence via the Delaware River and canal to Honesdale, where railroad connections were made with the coal fields, was the only important private canal within the state. The Wurtz brothers of the Lackawanna region and Philip Hone, mayor of New York, sought to bring coal to the Hudson. The company began digging in 1825 and soon ran through its resources, but the state legislature lent the company $800,000, which was repaid out of the profits.

Few lateral canals ever paid even their operating costs. Revenues declined for several reasons: the reduction in tolls, the decline in tonnage due to exhausted woodlands and the shift from wheat, and the competition from the railroads in the 1850's. Canal employees and local business interests, however, kept the lateral canals open until the 1870's. The people of the state voted in 1874 to keep open only the Erie, Oswego, Cayuga and Seneca, Black River, and Champlain canals. Shortly thereafter the rest were abandoned. The Delaware and Hudson Canal Company transformed itself into a railroad system connecting the coal fields with Montreal.

Canal policy became a major issue dividing the parties. The Whigs, drawing support from merchants, shippers, and contractors, unstintingly supported internal improvements of all kinds. The Democratic party split over the canal issue, the Barnburner faction insisting upon retrenchment and the Hunker wing demanding state aid. During the 1830's a campaign for double locks on the Erie Canal got under way, and in 1838 the Whigs authorized $40,000,000 for a gigantic program of aid for canals and railroads in almost every section of the state.

This debt increase seriously impaired the credit of the state. The Barnburners pushed through their famous "stop and tax law" of 1842 which brought all construction to a halt for four years. The Democrats wrote into the Constitution of 1846 several provisions designed to limit major expenditures unless approved by the people. They even assigned canal revenues to maintenance expenses and set up a sinking fund for retirement of the canal debt.

The Whigs were eager to complete the enlargement of the Erie Canal. But how were they to surmount the constitutional barriers? Governor Washington Hunt in 1850 devised a clever scheme whereby the comptroller would sell canal revenue certificates worth $9,000,000. Twelve economy-minded senators resigned their seats in 1851 in order to leave the Senate without a constitutional quorum. The Whigs, however, won many seats at the fall election, and a majority of the "resigners" were retired from office. Thereupon, the comptroller was empowered to sell canal revenue certificates worth up to $3,000,000. The Court of Appeals found this act invalid but the canal supporters would not give up. In 1853 Governor Horatio Seymour, a procanal Democrat, called a special session of the legislature to submit an amendment authorizing loans of not more than $2,250,000 in each year during the next four years. It was overwhelmingly approved. Many citizens voted for the measure because they believed that the New York Central Railroad discriminated against upstate shippers in noncompetitive points in favor of through freight from Buffalo and Chicago.

The natural waterways of New York State—lake, river, sound, and ocean—carried a volume of freight far exceeding that of the canals and railroads. Indeed, the chief function of turnpikes, canals, and railroads before 1850 was to connect navigable bodies of water.

The lakes and rivers of New York were crowded with a variety of vessels. Over nine thousand schooners, barks, brigantines, and brigs cleared Buffalo harbor in 1855. The buckets of ten elevators unloaded the holds of these vessels speedily and efficiently. Traffic on Lake Ontario, although smaller in volume, grew, especially after 1833, when the Canadian government opened the Welland Canal, allowing ships to pass around Niagara Falls. By 1860 tonnage carried on the Great Lakes was second only to that on the Atlantic Ocean in the western hemisphere.

Lake Champlain carried much less freight than either of the Great Lakes bordering on New York. High-quality iron ore was sent down to the forges surrounding the lake and as far south as the iron and steel forges of Troy and Albany, but lumber was the major item on Lake Champlain as well as on the other lakes. By 1850 the steamboat had supplanted the sailing vessel on the lake.

The Hudson River, called the "American Rhine" by admiring foreigners, remained one of the nation's major arteries. About two hundred vessels plied between Albany and New York in 1827, and 163 ships were carrying flour, pork, lard, butter, and wool between Albany and Boston in 1828. The steamboat gradually outmoded the sailing vessels, first in the passenger traffic and after 1840 in freighting. By 1840 there were over one hundred steamboats on the Hudson, some of them making the trip from Albany to New York in eight hours. Even after the railroads took most of the passenger traffic, barges and canal boats towed by steamboats carried the bulk of farm produce during the summer months.

The steamboats engaged in rate wars in order to gain customers. The owners of the major lines organized the Hudson River Steamboat Association to fight interlopers breaking the three-dollar fare from New York to Albany. They paid Cornelius Vanderbilt a bonus of $100,000 in addition to a yearly retainer of $5,000 to withdraw from the Hudson River business. Steamboat captains also competed in speed, tying down the safety valves and skipping the smaller landings. Not infrequently the boilers blew up and the ships burned. Accidents, however, did little to deter steamboat travel, which Americans found the cheapest and most pleasant means of travel.

Long Island Sound was the major channel down which the trade and travel of lower New England flowed to Manhattan. The curiously indented coastline of Connecticut and Rhode Island hampered the construction of a shore-line railroad that could serve Bridgeport, New Haven, New London, and Providence. Furthermore, boats offered passengers greater comfort and the chance to sleep. Each of the cities on the sound and a few beyond hoped to monopolize the transfer trade between Boston and New York. At first, Providence took the lead, but Stonington, Norwich, and Fall River made their bids. In 1847 Fall River capitalists began the historic Fall River Line to New York City. Competition of the most savage sort broke out as rival lines and cities tried to gather in a larger share of the through traffic. Not until 1881 did the various lines enter into a lasting agreement.

The life of Cornelius Vanderbilt was an epic of the Steam Age. As a youth he rowed passengers from his native Staten Island to Manhattan, then extended his operations throughout New York harbor and up and down the coast. In 1818 he became a steamboat captain for Thomas Gibbons, who was challenging the steamboat monopoly of New York waters granted to the Livingstons. Ten years later Vanderbilt felt confident enough to establish his own steamboat route. In the next three decades he won the soubriquet of "Commodore" because of his shipping activities, which, incidentally, netted him a fortune of over $20,000,000. Until he was bought out by his rivals, he ran his boats from Manhattan to points in Jersey, along Long Island Sound, and up the Hudson. During the 1850's Vanderbilt operated a line of ships to Nicaragua and Panama and engaged in the transatlantic shuttle. In the same period he became interested in the Harlem Railroad and other railroads connecting with his ships. The hard-driving Commodore retired from shipping in 1864 and directed all his energies to building up a railroad empire.

During the 1830's many New York communities became enthusiastic supporters of railroads. In general, however, the wealthy men of New York City showed much more caution in promoting railroads than did the capitalists of Boston, Philadelphia, and Baltimore. Domestic and foreign commerce was thriving, and few merchants thought the railroad would ever displace the Erie Canal as a freight carrier. Furthermore, the state legislature discouraged railroads paralleling the Erie Canal from carrying freight.

The first railroad in New York was the famous Mohawk and Hudson between Albany and Schenectady. On August 9, 1831, thousands of spectators watched the tiny "De Witt Clinton" draw three coaches over the wooden scantlings or rails, reinforced on top by strips of iron a half-inch thick and two inches wide. The managers quickly adopted improvements. New long cars replaced the first crude bodies adapted from the stagecoach, and more powerful locomotives proved more reliable.

Even before the completion of the Mohawk and Hudson line, the legislature granted a charter to the Saratoga and Schenectady, which rapidly built a line to the fashionable watering place. By 1833 two trains left Albany each day for Schenectady to connect with cars leaving for Saratoga Springs. Some citizens of Troy who wanted to get control of the passenger traffic to Saratoga organized the Rensselaer and Saratoga Railroad in 1831 and also captured control of the Schenectady and Saratoga. These moves infuriated the businessmen of Albany. In 1836 Troy citizens organized the Schenectady and Troy, one of the few steam railroads financed, constructed, and operated by a municipality. This venture, however, failed to divert the passenger traffic to Troy because the Utica and Schenectady Railroad threw its business at Schenectady to the Mohawk and Hudson line. In 1852 the Common Council of Troy, under pressure from the taxpayers, sold their road to Edwin D. Morgan, president of the Hudson River Railroad, who almost immediately transferred the line to the newly formed New York Central.

Promoters projected a series of short lines across the state. The Utica and Schenectady opened in 1836 and made handsome profits, although its charter prohibited it from transporting freight. The next links, the Syracuse and Utica and the Auburn and Syracuse, began to operate trains in 1839. Two years later the Auburn and Rochester was completed, touching the villages of Geneva and Canandaigua. The direct road between Syracuse and Rochester was not opened until 1852, but it soon supplanted the earlier route. Meanwhile capitalists in Rochester had constructed a line westward to Batavia. When the Attica and Buffalo made connections with the Rochester and Batavia in 1842, the chain across the state was complete.

The all-rail route from Albany to Buffalo posed many problems, especially uncertain schedules and frequent changes of cars. In 1842 representatives of the various lines agreed to arrange through trains. The ban on freight carriage was irksome to railroads and shippers alike. In 1847 the legislature permitted the railroads to carry freight provided they paid equivalent tolls to the canal fund. Shippers kept complaining about the high rates, and after considerable agitation the tolls were repealed in 1851.

Finally, in 1853, Erastus Corning, an Albany merchant, consolidated the eight short lines across the state into the New York Central. Shippers of high-class and perishable freight immediately began using the railroad instead of the Erie Canal. By 1858 the canal boats had lost all but two major types of freight—lumber and grain products.

During this period Troy and Albany were competing to become the chief terminal for railroads stretching across from Boston and up from New York. Boston capitalists had extended the Western Railroad to the New York State line, where it connected with the Albany and West Stockbridge line, which was largely financed by the city of Albany. As a result of this connection Bostonians could travel by rail to Buffalo as early as 1842. New York merchants realized that their rivals had stolen a march on them. Western storekeepers could visit the warehouses of Boston long before the ice had melted in the Hudson River.

At first the businessmen of New York City paid little attention to Boston's advantage. They failed to throw their full support to railroads connecting this great seaport with the western waterways. The New York and Harlem, chartered in 1831, pushed northward at a snail's pace. The Hudson River Railroad was hardly more than a paper enterprise until 1845, when citizens of Poughkeepsie stirred up action. Then promoters collected $3,000,000 and hired John B. Jervis, the most famous engineer of the day. Jervis built a water-level route on the east bank and by 1851 trains were running into East Albany. A few months later the New York and Harlem, following an inland route, also reached East Albany.

Meanwhile, Troy was trying to make rail connections with Boston and New York. Passengers and freight could cross the Hudson at Troy by bridge whereas at Albany they had to undergo the inconvenience, expense, and danger of crossing the river by ferryboat. The businessmen of Troy fought the proposal for a bridge at Albany in 1841 and again in 1845, 1854, and 1856 by lining up most of the steamboat and canal interests. These latter feared that bridge piers would obstruct navigation to the upper Hudson. The victory of Albany became certain when the completion of the Pennsylvania and the Baltimore and Ohio railroads threatened to divert passenger travel and high-class freight away from New York City. The political allies of the New York Central forced through a charter for a bridge at Albany in 1856 but the span was not completed until 1866.

The citizens in the southern tier of counties joined the chorus for railroad facilities. In 1832, over the opposition of the "Canal Ring" in Albany, Eleazur Lord and a number of other promoters took out a charter for the Erie Railroad, which was to run across the state from Piermont to Dunkirk. Difficulties of every description beset them. The hilly terrain and river crossings troubled the engineers. The region had a sparse population, without a single city of more than three thousand inhabitants along the route. Capital was hard to raise, especially after the Panic of 1837 forced the Erie into bankruptcy. The state of New York advanced $6,000,-000, and the local governments along the route gave much aid. After its reorganization in 1847, the Erie forged ahead rapidly, and by 1851 trains carried Fillmore's cabinet to Dunkirk over the longest continuous railroad line in the world.

Troubles continued to bedevil the Erie. The poor location of its terminals hampered smooth operations. The thirty-five-mile trip by steamboat from Piermont to New York City was inconvenient and, in winter, dangerous. Later, the railroad built an extension to Jersey City. Dunkirk was also a bad selection since most freight coming down the Lakes made for Buffalo. The Erie later made connections with Buffalo over two locally built roads—the Buffalo and Cohocton and the Attica and Hornellsville. Overcapitalization and poor management proved more disastrous to the company than its awkward terminals and nonstandard six-foot gauge. Heavy freight traffic could not save the line from bankruptcy in 1857, when the railroad fell into the hands of Daniel Drew. For the next dozen years its history is an epic of mismanagement and corruption in which Drew, Jay Gould, Jim Fisk, and other scoundrels dissipated the road's dwindling assets.

Citizens in the north country benefited from the desire of Boston interests to secure an independent route to the Lakes. In 1850 the Northern Railroad linked Lake Champlain and Ogdensburg, but the line proved a disappointment to its backers in Boston. The Watertown and Rome Railroad was completed by 1851, and by the end of the decade had reached Potsdam and Ogdensburg.

During the 1850's several north-south lines were built connecting the New York Central and the Erie railroads. The most important among these railroads, projected southward from Albany, Utica, Syracuse, Rochester, and Buffalo, was the Albany and Susquehanna, later the major segment of the Delaware and Hudson Railroad. This railroad, relying a great deal on local aid for capitalization, reached Oneonta in 1865 and Binghamton a short time later.

New York's basic railroad pattern was established by 1860, and practically all sections of the state had railroad service. The Long Island line, for example, opened the region of that name. During the 1850's the two cross-state lines—the New York Central and the Erie—were gradually taking more traffic from the Erie Canal and helped to continue New York City's firm grasp on the western trade.

Most farmers and villagers, however, continued to rely upon the miserable roads for ordinary transportation and travel. The roads were under the care of the town commissioners of highways, who laid out roads, directed repairs, and erected bridges. They also divided the towns into road districts, and the overseers of highways in charge of these districts supervised road maintenance. They had power to assess upon each resident several days of labor on the road, but they did not have the equipment, technical knowledge, or skilled labor to keep the roads in good shape.

Practically all of the privately owned toll roads failed to earn enough revenues to pay for repairs. The turnpikes faced competition from several rivals: the canal system carried much freight; the railroads in the 1830's attracted the through passenger traffic from the stagecoach; and the counties in the 1830's were beginning to show more interest in improving the public roads.

Shortly before the mid-century mark the movement for plank roads swept the state. The first plank road, which ran from Syracuse to Oneida Lake, proved so popular that in 1848 the legislature passed a general plank road act. Enthusiasts secured charters for over 182 companies within the next two years. Plank roads were easily built upstate, since ample lumber was still available. Local businessmen financed plank roads in every direction, hoping to enlarge the trading region of their city or town.

Unfortunately plank roads quickly deteriorated and became dangerous for horses to use. The heavy wagons broke the planking and decay quickly rotted away the boards. Like their predecessors, the turnpikes, the plank roads seldom earned enough revenue to pay for repairs. The growing scarcity of timber, and of money after the Panic of 1857, ruined most plank road companies.

Improvements in communication instituted during this period were so marked as to be revolutionary. Mail service was greatly improved. The railroads provided faster service than the stagecoach companies. After some delays the government facilitated the delivery of mail in other ways. The establishment in 1851 of the three-cent rate for prepaid letters increased the volume of mail. In New York City the government charged the recipient two cents for each letter delivered; not until 1863 was there free city delivery. Postal receipts from New York State amounted to about 22 per cent of the national total, reflecting the great amount of business transacted in the state.

The delivery of parcels was carried on by scores of small companies, especially within New York City and the other urban centers. Four large companies controlled most of the important intercity business of the nation. The American Express Company, one of the largest, had close ties with the New York Central lines.

The invention of the magnetic telegraph in 1844 emancipated communication from transportation. Soon after the successful demonstration by Samuel F. B. Morse, promoters rushed to construct intercity lines. In 1846 Ezra Cornell of Ithaca built, under contract, a line from New York to Albany. This was extended by the end of the year to Buffalo. Cornell constructed a line to Michigan and sank his capital into a line paralleling the Erie Railroad. But this line across the "southern tier" was no more successful than the railroad, and it went bankrupt in 1852. Hiram Sibley of Rochester, who controlled the line from Albany to Buffalo, arranged a merger in 1856 with Ezra Cornell's interests. The reorganized company took the name of Western Union and established a virtual monopoly of wire services. By the end of the Civil War, Sibley and Cornell were millionaires.

Plank roads, railroads, canals, steamboats—all had revolutionary effects on the economy of New York. The predominantly self-sufficient farmer of pioneer days was gradually transformed into a specialized commercial farmer sensitive to every shift in the markets. The isolation of many rural communities was breaking down as citizens and goods flowed freely in and out. Merchants in both the upstate and metropolitan region, recognizing the crucial role of canals and railroads, looked with satisfaction upon the finest and most actively expanding transportation network in the country. New York State grew steadily in population, wealth, and trade, thanks largely to the splendid system of water and rail transportation promoted by its citizens in this period.

The Businessman

*Free institutions, general education, and the ascendancy of
dollars are the words written on every paving-stone along
Fifth Avenue, down Broadway, and up Wall Street. Every
man can vote, and values that privilege. Every man can read,
and uses the privilege. Every man worships the dollar, and is
down before his shrine from morning to night.*
—Anthony Trollope, *1862*

BUSINESS—commerce, finance, and manufacturing—grew enormously
between 1825 and 1860. Domestic commerce expanded almost explo-
sively with the extension of canals and railroads, the development of the
trans-Appalachian region, and the growth of manufacturing. Foreign trade
was a declining fraction of the total business transacted in the United
States, although exports and imports made impressive gains. To put it
another way, the merchants of New York City in 1815 faced the sea—
in 1860 they looked inland.

The big merchants were the leading citizens in the cities and towns of
New York. Those on Manhattan Island directed the flow of farm products
to Europe and the distribution of finished goods manufactured abroad
or in the factories of the Northeast. By 1825 specialization had nearly
outmoded those merchants who not only owned their own ships and
engaged in foreign trade but also bought and sold goods at wholesale and
retail, and performed banking and insurance functions for others. Some
commission merchants, brokers, importers, jobbers, began to specialize
in certain commodities or to perform only one function.

Commission merchants were mainly interested in selling goods con-
signed to them by outsiders. A few specialized in dry goods, flour, hardware, and the like, but most commission houses dealt in any product that
came along. The broker or factor brought buyers and sellers together,
taking no title to the goods. In addition, there were auctioneers, bankers,
and agents of various kinds.

The auction system played an unusual role in the import trade during the 1820's and 1830's. Under New York law all goods offered at auction had to be sold. Almost one-half of the goods imported in the 1820's was sold at auction, sometimes at a loss, to the import houses. Auctioneers handled a smaller share of the nation's imports during the 1830's and thereafter their business fell off sharply.

Jobbers or wholesalers, the main customers at the auctions, funneled goods to the country storekeepers who swarmed to Manhattan to seek out the best bargains. After 1840 some of the small storekeepers in more distant regions began using the jobbing centers in the West such as Cincinnati and Chicago and in the South such as Mobile and Augusta. To counter this competition, some of the mercantile houses in New York sent traveling salesmen directly to the small stores.

The consumer received goods through retail stores, public markets, and peddlers. Retailers were normally not specialists and carried a heterogeneous stock of goods. In New York City and the larger upstate centers some specialty shops emerged, the drugstore usually in the vanguard. Men's clothing shops were first established in New York City in the 1830's. The most important store in New York City was the "palace" of A. T. Stewart, an Ulsterman who made a fortune selling textiles in his department store. Stewart was one of the first to adopt the policy of one fixed price, which soon became common practice in the larger establishments. Lord and Taylor and R. H. Macy also founded their stores in this period.

Upstate, the merchants were usually the wealthiest citizens in their communities. They not only sold to consumers but also stored and transported goods obtained, often by barter, from the farmers. They stocked their shelves with products as diverse as textiles and tropical foodstuffs. The importance of the country storekeeper was widely recognized. He was buyer of farm produce, seller of imports, banker, promoter of turnpikes, sponsor of local manufactures, not to mention his duties as civic and social leader. Thurlow Weed described the significance of the general store in one of the counties of the southern tier:

I remember the stir which a new store, established in Lisle (some seven or eight miles down the river [Tioughnioga]) by the Rathbuns, from Oxford, created in our neighborhood. It was "all the talk" for several weeks and until a party of housewives, by clubbing together their products, fitted out an expedition; vehicles and horses were scarce, but it was finally arranged; A furnishing a wagon, B a horse, C a man, and D a boy to drive. Four matrons with a commodity of black salts, tow cloth, and maple sugar, went their way rejoicing, and returned triumphantly at sunset.

The history of American foreign commerce and merchant marine in this period is virtually identical with the story of New York port. In 1860 the metropolis was handling over two-thirds of the imports and one-third of the exports of the United States. New York City dominated the passenger and immigrant traffic across the North Atlantic, the import trade, the export trade in cotton, coastwise freighting, and the trade with California and the Orient.

Seaborne trade expanded rapidly in the nineteenth century. The textile mills of Lancashire demanded more cotton; the primary-producing regions of the South wanted more and more manufactured goods; and a growing number of immigrants sought passage across the North Atlantic. The tonnage of the United States on the various routes rose from 1,191,776 tons in 1830 to 5,353,868 tons in 1860, an amount almost equal at the later date to that of the British Empire.

The low cost and good design of American ships were matched by the acumen of owners and seamanship of captains. After 1815 wholesalers, importers, and exporters found it economical to patronize common carriers or to charter vessels rather than to sail their own ships. The most common type of shipping enterprise was the small firm owned by the shipmaster or by a family and operating one to three ships. American ships operated at a low labor cost because able officers drove the seamen hard.

The number of persons crossing the North Atlantic to America rose from 10,311 in 1820 to a record of 460,474 in 1854. Over 90 per cent were emigrants who for a fare of twenty dollars had the use of a bunk measuring six or seven by two feet and who provided and cooked their own food. Most emigrants chose the general trading vessels, particularly those carrying cotton to Liverpool. Cabin passengers, who paid $150 for the trip, took passage on the luxurious packets which averaged twenty days eastbound and thirty-five days westbound from Liverpool to New York. Packets also carried many emigrants in steerage and captured most of the high class freight.

By 1860 the American people were buying most of their clothing materials through New York firms. Textile imports, comprising one-third of all imported goods, were the outstanding feature of New York's whole business as a seaport. The merchant houses of Manhattan had a virtual monopoly on woolens and cotton goods from England, linens from Ireland and Hamburg, and silks and laces from France.

The flood of British textiles led to tariff demands by textile operators in New England. Congress placed tariffs on cotton and woolen goods in 1816 and 1832, which helped native manufacturers to produce goods, especially in the cheaper grades. By 1860 domestically produced textiles, sometimes referred to as "domestics," were triple the amount of imported textiles in monetary value. At first Boston houses controlled the trading in "domestics," but after 1840 the business drifted to Manhattan, the mecca for country storekeepers from the West and the South.

Iron and steel products were eyed favorably by shipowners because they were second in tonnage although sixth in value. British steel mills and foundries were able to lay down these products in New York at a cheaper price than the infant ironmakers of the United States. The bulk of sugar and coffee, second and third in value among all imports by 1860, also came to New York.

Cotton continued to provide most of the outbound cargo. In 1852 tonnage engaged in the transport of cotton constituted almost one-half of the fleet registered for foreign trade. New York firms profited in many ways from the cotton trade. The commission merchants, or factors, resident in the southern towns were usually agents of the New York firms. Because of their connections with New York and Boston banks they could extend liberal credit to the planters. Underwriters associated with New York insurance companies received premiums for insuring the bales in storage or transit. If the cotton was transshipped at New York, a series of persons benefited: draymen, storekeepers, commission merchants, cotton brokers, weighers, packers, stevedores, laborers, insurers, and of course, shipowners. If the cotton passed directly to Europe, shippers, insurers, and bankers of New York still profited.

The coastwise carrying trade employed thousands of craft whose tonnage in the aggregate exceeded that engaged in trade with foreign countries. Schooners operated up and down the coast from Maine to North Carolina with New York harbor the center of their activities. The growing population of New York City demanded more and more products: foodstuffs from nearby points in New Jersey and Connecticut; building materials such as lumber, granite, and lime from Maine; tar and turpentine from North Carolina; coal from Pennsylvania; tobacco and flour from the Chesapeake region. In return, the schooners carried a heterogeneous assortment of goods: foodstuffs such as sugar, tea, and wines; textiles, both imported and domestic; ironware, and so on. New York exchanged many manufactured products, such as textiles, ironware, and shoes, with Boston, its only serious rival in the import trade.

Large square-rigged ships—tramps, traders, and packets—served the ports in this country below Cape Hatteras. Over a score of packets operated regular schedules between New York and New Orleans and Mobile. The outbound ships carried general freight; the inbound, chiefly cotton, hides, furs, lead, wheat, and tobacco.

Ship operators of New York City dominated the trade with Latin-American and Caribbean countries, Cuba and Puerto Rico providing the most business. The Cuban planters sent their sugar to New York to be refined and relied upon New York merchants and bankers for credit. Political disturbances and British competition limited trade with the South American republics except in Brazilian coffee, Argentine hides, and Peruvian guano.

The more distant trades—those to China, India, and Africa—were be-

coming relatively less important during this period. Furthermore, Boston
provided stiff competition. Its shippers carried on most of the trade with
India, although the tea from China generally arrived in New York. Incidentally, New York ports such as Sag Harbor and Hudson contributed
only a few ships to the great whaling fleet which comprised almost one-
fifth of the nation's registered marine in the 1840's.

The merchant marine experienced a boom between 1847 and 1857
due to the general prosperity of the country and also to a combination
of unusual conditions. The British Parliament, by repealing the Corn
Laws in 1846, opened up a large market for grain. The annexation of
California in the same year and the gold rush a few years later created a
heavy demand for shipping space for passengers and for their provisions.
In 1856 the British government diverted many of its deep-sea ships to
supply the troops in Crimea, and the tea trade between China and Great
Britain employed many fast American clippers.

This boom only delayed the spectacular decline in the American maritime industries after 1857. First and most basic of all, rising costs in the
building and operating of ships were ending the American advantage
over foreign builders and ship operators. The collapse of the California
boom also released many ships. The Panic of 1857 caused a general business recession and aggravated the problem of surplus tonnage. The Civil
War ruined the cotton trade, which was the mainstay of the merchant
marine, and many shipowners lost their vessels to enemy action or transferred them to foreign registries. The sailing packet service declined
rapidly because of the competition of the iron-hulled steamships. Eastbound passengers deserted the sailing packets by 1860, and immigrants
to the United States found steamships faster and safer.

By 1863 the decline in American merchant marine had reached the
point where less than 50 per cent of the nation's commerce, in monetary
terms, was carried in American vessels.

Mechanical and structural innovations—steam power, screw propeller,
and the steel ship—foretold a revolution in ocean transport in which
Americans were to play a distinctly secondary role to the British, who
quickly took the leadership in steamship travel on the high seas. Their
marine engines were the most advanced in the world; their iron and steel
industry made the cheapest hulls; and the British government fostered
steamship lines by subsidies. In 1839 Samuel Cunard started his famous
line from Liverpool to Boston and, after 1848, extended service to New
York.

The high cost of American-built steamships as compared with sailing
vessels discouraged their construction and made competition with British vessels difficult. American designers were also technologically behind the British. Nevertheless, Congress decided in the late 1840's to

grant subsidies to steamship lines to Le Havre, Bremen, Liverpool, and San Francisco. Edward Collins, king of the packet-owners operating out of New York City, won a generous subsidy and in 1850 began operating four large wooden paddle-wheel ships to Liverpool. Like many Americans, Collins was obsessed with the desire for speed, even at the expense of profits. Two tragic accidents and poor management caused Congress in 1857 to cut the subsidy, and the next year the Collins line went bankrupt. The only subsidized line that proved a success was the one from New York to California.

By mid-century the merchants and bankers of New York City had won supremacy in American finance. The banks, commission merchants, and mercantile houses granted credit to inland jobbers and to country store-keepers, who in turn "carried" their customers until the crop was in. This intricate system worked moderately well in good times, but periodic panics obstructed the free flow of credit and forced even some of the stronger firms into bankruptcy.

Americans, of course, yielded world leadership to the great financial houses of London. Several British houses, notably the famous Baring firm and W. & J. Brown (later Brown, Shipley and Company), specialized in the lucrative Anglo-American trade. In this country the house of J. P. Morgan owed its early growth to the handling of English investments in the American wheat trade.

Not only did the banking business of the state grow in volume but it also changed its character. Capital resources grew slowly before 1850, then more than doubled within a decade. The most striking change was the rapid increase in bank deposits as compared with the slow rise in the number of notes they issued. Unfortunately, neither bankers nor state officials realized that deposits as well as notes needed to be covered by a reserve. When the Panic of 1857 struck, many banks could not redeem their notes. The national banking system set up in 1863 partially met this need by requiring a specific minimum reserve, making stockholders liable, and providing for the regular examination of accounts.

Before 1838 banks were a quasi-monopoly granted by special act of the legislature for periods of thirty years or more. Politicians and busi-nessmen sought charters because of the high profits and the opportunities to use the bank funds in various ventures. With the granting of a new charter there often took place a wild scramble to secure the stock of that bank. Lobbyists tried to logroll other charters through the legisla-ture. The administration of the banks frequently revealed poor judgment and sometimes downright dishonesty. In 1827 the legislature prohibited directors from borrowing more than one-third of the paid-up capital, from paying dividends except out of profits, and from operating until the capital had been paid in. It also fixed the maximum interest rate at 6 per cent. Total debts could not exceed three times the paid-up capital exclusive of the specie actually on hand. Such regulations hint at the sort of abuses which had taken place.

Two years later the legislature tried to protect the noteholder against loss by setting up a safety fund to which all banks had to subscribe a total of 3 per cent of their capital. If this fund were not sufficient, the state authorized further assessments. This law of 1829 provided for three commissioners to supervise the system and to make periodic inspections of the banks. The bankers of New York City generally opposed the scheme on the ground that since most of their business was deposit and discount, their institutions would be paying assessments to bail out mismanaged country banks. In fact, the existence of the safety fund encouraged rural banks to increase their note circulation.

During the 1830's banking questions plagued state politics as well as Jackson's administration. Some of the Democrats who followed Old Hickory against Nicholas Biddle, head of the Second Bank of the United States, were actually in favor of the banks chartered by the state of New York. Other Democrats opposed all "chartered monopolies" on principle. During the height of the boom promoters founded more banks and created more credit. When the crash came in 1837, blame was heaped upon the bankers. In 1838 Governor Marcy exploited the strong antimonopoly feeling by urging the passage of a free banking system under which any group with the required capital might enter the banking business without special legislation. This act, according to Bray Hammond, was the "most important event in American banking history" since it created a distinctly American system of banking. Before 1838 the state governments granted charters to banks only by special legislative acts, partly because banks were virtually organs of the state and partly because entrenched groups had sought exclusive privileges.

In addition to the free banking feature the act of 1838 provided a new device for ensuring the safety of bank note issues. Banks were required to deposit stock of the state, United States, or other states, or bonds and mortgages with the comptroller before they could secure notes for issue. Within the next eleven years the comptroller sold at a severe discount the securities of thirty-one free banks that failed. During 1840–1842 eleven banks covered by the safety-fund system failed, largely due to mismanagement, laxity on the part of the bank commissioners, and the pressures engendered by the depression following 1837. The comptroller therefore levied additional assessments upon the solvent banks in order to pay off the notes of the defaulting banks. The losses had been so great that the state was obliged to advance funds. In 1842 the legislature provided that in the future the safety-fund system would be responsible for only the notes and not the deposits of the bankrupt institutions.

In 1851 a state banking department was established, with a superintendent in charge. He had general administration over both types of banks: the "free banks," of which there were 136 in 1850; and the safety-fund banks, numbering seventy-three at the same time. The number of safety-fund banks gradually declined as their charters expired, but many reorganized under the free banking law. State bank notes became relatively unimportant after 1866 when the federal government drove them out of existence by levying a 10 per cent tax.

The National Banking Act of 1863 used the bond-deposit principle as the basis of note protection despite the better history of the safety-fund system. Not until the twentieth century did lawmakers take steps to protect depositors as well as holders of bank notes.

Capital needs were met not only by banks but also by other agencies, such as investment houses or banks, savings banks, and insurance companies. Financial institutions rose up to float and to market stocks and bonds. Private banking houses competed with commercial banks in selling public and private securities.

The early stock exchanges facilitated the trading in securities. The New York Stock Exchange, founded in 1817, became the major center for security transactions. It had a membership ranging from seventy-five to one hundred, and its exclusiveness led outsiders to organize a rival group in the 1830's. The Panic of 1857 effected a revolution among the membership by wiping out many of the older and conservative men. The younger financiers who came to the fore found great opportunities for speculation during the Civil War.

The Exchange did not dominate new financing, since corporations either floated securities directly or through commercial and investment banks. The expansion of railroad corporations created millions of dollars of securities which needed a market for traders. After 1840 the investment and speculative activity of the nation became concentrated in New York City. The invention of the telegraph, the improvements in transportation, and the growth of commerce contributed to this concentration. Furthermore, country banks placed more of their demand deposits in Manhattan banks, which led to the diversion of much of these reserves into the call money market. Ample supplies of call money, which were borrowed subject to return on demand, provided funds to investors, and increased the earnings of country banks. Brokers were thus able to borrow capital at relatively low rates. Unfortunately call money was hard to collect in the event of panic, and in the Panic of 1857 some of the banks were forced to call in loans quickly in order to return demand deposits to country banks. The hasty liquidation of securities accentuated the depression and underlined the importance of providing a more flexible system of bank reserves.

Savings banks were intended to receive the deposits of wage earners and thus encourage thrift. The law required that the nonsalaried directors limit their investments to mortgages, public securities, or other high-grade investments. By 1859 the legislature had created seventy-five savings banks and placed them under the jurisdiction of the superintendent of the Banking Department.

Various kinds of insurance were developed to meet the expanding needs of business and to provide more security for individuals. By 1815 New York had several companies specializing in marine insurance. They insured ships, cargoes, and the earnings of the voyage. Frequently they banded together to cover highly valuable cargoes. The Atlantic Mutual Insurance Company handled the bulk of marine insurance in 1860. Fire insurance companies prior to 1834 were joint-stock concerns specifically chartered by the legislature. As a result of the great fire in New York City in December 1835, in which many companies were ruined, there was a movement toward mutual insurance companies throughout the state. During the 1840's and 1850's life insurance companies grew rapidly. They were gradually working out sound methods of computing life expectancies and were developing the system of selling policies through agencies.

In 1853 mismanagement and fraud forced legislation regulating both fire and life insurance companies. The state comptroller was to receive annual reports, and out-of-state companies were not permitted to operate within the state without depositing with the comptroller a copy of their charter, a statement of their condition, and some securities as a bond.

New York had established its industrial supremacy by the time of the Civil War. Whether one considers value of output, number of workers employed in manufacturing, or the diversity of industrial production, New York scored first. Several factors greatly aided the growth of manufacturing in the Empire State. New York had plenty of labor, especially of the unskilled variety. In addition, the thousands of skilled artisans and craftsmen who settled in New York introduced new industries and processes. The unrivaled transportation network meant that entrepreneurs could secure raw materials easily and could sell their products in an ever-expanding market. Furthermore, in New York more capital was available for investment than anywhere else in the United States. Finally, the dynamic character of New Yorkers, who were pace setters in commerce, agriculture, and transportation, naturally found expression in manufacturing. In New York, according to the census for 1855, some 214,000 workers in over 24,000 establishments turned out goods worth more than $317,000,000.

Manufacturing increased enormously between 1825 and 1860, although the speed of this development varied from industry to industry. Three methods of production were used, singly or in combination: handicraft production in larger shops, the domestic or putting-out system, and the factory system.

The merchant capitalist was the key figure behind the handicraft and domestic systems. He raised the money, organized production, and found markets for the output. He became the distributor of the output of the handicraft shops, which grew in size as the more energetic among the craftsmen began hiring more journeymen and apprentices.

In the domestic or putting-out system the merchant-capitalists bought wool or other raw materials, farmed them out to families to work up in their own homes, and sold the product to distant buyers. The domestic system was well adapted to the making of clothing and shoes. The skilled tailor could take work home to his wife and children to complete. Home sewing machines, developed in 1846, were used for the routine sewing. Thousands of women in both the rural and urban regions of New York carried on this type of work.

In many parts of New York woolen cloth continued to be woven on hand looms after the carding, finishing, and spinning of wool had moved to the factory. In 1849 in Washington County there was a curious combination of the factory and the domestic system. The small mills manufactured cloth and flannel. They also made batches of wool into rolls on the carding machines. These rolls were taken by families to spin into yarn to use in knitting, weaving carpets, and making flannel.

In 1825 household or domestic manufacture continued to be the chief method of making goods in rural New York. In addition, many towns and cities had craftsmen, such as cobblers, blacksmiths, coopers, hatters, weavers, tailors, and tanners, who had taken up permanent residence. There were also neighborhood industries, notably gristmills and sawmills. Other small industries were ironworks, potash plants, distilleries, and tanneries.

After the Revolution the per-capita value of household manufactures began to decline, although the Napoleonic Wars revived the home manufacture of textiles. After 1815 cheap factory-made textiles from Britain cut down household production in cities. The state total for woolen cloth produced in the home reached its peak in 1825, but only because the expansion of the industry in the northern and western counties outweighed the losses along the Hudson and Erie Canal.

Household textile manufactures dropped nearly 50 per cent from 1825 to 1835. During the next decade household production fell more slowly, perhaps because of the Panic of 1837. But between 1845 and 1855 practically all the housewives of New York State put away their spinning wheels as railroads penetrated the inland towns and factories arose in all parts of the state. By 1845 officials of the New York State Agricultural Society were complaining that housewives were no longer making homespun for prizes at the state fair.

Remarkable technical advances, originating in Great Britain, were transforming production in many fields. Prior to 1840, when water power was the prevailing method of driving machinery, small mills with inefficient undershot wheels were established on small streams such as the Oriskany and Sauquoit creeks in Oneida County. During the 1840's hydraulic turbines began to replace the slow-moving water wheels and to make possible the erection of factories away from streams. As early as 1846 textile mills driven by steam power were erected in Utica, utilizing the coal brought up from Pennsylvania over the Chenango Canal. Steam power was introduced rather slowly because of the cost of installation and of maintenance.

The adoption of the corporate form facilitated industrial expansion, especially in the 1850's. Promoters of banks in the 1790's and thereafter had discovered the special advantages of incorporation: continuity of operations, ease of raising capital in small amounts from many investors, and limited liability. Subsequently, turnpike and bridge companies and later the manufacturers turned to the legislature for charters of incorporation. The scandals attending the granting of charters led the radical Democrats in the 1830's to demand general laws of incorporation whereby any groups meeting the minimum requirements might secure a charter. The constitutional convention of 1846 adopted the principle: "Corporations may be formed under general laws; but shall not be created by special act, except for municipal purposes." Two years later the legislature provided for general incorporation and in the next decade there was a rush by manufacturers to secure charters.

The factory system, that is, mass production with integration of processes and a heavy investment of capital, grew rapidly in New York during this period, especially for textiles—cotton, wool, silk, and hemp. New York merchants followed the lead of Bostonians in setting up textile factories. Benjamin Marshall, a Scot who had made a fortune in the importing business in New York City, purchased the properties of Benjamin Walcott in Whitestown in Oneida County and produced a high quality cotton cloth. In 1836 another group of New York capitalists established the Harmony Cotton Manufacturing Company at Cohoes.

Cotton factories were concentrated in Oneida, Albany, Rensselaer, and Dutchess counties. Woolen mills were scattered more widely over the state, with the largest ones in Oneida County. The silk industry made little headway despite the silk-worm craze, the backing of farm journals, and some public assistance. After 1850 Amsterdam emerged as an important center of carpet manufacture, and its neighbor, Cohoes, saw the beginnings of the knitwear manufacture, later to become so important in the Mohawk Valley. Factories making rope out of hemp grew up in many cities and towns.

The manufacture of clothing for sale, which in the twentieth century has been the most important industry in the state, employed a larger number of workers than any other branch of manufacturing. A majority of them were immigrant women living in New York slums. Sailors were the first important customers. As the product improved in quality, members of the middle class began to buy ready-to-wear clothing, which was much cheaper than custom-made clothes. Master tailors providing both capital and managerial direction developed into clothing manufacturers. They were able to utilize labor more effectively and more cheaply by making hundreds of suits of standard sizes and shapes. New York City was the center of the industry but Rochester had several important factories.

The metallurgical industries employed approximately thirty-four thousand workers in 1855. Iron of excellent quality was abundant in the Champlain region, where many furnaces fringed the shores of the lake. Charcoal remained the only fuel for smelting until the 1830's, when new processes utilizing coal came into use. Troy and New York City were the major centers for the fabrication of iron and steel. Perhaps the leading personality in the industry was Henry Burden, a Scotch engineer, who became superintendent of the Troy Steel and Iron Company. Burden invented several processes which enabled him to manufacture horseshoes in four seconds and compress puddled iron into rough bars. Troy used iron and steel in the manufacture of stoves and vehicles, while the foundries of New York City produced marine engines, locomotives, stoves, and omnibuses. The skillful metalworkers of Manhattan likewise led in the use of silver, copper, precious jewels, and gold.

Leather and leather goods factories employed over nineteen thousand workers in 1855. Farm families continued to tan some skins, but more often they took the skins to the neighborhood tannery. The large tanneries kept moving westward as the hemlock stands in the eastern Catskills were depleted. Hides were brought in from all parts of the country, and from as far as South America. In New York City the boot and shoe industry, following the example of New England, was slowly turning toward factory production. Merchant capitalists engaged contractors, who in turn hired journeymen to perform specialized operations. The availability of thousands of immigrant cobblers in New York City slowed down the shift of production to factories. Other leather goods industries developed in several communities—Gloversville and Johnstown, for example, became outstanding in the manufacture of gloves.

Extensive woodworking industries were carried on in almost every corner of the state. Great quantities of lumber went into the construction of buildings in the cities. Steamboats, locomotives, and factories burned up large amounts of wood as fuel.

Wood was also used for furniture, household utensils, and farm implements. In New York City, German cabinetmakers turned out quality pieces as well as enormous quantities of cheap tables, chairs, beds, and chests. Duncan Phyfe, a Scot living in New York City, was the leading designer of furniture in this period. New York City also became the main center of piano production in the United States. During the 1830's German craftsmen gradually supplanted native workmen in this industry; most of them remained wage earners, but a few like Steinway set up independent shops.

New York, premier in printing and publishing, was also the leader in manufacturing paper. At first, rags were the raw material for paper production, but after 1850 manufacturers found it possible to use spruce and balsam. The pulp and paper business was located chiefly in Watertown and in towns along the upper Hudson River.

The production of prepared foods and beverages exceeded in value that of any other branch of industry. As wheatgrowing declined in eastern New York, the center of flourmilling moved westward and centered in Rochester, which had twenty-one mills in 1835. The output of Rochester mills in 1851 exceeded 500,000 barrels, but in the 1850's Oswego and Buffalo began challenging Rochester's millers. These cities milled some of the wheat coming down the Lakes, whereas Rochester relied upon the declining output of the Genesee Valley.

New York City, led by its German citizens, captured control of the refining of sugar. The Stuart brothers from Scotland were the first to introduce the use of steam, which permitted refineries to grow in size and output. In 1854 ten large refineries employed over one thousand men.

New York produced over seven million bushels of salt, or 59 per cent of the national output in 1859. The salt springs near Syracuse, once a source of power for the Onondagas, came under the jurisdiction of the state in 1795. The state leased lots to saltmakers, requiring them to pay a duty of four cents a bushel. Large castiron kettles, holding about one hundred gallons each, were used to boil out the salt. Salt manufacturers at Syracuse had several advantages over their competitors in other states: nearness to eastern markets, low capital investment, and access to wood and coal needed to keep the fires going.

Slaughterhouses were found in all the cities of New York, with the largest ones in Albany, Buffalo, and New York. The butchers relied upon livestock driven in from the countryside, but after 1850 butchers supplemented local sources with cattle brought from the Midwest over the New York Central and Erie railroads.

The popularity of fermented and distilled beverages nourished an important industry and employed thousands. Whatever success the temperance movement had in cutting down consumption among natives was more than offset by the influx of whisky-loving Irish and beer-drinking Germans. The consumption of beer rose sharply and was paralleled by a decline in the use of rum. Whisky remained a favorite drink among all classes. Albany, Troy, Hudson, and New York City had large breweries and distilleries which in 1840 accounted for one-tenth of the nation's production.

The East River yards contained the greatest concentration of shipbuilding activity in the United States. During the heyday of the wooden ship no city in the world could match the ships of New York for strength, speed, beauty, and comfort. Other cities in the state engaged in boat construction on a minor scale: Rochester was pre-eminent in building canal boats until about 1850, when Syracuse took the leadership, and Buffalo's builders turned out many lake schooners for the expanding lake marine.

The fact that New York yards had to import oak and pine from a distance proved little hindrance. Manhattan and Brooklyn shipbuilders had the advantage of being close to the shippers and merchants. These shippers demanded ships of high quality and of many kinds; furthermore, their vessels needed periodic repair, which provided the yards with a good share of their annual business. Many of the ablest builders in the world gravitated to New York to find scope for their talents. The yards of New York were also advanced technically, using labor-saving devices such as steam sawmills to cut timber.

Perhaps the most famous of the shipyards which dotted the shore line below Corlear's Hook (near the present Williamsburg Bridge), was that founded by Henry Eckford, a Scot who had learned the business of building ships in Quebec. When he died in 1832, after winning a fine reputation overseas for his naval vessels, the yard came under the control of Isaac Webb, from Connecticut. His son, William H. Webb, dominated the industry between 1840 to 1860. European navies sought his ironclads while the Black Ball Line purchased his packets. Jacob Westervelt, David Brown, and Stephen Smith were builders whose ships were well regarded for their speed, performance, and stamina.

The shipbuilding industry was extremely sensitive to the ebb and flow of business trends. The slightest ripple in confidence caused merchants and shippers to defer building. The Panic of 1837 virtually ended shipbuilding for two years, but the opening of a new trade route, such as the

California trade in 1850, caused a rush for many ships. Allied trades such as sailmaking and caulking prospered or declined in sympathy with the shipyards.

Shipbuilders had to be alert to changes in trade routes and to technical developments. The ablest brains devoted their major energies to the design and construction of wooden ships. More than 95 per cent of the American merchant marine consisted of sailing ships as late as 1863. Their greatest achievement were the clippers, with three masts, a long hull, and concave bows. These were in demand during the 1850's for the trade with California, China, and Australia. No sailing ship ever equaled the record set by the *Flying Cloud,* Donald McKay's superb creation, which sailed from New York around the Horn to San Francisco in eighty-nine days.

Despite such records, the superiority of steam became evident. Steamboats had captured the passenger and much of the freight traffic on rivers and inlets long before 1825 and mariners were taking their steamboats out on the high seas in the 1830's. The arrival of two English-built steamships within four hours in 1838 caused New Yorkers to take more interest in ocean-going steamships. Unfortunately the East River shipbuilders committed themselves tenaciously to paddlewheels ill suited to the buffeting of high seas, and they failed to adopt the screw propeller which British builders had utilized on the Clyde River at an early date.

The decade of the 1850's was the high point of activity for shipbuilders in New York. The great yards were turning out a wide variety of vessels: packets for the North Atlantic shuttle, clippers for the California trade, warships for several European and Latin American navies, steamships for the Collins Line, and a host of craft for river, bay, coastal, and oceanic traffic. Over two thousand workmen, mainly native Americans, were employed in the shipyards of New York City.

The economy of New York by 1860 displayed signs of approaching maturity. Its farmers, who had almost completed the task of transforming forest into farmland, were also well on their way toward becoming businessmen. The merchants on Manhattan had earned handsome profits acting as middlemen between the wheat and cotton growers of the nation and the textile and steel manufacturers of England. Upstate, merchants in hundreds of communities were performing similar functions and winning wealth and power. Other New Yorkers had nursed into manhood impressive financial institutions, which remained, however, distinctly subsidiary to those of London. Equally promising for the future was New York's industrial development, which was already noted for its output and diversity. The businessmen of New York between 1825 and 1860 definitely established the primacy of the Empire State in commerce, finance, and manufacturing.

Chapter 22

The Rise of the Dairy State,

1825-1860

Latterly—all the Rage for emigration, has been to the far west—to Michigan, Indiana, Illinois, etc. And of the settlers already here [Delaware County] abundance of them are in a mind to sell out and push on farther west.
—SAMUEL A. LAW, *1833*

THE expanding network of turnpikes, canals, railroads, and plank roads unleashed two revolutionary forces in New York agricultural history—the "pull" of the growing urban market and the pressure of western competition. The farm family of 1860 was spending an increasing amount of its time producing goods for a distant market and less for its immediate use than it had in pioneer days, and it became more dependent upon the storekeeper for goods. By 1860 practically all farm women purchased cotton and wool goods instead of making them at home.

Price fluctuations became increasingly important for the farming population between 1825 and 1860. Prices rose from the low level of the early 1820's until the middle 1830's, and the farmers shared in the general prosperity. The growing urban population and the construction of canals, railroads, and factories stimulated the demand for raw materials and foodstuffs. After the Panic of 1837 farm prices remained low until the late 1840's, when events in Europe (the Crimean War and the repeal of the Corn Laws in England) coupled with the expansion of American railroads and industry pushed prices upward. Another panic in 1857 again brought prices down.

Since each farmer tended to produce whatever products would leave him the greatest margin of profits, a bewildering number of individual and local adjustments took place. Thus many farmers in the Hudson and Mohawk valleys turned to butter and cheese when the wheat midge, rust, and Hessian fly made wheat raising unprofitable in the 1830's. Cheap western wool after 1845 caused many upland farmers to swing over to dairying. A few farmers concentrated on special crops such as flax, hops, barley, broomcorn, and fruit. Those living near cities engaged in market gardening and milk production.

Yet wheat remained the most important cash crop and did not yield first place to dairying until after 1850. The great increase in wheat production in the Genesee Valley after 1825 more than offset the rapid decline in the eastern part of the state. The rich fresh soils of the western counties yielded more than twice as much wheat per acre as the worn-out and infested fields in the Hudson and Mohawk valleys. The heyday of the Genesee Valley as one of the nation's major grain centers came to an end in the late 1850's when the midge ruined the crop.

Corn, oats, barley, rye, and hay became more important as wheat declined. Corn, used by farmers to feed their growing herds of cows and hogs, remained the most useful crop, as it had been during the pioneer days. Oats were useful on the farm and also brought in cash from operators of stagecoach lines and contractors building railroads and canals. These businessmen owned many horses. New York farmers in 1840 raised over half of all the barley grown in the United States and sold much of it to the breweries. Distilleries also took a large part of the rye crop, which was grown chiefly in the Hudson Valley counties.

New York had become the leading potato-producing state by 1840. The blight cut output in half within the next ten years, but farmers continued to plant potatoes for the growing city market.

Certain localities became well known for special crops. The Hoosic Valley in Rensselaer and Washington counties was the center of flax production. Otsego County raised over one-third of the state production of hops, and New York State accounted for more than 90 per cent of the nation's total production in 1860. Hopgrowing fitted in well with dairying but it was a highly speculative undertaking. "Hop money" built many imposing farmhouses, some of which can still be seen in the vicinity of Waterville and Cooperstown.

The average farmer of this period gave his orchard practically no care. Since most apples and other fruit went into cider or fermented drinks, it made little difference what variety he raised. Farmers often made from twenty-five to fifty barrels of cider for family use. By 1850 the owners of extensive orchards in the Hudson and Mohawk valleys were selling their apples to buyers from the seaboard cities.

Horticulture as such did not gain any real support until after the Revolution. European-trained gardeners employed by gentlemen farmers such as the Livingstons of Columbia County first introduced new and improved varieties of vegetables and fruit. Later the Downing family of Newburgh established a famous nursery, and Rochester during the 1850's claimed the title "The Flower City." The Mount Hope Nursery of Ellwanger and Barry, covering 440 acres, was the largest in Rochester—indeed, in the world. The extension of both the Erie and the Harlem railroads greatly expanded the region in which vegetables and perishable fruits could be profitably grown for marketing.

The insistent demands for wool and dairy products, the expansion of canals, railroads, and highways, the excellent pastures, and the decline of wheat culture turned a majority of farmers to animal husbandry. By 1850 the wheat crop yielded first place to dairy products in terms of value.

The high point of the sheep industry came between 1830 and 1845, when some upland counties, such as Washington, boasted as many as six sheep per capita. During the 1840's the western growers, especially in Ohio, began to ship their wool to the New York and the New England wool manufacturers. They could undersell the New York sheep raiser because their costs were lower. The Walker Tariff of 1846 repealing the duty on the higher grades of wool caused a panic among the woolgrowers of New York. Between 1845 and 1855 the number of sheep pastured in most counties dropped by more than 50 per cent. The stimulus given to sheep raising during the Civil War could not halt the steady decline of this industry.

New York ranked first in beef production between 1840 and 1850. Many of the farmers in the lower Hudson Valley raised beef cattle, which they bought as two- or three-year-olds from drovers coming from the north or west. The farmers fattened the cattle through the winter and the following summer, and then drove them to market. Daniel Drew, the Wall Street plunger, began his career driving cattle from the Mohawk and Cherry valleys to Manhattan slaughterhouses. Just before he marketed his cattle, the wily Drew fed them large amounts of salt which caused them to drink heavily, thus increasing their weight. This trick gave rise to the term "watered stock," now used in connection with the sale of securities. Other drovers picked up animals in the Genesee country and drove them to Albany, a leading beef-packing center. During the 1850's the railroads began to flood the East with cattle raised on the prairies, pushing New York down to third place in beef production by 1860. After the Civil War the refrigerator car greatly simplified the shipment of fresh meat from the West to the eastern markets. Western competition was also responsible for the decline of hog raising in New York during this period.

The rise of the dairy industry was by far the most significant development in the agricultural history of the state between 1825 and 1860. Farmers discovered that cows were their most reliable money-makers, since both the domestic and foreign market kept demanding more dairy products. Dairying had several advantages. Manure helped restore soil fertility, and butter-making and milking utilized the labor of women and children, which the decline of home manufacture of cloth had released. Farmers found it easy to store cheese and butter and to carry them to market.

The production of butter was the backbone of the dairy industry, both in the value of the product and in the number of farmers engaged. Orange County led all other counties in butter-making from colonial days until 1845, when it turned to selling fluid milk to New York City. In the fall of the year buyers visited the farms and, after testing the butter, made their offers. Having accepted an offer, the farmers loaded their firkins of butter on their wagons and delivered them to depots along the canal and railroad.

Butter-making was more evenly distributed throughout the state than cheese production, which was concentrated in central New York. The fame of Herkimer County cheese has come down to us from this period, when this county produced almost one-fourth of the state's supply. To meet the growing demand for cheese, especially by English importers, New York farmers made several improvements and changes. More attention was paid to testing cows to determine the quantity and quality of output. Better breeds such as Durhams, Ayrshires, and Herefords were imported to improve the degenerate "native cattle." The introduction of English grasses and the provision for better shelter and forage in the winter also increased milk production. Farmers gave increased attention to the improved cheese presses and techniques of dairying recommended by county agricultural societies and farm journals.

Perhaps the outstanding development was the rise of the cheese factory. In 1851 Jessie Williams, a farmer near Rome, began to take in the milk from his neighbors to make into cheese. His success in finding a ready market prompted other farmers to follow his example. During the 1860's the cheese factory movement spread to many sections of New York, and thereafter to Ohio, Michigan, and Wisconsin. Factories could use large presses, relieving the family of the drudgery of stirring and pressing. Skilled managers could produce a uniform product of superior quality at lower cost than the housewife.

The spread of cheese factories facilitated the organization of marketing. In 1858 producers in Herkimer County set up a marketing society, which led to the establishment, in 1871, of the state-wide Dairymen's Board of Trade.

The influence of the urban market and the railroad is clearly illustrated in the growth of the milk industry. Before the construction of the railroads enabled farmers to send fresh country milk to market, a great deal of the milk drunk in New York City came from the immediate vicinity. An unusual source was so-called distillery milk, that is, milk from cows drinking the swill of distilleries. This milk was widely sold. The barns attached to the distilleries were incredibly dirty, since the cows never left their filthy pens. Their only food was the thirty to forty gallons of hot mash they drank each day. The diseased animals produced a "blue, watery, insipid, unhealthy secretion" whose food value was questionable. Sometimes the dairyman put in chalk, sugar, flour, molasses, starch, and coloring matter in order to conceal the water which they had added in generous amounts. Physicians kept up a running warfare against this milk, blaming it largely for the alarmingly high infant mortality. One out of two children failed to reach his fifth birthday. Little was done before the Civil War to clean up this source of malnutrition and disease.

Country milk gradually took command of the New York City market after railroads were built. Shipments over the Erie Railroad rose from 385,505 quarts in 1842 to 24,414,608 quarts in 1861. Many dairy farmers made handsome profits, averaging, according to one estimate, over thirty dollars a year on each cow.

Farm management practices of the ordinary farmer continued to be soil-depleting and slovenly. In 1852 one observer estimated that one-twelfth of the farmers improved their lands, one-fourth cultivated their lands in such a way as to prevent deterioration, and the rest "skinned" the land. Almost every county reported serious soil exhaustion and falling crop yields. Tenant-operated farms were particularly neglected. The *Cultivator* in 1838 described the native cattle as "small, short-bodied, thin and coarse haired, steep rumped, slab sided, and have little aptitude to fatten."

Substantial advances, however, took place both in the spread of agricultural knowledge and in its application. No figure contributed more to this advance than Jesse Buel, who transformed a brier-covered, sterile piece of land west of Albany into a farm famous for its productivity and beauty. In 1834 Buel founded the *Cultivator,* a journal which preached the benefits of scientific agriculture. His own profitable experience added weight to his arguments for manuring, draining, deep plowing, crop alternation, and the substitution of fallow crops for naked fallows. After Buel's death the *Cultivator* was merged with the *Genesee Farmer,* which Luther Tucker had founded in 1831. Later, in 1853, Tucker brought out the first issues of the *Country Gentleman.*

Other journals helped to spread the advantages of improved farm management. The *New Genesee Farmer,* established in 1839, rivaled the influence of its namesake. In 1865 it was merged with the *American Agriculturist.* Another important journal was *Moore's Rural New Yorker,* founded in Rochester in 1850, and offering its readers a broader coverage than purely agricultural articles. The New York State Agricultural Society contributed to the advance of scientific agriculture by publishing an annual volume of *Transactions* starting in 1841, which included reports from county societies, reprints from foreign journals, and general information about agriculture in New York.

The establishment of the New York State Agricultural Society in 1832 was another project ardently supported by Jesse Buel. After years of agitation, the state legislators finally agreed in 1841 to subsidize county societies and to authorize a state fair as well. The annual state fair drew large crowds, who inspected the specimens of fruit and vegetables, livestock, and tools. The side shows and horse races made it an exciting day for the family when the farmer visited the fair. County societies, revived by the act of 1841, spent most of their energies sponsoring the local fair at the county seat.

Educating young people in agricultural principles and farm practice was another aim close to the heart of Buel and other leaders. Before 1825 Elkanah Watson had been urging the establishment of a "pattern farm" where young men could study latest methods. Buel from 1823 onward pressed for state aid for an agricultural school, but, he sadly noted, the "farmers are the principal opponents." During the 1830's and the 1840's the friends of the agricultural school attempted without success to raise funds by private subscription. Several manual labor schools got under way but soon foundered for lack of support.

During the 1850's several leading New Yorkers renewed the campaign for a state agricultural college. Dr. Amos Brown of Ovid started an agricultural school in 1852 and five years later received a state loan of $41,000. This school, however, failed to survive. Meanwhile, Charles Cook of Montour Falls attracted to his town the People's College originally sponsored by Horace Greeley, and he succeeded in persuading the legislature to grant to his institution the proceeds of the Morrill Land Grant Act. This famous law of 1862 provided for a federal grant of public land to each of the states as an endowment for education in agriculture and in the mechanic arts. Since Cook was unable to meet the state requirements in regard to staff, buildings, and equipment, the grant was transferred to Cornell University at the time of its founding in 1865.

As the circulation of farm journals rose, as more fairs were held, and especially as new methods increased farm yields and income, more and more farmers put into practice the latest information about drainage, fertilizers, rotations, and breeding. Fertilizers such as gypsum began to be used to enrich the soils, and although few farmers realized the value of a regular rotation, many began to plan fallow crops instead of allowing the field to grow up to brush. Machinery gradually came into wider use in New York State—and throughout the nation. Americans were spurred to invent, improve, and adopt new tools and machines because land was cheap relative to labor. By 1840 the cast-iron plow had completely replaced the old wooden plow, enabling the farmer to do more work with half the number of oxen and horses. Most plows were of local manufacture, although a few brands such as the "Livingston County" were widely distributed. New soil-working implements, such as rollers, corn planters, and cultivators, came into use. The greatest improvements in the manufacture of farm machinery took place after 1840. The revolving rake displaced the hand rake. Hand mowing gave way to the mowing machine on level fields, and harvesting was speeded up with the adoption of the threshing machine and the reaper.

Important as these advances were, they did not eliminate the need for much hand labor. The family, as always, continued to supply the largest part. The menfolk did the field work, and the women took care of the house, churned the butter, and made the cheese. The more prosperous farmers employed dairymaids and hired laborers. Ten dollars a month plus board and room was the average wage, although harvest hands received appreciably more. Farmers complained, then as now, how hard it was to find good workers who would not get drunk on Saturday night.

Lumbering continued to be important in rural New York. Not only did the majority of farmers rely upon the forests for their fuel, fencing, and building materials, but settlers on the northern and southern slopes of the Adirondacks, in the Catskill regions, and along the headwaters of the Susquehanna and Allegheny rivers were fully as interested in lumbering as in agriculture, and during the winter these men often set out for the lumber camps to cut timber and haul it to streams. Some observers, including Horace Greeley, complained that lumbering retarded the development of orderly agricultural life. The dangerous work tended to roughen character as well as speech. There were many complaints by absentee landowners that woodsmen were stripping their forest lands.

Lumbering became big business on the major rivers. In 1851 more than 26,000,000 feet of lumber piled up at the great boom at Glens Falls, and this figure was increased eightfold in the next twenty years. Lumber was needed for housing in the cities, for fuel for steamboats, locomotives, and homes, and for the manufacture of ships, tools, and carriages. By 1850 New York led all other states in lumber production.

Rural decline, as evidenced by worn-out fields, abandoned farms, and population decline, was in evidence in much of the hill country by the time of the Civil War. The census of 1860 showed that scores of townships had actually lost population during the previous quarter century. This was for a variety of reasons. Sheep raising and dairying, which required large acreage, crowded out small farmers. Those farmers who had enough capital to buy machinery found it profitable to cultivate more land. Small villages, which had grown up around the meetinghouses or taverns, were also losing population. Country storekeepers complained that farmers would drive twenty to thirty miles to find bargains in the city. Small gristmills and sawmills began to disappear, partly because of the lack of raw material in the vicinity, partly because the larger commercial mills could offer better services at lower prices.

Fresh lands to the west and the lure of jobs in the cities caused thousands of young people to leave the old homestead. The desire to migrate was hard to repress in persons accustomed to moving from one frontier to another. The newspapers and farm journals carried enticing stories of cheap and fertile lands in Michigan and other western states. The western "fever" was contagious, and the success of former neighbors who had gone west made those who remained behind restless. By 1850 there were 385,954 former New Yorkers living in the Old Northwest (Ohio, Indiana, Illinois, Michigan, Wisconsin). Emigration was so extensive that public officials and editors predicted a deserted countryside. They warned farmers of the perils and disappointments faced by the frontiersmen.

The city rivaled the western prairies as the magnet for ambitious youth. The monotonous round of field labor and chores, enlivened only by sermons and an occasional social gathering or county fair, offered little hope of prosperity and no chance for fame. Furthermore, the financial opportunities in cities had great appeal. Did not a Staten Island farmer, Cornelius Vanderbilt, amass a tremendous fortune in shipping and later in railroads? The list of upstate farmboys who made good in the city is impressive: John D. Rockefeller, Daniel Drew, Jay Gould, Russell Sage. The educational system also tended to divert young people from the farm. The colleges, with their classical curriculum, ignored agriculture and trained graduates for the law, ministry, and teaching. Those graduates of the academies who did not go on to college drifted into clerical positions, business, and elementary-school teaching. Not without reason did one farm leader exclaim: "Educate them! Why the moment you educate them they will leave the business."

The extension of the railroads into the Middle West and the rate wars arising from the competition for the control of the meat and grain shipped from Chicago to the seaboard robbed eastern farmers of their geographical advantage. For example, in 1857 the New York Central and the Erie railroads carried cattle and sheep from Chicago to New York for thirty-five dollars a carload, while noncompetitive points in the Genesee Valley had to pay as much as eighty-five dollars a carload to transport their stock to the metropolitan market. New York farmers were to complain again and again throughout the century that the railroads were overcharging them and subsidizing their western rivals.

Lack of capital prevented some farmers from buying improved livestock and farm machinery and from making permanent improvements. Credit was not easily secured for such purposes, since many farmers already owed money either to the landed proprietors or to the trust and insurance companies. During the 1830's many farmers in the western part of the state tried to secure the deeds to their farms by becoming mortgagors, rather than remaining as purchasers under contracts. The New York Life Insurance and Trust Company and the Farmers' Loan and Trust Company lent money at 7 per cent on improved real property. Few farmers were able to discharge their mortgages within the time limit, but the trust companies avoided foreclosures wherever possible. The experience of these companies confirms the general complaint that money was scarce.

The majority of farmers continued to make a living by readjusting their activities to the demands of the market. They won national leadership in all phases of the dairy industry and in such minor crops as potatoes, flax, and hops. As late as 1850 New York's cattle growers, sheep raisers, and wheat farmers kept the state among the top producers of these products. Jesse Buel and his associates were pace setters in the national movement for scientific agriculture and agricultural education. In every county were progressive farmers who rotated their crops, used fertilizers and drain tiles, and purchased better livestock and machinery. By 1860 New York farmers on the whole had made a successful transition to commercial farming.

Immigration and Labor

Yet we have our Five Points, our emigrant quarters, our swarms of seamstresses to whom their utmost toil in monotonous daily drudgery give only bare subsistence, a life barren of hope and of enjoyment; our hordes of dock thieves, and of children who live in the streets and by them. No one can walk the length of Broadway without meeting some hideous troop of ragged girls, from twelve years down, brutalized already almost beyond redemption by premature vice, clad in the filthy refuse of the rag-picker's collections, obscene of speech, the stamp of childhood gone from their faces, hurrying along with harsh laughter and foulness on their lips . . . ; with thief written in their cunning eyes and whore on their depraved faces.—GEORGE TEMPLETON STRONG, *1851*

NEW YORK maintained, in fact, increased, its lead in population after 1825. The state's population doubled between 1825 and 1855; this was approximately the same rate as that for the nation. This gain occurred despite a heavy westward emigration. In 1860 there were 867,032 natives of New York living out of the state, most of them in the region of the Old Northwest. Of course, many citizens of Connecticut, New Jersey, and other states moved to New York, but the Empire State lost three people for every one it gained from other states.

The high birth rate and immigration from Europe accounted for the rapid growth of population, which rose from 1,372,812 in 1820 to 3,880,735 in 1860. The thousands of immigrants, most of whom came as young adults, and native citizens as well, generally reared good-sized families. The census for 1865 shows that 25 per cent of all families had more than three children. It is interesting to note that another quarter of all families had no children at all.

Perhaps the most significant development was the growth of urban population. New York City's population almost quadrupled between

1825 and 1855, and the metropolitan area was well over a million at the opening of the Civil War. Other cities made similar gains. The following figures are representative:

Table 4. Urban population, 1825 and 1855.

	1825	1855
Albany	15,971	57,333
Brooklyn	10,791	205,250
Buffalo	5,141	74,214
New York City	166,086	629,810
Rochester (1828)	9,469	43,877
Syracuse	3,833	25,107
Troy	7,859	33,269

People living in cities of more than ten thousand totaled almost 30 per cent of the state's population in 1855. This figure understates the urban drift, since it excludes communities below the ten-thousand figure. In contrast, the rural population was no longer growing. In fact, hundreds of townships had fewer residents in 1860 than in 1830. So extensive was the flight from the land to the cities and to the west that public officials and farm editors expressed much concern at the trend.

The Negro population grew slowly, numbering only 45,286 in 1855, or about 1.3 per cent of the population, a percentage much lower than that in colonial times. Most Negroes lived in New York City and Brooklyn. The Negro suffered much inequality both within and outside the law. The Constitution of 1822 discriminated against free Negroes by requiring them to meet a property qualification higher than that required for white voters. Although the property qualification for whites was abolished in 1826, that for the free Negroes was retained. On three occasions, 1846, 1860, and 1867, the public refused to approve a constitutional amendment permitting equal suffrage rights for Negroes. It required the Fifteenth Amendment to eliminate the property qualification imposed on Negroes. In addition to legal inequities, the Negroes met the usual round of discrimination and lack of opportunity. The Irish immigrants in particular fought desperately for the jobs as manual laborers, waiters, and domestic servants which previously had offered Negroes their best opportunities for employment.

The proportion of native-born New Englanders in New York declined steadily after 1825, although Yankee stock remained the largest single element in the racial composition throughout the nineteenth century. The slackening of immigration from New England, however, was more than offset by the inrush of Europeans. By 1855 the foreign born composed over one-fourth of the population of the state and nearly one-half of the inhabitants of Manhattan.

Over 90 per cent of the immigrants to the United States before the Civil War came from western and northern Europe, and especially from Ireland and Germany. A considerable migration of English, Scotch, and Welsh reached New York, but their numbers were much smaller than the Irish total. Smaller contingents of Scandinavians, Swiss, and Netherlanders also settled in the state.

Tremendous economic changes were uprooting the population of Europe during the nineteenth century. With the collapse of the last vestiges of feudalism and the spread of the industrial revolution, factory enterprises gradually displaced handicraft production, and thousands of artisans migrated to America. The spread of commercial farming led to the enclosure movement in England and Scotland, dispossessing thousands of small farmers. Moreover, the period of relative peace after 1815 and the slight improvements of public health, in combination with the high birth rate, created a sharp increase in European population.

Conditions in Ireland in the first half of the nineteenth century were deteriorating rapidly. Tenant farmers found their rents rising and their leases becoming less secure because landlords were shifting from grain to sheep raising. The cotters, or landless farm laborers, relied almost entirely for their food on their potato patches. In 1845 disaster struck when the potato "rot" wiped out the food supply of most of the rural population. The cotters flocked to the seaports, and tenants by the thousands gave up their farms or were evicted for nonpayment of rent. Landlords, philanthropists, and even local governments granted funds to some of the dispossessed people to leave their island home. New York City was one of the main goals, and by 1860 over 200,000 Irishmen were living in that city.

The magnet pulling Europeans to America was the opportunity to better themselves. Here were many jobs on the canals and railroads, and the construction of houses, stores, and factories required an even greater number of workers. The farmers of New York kept demanding more "greenhorns" to bring in the harvest and to milk the cows. But New York, like the other states, offered more than work. Here the immigrant could worship as he pleased; he could earn the right to vote; he was free from rigid police supervision and the draft. Best of all, he, or at least his children, could climb up the economic and social ladder.

The attractions of the New World were to be enjoyed only by those willing to endure many hardships. At every step the immigrants ran into sharpers and swindlers among the tavern keepers, ship captains, ticket sellers, and employment agents. They usually had to spend some time in the water-front inns of Liverpool, Hamburg, and Le Havre waiting for their sailing vessels. The two-month voyage was the next grueling ordeal. Weakened by poor food, overcrowding, lack of ventilation and sanitary arrangements, the passengers often contracted cholera, typhus, small pox, and dysentery. Representatives of private agencies—runners, boardinghouse-keepers, and employment agencies—were waiting on the docks of New York City to serve, and often to exploit, the newcomers.

Thousands of diseased and destitute foreigners swamped the hospitals, almshouses, prisons, and orphanages of New York City. Investigations showed that swindlers were stripping many immigrants of their few possessions. To deal with this desperate situation, the state legislature created the Board of Commissioners of Immigration, which was authorized to reimburse local communities for looking after the welfare of indigent foreigners. The board was partly financed by levying a head tax on each immigrant. The commissioners had to appease politicians, combat the boardinghouse-keepers, and stretch their limited funds over a large number of immigrants. Their major accomplishment was the acquisition of Castle Garden as a central landing depot for all immigrants. This action curbed some of the worst abuses, since immigrants could buy tickets from accredited travel agencies and secure reliable information about jobs and routes from state officials. Immigrants were also helped by emigrant-aid societies set up by the various nationality groups.

Several enclaves of foreigners developed in New York and other cities. The Irish on Manhattan tended to concentrate in the dilapidated dwellings on the Lower East Side behind the wharves and warehouses. The Germans at the half-century mark lived farther up the island centering in the region between Grand Street and Fourteenth Street. In the upstate cities, immigrants usually moved into the worst sections.

Immigrants did not easily forget the homeland with its precious memories of childhood and its remaining family ties. For example, on the feast of their patron saint, the Friendly Sons of St. Patrick and the Ancient Order of Hibernians assembled to celebrate their origins with song and oratory. In 1846 the poverty-ridden Irish community of New York collected over $800,000 for famine relief in Ireland. Despite these evidences of old loyalties, homesickness gradually vanished under the pressures of daily living. The job, the saloon, the parish church, the fraternal society, and especially the family created new loyalties. Each nationality group built up a complex of organizations which performed a vital function in adjusting their group to everyday living in America.

The foreign-language press, next to the job and the school, was the greatest force for Americanization. Although these journals sprang up to serve as clearinghouses for information and to perpetuate memories of the old country, their editors gradually copied most of the features of the American press, fostered community services, and debated the controversial issues of the day. To illustrate, the *Irish-American* championed the cause of Irish freedom, defended the Catholic church against every attack, and fought such "fanatical" reforms as temperance and abolition.

Naturalized citizens became a potent force in New York politics. The Democratic party welcomed the foreigners and generally won their support. The Whig party held few attractions because of its tendencies toward nativism, temperance, and aristocracy. Some Germans, especially those of liberal views, swung to the Republicans in the late 1850's because of that party's opposition to the extension of slavery.

The Irish in New York City created the greatest Irish community outside of Dublin. Naturally enough, the immigrants, finding themselves in the midst of a strange culture, continued their clannish habits, especially when they experienced the animosity of some Protestants fearful of papal supremacy, the hostility of native workmen resentful of competitors for jobs, and the complaint of taxpayers disturbed by the bulging relief rolls. The Roman Catholic church became the rallying point for most sons of Erin. Exhausted by hard physical labor and crowded into squalid tenements, many workmen turned to barrooms and saloons for recreation. Many, perhaps hopeful of a chance to settle accounts with Great Britain, joined the militia, and Irish units gave a good account of themselves in the Civil War. Politically they were Democrats and backed Tammany Hall, which in turn rewarded the faithful with jobs and relief. Although the top places on the ticket were reserved for native Americans, the Irish soon made their influence felt, winning minor posts and receiving favors as contractors and licensed saloon keepers.

The upstate cities by mid-century were also becoming cosmopolitan. For example, the census of 1855 showed that 44 per cent of the people of Rochester were foreign born. If one adds to this group their children, the total comes to well over half of the population. The largest foreign-born element in Rochester and Buffalo was German-speaking.

Buffalo's German colony numbered almost 30,000 out of a city total of 74,000. The German-American social pattern was more varied than that of the Irish, reflecting, as it did, the large number of religious, class, and regional distinctions in the German states of Europe. Protestants ranged from ultra orthodox Lutherans to Pietists, with the Evangelical Lutherans predominating. Sermons, hymns, and school instruction in the German language kept alive the spirit of the Old World.

German Catholics constructed several churches in Buffalo, but these religious organizations accepted the orders of Irish-born Bishop Timon with great reluctance. Considerable friction developed between the Germans and Irish of the immigrant generation in many parts of the state. The Germans prided themselves upon their thrift, sense of order, and culture. The Irish regarded themselves as peculiarly gifted to administer the Catholic church and to direct the Democratic party.

English (102,286), Canadian (47,842), and Scottish (27,523) immigrants made a much easier adjustment than either the Irish or the Germans. They readily joined the churches and other societies of the old American stock, who approved their Protestant background, ability to speak English, and Victorian habits. Immigrants from England did not establish many distinctly British societies and churches although the Sons of St. George appeared in the major cities. The Scots joined the Sons of St. Andrew's and occasionally sported kilts, but in general they did not parade their national origins. The Canadian-born were even less group-conscious, although the minority of French Canadians who settled along the border tended to keep their distinctive culture.

Citizens of native birth and parentage continued to dominate the countryside, to provide most of the middle class, and to furnish the business and political leaders in the cities. The friction between the Yankee element and the pre-Revolutionary stock noticeably lessened. Intermarriage, the religious revivals, the spread of the school system, and the influx of the Irish and Germans in the 1840's and 1850's gradually fused together the diverse elements of native birth.

Nativism, or antiforeign feeling, on the part of the old stock was a mixture of prejudice and threatened interests. The basic emotion was fear, fear that the foreign tide would submerge traditional customs and institutions. Old-stock New Yorkers identified themselves as the custodians of the American heritage, which they defined rather narrowly as Protestant and Anglo-Saxon.

The rise of Catholicism was a threat to Protestant control. The Irish and Germans ignored the Puritan Sabbath, fought the prohibition crusade, and called for the banishment of the King James Bible from the public school. The demand by Bishop John Hughes for a share of public funds for the parochial school system was regarded as an aggressive move and brought forth strong nativist resentment.

The increase in immigration presented many political problems. Whigs, irritated by the aliens' preference for the Democratic party, charged the Catholic clergy with political meddling, conveniently forgetting the political activities of many Protestant clergymen. Believers in democracy were critical of the papacy for its promonarchical stand in the suppression of such apostles of republicanism as Kossuth and Garibaldi. They also disliked the authoritarian structure of the church and the powers of the bishops. The interdiction of St. Louis' Church in Buffalo by Bishop Timon in 1851 and the excommunication of recalcitrant church trustees in 1854 by the papal legate gave Protestants and democrats the opportunity to condemn as undemocratic the organization of the Roman Catholic church. The Buffalo *Commercial Advertiser* commented, "For refusing to do what the laws will not permit and what is clearly against the fundamental principles of a republican government, these good citizens [the trustees of St. Louis] have launched against them 'the major excommunication'!"

Nativist sentiments were clearly evident in the signs which read "No Irish Need Apply" and in the barrage of articles and books critical of foreign customs and institutions. Some violence occurred, but fortunately New York was spared the disgraceful anti-Catholic riots which took place in Pennsylvania and Massachusetts. By mid-century nativism was a strong political force giving rise to the Native American, or, as it was more often called, the Know-Nothing party. As is indicated in the chapters on political history, nativism as a political issue was short lived and after 1856 became subordinated to the greater question of slavery extension.

The assimilation of foreigners was a slow process, lasting for several generations. Some immigrants never made more than a superficial adjustment to American life because they were unwilling to abandon their native tongue and characteristic habits. Many of the younger immigrants, however, and most of the children adopted American ways and customs enthusiastically. They sent their children to the public schools and tried to get ahead as fast as they could.

All in all, the most remarkable feature of immigrant life was the rapidity of Americanization, contradicting the complaints of nativists that the foreign elements refused to give up their outside loyalties. The forces of assimilation were powerful and continuous: the public school, the press, the political parties, contact with Americans on the job and at play, the conflict between the older and younger generations. All these factors eroded the sense of religious or national solidarity and operated to create "Americans."

Generalizations about labor and labor conditions are somewhat hazardous and always subjective. From a modern viewpoint labor conditions ranged from bad to terrible. Horace Greeley's *Tribune* in 1845 commented pithily:

The average earnings of those who live by simple labor in our city—embracing at least two-thirds of our population—scarcely, if at all, exceed one dollar per week for each person subsisting thereon. On this pittance . . . three hundred thousand persons within sight of Trinity steeple must pay city rents, buy their clothing, and obtain such medical attendance, religious consolation, mental culture, and means of enjoyment as they have.

Despite these conditions, over 200,000 Irish, Germans, and Englishmen, not to mention thousands of native Americans, voluntarily chose to settle in the slums of New York City between 1845 and 1860. What prompted them to settle there? For the most part, hope for a more prosperous future as well as escape from even worse conditions.

The bottom of the working scale was occupied by sweated women, overworked children, and day laborers. Long hours, low wages, and abominable working conditions belied a land of opportunity, but fresh recruits stepped off the ships every month.

Servants were the most numerous members of the unskilled workers. The boardinghouses, hotels, and mansions of the wealthy required large numbers of housekeepers, chambermaids, nurses, charwomen, laundresses, cooks, and waiters. In the 1840's servant girls in New York City averaged six dollars per month, in addition to board and lodging. The keen competition between Irish and Negroes for positions as servants and manual laborers broke out at times into fights and riots.

The needleworkers who sewed garments in their own homes were even worse off than the servants. Earnings were only a pittance, since contractors found plenty of workers at almost any wage. Immigrants and the wives of laborers and farmers were eager to make an extra penny. One observer estimated in 1867 that thirty thousand women in New York City worked a twelve- to fifteen-hour day for about thirty cents a day.

Much unskilled labor was needed in the city and on the farm. Laborers unloaded ships, boats, and carts, carried coal, ice, and bricks, took care of the horses and stables, and handled countless odd jobs. Around New York City and Buffalo, Germans and Scots worked as gardeners on the estates of the well-to-do and raised vegetables for the city markets. Dairy farmers needed men to take care of the cows and girls to churn butter. During the 1840's farm laborers averaged ten dollars a month in addition to board and room. Hired men, servant girls, and unskilled labor in general were driven mercilessly from before dawn to after dusk.

Sailors received upwards of twenty-five dollars a month, but after 1830 the harsh discipline deterred many natives from shipping out. Their places were filled by foreign sailors who found wages and food on American ships superior to those in other marines. Seamen often got into the clutches of "shipping masters" who advanced money at usurious rates. The masters would then force sailors to sign for voyages in order to pay off their indebtedness.

The skilled craftsmen—coopers, carpenters, masons, shipwrights, printers, plasterers, cabinetmakers, jewelers, bricklayers—had been the aristocrats of labor, but new developments were undercutting their economic position. The merchant capitalists were displacing the artisans as the center of power. They bought raw materials and sought to reduce labor costs by cutting wages and by hiring unskilled labor. The shoemakers and printers were the first to experience this threat to their craft. Capitalists subdivided the work and hired boys, apprentices, women, and children to perform the simpler operations. Craftsmen in the building trades also disliked the competition of immigrants, who weakened their bargaining power and broke down the apprenticeship system.

During the 1850's revolutionary changes were affecting the clothing and shoemaking industries because of the introduction of the sewing machine. Capitalists bought the machines and erected small factories, undercutting the independent craftsmen. Most shoes and clothing, however, were still made by cobblers and sweated seamstresses as late as 1860.

The textile workers of New York have attracted much less attention from historians than the workers in the more advanced cotton and wool manufacture of New England. In general, the first factory workers were women and children drawn from neighboring farms. By 1850 a permanent factory population, including many British immigrants, had grown up. In 1855 the male minority received an average of nineteen dollars a month; the women about nine dollars in cotton mills and almost twelve dollars in woolen factories.

The mixed attitude of alarm and condescension shown by the rising business leaders reflected the awakening of labor to its low condition. Discontent was widespread, but the labor movement was troubled by conflicting aims. The ablest leadership came from skilled workers, who demanded better pay and improved working conditions. Some intellectuals tried to capture the labor movement as a means of accomplishing a general reform of society, a goal which interested the rank and file very little.

In 1829 the workmen of New York City formed an organization to fight the plan of employers to lengthen the working day beyond ten hours. Their success in this undertaking led the leaders to put up a slate of workingmen in the fall election. Workers had many grievances, which they hoped could be corrected by legislation. Their children often grew up in ignorance because the Public School Society of New York City, which was a private association organized in 1826, was unable to provide adequate schooling. Furthermore, parents unable to pay the fees disliked the requirement that they must sign a pauper's oath if they wished their children to attend school. Worse still, workers sometimes were jailed for petty debts and were forced to turn out for militia service while the rich avoided it by paying a small fine. No law protected wages when employers went bankrupt, and the rise of chartered monopolies, especially in banking, disturbed the laboring man, who felt a new aristocracy of wealth was dominating the country and robbing the worker by the manipulation of currency.

The success of the Working Men's party in electing several of its candidates to office created a furor among the conservative classes of New York City. Editors branded it the "dirty-shirt party." One of its leaders, Fanny Wright, was delicately described as "the Red Harlot of Infidelity . . . madly and triumphantly stalking over the city." The usual difficulties of third parties troubled this organization. Factionalism emerged when the colorful but doctrinaire leaders insisted on having their own way. Thomas Skidmore, the first leader, tried to impose upon the movement his pet ideas of agrarianism. The average workingman was only mildly interested in Skidmore's proposals that every adult should receive a free grant of 160 acres and that no one should be allowed to own more than that amount of land. Late in 1829 Skidmore seceded from the party after his proposal for continued mass meetings was turned down in favor of party organization on the ward level.

Three English-born "free enquirers" took over control of the movement and stressed the need for the establishment of a national system of education. Robert Dale Owen, the son of the famous British reformer, urged that all children be placed in government boardinghouses and receive the same clothing and training. Fanny Wright, an attractive and statuesque brunette, advocated political and social equality for everyone, white or black, male or female. Her questioning of the divine inspiration of the Bible and her belief in greater sexual freedom made her the favorite target of outraged clergymen and news-hungry editors. George Henry Evans, who edited the official paper, the *Working Man's Advocate,* was a champion of free public education and later became the chief theorist of agrarian reform.

These educational ideas met resistance among conservatives and among ordinary workmen who wanted to bring up their own children. In 1830 the opponents of Owen and Wright got control of the party at the state convention in Salina and endorsed two Tammany men for governor and lieutenant governor. The labor vote in 1830 was split three ways and the Working Men's party disappeared.

This early labor party scored some gains despite its rapid collapse. It brought to public attention the grievances of the working classes and it stimulated the politicians of Tammany Hall to adopt some of its planks in order to keep the labor vote. Within a decade the legislature passed legislation ending imprisonment for debt and abolishing compulsory militia service. It also passed mechanics' lien laws to give the workers protection against defaulting employers. The movement for free public schools also received a great impetus.

Labor organizations led by the printers and shoemakers multiplied rapidly in the boom years between 1830 and 1837. By 1833 there were at least fifteen organized trades in New York City and a central body called the Trades' Union. The tailors and other unions won important gains over the stiff opposition by employers, who turned to the courts for protection. In 1835 shoemakers in Geneva refused to work for any master who did not observe union rules, including the closed shop. Their employer hauled them into court for criminal conspiracy. Chief Justice Savage ruled, "It is important to the best interests of society that the price of labor be left to regulate itself. . . . Competition is the life of trade." This decision was cited as precedent for a ruling against tailors in New York City the following year. Over twenty-five thousand workers met to protest the sentence imposed upon the tailors.

A convention of mechanics, farmers, and workingmen opened in Utica on September 15, 1836, to protest the court decisions and to form an Equal Rights party. The new party prevented Tammany from winning control of the congressional and legislative delegations in the fall elections. The labor leaders were opposed to the conservative wing of the Democratic party, which had granted many banking monopolies.

The Panic of 1837 threw thousands out of work and brought dire poverty to many families. Within a year it was estimated that approximately one-third of the working class were jobless. The infant trade unions could not keep alive and their newspapers disappeared. In February 1837 a crowd of unemployed workers stormed the Manhattan store of Eli Hart and Company, which was accused of hoarding flour in order to push the price upward.

The decade of the 1840's was a "hungry" time for the working classes of New York. Unemployment was widespread and the wave of immigration after 1845 swelled the ranks of the jobseekers. In the search for jobs various elements clashed: Negroes versus Irish; natives versus foreign born; skilled craftsmen versus unskilled. The artisan looked with dismay upon the growing use of machinery, whose "occult power" threatened not only their skills but in some cases their jobs as well. These years of turmoil undermined labor solidarity and destroyed union organizations.

Intellectuals on the fringes of the labor movement tried to interest the workingmen in various panaceas: land reform, associationism, and co-operatives. The utopian reformers differed violently among themselves but they did agree that labor unions were largely a waste of time. They urged the abolition of capitalism and the inauguration of a new social order in which there would be universal freedom, peace, and prosperity.

Of the utopian proposals, the agitation for land reform probably had the most lasting influence upon the labor movement. Its champion was George Henry Evans, who declared that land monopoly was the main obstacle preventing mankind from achieving the republican equality envisioned by the Declaration of Independence. The degradation of the working class could be avoided only if a homestead law gave every citizen his rightful heritage—a portion of the public domain. The opportunity to secure a farm would prevent a labor surplus in the eastern cities and thus check exploitation by employers. In fact, factories would wither away, since farmer-artisans would exchange commodities.

Evans showed much ingenuity in spreading his ideas to the public. He formed the National Reform Association, which held public meetings; he published *Young America;* and Horace Greeley opened the columns of the *Tribune* to articles on land reform. In 1845 Evans wrote a famous circular entitled "Vote Yourself a Farm." The land reformers seized upon the antirent war in the Hudson Valley as an argument for their cause. They attempted to capture control of the antirent organizations, but the farmers disliked the doctrinaire attitude of the land reformers and ousted them from their movement.

The crusade for land reform made many converts upstate. Strangely enough, Gerrit Smith, the greatest landholder in New York, swung over to National Reform. Not only did he urge the adoption of a homestead bill in Congress, but he also gave away thousands of parcels of land in northern New York to Negroes and poor whites. Unfortunately most of the recipients were unable to make a living on the forested slopes of the Adirondacks.

The weight of evidence indicates that cheap land in the West did not operate directly as a "safety-valve" for discontented labor in New York and other eastern cities. Although hundreds of thousands of New Yorkers moved to western states, relatively few wage earners and artisans in New York's cities became farmers in the West. The odds were formidable. Few workingmen could save enough money to buy land, machinery, and stock or knew how to open up a new tract or to cultivate an old farm. Western towns and cities were probably a greater "safety-valve" for labor than were western farms. Almost 70 per cent of those listed in the Rochester directory of 1827 had moved on before the listing of 1834. Presumably most of this floating population moved to western cities.

Associationism was the theory of production developed by Charles Fourier of France. Albert Brisbane read Fourier's writings and became his leading American disciple. Horace Greeley also became a convert, and the *Tribune* carried many articles by Brisbane explaining and promoting the theories of Fourier. According to this theory, society should be organized in "groups" living together as both partners and stockholders of a co-operative community. Several phalanxes were set up in New York State, but they failed in short order. Scarcity of capital and difficulties of apportioning control between stockholders and working members were the major causes of their collapse.

Producers' and consumers' co-operatives won considerable support among workingmen, particularly among those of German background. In New York City, the coopers, cabinetmakers, and tailors organized co-operative shops. The consumer co-operatives tried to reduce the cost of living by eliminating the middleman. Both types of co-operatives waned. They lacked capital, experienced leadership, and, particularly, a stable membership. In general, native workmen preferred direct action through strikes than slow gains through organizing co-operatives.

The discovery of gold in California created a boom marked by rising prices and the revival of unionism. Carpenters, bakers, shoemakers, bricklayers, and plasterers in New York City organized and won higher wages. In Rochester the blacksmiths, tin-plate makers, machinists, iron-workers, carpenters, printers, and even seamstresses formed unions by 1853 and secured substantial wage increases.

The unions of the 1850's were craft unions, which excluded unskilled workers and sought to protect their position by apprenticeship rules and initiation fees. They also tried to apply the principle of collective bargaining to the whole trade. The tailors and printers of New York City drew up a fair wage schedule and invited employers to sign agreements maintaining the rate. The printers were the first to set up a strong national union to regulate the scale of wages in different localities.

The depression of 1854–1855 and the Panic of 1857 again shattered most unions. Unemployment brought acute distress, and in the fall of 1857 thousands of workers met in Tompkins Square in New York City to demand work. Several unions reorganized in 1859 but received another jolt at the outbreak of the Civil War.

The working class, on the whole, remained remarkably conservative throughout this period. During the 1850's Marxian socialism made a bridgehead in the German settlements. John Weydemeyer in 1853 founded the *Amerikanischer Arbeiterbund* in New York City. To attract trade union support the *Arbeiterbund* called for the ten-hour day, the abolition of child labor, free higher education for all, and no temperance legislation. But enthusiasm waned, since German workmen, like native Americans, preferred simple unionism to ideological crusades.

Comparisons between the level of living of the "typical" workingman of New York a century ago and today are perhaps fruitless since such revolutionary changes have taken place in the entire social structure as well as in the amount and quality of goods consumed. Moreover, data on annual incomes for this period are fragmentary. Lack of accurate information on unemployment makes any estimate of total earnings pure guesswork. One estimated budget for a New York City worker's family of four in 1853 (Table 5) assumed an income of twelve dollars a week. Yet common laborers in that city seldom made more than six dollars, and only a few artisans reached twelve dollars. At the bottom of the scale the woman needleworkers often received under one dollar a week.

Food accounted for almost half of the expenditures of a workingman. Another fourth went for shelter and most of the rest for clothing. The workingmen and their families found whatever recreation they had in their homes or in the streets. In general, the workingmen had better food and clothing but poorer housing in 1860 than in 1825. Their children also had somewhat better educational opportunities. Low though the standards were, the American workingmen at this time had more food, better housing, and better clothing than their European counterparts.

The laboring class felt progressively less secure despite the slight increase in their real earnings. This was especially true among the skilled craftsmen, who had lost bargaining power and status over the decades because of heavy immigration and the introduction of machinery. The repeated financial crises and depressions brought more distress to the completely urbanized workingmen than to semirural artisans of an earlier day, who often grew a portion of their own food.

Businessmen and journalists took pride in the booming cities of the Empire State. They pointed to the doubling of population every two decades, the elegant mansions of the merchants, the new factories, and the large number of houses and stores being built. What they ignored were the noisome slums, dirty streets, and the failure of city administrations to provide adequate water, police, and fire protection.

Table 5. Standard workingman's budget, New York City, 1853.

Groceries	$273.00
Rent	100.00
Clothing, bedding, etc.	132.00
Furnishings	20.00
Fuel	18.00
Lights	10.00
Taxes, water, commutation	5.00
Physicians' and druggists' charges	10.00
Traveling	12.00
Newspapers, postage, library fees	10.00
	590.00
Church, charity, etc.	10.00
Total annual expenditures	$600.00

Source: New York *Times*, Nov. 8, 1853. The expenditures are for a family of four, "living moderately" (cited by Edgar W. Martin, *The Standard of Living in 1860* [Chicago, 1942], p. 395).

The city dwellers faced hazards fully as formidable as those met by pioneers in the Genesee Valley. Their main enemies were poor housing, disease, crime, dangerous work, or no work at all.

New York City had greater difficulty than upstate cities in providing shelter, since business enterprises and population on Manhattan could expand in only one direction. At the beginning of this period the merchants lived in comfortable residences close to the business district at the lower tip of Manhattan. Gradually as the business district pushed up Broadway the well-to-do built new mansions farther north. Brick and stone were preferred to wood because fire was a constant threat.

Many of the new houses built in the decade before the Civil War were "colony houses," with a frontage of only twenty feet. A hall and an office occupied the first floor, three connecting rooms with sliding doors the second floor. An attic story was sometimes hidden behind the French "mansard" roof. Upstate, some Georgian features, such as dormer windows and red-brick construction, lingered on, but the white porticoes fronting or surrounding the house were by far the most popular and distinctive features.

The houses of the wealthy in New York City frequently touched one another because land was expensive. They were nearly uniform in appearance, with iron railings, marble facing, plate-glass windows, and silver plates at the door. The interior arrangements were also much alike: the drawing room, library, and dining room on the principal floor, the bedrooms and nursery upstairs. They were heated with coal and lighted with gas or oil lamps. Few had hot and cold running water, water closets, or baths. New York City in 1855 had only 1,361 baths and 10,384 water closets, and Albany had only 19 baths.

More numerous but less conspicuous than the mansions of the rich were the homes of the small businessmen, professional people, and well-to-do farmers. Usually these were wooden houses with a parlor or sitting room, a kitchen, and bedrooms enough so that there was a spare room for guests. Wood stoves were used for heating and oil lamps were gradually replacing candles. The family usually gathered in the sitting room, which also served as dining room. A rag carpet covered the soft pine floor, and mottoes, steel and wood engravings decorated the walls.

The housing problem, particularly for the working class, grew constantly more acute because population growth exceeded the rate of construction. Density of population per acre and average block density in New York City rose steadily from 1825 to 1850. Clerks and laborers erected shanties on the outskirts of town. Speculators built cheap tenements and packed as many people as possible in each building. The tenement houses were usually double buildings with two suites on each floor of the front part. An alley led to the rear house with a similar arrangement. Hallways, stairs, and bedrooms were dark. One tenement housed 146 families with an average of six persons to a single ten-by-twelve room. Agents also cut old mansions that had been abandoned by the merchants into dozens of small apartments, filling them from cellar to garret. In 1850 some twenty-nine thousand persons were living in cellars without light, ventilation, or heat.

Rents were high, although the tenants got little more than a roof over their heads. The usual rate for a living room and dark bedroom was six dollars a month. Tenants had to carry water from outside wells and seldom had indoor toilet facilities. Certain neighborhoods became notorious for their crime. The Five Points off Broadway near Worth Street was internationally famous. Charles Dickens visited the region and described the buildings known as the "Den of Thieves," the "Old Brewery," and "Murderer's Alley." Upstate cities also had their rookeries in the center of town and two-room shanties on the outskirts.

Streets, sidewalks, and sewers were neglected. Only a few thoroughfares were paved, usually with macadam, gravel, or wooden blocks. Streets were the dumping place for trash and garbage as well as the manure of horses and cattle on their way to the slaughterhouses. Ordinances called upon each property owner to clean his section of the street, but the hordes of pigs proved more conscientious. Sewers were luxuries afforded by the cities in only a few places, and heavy rains frequently flooded cellars. New York City had a few gas lamps for street lighting by 1830, and Rochester had sixty gas lamps in 1843. Gas lamps, however, were the exception. Late travelers had to rely upon the fitful light from the few oil lamps.

The average resident of the cities walked to work. The rich owned their own carriages, but families with moderate incomes rented carriages from the livery stables for special occasions. Horsecars became common in the larger cities during the 1850's. By 1858 the five main lines on Manhattan were carrying nearly 35,000,000 passengers annually, and promoters wheedled and bribed the Common Council to grant more franchises. Omnibuses with a capacity of a dozen or so passengers served other streets. Hackney drivers charged such exorbitant rates that few could afford to patronize them. In 1860 the streets of New York were already famous for their congestion.

The outbreaks of fires were the most urgent concern of city dwellers. The damage caused each year was heavy, not counting the thousands of dollars paid for premiums on fire insurance. Practically every city experienced one or more disastrous conflagrations which left thousands homeless. For example, in 1835 thirteen acres of buildings around Hanover Square in New York City were gutted. Despite their losses, businessmen reconstructed the devastated areas within a short time.

The city governments provided a certain amount of loose supervision over the volunteer fire companies. The New York Fire Department had a Board of Fire Wardens and a chief engineer. But its 3,700 firemen were volunteers, and the department's funds came from donations, festi-

vals, concerts, fines, and other sources. The firefighters, sporting red
flannel shirts and broad leather belts, were unable to do much more
than prevent the spread of the flames to neighboring buildings. All too
often members of rival companies fought each other for possession of
wells and hydrants, pocketed valuables in burning buildings, and drank
up large amounts of whisky.

Most property owners preferred to risk fire rather than to pay taxes
for a public water system. The increase in population, however, required
additional supplies of fresh water. Finally in 1835 New Yorkers voted to
bring the water of the Croton River to Manhattan, and seven years later
torchlight parades and banquets celebrated the completion of the Croton
dam and aqueduct. The taxpayers of Rochester, however, persuaded the
Common Council to put off construction of a municipal waterworks
until after the Civil War.

The lives and property of city dwellers did not receive adequate
police protection. There was little discipline, and no uniformed force
existed before 1845. New York City had two elected policemen in each
ward plus a group of marshals appointed by the mayor, and at night a
"watch" of citizens patrolled the streets. In 1844 the state legislature
authorized the organization of a regularly paid police force on a twenty-
four-hour basis. The mayor appointed the chief of police and subordinate officers with the advice of the aldermen, until the revised city
charter of 1853 created a Board of Commissioners to appoint officers.
The same year the commissioners finally compelled the policemen to
wear official uniforms consisting of a blue cap, a blue coat with swallow-
tail and brass buttons, and gray pantaloons. These uniforms gave the
policemen more authority and also made it more difficult for them to
slink away in the event of trouble.

Politics and corruption were to mar the administration of the police
force from the outset. Charges that the police were the tools of Tammany Hall and the Democratic politicians caused the Republican majority in the state legislature to create its own police force for the city.
Mayor Fernando Wood resisted this invasion of home rule, and his
forces gave the officers under the state board a good pummeling in
1857. For a time, the two police forces spent more time challenging
each other than in tracking down criminals. State authority, however,
was vindicated by the Court of Appeals.

Drunkenness was the most common cause of arrest, followed by petty
thievery and prostitution. The young unmarried immigrants who frequented the barrooms got carried away with argument and sometimes
engaged in fights and riots. Police found it safer and more profitable
to pick up drunkards than to interfere with gambling dens and houses
of prostitution which enjoyed their "protection."

Native Americans pointed with scorn to the apparently high rate of crime, vice, and pauperism among the foreign born. The difference between native and foreign born was not so great when similar age groups are compared. No doubt the slum environment and the inadequate police force accounted in part for the high incidence of crime. Furthermore, many children grew up without family or religious guidance because of the death, illness, or absence of parents.

Illness and premature death struck hard at city dwellers and farm families alike. Children in particular suffered severely. In 1857 two-thirds of the registered deaths in New York City were for children under the age of five. Epidemics of typhoid, typhus, and cholera created panic among the slum dwellers, but they accepted more resignedly the ravages of tuberculosis, the most deadly killer of urban and rural population.

The number of doctors in New York City—roughly one for each 576 persons in 1855—was adequate, but their training and knowledge was deficient. A minority had attended medical college for a year or two and absorbed some information from lectures. The rest observed the techniques of older physicians before hanging out their shingles at the age of nineteen or twenty. These doctors were grossly ignorant of the causes and remedies of disease. The important exceptions among the major diseases were smallpox and malaria, controllable by vaccination and quinine, respectively. In general, the average physician relied upon bloodletting, cathartics, and emetics.

Most sick people did not consult doctors, relying instead upon nature and family remedies. When these measures failed to restore health, they turned to the patent medicines advertised in every paper. There were pills with impressive titles, glowing testimonials, and miraculous powers. A typical product was Tarrant's Cordial Elixir of Turkey Rhubarb, which, so it was claimed, cured indigestion. Frequently these panaceas contained enough alcohol to induce a temporary feeling of well-being.

The ailing public welcomed new therapeutic systems such as the present generation hails the "wonder-drugs." During the 1830's the exponents of the Botanic System evolved by Samuel Thomson prescribed herbs in place of the standard remedies of bloodletting and calomel. During the 1840's the science of homeopathy swept New York State, making thousands of converts. This system claimed that patients should be given drugs which produced effects on a healthy person similar to the symptoms of the disease treated. With the discovery of anaesthetics, surgery took a major step forward in comparison with other branches of medicine. Surgeons were enabled to make hitherto impossible abdominal operations, but, since infection usually set in, few patients lived to boast of their operations.

Parks were seldom considered a municipal function before 1850, and urban congestion was not a serious matter except in New York City. Typically, the street plan for Manhattan of 1811 did not include any open spaces. As congestion increased, the demand for parks grew. In 1851 Mayor Ambrose Kingsland recommended to the Common Council the purchase of a tract on the East River, but business groups objected because of the cost and the blocking of river frontage. In 1853, the legislature authorized the Common Council to open a park between Fifth and Eighth Avenues and running from 59th to 106th Street. Six years later the park was extended to 110th Street. Politicians got hold of the project, which offered considerable opportunities for contracts and patronage, but the legislature took control from the city commission in 1857 and provided for an eleven-man board appointed by state officials. On the new board of commissioners was Andrew Green who was to become the greatest public servant in New York City during the last half of the nineteenth century.

In many respects the cities of New York before 1860 were hardly more than overgrown towns. In fact, most adult residents had come from farms and villages in New York and in Europe. Silently but rapidly the cities created urban manners and institutions as society became more complex and more impersonal. Men found it necessary to live long distances from their work. People took less interest in the affairs of their next-door neighbors.

Cities made some progress toward accepting social responsibility, but acted only under extreme pressure. Fire and police protection improved, more children attended schools each year, and some advances took place in street lighting, water systems, and sewers. These strictures of urban life might leave the impression that residents were entirely insensitive to distress. Such was not the case, as the rise of various humanitarian and philanthropic organizations bears ample proof (see Chapter 24 as well). Perhaps the comments of Anthony Trollope, a visitor from the most urbanized country of the era, suggest that New Yorkers were becoming alive to their social responsibilities:

Perhaps . . . in no city has more been achieved for humanity by the munificence of its richest citizens than in New York. Its hospitals, asylums, and institutions for the relief of all ailments to which flesh is heir, are very numerous, and beyond praise in the excellence of their arrangements.

Religion and Reform

I have got beyond Temperance to the Cold Water Society—
no Tea, Coffee or any other slops—only pure Water to drink
and coarse fare to eat.—JOSIAH BISSELL, *1830*

THE religious history cf New York between 1825 and 1860 is one of
the most fascinating chapters in the history of Christian expansion.
Seldom have so many religious talents been at work in such a short
period of time. The roll call contains impressive names such as Charles
Finney and eccentric figures such as John Humphrey Noyes. An outstanding development was the growth of Roman Catholicism to the point
where its communicants were more numerous than those of any single
Protestant denomination. Although Protestantism splintered into a bewildering number of sects, it remained the dominant religious force.
New York, in fact, was the nerve center of the movement called by Dr.
Dixon Ryan Fox the "Protestant Counter-Reformation" (1800–1850),
which not only sponsored extensive missionary campaigns on the frontier but also re-established the hold of orthodoxy upon the major denominations.

The people of New York were definitely more religious minded in
1860 than in 1825, whether regarded from the standpoint of numbers
or intensity of belief. Evangelical Christianity routed deism and "free-
thinking"—so common before 1800—enrolled an increasing percentage
of people within the state, and also provided hundreds of missionaries
for the Pacific Northwest and Asia.

A basic core of belief lay beneath the surface disagreements of
Protestantism. Practically all churches agreed that the Bible was divinely
inspired and was therefore the final authority on all matters of faith.
Christians of almost every variety held that the moral law undergirded
the universe, which was God's own handiwork. Most Protestants believed
that a better world was coming. Those more secular in thinking sub-
scribed to the theory of inevitable progress; those who believed in the

literal validity of the Bible expected that Christ would soon come again. All expected improvements in society since morally responsible individuals would perform good works to help establish the Kingdom of God on earth.

All churches, with the exception of the Roman Catholic, the Protestant Episcopal, and the Unitarian, considered conversion a more or less dramatic transformation of the individual from a state of sin to a state of grace. To stimulate this conversion most Protestant churches relied upon revival meetings at which preachers invoked divine guidance and called on men to repent. Perhaps the somewhat unfriendly comments of George Templeton Strong of New York City in 1858 will explain the impact of revivals upon the population:

One should think and speak cautiously of any thing which so many good men receive as a special manifestation of the Holy Spirit, but I confess that this movement does not commend itself to me. It is becoming daily more and more heated and morbid. Irreverence, presumption, indecency, and other symptoms of a mere epidemic religious fever multiply as the revival develops. . . . The great object of the meeting seems to be to drug men up to a certain point of nervous excitement and keep them there. Was told today on good authority of an incredible hymn said to be popular among "revived" Methodists, of which this is one verse:

> Ye Saints rejoice, give cheerful thanks,
> For Awful Gardner's joined your ranks.
> And, while the lamp holds out to burn,
> There still is hope for Patrick Hearne.

Why was upstate New York so receptive to religious appeals? First of all, the population, largely Yankee in origin, was greatly influenced by the religious movements in New England. The Second Great Awakening in Connecticut, beginning late in the 1790's and continuing for several decades, was carried to New York by settlers and by missionaries sent out by benevolent societies. As a result, revivalism had appeared in New York long before 1825. Secondly, the gradual shift to commercial agriculture enabled the children of the pioneers to have more leisure for education and religion. Thirdly, leaders of great power and religious intensity emerged to direct the movement.

Charles Grandison Finney was the outstanding religious figure of this period. Born in a Connecticut manse, he grew up on the frontier of central New York. At first he turned to the law, but the inner spirit called the handsome orator to the ministry. He attracted national attention in 1825 by leading a revival at Western, a small town near Rome. The excitement spread to Rome, Utica, and throughout Oneida County. People in other sections beseeched Finney to visit their churches and set sinners free. In 1830 Finney moved to Rochester and conducted one of the most significant revivals in American history. More important than the thousands of converts were the deepening of the faith of older members and the training of hundreds of lesser leaders.

The evangelist moved to New York City in 1832, answering the call of the Tappan brothers, two silk merchants who used their wealth to promote benevolent societies. Finney failed to stir the metropolis as deeply as he had the upstate regions. His preaching led to the formation of several "free churches," which charged no rent for the pews. His articles appearing in the New York *Evangelist* spread his views across the country.

Finney was not an original thinker in theological matters; rather he reflected changes already cracking the iron front of orthodox Calvinism. He neatly bridged the old doctrinal debate over the relative merits of faith and works by stating, "Genuine faith always results in good works and is itself a good work." A sinner, therefore, could not by his own will cast out sin. For Finney and his followers, the regeneration of the individual led to the reformation of society.

Finney was more original in devising new methods of conducting his revivals. He adopted a direct, extemporaneous style of preaching. Harsh invective would burst out at times: "Oh God smite that wicked man. . . . God Almighty, shake him over Hell." He prayed for sinners by name, encouraging them to come forward to the "anxious seat," where the congregation might watch their soul searchings. Finney was a skillful leader and seldom permitted the meetings to get out of control. But scores of less skillful evangelists followed his methods and actually encouraged groaning, shouting, and other sensational excesses.

The conservative clergy opposed the "new methods," pointing with outraged finger to the emotional excesses, to the un-Christian invective, to the dangerous practice of allowing women to participate in public and private meetings, and to the charlatans who disgraced the cause of religion. Even more serious was the belief that some evangelists spread heresy and caused divisions within local churches and denominations.

Revivalism reached its peak in the early 1830's, although stirring revivals later swept the churches in 1843 and 1857. There were several reasons for the gradual decline of the revival in New York. The Irish and German immigrants showed little interest. As denominational loyalties grew stronger, churches relied more on settled clergymen rather than on itinerant evangelists, and the excesses of some revivalists disturbed the average church member. Many of the followers of Finney in the 1840's and 1850's drifted away from purely religious activities and threw themselves into abolition and temperance movements.

Probably the comment of William Reed about the revivalists is as sane and reasonable as we shall find: "They set the whole community in commotion, disturbed old sinners, rubbed the ears of lazy Christians and probably did some good, if not so much in converting sinners as in setting people to thinking."

Diversity was another American religious characteristic amply demonstrated in New York. The Empire State had the most cosmopolitan population in the country. As a result, a great variety of sects deriving from European sources was to be found among the inhabitants, who introduced and maintained churches with which they were familiar. To add to the complexity, New York was the birthplace of several new sects.

New York remained overwhelmingly Protestant in this period, although Roman Catholicism was making great gains, especially in New York City. The first religious census, in 1855, showed that Roman Catholics numbered 242,225 out of a total population of 3,466,212. The various Protestant denominations claimed only 457,971 members, but the majority of those not belonging to any church were Protestant in background.

The Methodists (140,196) and the Baptists (89,713) were the most aggressive of the major Protestant sects in seeking converts in the city and countryside. Both relied in the main upon uneducated clergy and laymen to spread their doctrines, which emphasized the importance of the individual's own efforts to win salvation.

The Presbyterians (92,712) and Congregationalists (25,946) stressed a trained clergy and doubted man's ability to free himself from sin. They opposed emotionalism even though the greatest revival of the period was set in motion by a Presbyterian, Charles Finney. Earlier in the century the two denominations had co-operated in setting up frontier churches and in supporting interdenominational agencies, but the Congregationalists began to show more denominational feeling, and they dropped out of the Plan of Union which had operated so largely to the advantage of the Presbyterians. In 1834 they organized a state association in New York, and in 1852 the first meeting of American Congregationalism was held in Albany.

Presbyterianism suffered a disastrous division in 1837. The members coming from New England found themselves at odds with the stern orthodox Calvinists of Scotch-Irish descent in Pennsylvania and the southern states. Having been reared in the Congregational church, they naturally favored congregational autonomy, and their views reflected the New England trend toward a more liberal theology. Their leaders shocked the conservatives because they damned slavery more vigorously than they warned of eternal damnation. An alliance of Presbyterians of the South, who were affronted at the charge that slaveholding was a sin, and of the Old School Presbyterians in Philadelphia and Princeton, who feared the spread of heresy, excised the presbyteries of Utica, Geneva, and Genesee as well as Western Reserve in Ohio. When the New School group organized a separate church, most of the membership within New York joined this new denomination. In 1850 it claimed 69,000 members in the state as compared with 23,000 members of the Old School.

The Protestant Episcopal church continued the gains begun before 1825 under the energetic leadership of Bishop Hobart. Its membership rose from 6,700 communicants in 1832 to 33,000 in 1859. Several factors favored the growth of this church: able leadership, the removal of the Tory taint, the stimulus provided by the High Church movement, the dignity and beauty of the service, and its appeal to fashionable and wealthy persons.

The Dutch Reformed church was centered largely in New York City. Its members and the Episcopalians claimed most of the families of wealth and position descended from the pre-Revolutionary population. Since most of the first generation of "new" families making their money in trade and manufacturing came from New England, they usually belonged to the Presbyterian-Congregational group.

Various German denominations, particularly the Evangelical Lutheran, expanded with the influx of Germans to this country after 1840. Large numbers of Germans settled in New York City, Rochester, and Buffalo.

Over 80 per cent of the Protestants belonged to these seven largest bodies. Other nationality and racial groups, such as the Welsh, French, and Negro, established denominations to which they had previously belonged. Among the smaller sects were the Free Will Baptists, Universalists, Unitarians, United Presbyterians (formed in 1858), Christians, and Friends.

A torrent of Irish and German immigration made the Roman Catholic church by mid-century the largest religious group in New York State. Most Catholics lived in cities, particularly the metropolis of New York, which had approximately 100,000 Catholics in 1850. In addition to the Irish and Germans, there were thousands of French, Italian, Swiss, and Spanish-speaking members. The Catholic clergy showed great ability in keeping most immigrant groups loyal to the church.

Catholic leaders faced many difficulties in ministering to their rapidly growing membership. Nevertheless, the number of congregations grew steadily, despite the lack of funds to construct church buildings, not to mention schools and orphanages. The poverty of many of its members, the hostility of some Protestants, the shortage of clergymen, the resentment by German and French Catholics of Irish domination, and the fight over state aid to education were some of the more troublesome problems facing the Catholic church.

Bishop John Hughes (1838–1864) was the most forceful and dynamic leader of Roman Catholicism in this period. Equally vigorous in disciplining lay trustees, in hitting back at nativists, and in setting up new churches, Hughes was particularly determined to reassert the traditional powers of the priesthood and bishops in church government. After several controversies, especially with German congregations, Hughes asserted his authority. The legislature in 1863 agreed to pass a church incorporation law ensuring control by the clergy. The law provided that a church corporation for the Catholic communion was to consist of the bishop, the vicar general, the pastor, and two lay trustees.

The common school system of New York City was not acceptable to Bishop Hughes for several reasons. The Public School Society, administering the schools for the city, was dominated by private directors of pronounced Protestant views. Furthermore, many teachers and textbooks were unsympathetic to the Catholic church, and the daily readings from the King James Version of the Bible were anathema to good Catholics. Church leaders organized a parochial school system in which Catholic doctrine as well as secular subjects were taught. But the shortage of buildings and trained teachers prevented the church schools from taking care of all the children of Catholic parentage. In 1840 Governor William Seward recommended that schools be established in which foreigners "may be instructed by teachers speaking the same language with themselves and professing the same faith." Catholic citizens of New York City immediately petitioned the Common Council for a share of the public school money. This action irritated the Public School Society and its backers, and in 1841 Samuel F. B. Morse ran for mayor on a Native American ticket. Bishop Hughes countered with the organization of a third party, called the Carroll Hall ticket, which held the balance of power in 1842. A new law of that year compromised the issue: the church schools received no public money, but the Public School Society made way for the publicly managed school system in New York City.

Nativism continued to harass the Catholic church throughout this period. The workingmen's fear of immigrant competition was the most important factor, but pauperism among immigrants and the political power exercised by the church in city elections were also influential in stimulating native Americans to organize secret societies, such as the Know-Nothings of the 1850's.

The Jewish synagogue, like the Catholic church, was a unifying force for its people. For most Jews life revolved around the congregation, which administered dietary laws, directed charitable and educational activities, and conducted the ceremonies associated with birth, marriage, and death. The Jewish community, centering in its one synagogue of 1825, gradually split up into several congregations, each ministering to Jews of differing backgrounds. It has been estimated that in 1860 New York City had twenty-seven synagogues.

The strange enthusiasms and peculiar cults of upstate New York have fascinated succeeding generations, but their importance has been greatly exaggerated. For example, Oneida Community and the Mormon church enrolled only a few hundred people within this state. One must repeat that these unusual movements do not compare in importance with the less spectacular but far more significant work carried on by the major denominations in organizing and maintaining churches for frontier farmers and city dwellers.

The Church of the Latter-Day Saints (Mormons) was the most important new sect originating in New York, but its later development took place almost entirely outside the state's borders. Joseph Smith professed that the angel Moroni appeared to him in Palmyra and told him that the Golden Plates of a new Bible lay buried near by. After digging up the plates, Smith (behind a curtain) dictated the Book of Mormon, which purported to describe the history of America from its settlement by one of the tribes dispersed at the Tower of Babel. Smith's miracles, prophecies, and revelations impressed a few neighbors, but most remained skeptical. A series of lawsuits and other troubles, combined with the attractions of the West, caused Smith to move, in 1831, to Kirtland, Ohio. Subsequently the Mormons moved to Illinois and Missouri and finally to Utah. In the 1840's and 1850's Mormon missionaries toured western New York and recruited several hundred candidates to live in the Desert Zion. The Mormon church, however, never took firm root in New York.

Another station along the broad "psychic highway" across central and western New York was Oneida Community, world famous for its experiments in communal living. Its success is wrapped up in the figure of John Humphrey Noyes, a genius at organization and leadership, who guided the community for several decades. He stated:

Our warfare is an assertion of human rights: first the right of man to be governed by God and to live in the social state of heaven; second the right of woman to dispose of her sexual nature by attraction instead of by law and routine and to bear children only when she chooses; third, the right of all to diminish the labors and increase the advantages of life by association.

Certainly these ideas were radical for his, or any, generation!

"Perfectionism" had won adherents in villages in central New York during the early 1840's. Its believers preached that true Christians could live without sin. In 1848 Noyes came to Oneida in central New York from Putney, Vermont, where his "Bible School" had shocked the neighbors by sharing everything in common, including the women.

Oneida Community was unique among "communitarian" communities within New York because it was an economic success and because it lasted for almost four decades. Fortunately for the group, Sewall New-house's trap for small animals provided the community with a steady income to supplement what they earned from farming. Outsiders were shocked by the system of "complex marriage" in which every woman was theoretically the wife of every man. Less controversial was the care of the children in the community nursery. The perfectionists at Oneida adopted other advanced ideas. Women were granted equality, wore bloomers, and bobbed their hair. As criticism mounted, the leaders of Oneida Community gradually abandoned their unusual practices. They permitted individual marriage and in 1879 divided the property among the members of the community.

The doctrine that Christ will return to the world to usher in the millennium has attracted Christian enthusiasts ever since the first century. In the 1830's and 1840's several thousand New Yorkers, as well as others in the northeastern part of the United States, adopted the views of William Miller, who preached that the world would come to an end in 1843 or 1844. After service in the War of 1812, Miller returned to his home in Washington County determined to prove that the Bible was pure revelation. He was a sincere, humble man, convinced that the symbols in the book of Revelations indicated that the world would come to an end about 1843. At first, few people were interested, although many Christians had a vague belief in the imminence of the Second Coming. Gradually Miller attracted more followers by his lectures and writings. As the date approached excitement grew. Thousands came to the tent meetings held in Rochester in 1843. Miller enjoyed a great triumph when Elon Galusha, the most prominent Baptist in the state, endorsed his conclusions.

As March 21, 1843 approached, the Millerites gathered together in protracted meetings to hail the millennium. Some neurotic individuals attached themselves to the movement and displayed hysterical behavior. Although nonbelievers have perpetuated a good deal of folklore about scandalous orgies, ascension robes, gatherings on hilltops, abandonment of business, and insanity in connection with the movement, the opponents of Miller showed the worst behavior by their attacks on Adventist meetings. Some followers slipped away after the fateful day passed without any cataclysm, but most of them accepted Miller's revised date of 1844. The stubborn continuation of the world after March 1844 naturally caused numerous defections, but the more resolute continued to hold on to their faith with some modifications. They decided to live as though the "Bridegroom" were coming at any moment. In 1845 Miller and his associates formed in Albany, an Adventist organization which later suffered from much internal strife. Another group of Adventists in western New York made a loose tie-up with the Seventh-Day Baptists of Maine and followed the westward-moving pioneers to the Middle West.

The rise of spiritualism provided the main religious excitement of the
1850's, as Millerism had in the 1840's. The latter had appealed to the orthodox, but spiritualism tended to attract religious liberals, such as the
Universalists. The liberals had drifted far from a literal interpretation of
the Bible and had seized upon scientific theories as the most fruitful explanation of the universe. Strangely enough, the mystical ideas in the
highly abstruse writings of the Swedish philosopher, Emanuel Swedenborg, furnished the basis for a revival as emotional as earlier manifesta-
tions.

Swedenborgianism combined many of the liberal religious doctrines
with the new sociological ideas of the time. By 1848 these concepts had
deeply penetrated the thinking of the Universalists and some of the Quakers. But until the Fox sisters allegedly made communication with the dead
it was too highly intellectual to appeal to the public at large. In March
1848 the two daughters of John Fox of Hydesville reported strange rap-
pings at night. More remarkable was their claim that they had communicated with a spirit who had answered their questions. The news of
this phenomenon spread rapidly after the two girls were introduced to
Rochester society. The spirits demanded public séances, and thousands
of people were convinced that the barrier between the quick and the dead
had been breached. Soon crowds were witnessing such phenomena as
table moving and the "speaking in tongues." Subsequently the Fox sisters admitted that they made the rapping sound by cracking the joints
of their toes, but the spiritualists claimed that the recantation had been
made under duress.

Spiritualism won many converts even among educated classes. William
Cullen Bryant, Horace Greeley, and Robert Dale Owen were inclined to
believe the phenomena of presentiments, second sight, and dreams. Intellectuals trained in the Swedenborg tradition received messages from
the great men of the past. These usually turned out to be platitudinous
homilies upon the necessity of following the rules of common sense. For
these people spiritualism was a way station to so-called free thought or
"modernism" in religion. The common people, however, looked for a direct
message from loved ones no longer on earth, and to fill this need there
sprang up a tribe of mediums, some of them obvious frauds and charlatans. Some spiritualist leaders encouraged experiments in unconventional
sex practices and as a result public opinion turned against them.

By 1855 the spiritualists claimed over a million converts throughout the
world, with perhaps a third of them in New York State. They published
over a score of magazines and had established centers in several parts of
the state. One legacy of the spiritualist movement is Lily Dale, a camp
meeting ground on the shores of Cassadaga Lakes.

The "burned-over district," a term applied to the region of central and western New York where habitual revivalism occurred, gradually lost its distinctive character as a spawning ground for religious aberrations. Several factors tended to diminish interest in religious extremism. The public and many reformers became intensely interested in political issues, especially the question of slavery. Neither the Catholic Irish nor the Germans showed much interest in cults; indeed, the growing strength of the immigrants created another issue, namely, nativism, which absorbed some of the energetic individuals formerly active in religious extremism. The excesses of emotionalism and the unfulfilled promises of the utopians caused many people to regard all religious enthusiasm with suspicion. Undoubtedly the Civil War diverted the minds of many from religious matters and, in general, caused a lowering in the moral tone. At any rate, New York after the Civil War lost its reputation as the nursery for strange cults.

The leaders of evangelical Protestantism, concentrating at first upon the regeneration of the individual soul, next turned their attention to the reformation of society. The Christian ideals of love, charity, and justice stirred their consciences and became the major inspiration behind virtually all the humanitarian reforms so characteristic of this period.

In this reform movement New York, particularly the upstate region, led the nation. No other section produced more leaders of the caliber of Theodore Weld, Charles Finney, Elizabeth Cady Stanton, Gerrit Smith, and the Tappan brothers in New York City. Probably the most irrepressible reformer was Gerrit Smith, whose career, like a seismograph, registered every tremor of the reform movement. Smith became interested as a young man in the benevolent societies, notably the Sunday School Union and the American Bible Society. Soon he branched out into temperance and abolition, the major concern of his adult life. But other reforms captured his fancy. He experimented with manual-training schools; he served as vice-president of the American Peace Society; he backed the crusade for women's rights; he clamored against tobacco, secret societies, and British rule in Ireland.

Alcohol was the rival of slavery as a target of the reformers. Intemperance was a public scandal, taking a heavy toll in unhappy homes, ruined health, and criminal behavior. A few individuals had denounced the liquor traffic and founded temperance societies before 1825, but these efforts had only temporary or local success. The temperance movement made headway only when evangelical religion placed behind the campaign its resources of consecrated leaders, able organizers, and a guilt-conscious fellowship. Stirred by Finney's words and responding to the appeals of Lyman Beecher from Litchfield, Connecticut, reformers began to organize local societies to combat Demon Rum. By 1827 the General Assembly of the Presbyterian church and the New York Synod of the Reformed Dutch church were urging the co-operation of their clergy. The next year the Methodists fell in line, reviving John Wesley's stern opposition to the manufacture and sale of ardent spirits by any member of that church.

The New York State Temperance Society, founded in 1829, directed a network of local societies which claimed over 100,000 members by the end of 1850. The state society sent millions of pamphlets and scores of lecturers to paint the horrors of drunkenness and its high cost to society. Members of the local societies pledged themselves to abstain from the use of ardent spirits in the home, at work, and at social functions. Pressure was brought upon tavern keepers and grocers to curtail or end the sale of liquor.

The leaders kept driving the temperance movement further toward total abstinence and toward state-wide prohibition. One of their first goals was tightening the license system. Village trustees had interpreted loosely the state excise law of 1801 which limited tavern licenses to those establishments considered "absolutely necessary for the benefit of travelers." In fact, many places were selling liquor without benefit of a license. In Brooklyn and other villages temperance advocates demanded strict enforcement of the law. For example, George Hall in 1833 got control of the Brooklyn Board of Trustees and drastically cut down the number of licenses granted to taverns. His enforcement of the law wiped out a host of grogshops, to the dismay of Irish workingmen.

The substitution of abstinence for temperance as the goal was virtually a brand new reform which some temperance advocates could not approve. The conservatives, however, could not prevent the state society in 1836 from pushing through a resolution requiring "total abstinence from all that can intoxicate." Other moderates disliked the attack on the use of wine at the communion table.

The temperance movement picked up speed in the 1840's with the formation of the Washington Temperance Society, made up of "reformed inebriates." Led by John B. Gough, a brilliant but controversial figure, the Washingtonians enthralled thousands with their confessions of shame and degradation. Other temperance enthusiasts joined the Sons of Temperance fully equipped with regalia and boasting an elaborate ritual.

Despite all this agitation, drunkenness continued to be a problem, especially after the hard-drinking Irish and beer-drinking Germans poured into the urban centers and augmented the ranks of native tipplers. The temperance forces in 1845 pushed through the legislature a local option bill, and within a year over 80 per cent of the towns voted for no licenses within their borders. Tavern keepers, brewers, distillers, and "wets" took alarm and secured the repeal of this law in 1847.

The temperance and abstinence movement in the early 1850's was

movements
Temp.
abolition

swinging over to a campaign for prohibition. The "drys" enlisted a majority of the farmers, the evangelical Protestants, and the native born. Horace Greeley thundered against the six thousand licensed and one thousand unlicensed grogshops in New York City. The Whig politicians embraced the prohibition cause and put through an act in 1854 which the Democratic Governor Horatio Seymour roundly vetoed. The next year a prohibition statute received the approval of Governor Myron Clark but was declared invalid by the Court of Appeals. The prohibition act of 1855 met open defiance in the cities, where officials, aware of the political power of saloon keepers and the foreign born, refused to aid in its enforcement or that of other regulatory laws. An investigation in 1858 showed that over 3,400 saloons were open on Sunday in violation of the law.

Temperance agitation did score some victories. Drinking to excess was definitely frowned upon in many circles, and some communities succeeded either in restricting or banning the sale of spirits.

Some temperance apostles also attacked the use of tea, coffee, and tobacco and questioned the eating of meat and spices. Although these campaigns won few supporters, they illustrate the lengths to which some of the reformers went. Sylvester Graham wrote to Gerrit Smith that a diet of whole wheat would "sanctify the race" and "make the whole human family better and happier, by the removal as far as possible, of *every* evil —physical, physiological, mental, and moral."

Abolition, the greatest reform movement of the period, enlisted a large number of its leaders and supporters in New York. An earlier generation had taken steps toward gradual emancipation of the children born to slaves in New York State and had passed a law in 1827 providing for the completion of that process. Meanwhile the religious groups backing the various benevolent societies—Sunday School, temperance, Bible, and so on—began to express concern over the plight of the slave. The success of the British reformers in securing emancipation in the colonies by 1834 inspired American humanitarians to emulate their example.

Arthur and Lewis Tappan, wealthy merchants of Manhattan, had been prominent figures in the benevolent societies of the 1820's. They invited Charles Finney to come to New York City to revive the churches and to join in their humanitarian activities. In 1831 the Tappan brothers laid plans for a national antislavery society to sponsor local chapters, send out agents, circulate periodicals, and stir up the conscience of the Protestant churches. At first the Tappans stirred up more hostility than support. But in 1833 they won the aid of James Birney, brilliant Kentucky landowner, and Theodore Weld, one of Finney's outstanding converts, and the American Anti-Slavery Society was formed. Weld, after his conversion in Utica, had promoted a manual-labor school at Whitestown and preached temperance sermons. In 1833 Weld accepted the task of organizing a group of seventy men who would give abolition lectures and help form local societies.

Abolition propaganda made gains despite the opposition of conservatives and laborers. By 1834 there were at least two hundred local societies and several abolition journals in New York. A decisive factor was the Utica Convention of 1835, called in that city despite the opposition of the Common Council. Hardly had the six hundred delegates assembled when a mob rushed into the meeting. The delegates were forced to adjourn to Peterboro, where Gerrit Smith gave them haven. Smith, who had already shown interest in many reform movements, threw his full weight behind their movement because of the attack upon basic civil rights.

The next year Smith was appointed by the American Anti-Slavery Society as one of its seventy agents. Through the efforts of these agents, abolition sentiment, which had taken root first in the Presbyterian church, spread into the Methodist and Baptist denominations.

By 1838 many abolitionist leaders were entering politics, since they realized that resolutions and appeals to morality would not eliminate slavery in the United States. At first they sent petitions to Congress urging the end of slavery in the District of Columbia and in the territories. Their second step was to organize the Liberty party, which made a poor showing in 1840 and 1844 and later merged with the Republican party. The abolitionists suffered from many internal quarrels which led to numerous splits and divisions in the movement.

Only a tiny fraction of New Yorkers became abolitionists, but a large number gradually swung to the stand of opposing the extension of slavery into the territories of the United States. Antislavery sentiments increased and influenced many members of the major parties. The political effects of the movement are dealt with in Chapter 19.

Several dramatic episodes connected with the Underground Railroad stirred up great excitement. The Jerry Rescue of 1851, in which leading citizens took a fugitive slave away from the United States marshal in Syracuse, illustrate the desperate lengths to which abolitionists went to thwart the processes of the law. They denounced the Fugitive Slave Law as immoral and invalid on the ground that it denied the Declaration of Independence. Many conservative citizens disliked the fanaticism of the abolitionists and feared that their tactics would subvert law and order. In general, the Irish immigrants and unskilled labor also opposed emancipation because free Negroes might compete with them for jobs.

The abolition crusade left many scars in New York State. Both the Republican and Democratic parties were split, and the Presbyterian and Methodist denominations underwent schisms on this issue. Abolitionists did little to help the free Negroes in New York, who were kept in menial positions and denied equal educational and legal rights. Negroes were often segregated in schools and transport; they were barred from professions; they were discriminated against in business.

Other evils besides intemperance and slavery pricked the consciences of the reformers. John R. McDowall, a Presbyterian clergyman in New York City, helped to organize the New York Magdalen Society to rescue females who had "deviated from the paths of virtue." Other reformers organized the American Society for Promoting the Observance of the Seventh Commandment, with local branches in many cities. By 1837 this organization, which changed its name to the New York Female Moral Reform Association, claimed 250 auxiliaries, most of them within New York State.

Women in New York as well as the other states were treated as second-class citizens. They could not vote, enter most professions, secure higher education, or claim adequate legal control over their property or their children. The legislature in 1848 gave married women the same rights of inheritance as those enjoyed by single women.

Meanwhile, a handful of feminists began to demand equal rights for women in all spheres of activity. Most of the early feminists had been active in the temperance and abolition movements, which were split wide open on the question of participation of women. At a dramatic convention held in Seneca Falls in 1848, a call was sounded for a Declaration of Sentiments for equality of women. But opposition greeted the feminists on every side. Conservatives and religious leaders deplored the revolutionary demands as a threat to family life and political stability. Some champions of abolition and temperance stubbornly resisted the admission of women as equal partners. Perhaps most discouraging of all was the indifference or outright hostility of most women in the state.

During the 1850's, however, the feminists scored several triumphs, in addition to developing some of their great leaders of the future. Susan B. Anthony emerged as a national leader, equally effective in organizing local societies as in lobbying at state capitals. In 1860 the New York legislature passed the "Earnings Bill," which secured to a married woman the property she had acquired by inheritance or by her labors. Wives were declared to be joint guardians of children, and they were also legally entitled to receive a life estate in one-third of real estate upon the death of their husbands intestate.

Feminists also tried to reform women's clothing. Elizabeth Smith Miller, who inherited the spirit of reform from her father Gerrit Smith, designed a new costume consisting of a knee-length skirt and loose trousers gathered at the ankle. Mrs. Amelia Bloomer of Seneca Falls had the courage to introduce this garb in public and to urge its adoption in her little periodical The Lily. Whenever the Bloomer girls appeared in public, men stared and some jeered. Children ran after them chanting derisively:

Hi Ho
In sleet and snow
Mrs. Bloomer's all the go.
Twenty tailors to take the stitches
Plenty of women to wear the britches.

As a result of this reception the women reformers gave up the fight and
returned to trailing skirts. A hundred years later a Broadway musical
comedy, later televised to the nation, added to the fame of Amelia
Bloomer and her Bloomer girls.

The crusade for world peace, like the drive for abolition, owed its first
impetus to the Quakers, but it also required the dynamism of revivalist religion to attract wide public support. David Low Dodge had written
peace tracts as early as 1809 and a few years later organized the New
York Peace Society. In 1828 this group became a branch of the American
Peace Society. Although its leadership came from New England, Gerrit
Smith and the Reverend Samuel May of Syracuse were active in the
cause.

The appalling conditions of the insane and criminal classes won the
sympathy of a few reformers. The mildly insane ordinarily lived at home;
the more dangerous were often locked in miserable unheated garrets or
sheds; the pauper insane were thrown into jail or into the county poorhouse. Ordinarily the directors of poorhouses were political appointees
and not qualified to handle the mentally sick. They often chained the insane in dungeons and beat them at the slightest provocation. Dorothea
Dix in her masterly report of 1844 cited an official who boasted that he
fed his charges on less than four cents a week.

Bloomingdale Asylum on Manhattan opened its doors in 1821 to take
care of insane paupers sent to it from towns and counties throughout the
state. Although it was founded and operated by a private group, it received annual grants from the state. Since its capacity was only two hundred, however, it could not handle more than a fraction of the cases. In
1831 Governor Throop urged the creation of an asylum for acute cases
of the pauper insane. After five years of delay the legislature established
the State Lunatic Asylum at Utica. This institution, the first charitable
institution owned, operated, and controlled by the state, made a pretense
of giving humane treatment. Wherever possible, patients were taken out
of cells, allowed to work on the land, and provided with amusements.
Three years later the state set up another asylum on Blackwell's Island.
However, these hospitals could handle only a small number of people.
The great majority of the indigent insane remained in the congested
poorhouses.

A few counties during the 1840's and 1850's set up separate buildings
for their insane, but they could offer little in the form of special treat-

ment. An exposé in 1865 induced the legislature to establish Willard Hospital for the Chronic Insane at Ovid in 1867.

Conditions in the local jail paralleled those of the poorhouse. The city or county jail had large rooms holding a hodge-podge of drunkards, thieves, hardened criminals, debtors, insane, and juvenile offenders. Guards were often brutal; the food was indescribably poor; usually there were no bathing facilities. The underlying principle behind the administration was retribution. In 1854 Governor Seymour blasted these jails as nurseries of crime.

Auburn Prison attracted world-wide attention for its method of handling prisoners. Finding that solitary confinement led to insanity, its authorities in the 1820's worked out a system of congregate work by day and separation at night. Guards maintained strict silence at all times and applied the whip unsparingly. Other states copied the Auburn plan because the work of the prisoner paid a good share of the operating expenses. Although New York and Pennsylvania led the world in penal reform in the 1830's, the modern observer would consider the discipline severe, if not brutal. No prisoner was allowed to speak with his fellow inmates or communicate with the outside world. His cell was tiny (7 feet by 3 feet 6 inches), and the food was largely porridge and soups. Flogging was common until state law prohibited it in 1847, and jailors devised cruel punishments, notably the "yoke" and the "shower-bath." In 1853 the warden of Auburn Prison admitted that over two hundred prisoners had undergone the latter penalty, which provided for prolonged immersion. Sing Sing on the Hudson followed the Auburn system. In spite of the severity of this system, conditions in the overcrowded county jails were much worse.

Many reformers, particularly Quakers such as Thomas Eddy and John Griscom, directed their attention to providing special institutions for dependent, delinquent, and neglected children. One of their first acts was to put into operation the House of Refuge for the Juvenile Delinquents in the City of New York, in 1842, the first juvenile reformatory in America. The state granted it financial support and in 1849 set up a similar institution in Rochester for the western counties of the state. Humanitarians in many localities founded orphanages throughout the state; the number rose from two in 1825 to over sixty by 1866. Both the state and local governments gave financial support to these private institutions. The increase in state support led the legislature in 1867 to establish a central supervisory body which would raise standards and prevent the waste of public funds.

Vagrant children roaming the streets of New York City were a problem to the police department as well as a concern to the reformer. Chief of Police George Matsell reported in 1850, "The degrading and disgusting practices of these almost infants in the schools of vice, prostitution, and rowdyism, would certainly be beyond belief." Public-spirited citizens organized the New York Juvenile Asylum in 1853 to receive children between the ages of five and fourteen. The directors placed many of the children out at employment and gave them moral and industrial instruction. The Children's Aid Society founded by Charles Loring Brace in 1853 opposed the trend toward placing children in institutions and attempted to place the children in farm families. His success led reformers in other cities to organize similar societies. The Protestant character of these "placing-out" societies alarmed Roman Catholics, who charged them with taking Catholic children and rearing them in Protestant homes. As a result they organized protectories in New York City and Buffalo.

Pauperism increased in seriousness with urbanization and immigration. Whereas in 1823 there were only 22,111 recipients of public poor relief in a population of approximately 1,500,000, in 1855 there were over 204,000 paupers in the population of approximately 3,400,000. A majority of the paupers lived in cities and a large proportion of them were foreign born.

Reformers, notably the Quakers, were the first to express concern over the plight of the urban poor. In 1819 the Society for the Prevention of Pauperism in New York City made a thorough survey and assigned most of the blame to intemperance. They urged the suppression of grogshops, the establishment of a savings bank, the appointment of members to visit residents in their neighborhoods, and the erection of houses of industry for the unemployed.

Meanwhile the legislators were wrestling with the larger problem of reforming the old poor law of New York. The agitation in Britain and the urgings of reformers caused the legislators in 1824 to direct Secretary of State John Yates to study the question and to report his recommendations. The Yates Report of 1824, the first comprehensive survey of poor relief in the United States, listed four methods in use in New York: the town poorhouse, home relief, the contract system, and the auction system. Under the contract system all the poor of a town were placed under the care of one or more householders at a fixed rate per month or week. Under the auction system the authorities "sold" the town poor to the lowest bidder. The latter was seldom accused of overfeeding his charges.

The Yates Report proposed that the county poorhouse become the center of the relief system. Presumably the new system would be more economical since paupers would have to work on the county farm for their keep. Furthermore, the intentional rigors of the workhouse would deter some people from applying for relief. In 1824 the legislature made it mandatory for sixteen counties to set up poorhouses and permissive for thirty-eight others. Within a decade almost all the counties had adopted the new scheme.

The workhouse system soon earned many enemies. A committee of the State Senate in 1856 described the poorhouses as

badly-constructed, ill-arranged, ill-warmed and ill-ventilated. The rooms are crowded with inmates; and the air, particularly in the sleeping departments, is very noxious, and to visitors, almost insufferable. In some cases, as many as forty-five inmates occupy a single dormitory, with low ceilings and sleeping boxes arranged in three tiers one above another.

Sickness was common and few workhouses had hospital facilities. The moral atmosphere was low since all kinds of people—male and female, insane and sane, crippled and able-bodied, diseased and well, vicious and virtuous—were crowded together in rooms and garrets. The keepers neglected their charges and permitted conditions that would shock humanity.

The committee urged the return to home relief, the removal of children and insane from the workhouses, better regulation of conditions, and constant supervision by the state of all charitable and reformatory institutions. Unfortunately, the legislature did not adopt any of these recommendations until after the Civil War.

The reform movement was a powerful force shaping the lives of New Yorkers. Since almost all of the reform leaders were intensely religious, they felt that Providence was behind them and they also believed they were participating in the onward march of Progress. A relatively small group of clergymen and philanthropists dominated the various societies seeking to abolish slavery, Christianize the Polynesians, close the grogshops, and the like. In the main, associates of Finney, who were carrying forward the work pioneered by Quakers, were in the vanguard of this movement.

The reformers won many victories despite their lack of numbers, their constant feuds, the hostility of conservatives and vested interests, and the indifference of the public. They themselves suffered several shortcomings, including a lack of humor and, sometimes, a deficiency of common sense. They often rushed to attack the results and not the causes of social evils. The individualistic tradition severely limited the possibilities of using collective solutions. Most important, the reformers found that an adolescent economy undergoing the stresses of industrialization could not afford to give all members of society a decent living.

Their achievements were nonetheless real and lasting. Many powerful organizations took root; the public was educated to demand improvements; public authorities recognized their responsibility to the handicapped and dependent classes; the downtrodden and defenseless found leaders to champion their cause. The Empire State was taking the first faltering steps toward making adequate provisions for public welfare.

Education and the Arts

The blab of the pave, tires of carts, sluff of boot-soles, talk of
   the promenaders,
The heavy omnibus, the driver with his interrogating thumb,
   the clank of the shod horses on the granite floor.
                        —WALT WHITMAN

THE citizens of New York were making great strides in education and the various branches of art and literature in the same period that they were winning undisputed leadership in commerce, transportation, finance, and manufacturing. The growth of free public schools on the elementary level and the development of the daily newspaper were significant in making New Yorkers better informed citizens. New York City, which in 1825 was a cultural center on a level with Boston and Philadelphia, gradually outstripped its rivals by the time of the Civil War. In painting, music, architecture, journalism, and the theater, New York City set the pace for the nation. In publishing and in literary pursuits, New Yorkers were slowly forging ahead of their rivals in the Boston-Cambridge area.

Great progress toward a public school system was made between 1825 and 1860, but the main developments were quantitative rather than qualitative. Education for the average boy or girl ended in the elementary school, which enrolled over 90 per cent of all students in 1860. The curriculum offered little beyond the traditional three R's. State supervision of elementary schools became more rigid, especially for the city systems that developed. During the 1850's the public high school began to challenge the dominant position of the private academies, which had always received some public support. Standards for teachers and physical conditions for students remained low.

The law of 1812, the basic educational provision until 1849, provided that the common school fund of the state should be apportioned among the different towns according to the population. The supervisors of each county were to levy upon each town a sum matching the state grant.

Additional funds to pay teachers' salaries were to be raised by a rate bill levied upon those sending children to the school in proportion to the number of days such children were in attendance.

Unfortunately, not all children received a free education and schooling was not compulsory. Thousands of children had to work to support themselves and their parents. For example, in Rochester in 1839 there were over one thousand children (about one-fourth of those in the age range five to sixteen) not attending any school. The worst defect in the law of 1812 was the requirement that indigent parents sign a pauper's oath if they wished the rate bill waived. Since many parents were too proud to sign such a statement, they kept their children at home. The superintendent of schools of New York State estimated in 1846 that over forty-six thousand children were not attending schools.

Sentiment for free public schools began in the cities and spread to the countryside. During the 1840's several cities followed the leadership of Buffalo and New York City in setting up systems of free public schools. The working-class leaders, residents of New England background, and the reformers were the strongest advocates. Opposition to public schools was strong, since many farmers and persons of wealth feared higher taxes. Roman Catholics, who thought such institutions were "godless" or tainted with Protestantism, or both, resented paying taxes for public schools and wished to use the money for schools maintained by their church. Private schools naturally feared the competition of a free public school system.

Between 1849 and 1851 a memorable battle was fought between the friends and foes of public schools. The legislature, heeding the petitions of thousands of residents, passed an act in 1849 establishing free schools throughout the state. The lawmakers considered this act so important that they referred it to the people. Well over two-thirds of the voters gave it their approval, but many New Yorkers took a second view when their tax bill came in. Furthermore, the act did not work well in practice. Real property was hit hard while corporate and personal property escaped taxation. Some twenty thousand citizens, especially in the rural districts, asked the legislature to repeal the act. The law was resubmitted to a vote and again sustained, though by a decreased majority.

The legislature passed a compromise act in 1851 which provided for the imposition of rates upon parents of children attending the public schools. At the same time they appropriated $800,000 for the schools, which meant, in effect, that most rural districts received enough state aid to avoid rate bills.

Friends of education kept fighting for more support and better direction of the school system. In 1854 the legislature removed the supervision of the schools from the secretary of state and created the office of Superintendent of Public Instruction. This led to closer supervision of local schools and higher standards. Finally, in 1867, the hated rate-bill system was abolished.

Economy was the watchword for trustees of school districts, who tried to secure teachers at the lowest possible salaries. During the 1820's some schools adopted the Lancastrian system, whereby the teacher worked with the more advanced students, who, in turn, heard the recitations of the less advanced. After a short trial period the Lancastrian system was quietly dropped. A more successful way of reducing expenses was the replacement of male teachers with female teachers, at half the cost. By 1866, when over 80 per cent of the common-school teachers were women, Superintendent Victor Rice enthused, "To teach and train the young seems to be one of the chief missions of woman. Herself high-minded, the minds of those with whom she comes in daily contact unconsciously aspire. Gentle herself, she renders them gentle."

The combination of low pay, hard work, insecurity, and political favoritism meant a transient and incompetent set of teachers. Teacher turnover was very high. In 1844 one observer estimated that twenty-six thousand people were hired to fill sixteen thousand positions. The emotion-charged words of Superintendent Samuel Young in his annual report for 1843 strips the "little red school house" of some of the nostalgic charm with which it has been invested by the passing years:

The nakedness and deformity of the great majority of the schools in this State: the comfortless and dilapidated buildings, destitute, in many instances, of the ordinary conveniences and decencies of life; the unhung doors, broken sashes, absent panes, stilted benches, gaping walls, yawning roofs, and muddy and moldering floors . . . and many of the self-styled teachers, who lash and dogmatize in these miserable tenements of suffering humanity, are shown to be low, vulgar, obscene, intemperate, ignorant, and profane, utterly incompetent to teach any thing that is good.

The statistics of Superintendent Nathaniel Benton in 1846 indicate that Young was not carried away by rhetoric. In the nine thousand districts inspected, 2,760 buildings were in bad repair; 6,462 had no playground; and over 5,000 had no privy accommodations at all. Furthermore, the average wage per month for male teachers was $14.00, and for females, $7.50. Improvements came with discouraging slowness. In 1865 Superintendent Victor Rice noted with satisfaction that he had succeeded in repairing many schools and had supplied them for the first time with proper cleaning equipment.

The basic requirement that teachers should possess an adequate knowledge of subject matter and understand how to handle children intelligently only slowly won support. The various state superintendents of common schools continually urged the legislature to improve teaching standards. In 1827 New York became the first state to appropriate money regularly to train teachers in the academies, and the law of 1835 established teachers' departments in eight academies, one in each senatorial district. These academies, however, failed to provide sufficient teachers to meet the need, and in 1844 the first normal school was set up at Albany. The idea of in-service training for teachers took hold, and Teachers Institutes lasting for two to six weeks were held. Common problems and newest methods were discussed.

By 1860 few schools had deviated from the traditional curriculum of spelling, writing, arithmetic, geography, composition, and patriotic history. The Bible was read regularly until the protests of the Roman Catholics against the King James Version led to its withdrawal. But *McGuffey's Readers* continued to provide students with a daily dose of morality. Some of the more progressive elementary schools in the cities offered courses in bookkeeping, natural philosophy (science), and French. The acquisition of factual information and the disciplining of the mind by memorization were the goals and methods of almost all teachers.

Secondary education remained almost entirely in private hands until the decade of the 1850's. The Board of Regents and various local authorities had already fostered development of a number of academies which prepared young men for college and trained teachers for the common schools.

The Regents acted with discrimination in granting charters to academies, requiring sponsors to show evidence of sufficient funds, suitable buildings, and public need. Unfortunately, promoters who were unable to meet these requirements could by-pass the Regents and secure charters from the state legislature. During the 1820's there was a rush for new charters, and every village and town with any pretensions sought to establish an academy. The poverty of pioneer days was passing and the Finney revivals stimulated Christian concern for securing trained young people to spread the Gospel. Yankee schoolteachers brought with them a strong faith in education.

When it created the University of the State of New York, the legislature also directed the Regents to encourage the establishment of academies. As early as 1786 the legislature had ordered the surveyor general to mark one lot of unsold land in each township for "Gospel and schools" and one lot for the promotion of literature. The revenue from these lots of land was given to the academies, but this fund was very small until it received an additional $150,000 from the Canal Fund in 1827. Money was apportioned according to the number of students pursuing classical studies or the "higher branches of English education." The total amount of aid to the academies was small and in 1840 averaged only $339. The Board of Regents also made special grants for the purchase of books, maps, and globes. Eight academies, which maintained departments for the education of common-school teachers, received special funds.

Academies were not coeducational as a rule. In general, seminaries were established for girls and academies for boys. Perhaps the outstanding seminary was the Troy Female Seminary founded in 1821 by Mrs. Emma Willard. Seminaries commonly offered genteel instruction in music and painting and other "accomplishments" suitable to the young lady of leisure.

The academies, however, responded to the growing demand for the practical subjects such as bookkeeping and teaching methods. Each year the list of such subjects grew. A considerable number of students came to elect courses in science or history and philosophy and did not follow the classical college-preparatory course. City schools designed for artisans and tradesmen specialized in practical subjects.

In 1850 unchartered private schools enrolled almost as many students as the chartered academies. Hundreds of small schools sprang up only to disappear within a year or so. As the Rochester *Republican* noted in 1837, "an educated young woman needs only a suitable room and some apparatus, and then begins operation at once." A majority of these schools catered to girls and became known as select schools. Although a few tried to enhance the young ladies' graces, most of them were primarily concerned with teaching the three R's. As the district public schools became free and as their standards of instruction rose, these select schools gradually declined. The strongest ones began to call themselves seminaries.

The academies in New York State reached their peak in 1855 with an enrollment of over 36,000 students, as compared with only 2,445 in 1825. Attendance varied from town to town, but apparently no more than 10 to 20 per cent of the boys and girls (ages twelve to sixteen) were enrolled in 1850. After 1855 academies declined steadily until about 1900. Most of the 12,272 students in private academies at the later date were studying under Roman Catholic auspices.

A demand for free instruction at the secondary level rose in New York State during the decade prior to the Civil War. In some communities the public demanded that the academies offer free tuition to students coming from the towns. "Free academies" were established in New York City and elsewhere. For example, Rochester set up a central high school in 1857. By 1860 there were twenty-two free, public high schools in the state. Most of these schools bore the name of free academies, institutes, and classical schools. Despite the rise of the high school, the private academies dominated secondary education before the Civil War.

Higher education was not a field in which New York led the nation. More New Yorkers went to out-of-state schools than the number of non-New Yorkers who studied at colleges in this state. The tiny fraction of the population which entered college (fewer than one per thousand citizens of New York as compared with almost seventeen per thousand citizens of the United States in 1952) remained almost stationary from 1833 to 1863. In the latter year there were only 1,305 students in the "literary" colleges and 897 in the medical colleges.

The most noteworthy development in higher education was the founding of several of our most important colleges under denominational inspiration. The education of clergymen was the main goal of the various denominations. St. Johns (1870) was Roman Catholic; Madison (now Colgate) and Rochester were established as the result of a Baptist feud in 1846; St. Lawrence (1856) was Universalist, and Alfred (1857) was Seventh-Day Baptist. In 1860 the Protestant Episcopal church founded St. Stephens (now Bard) to supplement Hobart and Columbia. New York University (1831) was nondenominational and owed its origin partly as a protest against the conservatism and Episcopal exclusiveness of Columbia. The Methodist Episcopal church founded Genesee College at Lima in 1851 and in 1871 moved it to Syracuse to be reopened as Syracuse University. Presbyterian influence remained strong at Hamilton and Union, founded before 1825. Cornell University, chartered in 1865, opened its doors in 1868. It was one of the first colleges in the state to provide coeducation and to avoid all sectarian ties.

The United States Military Academy at West Point was opened in 1802 with ten cadets. Major Sylvanus Thayer, who served as superintendent from 1817 to 1833, built up the academy into a first-rate military school. Many of the famous generals of the Civil War—Lee, Grant, Jackson, Sheridan, Early, Jefferson Davis—received their training in the castellated Gothic structure on the heights overlooking the Hudson.

Both old and new colleges needed money desperately. Their presidents spent much of their time seeking benefactors. The most munificent donation of the time (over $600,000) was made to Union by President Eliphalet Nott. The state legislators made grants to several institutions, but they became increasingly less generous, preferring to devote tax money to free public schools. Tuition, often only thirty dollars a year, brought in little revenue and could not be increased because the students, the majority of them the sons of farmers and parsons, could not afford to pay more.

The basic aim of the colleges was to train men for positions in church and state, and therefore the colleges stood for conservatism in politics and orthodoxy in religion. Trustees and faculty were agreed that the primary function of the college was to preserve and perpetuate the knowledge of the past, not to stimulate new ideas in immature minds.

Students prepared for admission by attending the academies or by studying with a private tutor. Colleges normally required applicants to be fourteen or older and to show some proficiency in Latin, Greek, English, and arithmetic.

The college course of study for the first three years consisted largely of drill in Latin, Greek, and mathematics. The fare for juniors was broadened to include some science and modern languages. Seniors escaped with less study of the ancient languages and mathematics but took prescribed courses in moral philosophy, political economy, science, and rhetoric. The president frequently gave the course in "evidences of Christianity" for seniors.

Cracks were beginning to appear in the iron front of the classical curriculum, despite the resistance of the conservatives. Union was the first college to place scientific instruction on a level equal with the classical course. Students could substitute modern languages for Greek and Latin and had several free electives. In the face of competition from New York University, Columbia in the 1830's added a "scientific and literary course" to train young men for mercantile and engineering pursuits. The new institution in Rochester allowed students several options. Among the new subjects in the curricula of various colleges were laboratory science, Romance languages, English literature, and history.

Faculty members were gentlemen, often clergymen, of unquestioned probity, great industry, and uncertain scholarship. Teaching was dull and uninspired, since memorization of the text was standard procedure. Teachers relied upon the prescribed textbook as the final authority and insisted upon the right answers instead of encouraging students to ask the right questions. Salaries were low—customarily less than one thousand dollars a year. The professors were expected to advise students, preach an occasional sermon, and police the dormitory. The daily routine was laid out as carefully as the curriculum. The following was the schedule at Hamilton College in 1813: prayers at six o'clock, summer and winter; recitation for one hour before breakfast; study hours before and after lunch, interrupted by two other recitations; dinner, followed by evening prayers.

Students frequently defied the stern and elaborate regulations adopted by the faculty. Their pent-up physical energies had no way of expressing themselves in organized athletics or planned social functions. Most misconduct was merely mischievous, such as placing cows in the rooms of tutors, ringing the chapel bell, and tearing down fences. Occasionally, however, students engaged in pitched battles with town boys, burned the college buildings, and stoned the professors. George Strong noted in his diary in 1835, "Lucky for the faculty that curses do not kill or else the faculty of Columbia College would have been swept from the earth."

Undergraduates showed considerable initiative in organizing and managing literary societies. On most campuses such societies enrolled practically the entire student body. Their chief purpose was to criticize literary compositions and to debate contemporary issues. The Phoenix Society at Hamilton College in 1825 debated these issues. Should the United States aid the Greeks to win their independence? Should students become engaged or marry? Does education cramp genius? In addition, the societies bought and collected libraries, a function most colleges neglected before 1850.

Despite their very real achievements, the societies gradually lost influence and after 1850 began to disappear, largely because the Greek-letter fraternities, originating at Union, spread to many colleges. Both the societies and the fraternities reflected student activities and values which the classroom could not satisfy. Their rise marks the growth of a secular spirit which defined success in terms of wealth, skill at games, and social distinction.

New York was a laggard in promoting education for women either in women's colleges or in coeducational institutions. Elmira Female College (1855) was the first institution for young ladies in this state. Vassar opened its doors in 1865. Coeducation had to wait until after the Civil War.

The establishment of professional schools was a significant development of this period. Many colleges, including St. Johns, St. Lawrence, Alfred, Rochester, and Madison, established theological departments. Independent theological schools also sprang up as denominational loyalties hardened. The Lutherans pioneered with Hartwick Seminary in 1816; the Presbyterians set up Auburn in 1820; and the Episcopalians founded the General Theological School in New York City in 1822. The division in the Presbyterian church prompted the New School Presbyterians to set up Union Theological Seminary in 1837 as a protest against the conservatism of "Old School" Princeton.

In engineering education New York State was a leader. The Erie Canal has been called America's first school of engineering, since many early engineers received practical training building locks and running surveys for that canal. Stephen Van Rensselaer, who took a keen interest in geology and other scientific matters, secured a charter in 1826 for the Rensselaer Institute. Its aim was "to qualify teachers for instructing sons and daughters of farmers and mechanics . . . on the application of experimental chemistry, philosophy, and natural history to agriculture, domestic economy, the arts, and manufactures." At the start, candidates received a degree in civil engineering after one year's study. In 1849 President Franklin Greene completed the reorganization of the school and extended the course of study for a degree in civil engineering to approximately four years. The United States Military Academy at West Point also trained men in engineering.

The aspiring lawyer continued to receive his training in the office of an established attorney and then passed an easy bar examination. A few law schools were started: at New York University in 1835; Albany in 1851; Columbia in 1858. Earlier, some colleges had professorships of law. The famous Chancellor James Kent lectured at Columbia from 1823 to 1847.

Medical colleges were more numerous than law schools, although most hopeful students were still trained in the office of an older physician. New York University set up a college in 1837 to compete with the College of Physicians and Surgeons. Albany Medical College (1839) and the University of Buffalo (1846) served the eastern and western parts of the state. The course of study was rather limited, and although the students listened to lectures, they received no laboratory training.

Adult education depended largely upon various voluntary associations and libraries. Informal groups and societies which had sponsored occasional lectures before 1825 multiplied during the lyceum movement in the 1830's. The lyceum was a local association of neighbors interested in self-improvement. It collected books and scientific specimens and sometimes had an assembly room, but its main function was the sponsorship of lectures. Talks on science were the most popular, but literary figures, such as Emerson, and politicians also swung around the lyceum circuit. New York took the leadership in lyceums, establishing the first state federation and providing the first president for the national federation in the person of Stephen Van Rensselaer.

Similar societies grew up under a variety of names: literary institutes, forums, Franklin institutes, manual labor schools, and young men's societies. There were several mechanics institutes which sponsored lectures on scientific and literary subjects. The Albany Institute, the successor to the Albany Lyceum, amassed a library and an art collection.

New York led the other states in the total number of professional, district, and academy libraries. The State Library, founded in 1818, became a leading reference library. Its directors persuaded the legislature to appropriate funds for legal works and for historical collections on the colonial period. The finest reference library in America at the time resulted from the bequest of John Jacob Astor in 1848 which enabled Director Joseph Cogswell to ransack the book markets of Europe. The Astor Library became the nucleus of the New York Public Library.

The establishment of small book collections in almost all of the ten thousand common school districts was one of the most interesting developments of this period. Governor De Witt Clinton in 1827 had urged that money be granted to each district for this purpose, and in 1836 the legislature set aside an annual grant of $55,000 which enabled the districts to collect over 1,600,000 volumes by 1853. Undoubtedly these libraries helped to raise the cultural level, but neglect and apathy limited their usefulness. Several of the superintendents of schools deplored this situation. In 1861 Superintendent Van Dyck noted that the libraries in the rural districts were "almost totally unused, and rapidly deteriorating in value."

Academy and workingmen's libraries provided facilities to many groups. The Regents made small grants to the academies for the purchase of books, but during the 1850's the average academy library had only five hundred volumes.

New York City became the center of American journalism, and newspapermen throughout the nation looked to its papers for ideas and suggestions for technical improvements. The journalistic opportunities in the metropolis attracted such able men as Horace Greeley and William Cullen Bryant.

The most notable development was the penny press, which had originated in London. Publishers could now sell a larger paper for less money primarily because circulation increased so enormously. Not only were there more people to buy papers but more of the urban masses could read and afford a couple of cents for a journal. Technological improvements such as the double-cylinder and rotary presses enabled printers to make thousands of impressions per hour.

The New York *Sun*, founded by Benjamin Day in 1833, was the first successful penny journal. Day built up circulation by interlarding the usual political and foreign items with sex scandals, animal stories, and even such hoaxes as the discovery of batlike people on the moon. James Gordon Bennett, a Scottish immigrant, soon applied a similar formula to the New York *Herald*. For over thirty years he skillfully mixed together the ingredients of sensationalism, comprehensive coverage, and political conservatism. Although his rivals accused him of degrading the public taste, they copied his techniques for gathering news rapidly and for using pictorial devices.

The greatest editor of the period and possibly in American history was Horace Greeley, who made the New York *Tribune* a national newspaper. Greeley, an upstate printer, attracted the attention of the Whigs with his brilliant editorials for Harrison in the campaign of 1840. The next year he founded the *Tribune*. Unlike Bennett, Greeley was extraordinarily sensitive to moral issues. In fact, he pursued reforms to the point of eccentricity. At various times he crusaded for temperance, feminism, free homesteads, public education, abolition, and even vegetarianism. Conservative Whigs detested his reformism but welcomed his ability to gain support for the Whig program among workmen and farmers. The *Tribune* offered comprehensive news, collected and edited by the ablest staff of the time. Among Greeley's gifted columnists were the literary interpreters Margaret Fuller and George Ripley; the world traveler Bayard Taylor;

the agricultural expert Solon Robinson; and his managing editor, Charles A. Dana. Greeley's editorials were forceful and distinguished for their moral earnestness. The *Tribune*'s editorial page was one of the most effective and popular of that time, or perhaps of any time.

Henry Raymond and several newspapermen on the *Tribune* disliked Greeley's penchant for fads. In 1851 they founded the New York *Times*, which from the outset cultivated an austere and dispassionate tone and prided itself upon its coverage, especially of foreign news. Raymond offered articles of interest to all the family. By 1860 the circulation of the *Times* exceeded that of the *Tribune*.

William Cullen Bryant was the leading voice of liberalism. Taking charge of the editorial page of the *Evening Post* in 1826, Bryant preached the liberal cause for over fifty years. He attacked monopolies such as the Second United States Bank, defended the right of workingmen to form unions, and spearheaded the antislavery faction of the Democratic party. The Kansas-Nebraska Act of 1854 caused him to swing over to the new radical group, the Republicans.

In the upstate region Albany had the most distinguished papers, the *Argus* and the *Evening Journal*. The *Argus* was one of the leading Democratic journals in the country and was the unofficial organ of the Albany Regency, the clique of powerful politicians who dominated the Democratic machine in the 1820's and 1830's. Edwin Croswell, editor after 1824, leaned to the Hunker wing, which refused to take a strong stand against slavery. This conservative position caused the Barnburner Democrats to found a rival paper, the Albany *Atlas*.

Thurlow Weed, the outstanding figure in upstate journalism, grew up in central New York and worked on several newspapers before he made his reputation as a leader of the Anti-Masonic movement. In 1830 he founded the Albany *Evening Journal*, the chief spokesman for the Whig party. Weed was a tireless and captivating leader whose activities won him the title of "Wizard of the Lobby." His political friends granted him lucrative contracts for state printing. The *Evening Journal* was one of the first to urge the formation of the Republican party in New York.

Other groups—religious, labor, reform—established journals and magazines to spread information among their followers and to attract more supporters.

In the literary realm, Cooper and Irving continued to write after 1825, but their best works were completed before 1830. After their eclipse, literary leadership passed for a time to writers in Concord and Boston.

New York, however, fathered two of the greatest authors in the "American Renaissance" of the 1850's—Walt Whitman and Herman Melville. Neither was a writer limited to local subjects, although Whitman delighted in describing the turbulence of his beloved Manhattan. Whitman's message was national in scope, and Melville treated questions of universal significance.

Whitman's ancestry was a mixture of Dutch and Yankee, Quaker and Calvinist. Rural Long Island and the busy Manhattan streets provided the major stimulus of his poetry. He lived intensely, observing mankind on every side from his varied positions as carpenter, schoolteacher, editor, nurse, and "loafer." Whitman preached the basic goodness of human nature. He was confident of man's ability to express his goodness in individual feeling and collective action. He exulted in physical vigor, gloried in this nation of pioneers and honest workmen, delighted in the cosmopolitan character of Manhattan, and celebrated the political sagacity of the "divine average" man. Whitman developed a rough-hewn idiom more suited to his robust song than the traditional meters and rhymes. He tried to catch the cadences of popular speech and the rhythms of the breaking waves. His *Leaves of Grass*, first published in 1855, is one of America's proudest literary accomplishments and possibly the greatest work of any New York author.

Herman Melville's works belong to the literary history of New York even though his deepest impressions came from the islands of the South Seas. He was reared in Albany, where his mother's family, the Gansevoorts, were prominent. As a youth Melville shipped to Liverpool as a common seaman and later served on two whaling ships in the South Pacific. His adventures among the Polynesians provided rich material for several novels and caused him to question the prevailing doctrines of mid-century America—the moral universe, progress, and the free individual. Melville became preoccupied with the quest for the secret of human woe. He felt that life is a clash between good and evil and that man's fate is to fight evil. His greatest novel, *Moby Dick*, published in 1851, describes the pursuit of the white whale by Captain Ahab, who realizes that he can never conquer his nemesis. The public showed only a passing interest in Melville's theories, and the author spent most of the remainder of his life working as a clerk in the customs service in New York City.

The art historian Oliver Larkin declares that art had come of age in America by the 1820's. Painters were moving from an objective reproduction of topography and from mere likenesses of well-to-do merchants to a more lyrical and allegorical level. Moreover, American artists were beginning to display some independence from European themes. Samuel F. B. Morse in 1827 spoke to the National Academy of the Arts of Design on its first anniversary. He asserted, "Our own soil must warm into life the seeds of native talent."

Painting prior to 1825 was largely derivative. Portraitists of the early republic followed the precepts and techniques of Benjamin West, an expatriate who had become head of the Royal Academy in 1792. West had urged painters to infuse their canvases with elevating patriotic messages. John Trumbull, a Yankee and a pupil of West, was the first major painter to set up his studio in New York. He executed several official portraits and historical scenes for municipal and federal authorities. Perhaps his most famous picture is his "Declaration of Independence." Trumbull was president of the New York Academy of Fine Arts, an organization dominated by wealthy citizens.

New York City attracted a large number of the nation's painters. The rising men of trade and finance celebrated their success by ordering portraits for their parlors. Artists from England and the Continent tended to settle in New York. Landscape painters discovered scores of arresting panoramas in the Hudson Valley and nearby Catskills.

Several English-trained artists settled in New York before 1825. During the 1790's Saint-Mémin, the Robertson brothers, and Francis Guy created topographical views of New York and environs. Guy's "Tontine Coffee House" is animated with the commercial activity of lower Manhattan. William G. Wall anticipated the Hudson River School with his *Hudson River Portfolio*. Wall had tramped up and down the valley with his sketchbook, capturing some of the grandeur as well as the softness of the topography. The plates in the portfolio document the Hudson River from the Adirondacks to the sea.

Portraiture overshadowed landscape painting largely because an artist could sell ten portraits to one landscape. The outstanding artist upstate was Ezra Ames, whose fine "George Clinton of 1812" made his reputation. Ames settled in Albany, painting many portraits until his death in 1836. John Vanderlyn, a pupil of Gilbert Stuart, observed the artists in France and Italy and infused his pictures with a Gallic flavor. His nude "Ariadne" aroused criticism among the prudish-minded citizenry. Samuel F. B. Morse achieved an occasional brilliance in the 1820's and 1830's with such pictures as his portrait of Lafayette and his landscapes of Cooperstown. Telegraphy, however, absorbed his talents and hindered his full development as an artist. Henry Inman painted delicate miniatures and large official canvases and helped found the National Academy of Design.

The first important school of landscape painters found inspiration in the legend-haunted Hudson Valley and the Catskills. Washington Irving in his *Sketch Book* had invested the region with romance and folklore. Cooper, Bryant, and other writers had painted word pictures of its beauty, and foreign travelers waxed enthusiastic over the vistas along the "American Rhine."

The Hudson River School enrolled several painters of considerable talent and imagination. The founder was Thomas Doughty of Philadelphia, who settled in Newburgh. Doughty's pictures emphasized the tranquil features of the Hudson. More talented was English-born Thomas Cole, who injected a dynamic note and later a touch of mysticism into his landscapes. Asher Durand turned his skill in engraving to a detailed rendering of the crags and trees of the Catskills. Like Cole, he exhibited a mastery of light and color. Most popular of all these painters was John F. Kensett, who skillfully harmonized colors in his poetic conceptions of the Hudson. Frederick Church in his early period constructed detailed compositions distinguished for draughtsmanship, but he deserted the Hudson Valley to seek grandiose themes in South America, Labrador, and the Holy Land. In the decade before the Civil War, George Inness painted river scenes in the tradition of Thomas Cole. Thereafter he tended to follow the French landscapists by introducing more subjectivity into his work.

Some painters tried their hand at genre, seeking to interpret mankind by depicting men in their simple everyday activities. John Quider took the legends of Cooper and Irving for many of his themes. The most faithful chronicler of provincial life in New York was William S. Mount of Setauket, Long Island. Mount traveled over Long Island sketching Negro workingmen, tavern keepers, and field hands. His stated purpose was to "paint pictures that will take with the public."

Popular art developed rapidly with improvements in lithography and the rise of universally accessible journalism. Nathaniel Currier, the operator of a lithograph print shop, formed his famous partnership with James Merritt Ives in 1857. Ives supervised the pictorial representation of thousands of commonplace subjects—"every tender domestic moment, every sign of national progress, every regional oddity, every private or public disaster from a cut finger to a forest fire."

Native sculpture developed slowly despite the requirements of public buildings and the increasing demand by businessmen for monuments in the cemetery and busts in the parlor. Erastus Dow Palmer of Albany mastered the art of cameo and wood carving before he turned his talents to sculpture. His "Indian Girl" and "White Captive" are graceful conceptions, less mannered than many statues fashioned by expatriates in Rome and Florence. John Quincy Adams Ward, a resident of New York, favored "simplified realism" in his marbles. "Indian Hunter" in Central Park is his best-known work.

Architecture in New York, in common with the rest of the nation, drew its inspiration from English and Continental examples. In the generation after the Revolution the Georgian, or postcolonial style, was adopted for many public buildings and private mansions. Gradually the classical revival gained momentum until in the 1830's and 1840's its modes were widely adapted throughout the state. The Gothic revival, best expressed in Trinity Church, won many adherents during the 1840's. Other styles borrowing from the Egyptian, Byzantine, and Italian also made their appearance. Builders and architects mixed together the various fashions in architecture, drawing strange silhouettes of the city skylines.

The Georgian tradition continued for several decades after the Revolution. Philip Hooker of Albany almost singlehandedly designed the public buildings of that city—the capitol, the City Hall, the leading churches, banks, schools, and the theater—and his influence spread westward. A fine example of his work is preserved in the graceful steeple of the Hamilton College Chapel (1828).

Early in the century, however, the architectural triumphs of Rome and Greece began to intrigue Americans, notably Charles Bullfinch of Boston and Thomas Jefferson. The latter was greatly impressed by the Roman ruins in southern France and persuaded his native state of Virginia to erect a capitol in the form of a Roman temple. Later he applied the classic principles of regularity and simplicity to the grounds of the University of Virginia. Less well known but equally interesting to New Yorkers is the ground plan of Union College, drawn up in 1813 by James Ramée, a refugee architect from Revolutionary France. The college buildings surround a broad mall dominated by a classical rotunda.

The classical style, commonly known as "Greek Revival," enjoyed widespread popularity, especially in the period between 1830 and 1850, for several reasons. Jefferson and his followers favored this style as best suited to republican simplicity. The Greek struggle for independence against the Turks during the 1820's aroused much interest in the Greek heritage. Nationalists, eager to escape from dependence upon English models, hailed the Greek Revival. College-trained men were well acquainted with the cultural achievements of Greece and Rome. Builders and carpenters found the Greek architecture readily translatable into wood. It looked impressive and did not add very much to costs. By 1830 such guides as Benjamin's *Practical Home Carpenter* were describing the technique of making mantelpieces, windows, doors, and corners in the Attic tradition.

Public buildings were often modeled after the Parthenon. The New York Custom House and the Rensselaer County Courthouse, both of 1827, had Doric columns for their porticoes. The most magnificent reproduction of a Greek Temple was the Utica State Hospital, which was fronted by a four-story Doric portico.

The mansions of the wealthy and the homes of substantial citizens in villages and countryside often adopted the Greek style. The General Spinner House (1840) in Mohawk had a Doric colonnaded porch and

a square cupola. Those unable to afford a projecting portico sought to
gain the same effect by placing pilasters in the gable end of the house.
Some built cornices which projected outward to make a pseudo pedi-
ment. Sometimes Greek features were added to earlier structures.

Pointed architecture, typical of the Gothic revival, found expression
in New York before the Civil War. The popularity of Scott's novels revived interest in the medieval period, which evangelical Christianity
and the Enlightenment had long equated with "barbarism." The growing
Catholic population naturally approved of the Gothic for St. Patrick's
Cathedral, which was begun in 1853. The High Church movement in
the Episcopal church also turned to medieval architecture for its models.
The vestry of Trinity Church commissioned Richard Upjohn to construct
the third Trinity Church in 1841 in the Gothic style. Ten years later St.
Paul's of Buffalo, another Gothic church by Upjohn, opened its doors.

The Gothic Revival spread more slowly to residential and commercial
buildings. Several merchants followed the example of James Fenimore
Cooper and added battlements, towers, turrets, pinnacled roofs, and
other medieval ornaments to their houses.

Perhaps the most fantastic development in architecture was the rage
for octagonal houses advanced by Orson S. Fowler, the eminent phrenol-
ogist. Fowler built a huge octagonal house near Fishkill and insisted that
the almost cylindrical shape was the most attractive, made the most
efficient use of space, and eased the work of the housewife.

Andrew Jackson Downing, a Newburgh nurseryman turned landscape
gardener, was a leading theorist of house design, especially for the
wealthy. Downing urged that the house should harmonize with its surroundings and that each home should express the individuality of its
owner. His advice, though sound, may have contributed to the chaotic
eclecticism which dominated New York architecture in the period before the Civil War.

Few citizens of New York engaged in or appreciated the more serious
expressions of music, although some gentlemen of wealth and culture
such as George Templeton Strong (who in June 1851 attended the opera
at Castle Garden three times in one week) enjoyed instrumental and
operatic music. Practically all the directors and performers of classical
music were Germans or Italians. Lorenzo Da Ponte, Mozart's librettist,
made a strenuous effort to attract the public to his Italian Opera House.
Although this venture failed, opera companies visited New York frequently. In 1842 the New York Philharmonic Society was organized and
gave the first of its annual concerts. Strong noted on November 18, 1843,
"Great crowd: all the aristocracy and 'gig respectability' and wealth and

beauty and fashion of the city there on the spot an hour beforehand."
The Academy of Music, established in 1854, sponsored concerts by foreign and native performers and offered some training to aspiring musicians. The singer Jenny Lind and the violinist Ole Bull were the most
famous of the scores of artists who toured the major cities of the state.

The larger cities had community choruses presenting serious, usually
religious, music. The New York Sacred Music Society in 1831 was the
first organization in the United States to perform Handel's *Messiah* in
its entirety. In Albany, Professor Ferdinand Ilsely put on a performance
of *The Creation* in 1839 and a decade later Haydn's *The Seasons*.

Music as folk art and light diversion also had its place. Most upper
class and many middle class homes had pianos made by Steinway,
Knabe, or Chickering, on which their daughters played. Men preferred
to master the fiddle so indispensable in country frolics. Group singing
delighted young and old, native and foreign born, farmer and city
dweller. The German immigrants were noted for their choruses and
Sängerfest.

The theatrical capital of the United States was New York, and Park
Theatre, opposite City Hall, was the foremost stage. Several other play-
houses, especially the Bowery, vied with the Park, but the leading stars
usually took engagements at the latter house. Upstate, each of the larger
cities from Albany to Buffalo enjoyed dramatic performances. The repertoire included a generous amount of Shakespeare and the English
dramatists of the seventeenth and eighteenth centuries. Plays by American authors, however, were gradually introduced, partly through the
encouragement of Edwin Forrest, the outstanding native actor. *Rip Van
Winkle* and *Uncle Tom's Cabin* were the two most popular native
dramas.

The theater faced a multitude of problems. Fire was a constant threat
and riots were not infrequent. The censure of clergymen hampered
managers, especially in the upstate cities. The peccadillos of some actors
and the raffish hangers-on of the theater provided the clergymen with
some ammunition for the charges of immorality. Financial troubles beset
every manager and forced many ventures into bankruptcy. The most
successful managers were Stephen Price and his partner, Edmund Simpson, who operated the Park Theatre between 1808 and 1840. Price
adopted the practice of importing celebrities from England in order to
attract audiences. Unfortunately, the huge fees demanded by the "stars"
made it difficult to pay others in the cast decent salaries. During the
1850's two directors infused the theater with fresh interpretations. William Burton, a comedian in his own right, cleverly adapted Dickens to
the stage and presented English comedies and burlesques. His great rival

was James W. Wallack, who formed a strong organization in 1852. Wallack insisted upon polished well-balanced performances even at the cost of subordinating or abandoning the starring system.

Edwin Forrest, our first native actor of top rank, delighted the pit with his passionate posturing and robust gestures. Fanny Kemble in the 1830's won the hearts of New Yorkers with her grace and animation. After Fanny's marriage, Ellen Tree was the favorite actress. Of course, the young blades gave a warm welcome to Fanny Elssler, the toe dancer, who caused a sensation in New York in 1840. Edwin Booth, son of the eminent actor, Junius Brutus Booth, began his distinguished career in New York in 1850.

By 1865 New York was taking the lead in most aspects of our native cultural expression. The metropolis on the Hudson attracted and sheltered the ablest and largest group of musicians and actors, painters and architects, journalists and publishers in the country. Even in belles lettres New York was edging ahead of Boston. In education New York was trying to make up for its laggard beginnings. The main features of the educational pattern were the establishment of free public education on the elementary level; the rise of the public high school; the private control of higher education, supplemented by normal schools and the agricultural college at Cornell; and the wide variety of professional and vocational schools.

The citizens of both metropolitan and upstate New York were conscious of their leading position in the economic and cultural life of the nation. Gradually the citizens of Manhattan began to regard their city as more than a purely state or regional capital. Charles Briggs, the editor of the *Broadway Journal,* noted in 1845 that "New York is fast becoming, if she be not already, America, in spite of South Carolina and Boston."

New York and the Civil War

The fury of the low Irish women in that region was note-worthy. Stalwart young vixen and withered old hags were swarming everywhere, all cursing the "bloody draft" and egg-ing on their men to mischief. . . . If a quarter one hears be true, this is an organized insurrection in the interest of the re-bellion and Jefferson Davis rules New York today.
　　　　　　—GEORGE TEMPLETON STRONG, *July 13, 1863*

CONFUSION, indecision, and instability marked the period between the election of Lincoln and his inauguration. Most citizens could not make up their minds as to what should be done about the seceding states. The great majority detested the abolitionists as troublemakers and favored some kind of compromise. Governor Edwin D. Morgan in his inaugural address in January 1861 urged conciliation, and even Horace Greeley for a time favored allowing the "erring sisters" to depart in peace.

The outbreak of hostilities on April 12 stimulated and solidified Union sentiment. Even Mayor Wood and many other sympathizers with the South came out publicly for upholding federal authority. Upstate, citizens showed a similar surge of patriotic feeling as young men rallied to the colors and their elders organized relief agencies. Governor Morgan's appeal for volunteers and for supplies met enthusiastic response. Recruits were organized into companies and sent off to Washington and the front. Various relief agencies sprang up to help the soldiers and their families.

The outburst of patriotic feeling, however, stilled partisan clamoring for only a few months. The fall elections revived old local differences, although the conduct of the war and other national policies transcended state issues for the duration of the war. Both parties suffered from factionalism. Some Democrats were such ardent supporters of the war that they joined with the Republicans to form the Union party. Some

335

Democrats, on the other hand, were such violent opponents of the war that they bordered on treason. Most Democrats, including such imminent leaders as Horatio Seymour and Samuel Tilden, were in favor of maintaining the Union by force but were highly critical of Lincoln's drastic measures to achieve that end. The Republicans had two major wings: the moderates led by Weed, Morgan, and the administration who stressed the importance of preserving the Union; and the radicals, led by Horace Greeley, who wanted immediate emancipation of the slaves.

In the fall of 1861 Governor Morgan, one of the outstanding governors of the North, won re-election with ease and continued his strong support of Lincoln. The Republicans also won the mayor's office in New York City, largely because Fernando Wood and his Mozart Hall faction split with Tammany Hall and divided the Democratic vote.

During 1862 Democratic spokesmen continued to attack the Republicans for violations of civil and political rights by means of arbitrary arrests and the suspension of habeas corpus. They called the Emancipation Proclamation an unconstitutional exercise of power and a threat to free labor in New York. The Republicans countered with the charge that the Democrats were disloyal or, at the very least, guilty of encouraging the rebels and of hampering the war effort. The Democrats surprised everyone, including themselves, by suppressing their differences and putting forward Seymour for governor. A strong believer in Jeffersonian principles, Seymour attacked the Republicans for violating civil rights. Horace Greeley and the radical Republicans captured control of their convention and chose General James S. Wadsworth as gubernatorial candidate. Seymour attracted many independent voters because of his distinguished career as governor in 1853–1854, and he defeated Wadsworth by a comfortable margin.

During the winter of 1862 and the following year enthusiasm for the war waned and demands for peace rose. The indecisive battles and heavy casualties were probably the most discouraging factors, but rising prices and disruption of family life by the war were also important. Most galling of all was the draft act and its bungling administration. After the initial rush of volunteers had subsided, the state, counties, and wards tried to encourage enlistments by granting bounties. These incentives were not sufficient, and in July 1862 the state legislature passed a weak draft law. When this law produced few soldiers, Congress in March 1863 enacted a conscription act to secure more recruits. All males between twenty and forty-five were to register for military service, and each loyal state was directed to provide soldiers in proportion to its percentage of the total population, with deductions for previous enlist-

ments. A draftee could commute service upon payment of $300 or evade service altogether by securing a substitute.

The draft began in New York City on Saturday July 11, 1863. On Sunday citizens had time to wonder who would be called next, to drown their sorrows in alcohol, and to organize a protest movement. The next morning a mob ran wild and drove the provost marshal from his office. During the next three days they sacked stores, burned the homes of abolitionists and Negroes, and lynched stray Negroes. Millions of dollars' worth of property was destroyed before federal troops restored order.

Citizens had some justification in resisting the draft, the first imposed by the federal government. It was particularly burdensome to the poor, who could not afford to buy exemption or to hire substitutes. Moreover, workingmen saw little sense or justice in fighting for emancipation of the Negroes, their chief rivals for unskilled jobs along the wharves and streets. Also, the draft law was unfairly administered. Investigations confirmed Governor Seymour's contention that the enrollment quotas for New York City were excessive. Seymour's enemies charged him with encouraging sedition and resistance by his speeches against conscription. Seymour's subsequent defenders have upheld his right to denounce an unfair law and its bungling administrators. They quite properly point out that Seymour did not countenance disorder and that he took vigorous action to restore order.

Victories at Gettysburg and Vicksburg aided the Unionists in the fall elections of 1863. The Democrats continued to urge conciliation with seceding states, to condemn conscription, and to protest arbitrary arrests. They lost control of the legislature and the mayor's office in New York City when C. Godfrey Gunther, an independent Democrat, defeated the newly formed alliance between Mozart and Tammany Halls. Governor Seymour in the last year of his term faced a hostile legislature. Although Seymour had to placate the powerful peace faction within the Democratic ranks, his own desire for conciliation with the South was sincere. The peace faction was particularly strong in New York City, which from the elections of 1860 to Appomattox provided more moral support to the Confederacy and more opposition to the war than any other important section of the North. Important officials, notably Mayors Fernando Wood and Godfrey Gunther, influential journals, such as the *Day-Book*, and the *News*, various organizations, some loosely connected with the Democratic party, and several huge mass meetings joined the agitation for peace. The "restoration of the Union as it was and the maintenance of the Union as it is" was a favorite slogan of the peace Democrats.

Radical Republicans in 1864 tried to replace Lincoln with Frémont,

but military victories in the late summer assured Lincoln of renomination. The Radicals, however, succeeded in loosening Weed's control over the state convention and in nominating Reuben Fenton for governor. The Republican ticket won by a narrow margin.

The end of hostilities relieved Fenton of many problems, although the assassination of Lincoln embittered the controversy over peace terms. For a time the more conservative Republicans rallied to the support of President Andrew Johnson, who tried to bring the southern states back into the Union on moderate terms. The Radicals demanded a more drastic program of reconstruction and gradually captured control of the party machinery.

The contributions of the Empire State to the war effort were massive and impressive. New York State was the leading state in population and wealth, and New York provided the greatest number of soldiers, the greatest quantity of supplies, and the largest amount of money. In addition, New York's citizens paid the most taxes, bought the greatest number of war bonds, and gave the most to relief organizations. Enlistment bounties alone cost the state over $43,000,000.

On the battlefields as well, citizens of New York distinguished themselves. More than forty generals hailed from New York, some of them in posts of great responsibility. The United States Navy naturally attracted many volunteers from the ocean and lake marine. Captain John Worden was in command of the *Monitor*, which sailed from Brooklyn to the famous engagement with the *Merrimac*. Altogether, New York sent 464,701 men into the army. Deaths, counting those who died after discharge from maladies contracted in the service, exceeded fifty thousand. These losses hit every section and every class in the state. The cities quickly recouped their population losses through immigration from Europe and from the countryside, but the towns, villages, and farms of New York slowly recovered from the blows of the war.

The Civil War stimulated business in New York, but its impact upon various segments of the economy was uneven. Manufacturing continued its rapid expansion, although certain industries lagged behind. Domestic commerce multiplied in volume but foreign commerce barely held its own. Railroads and canals could hardly handle the increase in traffic, but, on the other hand, the merchant marine was almost ruined. Businessmen in general prospered but labor suffered from the inflation. Agriculture flourished but the decline in rural population presented serious difficulties.

The financial panic of 1860–1861 brought bankruptcy to scores of business houses and unemployment to thousands of workers. By the summer of 1861 over one-fourth of the jobbers of Manhattan had gone under, but a revival in business during the fall brought prosperity to

The headquarters at Newburgh where Washington announced the end of the war for independence. The house was built in 1750–1770. (New York State Department of Commerce.)

Fort Ticonderoga, scene of episodes of the French and Indian War and the American Revolution, built in 1755 and reconstructed early in the present century. (New York State Department of Commerce.)

Left: Portrait of Governor Peter Stuyvesant, painted from life by an unidentified artist. (New-York Historical Society, New York City.) *Right:* Portrait of Joseph Brant (Thayendanegea), painted by Gilbert Stuart in 1786. (New York State Historical Association, Cooperstown.)

Section of a Dutch overmantel, painted for the home-tavern shown in the painting. The house was built in Leeds by Marten Van Bergen in 1729. (New York State Historical Association.)

The Le Ray de Chaumont house, built in 1806–1808 in Le Raysville. (David F. Lane photo.)

Johnson Hall in Johnstown, built 1762–1763 by Sir William Johnson. (John Vrooman photo.)

The Dutch church at Church and Market Streets in Albany, 1805, from a colored
lithograph by James Eights. (New York State Historical Association.)

A view of Trinity Church and Wall Street in New York City about 1829, from a
drawing by C. Burton. (New-York Historical Society.)

A drawing of West Point Military Academy in 1828, by George Catlin. (New-York Historical Society.)

Oswego, probably about 1850, from a colored lithograph. (New York State Historical Association.)

The Angel Moroni on Hill Cumorah near Palmyra, associated with Joseph Smith and the Book of Mormon. (New York State Department of Commerce.)

Shaker Church Family Meeting House, built in 1824, in New Lebanon. (N. E. Baldwin photo, New York State Museum.)

An engraving of New York City in 1856, looking south from 42nd Street. In the foreground are the old reservoir and the Crystal Palace. (New-York Historical Society.)

Burning of the City Hall, New York, in 1858, a lithograph by Currier and Ives. (New-York Historical Society.)

Oil painting of the Smith and Dimon shipyard in 1833, in New York City, by James Pringle. (New York State Historical Association.)

Water color of a canal boat on the Erie Canal near Pittsford in 1837, by George Harvey. (New York State Historical Association.)

The "De Witt Clinton" pulling the first steam-powered passenger train in New York State from Albany to Schenectady on August 9, 1831. (New York Central System.)

Left: Benjamin West's portrait of Robert Fulton, 1806, who built the *Clermont,* the first of a line of commercial steamboats. *Right:* Life mask of Governor De Witt Clinton, a major supporter of the Erie Canal, by John H. I. Browere. (Both, New York State Historical Association.)

HUDSON RIVER
Steam-Boat Line.

Constitution,
Captain W. J. WISWALL.

Constellation,
Captain R. G. CRUTTENDEN.

DAILY.

THESE new and splendid Boats will be despatched, DAILY, from New-York and Albany, during the summer months; commencing their regular trips, under this arrangement, on Monday the 5th June. Leaving the wharf, foot of Cortlandt-street, New-York, at 10 o'clock A. M. and the wharf near the Steam-Boat Office, South Market-street, Albany, at 9 o'clock.

When practicable the Boats will come to at the wharves of Newburgh, Poughkeepsie, Catskill and Hudson. At Rhinebeck and Kingston a convenient barge will constantly be in readiness to receive and land passengers. At the other intermediate places, passengers will be received and landed whenever it can be effected with safety.

These Boats are of the first class, and for extensive and airy accommodations, speed, and quiet motion of their engines, and skilful management, are not surpassed by any boat navigating the Hudson River; and the proprietors assure the public that the most assiduous attention will be paid to the safety and comfort of Passengers.—Agents for this Line,

A. N. HOFFMAN, *No.* 71 *Dey-street, New-York.*
T. BARTHOLOMEW, *South Market-street, Albany.*

Broadside for the Hudson River Steam-Boat Line in 1826. (New York State Historical Association.)

Left: Photograph of Herman Melville. (New York Public Library.) *Right:* John Rogers' sculpture of Joseph Jefferson as Rip Van Winkle. (New-York Historical Society.)

Broadside announcing a concert by traveling performers in 1829. (New York State Historical Association.)

Left: Oil portrait of Thurlow Weed, "the Dictator" of the Whig party, by Asa W. Twitchell. (New York State Historical Association.) *Right:* Photograph of William H. Seward by Mathew Brady. (New-York Historical Society.)

Thomas Nast's drawing of the Seventh Regiment of the New York National Guard marching down Broadway during the Civil War. (*Harper's Weekly.*)

Bag-making bee at the Oneida Community in the 1880's. The man with the black beard is reading to the group. (Photographic collection of S. R. Leonard, Sr.)

The home of the Eastman Company, now the Eastman Kodak Company, in Rochester in 1891. (Eastman Kodak Company.)

Octagon house built in 1860 by Paul Armour in Irvington-on-Hudson, now owned and occupied by Carl Carmer. The veranda and dome were added after 1870. (George Karfiol photo.)

The W. K. Vanderbilt chateau at 660 Fifth Avenue, New York, designed for the Commodore's grandson by Richard Morris Hunt in 1881. (Brown Brothers.)

"After the Battle," cartoon from *Puck*, 1898. Republican Thomas Platt says to Tammany leader Richard Croker, "Well, so long! See you at Philippi in January!"

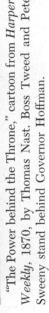

"The Power behind the Throne," cartoon from *Harper's Weekly*, 1870, by Thomas Nast. Boss Tweed and Peter Sweeny stand behind Governor Hoffman.

Theodore Roosevelt greets the "Rough Riders" in 1910 after returning from a trip abroad. (Museum of the City of New York.)

The "million-dollar staircase" in the state capitol in Albany, designed by Henry H. Richardson, completed in 1898. (New York State Department of Commerce.)

Edith Wharton, many of whose novels portrayed New York society. (New-York Historical Society.)

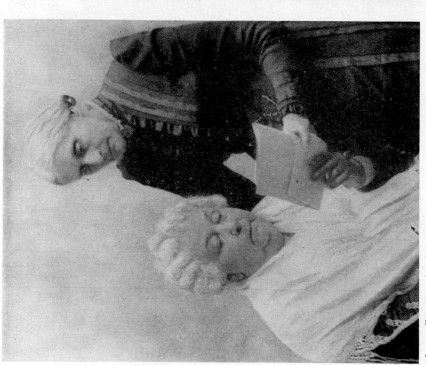

The suffragette leaders Elizabeth Cady Stanton and Susan B. Anthony. (Susan B. Anthony Memorial, Inc.)

Left: The Chapel at Hamilton College in Clinton, designed by Philip Hooker and completed in 1828. (Hamilton College.) *Right:* The library tower at Cornell University, overlooking Cayuga Lake. (Cornell University.)

The Museum of the Brooklyn Institute of Arts and Sciences, designed by McKim, Mead & White and begun in 1897. The steps have since been removed. (McKim, Mead & White.)

Some of the buildings at the Farmers' Museum at Cooperstown. (New York State Historical Association.)

Lew Fields and Joseph Weber in *Twirly Whirly* at the Fields Music Hall in 1902. (The New York Public Library Theatre Collection.)

The Four Cohans. (The New York Public Library Theatre Collection.)

Left: Ethel Barrymore in *Lady Frederick* in 1908. (The New York Public Library Theatre Collection.) *Right:* Lynn Fontaine and Alfred Lunt in *The Taming of the Shrew* in 1935. (Vandamm Studio.)

Helen Hayes and George Zucco in *Victoria Regina*, 1935. (Vandamm Studio.)

Charles Evans Hughes campaigning for governor of New York State at a county fair in 1908. (Brown Brothers.)

Left: Governor Alfred E. Smith. (Museum of the City of New York.) *Right:* Robert Moses.

President Roosevelt, Governor Lehman, and Mayor La Guardia drive to ground-breaking ceremonies of the Brooklyn-Battery Tunnel in 1940. (Franklin D. Roosevelt Library, Hyde Park.)

"One More Decoration," Rollin Kirby cartoon of Thomas E. Dewey for the New York *World Telegram*, 1937. (Museum of the City of New York.)

Loading apples near Kinderhook. (New York State Department of Commerce.)

Gathering sap for maple syrup on a farm near Lake Placid. (New York State
College of Agriculture at Cornell University.)

Logs for pulp near Glens Falls. (New York State Department of Commerce.)

Cows coming home for milking at a Kanona farm, Steuben County. (Standard Oil Co., N.J.)

Watkins Glen. (Finger Lakes State Park Commission.) *Right:* Ausable River, with Whiteface Mountain in the distance. (New York State Department of Commerce.)

The Brooklyn Dodgers at Ebbets Field in the 1955 World Series. (Brooklyn National League Baseball Club.)

The Thruway in the Mohawk River Valley near Fort Plain. (New York State Thruway Authority.)

The General Electric Research Laboratory near Schenectady. (General Electric Company.)

Dress operators, members of the I.L.G.W.U. (Harry Rubenstein.)

Left: Plant of the American Radiator and Standard Sanitary Corp., in Buffalo. (American Radiator Company.) *Right:* Hand-blowing operation in "A" Factory at Corning. (Corning Glass Works.)

Grain elevator at Albany, reputedly the largest in the United States. (Standard Oil Co., N.J.)

A lock on the Barge Canal. (Wide World Photo.)

The George Washington Bridge. (The Port of New York Authority.)

Displaced persons arriving in New York harbor after World War II. (The New York *Times*.)

The port of Buffalo. (Buffalo Chamber of Commerce.)

New York International Airport. (The Port of New York Authority.)

A view of the East River and Manhattan skyline, showing the Manhattan and Brooklyn bridges. (The Port of New York Authority.)

The United Nations buildings. (The Port of New York Authority.)

the survivors. Prices firmed after the initial declines and made sharp advances, especially after the government began to issue legal tender notes (greenbacks) in March 1862. By 1865 the price level measured in terms of paper money had more than doubled the prewar level.

Banks and insurance companies flourished. Most banks were able to pay at least 7 per cent in dividends. After some hesitation many state banks agreed to reorganize under the liberal provisions of the National Banking Act of 1863. The legislature facilitated the shift by an enabling act in 1865, which permitted state banks to become part of the national system without the necessity of formal dissolution and the consequent inconvenience of a distribution of their capital and earnings. In 1865, 183 banks joined the national system. Savings banks, appealing to the wage-earning class, made important gains. In New York City over 100,000 new depositors came forward, and in the rest of the state an even greater number of new depositors took advantage of the high rate of interest—6 per cent or more.

Foreign trade underwent severe shocks and drastic changes. In general, its relative share of the total business transacted within the United States gradually declined. The value of exports from New York City in 1865 was double that of 1860, merely keeping pace with the general advance in the price level. In contrast, imports declined sharply, largely because of the high wartime tariffs. Cotton, formerly the banner export from New York, dwindled to a small trickle, but a torrent of wheat from the new farms in the upper Mississippi Valley filled the holds of vessels leaving the docks of Manhattan for England.

The merchant marine, which during the 1850's had failed to make the shift from wooden sailing vessels to iron steam-driven ships, virtually collapsed during the war. Confederate raiders and high insurance premiums caused many shipowners to transfer their ships to British registry. Whereas in 1860 two-thirds of the trade of New York was in American ships, by 1863 only one-fourth remained in domestic bottoms. This trend continued until by the end of the century only a small fraction of vessels operating out of New York were American owned and operated.

Internal commerce expanded much more rapidly than foreign trade. The Erie Canal remained the backbone of heavy freight transportation (mainly grain and lumber) between the Lakes region and the port of New York. It carried twice as much of the lake traffic received at Buffalo as the New York Central and the Erie railroads combined. Buffalo became a major port, handling millions of bushels of grain each year.

Rail traffic increased more rapidly than canal traffic. The railroads not only were the principal passenger carriers but also the main agency for local freight within the state. Westbound freight, consisting largely of merchandise, deserted the canal boats for the railroad and eastbound

perishables traveled by rail. The railroads reinvested most of their profits in better equipment and improved roadbeds. The New York Central speeded up its construction of a double track, completing the section from Rochester to Buffalo in 1863. Improved engines enabled the railroads to double the length of the trains. The biggest railroad project during the war was the construction of the Atlantic and Great Western running from Salamanca to the West. This railroad connected with the Erie Railroad, a heavier freight handler than the New York Central.

The manufacturers of New York turned out immense quantities of supplies for civilian and military purposes. In general, production had become centered in the factory, but much of the clothing and shoes continued to be made by women's labor in the home. Woolen and shoe factories enjoyed unusual growth because of heavy army demands. Cotton textiles suffered because of the scarcity of raw cotton. Some new, war-stimulated industries, such as Western Union Telegraph, made handsome fortunes for their owners. Millers and pork packers also found their business more active.

The working classes and certain elements in the middle classes were hard hit by the rising cost of living. Coal, selling for about five dollars a ton before the war, rose to more than ten dollars in 1863 and still higher the following year. Citizens in upstate cities joined with residents of Manhattan in denouncing the coal "famine," apparently engineered by the railroad and canal companies. Coffee, tea, sugar, whisky, and beer doubled in price. Rents lagged behind only because of the decline in population. Nevertheless, in 1864 the New York *Tribune* criticized William B. Astor for raising his rents 30 per cent. Because of a shortage of metallic currency, individuals bought and sold with stamps and personal notes, and ferry, state, railroad, and industrial companies issued "shinplasters" or tokens. For example, the city of Rochester issued $160,000 in shinplasters during the war. The *United States Economist* on November 29, 1861, noted, "In this State alone, the different forms of shinplaster currency must be numbered by many thousands."

The real wages of labor lagged well behind the rise in prices. The miseries of poverty, widespread before the war, became even worse. So bad did the conditions become in 1864 that the officers of the Russian fleet in New York harbor were moved to contribute $4,760 to buy fuel for the poor. Contractors in 1861 took advantage of the labor surplus in New York City to cut wages from the prewar level of about $1.25 a day to eighty-five cents. Hardly had the working class made its adaptation to the reduced wages when prices shot upward. In desperation, workingmen began to organize unions and to call strikes. By the fall of 1862 German cabinetmakers, painters, printers, and stage drivers were striking for higher wages. Limited successes led other workers to organ-

ize. Streetcar drivers in New York City lost their bid for an eleven-hour day, but machinists won a 25-per-cent increase over the two dollars a day they had been getting, and bakers won a twelve-hour day in 1863. Newspaper publishers, however, defeated the strong printers' union in a strike in 1864. The unions in Rochester and other centers also failed to win raises commensurate with the rise in living costs.

Working conditions for women grew progressively worse. Most employed women on Manhattan worked an eleven-hour day or longer for clothing contractors at a wage of from one dollar to three dollars a week. Inexperienced women were often defrauded of the little they did earn.

Employers fought unions by various means. Usually they refused to agree to terms and tried to hire new workers. In order to keep ample supplies of labor on hand, they urged the government to encourage immigration. In 1864 Congress authorized agents to recruit labor abroad and exempted immigrants from conscription in the army. Mayor Gunther of New York City protested:

At a time when nearly 50,000 operatives in this city alone are contending against the oppression of capital, and the wages paid are inadequate for their support, is it just to them or to the European laborers to bring the latter into a conflict for existence with the former for the benefit of employers?

Easy money, war excitement, and disrupted family life upset the normal pattern of behavior for many citizens. Saloons and resorts were crowded by patrons eager to forget their troubles. Luxury shops catered to the new rich, who flaunted their finery in public places. This frivolity and extravagance evoked much censure. Some may have been amused, but few could approve of the masquerade ball where the hostess appeared in a corona of diamonds which was lit up with jets of gas fed by a "gasometer" attached to her hoop skirt.

Graft and corruption of all sorts flourished during the war, reaching a peak in the postwar era. Contractors earned a reputation for sharp practice if not downright thievery. The extent of corruption was partially revealed in the great libel case of George Opdyke against Thurlow Weed. Opdyke, a former mayor of New York City, had made a fortune by a secret partnership in various contracts with the government. Weed, smarting from attacks upon his own integrity, exposed some of these transactions and charged that damage claims in a certain gun factory were fraudulent. Opdyke failed to convince the jury that Weed was guilty of libel.

But New Yorkers were not without their capacity for generosity and self-sacrifice. Individuals from Buffalo to New York set up organizations to care for wounded veterans and needy dependents of soldiers. Women sponsored charitable fairs, bazaars, and concerts. The most important single organization was the United States Sanitary Commission, in which several New Yorkers held key positions. This civilian organization helped to tend the wounded soldiers and ministered to the comfort of soldiers. Counties, cities, and towns granted millions of dollars for the relief of indigent families and soldiers. The Common Council of New York City set aside a special fund which was distributed through ward committees. In addition, the legislature appropriated large sums to transport sick and wounded soldiers to their homes. The state also set up a temporary home for soldiers in 1865. Later the Grand Army of the Republic established a home for veterans at Bath which the state took over in 1878.

Older charities also needed more money to meet rising costs. High employment cut relief rolls in some communities, but the sharp increase in orphans and broken families created a financial as well as a social problem. Indeed the problem of child dependency became so acute that in 1867 the state set up the Board of State Commissioners of Public Charities.

Public authorities were much concerned over the distressing increase in crime. Children from broken families often became delinquent and some of them drifted into serious crime. Draft calls absorbed most of the young men in the state, who found in the army an outlet for their excess energies. One result was the decline in the number of male inmates of penitentiaries and jails. On the other hand, the number of female convicts kept rising. Morals in general deteriorated with the increase in drunkenness, prostitution, and gambling.

Neither the outbreak of war nor the Emancipation Proclamation brought better times for the Negroes of New York. A free man in theory, the Negro was actually a social and economic outcast. Segregation was the rule in New York City, in the schools and elsewhere. The unskilled laborers, largely Irish, heaped upon the colored people and their abolitionist friends the blame for inflation, the draft, high taxes, and casualties. Prejudice against the Negroes was common among most citizens of New York. For example, in 1860 the voters turned down by a wide margin an amendment granting the Negro the right to vote without meeting property qualifications. Mayor Fernando Wood of New York openly attacked the Negroes as inferior, and representatives of New York City in both the state and national legislatures undoubtedly reflected local opinion in opposing the passage of the Thirteenth Amendment.

Public schooling suffered from lack of funds, while the number of children of school age steadily increased. The caliber of teachers declined, too, as young men left for the army. The draft, naturally, brought about a decline in college enrollments. During the war years two New

York philanthropists, Ezra Cornell and Matthew Vassar, founded the colleges named after them.

The Civil War affected the religious, political, and economic life of New York in many ways, disorganizing many social institutions. In general, the humanitarian movement lost in scope as most reformers concentrated all their energies on the war and on emancipation of the slaves. Political parties regrouped as citizens quarreled over the conduct of the war and the objectives of Lincoln and Johnson. Inflation and uneven war prosperity widened the cleavage between rich and poor. Perhaps most significant of all was the fusing together of various nationality groups. The patriotism and courage of the immigrants helped to diminish nativist prejudices against them. Conversely, the newcomers as well as the older native stock tended to identify their loyalties more closely with those of the nation.

BOOK II

1865 - 1956

✻

Introduction

IN THE hundred years since the Civil War, New York was transformed from predominantly a land of agriculture into a rich industrial commonwealth. In the process, the farm was subordinated to the factory and the standards of an agrarian society were supplanted by the mores of an urban and industrial society. Even those who remained on the land did not escape the effects of this revolutionary transformation, for both the methods of farm production and the character of the farmer's market combined to make him a commercial specialist and agriculture a modern business enterprise. The self-sustaining farm community tended to disappear, and the farmer as an economic individualist ceased to exist.

The social and economic status of the workingman was also basically altered. The craftsman became an urban factory worker who had little control over his wages and working conditions. His special skills no longer enabled him as an individual to bargain effectively with his employer, and the hostility of both the government and the nonlaboring public to trade-unionism made it difficult for him to improve his lot by joining with his fellows in any collective effort. Not until after 1914 did he by means of strikes and political action make progress in improving his status.

Trade and transportation underwent a similar revolution. By the end of the nineteenth century New York had six thousand miles of railroad track; and the state's railroads played an indispensable part in the development of urban centers, the exploitation of mine, field, and forest, and the distribution of a wide variety of New York products to state, national, and world markets. With the coming of the automobile, the state was gridironed with improved highways that afforded an increased opportunity for freight and passenger traffic and contributed to the decline of isolation and provincialism. More recently the growth in air traffic within the state and from the state to all parts of the world has provided still another chapter in the continuing history of New York transportation.

The economic revolution has been paralleled by equally sweeping changes in the cultural life of New York's citizens. What were once regarded as pursuits open only to the members of the upper and well-to-do classes have been made available to individuals from every walk of life. These pursuits, covering a wide range of activities, have attracted an ever-increasing number of the state's people who have time and inclination to develop artistic and other cultural interests.

Finally, New York's government has been altered beyond recognition during the past century. During the decades after the Civil War, politics in the state, as in the nation, declined in prestige. In the state and in its leading cities this was largely an era of boss domination, corruption, and favors for special interests. Here and there were voices of protest, but it was not until the opening of the twentieth century that New York undertook its pioneer reform programs and that outstanding statesmen such as Charles E. Hughes, Alfred E. Smith, Franklin Delano Roosevelt, and Thomas E. Dewey addressed themselves to issues pertaining to the education, health, security, and social and economic well-being of all the people that a new chapter was written in the political history of the state.

PART FOUR

Politics from the Gilded Age
to the Present

✤✤✤✤✤✤✤✤✤✤✤✤✤✤

Boss Rule

*Q. Was it common report around the State House, and in
Albany generally, that certain men made it their special vocation to see members, and to control their votes by giving them
money?*

*A. Yes, sir; and it was understood in the Lower House that
there was an organization formed of men of both parties, Republicans and Democrats, called the Black Horse Cavalry,
composed of twenty-eight or thirty persons, who would all be
controlled by one man, and vote as he directed them. Sometimes they would be paid for not voting against a bill, and
sometimes they would not be desired, if their votes were not
necessary.*—WILLIAM M. TWEED, *testimony before committee
of New York City aldermen, 1878*

AT THE conclusion of the Civil War, the state constitution, which had
been adopted in 1846 and reflected Jacksonian democracy's distrust of
both centralization and appointive offices, provided politicians with unexampled opportunities for plunder and deprived the electorate of
almost all the advantages of self-government. New York had a governor,
a legislature, and numerous commissions and boards, but it did not have
officials who could be held accountable by the voters. Governors attributed maladministration to the legislature; the members of the Assembly and Senate reflected local rather than state interests; and
civil servants or bureaucrats correctly assumed that their jobs were nothing more than rewards for the services that they had rendered to the
party in power. At every level of government there were those willing
to sell their influence to the highest bidder, and during the postwar years
there was never a shortage of bidders.

The governor, while enjoying more prestige than any other state
official, was in many respects little more than a figurehead. He served
only a two-year term and was unable to control his most influential sub-

ordinates, for the heads of all the executive departments were elected by the voters. As a consequence, such officials as the lieutenant governor, secretary of state, comptroller, attorney general, treasurer, state engineer, canal commissioner, and prison inspector were frequently members of the opposition party. To compound the confusion, most of these officials did not serve concurrent terms with the governor. The governor, moreover, had relatively little control over the legislature. It required only a two-thirds vote of those present in the Senate and Assembly to override his veto, and he was not permitted to veto separate items in appropriation bills.

The legislature was by far the most powerful branch of the government. The Senate, or upper house, consisted of thirty-two members who were elected for a two-year term from each of the state's thirty-two senatorial districts. The Assembly, whose members served for only one year, was made up of a representative from each of the 126 Assembly districts. A large part of each legislative session was devoted to the consideration of appropriation bills. Of the $12,000,000 in expenditures authorized by the legislature of 1865, $6,000,000 was for the war, $2,000,000 for the payment of the bonded debt, $1,000,000 for work on canals, and only $3,000,000 for current operating expenses. Most of the money spent by the state was provided by a general tax on real and personal property. Some money was also raised by taxes on banks and corporations. In 1885–1886 an inheritance tax and a tax on the organization of corporations were adopted, and with the passage of the Raines bill in 1896 a large amount of revenue was furnished by the state liquor tax.

Because the interests of the senators and assemblymen were largely confined to the localities that they represented, few members of the legislature were prepared to deal with broad issues and statewide problems. Many of the bills passed in every session were concerned with private claims or local improvements. Such measures were invariably passed by logrolling, and they were usually designed to increase the political capital—and on occasion the financial resources—of their sponsors. Little attempt was made to deal with the complex problems raised by the rapid growth of industrial and finance capitalism during the postwar years, and some legislators were more interested in blackmailing than in regulating the state's corporations. Several legislators received bribes for voting for bills favorable to certain business interests, while a bipartisan coalition known as the "Black Horse Cavalry" voted for "strike" bills which were ostensibly antibusiness in intent but were actually brought forward because the "cavalry" knew that it would be bought off by the concerns at which the strike bills were directed.

The legislature was divided along geographical as well as party lines, and usually regional and party interests coincided. The Republicans attracted the bulk of their votes from the upstate rural areas, while Democratic strength was concentrated in New York City and Brooklyn. Although the Democrats were able on occasion to win gubernatorial elections, it was only under the most unusual circumstances that they could obtain control over both branches of the legislature. Republican supremacy in the Assembly and Senate was in part the result of gerrymandering and a system of apportionment that penalized urban voters. The basis of Republican strength in the legislature is illustrated by the fact that in 1879 one Kings County senatorial district had 292,000 inhabitants and a New York City district 235,000, while two upstate districts had populations of 89,000 and 90,000.

The Republican legislatures consistently refused to grant home rule to the state's cities. This policy not only reflected the prejudices of assemblymen and senators from farm districts, but it also enabled the Republicans in the state government to name city officials who otherwise would have been appointed by Democrats in New York City and Brooklyn. In 1857 the New York City and Brooklyn police departments were placed under state control, and in 1866 similar measures were adopted for the two cities' health and excise departments. Of the 808 acts adopted by the legislature in 1870, 212 applied to villages and cities. Of the 212, thirty-four concerned New York and an even larger number referred to Brooklyn.

Partisan control and a relatively rapid turnover in personnel helped to reduce the judiciary to the level of incompetence that characterized the other branches of the state government. Judges were elected by popular vote for the comparatively short period of eight years. The Supreme Court, which consisted of thirty-three justices, exercised appellate jurisdiction in eight general terms. The Court of Appeals was made up of four elected judges and four Supreme Court justices who served one-year terms on a rotating basis. The organization of the appellate tribunals produced constant conflicts, while the annual changes in the make-up of the Court of Appeals created both confusion and an inability to dispose of the backlog of cases. Although the judiciary included some enlightened and disinterested jurists, it was by and large a political institution whose members were selected for their availability rather than their ability.

Every autumn the Democratic and Republican parties waged bitter and relentless campaigns for control over some part of the state government. Both parties were "plunderbunds" whose principal objective was to get at the booty that was theirs for the taking after a victory at the polls. Victory meant jobs for the faithful who had got out the vote and an opportunity for graft for those who got the jobs. For the electorate it meant little more than a change in names without a change in policies. Upstate Republicans could be as corrupt as Tammany Democrats, and officials from both parties received kickbacks from contractors, falsified their accounts, and exacted political contributions from their subordinates on the public payroll. At the height of a spirited campaign politics often seemed little more than a game to outsiders, but to politicians it was a business whose profits were frequently as large as they were illicit.

The only major issues on which the two parties disagreed concerned the nation rather than the state, and their platforms were usually nothing more than carbons of the collection of statements pieced together at the quadrennial conventions of their respective national organizations. During campaigns for state office Democratic and Republican orators held forth in city auditoriums or at country crossroads on the significance of the tariff, currency, and Reconstruction. Corruption in the state government was the only state issue—as contrasted with national issues—that invariably received the attention of the politicians, but it was not an issue on which the leaders of the rival organizations basically disagreed. Both parties condemned corruption, and both were corrupt. At every election the "outs" begged the voters to "throw the rascals out." If the voters responded, the roles of the two parties were reversed, but the substance of the roles rarely changed. Victory at the polls enabled a politician to be corrupt; defeat compelled him to denounce corruption. Whether calling their opponents thieves or lecturing the voters on national policies, Democratic and Republican politicians appealed to the electorate with all the clichés of American political warfare. Every effort was made to keep old hatreds alive, and symbols that recalled past glories were substituted for reasoned arguments of current issues.

Both parties were machines, and each machine was ruled by a boss or by a group of bosses. Aided by numerous lieutenants, most of whom held public office, the state boss was in a position to exert a decisive influence on local politics, the legislative and appointive processes at Albany, and the distribution of federal patronage in New York State. He played a major part in the selection of his party's nominees for state office, and his henchmen helped to pick candidates for local and county offices. He and the machine that he bossed got out the vote on election day, collected campaign contributions, protected the economic groups supporting the party from hostile legislation, saw that government contracts were awarded to those firms that gave the machine its financial support, settled disputes over patronage within the party, disciplined the organization's dissidents, and served as the continuing force that held the party together despite changes in state administrations.

Because of the rivalry between the Democratic organizations in Brooklyn and New York City, it was exceedingly difficult for any single individual to dominate the party on a state-wide basis. From 1870 until the turn of the century Hugh McLaughlin bossed Brooklyn's Democrats and successfully resisted all efforts of Tammany Hall to take over his highly efficient and effective organization. Tammany, in turn, was run by William Marcy Tweed until his imprisonment in the early 1870's, when he was succeeded by "Honest" John Kelly. Both Democratic machines received the overwhelming support of Irish immigrants and Irish-Americans, and both were so firmly entrenched that they could not be destroyed by the various reform groups within the party. Despite the rivalry between the Tammany and McLaughlin organizations, Tweed was able to rule both his party and the state from 1868 to 1871, and Samuel Tilden exercised equally effective—but immeasurably more honest—control over the Democratic party during his term as governor from 1875 to 1876.

The Republican state machine enjoyed a marked advantage over its Democratic counterpart. It could generally count on a majority in both houses of the legislature, and Republican presidents during the postwar years provided it with the federal patronage within the state. The Post Office Department had more workers in New York than in any other state, and the federal Custom House in New York City was the largest in the nation. As a consequence, the Republican leadership in New York was assured a large supply of jobs for the organization's hacks even when the party lost control over the state government. With his election to the governorship in 1864 and again in 1866, Reuben E. Fenton became the acknowledged boss of the Republican party in New York. By 1870, however, Fenton had been forced to relinquish his position to Roscoe Conkling, who remained the ruler of New York's Republicans until after his resignation from the United States Senate in 1881.

During Fenton's two terms as governor the Reconstruction controversy in Washington preoccupied the Republicans in Albany. For a short time the state party was split between President Johnson's Conservative supporters who were led by Thurlow Weed and Henry Raymond of the *Times*, and the Radicals who backed the Sumner-Stevens program for the South and whose acknowledged leader was Fenton. This interlude of factionalism ended with the triumph of the state's radicals, who succeeded in re-electing Fenton governor in 1866 and in selecting Conkling as United States senator in 1867. Despite the Republicans' preoccupation with national issues, Fenton's administration was not devoid of local accomplishments. The legislature made provisions for the establishment of Cornell University, opened the public schools to even the poorest New Yorkers by abolishing the rate-bill system, and legally established an eight-hour working day. The law providing for the latter, however, contained enough exceptions to make it almost meaningless.

The most dramatic and least edifying events of the Fenton administration occurred in the legislature at the climax of the Erie Railroad war. In 1867 Commodore Cornelius Vanderbilt secured control of the New York

Central system, and he temporarily gained control of the Erie Railroad and removed Daniel Drew as the line's treasurer. But Drew soon re-established himself in power. Within a short time he, Jay Gould, and James Fisk were conducting a rate war with the Central. When Vanderbilt sought to regain control of the Erie, Drew responded by issuing worthless stock. Vanderbilt bought between six and seven million dollars' worth of Erie securities, while Fisk gleefully declared, "If this printing press don't break down, I'll be damned if I don't give the old hog all he wants of Erie." As soon as Vanderbilt discovered that Erie's bosses could print stock faster than he could buy it, he secured a warrant for their arrest on the ground that they were illegally issuing certificates in defiance of a court order. The Erie triumvirate then fled to Jersey City with more than $6,000,000 in cash and procured a judge to set aside the warrant for their arrest. At this point Gould was sent to Albany to bribe the legislature into approving Erie's illegal stock issues. Vanderbilt soon arrived at the capital with money to buy off Gould's supporters in the Senate and Assembly. What promised to be a saturnalia of corruption was avoided only after Vanderbilt decided that it would be cheaper to accept a compromise than to meet the prices demanded by the more avaricious legislators. Under the new arrangement Drew and Gould took over the Erie, and, with the aid of Tweed, they systematically robbed the road of its remaining assets.

Tweed's interests were not confined to Erie, for he soon became the most powerful political leader in the state. A chair maker by trade, he entered politics after he had built up a following among the members of his volunteer fire company in New York City. Serving first as Tammany leader of his district and then of his ward, he was elected in 1859 to the county Board of Supervisors. Four years later he became deputy street commissioner. As supervisor he demanded and received bribes in return for authorizing the payment of bills owed by the county, and as street commissioner he obtained a kickback of 10 per cent or more from all contractors employed by his department. By the end of the Civil War he was a grand sachem of Tammany and chairman of its general committee. Both his followers and opponents knew him as "Boss" Tweed.

After 1869 the Tweed Ring's control of New York City's government was virtually absolute. Mayor A. Oakey Hall served as the Ring's front man; Comptroller Richard B. ("Slippery Dick") Connolly and Chamberlain Peter B. Sweeny were Tweed's first lieutenants and archmanipulators; and such corrupt judges as George G. Barnard and Albert Cardozo protected the machine in the courts. On election day Tweed's candidates were assured of majorities by ballots stolen from the opposition, Tammany repeaters, and the votes of recently arrived immigrants who were illegally naturalized by Ring judges at the rate of a thousand a day. The profits of Ring rule for Tweed and his cohorts were provided by contracts to their favored associates, bribes from anyone who wished to obtain something from the city government, and outright thefts from the city treasury. Tweed and his henchmen were able to steal more than $8,000,000 from the City of New York in a single year, and the total amount pilfered by the Tweed Ring has been put at anywhere between $45,000,000 and $75,000,000.

Tweed made his first bid to extend his control beyond the city in 1866 when John T. Hoffman, the Tammany mayor of New York City, was named the Democratic candidate for governor. Although Hoffman received the unlimited support of Tammany's naturalization mills, he was defeated by Fenton. In 1867 Tweed "elected" himself a state senator and renewed his assault on the government at Albany. The next year, in what was probably the most corrupt election in the history of New York, Hoffman was elected governor. Hordes of immigrants, fraudulently naturalized by Tammany judges, built up a huge down-state majority for Hoffman. In several of the city's election districts Hoffman's vote was considerably larger than the total registration. Andrew D. White, an upstate Republican and president of Cornell, charged that "the gigantic frauds perpetrated in the sinks and dens of the great city" determined the outcome of the election, and Roscoe Conkling attributed Hoffman's victory to "many thousand forged naturalization papers . . . , repeating, ballot-box stuffing, ruffianism, and false counting." Despite such allegations, Hoffman's victory was not successfully challenged, and Tweed had his choice in the governor's chair.

In 1869 Tweed's domination of the state government was undisputed. The Democrats captured both the Senate and the Assembly, and in the following year Hoffman was re-elected governor. Although the Republicans regained control of the legislature in 1870, Tweed quickly overcame this obstacle by buying off some of the more pliant members of the opposition. The results of Tweed's rule were soon apparent. In 1869 Governor Hoffman appointed Barnard and Cardozo to the general term of the Supreme Court, and the legislature provided the means for increasing Tweed's already swollen income by raising New York City's taxes and by adopting a bill that assured Gould of continued control over the Erie. In 1870 Tweed sponsored a new charter for New York City that was adopted with only two opposition votes in the Senate and five in the Assembly. Under the terms of the Tweed charter, the state commissions in the city were abolished, the appointive power was concentrated in the hands of the mayor, and the Street and Aqueduct Departments were replaced by a Department of Public Works which Tweed soon dominated. To secure the Republican votes necessary for the adoption of the charter cost Tweed large amounts of money, and it was charged that five Republican senators obtained $40,000 each for their votes, that six Republican senators received $10,000 each, and that Tweed's representative handling bribes in the Assembly had some $600,000 at his disposal. But Tweed got his money's worth, for the new charter enabled him and his henchmen to carry out the most spectacular bit of looting ever perpetrated on an American city.

Tweed's prestige increased with his power. He lived and entertained sumptuously in a Fifth Avenue mansion; he was widely acclaimed as a generous benefactor of the city's poor; and plans were under way to erect a statue of him in New York harbor. A group of leading citizens that included John Jacob Astor and Moses Taylor stated publicly that there were no irregularities in the administration of the city's finances, and the New York *World* wrote, "There is not another municipal government in the world which combines so much character, capacity, experience, and energy as are to be found in the city government of New York under the new charter." There were, however, many New Yorkers who refused to accept this view. Samuel J. Tilden, who was state chairman of the Democratic party, condemned Tweed's methods but refused to break with the Ring until he had obtained incontrovertible evidence of its corrupt methods. In the city, a rival organization known as the Young Democracy ran candidates against Tweed's nominees. The New York *Times* maintained an unremitting editorial offensive against the Ring and its boss, and Thomas Nast exposed and highlighted the machinations of Tweed and his cohorts in a series of devastating cartoons in *Harper's Weekly*. Tweed feared Nast's cartoons far more than he did the *Times*'s editorials, and on one occasion he said: "I don't care what people write, for my people can't read. But they have eyes and can see as well as other folks."

Despite attacks from within and without his party, Tweed's position remained unassailable until the spring of 1871, when a disgruntled member of Tammany named James O'Brien turned over to George Jones, editor of the *Times*, transcripts that revealed corruption in the state comptroller's office. When Jones began publishing the transcripts in July 1871, the public response was immediate. Indignation meetings were held; a Committee of Seventy was organized to drive the Ring from power; and steps were taken to institute legal proceedings against Tweed and his cohorts. Tilden, whose relation to Tweed up until this time had at best been equivocal, made no overt move against the boss during the summer of 1871. But by September he had become convinced that there was enough evidence to smash the Ring, and within a short time he had placed himself at the head of the anti-Tweed forces. In the ensuing months Tilden uncovered masses of evidence against Tweed, drove the members of the Ring from the Democratic party, successfully ran as an anti-Ring candidate in 1872 for the Assembly, served as the key witness at the trials of the leading culprits, and provided the prosecution with funds, moral support, and legal advice. More than any other individual, Tilden was responsible for the overthrow of Tweedism.

Although Tilden and his fellow reformers were able to destroy the Ring, they were not so successful in punishing its members. Sweeny and Connolly escaped to Europe, Mayor Hall was saved by a hung jury, and the Ring judges either resigned or were removed by impeachment proceedings. Tweed was sentenced to jail for twelve years, but he was released at the end of a year when the Court of Appeals threw out the lower court's decision on a technicality. Rearrested, he escaped from jail in 1875 and fled the country. Arrested for the final time in 1876 in Spain, he was returned to the United States and confined in the Ludlow Street jail until his death in 1878.

Despite the excesses of the Tweed Ring, Tammany Hall did not have a monopoly on corruption during the postwar years. It is worth remembering that upstate Republicans accepted bribes from Tweed and that the ethical standards of New York's businessmen in this period were little, if any, better than those of its politicians. Corruption was, moreover, a national development rather than a New York phenomenon. Grant's administration was more corrupt than any other in the nation's history; dishonest politicians and businessmen combined to plunder all the southern states during the Reconstruction period; and officials of such northern states as Pennsylvania stole as much and as often as those of New York. None of these facts excuses the behavior of Tweed and his henchmen, but they do indicate that New York's experience was anything but unique and that the Tweed Ring should be viewed as one more manifestation of the breakdown in the nation's moral standards in the decade after Appomattox.

The revelations concerning the Tweed Ring discredited the Democrats and enabled the Republicans to regain control of the state government. John A. Dix, the Republican candidate, defeated Francis Kernan, who was the choice of the Democrats and Liberal Republicans, for the governorship, while Grant ran far ahead of the Democratic-Liberal ticket in New York. In addition, the Republicans obtained large majorities in the Assembly and Senate. The two most notable achievements of the Dix administration were a new charter for New York City that removed some of the more obnoxious features of the Tweed charter and a series of constitutional amendments that were proposed by a commission appointed in 1872 and approved by the voters in 1874. The changes in the constitution included amendments that abolished property qualifications for Negro voters, instituted electoral reforms, forbade extra payments to state contractors, allowed the governor to veto individual items in appropriation bills, required a two-thirds vote of the full membership of each house to override the governor's veto, permitted the sale of the state's lateral canals, and increased the term of the governor from two to three years (twenty years later the two-year term was re-established). Many of these amendments had been proposed by the constitutional convention of 1867, but they had been rejected by the state's voters.

Although the constitutional amendments adopted in 1874 eliminated a number of obvious abuses, they did not basically alter the state's framework of government. New York's government was still decentralized; the victors still got all the spoils; officeholders were still able to escape responsibility; and the citizens of the most powerful industrial and financial state in the Union still lived under a constitution that had been framed to meet the needs of an overwhelmingly agrarian population. Advocates of honest government had overthrown the Tweed Ring, but they had done little to prevent the emergence of similar organizations in the future. As in the past, New Yorkers would continue to be subjected to machine rule, with brief interludes of honest and efficient administration.

Democratic Ascendency

The principle of selecting the subordinate employes of the State on the ground of capacity and fitness, ascertained according to fixed and impartial rules, without regard to political predilections and with reasonable assurance of retention and promotion in case of meritorious service, is now the established policy of the State.

*—*Grover Cleveland, *January 1, 1884*

THE downfall of the Tweed Ring marked the end of an era of flamboyant corruption, and in the ensuing years New York's government was administered by a succession of able Democratic governors who compiled a record of solid, if not spectacular, achievements. From 1875 to 1895 Samuel J. Tilden, Grover Cleveland, and David B. Hill won national reputations as state executives and helped to make New York the most powerful single force in the Democratic party. During the same period the Republicans controlled the governorship for only one term and failed to produce any official whose stature was comparable to that of the Democratic leaders. Roscoe Conkling bossed the Republican party for several years, but his major triumphs occurred in Washington rather than in Albany, and after his downfall in the early 1880's it took Thomas C. Platt some ten years to rebuild the state Republican machine.

Tilden's contribution to the overthrow of the Tweed Ring marked the first of a series of developments that were to lead him to the threshold of the White House. In 1870 he had been a fairly prominent, though pedestrian, politician. Two years later he was known throughout the nation as a crusader for good government, and by 1874 he was his party's obvious choice for the governorship. Dix, who was renominated by the Republicans, campaigned on his record, while Tilden put himself forward as a reform candidate who would rid the state of corruption. With the support of Hugh McLaughlin and "Honest" John Kelly, who had succeeded Tweed as head of Tammany, Tilden piled up hugh majorities

361

in Kings County and New York City. Further assistance was provided by the nation-wide swing to the Democrats in the off-year congressional elections. Tilden carried the state with a plurality of fifty thousand. In addition, the Democrats obtained a substantial majority in the Assembly, won eighteen of New York's thirty-three congressional seats, and elected their candidate mayor of New York City.

Before assuming the governorship Tilden had devoted himself to a lucrative law practice. One of the richest corporation lawyers in the nation, he had a list of clients whose names read like a who's who of American business. But he also had ample time to devote to politics. He had written campaign pamphlets for the Democratic party before he was old enough to vote, and in subsequent years he served as corporation counsel for New York City, a member of the Assembly, and a delegate to the constitutional convention of 1846. After the Civil War he became state chairman of the Democratic party, and in 1868 he managed Horatio Seymour's unsuccessful campaign for the presidency.

Despite Tilden's success in both law and politics he possessed few of the characteristics generally ascribed to party leaders. He was cautious to the point of timidity, and at the major crisis of his political career his indecision probably cost him the presidency. But he was also a cold and calculating man who had to rely on his brains and knowledge rather than his personality to achieve his objectives in public life. He perhaps knew more about New York politics than did any of his contemporaries, but he was uninterested in political theory and the broader aspects of the problems confronting the state and nation in the postwar years. Although his contemporaries considered him a reformer, he never broke with his party on any major issue, and no important progressive measures were identified with his name. Rather, he built his political reputation on his opposition to corruption. This made him more than a politician and something less than a statesman.

In his first message to the legislature, Tilden advocated economy and honesty in government and devoted enough attention to national affairs to convince many observers that he had at least one eye on the White House. His message proved an accurate forecast of the years he was to spend in Albany. As governor he continued to take an active part in the cases against Tweed and his associates, pushed the impeachment proceedings against the Ring judges, reduced the state's taxes by approximately 50 per cent, appointed a commission to draw up some general rules for the administration of the state's cities, and induced the legislature to enact four laws that were designed to eliminate corrupt practices in the city and state governments. His most notable achievement, however, was the destruction of the notorious Canal Ring. It was this, more than anything else that he did in Albany, that won him a national reputation and was responsible for his receiving the Democratic nomination for the presidency in 1876.

The Canal Ring was a bipartisan alliance whose members illegally pocketed a share of the money appropriated for repairs on the Erie Canal and its feeders. By assuring a few favored firms of canal work at prices far beyond cost and a reasonable profit, the Ring was able to obtain from the contractors a percentage of the funds paid by the state for canal repairs. Tilden alluded to the Canal Ring in his first message as governor, but as in his attack on the Tweed Ring, he refused to take the offensive until he had obtained enough evidence to ensure convictions in court. By March 1875, when he had completed his research, he delivered to the legislature a detailed account of the machinations of the Canal Ring. Despite the opposition of the Ring's adherents in both the Senate and Assembly, the legislature authorized the governor to appoint a commission of investigation. Under the chairmanship of John Bigelow, the commission in its three-thousand-page report of February 1876 substantiated all of Tilden's charges. Suits were immediately instituted against the Ring's leaders and their accomplices. Although some of the guilty managed to escape jail, Tilden succeeded in smashing the Canal Ring and saved the taxpayers millions of dollars. Perhaps even more significant in an age of extreme partisanship was the fact that all but two of the men indicted for canal frauds were Democrats.

Tilden was succeeded by Lieutenant Governor Lucius Robinson, a Democrat who became governor following his victory in the fall elections of 1876. Although pledged to carry out Tilden's program, Robinson was hampered by a hostile legislature and the increasing enmity of Kelly's Tammany machine. When Kelly was unable to block Robinson's renomination in 1879, he ran on an independent ticket and drew enough votes from the Democrats to enable the Republicans to take the election.

While control of the Democratic party was passing from Tweed to Tilden, Roscoe Conkling was emerging as one of the most powerful men in the federal government and the undisputed leader of the New York Republican machine. A handsome man of undeniable ability, an artist in the use of invective, and a master of spread-eagle oratory, Conkling subjected his Republican followers in New York to a degree of discipline that would have won him rapid advancement in the army of Frederick the Great. He shunned theories and principles, despised reformers, and believed that the spoils system was the cornerstone of party government. He fought his opponents in his own party as viciously as he did the Democrats, and those who dared to question his leadership were summarily dispatched to a political Siberia in which there were no jobs for party workers. In what has been accurately termed "the age of the spoilsman" Conkling was the greatest spoilsman of them all.

Before Conkling was twenty-one, he had been admitted to the bar, become a worker for the Whigs, and been appointed district attorney of Oneida County. Joining the Republican party soon after its organization, he was elected mayor of Utica in 1858, and in the following year he entered the House of Representatives. Re-elected to the House in 1860, he was defeated in 1862 and re-elected in 1864 and 1866. In Congress he won a reputation as a spectacular and persuasive speaker, and in the immediate postwar years he was a member of the Radical, anti-Johnson bloc in the House. In 1867, despite the opposition of Governor Fenton's faction, he was elected to the United States Senate over Ira Harris, the incumbent and choice of the organization. By 1870 the Fenton forces had been completely routed, and Conkling was the boss of the New York Republicans.

Conkling's control over the state Republican organization was made possible in large part by his friendship with President Grant. He never missed an opportunity to extol Grant, and the President reciprocated by giving him sole authority over the distribution of the federal patronage in New York. Conkling's position as one of the largest—if not the largest—employer in New York enabled him to dictate to Republican state conventions, name his party's candidates, and secure his own re-election to the Senate in 1873 and 1879. As long as he was able to control the more than seven thousand federal jobs in New York, he was in a position to destroy the political career of anyone who sought to challenge his leadership. Some indication of the esteem in which he was held by Grant and of his own estimate of the power that he wielded is revealed by the President's offer to make him a Supreme Court justice and Conkling's decision to remain in the Senate.

By the mid-1870's Conkling was at the height of his power. He had built up his own national machine of Republican workers who came to be known as Stalwarts. Opposed to the Stalwarts were James G. Blaine's Half-Breeds. Both factions professed undying loyalty to Republicanism, but they were unable to agree on the division of the party's spoils. The leaders of the rival wings of the party were both candidates for the Republican presidential nomination in 1876; but although Blaine led on the early ballots and Conkling managed to obtain as many as ninety-nine votes, the convention eventually nominated Rutherford B. Hayes of Ohio. The Republican candidate had the reputation of being a reformer, and when he defeated Tilden in the disputed election of 1876, Conkling for the first time in his career was faced with the prospect of dealing with a president who was opposed to many features of the spoils system.

On April 22, 1877, Hayes wrote in his diary, "Now for Civil Service Reform," and on June 22 he issued an executive order stating that no civil servants "should be required or permitted to take part in the management of political organizations, caucuses, conventions, or electoral campaigns" and that "no assessments for political purposes" on office-holders should be permitted. A report of a commission headed by John Jay had already made clear that the workers in the New York Customs House were bribed to undervalue imports, paid regular political assessments, and took an active part in every form of political activity. The political implications of both the President's order and the Jay report were apparent to every member of the New York Republican machine, for the Custom House was managed by Collector Chester A. Arthur and Naval Officer Alonzo Cornell; and both men were Conkling's lieutenants.

Conkling's determination to oppose the President's program was clearly revealed by the proceedings of the Republican state convention of 1877. In a speech approved in advance by Conkling, Thomas C. Platt attacked Hayes, praised the "working and fighting soldiers of our political army," and castigated the "political Pecksniffs" who urged reforms. George William Curtis, the editor of *Harper's* and the outstanding Republican advocate of reform in the state, replied to Platt with a defense of the President's civil service program. Conkling's speech answering Curtis was probably his most famous oratorical effort, and it certainly ranks as one of the most vitriolic and sarcastic addresses ever delivered by a leading American political figure. In it, after disposing of civil service reform and the administration in Washington, he turned his attention to reformers in general and Curtis in particular. His opponents, he insisted between sneers, were "man milliners, the dilettanti and carpet knights of politics." They were, he continued, "wolves in sheep's clothing. Their real object is office and plunder. When Dr. Johnson defined patriotism as the last refuge of a scoundrel, he was unconscious of the then undeveloped capabilities and uses of the word 'Reform'!" Then, turning toward Curtis, Conkling succinctly and vividly stated his political philosophy with the assertion that reformers "forget that parties are not built up by deportment, or by ladies' magazines, or gush!" When Conkling concluded his speech, the next move was the President's.

Hayes did not hesitate to meet Conkling's challenge, and in October 1877 he nominated Theodore Roosevelt, Sr., customs collector and L. B. Prince as his associate naval officer in New York. By appealing to his colleagues in the Senate to exercise "senatorial courtesy" (by which no appointee was approved if opposed by the senator from the state in question) Conkling was able to prevent the confirmation of both nominees. After Congress adjourned in July 1878, Hayes suspended Arthur and Cornell and selected Edwin A. Merritt and Silas W. Burt to succeed them. Meanwhile senatorial courtesy had begun to wear thin as the dangers of factionalism became more apparent, and in February 1879 Merritt and Burt were confirmed by the Senate. Despite this defeat, Conkling soon resumed the offensive. His state organization elected

Cornell governor of New York in 1879, and in the following year he went to the Republican national convention determined to secure a third term for Grant. But once again he was defeated as the nomination went to James A. Garfield of Ohio, a Half-Breed. As a consolation prize for the Stalwarts, Arthur was made the party's vice-presidential candidate. In spite of Conkling's request that he refuse the nomination, Arthur accepted it.

Garfield proved no more acceptable to Conkling than had Hayes. Not only did the new president make Blaine his secretary of state, but he also named William H. Robertson, who was the acknowledged leader of the anti-Conkling Republicans in New York, to the post of collector of the New York Customs House. Conkling, with the assistance of Platt, who had been elected to the United States Senate in January 1881, immediately set to work to block Robertson's confirmation by the Senate. But he was no more successful in 1881 than he had been in 1879. When he realized that he faced inevitable defeat, he decided to resign his seat, return to Albany, and vindicate himself by securing his immediate re-election to the Senate. He induced Platt to join him, and in May 1881 both men resigned. At this point their plans miscarried. To the surprise of almost everyone and in spite of a special trip that Vice-President Arthur made to Albany to support his fellow Stalwarts, the Republican legislature refused to re-elect Conkling and Platt.

Despite this defeat, Conkling retained enough power and prestige to control the Republican state convention of 1882. Cornell, who had been the organization's choice in 1879, had compiled a good, if not outstanding, record as governor, but three years later Conkling was prepared to go to any extremes to prevent his renomination. Cornell had refused to use his influence and prestige to secure Conkling's and Platt's re-election to the Senate in 1881, and now Conkling ruled that Cornell would not be allowed to succeed himself. Through the use of corrupt methods that reminded more than one observer of the heyday of the Tweed Ring, Conkling compelled the convention to nominate Charles J. Folger. Although Folger was personally honest, the fashion in which he had been nominated outraged the reform groups in the party, and the Republicans entered the campaign of 1882 hopelessly split.

The Democrats appeared as divided as the Republicans. The two leading candidates were Roswell P. Flower, a banker from Watertown and New York City, whose principal political asset was his ability to make generous financial contributions to the campaign, and General Henry W. Slocum of Brooklyn, an inveterate office seeker, who had served under Sherman on the march to the sea. Slocum was backed by Boss McLaughlin's Brooklyn machine and by the Tilden organization, which was controlled by Daniel Manning, owner of the Albany *Argus*. Flower was supported by diverse groups, but his preconvention strength was considered equal to that of Slocum. Tammany, under the direction of Kelly, was prepared to jump to the winning side as soon as it was apparent which side that would be, while the County Democracy, an anti-Tammany organization, was opposed to both candidates. When the convention opened it was apparent that the supporters of Flower and Slocum were evenly divided. On the first ballot Slocum received 98 votes to Flower's 97, while on the second ballot they were tied at 123 with Grover Cleveland, a reform mayor from Buffalo, in third place with 71 votes. On the third ballot the County Democracy broke the deadlock by casting all its votes for Cleveland. The Flower delegates quickly followed, and Tammany belatedly jumped on the bandwagon. Although Slocum's supporters stood firm, they were unable to prevent Cleveland's nomination. The outcome of the campaign was a foregone conclusion, for even a weaker candidate than Cleveland proved to be would have been assured of a victory over the divided and dispirited Republicans. Out of a total of more than 900,000 votes, Cleveland had a plurality of almost 200,000.

Cleveland's early career was similar to that of many other young lawyers with an interest in politics. The son of a Presbyterian minister, he had been born in New Jersey, spent his youth in upstate New York, and became an able, if not distinguished, lawyer in Buffalo. Aligning himself from the outset with the Democratic party, he served successively as ward supervisor, assistant district attorney for Erie County, and sheriff of Buffalo. It was, however, his election in 1881 as mayor of Buffalo which gave him an opportunity to gain more than a local reputation, for his administration was distinguished by its efficient honesty and the frequency with which he vetoed the bills adopted by a graft-ridden board of aldermen. Before his nomination for governor, he was widely known as the "veto mayor," and at the convention of 1882 his candidacy was supported by a well-organized group of experienced politicians from the vicinity of Buffalo.

In an age of spectacular politics and colorful politicians, Cleveland impressed most observers with his stolidity. A heavy-set man with a powerful physique, he had a personality that matched his appearance. Firm, forthright, and deliberate, he never hedged and he seldom compromised. Cynics thought his honesty both old fashioned and naïve, but the voters considered it his outstanding attribute as a politician. He had a deep-seated sense of right and wrong, and this fact more than any other determined his stand on the questions that confronted him. At a time when almost every public figure belonged to this or that machine, he remained an independent.

During his first year as governor when both branches of the legislature were Democratic, Cleveland maintained the reputation that he had earned as the "veto mayor" of Buffalo. He not only refused to approve innumerable private and local bills, but he also used the veto power to prevent the enactment of the various jobs and steals that were devised by either upstate Republicans or downstate Democrats. Of all his vetoes, none attracted more attention than that of the Five Cent Fare bill. Backed by Tammany Hall and several reformers, this measure lowered the fares on a New York City elevated railroad system that was controlled by the notorious Jay Gould and was as profitable as its management was corrupt. On the surface it seemed an eminently desirable bill, but Cleveland vetoed it on the ground that it violated the contract that had been made in the franchise issued to the company. Because of the cogency of the argument advanced by the governor in his veto message, many original supporters of the measure reversed their stand; and Theodore Roosevelt, who was serving his second term in the Assembly and who had voted for the bill, publicly stated that he had been wrong and that Cleveland was right. But Tammany was not prepared to make a similar admission, and within a short time there was open warfare between the governor and John Kelly.

The split between the governor and Tammany was precipitated by Cleveland's determination to increase the efficiency of the immigration department and the harbor masters. Both were branches of the state government in New York City, and both provided Tammany with patronage. After Cleveland's proposed changes had been adopted in modified form, he named a McLaughlin lieutenant rather than a Tammany man to the important post of immigration commissioner. The nominee's confirmation was blocked, however, by Senator Thomas F. Grady, a Kelly henchman, who was supported in his opposition to the governor's choice by a bipartisan alliance of Tammany Democrats and upstate Republicans. Refusing to be blackmailed into changing his nominee, Cleveland withdrew every Tammany name from his list of appointees for state jobs, and in October 1883 he wrote Boss Kelly: "I am anxious that Mr. Grady should not be returned to the next Senate. I do not wish to conceal the fact that my personal comfort and satisfaction are involved in the matter. But I know that good legislation, based upon a pure desire to promote the interests of the people and the improvement of legislative methods, are also deeply involved." Mr. Grady was not returned to the next Senate. Cleveland had earned the enmity of Tammany for the remainder of his term in Albany, but he had also won the respect of reformers throughout the state and the nation.

As governor, Cleveland did not sponsor any basic changes in the framework of government, and he showed little interest in expanding the state's responsibilities and services. But he gave the citizens of the state an honest, efficient, relatively nonpartisan administration; and this was far more than they had received from most of his predecessors. During his first year in office, he set new standards for appointments to state positions, drastically reduced the number of officeholders, and supported a civil service bill which had been introduced by Theodore Roosevelt and was adopted by the legislature. In the following year, when Tammany was in open revolt and the Republicans controlled the legislature, he repeatedly co-operated with Roosevelt to promote reform legislation. Roosevelt sponsored and Cleveland approved bills to transfer several county officials from a fee to salary basis, to concentrate the appointive power for cities in the hands of the mayors, and to deprive the aldermen of the right to confirm a mayor's appointments. The same session of the legislature adopted a bill providing for the compulsory inspection of financial institutions and appropriated approximately a million and a half dollars for the establishment of a state reservation at Niagara Falls. Cleveland's record as governor was impressive by both New York's and the nation's standards. It was the principal reason why he was named the Democratic presidential candidate in 1884 and why he attracted enough independent-Republican—or Mugwump—votes to be elected.

When Cleveland resigned as governor on January 6, 1885, he was succeeded by Lieutenant Governor David B. Hill. Elected city attorney by the Democrats of Elmira in 1865 when he was twenty-two, Hill had served as a delegate to the Democratic state convention in 1868, as a member of the Assembly in 1870 and 1871, and as chairman of the party's state convention in 1877 and 1880. He was elected mayor of Elmira in 1882. In the same year he had received a larger plurality for lieutenant governor than Cleveland had for governor. Cleveland and Hill had little in common except their party affiliations. A man of undoubted intelligence, Hill lacked Cleveland's devotion to principle and willingness to subordinate partisan considerations to the general welfare. He was a businesslike administrator, who was personally honest in financial matters. But he was also a spoils politician who was willing to go to almost any extreme to ensure a victory for himself and his party. Unlike many other politicians of the day, he had no apparent desire to use his official position to acquire a fortune. Power was an end in itself, and he sought it relentlessly. Although he lacked the kind of outgoing personality that is usually the hallmark of a political leader, this was more than offset by his industry, the ingenuity with which he united diverse interest groups, and his ability as a campaign strategist. Ruling his party and state for almost a decade, he was one of the most successful bosses in New York's entire history.

As soon as Hill assumed the governorship, he set to work to secure his election to a full term in the fall elections of 1885. At first few observers accorded him more than an outside chance, but he assiduously cultivated party leaders in every section of the state. At the same time, realizing that he would never receive the support of reform elements in the party, he appealed to the machine groups by openly encouraging the discontent arising from President Cleveland's refusal to turn the federal bureaucracy over to the Democratic regulars at the outset of his administration. When the Democratic convention met, Hill was backed by every major faction in the party except the County Democracy, and he was nominated on the first ballot. Throughout the campaign, he spoke to large and enthusiastic audiences as an unabashed partisan. His war cry, "I am a Democrat," announced to all that he had no sympathy with Cleveland's views on civil service and that he neither expected nor wanted the votes of the Mugwumps. Although Ira Davenport, the Republican candidate, was no match for Hill as a campaigner, he undoubtedly would have carried the state if the Republicans had not lost approximately thirty thousand votes to the Prohibitionists. Many contemporaries considered Hill's election by a plurality of only eleven thousand more an accident than a victory, but he was re-elected governor in 1888, and he was elected to the United States Senate by the legislature in 1891.

Hill's success as a party leader can be attributed in large measure to his skill in bringing together diverse—and often hostile—groups that had little in common besides their loyalty to him. New York's Democrats were divided up among machines whose leaders seldom agreed on anything except the desirability of supporting Hill. Tammany Hall, whether it was ruled by Kelly (until his death in 1886) or by Richard Croker, his successor, repeatedly produced large majorities for Hill. At the same time he could count on the backing of McLaughlin's Brooklyn organization, and he always maintained friendly relations with the party's upstate bosses. In addition, he was careful never to alienate the labor vote. In 1887 Henry George had campaigned for mayor of New York City on a labor ticket; and although he lost the election to Abram S. Hewitt, the Democratic candidate, he polled more votes than Theodore Roosevelt, the Republican nominee. The implications of this election were not lost on Hill. His campaign speeches contained many kind words for the workingman; as governor he consistently refused to approve any bill permitting prisoners to do any work that might jeopardize the jobs of free laborers; and during his two terms at Albany more labor bills were adopted than in any preceding administration.

In his campaigns against the Republicans, Hill was always able to capitalize on the liquor issue. The Republicans, caught between the upstate "drys" and the urban "wets"—particularly the Germans—were compelled to take a more or less equivocal stand on the question of the state's regulation of the sale of alcoholic beverages. As a consequence, the Prohibitionists were always able to attract some votes from the Republicans in the rural districts. The Democrats, with nothing to gain by temporizing on this issue, openly appealed to the wets and took a strong stand for what they preferred to call "personal liberty" (or the right of any individual to drink as much as he wished). Hill always received generous campaign contributions from the state's liquor firms, and the Republicans' loss of votes to the Prohibitionists was undoubtedly one of the important factors in his party's successive victories at the polls.

Although Hill could defeat the Republicans on a state-wide basis, he was not able to break their hold on the Senate and Assembly. During his two terms as governor he was in constant conflict with a succession of Republican legislatures that sought to embarrass him by passing reform bills that they knew he would veto. Hill, for his part, usually played the role assigned him by the opposition. Thus, in 1888 he vetoed a bill for the prevention of bribery at elections, and in both 1888 and 1889 he vetoed the Saxton bill for the Australian, or secret, ballot. Under the terms of the Saxton bill, official ballots that were to be marked in secrecy would replace the ballots which the parties printed in different colors and which enabled poll watchers to know how every vote was cast. Public opinion, however, favored electoral reform, and Hill soon realized that he would have to make some concessions. Accordingly, in 1890 he recommended that the Corrupt Practice Act, which required every candidate for an elective office to file expense accounts, be extended; and when the legislature followed his advice, he signed the bill. In the same year he approved a revised version of the Saxton bill. The amended bill provided that in addition to the official ballot every voter be issued a "paster," or party ballot, which could be pasted over the regular list of candidates. The "pasters," whose use had been proposed by Hill and which he defended on the ground that they were needed by illiterates, effectively circumvented the Saxton bill's requirement for secrecy.

Soon after Hill had assumed the governorship it became apparent that he considered himself Cleveland's rival for the control of the party. As a spoilsman he had no sympathy for the President's interest in civil service reform, and within a short time he had become the spokesman for those who complained that the party's regulars were not receiving a large enough share of the federal patronage. By 1888 Hill had undisguised presidential ambitions, but he was not yet ready to make his bid, and Cleveland was renominated by acclamation. Following the election, in which Hill was re-elected governor and Cleveland was defeated because of his failure to carry New York, it was charged—but never demonstrated —that the governor had sabotaged the national ticket. In any event the breach between the two men steadily widened. Although Hill was elected to the United States Senate in the spring of 1891 (for the remainder of the year he served as both governor and senator), he was unable to dislodge his rival as head of the party, and in 1892 the Democrats for the third time selected Cleveland as their presidential candidate.

The Democrats did not lose control of the executive branch of the state government until 1895, but they had prepared the way for their own defeat some years before this. In 1891 they elected Flower governor and won the Assembly sixty-seven to sixty-one. The Senate, however, remained in doubt, for each party had fourteen seats while the outcomes of the election in four districts—Troy, Onondaga, Steuben, and Dutchess—were in dispute. The Court of Appeals awarded the Troy seat to the Republicans and the Onondaga seat to the Democrats, left the Steuben contest to the Senate, and ruled that the Dutchess return (which gave the seat to a Democrat) was illegal. Despite the court's decision, Deputy Attorney General Isaac H. Maynard and the state Board of Canvassers awarded Dutchess to the Democrats. With a sixteen-to-fifteen majority the Democrats then organized the Senate and voted to seat their party's candidate from the Steuben district. The Democrats had achieved their immediate objective, but they had also managed to antagonize all but their most rabid partisans. In an apparent effort to enrage public opinion still further, Flower appointed Maynard a judge of the Court of Appeals. In 1893, when Maynard was a candidate for the same post, he was defeated by a plurality of more than 100,000. Democratic misfortunes were climaxed by spectacular revelations concerning the alliance between crime and Croker's Tammany machine in New York City. The Reverend Charles H. Parkhurst found ample evidence on his tours of the city that Tammany was filled with "a lying, perjured, rum-soaked, and libidinous lot," while the testimony before the legislature's Lexow committee in 1894 demonstrated that the police and Croker's henchmen exacted regular tribute from New York's prostitutes, brothel keepers, criminals, and saloon owners.

When the Democrats held their state convention in 1894, their "theft" of the state Senate, Hill's refusal to resign the governorship after his election to the Senate, the disclosures concerning Tammany rule in New York City, and the voters' inclination to attribute the hard times following the Panic of 1893 to the party in power all combined to make the outcome of the gubernatorial election a foregone conclusion. The delegates, who behaved as though they were attending a wake, turned to Hill in desperation. Although he at first attempted to check the movement to draft him, he reluctantly agreed to be the party's candidate. In accepting the nomination, he stated that having been honored by the party when he "solicited its favors, in the days of its sunshine and prosperity," he would not "desert it now in the hour of its danger and this great emergency." Hill exaggerated neither the danger nor the emergency, and in November he was overwhelmingly defeated by Levi P. Morton, the Republican candidate. Morton's victory marked the end of twelve years of Democratic rule and the beginning of a decade and a half of Republican control of the state government.

In 1894 the voters approved a new constitution that had been drawn up by a convention which was presided over by Joseph H. Choate and whose members included Elihu Root, William C. Whitney, John Bigelow, and Andrew H. Green. The Constitution of 1894 (which, with amendments, is still in effect) reduced the governor's term to two years, increased the Senate's membership from thirty-two to fifty and the Assembly's from 128 to 150, provided for a new system of apportionment that continued in different form the rural counties' overrepresentation in the legislature, and sought to divorce state from local politics by providing for state elections in even years and municipal elections in odd years. In an effort to speed up and standardize the administration of justice, the new constitution consolidated the minor courts in Brooklyn, New York City, and Buffalo with the Supreme Court, abolished the general terms, established four appellate divisions of the Supreme Court, and increased the number of Supreme Court justices in each district. An effort was also made to furnish cities with minimum guarantees against state encroachment. Cities were divided into classes, and any bill relating to less than all the cities of a class had to be approved by those cities that were directly affected. If approval was withheld, the measure could become law only if it was repassed by the legislature. Other important provisions of the constitution forbade the cutting of any timber in the state's forest preserve, set up rigid standards for voting, and provided for competitive appointments to the civil service under the merit system. Although the Constitution of 1894 did not increase centralization of administration by reducing the number of elective offices, it did remove a great deal of the chaos and many of the abuses that had been characteristic features of New York's government under the Constitution of 1846.

During the two decades preceding the adoption of the Constitution of 1894, New York had been almost continuously ruled by Democratic governors and Republican legislatures. The national reputations and executive abilities of Tilden, Cleveland, and Hill tended to obscure, but did not obviate, the fact that the control of the government was usually shared by the two parties. Although this division of power frequently provided the citizens of the state with nothing more rewarding than a stalemate, it should not be assumed that this was an entirely negative period. Every session of the legislature adopted, and every governor approved, bills that in the long run were to be far more important than the innumerable jobs and deals that consumed so much of the time of a New York politician. Ranking high on any list of such bills was the act for civil service reform. Adopted in 1883, this measure followed closely the provisions of the law enacted earlier in the same year by the federal government. Many years elapsed before the merit system became firmly established, but the law of 1883 marked the first breach in the wall of partisan privilege that had been erected by the spoilsmen.

The state also showed an increasing interest in the regulation of economic affairs. In its famous report to the legislature in 1880, the Hepburn committee not only described in detail the effects of the various forms of rate discrimination practiced by the railroads, but it also anticipated most of the findings of the congressional investigations that preceded the enactment of the Federal Interstate Commerce Act in 1887. After considerable delay and protracted debates, the legislature of 1882 created a three-man railroad commission which had the power to investigate complaints and advise the legislature but was not given any regulatory functions. Several bills, all of which proved ineffectual, were also adopted to regulate insurance companies, and a statute in 1887 provided for the supervision and administration of trust companies. The members of the Senate and Assembly, moreover, revealed an increasing concern over the lot—and the votes—of the state's workingmen. The legislature established the office of factory inspector (1886), made twelve hours the maximum work-day for employees on elevated and street railways in cities with a population of more than fifty thousand (1886), prohibited the employment of children under thirteen in factories (1886), created a state Board of Arbitration to settle disputes between employers and employees (1887), and forbade corporations to pay their employees in "store orders" (1889).

An equally significant extension of state authority occurred in the field of conservation. Despite the creation of a state park commission in 1872, little was done to conserve New York's physical resources until 1883, when the legislature withdrew from sale forest lands that had been acquired in tax arrears. Within two years the legislature had authorized the establishment of a state forest preserve in the Adirondacks, set up a state forestry commission, and appropriated the funds for a park at Niagara Falls. Successive legislatures adopted bills regulating the forest preserves, and in 1892 Adirondack Park was created. Although timber cutting was permitted in both the forest preserve and Adirondack Park during Governor Flower's administration, this policy was reversed by a provision in the Constitution of 1894. New York was far more fortunate than most states in having officials who had enough foresight and courage to prevent powerful private interests from destroying some of the state's most valuable possessions.

Most of the progressive measures adopted by New York from 1874 to

1894 soon proved inadequate, and in subsequent years they were substantially revised and expanded. But taken collectively, they add up to a program of considerable breadth and vision for the period in which they were enacted. In an age which is frequently remembered only for its party battles and bosses, New York began the erection of that structure of social legislation that today is among its most distinctive features.

From Platt to Progressivism

*In New York State, United States Senator Platt was the abso-
lute boss of the Republican party. "Big Business" was back of
him; yet at the time this, the most important element in his
strength, was only imperfectly understood. It was not until
I was elected Governor that I myself came to understand
it.*—THEODORE ROOSEVELT

DURING the two decades preceding World War I reformers played a
major—if not decisive—role in New York's government and politics.
Although Thomas C. Platt bossed the Republicans until the turn of the
century and Tammany continued its domination over the Democrats, both
parties contained sizable blocs of progressives. Theodore Roosevelt and
Charles Evans Hughes were outstanding Republican governors, while in
the legislature Robert Wagner and Alfred E. Smith demonstrated that
Tammany Democrats could also be reformers. By 1914 New York had
not reached the millennium, but it had adopted a body of forward-looking
legislation that placed the state in the front ranks of the progressive movement.

When Levi Morton defeated David Hill for the governorship in 1894,
the voters of New York exchanged one machine for another. Morton
was Platt's candidate, and Platt headed one of the most efficient political
organizations in the state's history. On the other hand, his rule was of
relatively short duration. He did not obtain control of the state government until the mid-1890's, and after 1900 his power declined rapidly.
Before he died in 1910, he was completely out of touch with his party and
his times, and to many he seemed an anachronistic symbol of a political
age that had been destroyed by progressivism.

Like many other party leaders, Platt devoted most of his adult life to
the business of politics. He was born in 1823 in Owego, Tioga County
(one of the southern tier counties), and as a young man he opened a
drugstore which soon became the informal headquarters for Tioga's Re-

publican politicians. After taking an active part in the Frémont campaign, he was made county clerk in 1858, and in the 1860's he became chairman of the county Republican committee. He used his position as the party's leader in Tioga to support Fenton, but within a short time he had shifted his allegiance to Conkling. He helped Conkling manage the state convention in 1870, and for the next eleven years he faithfully followed his own and his party's boss. He voted as Conkling directed during his two terms in the House; he resigned from the Senate with Conkling in 1881; and he returned to Albany—and defeat—with Conkling in the same year. It was his willingness to stand by Conkling in 1881 that earned him the nickname "Me-Too Platt."

Within a few years of their rejection by the New York legislature, Conkling had been relegated to political obscurity and Platt was boss of the state Republican machine. During Arthur's administration Platt obtained control over some of the federal patronage, and in 1884 he made peace with the party's national organization by announcing that he favored Blaine's nomination for the presidency. Four years later he helped to carry the state for Harrison. It was not, however, until 1894 that his machine took over the state government. In 1897 he avenged the humiliating defeat of 1881 by securing his election to the Senate, and in 1903 he still retained enough influence in the organization for re-election.

Like every other boss, Platt derived his power from his ability to reward the faithful with jobs and favors. All the jobs went to loyal party workers, and the favors were granted to those business firms that helped to finance the Republican organization. As the state's Republican leader, he always attempted to distribute the largesse at his disposal in such a way as to promote party harmony and to prevent the organization from being disrupted by factionalism. Known to both his followers and opponents as the "Easy Boss," he preferred compromise to the type of intraparty conflict that had led to his own and Conkling's downfall. He viewed irregularity as the gravest of political sins, but he also realized that the New York Republicans had to appeal to reform as well as machine groups to win elections. Thus in 1891 he unsuccessfully attempted to secure the nomination for governor of such a well-known Republican as Andrew D. White, and in 1898 he backed the unpredictable Roosevelt for the highest office in the state. His answer to the curse of factionalism was not to crush rebellions but to appease the rebels.

The major decisions concerning the conduct of the Republican machine were invariably reached at conferences which Platt held every Sunday at the Fifth Avenue Hotel in New York City. Party leaders from every section of the state regularly attended what came to be known as "Platt's Sunday school classes." Because Platt's suggestions were always approved by his lieutenants at these sessions, the corner of the lobby in which he instructed his willing students was usually referred to as the "Amen Corner." It was at the Amen Corner that the party's nominees were selected, platforms drawn up, jobs distributed, and directives formulated for legislators and governors.

From 1895 to 1899 Platt was at the height of his power in New York. Republican legislatures unfailingly did his bidding, and the occupants of the governor's office were his personal selections. Morton, whom Platt considered the "safest governor that New York ever had," displayed some interest in civil service reform, but he never got out of hand, and in a crisis he always followed the boss's orders. Particularly consoling to Platt was Morton's belief that the legislature was an autonomous branch of the government and that the governor should use his veto power only under the most unusual circumstances. He also revealed his "safeness" by permitting the machine to revive the abuses in canal administration that had been eliminated some twenty years earlier by Tilden.

Frank S. Black, who was elected governor in 1896, equaled or surpassed Morton's loyalty to the machine. In addition to continuing his predecessor's canal policies, he substituted what he called "starchless civil service" for the merit system and appointed some of the organization's most disreputable and notorious hacks to positions of responsibility. Of all his appointments, that of Louis Payn as superintendent of insurance provoked the greatest public indignation. A veteran member of the "Sunday school classes" and an avowed lobbyist, Payn was such an obviously obnoxious selection that even some of the Republican regulars in the state Senate refused to vote for his confirmation.

When the members of the Sunday school class decided that a bill was a "party measure," legislative approval was a virtual certainty. High on any list of such measures was the Raines Liquor Tax bill. Although originally opposed by Republican senators and assemblymen with urban constituencies, it was adopted by the legislature in 1896 because of pressure exerted by Platt. It provided for high license fees for saloons and hotels in cities, restricted the sale of liquor on Sundays to hotels, divided the revenue from liquor taxes between state and local governments, and placed the administration of the law under state authority. Prohibitionists favored the law as a temperance measure; Platt backed it as a device which would create additional state jobs for his followers and provide the state with funds that would be supplied in large part by cities in which there were many Democrats and few Republicans. In neither of these expectations was he disappointed. On the other hand, he did not anticipate that the law would also result in a marked increase in prostitution. To circumvent the Sunday restrictions, many saloons bought a few beds and called themselves hotels. Having the beds, the "Raines law hotels" put them to use, and soon many saloons were also brothels.

The Greater New York bill was another "party measure" that was adopted in large part because of Platt's influence over Republican officials in Albany. For some thirty years several interested individuals (the most persistent of whom was Andrew H. Green) had been agitating to enlarge New York City so that it would include all the communities in the state bordering on New York harbor. It was not, however, until Platt took up the cause that substantial progress was made. In 1890 the legislature authorized a committee to investigate the problem, but no move was made to implement the committee's report favoring the project. Although a plebiscite in 1894 revealed that a majority of the voters in the area affected by the proposal favored a consolidated city, the legislature continued to withhold its approval. But when word went out from the Amen Corner in 1896 that the organization favored consolidation, the legislature adopted a bill creating a commission to draw up a charter for Greater New York. Behind Platt's decision to support the bill was his conviction that the enlarged city would be ruled by commissions that would be appointed by the governor and staffed by Republicans.

The Greater New York bill aroused more opposition than any other measure sponsored by Platt. Several upstate Republicans were alarmed by the prospect of a single huge city that could dominate the state; many Brooklyn citizens objected to the destruction of their city's identity; the McLaughlin machine viewed the bill as a device for extending Tammany's authority to Brooklyn; and New York City businessmen feared that the annexation of relatively undeveloped areas would increase their tax burdens. In addition to those Republicans who took their orders from Platt, the bill was supported by Tammany politicians who looked forward to controlling the patronage of the greater city and by many New Yorkers who were thrilled by the idea of such a magnificent metropolis. Despite extraordinary pressure exerted by Platt, some Republican legislators refused to support the bill, and it was passed in 1896 only because of the votes it received from Tammany. When Morton expressed some doubts concerning the feasibility of a Greater New York, Platt had to "rowl" him "with a fierceness that hurt" to induce him to sign the bill. In 1897 a charter for the enlarged city was approved by the legislature and on January 1, 1898, Greater New York began its official existence. The original charter for Greater New York provided for the division of the city into five boroughs (Bronx, Brooklyn, Manhattan, Queens, Richmond), each of which had a president elected by the respective borough's voters. The Board of Aldermen, with sixty-five members, was the city's legislative body. The mayor, comptroller, and president of the Board of Aldermen were elected on a city-wide basis, and together with the borough presidents constituted the Board of Estimate and Apportionment which was empowered to make policy for the city and to have authority over the city's finances.

Platt's practically autocratic control over the state government ended with the election of 1898. Although most of the party's regulars favored Governor Black's renomination, the Easy Boss realized that public indignation over the canal scandals, the Payn appointment, and starchless civil service required the selection of a candidate who was acceptable to independent voters and who had not been identified with the Republican regime at Albany. Under the circumstances Platt felt compelled, however reluctantly, to back Roosevelt as Republican nominee. Above all else Platt needed a winner, and Roosevelt alone seemed capable of leading the party to victory. His exploits in the Spanish American War, following his service as assistant secretary of the navy, had made him a national hero; his record as a state assemblyman, federal civil service commissioner, and New York City police commissioner had established his reputation as a reformer; and his family background as well as his education at Harvard served to convince many independents that he was above the machinations of the organization supporting him. The hacks and wheelhorses in the Platt organization may not have liked him, but they had to put up with him. They could, moreover, console themselves with the thought that he had never broken with the party and that he had even stuck by Blaine in the Mugwump revolt of 1884. Events were also to demonstrate that in spite of his reputation as a reformer and moralist, Roosevelt could be as practical a politician as any veteran of the Amen Corner. The machine's leaders were to learn that the difficulty was not so much that he was a reformer, but that he was an ambitious man who would not participate in any movement which he could not also lead.

In the first weeks of the campaign of 1898, Roosevelt "fairly pranced around the state," giving speeches on the glories of the Spanish American War and imperialism. The voters clearly resented his refusal to discuss state issues; and although Augustus Van Wyck, the Democratic nominee, was a weak candidate, he seemed strong enough to defeat a thoroughly discredited Republican party. But in the middle of the campaign Croker played into Roosevelt's hands by announcing that Supreme Court Justice Joseph F. Daly, a veteran with twenty-eight years' service on the bench, would not be renominated. Reformers in both parties were shocked by this blatant attempt to make loyalty to Tammany the only qualification for election to the judiciary, and Roosevelt immediately made Crokerism the major issue of the campaign. In all likelihood it was his militant stand against Tammany that enabled him to win the election, with a plurality of approximately eighteen thousand votes.

Roosevelt considered himself "the best governor within my time, better than either Cleveland or Tilden." Although he was never as much of a reformer as he liked to imagine, he had considerable justification for this typically immodest estimate of his accomplishments. Some of his appointments reflected Platt's influence, but many others did not. Despite the opposition of the machine, he dismissed Payn as superintendent of insurance, and he supported the enactment in 1899 of a civil service law which unified the state system and required appointing officers to fill any vacancy with the first candidate on the eligible list. In addition, a number of labor bills were adopted during his administration. Laws were enacted to regulate work done on a piece-rate basis by tenement-house dwellers in their homes, to safeguard women and children in industry, to create a tenement-house commission, to increase the number of factory inspectors, and to improve working conditions in the building trades, restaurants, hotels, and drugstores. Although Roosevelt was inclined to take all the credit for such legislation, he did in fact support many labor reforms, and on occasion his influence over the legislature proved decisive.

In Roosevelt's opinion the adoption of the Franchise Tax bill in 1899 was the most important contribution that he made as governor. Although he did not sponsor the measure, he gave it his enthusiastic support and deserves most of the credit for its enactment. Under the terms of this bill, public service corporations, which in the past had not paid taxes on franchises for the streets they used, were to have the value of their franchises taxed as real estate. For understandable reasons corporations affected by the bill did all within their power to defeat it. Because many of these corporations contributed to the Republican party, the Platt organization also opposed the bill. But it was favored by the voters, and to appease public opinion the machine decided to let it pass in the Senate and then permit it to die in the Assembly. Roosevelt responded to these tactics with a barrage of special messages favoring the tax. Through constant pressure he was able to obtain its passage on the final day of the session. When it reached the governor's desk, it contained certain objectionable provisions that had been inserted by the measure's opponents in the hope that Roosevelt would disapprove of them and would therefore veto the bill. Roosevelt, however, called an extra session of the legislature and secured the passage of a measure satisfactory to him. The Franchise Tax bill was a victory for reform. Roosevelt, in this instance at least, had defied, outmaneuvered, and defeated Platt.

If Roosevelt was a reformer, he was also a politician who knew when and how to compromise. He eliminated fraud in the administration of the state's canals, but he made no move to punish the members of his own party who had profited from the canal frauds. He removed Payn as superintendent of insurance, but he named another member of the machine to the same post. He prided himself on his independence, but he never broke with the organization. Throughout his administration he and Platt maintained an uneasy truce. Each needed the other, for both realized that open warfare would wreck their careers. The result was a *modus vivendi* that gave the governor considerable latitude in the formulation of policy and enabled the boss to retain his control over the day-to-day operations of the machine.

Although Roosevelt made several concessions to the party's professional politicians, he did not make enough to please Platt, and in 1900 the boss maneuvered the governor into accepting the Republican nomination for the vice-presidency. Roosevelt's shift from state to national politics did not, however, end Republican rule in New York. Benjamin B. Odell, Jr., a Platt lieutenant who had served in Congress and as chairman of the Republican state committee, was elected governor in 1900 and re-elected in 1902. In 1905 he was succeeded by Frank W. Higgins, an upstate Republican businessman who had been lieutenant governor during Odell's second term.

During the Odell and Higgins administrations there were a number of changes in the leadership of the Republican party. Odell took over the party's machinery in the state, and President Roosevelt rather than Platt distributed the federal patronage in New York. Deprived of the two most important sources of his power, Platt was reduced to a position of relative insignificance in state and national politics. Odell, however, was unable to maintain his hold over the state organization. When Higgins became governor, he indicated his independence by helping to defeat Odell's candidate for the speakership of the Assembly, and by the end of his term the party was controlled by a loose alliance of local bosses.

During the same years equally significant changes occurred in the high command of the Democratic party. Following Seth Low's victory in 1901 over the Tammany candidate for mayor of New York City, Croker relinquished his position as leader and retired to his estate in Ireland. For a short time Tammany was ruled by a triumvirate, but by 1902 Charles E. Murphy had emerged as undisputed leader. Murphy, who was to hold this position until his death in 1924, exercised fully as much power as his predecessors had; but he was more sensitive to public opinion than were most Tammany leaders and he permitted the organization to back certain reform measures that were designed—among other things—to improve the lot of Tammany's poorer constituents. One of Murphy's first acts was to extend Tammany's control to Brooklyn, and in 1903 his lieutenant, Patrick McCarran, overthrew the McLaughlin machine. But within a short time Brooklyn Democrats had driven the invaders from the borough, and in subsequent years they were able to prevent the tiger from recrossing the bridge.

As governor, Odell provided the state with an unimaginative administration that was characterized by its economy and efficiency. Under his direction, the number of state offices was reduced, several departments were consolidated, a roadbuilding program was undertaken, work was begun on the conversion of the Erie Canal to the Barge Canal, and Seth

Low's demands for home rule for New York City were supported. At the same time, Odell endeared himself to the taxpayers by cutting the state's expenditures (as well as its services) and by substituting indirect for direct methods of taxation. During Higgins' administration Odell's tax and economy programs were continued, and the government strengthened its control over working conditions within the state. In 1905 the voters approved a constitutional amendment that permitted the legislature to regulate wages, hours, and working conditions for laborers employed by the state or on public contracts, and in the same year the legislature passed a law (which was later invalidated by the Supreme Court) regulating the hours of labor of men in bakeries. To contemporaries, however, every other event of the Higgins administration was overshadowed by the results of the legislature's investigations of New York City's gas and insurance companies.

The inquiry into the conduct of the city's gas companies was undertaken in response to consumers' repeated complaints of high rates. Despite the opposition of the gas lobby, the legislature in 1905 appointed a committee headed by Senator Frederick C. Stevens to investigate the companies' policies. Charles Evans Hughes, a New York City attorney, was made committee counsel. The testimony elicited by Hughes's skillful examination of witnesses revealed that the companies comprising the so-called gas trust had eliminated competition within the city, were grossly overcapitalized, charged exorbitant rates, made enormous profits, and sold an inferior product. In his report at the conclusion of the investigation Hughes proposed that in the future gas be sold at seventy-five cents per thousand cubic feet instead of at $1.00 or $1.25, that the price of electricity be reduced from fifteen to ten cents per kilowatt hour, and that the supervision of the gas and lighting companies be intrusted to a public service commission "with inquisitorial authority, competent to make summary investigations of complaints, to supervise issues of securities and investment in the stocks or bonds of other companies, to regulate rates and to secure adequate inspection, or otherwise to enforce the provisions of the law." Although these proposals were adopted by the legislature, the gas bill was not enacted until 1906, and then the statutory price was set at eighty rather than seventy-five cents.

Within a few months of the gas investigation the Armstrong committee began its examination of a group of New York City insurance firms. In the course of the hearings Hughes uncovered a trail of corruption and misrepresentation that made the gas companies look like models of business ethics. Under Hughes's questioning a succession of highly paid and hitherto respected insurance executives admitted that they retained control over their companies through extralegal devices, made regular campaign contributions to the Republican party, bribed legislators of both parties, paid out large sums to corrupt the press, maintained lobbyists at Albany and other state capitals, arranged illegal loans between their companies and banks on whose boards they served, speculated with their companies' funds in other enterprises, falsified their books, and knew virtually nothing about the actual conduct of the insurance business. By the time the four-month investigation had ended, several insurance executives had fled the country, almost all of them had been convicted by their own words of fraudulent practices, the superintendent of insurance (who had been appointed by Roosevelt) had resigned in disgrace, and Hughes had become one of the state's most prominent Republicans. In 1906 the legislature, following the recommendations made by Hughes's report on the investigation, adopted bills regulating the state's insurance companies, prohibiting corporations from contributing to political campaigns, and requiring lobbyists to register and make public the nature of their work.

The reputation that Hughes earned as a skillful and fearless investigator made him the outstanding candidate for the Republican gubernatorial nomination in 1906. Although he was not acceptable to the party's regulars, they agreed to his nomination because they realized that no one else had even an outside chance of defeating the Democrats. To oppose Hughes the Democrats nominated William Randolph Hearst, who in 1905 had headed an independent ticket in the New York City mayoralty election. The ensuing campaign was one of the most bitter in New York's history, and Hughes was the only Republican on the state ticket to be elected.

When Hughes became governor, he had no political past. He had never held any office before his appointment as counsel for the gas investigation, and he had never given the Republican party anything beside his vote. After graduating from Brown University and Columbia Law School, he entered private practice in New York. Following a short interlude of teaching at Cornell, he returned to the city and the law. Although he won several notable cases as a trial lawyer, he was known by almost no one outside the legal profession before he began his career as an investigator. In 1905, during the insurance hearings, he was nominated by the Republicans as their candidate for mayor of New York City. Although it was understood that he would not have to campaign and that he could continue as counsel for the Armstrong committee, he believed that the nomination would place him in an ambiguous—if not compromising—position, and he refused to be a candidate. He made no effort to secure the gubernatorial nomination, and when he assumed office in January 1907, his only commitments had been made to the voters during the campaign.

Hughes was not a party leader, and during his two terms as governor he was usually opposed by the regular Republican organization. He was, however, a successful executive who repeatedly defeated the politicians by violating all the rules of politics. He refused to compromise on matters of principle, he placed the general welfare ahead of party welfare, and he appealed to the voters directly whenever he wished their support. He was, moreover, a progressive in an age of progressivism. While most state Republican leaders continued to act as if nothing had changed since the days when Roscoe Conkling had bossed the party, Hughes won widespread popular support for his espousal of a series of reforms that were designed to eliminate economic and political abuses. During the progressive era, Roosevelt was the only New Yorker to gain greater renown as a progressive; but Roosevelt owed his reputation to his activities in Washington rather than in New York, and his reform record as governor did not match that of Hughes.

Soon after becoming governor, Hughes alienated the party's bosses by refusing to accept their candidates for the major appointive positions in the state government. When Roosevelt at the request of the organization intervened in the dispute, Hughes let it be known that it was his—and not the President's—responsibility. Although Hughes's prestige enabled him to force the machine into accepting many of his nominees, he ran into a solid wall of opposition when he sought to remove Otto Kelsey as superintendent of insurance. John Raines, William Barnes, Jr., and other regulars protested that Kelsey had never even been accused of dishonesty. While conceding this point, Hughes maintained that the superintendent of insurance was incompetent and would have to go. To the party's professionals this seemed a revolutionary and irrelevant basis for judging a public servant. Raines announced that he would "fight Mr. Hughes tooth and nail for the rest of the session," and on May 3, 1907, the Senate rejected the governor's request for Kelsey's removal. Hughes had lost his first battle, but he was engaged in a war.

Despite the opposition that Hughes had aroused among the party's professionals, he was able to force the legislature to approve his plan for a thorough reorganization of the state's program for the supervision of public utilities. Although the state commission of gas and electricity had been established on his recommendation in 1906, he soon became convinced that the problem of economic regulation required a more comprehensive solution. Accordingly, in his first message to the legislature in 1907, he proposed that the Board of Railroad Commissioners, the Commission of Gas and Electricity, and the Rapid Transit Board of New York City be replaced by two public service commissions, one of which would have authority over New York City and the other over the rest of the state. Each of the commissions would be authorized to investigate the affairs of the companies under their jurisdiction, fix rates, set minimum standards of service, "provide for the safety of employees," and "generally to direct whatever may be necessary or proper to safeguard the public interest and to secure the fulfillment of the public obligations of the corporations under its supervision." When these proposals were incorporated in the Page-Merritt bill, there seemed little possibility that the measure could be passed over the opposition of both the leaders in Hughes's own party and the state's most powerful business groups. The governor, however, took his case to the people in a series of speeches that he delivered in every part of the state. Old Albany hands laughed at the governor's naïveté, but the voters responded by deluging the legislature with mail favoring the measure. Three weeks after Hughes had started his speaking tour the Page-Merritt bill became law. A reporter wrote that the governor had forced "an insolent and hostile legislature to its knees."

In his second year in office Hughes again demonstrated that it was possible for a governor with popular support to defeat a recalcitrant legislature. At his suggestion the Agnew-Hart bill was drawn up to repeal an existing statute that legalized bookmaking at the state's race tracks. Although he had no moral objections to either gambling or horse racing, the state constitution forbade gambling, and it was for this reason that he advocated the repeal of the law in question. The Agnew-Hart bill passed the Assembly, but it was bitterly opposed in the Senate. Hughes then made a direct appeal to the voters for their support, but the measure failed in the Senate by a tie vote, and the legislature immediately adjourned. The governor countered by ordering a special session to reconsider the measure. Meanwhile, the death of a senator made it necessary to hold a special election in the Niagara-Orleans district. Hughes stumped the district for the candidate favoring the Agnew-Hart bill. His candidate won the election and provided the vote needed to pass the bill in the special session of the legislature.

By the end of his first term Hughes had alienated everyone but the voters. The bosses would have shelved him if they had dared, but his popularity made this an impossibility, and he was renominated for a second term on the first ballot. Opposed in the campaign by Lewis S. Chanler, the Democratic lieutenant governor, Hughes was re-elected by a larger plurality than he had received in 1906. Throughout most of his second term, he sought to secure reforms in the state's governmental and electoral machinery. In his messages to the legislature and in numerous speeches to the voters he advocated direct primaries, the short ballot, and the abolition of the Senate's check on the governor's power of removal. Despite the persistence with which he argued for these proposals, they were not approved by the legislature until some years after he had left office.

In addition to the major reforms that Hughes championed were a number of other acts that revealed his progressivism. He created commissions to investigate economic and political abuses, obtained a more equitable apportionment of the Senate and Assembly seats, co-operated with Assemblyman Al Smith to secure the adoption of a bill limiting campaign expenditures, and was instrumental in the enactment of a bill for the regulation of telephone and telegraph companies. He also had an outstanding record as a friend of labor. Under his sponsorship New York in 1910 passed the nation's first workmen's compensation law (which was later invalidated by the Court of Appeals), and in his two terms as governor he signed fifty-six laws that were designed to assist and protect workers. When he retired, a New York City labor paper wrote that he was "the greatest friend of labor laws that ever occupied the Governor's chair at Albany." More important, however, than any bill or bills that he sponsored was the fashion in which he revitalized democracy in New York. In October 1910 the New York *Evening Post* wrote:

This new breath which he breathed into our political methods came largely from his steadfast reliance upon reason and justice. No public man ever treated a democracy more consistently as a fair-minded court that could be prevailed upon to see where the weight of argument lies and what is the right thing to do. . . . We gratefully acknowledge that he has ennobled our public life and quickened our hope in democracy.

In October 1910 Hughes resigned as governor to become a justice of the United States Supreme Court. In the fall elections of the same year the Democrats elected John Alden Dix governor and won control of both branches of the legislature. On assuming office Dix recommended a comprehensive program of progressive legislation that included proposals for direct primaries, popular election of United States senators, an income tax, factory inspection, and an increase in corporation taxes. The legislature, however, ignored almost all his suggestions. During his first year in office the regular business of the legislature was postponed for months because of an intraparty struggle over the selection of a United States senator. Tammany's candidate, William F. Sheehan, was opposed by a group of Democratic independents headed by Franklin D. Roosevelt, who was serving his first term in the state Senate. It was not until the end of March that this dispute was settled with the selection of a compromise candidate. By this time the Democratic majorities in the Assembly and Senate were so hopelessly divided that they were unable to agree on any of the governor's proposals. In the following year the Republicans, who had regained control of the legislature, were equally unco-operative. By the end of his term Dix had alienated both the reformers and regulars, and he was not renominated by the Democrats.

William Sulzer, who was elected governor by the Democrats in 1912, was a Tammany candidate from New York City. But he was also a mercurial man who on more than one occasion had defied the machine. He had a remarkable hold on the city's voters, and he had served five years in the Assembly and eighteen in the national House of Representatives. Throughout his legislative career he had sponsored numerous progressive measures, and as governor he urged the adoption of a sweeping program of reform.

Sulzer began his term as governor with the statement: "I am free . . . and shall remain free. . . . No influence controls me but the dictates of my conscience." But Boss Murphy had other ideas. Before taking office Sulzer had informed the boss that he intended to be governor in his own right, and Murphy had reportedly answered, "Like hell you are." Sulzer, refusing to be intimidated, ignored Tammany applicants for jobs. When he rejected the machine's candidate for highway commissioner with the assertion, "I am the Governor," Murphy replied, "You may be the Governor, but I have got the Legislature, and the Legislature controls the Governor, and if you don't do what I tell you to do, I will throw you out of office."

As soon as Murphy realized that he could not rule the governor, he prepared to destroy him. On August 11, 1913, a legislative committee that had been appointed at Murphy's instigation reported that Sulzer had falsified the accounts of his campaign expenditures. On the following day the Assembly voted to impeach him. In September he was tried on eight charges by a court of impeachment consisting of the members of the Senate and Court of Appeals. He was convicted on three of the charges, for a majority of the court ruled that he had misrepresented the expenditures of his campaign funds, had committed perjury, and had suppressed evidence. On October 17 he was removed from office. A victim of political vengeance, Sulzer had been convicted of crimes that he had committed before becoming governor. In the final analysis he was removed because he refused to obey Murphy's orders.

When Sulzer was forced from office he was succeeded by Lieutenant Governor Martin H. Glynn. Although he received far more co-operation from the legislature than had either Dix or Sulzer, he was unable to provide the state with the type of executive leadership that had been so notably lacking since Hughes had resigned from office. Glynn ran for a second term in 1914, but he was defeated by Charles S. Whitman, a Republican who had attracted considerable attention throughout the state as a crusading district attorney.

The repeated conflicts between the executive and legislative branches of the government during the Dix, Sulzer, and Glynn administrations tended to obscure the fact that it was in this period New York adopted a series of significant labor laws. These statutes, which were largely concerned with conditions affecting workers in New York City, received the wholehearted support of Tammany Hall. Murphy never displayed any interest in reform as such, but he recognized the need for backing legislation that would aid and protect his constituents. He was, moreover, represented at Albany during these years by two of the ablest statesmen ever produced by Tammany Hall. Robert F. Wagner was the leader of the Senate Democrats, and Alfred E. Smith occupied a similar position in the Assembly. Both men were machine Democrats, faithful followers of Murphy, and outstanding reformers.

Although Tammany assemblymen and senators in the past had backed measures designed to aid the workingman, it was not until 1911 that its representatives at Albany took the lead in developing a comprehensive program of labor legislation. In that year, following the death of many girls in the Triangle Shirt Waist factory fire in New York City, the legislature appointed the State Factory Investigating Commission. With Wagner as its chairman and Smith as vice-chairman, the commission spent two years examining every phase of the conditions of labor in New York's factories.

Both Smith and Wagner were skilled legislative leaders, and it was largely through their efforts that almost all the recommendations made by the Factory Commission became law. During the first year of the commission's existence the legislature adopted measures to regulate sanitary conditions and eliminate fire hazards in factories. The legislature also adopted a "one-day-of-rest-in-seven law" and set up a series of regulations to protect women and children in industry. In 1913, when Wagner was president pro tem of the Senate and Smith speaker of the Assembly, the legislature enacted virtually all the Factory Investigating Commission's recommendations that had not already been made law. Among the most important labor laws passed in 1913 was the Workmen's Compensation Act. The 1913 session of the legislature also enacted ballot reform and direct primary bills and ratified the amendment to the federal Constitution for the direct election of United States senators. Finally, in 1915, Wagner and Smith, although members of the minority party, were largely responsible for the legislature's enactment of the Widowed Mothers Pension bill. When Smith retired from the Assembly in 1915 to run for sheriff of New York County, he and Wagner had compiled a record that has never been surpassed in the history of the New York legislature. Their contribution to the welfare of the workingman is indicated in part by a statement in 1913 of the New York State Federation of Labor:

Your legislative committee desires to call the attention of the delegates to the . . . unprecedented number of labor laws placed on the statute books of this State. No Legislature in the history of the State Federation surpassed the session of 1913 in the passage of so many or so important remedial measures for wage-earners of New York State, and we doubt if any state in the

Union can now compare with our Empire State in its present code of labor laws. The result this year is due to the State Factory Investigating Commission, of which Senator Wagner is chairman and Speaker Smith vice-chairman.

Despite the great variety of reforms adopted by the legislature in the period before World War I, little was done to provide the state with an efficiently centralized government and responsible officials. In 1915, however, a constitutional convention presided over by Elihu S. Root sought to remedy this deficiency with a series of amendments that made the governor the chief executive in fact as well as in name. The proposed constitution gave the governor the power of appointment and removal over practically all executive officers except the attorney general and comptroller, both of whom remained elective; more than 160 boards and commissions were consolidated into seventeen departments; the piecemeal approach to appropriations was supplanted by an executive budget; and the tax system was made uniform throughout the state. These changes did not ensure good government, but they did make responsible government possible. On the other hand, they were not completely acceptable to any of the major interest groups within the state. Rural Republicans objected to a system of taxation that would have eliminated many of the abuses from which they profited. Many Democrats were opposed to the continuation of a method of apportionment from which the Republicans benefited and to those provisions that gave the governor control over both appointments and the preparation of the executive budget. Progressives maintained that the proposed framework of government was the product of reactionary theories that had been propounded by Root and his fellow conservatives. Trade unions feared that the new constitution would deprive them of many of the rights that they had recently acquired. The amendments prepared by the convention were submitted to the voters in three parts, and each part was overwhelmingly defeated.

During World War I, the state government turned from domestic reforms to plans to aid the defense of both the state and the nation. Although the preparedness program was for the most part the responsibility of the federal government, the legislature in 1916 adopted the Slater Act for military training of high school boys and the Stivers Act for militia conscription. During Whitman's second term (1917–1918), state problems were completely subordinated to those of the nation. Following the United States declaration of war, a commission was established to control the production and distribution of food; a compulsory work law was adopted; the military training program for school and college students was expanded; and a bill designed to prevent sabotage was enacted.

The war years also witnessed the final victory of the woman's suffrage movement in New York. In the period following the Civil War, the various national organizations demanding the vote for women drew their most enthusiastic support and most of their funds from New York. Elizabeth Cady Stanton and Susan B. Anthony were in this period the acknowledged leaders of the movement in both the state and the nation. In 1872 Miss Anthony attracted nation-wide attention not only by insisting on voting, but also by refusing to pay bail following her arrest after she had voted and by refusing to pay the fine imposed on her by the judge who tried her case. But this was an incident—although a spectacular one —in a protracted campaign waged by a number of courageous women who annually petitioned their representatives in Albany, held countless meetings, made innumerable speeches, wrote and distributed propaganda, haunted the halls of the state capitol during every legislative session, and pestered every prominent man they managed to meet. At the state constitutional conventions of 1867 and 1894, they unsuccessfully sought an amendment granting women the right to vote, and they worked tirelessly for a similar amendment to the federal Constitution.

Despite their energy and pertinacity, the suffragettes had little to show for their efforts, and it was not until the first decade of the twentieth century that the movement began to gain the support that was to ensure its success. Several new organizations, made up of either men or men and women, were formed to assist the National American Suffrage Association, which carried on the earlier tradition of agitation, and the National Woman's party, which was formed in 1913 and pursued a consistent policy of militancy. Moreover, for the first time several wealthy women began to give their support to a crusade that in the past they had either ignored or ridiculed. Although Miss Stanton died in 1902 and Miss Anthony in 1906, there were now many others to carry on their work, and Miss Carrie Chapman Catt emerged as the generally acknowledged leader of the movement in both the state and the country.

By 1910 the suffragettes were committed to an aggressive campaign that was as spectacular as it was effective. The old methods were not abandoned, but many new ones were added. Suffragette societies were organized along the lines of political parties; huge parades were held in New York City; motorcades toured the state distributing literature; street-corner speakers urging the vote for women became a commonplace in large cities; a one-day strike of women was threatened; and almost any stunt that would attract publicity was used. These tactics and the long campaign of education that had been carried on by earlier suffragettes finally produced results. A bill for amending the state constitution was passed by the legislature in 1913 and repassed in 1915, but was rejected by the voters at the polls. The process was immediately repeated, and this time it proved successful. The legislature passed the bill in 1916 and 1917, and the voters approved it in the fall of 1917. Two years later the nineteenth amendment to the federal Constitution, providing for woman suffrage, was submitted by Congress to the states; and on June 10 the New York legislature, meeting in special session, unanimously ratified this amendment.

When the United States entered World War I, New York's reformers were left with a great deal of unfinished business, but they could also look back on several notable achievements. They had given the state's citizens an opportunity to increase their control over the government, made the state's administrative machinery more efficient, regulated a number of different types of business enterprises, reduced fraud and corruption in public life, and enacted a series of labor laws that were as advanced as those of any other state in the Union. As remarkable as these accomplishments were, they were to prove merely a prelude to the greatest era of reform in the state's history.

Al Smith and Reform

*Law, in a democracy, means the protection of the rights and
liberties of the minority. . . . It is a confession of the weakness of our own faith in the righteousness of our cause, when
we attempt to suppress by law those who do not agree with
us.*—ALFRED E. SMITH, *1920*

THE end of World War I marked the advent of one of the most reactionary periods in the history of the United States. Americans, apparently
weary of crusades at home and abroad, rejected the ideals of the progressive era and made the worship of business prosperity the new secular
religion. The federal government sought to aid rather than regulate
business; organized labor declined in numbers and militancy; the Ku Klux
Klan ranged over many states in the South and West; and individuals
holding unorthodox economic and social views risked jail sentences, de-
portation, or (in the case of Sacco and Vanzetti) their lives. Conservatism
had supplanted progressivism, and the mass of Americans viewed the
new order with equanimity, if not approval. In the midst of the compla-
cency and reaction of the 1920's, however, New York remained an island
of progress and reform.

The history of New York's government during the postwar decade is
in all essentials the story of Alfred E. Smith and the programs that he
initiated and completed as governor. Although there was no area of state
activity that was not influenced by his policies, his major accomplishments
were the establishment of a system of centralized and responsible government, the adoption of a body of welfare legislation that surpassed that of
any other state, and the revitalization of the democratic spirit when democratic thought and practices appeared to have reached their nadir. His
conduct of the government made New York a model for every other state
in the Union and served as an outstanding example of the continuing
strength of progressivism in an age of conservatism.

Long before Smith became governor, many American politicians had been able to convert their humble origins into a major political asset. The folklore of politics, however, also required that a poor boy who wished to become president be born of Protestant parents on a farm or in a village, and Smith was a Catholic from the slums of the nation's largest city. His story, nevertheless, was in many respects the urban counterpart of the classic legend. As such, it was one more indication that the frontier had ended and that America's future would increasingly be determined by its cities rather than by its countryside. But not all Americans were prepared to concede these points, for when Smith ran for the presidency in 1928, he was overwhelmingly rejected by rural, Protestant America. The final chapter of the American success story had not yet been rewritten for poor boys from the city, and it was perhaps appropriate that Smith was defeated for the presidency by a candidate who had been born in a cottage in Iowa. It was to New York's credit that in successive elections a majority of its voters had not permitted the prejudices of an earlier America to obscure Al Smith's thoroughly American attributes and achievements.

Born in 1873 on Manhattan's Lower East Side, Smith grew up in the shadow of the Brooklyn Bridge. In what he in later years referred to as "the old neighborhood," first and second generation Irish outnumbered all other national groups, and everyone's life was either directly or indirectly affected by St. James Roman Catholic Church, poverty, and Tammany Hall. If this region—as outsiders insisted—had more than its share of criminals, prostitutes, and drunkards, it also had hard-working, law-abiding families like the Smiths. If some boys became ne'er-do-wells, others like Al Smith became altar boys. If life in the slums was often hard and frustrating, there were also interludes of swimming in the East River, Sunday excursions to Coney Island, parties at the church, political outings and chowders, amateur theatricals, and family visits to the beer garden. The old neighborhood may have hardened and embittered some of its inhabitants, but it helped to make Smith both a sentimentalist and a realist. As an adult, he looked back with nostalgia on a boyhood that was as American as that of any farmer's son. At the same time he sought to do all within his power to prevent other Americans from being subjected to the evils that he had endured as a child.

Like many other East Side boys of his generation, Smith began work when he was still a child and entered politics as soon as he came to manhood. At twelve he was selling papers. Three years later he left school for a job with a trucking concern. Before he was twenty-five, he had worked as a shipping clerk in an oil factory, a salesman in the Fulton Fish Market, and a shipping clerk in a Brooklyn pumpworks. Meanwhile he had joined the local branch of the Tammany organization and had attracted the attention of the district leader. As a consequence, in 1895 he was appointed subpoena server in the office of commissioner of jurors, and in 1903 he was elected assemblyman. By 1915, his last year in the Assembly, he was recognized by both Democrats and Republicans as an outstanding legislator and reformer, while his work in the constitutional convention of the same year revealed that he knew as much about the operation of New York's government as did any politician in the state. He served as sheriff of New York County in 1916–1917 and as president of the New York City Board of Aldermen in 1918. Elected governor in 1918, he was defeated for the same office by Nathan Miller in the Harding landslide of 1920, but was re-elected in 1922, 1924, and 1926. His active political career ended in 1928 when he was defeated for the presidency by Herbert Hoover.

The turning point of Smith's life was his election to the Assembly. He once wrote that the "state legislature was a great university of learning," and he might have added that he was one of the ablest and most diligent students ever to attend its classes. During his first three years in the Assembly he was by his own admission almost completely unaware of "what was going on." But he kept his mouth shut, studied every bill that was brought to a vote, and took care of his constituents in the old neighborhood. By 1907 he was participating in the debates; in 1911 he was made majority leader; and two years later he served as speaker. It was in the Assembly that he first met men from other parts of the state, learned his trade as a politician, and acquired his mastery of every phase of the state government. It was in the Assembly, moreover, that he had his first opportunity to impress politicians from both parties with his liberalism, industry, fair-mindedness, sense of humor, and ability as a speaker. During his last year in the Assembly when he was running for sheriff, the New York *Tribune,* a Republican paper, wrote that "in the past ten years there has been no Republican, Progressive or Democrat in the State Legislature who has rendered as effective, useful, downright valuable service to this town as ex-Speaker Smith." His record, the *Tribune* continued, revealed that he was "a true leader, a genuine compeller of men, a man of wit and force with an instinctive grasp of legislative practice."

If Smith went to college in the Assembly, he did his postgraduate work at the constitutional convention of 1915. Serving with some of the most prominent men in the state, he again acquired new friends and new knowledge. He won the respect of such outstanding Republicans as Elihu Root, Henry L. Stimson, and George D. Wickersham, while the diversity of the subjects considered in the debates provided him with facts and ideas that he was to use throughout his four terms as governor. But the convention profited as much from Smith as he did from it. Despite the fact that he was a member of the minority party, the information that he supplied on more than one occasion determined the programs adopted by the majority.

Whether serving as an assemblyman, as a delegate to the constitutional convention, or as governor, Smith was at all times a pragmatist. Relatively uninterested in economic and political theories, he always preferred the specific to the general. He did not read widely and he was not well informed on subjects that had not been part of his personal experience. But he had a systematic mind, a phenomenal memory, the ability to grasp the details and broader implications of public questions, and a desire to get things done. When confronted by a particular problem, he was not influenced by precedent or ideological considerations, but by his estimate of the possible results of a course of action. As a result, he was never a doctrinaire, and as he grew older he became less and less a partisan.

As a practical reformer Smith was always more than a match for his conservative opponents. For example, when he urged state intervention to relieve the postwar housing shortage, the Republicans accused him of being a socialist. To Smith this was not only untrue but irrelevant, for the heart of the matter was that people needed low-priced homes and private enterprise could not or would not build them. When he advocated that the governor be granted executive authority and responsibility, he was accused of a desire to become a dictator, and some Republican leaders went so far as to call him a king. But to Smith the only issue was that the existing system of administration was inefficient and the system that he proposed was not. This type of liberalism made him a disconcerting political figure to almost everyone but the voters. When his opponents argued that his recommendations violated hallowed theories and traditional views, he replied with speeches that explained to the voters how and why they would benefit from his reforms. The people proved as practical-minded as Smith, and on successive election days they endorsed both him and his policies.

Despite Smith's effectiveness as a reformer, he remained a loyal member of Tammany Hall throughout his life. As a young assemblyman he took his orders from the organization, and as speaker in 1913 he led the Tammany movement in the Assembly to impeach Sulzer. But as he moved up the political ladder he demanded and received increasing freedom from the machine. He was fond of Murphy, and the boss was proud of him. There is no evidence that they ever fought or that Smith ever resented Murphy's leadership. Smith considered the boss a "good adviser" and wrote that "if he placed his confidence in a man he allowed that man to make the decision." Murphy placed his confidence in Smith and made no apparent effort to determine state policy when his former protégé was serving as governor. When Murphy died in 1924, Smith assumed leadership of the party in the city and refused to let Tammany renominate John F. Hylan for a third term as mayor. Hylan was allied with Hearst, whom Smith despised, and in 1925 the governor succeeded in securing the nomination and election of James J. Walker as mayor of New York City. Smith's support of Walker proved to be a major political blunder. As likable as any man in New York politics, Jimmy Walker was altogether casual about moral obligations and had no apparent sense of civic duty. He usually did not get to work before three in the afternoon, and he spent many of his evenings in night clubs. Moreover, during his administration, Tammany revived practices that recalled the Tweed Ring. Favors were sold to members of the machine or to the highest bidders; criminals and politicians formed a mutually profitable alliance in which the former paid the latter for protection; and the city was forced to the brink of bankruptcy. While Smith was making the state government a model of efficiency, Walker was permitting—if not encouraging—every form of political thievery in the city. Walker's record revealed that Smith, instead of changing Tammany, had risen above it. The tiger was as voracious as ever.

Smith's refusal to play machine politics may not have been altogether altruistic on his part, for he realized from the outset that he needed more than Tammany votes to win elections. Instead of giving the largest political plums to the Democratic regulars, he sought to make merit the principal basis for appointment. He advocated policies that were enthusiastically supported by reform and civic groups in both parties. In an immediate sense, these tactics appeared to be poor politics, but from a long-term view they proved just the reverse. Over the years he attracted many independents who were more interested in good government than in the welfare of a particular political party. But it did not stop there, for, in the words of Warren Moscow, "The Smith hold on the voters became catching. . . . They started voting for Al and his brown derby and found it easier and easier as the years went by to vote also for the party he headed." The votes of the independents, however, never alienated those of Tammany, and in successive campaigns he was endorsed by both reform and machine groups. His ability to keep such unlikely bedfellows in the same bed was ascribed by William Allen White to the fact that he retained his old friends with his heart while winning new ones with his head.

One of Smith's most important political assets was his conviction that honest politics were the best politics. This involved more than money honesty, for in Smith's case it also meant an attempt to avoid equivocation in the discussion of issues. Thus, he opposed prohibition when it might have been to his immediate advantage to temporize. He reversed his stand on woman suffrage and publicly stated why he had changed his mind. He never talked down to the voters; he used facts to prove his points; and he did not resort to political shibboleths. Many of his speeches were detailed expositions of the state's finances, and observers continually marveled at his ability to make statistics interesting. In seeking approval for a bond issue, a constitutional amendment, or a bill pending in the legislature, he invariably took his case to the people in speaking tours and radio addresses. In this fashion he not only secured the adoption of almost all of his proposals, but he also helped to make New Yorkers the most enlightened body of voters in the nation.

Smith's skill as a politician was repeatedly demonstrated by his ability to overcome the opposition of successive Republican legislatures. Whenever one of his proposals was rejected by the legislature, he would appeal to the people for their support. This technique was usually successful, for on many occasions public opinion forced the legislature to reverse its original stand. The legislature also proved of invaluable assistance to him in his campaigns for re-election. "Let's look at the record" was a constant refrain in his campaign speeches, and the record consisted of a list of Smith's proposals that had been defeated by Republican majorities in the Senate and Assembly. Legislative opposition always assured him of an adequate supply of issues, and on one occasion he said, "If the Republicans had not used partisan obstructive tactics against me, I should have been in private life long ago." Perhaps he overestimated the assistance he received from the Republicans, but the fact remains that by campaigning against the record of the legislature he won every gubernatorial election but that of 1920, defeating Whitman in 1918, Miller in 1922, Theodore Roosevelt, Jr., in 1924, and Ogden Mills in 1926. Some conception of both his effectiveness as a campaigner and the popularity of his policies can be gained from the fact that in 1924, when the Republican presidential candidate ran more than 850,000 votes ahead of his Democratic opponent in New York, Smith carried the state by 108,561 votes.

During Smith's first term as governor the United States was in the midst of a campaign against radicalism that made it dangerous for anyone to express opinions that were not in accord with those of the most conservative groups in the country. Although many Americans from all walks of life were stigmatized and persecuted for their views, the principal targets of the antiradical campaign were Communists, members of the Industrial Workers of the World, and Socialists. New York, too, succumbed to the pressure of the professional flag wavers, and in 1920 the Republican majority in the Assembly refused to seat five Socialist assemblymen on the ground that the legislature had the right to pass on its own membership. Smith had no use for the theories espoused by Socialists, but he was deeply concerned with the rights of minorities and the preservation of the democratic process in America. He thought that both were threatened by the Assembly's action, and when he was unable to prevent the expulsion of the Socialists, he issued the following statement to the press:

Although I am unalterably opposed to the fundamental principles of the Socialist party, it is inconceivable that a minority party, duly constituted and legally organized, should be deprived of its right to expression so long as it has honestly, by lawful methods of education and propaganda, succeeded in securing representation, unless the chosen representatives are unfit as individuals.

It is true that the assembly has arbitrary power to determine the qualifications of its members, but where arbitrary power exists it should be exercised with care and discretion, because from it there is no appeal.

If the majority party at present in control of the assembly possesses information that leads them to believe that these men are hostile to our form of government and would overthrow it by processes subversive of law and order, these charges in due form should have been presented to the legislature and these men tried by orderly processes. Meanwhile, presumably innocent until proved guilty, they should have been allowed to retain their seats.

Our faith in American democracy is confirmed not only by its results but by its methods and organs of free expression. They are the safeguards against revolution. To discard the method of representative government leads to misdeeds of the very extremists we denounce and serves to increase the number of enemies of free government.

The legislature's efforts to enforce conformity were not confined to the expulsion of the Socialists, for in 1919 the Senate and Assembly established a joint legislative committee, under the chairmanship of Senator Clayton R. Lusk, to investigate "enemies of the government." All such enemies proved to be radicals, and the committee's report to the legislature in 1920 recommended that public school teachers be required to take a loyalty oath and that no private school be granted a license by the state until its curriculum has been approved by the Board of Regents. The committee also recommended that the courts be empowered to remove from the ballot the name of any party whose ideals did not conform to those of the United States. The legislature passed bills embodying each of these proposals, and Smith vetoed each bill. In his three veto messages he took his stand as an unreconstructed Jeffersonian democrat. His statement explaining his veto of the licensing bill for private schools still stands as a model to which Americans can aspire:

The mere statement of the provisions of this bill is sufficient to demonstrate that in details it is wholly impossible of just enforcement. . . . In effect, it strikes at the very foundation of one of the most cardinal institutions of our nation—the fundamental right of the people to enjoy full liberty in the domain of idea and speech. To this fundamental right there is and can be under our system of government but one limitation—namely, that the law of the land shall not be transgressed, and there is abundant statute law prohibiting the use of free speech. It is unthinkable that in a representative democracy there should be delegated to any body of men the absolute power to prohibit the teaching of any subject of which it may disapprove. . . .

The clash of conflicting opinions, from which progress arises more than from any other source, would be abolished by law; tolerance and intellectual freedom destroyed, and an intellectual autocracy imposed upon the people. . . . The safety of this government and its institutions rests upon the reasoned and devoted loyalty of its people. It does not need for its defense a system of intellectual tyranny which, in the endeavor to choke error by force, must of necessity crush truth as well. The profound sanity of the American people has been demonstrated in many a crisis, and I, for one, do not believe that governmental dictation of what may and may not be taught is necessary to achieve a continuance of the patriotism of our citizenship, and its loyal support of the government and its institutions.

Because of Republican opposition in the legislature, Smith was able to accomplish relatively little in his first term as governor. The Republicans, having controlled the governor's office for nineteen of the preceding twenty-three years, viewed Smith's election in 1918 as more or less an accident. They were prepared, therefore, to wait him out until 1921, when they were confident that a member of their own party would again be governor. During this period of comparative inactivity Smith devoted his attention to the preparation of a blueprint for the reorganization of the state government. In January 1919 he appointed a Reconstruction Commission to study postwar problems and methods for eliminating governmental inefficiency. The commission was a nonpartisan body whose members represented major civic, professional, and economic groups in the state. When the legislature refused to appropriate funds for the commission's expenses, the members of the commission paid the money out of their own pockets.

The commission's report on governmental reorganization, which was submitted in October 1919, was similar in many respects to the amendments proposed by the constitutional convention of 1915. The report called for the consolidation of the state's numerous executive boards and agencies into a small number of departments whose heads were to be appointed by the governor with the consent of the Senate. The department heads were to be responsible to the governor and to serve as his cabinet. The governor, lieutenant governor, and comptroller were to be the only elective officials in the executive branch of the government, and each was to serve a four-year term. As an additional device for centralizing authority and responsibility in the hands of the governor, the commission recommended the establishment of an executive budget. Under this arrangement the governor with the assistance of his cabinet would prepare a consolidated budget that would contain provisions covering the state's total expenditures and revenues in any given year. The over-all plan outlined by the commission made the executive branch of the state government a pyramid with the governor at its apex. Each department head would be responsible for his department, and the governor was responsible for the department heads.

By repeated appeals to the voters Smith was able to secure the adoption of constitutional amendments that carried out almost all of the Reconstruction Commission's recommendations. In 1920 the Senate and Assembly approved proposals for the consolidation of 187 executive agencies into nineteen departments, the establishment of the cabinet system, and a reduction in the number of elective officials. Constitutional amendments, however, had to pass two legislatures not having the same Senate before they could be submitted to the voters, and in 1921 the Assembly failed to repass the reorganization amendments. But in 1922 Smith made reorganization the principal issue of the gubernatorial campaign, and his victory was in large part responsible for favorable legislative action on the amendments in 1923. The amendments were passed for the final time in 1925, and they were overwhelmingly approved by the voters in the fall of the same year. At this point, Republican legislative leaders threatened to sabotage the entire program by making an opponent of reorganization chairman of the commission that had been created to prepare bills to implement the new amendments. Smith immediately countered by suggesting that Charles Evans Hughes, who had advocated governmental reorganization as early as 1909, be made chairman of the commission. As Hughes was one of the most respected men in public life and a member of their own party, the Republicans had no alternative but to accept the governor's suggestion. The Hughes commission's report was adopted without change by the legislature in 1926, and in January of the following year the plan went into effect. When the long and tortuous struggle for reorganization was finally finished, it was Smith who deserved the major share of the credit. He had appointed the Reconstruction Commission; he had used every conceivable opportunity to explain the amendments to the voters; and he had pushed, cajoled, and outmaneuvered the legislature.

The executive budget, like the consolidation amendments, encountered considerable opposition in the Senate and Assembly. Despite countless speeches by the governor and the educational work of numerous reform groups, it was defeated by successive Republican legislatures from 1923 through 1925. But its passage was urged by the Hughes commission, and this proved sufficient to secure its adoption. Smith later wrote, "Unable to escape the logic and the pressure, both houses of the legislature passed it in 1926 for the first time." It was repassed in 1927, approved by the voters in the fall of the same year, and went into effect on January 1, 1929. The new system gave the governor both control over and responsibility for the state's financial policies. The legislature's power at the same time was drastically curtailed. It could reduce the budget presented by the governor, but it could not increase expenditures unless it also provided the means for increasing the state's revenues.

The proposal for a four-year term for the governor was the only major recommendation made by the Reconstruction Commission that failed of adoption. Although Smith favored this change and campaigned for it on several occasions, he also believed that gubernatorial elections should not be held in the same years as presidential elections. But the legislature, which was controlled by Republicans who realized that, in the past, Republican presidential candidates had helped to elect Republican governors, passed a four-year amendment that provided for gubernatorial elections in presidential years. To Smith this provision completely killed the plan's effectiveness, for it made it exceedingly difficult for a voter to prevent his attitude toward national issues from influencing his views on state issues. Smith took his case to the people, and in 1927 the voters defeated the four-year amendment that had been adopted by the legislature. In the same election eight other amendments, all of which had been endorsed by Smith, received large majorities. Smith's ability to obtain the defeat of one out of nine amendments indicates perhaps more clearly than any other event both his effectiveness as an educator and the people's confidence in his judgment.

Smith's reform program was not confined to the reorganization of the government, for he was also in large part responsible for the improvement and expansion of a number of the services which the state rendered to its citizens. He considered the people the state's most valuable asset, and the various progressive measures that he sponsored as governor were all designed to provide a better life for the individual New Yorker. This could be said of some of Smith's predecessors, but few of them had such a broad view of the general welfare, and no governor was a more skillful politician. His interests ranged over every phase of activity within New York, and the reforms adopted during his administration were as diversified as the state.

Smith viewed education as one of the state's most important functions, and as governor he made constant efforts to improve the state's school system. His interest in education was undoubtedly stimulated by his inability to complete his own schooling. In his annual message of 1923 he asserted that "anyone desiring to have a proper understanding of the necessity for an education need only talk to the man who was denied it," and on the same occasion he insisted that it was the duty of the state to make sure that all children received the same educational opportunities. Realizing that it was impossible to "serve the cause of education without spending money to do it," he continually goaded the legislature into increasing the appropriations for the state's local school systems. In 1919 the legislature on his recommendation provided an additional $5,300,000 for salary increases for teachers; in the following year this figure was increased to $20,500,000. In 1925 he appointed a commission headed by Michael Friedsam to study the financial and administrative problems of the schools, and in 1927 the legislature adopted the Friedsam commission's proposals for increased state aid for education. Smith was also instrumental in raising the standards of the state's rural schools. In 1925, after repeated rebuffs from the legislature, he obtained an additional appropriation of $9,000,000 for schools in country districts. It was, moreover, under his direction that New York began to consolidate its rural school districts into larger units. A product of a Catholic church school on the Lower East Side of Manhattan, Smith did as much for upstate public schools as did any governor in the history of the state.

The reputation that Smith had earned as a friend of labor when he was an assemblyman was enhanced during the four terms he served as governor. Laws were passed to safeguard women and children in industry; the statutory work week for children was reduced; and in 1927 the legislature, following recommendations that Smith had made in every annual message since 1919, adopted a bill for a forty-eight-hour week. At the same time both the efficiency and effectiveness of the state labor department were increased under the outstanding administrations of Bernard L. Shientag as industrial commissioner and Frances Perkins as chairman of the Industrial Board. To Smith, however, all these accomplishments were overshadowed by the revision of the Workmen's Compensation Acts. In his last annual message Smith stated with justifiable pride that New York's Compensation Law was "perhaps the most liberal statute of its kind in the world."

During Smith's administration the state undertook an extensive program of public works that included new state office buildings, hospitals, prisons, parks, a bridge across the Hudson at Poughkeepsie, the elimination of railroad grade crossings, highways, a state health laboratory, and the expansion of the facilities of the Teachers College at Albany. Although Smith initiated many of these projects and supported all of them, he gave his greatest attention and enthusiasm to the expansion of the state's park system. When he assumed office in 1919, some thirty-five different boards and commissions were responsible for the various parks and historic sites throughout the state. Each received separate appropriations, and a co-ordinated park program was an impossibility. At Smith's instigation the legislature in 1923 created a Council of Parks, consisting of the chairmen of the various state park boards. In the following year he proposed and the voters approved a $15,000,000 bond issue for the construction of parkways and the purchase of additional land for parks. By his final term as governor he had greatly expanded the size of the state's recreational areas, placed the park administration on a businesslike, nonpolitical basis, and taken the first steps to develop a system of parkways.

Smith's conservation program went far beyond that proposed by any of his predecessors. In each of his five gubernatorial campaigns he advocated public ownership and operation of the state's water-power facilities. The Republicans, however, had already put into effect a plan which called for public ownership and private operation. Under the terms of the Machold Storage Law of 1915, the state was divided into a number of "river regulating districts," and the officials of each district were authorized to lease water-power sites to private companies. Following Miller's election as governor in 1920, a State Water Power Commission was established with authority to grant fifty-year leases to power companies. When Smith was re-elected governor in 1922 he sought to reverse the Republican policy, and in 1924 he succeeded in preventing the Water Power Commission from approving the application of two power companies for the use of the waters of the St. Lawrence River. Two years later the Water Power Commission, which had fallen under the control of the Republicans, proceeded to issue licenses to two corporations for power projects on the St. Lawrence. Meanwhile the legislature, on the recommendation of the Hughes commission, had transferred the authority vested in the Water Power Commission to a Water Power and Control Commission, two of whose three members were to be appointed by the governor. But the new law did not go into effect until January 1, 1927, and during the last month of its existence the old commission attempted to grant final approval for the St. Lawrence license. When Smith learned of the commission's intention, he announced that he planned to "take such action in the courts as may be necessary for the protection of the interests of the state." This threat scared off the companies, both of which withdrew their applications. For the remainder of his administration Smith dominated the Water Power and Control Commission, and no leases were granted to private power companies.

Although Smith prevented the transfer of the control of the state's power sites to private interests, he was not able to secure legislative approval for a public power policy. In his annual message in 1924 he recommended the creation of "a New York State Power Authority which shall be a public corporation, municipal in character, having no stockholders, deriving its powers from the state and having duties specifically imposed upon it to take over and develop the water power resources of the state." Although he repeated this proposal on numerous occasions to both the legislature and the voters, he failed of his objective. On two different occasions bills establishing a power authority were defeated by Republican legislatures. Smith considered the rejection of his plan for a power authority a major defeat for the people, and he warned them: "Do not give up your water power. . . . We are poor citizens if we allow the things worth most to get into the hands of the few."

Because any expansion of the state's services cost money, one of Smith's principal tasks was to persuade the taxpayers to accept higher taxes. In the past politicians had sought to make political capital out of economy, and it was generally thought that there was a direct ratio between an administration's frugality and its popularity at the polls. Smith, however, believed that the people were willing to spend money if they knew why they were spending it and were given adequate assurances that they would receive their money's worth. On repeated occasions he obtained popular support for increases in state expenditures by explaining to voters the benefits that would accrue from the policies that he advocated. By using this approach he was able to convince a majority of the voters that taxes should always be judged by the services that they purchased. The voters seldom disappointed him. In his autobiography he wrote:

It is a mistake to think that the people approve of reduced appropriations when in the process of reducing them the state or any of its activities are to suffer. What the people want is an honest accounting for every dollar appropriated. They want every dollar of public money to bring a dollar's worth of service to the state. They have no patience with waste and there is a great difference between large appropriations and waste.

Under Smith's direction the state's revenue program was completely reorganized. The property tax, which at one time had provided the bulk of the funds used by the state, was steadily reduced until by 1928 it was only one-half mill per dollar of assessed valuation. At the same time other sources of revenue were developed. The liquor tax, mortgage tax, and the fees for the registration of motor vehicles (all of which were introduced before Smith had entered office) helped to offset the decrease in the property tax. In his first year as governor the legislature passed an income tax, which eventually became the principal means of raising revenue, and in 1926 a franchise tax was adopted for state banks, trust companies, financial corporations, and national banks. To raise money for such long-term improvements as the elimination of grade crossings and the construction of state buildings and parks, Smith resorted to bond issues, each of which required the approval of the voters. Although Republican advocates of a pay-as-you-go policy generally opposed the bond issues, Smith in each instance obtained the support of a majority of the electorate. He maintained not only that it was good business to borrow money when interest rates were low, but also that bonds provided the most equitable method for distributing the costs of capital improvements whose benefits would be enjoyed by future generations of taxpayers.

Smith's fiscal policies proved advantageous to the state's communities. The decrease in the state property tax not only permitted towns and cities to raise their property taxes, but almost every form of state revenue was shared with the local governments. The precedent for the assignment of part of the receipts from a state tax to local governments was established with the passage of the Raines Liquor Tax Law in 1896, and the same policy was followed in the distribution of the proceeds from the mortgage tax, the fees for motor vehicle registration, the income tax, and the 1926 franchise tax on financial institutions. The amount of revenue from state administered taxes assigned to local governments rose from $9,318,000 in 1919 to $62,381,000 in 1928.

The state also assisted local governments with grants-in-aid. Although it was already an established practice for the state to help communities to finance their school systems, in this period the amounts granted were markedly increased and the program was extended to several other fields of local endeavor. The Lowman Act of 1920 provided for financial assistance for county roadbuilding programs; in 1924 the state granted money for the first time for local health units; in the following year a subvention was made for public health nursing; and in 1926 the legislature authorized aid for the construction of county hospitals and the maintenance of county health units. In 1919 state subventions accounted for only 2.8 per cent of the cost of local government. Nine years later the amount had risen to 9.3 per cent. Through grants-in-aid and the allocation of tax revenues, the state was able to promote local autonomy without producing local bankruptcy.

The aid program for local communities was just one of the many ways in which Smith employed the state's power to increase the people's power over their own affairs. Although his conservative opponents maintained that government intervention tended to destroy popular rights, he repeatedly maintained that the state's assumption of new duties and obligations strengthened rather than weakened political democracy. By making the state an active and immediate force in the lives of its people he helped to create one of the most alert electorates in the nation.

Toward a New Deal

1928
32

The country needs and . . . the country demands bold, per-sistent experimentation. It is common sense to take a method and try it: If it fails, admit it frankly and try another. But above all, try something.
— Franklin D. Roosevelt, *May 22, 1932*

FRANKLIN D. ROOSEVELT's two terms as governor were a transitional period in New York's history and in his own personal career. Elected in 1928 at the height of the boom, he completed his final year in office in 1932 at the depth of the depression. In the interval he had helped to prepare a New Deal for the state and the nation. In one sense, his governorship was an apprenticeship for the larger task before him, but in another it was a series of political skirmishes that were designed above all else to secure his election to the presidency.

Born in 1882 at Hyde Park, in Dutchess County, Roosevelt was a descendant of an old and respected New York Dutch family and the only child of well-to-do parents. His family belonged to the landed aristocracy of the Hudson Valley, and Theodore Roosevelt was a distant cousin. Educated at home by governesses and tutors, he took occasional trips abroad with his parents and devoted much of his time to nature study and naval history. At the age of fourteen he was sent to boarding school to complete his preparation for college. At Harvard, which he entered in 1900, he gave enough attention to his studies to graduate in about the middle of his class, but his principal interests appeared to be club life—he belonged to eight undergraduate clubs—and the Harvard *Crimson,* which he edited in his senior year. Although he attended Columbia Law School, he withdrew in 1907 before completing the requirements for the degree. In the same year he passed the bar examinations and went to work for the law firm of Carter, Ledyard, and Milburn. Three years later he entered politics.

When Roosevelt in 1910 agreed to be a Democratic candidate for the state Senate, his chances seemed hopeless, for the district in which Hyde Park was located had not sent a Democratic senator to Albany since 1884. Throughout his campaign, however, he appeared blissfully unaware of this fact, and to the surprise of almost everyone he defeated his Republican opponent by 1,140 votes. His victory was in large part the product of factors over which he had no control. He belonged to an established and well-known family in the district; he was related to the illustrious Teddy; and he was an indirect beneficiary of the growing cleavage between the conservative and progressive factions of the Republican party. In his first term at Albany, he led the revolt against the Tammany candidate for the United States Senate and astounded his colleagues by refusing to let Dutchess County accept its helping from the state's pork barrel. More than one politician wondered at his sanity.

His reputation as an anti-Tammany Democrat aided him in his successful campaign for re-election to the Senate in 1912. A year later it was undoubtedly one of the factors that helped him to secure a place in Woodrow Wilson's administration. Because Charles Murphy had sought to block Wilson's nomination in 1912, the President turned the patronage in New York over to independent Democrats and made Roosevelt, an early and enthusiastic supporter of the New Freedom, assistant secretary of the navy. In his new post Roosevelt demonstrated that he was an able and imaginative administrator. He cut red tape, reformed the Navy yards, eliminated middlemen in the purchase of supplies, was an outspoken advocate of "preparedness," helped establish the North Sea barrage during the war, and supervised the liquidation of the Navy's stores in Europe after the war. His reward for this outstanding record—not to mention the party's recognition of the fact that his name was Roosevelt —was the Democratic nomination for the vice-presidency in 1920. Despite the fact that all the signs pointed to an overwhelming Republican victory, he waged an intensive campaign in which he made more speeches than any previous candidate for the vice-presidency. The signs, however, were accurate. Following Warren G. Harding's election as president, Roosevelt retired from public life to enter business.

Less than a year after the election of 1920 he contracted poliomyelitis, and for the next seven years he devoted most of his energy to an attempt to regain the use of his legs. While making frequent visits to Warm Springs, Georgia, where he took regular exercises in the spring waters, he also managed to maintain most of the political contacts that he had established in the preceding decade. Throughout this period he was especially close to Al Smith. It was largely because of Roosevelt's insistence that Smith agreed to be the Democratic candidate for governor in 1922. Two years later Roosevelt was well enough to make the nominating speech for Smith at the Democratic national convention. In 1928 he again placed

Smith's name before the convention, and the New York governor became the party's choice for the presidency.

To be elected, Smith—among other things—had to carry New York. This, in turn, necessitated a strong state ticket. Herbert Lehman, who had contributed heavily to Smith's campaign and was relatively well known because of his philanthropic activities, had agreed to run for lieutenant governor. Although Roosevelt was Smith's choice for governor, he had repeatedly stated that he would not accept the nomination. But on the eve of the Democratic state convention, Roosevelt, who had been under constant pressure from Smith and other party leaders, agreed to run if he was drafted. The next day he was nominated by acclamation, and Lehman was selected as his running mate. Roosevelt's reluctance to accept the nomination was due ostensibly—and, to a large degree, actually —to his desire to continue his program of therapy under which he had already made enough progress so that he could walk with the aid of canes. There is reason, however, to believe that political considerations also colored his thinking. He had his eye on the presidency, which he and his closest advisers believed could not be won by a Democrat until 1936. But Smith persuaded him that he had a duty to the party in 1928, the Depression moved the Democratic presidential year up to 1932, and the rest is history.

Roosevelt's health became a campaign issue in spite of the efforts of responsible leaders in both parties to avoid the question. Although the press in general viewed his physical condition as an irrelevancy, there were persistent reports that he had been forced to "sacrifice" his health to Smith's political ambitions. Roosevelt eventually felt impelled to issue a statement denying such reports. Far more convincing, however, was the vigor with which he campaigned, for by election day he had made more speeches than his Republican opponent. Campaigning on his predecessor's program and the promise to complete it, he carried the state by 25,000, while Smith lost the state by more than 100,000.

Many explanations have been offered for Roosevelt's victory in 1928, but in all likelihood the most decisive factor was the dissension in the Republican party. Albert Ottinger, the Republican candidate for governor, who had been an able attorney general of the state and had demonstrated that he was an effective vote-getter with a large following in New York City, offended Hamilton Ward of Erie County, Republican nominee for attorney general. The Ward organization dragged its heels in the gubernatorial campaign.

When Roosevelt became governor, his most obvious political assets were his name, his record with the Navy in Washington, and his winning personality. A strikingly handsome man, he almost invariably impressed visitors with his buoyancy, easy manner, and self-assurance. In earlier years many observers, including Frances Perkins, thought him something of a snob, and Hugh Johnson at the outset of the Wilson administration had written disparagingly of Roosevelt's "Hah-vahd accent." But by 1929 he had a relaxed, informal manner that usually made individuals from every class and background feel that he was their friend. As effective before large gatherings as in small groups, he was an extraordinarily persuasive public speaker with a "radio voice" that still remains as a standard of perfection to which politicians aspire. He was cheerful without being a Pollyanna, and his awareness of the solemnity of his official position never had an adverse effect on his sense of humor or his seemingly infinite capacity for enjoying life.

Roosevelt was not a profound thinker, but he possessed an unusual ability to gauge and interpret public opinion. It was this ability, more than any other attribute, that made him a great popular spokesman and a successful party leader. This same ability could also make him overly cautious and inclined to temporize on controversial issues while he was governor. An ambitious man, he viewed Albany as a way station on the road to Washington. As a consequence, during his governorship he often gave the impression that he was using his admittedly brilliant talents as a politician, not to force a program through the legislature, but to further his own career by avoiding any moves that might alienate substantial voting blocs. As president, he was often and rightfully considered a daring innovator, but this was after he had achieved his goal and Albany lay behind him. A man who would eventually go down in history as a superb fighter, he preferred during his two terms as governor to win his victories at the council table rather than on the warpath.

Throughout his governorship Roosevelt was aided by a group of political advisers whose astuteness was matched by their desire to see him reach the White House. Foremost among these was Louis McHenry Howe, a former upstate political correspondent for the New York *Herald,* who managed Roosevelt's campaign for the state Senate in 1910, served as his special assistant when he was assistant secretary of the navy, was with him at Campobello when he was stricken with poliomyelitis, and stuck by him when he was out of politics in the 1920's. A small, frail man who preferred to remain in the background, Howe gave Roosevelt his complete loyalty. He was perhaps the greatest political strategist of his generation and deserves a large share of the credit for Roosevelt's rise to the presidency. James A. Farley was all that Howe was not. A big, jovial extrovert, who was justifiably proud of his ability to remember the names of the lowliest precinct workers, he was a former New York boxing commissioner who had become chairman of the Democratic State Committee. He had the confidence of organization Democrats throughout the state, and he was largely responsible for strengthening the party's machinery in the upstate counties. Of almost equal importance to Roosevelt was Edward J. Flynn, the Democratic boss of the Bronx and Roosevelt's secretary of state. A suave, well-educated politician who headed one of the most powerful and honest city machines in the state, he provided the governor with an invaluable counterweight against Tammany in New York City.

The new governor sought to fill the various divisions of the executive branch of the government with nonpartisan experts. Colonel Frederick Stuart Greene, who had become anathema to the politicians while serving as head of the Department of Public Works under Smith, was reappointed by Roosevelt. Several other Smith appointees were retained, and still others were promoted. Many of those selected by Roosevelt to serve in the state government within a short time became figures of national importance. Dr. Thomas Parran, Jr., commissioner of health under Roosevelt, in 1936 became surgeon general of the United States, while Frances Perkins, Samuel I. Rosenman, Harry L. Hopkins, and Henry Morgenthau, Jr., all held responsible state positions before becoming prominent New Dealers.

Roosevelt entered office pledged to complete the program initiated by his predecessor. Like Smith, he advocated state development, operation, and transmission of the hydroelectric resources of the St. Lawrence River, and like Smith he failed to obtain the legislature's approval of this proposal. In addition, he demanded the enactment of many labor laws, prison reform, more efficient use of the state's rural resources, and the reorganization of local government. Only a few of these and similar demands became law, while those that did seldom met the specifications set by the governor. He set up commissions to study and report on various parts of his legislative program. The results of this method were not always felicitous, for on many occasions a commission's recommendations proved unsatisfactory to either the governor or legislature.

Among the first and most notable achievements of the new administration was the preservation of the executive budget, which had become a part of the state constitution in 1928 and went into effect the following year. The legislature had reluctantly approved the executive budget, but it was still not prepared to relinquish its former hold on the purse strings. Accordingly, in 1929 it adopted an amended budget containing certain specified sums that could not be segregated by the governor without the consent of the chairmen of the Senate and Assembly finance committees. Although the provision concerning the segregation of the lump sums was valid under a law antedating the executive budget, to Roosevelt it seemed an invasion of the executive authority granted by the constitutional amendment of 1928. He therefore vetoed the lump-sum provisions (which covered appropriations for $56,000,000). When the legislature repassed this part of the budget over his veto, Roosevelt took his case to the courts. In November 1929 his position was upheld by the Court of Appeals, and for the first time in its history the state government was able to manage its finances on a businesslike basis.

Although the judiciary could safeguard the executive budget, it could not assist the governor in the other phases of his conflict with the legislature. The governor proposed, but the legislature disposed, and in the process neither side scored a clear-cut victory. For example, in his efforts to reform the state's long-range welfare program, Roosevelt's achievements fell far short of his goals. In 1929 the legislature adopted a public welfare law which shifted the emphasis from institutional to home relief, sought to remove the stigma from poverty, and made some provision for the medical care of the needy. Although this measure was hailed as an enlightened and forward-looking piece of legislation, it proved to be a statement of principles rather than a device for implementing them. In the following year, the legislature approved a social security bill that also represented more of an advance in theory than in practice. Those eligible for pensions under the new law had to have no means of support, to be seventy or over, and to have lived in a single welfare district for at least a year and in the state for a minimum of ten years. Qualified students of the subject condemned the bill on the grounds that the age level was too high and the residence requirements excessive. Roosevelt thought it at best a "stop-gap" measure. In similar fashion, while approving a bill raising construction and housing standards in New York City tenements and apartments, he agreed with critics of the law that it did not give adequate relief to those living in the old-law tenements.

Roosevelt also had to settle for considerably less than he wanted in the field of labor legislation. He did, however, secure the adoption of several bills that strengthened existing statutes or provided additional safeguards for the state's workers. Temporary injunctions in industrial disputes without a notice of a hearing were forbidden; provision was made for jury trials of alleged violations of injunctions; the workmen's compensation law was broadened to include disabilities not covered in earlier statutes; the eight-hour law for public work and the factory inspection law were both strengthened; and a law establishing a forty-eight-hour week with a weekly half holiday was enacted. Some of these laws were not all that Roosevelt desired (he referred to amendments to the Workmen's Compensation Act as "crumbs" thrown to him by the legislature). Equally important was the fact that despite repeated requests he was unable to induce the legislature to approve bills establishing "a fair-wage board on behalf of women and children," declaring that "the labor of a human being is not a commodity or an article of commerce," and creating a system of unemployment insurance.

Roosevelt's legislative program was designed to appeal to farmers as well as workers. Because most of his proposals lightened the farmer's local tax burden, they encountered relatively little opposition in the predominantly farm-oriented Senate and Assembly. At his instigation, the state increased its contributions for highway construction and maintenance, rural schools, and grade crossing elimination. In addition, more state money was provided for safeguarding rural health, and funds were appropriated for a soil survey of the state. The governor also took an interest in attempts to stabilize the milk industry. When the Emergency Committee of the New York Milk Shed drew up plans to organize the dairy farmers in New York and adjoining states into a co-operative marketing association, Roosevelt announced that he approved of the project and would give it his support.

Roosevelt's record as a legislative leader did not match his own as president of the United States. Like Smith, he sought to capitalize on the Republican legislature's opposition to his policies; but unlike Smith, he could not point to a long list of basic reforms. On more than one occasion Roosevelt appeared willing to settle for half a loaf, and the legislature, recognizing this fact, was inclined to give him just that. Moreover, during his second term his candidacy for the presidency not only necessitated long absences from Albany, but it also increased the apparent need for a relatively cautious approach to controversial issues. Walter Lippmann thought that he was merely a pleasant man who wished to be president, and the *Nation* stated that "his weakness and readiness to compromise have been as evident as his personal charm and absolute integrity." Both statements may have been excessively harsh, but they were not without some justification.

Despite the opposition of the legislature, it was Tammany politicians rather than Republican lawmakers who provided Roosevelt with his most vexatious political problems. In 1929 James J. Walker, the jovial, irresponsible Tammany mayor of New York City, was re-elected by a record plurality of 500,000 votes. In the preceding year the first in a series of bizarre events that were to lead to Walker's and Tammany's downfall had occurred when Arnold Rothstein, a notorious gambler and racketeer, was murdered. When the authorities failed to find his murderer, the press hinted that a thorough investigation was being prevented by leading Tammany politicians who in the past had had illegal dealings with the dead gangster. Then Representative Fiorello La Guardia in his unsuccessful mayoralty campaign in 1929 produced evidence that a Democratic magistrate in the Bronx had accepted a $20,000 loan from Rothstein. In 1930 the legislature took up the matter and passed a bill authorizing the governor to conduct an investigation of the city administration. Roosevelt, however, vetoed the bill on the ground that the constitution granted the right to make such an inquiry to the legislature rather than to the governor. The legislature did not accept the governor's invitation to proceed on its own. Meanwhile, Charles H. Tuttle, a Republican serving as United States attorney for the southern district of New York, obtained indictments for fraud against a number of the city's judicial and civil officials.

Throughout the spring and early summer of 1930, Roosevelt met the repeated demands of civic groups for an investigation of New York City either by repeating his earlier views on the limitations imposed on him by the constitution or by referring to the need for the "observance of the home rule principle." The Republicans, as well as many independents, thought it more likely that he did not wish to antagonize Tammany during an election year. In any event, he did not act until August, and he refused to take any steps that might have led to a full-scale inquiry. Instead, he appointed Attorney General Ward, a Republican, to supplant Thomas C. T. Crain, the Tammany district attorney in New York County, as the prosecutor in a case involving the sale of a city office. In addition, at his request the Appellate Division of the Supreme Court, covering Manhattan and the Bronx, began a general investigation of the magistrates' courts. To head this investigation, the court selected Samuel Seabury, Democratic candidate for governor in 1916, a former judge of the Court of Appeals, and a veteran fighter against Tammany rule.

The Republicans entered the gubernatorial campaign of 1930 determined to make corruption in New York City the sole issue. They, accordingly, nominated Tuttle for governor, and he proceeded to devote almost all his speeches to the evils of machine rule in the city. Roosevelt had been renominated by the Democrats; and while Tuttle talked of thieving Democrats, Roosevelt discussed the difficulties he had encountered in trying to force a reform program through a Republican legislature. Roosevelt carried the state with an unprecedented plurality of 725,000 votes, and the rest of the state-wide ticket was also elected. His victory, however, should not be attributed entirely to either the merits of his legislative program or to the Republicans' failure to capitalize sufficiently on the situation in New York City, but in part to the severity of the Depression. The Republicans in Washington had done little to restore prosperity, and in 1930 many New Yorkers, in effect, voted against Herbert Hoover's policies as president.

Following the election, the public's interest in the city's affairs was sustained by newspaper reports of official corruption uncovered by Seabury and Hiram C. Todd, the special assistant attorney general selected by Ward to conduct the prosecution of the case involving office-selling. By January 1931 it was apparent to all but the most partisan Democrats that every part of New York City's government should be thoroughly investigated. In his opening message to the legislature Roosevelt said, "It is not alone your right but your duty to conduct . . . an investigation if you determine that such course falls within your obligation to maintain the welfare of the state." In April, after examining Walker's replies to charges made against him by the City Affairs Committee, Roosevelt announced that he had not found "sufficient justification in these documents, as submitted, to remove the Mayor of the City of New York."

In March 1931 the Senate and Assembly adopted a resolution creating a joint legislative committee to conduct a general investigation of the affairs of New York City. State Senator Samuel H. Hofstadter served as committee chairman, and Seabury was named chief counsel. The so-called "Seabury committee" soon revealed that corruption in the city's government was far more extensive than even the anti-Tammany reformers had suspected. Seabury proved to be an extraordinarily astute cross-examiner, and the testimony that he elicited from reluctant Tammany witnesses revealed that there was no part of the city's government free from graft. City officials had formed corrupt alliances not only with business firms but also with some of the most notorious criminals in the nation. While the police provided protection for those who could pay for it, prominent members of the government gave contracts, franchises, and judgeships to their friends and associates or sold them in private transactions to anyone whose conscience and bank account enabled him to resort to bribery. Many officeholders had little knowledge of their duties and devoted only a few hours a week to their jobs in the city government. Many officials, including the mayor, were unable to explain satisfactorily how they had obtained sums of money far in excess of their salaries.

During the Seabury investigations Roosevelt approved the appropriation of $50,000 for the committee's expenses and gave the committee a free hand, but he made no move to interfere in the city's affairs until he was requested by Seabury and others to remove, first, Thomas M. Farley, sheriff of New York County, and then Mayor Walker. In February 1932 Farley, who soon became known as "Tin-Box Tom" because he insisted that the money he had accumulated beyond his salary came from a tin box in his possession, was removed from office following a hearing. In taking this step, Roosevelt went beyond any of his predecessors, for he was the first governor to remove an elected local official on the ground that the official was unable "to give a reasonable or credible explanation of the sources of . . . [his bank] deposits, or the source which enables him to maintain a scale of living beyond the amount of his salary." Walker was charged with—among other things—incompetence, accepting favors from corporations dealing with the city, owning convertible bonds in a corporation doing business with the city, using his official position to obtain a city franchise for a company with which his friends were associated, and being unable to give a satisfactory explanation of his nonsalaried income. The Walker hearings, which began on August 11, 1932, ended abruptly on September 2, the day after Walker had resigned as mayor. Following Walker's resignation, John P. O'Brien served as interim mayor until the election in 1933 of La Guardia on a Fusion ticket sponsored by Seabury. For the next twelve years La Guardia provided the city with one of the most colorful and exemplary administrations in its history.

Roosevelt's reluctance to take the initiative before the creation of the Hofstadter committee convinced many New Yorkers in both parties that he had subordinated the need for reform to his desire to further his own political career. The New York *Evening World*, which had earlier supported him, wrote that he had "lost a respect for which no victory can compensate." Charges of political plotting may have been true, but the fact remains that Roosevelt did alienate Tammany, for the city machine opposed his nomination for president. On the other hand, good politicians are lucky as well as wise, and Tammany opposition undoubtedly strengthened his candidacy in the West and South.

Roosevelt's handling of Tammany was in contrast to the straightforward fashion in which he met the problems arising from the Depression. At his instigation and under his direction, New York became one of the first states to adopt a comprehensive plan to relieve the suffering caused by economic disaster. Although the effect of the stock market crash of 1929 on the state and national economies was not immediately apparent, it was evident by 1931 that the United States was in the worst depression in its history. Never before had so many of New York's citizens been in want, and never before had the state been forced to deal with an economic crisis of such magnitude and complexity. From 1929 to 1933 the number of factory wage earners in New York decreased from 1,105,963 to 733,457, and total wages declined from $1,650,389,000 to $754,367,000. There were, moreover, many men who, while employed, were not working full time. In 1932 23.4 per cent of the state's male workers were employed on a part-time basis, while 32.6 per cent were wholly unemployed.

At the outset of the Depression privately financed charitable organizations assumed the major responsibility for the care of the needy. But these agencies now had neither the facilities nor funds for handling the huge number of destitute people demanding food and shelter. Despite the heroic efforts of the state's private relief agencies, charity could not keep pace with the onrushing tide of economic disaster. Even more ineffectual were the cheery—but not cheering—slogans issued by business and government officials who wished to convince people that the hard times could be dispelled by a strong dose of optimism. The Depression, however, was not a psychological phenomenon to the unemployed men selling apples on city street corners, the hungry people lined up at soup kitchens and milk stations, and the residents of crude huts in shanty towns on the edges of many cities.

When private agencies could no longer carry the relief burden, local governments took over the task. In the winter of 1930–1931, Rochester became one of the first cities in the state to put its unemployed to work. Organized by city officials and financed by city funds, the Rochester program provided the unemployed with jobs on public works at prevailing wages. A somewhat similar plan was adopted at approximately the same time by Buffalo, and many other cities and towns used public funds to supplement private charity. In New York City the problem of caring for the unemployed was complicated by a provision in the city's charter forbidding the use of public funds for outdoor relief. This obstacle was circumvented by relying on private charities to which the city contributed funds. Regardless of the method used, the question of where the money was to come from always remained. By the summer of 1931 most local governments faced bankruptcy because of their relief activities, and it was clear that the state would have to provide work and money for the needy.

Roosevelt was one of the first officials in the state and the nation to realize that the Depression had made private misfortune a public responsibility. In March 1930 (or less than five months after the Wall Street crash), he proposed a five-point program that called for a census of the unemployed, the co-ordination of public and private relief activities, local campaigns for the creation of new jobs, establishment of free employment agencies in every community in the state, and local public works projects. The following month he appointed a Committee on Stabilization of Industry for the Prevention of Unemployment, and under his direction the state expanded its public works program. Then, in August 1931, when it was evident that the state would have to intervene to save many of its local governments from bankruptcy and a large number of its citizens from starvation, he called a special session of the legislature to devise ways of meeting the emergency. In asking for relief legislation, he emphasized that old methods could not meet the new problems and that a bold course was essential:

In broad terms I assert that modern society, acting through its government, owes the definite obligation to prevent the starvation or the dire want of any of its fellow men and women who try to maintain themselves but cannot. . . . To these unfortunate citizens aid must be extended by government—not as a matter of charity but as a matter of social duty. . . . When . . . a condition arises which calls for measures of relief over and beyond the ability of private and local assistance to meet,—even with the usual aid added by the State—it is time for the State itself to do its additional share.

The legislature responded to the governor's requests with the adoption of the so-called Wicks Act. Although this measure bore the name of a prominent Republican member of the state Senate, it contained all the proposals made by Roosevelt in his message to the special session of the legislature. A Temporary Emergency Relief Administration, directed by three persons appointed by the governor, was established to supervise the distribution of state aid to local communities for work relief and home relief. The state was divided into welfare districts that consisted of cities, or of counties exclusive of any cities within their borders. Within each district, the local welfare commissioner served as the representative of the T.E.R.A. for the administration of the home relief program. Work relief was directed by an emergency work bureau whose members were appointed by the mayor or the county board of supervisors. Home relief was viewed in the broadest possible terms, for it included not only food and shelter but also clothing, light, medicine, and medical care. Those eligible for any form of relief were defined as "needy persons, who are unemployed or, if employed, whose compensation therefrom is inadequate to provide the necessaries of life and who have been residents of the state for at least two years . . . and . . . dependents of such persons."

During the first ten months of its existence, T.E.R.A. administered the expenditure of $48,696,595 for either work relief or home relief to 379,070 families, representing approximately 1,500,000 individuals. Conceived as a temporary expedient, T.E.R.A. was prolonged by successive legislative acts until 1937. Although T.E.R.A. never had enough money to help all the state's needy, it did succeed in working out an integrated program for the care of those who in more normal times were capable of caring for themselves. Because New York was the first state to adopt a plan to aid its communities during the Depression, it had to make many of its own precedents. As a pioneering venture, T.E.R.A. set the pattern for both state and federal governments during the Depression. It helped to remove the stigma of the dole from relief activities, put the unemployed to work on projects that added measurably to the state's physical assets, sought to use skilled workers in the trades that they had previously followed, standardized policy without destroying local administration, and made medical care an accepted part of the government's relief program. In short, it did for New York much of what the New Deal was soon to do for the nation.

When Roosevelt left Albany for Washington, he was far better prepared than most of his contemporaries realized to meet the greatest peacetime crisis in American history. Many New Deal programs did not seem so new to New Yorkers, for Smith had educated them as reformers and Roosevelt had shown them how to combat a depression. If, as is frequently said, the American federal system permits each state to act as a public affairs laboratory, it was New York which had conducted most of the experiments that prepared the way for Roosevelt's domestic policies as president. Some specific New Deal measures may have been unprecedented, but its spirit had been known and shared by New Yorkers for a decade before Roosevelt entered the White House.

The Little New Deal

*I fought only for legislation I considered sound and enlight-
ened: legislation which I believe is of benefit to all groups of
our people.*—HERBERT LEHMAN, *January 1, 1937*

WHEN Roosevelt became president of the United States, there was no
break in the continuity of New York's executive leadership, for Herbert
H. Lehman was a close friend and political associate of the retiring governor. On the surface the two men appeared to have little in common:
Lehman's self-effacing personality and quiet seriousness stood in marked
contrast to Roosevelt's buoyancy and exuberance. But both men came
from well-to-do families, and both possessed a sense of *noblesse oblige.*
Both men, moreover, were in substantial agreement on the issues before the people and government of New York. Lehman, like Roosevelt,
believed that the economic emergency required unprecedented action
by the state and that only government intervention could save American democracy and capitalism. Both men, in short, were New Dealers.

Lehman was the son of an immigrant from Germany who had made a
fortune in the cotton business in Montgomery, Alabama, before the Civil
War and had then moved to New York City where he had founded the
highly successful banking firm of Lehman Brothers. The future governor,
the youngest of eight children, was born in New York City in 1878, educated in private schools, and graduated from Williams College in 1899.
Returning to New York City, he became interested in welfare work,
taught three nights a week at the Henry Street Settlement, and entered
the textile firm of J. Spencer Turner Company. By 1906 he was vice-
president and treasurer of the concern, and two years later he was made
a partner in Lehman Brothers.

Following the outbreak of World War I, Lehman became widely known
for his philanthropic work. As treasurer and vice-chairman of the Jewish
Joint Distribution Committee, he bore the major responsibility for the
collection and distribution of $75,000,000 for aid to war sufferers. When

the United States entered the war, he served for a short time as an assistant to Roosevelt in the Navy Department, but in August 1917 he was commissioned a captain in the Army and assigned to the general staff. Advancing to the rank of colonel in the quartermaster service, he had charge of obtaining, shipping, and distributing supplies for the American Expeditionary Forces. In the immediate postwar period, he was a special assistant to the secretary of war, member of the Board of Contract Adjustment, and member of the War Department Claims Board.

By the 1920's Lehman was a proven administrator, a respected financier, and a prominent philanthropist. He was, moreover, an admirer of Al Smith, and he demonstrated his admiration with substantial campaign contributions. Smith, in turn, liked and respected Lehman, and in 1926 he made the banker the manager of his gubernatorial campaign. Two years later, when Lehman was both finance director of Smith's campaign for president and the Democratic candidate for lieutenant governor of New York, he gave the astonishing amount of $500,000 to Smith's campaign fund. Cynics might conclude that Lehman's generosity was responsible for his nomination for lieutenant governor. But in reality he was selected because he was Smith's friend, had an irreproachable record in his public and business life, and would presumably appeal to the so-called Jewish vote in New York City. Elected in 1928 by a narrow margin, he was re-elected in 1930 by a plurality of 565,000.

Lehman was one of the few lieutenant governors in the history of the state to view his job as other than a sinecure. He not only moved to Albany so that he could devote all his time to his position, but he also severed all his business connections as soon as he entered politics. Because Roosevelt's frequent trips to Warm Springs and his extensive presidential campaign took him out of the state on numerous occasions, Lehman had frequently served as acting governor. Roosevelt never underestimated the lieutenant governor's contribution to his administration, and several times he referred to Lehman as "my good right arm" and the "other governor." When Roosevelt was nominated for the presidency, he was determined that Lehman should be his successor. But Tammany, which had unsuccessfully sought to prevent Roosevelt's nomination for president, was firmly opposed to Lehman's candidacy. Once again, Tammany managed to end up on the losing side, for Roosevelt and Smith forced John F. Curry, the Tammany boss, to back down, and Lehman was nominated. In the ensuing election he piled up an 849,000 plurality over William J. Donovan, his Republican opponent.

As governor, Lehman was one of the most unusual figures to attain high office in the United States. He was entirely lacking in what political writers like to refer to as "color," and he never played politics in the accepted meaning of that term. His public record contains no evidence that he ever subordinated either the general welfare or his own principles to further his own political career. He was a poor public speaker who possessed neither Smith's easy, informal platform manner nor Roosevelt's natural oratorical polish. In small gatherings he did not try to be one of the boys, and it is unlikely that he ever slapped a back during all the years that he was in Albany. But if he possessed none of the attributes of the stereotype of the politician, he did possess qualities that consistently appealed to a majority of the state's voters. They voted for him, not only because he was transparently honest in his thinking as well as his acts, but also because he seemed remarkably free from partisan bias, was an excellent administrator, and knew how to be progressive without being radical. Everything about the man inspired trust. Even his opponents refused to accuse him of ulterior motives.

Following his election as lieutenant governor in 1928, the *Review of Reviews* wrote that it was "asserted, probably with good reason, that it was Lehman's popularity (in a city that has many more than half a million Jewish voters) that carried the State ticket for the Democrats, while they lost the Presidential ticket." As appealing as this statement has been to many subsequent political observers, it represents something less than the whole truth. Lehman was obviously popular with his coreligionists, but it was not only because they were coreligionists. Being Jewish is not enough to secure a candidate's election in New York. In 1928, Ottinger was defeated by Roosevelt in the same election in which Lehman was victorious, and in New York City's 1945 mayoralty election, Jonah J. Goldstein made a miserable showing. As significant as Lehman's strength in New York City is the fact that he generally ran far ahead of his ticket in upstate New York. Some of his supporters may have backed him because he was a Jew; many more voted for him because he was a statesman.

Although Lehman's "Little New Deal" for New York was in many respects similar to Roosevelt's domestic program for the nation, it was the president, and not the governor, who was accused by conservatives of being a radical and an impractical theorist. In part, Lehman's immunity to such charges can be attributed to his background, for it was difficult for the voters to imagine that a member of one of the most prominent banking houses in the nation was anything but a hardheaded businessman. In part, it was due to his modesty, for he never "personalized" his program. More important, however, than either of these considerations was the fact that Lehman proved himself a more efficient administrator than Roosevelt. While the federal government was piling up a larger debt each year, Lehman was converting an inherited deficit into a surplus. Nor was the Little New Deal ever disrupted by dissension and sudden changes in policy that on occasion characterized its parent in Washington. Throughout the difficult years of the Depression New York's government was relatively free from intramural bickering, confusion over the location of responsibility and power, and laxity in administration.

Only once in his public career was Lehman rejected by the voters of New York. In 1946, although running well ahead of his ticket, he was defeated for the United States Senate in what proved to be an irresistible Republican trend. For the rest he was invincible. In 1934, when he defeated Robert Moses for governor, his 808,000 plurality was only slightly below that of 1932. In 1936, he ran well ahead of Ogden Mills, with a plurality of 520,000. Two years later, campaigning for the first time for the new four-year term, he defeated Thomas E. Dewey by a plurality of 64,000. His relatively close victory in 1938 can be attributed in part to the fact that for the first time since 1932 the Democratic tide in the nation had passed its high point, and in part to Dewey's widespread appeal—particularly upstate—as a gang-busting prosecuting attorney. But even in 1938 the Lehman name had not lost its magic, for he polled a larger vote in New York City than any other preceding candidate.

During the Depression years Lehman, Roosevelt, and La Guardia maintained an informal alliance that was beneficial to all concerned. The three men shared a devotion to New Deal principles, and they enjoyed near-monopolies on their respective offices. Lehman's governorship extended from 1933 to 1942, Roosevelt's presidency was terminated by his death in 1945, and La Guardia was mayor of New York City from 1934 until 1945. Although La Guardia was elected mayor three times with at least nominal Republican support, he had little connection with the party. A political maverick, he often co-operated with both Lehman and Roosevelt, and his views on social and economic questions were almost identical with theirs. A man of undoubted honesty and one of the most unpredictable figures in American public life, he helped to make New York City a bulwark of the Democratic administrations in Albany and Washington. The only ostensible political tie between the three men was the American Labor party. A New York offshoot of Labor's Non-Partisan League, the new party in 1936 backed both Lehman and Roosevelt and in 1937 provided La Guardia with his actual margin of victory. Drawing most of its support from organized labor in New York City, the party's leadership was divided among union leaders and intellectuals, and in its early years most of its members were former Democrats.[1]

[1] By 1938 Communists had gained control of the Manhattan branch of the party, and within a short time the entire party was split into Communist and anti-Communist wings. In 1944 the latter group withdrew to form the Liberal party.

During the opening months of Lehman's first term as governor, the economic crisis became acute. Unemployment figures reached new highs, old and respected firms went into receivership, farmers destroyed their crops rather than sell them at a loss, and a succession of bank failures was dragging down the nation's financial system into ruin. On March 4, 1933, Lehman issued a proclamation closing all the banks in the state through March 6. On March 4 Roosevelt had been inaugurated as president, and he declared a national banking holiday on March 6. Under the plan adopted by the federal government, the more stable banks were quickly reopened, and within a relatively short time the nation's financial system was again operating on a more or less normal basis. The bank crisis was merely the first of many instances in which the federal government under the New Deal came to the aid of the states. In the ensuing years New Yorkers would increasingly look to Washington rather than to Albany for the help that they needed to survive the Depression.

New York's unemployed workers, like those of other states, were the direct beneficiaries of federal grants to states for either relief or jobs on public works. In New York, as in other states, federal funds for relief were distributed by the Temporary Emergency Relief Administration until 1935, when the federal government substituted work relief for direct relief. Jobs for the unemployed were provided by the Civil Works Administration (from 1933 to 1935), Works Progress Administration, and Public Works Administration. There were many other forms of federal assistance for New Yorkers. The Civilian Conservation Corps enabled young men from the city to work on roadbuilding and forestry programs; the Federal Surplus Relief Corporation (later, Federal Surplus Commodities Corporation) distributed food to the unemployed; the National Youth Administration gave part-time employment to many needy students; camps were established to house unemployed transients; and farmers were substantially aided by a succession of New Deal agriculture acts. These measures not only aided the unemployed, but they also greatly added to the state's physical assets. In 1936, in the course of a review of the joint endeavors of the state and federal governments in New York, Lehman said:

Federal grants, supplemented by State and Local appropriations, have made possible the enlargement of our great hospitals; they have made possible the construction of new bridges such as the one at Catskill, two at Buffalo, the Triboro Bridge in New York, and in many other parts of the State; they have made possible the development of health and recreational facilities such as the great spa at Saratoga; they have made possible the construction of hundreds of school buildings in this State; they have made possible a program for the conservation of our soil, the prevention of soil erosion and the development of reforestation. In every one of these activities Federal and State co-operation of some kind was necessary. In every one of these instances we could not, at least, for many years, have undertaken the work save through the co-operation of Federal and State governments and through the financial assistance received from the former.

From the inception of T.E.R.A. in 1932 until the agency was ended in 1937, $1,155,314,101 was spent by federal, state, and local governments for emergency relief in New York. Of this amount, 44 per cent was supplied by the federal government, 36 per cent by localities, and the remainder by the state. Most of the money was used for either home relief or work relief. Throughout its existence, T.E.R.A. provided home relief for a monthly average of 265,000 families and unattached individuals; and in February 1935, when the relief load was at its highest, 17 per cent of the state's population was receiving public assistance. Until April 1935, when the W.P.A. took over work relief, an average of approximately 149,-000 persons in New York were employed on public works projects, while at one point the C.W.A. had almost 350,000 New Yorkers on its payroll. In addition, from April 1933 to June 1937, 115,000 young men from the state were enrolled in the Civilian Conservation Corps. During the same period, T.E.R.A., acting as the agent for the federal government, distributed 331,000,000 pounds of food and 3,000,000 articles of clothing to the needy. Ten transient camps in New York provided more than 200,000 individuals with food, shelter, and medical care.

Despite the scope of the federal-state relief programs in New York, many who needed help did not receive it. Unemployment always outran the funds allotted to combat it. Moreover, the prominent role played by localities in the distribution of relief resulted in a distressing lack of uniformity in standards and procedures. Finally, the entire program was conceived and applied in such haste that it was impossible to avoid waste and inefficiency, and the shortage of personnel trained in relief administration was a constant problem. But when all this has been said, the fact remains that the job was done. And it was done in New York with a rare degree of humaneness and the almost total absence of partisanship.

The numerous changes in state and federal relief policies made imperative the reorganization of the administration of New York's welfare agencies. Accordingly, Lehman in 1934 appointed a commission headed by Allen Wardwell to "make a detached and impartial study and evaluation of the administration of unemployment relief." The commission's report formed the basis for legislation in 1936 for co-ordinating and centralizing the various parts of the state's relief administration. Under the new law, the Board of Social Welfare, which had succeeded the State Board of Charities in 1929, was authorized to adopt rules and regulations concerning relief that had the force of law and to appoint a commissioner of welfare to serve as executive officer of the Department of Social Welfare. After July 1, 1937, all the functions and responsibilities of T.E.R.A. were assumed by the department, and the local emergency-relief bureaus created under the Wicks Act were terminated.

The 1936 act also regularized home relief and ensured its continuance. The state was to pay 40 per cent of expenditures for home relief for any individuals who had lived in the state for the two years preceding the date of his or her application for assistance. A year later the residence requirement was further liberalized, and the state agreed to pay localities the total cost of home relief given to any person with a legal settlement [2] in any town or city within the state. The same law extended state responsibility to needy Indians on state reservations and provided that 40 per cent of the salaries of the employees of city and county public welfare departments should be furnished by the state. Finally, in 1940, the legislature adopted the Social Welfare Law, which codified and removed inconsistencies and ambiguities from existing statutes concerned with state, local, and private welfare work.

The welfare program adopted during Lehman's administration as governor reflected a basic change in the public's attitude toward the government's responsibility to the people of New York. Poverty, which had once been a mark of opprobrium, was now considered a misfortune for which the individual was not responsible. Public relief, which many people had earlier referred to as a "dole," was now generally accepted as a more equitable and efficacious method than private charity for relieving human misery. What had once been considered "socialistic" and "un-American" were now accepted as commonplaces, and among the constitutional amendments approved by the voters in 1938 was a provision stating that "the aid, care and support of the needy are public concerns and shall be provided by the state and by such of its subdivisions, and in such manner and by such means, as the legislature may from time to time determine." The nature and extent of these public concerns were indicated in the following provision:

Subject to the limitations on indebtedness and taxation, nothing in this constitution contained shall prevent the legislature from providing for the aid, care and support of the needy directly or through subdivisions of the state; or for the protection by insurance or otherwise, against the hazards of unemployment, sickness and old age; or for the education and support of the blind, the deaf, the dumb, the physically handicapped and juvenile delinquents . . . ; or for health and welfare services for all children, either directly or through subdivisions of the state, including school districts; or for the aid, care and support of neglected and dependent children and of the needy sick, through agencies and institutions authorized by the state board of social wel-

---

[2] Legal settlement was defined as one year's continuous residence in a town or city without having received public relief.

fare or other state department having the power of inspection thereof, by payments made on a per capita basis directly or through subdivisions of the state.

Although the Depression forced Lehman to devote much of his time and energy to emergency measures granting temporary aid to this or that economic group, he also sponsored a long-range reform program that was designed to assist the needy in good times as well bad. One of the most important features of this program was an unemployment insurance bill which became law in 1935 after being repeatedly recommended to the legislature by both Roosevelt and Lehman. With the passage of the Federal Social Security Act later in the same year, the state plan was integrated with that of the national government in an arrangement by which employers contributing to the New York fund were credited with such contributions up to 90 per cent of the federal unemployment compensation payroll tax. The enactment of the Social Security Act also made it possible for New York to participate in a federally sponsored program for the care of dependents.

Lehman had been urging reforms in the old-age security act of 1930, and in 1936 the legislature liberalized the provisions to conform to those of the national Social Security Act. In the following year the legislature adopted an omnibus bill that made the state eligible for federal grants to assist New York's programs for public health, aid to blind and dependent children, and child health and welfare services.

Lehman's record as a friend of labor surpassed that of any governor in the state's history. When he entered office in 1933, he outlined his labor program to the legislature; five years later all his major proposals were on the statute books. Patiently restating his views to successive legislatures, he achieved his objectives by convincing rather than browbeating his opponents. Because so many labor bills were passed during his administration, he usually enumerated rather than discussed his accomplishments in this field. Thus, after considering at some length the recently enacted unemployment insurance and social security laws in a campaign speech at Syracuse in 1938, he concluded his address with the following list of bills adopted by the legislature during the first six years of his governorship:

Minimum wages for women and minors;
Broadening of the Workmen's Compensation Law to cover occupational diseases;
A law protecting workingmen in labor disputes by insuring to them a right to trial by jury in case of alleged violation of an injunction;
A law governing contracts and terms under which labor injunctions may be issued by our courts;
The outlawing of the "yellow-dog" contract;
The outlawing of the vicious "kick-back";

The statutory declaration of policy that the labor of human beings is not a commodity or an article of commerce;

A law shortening the maximum hours of work per week of women in factories, mercantile establishments and hotels;

A law raising the age at which children may leave school to enter industry from fourteen to sixteen years;

Adoption of the eight-hour day and six-day week for institutional employees of the State;

Adoption of the three-platoon system of firemen in the city of New York;

A bill providing tenure to school teachers in rural areas and reducing the probationary period for such teachers;

A law prohibiting duress, intimidation or coercion of an employee through the medium of the payroll envelope;

A career law granting mandatory annual increments and salaries for each employee of the State within established grades;

The creation of a State Labor Relations Board and a State Mediation Board;

A law subjecting detective agencies supplying strike breakers and strike breaking service to the strictest regulation.

Throughout his administration Lehman was a constant supporter of the public school system. Despite the drain of relief expenses on the state's financial resources, he consistently allocated more state money for school aid than had been granted in the years before he entered office. He also pushed the central school program inaugurated by Smith, and he looked forward to the day when it would be "possible for every boy and girl in the State to have ready access to a modern school in which training is offered from the kindergarten through the senior high school." In reviewing his ten years of the governorship in the fall of 1942, he thought that his administration's important contributions to the state's school system were

the amendment to the education law requiring all children to attend school until sixteen years of age, the extending of teacher tenure to the village schools, increased State aid for transportation, raising of the professional requirements for district superintendents of schools, the licensing or registration of nursery schools and private trade schools, State aid for kindergartens, a minimum salary of $1,000 for rural teachers, changing the normal schools to teachers colleges, and amendments to many of the professional laws.

Lehman also had marked success in securing the adoption of his public utility program. Although he, like Roosevelt and Smith, was unable to carry out his plans for public power development on the St. Lawrence River, his proposals for the regulation of utilities were all approved by the legislature. Municipalities were authorized to establish, own, and operate gas and electric plants, and villages were granted permission to extend their lighting systems into adjacent regions. Both consumers and taxpayers were aided in a number of other ways. The Public Service Commission was given the right to establish temporary rates before the courts had decided on the matter; the utilities rather than the taxpayers were required to pay the cost of the Public Service Commission's investigations; utilities were compelled to transfer to the state all consumer deposits which remained unclaimed for fifteen years; and utilities had to pay consumers' interest on deposits every two years rather than on the withdrawal of deposits, as in the past. The state's regulatory powers were expanded by laws giving the commission power to remove all unjustified charges of utilities from operating expenses, requiring utilities to advertise for bids and to give the work to the lowest bidder, and extending the commission's authority over holding companies and concerns affiliated with them. Some indication of the over-all effect of this program is indicated by the fact that during Lehman's first six years in office reductions in annual utility rates totaled more than $46,000,000.

Lehman combined a deep-seated interest in reform with undoubted ability as an executive. His administration was seldom—and then only in campaign years—charged with inefficiency, and there was a minimum of friction among his subordinates. His political opponents might complain of his fondness for New Deal reforms, but they could find little to criticize in the way that he administered the government's finances. When he entered office, the Depression was making heavy demands on the state treasury, and an accumulated surplus of $99,303,000 for the fiscal year 1930 [3] had, by 1933, become a deficit of $94,428,000. In the next five years Lehman was able to wipe out the deficit, and in 1938 the state had a surplus of $6,469,000. For the remaining years of his administration, the state always operated well in the black, and in 1942 the state income tax was reduced 25 per cent. Lehman was a New Dealer in everything but his fiscal policies.

Lehman's outstanding record as a public financier was the product of careful planning and good fortune. It was achieved in part by drastic economies in administrative expenses. While grants-in-aid to localities and appropriations for state services were generally increased, the cost of administration was sharply cut. His success was also due in part to the large amount of federal monies received by New York during the Depression. Finally, he was able to accumulate a surplus by securing new sources of revenue. In the process New York City became the loser. When La Guardia became mayor, the city was practically bankrupt, and to obtain needed revenue he instituted cigarette, sales, and public utility taxes. But by the end of the 1930's the state had enacted cigarette and

[3] The fiscal year at that time extended from July 1 to June 30. In 1943, the beginning of the fiscal year was changed from July to April 1. Subsequent references in the above paragraph are to fiscal years.

utility taxes, and the city had to look for other forms of revenue. Although these taxes helped Lehman build up a surplus, the bulk of the state's revenue, as in the past, was derived from taxes on personal incomes, business, motor vehicles, liquor, and (after 1940) horse racing.

Lehman's appointments as governor provided little indication of his party affiliation. Positions at the policy-making level went to specialists rather than party leaders, while all other jobs in the executive branch of the government were filled with appointees selected and promoted on the basis of their civil service ratings. In addition to vetoing countless bills that would have undermined the civil service, he supported and signed measures prohibiting inquiry into the political affiliations of civil service employees, authorizing group insurance for those on the merit system, forbidding racial or religious discrimination in the civil service, and establishing minimum salaries with annual increments for those in both the competitive and noncompetitive classes. The New York *Times* wrote that Lehman deserved to be called the "Civil Service Governor"; the Civil Service Reform Association considered his record "excellent"; the Association of the State Civil Service Employees declared that he was "the outstanding champion of clean and efficient government in the United States" and "the greatest Governor the Empire State has ever had"; and the executive secretary of the National Civil Service Reform League stated that he was "a Governor who sincerely stands for the merit plan—not mere lip service such as most executives give it."

During Lehman's last two years in office his reform programs were forced into the background by the demands of World War II. A militant opponent of the dictators throughout the 1930's, he became an outspoken interventionist after the outbreak of the war. Before the United States became a belligerent, New York under Lehman's direction had created a State Guard to supplant the federalized National Guard, established local defense councils throughout the state, trained thousands of volunteers for civil defense, surveyed the state's industrial resources for war, and organized defense production clinics. Following the Japanese attack on Pearl Harbor, a State War Council with Lehman as its executive officer assumed the ultimate responsibility for directing New York's war effort. In addition to doing all within its power to expand military production, the council supervised programs for training warworkers, employed a variety of expedients to relieve the shortage of farm labor, and sought to strengthen the state's civil defense organization. An attempt was also made to prepare the state and its people for the postwar years. In 1942 Lehman appointed a Committee on Post-War Employment "to start planning now to provide for the security of our citizens after peace has come." Between three and four hundred million dollars from bond issues was earmarked "for use after the war in the construction of low-cost housing, grade-crossing eliminations and highways."

When Lehman resigned as governor on December 2, 1942,[4] to become director of the Foreign Relief and Rehabilitation Administration, he brought to a conclusion one of the outstanding administrations in the state's history. A rich man, he had spent his governorship converting the state government into an agency for aiding the poor. Rejecting the social Darwinist notion that the poor deserved their lot and that charity was nothing more than a handout to society's weak sisters, he believed that every human being, by the mere fact of being human, had certain rights and that it was the function of the government to guarantee such rights. In his farewell address, delivered in the midst of war, he restated the principles that had guided him throughout his administration:

My greatest satisfaction has come through the part which I have been privileged to play in enacting enlightened and beneficial social [and] labor legislation. New York State has been a leader in social progress. Our code of social and labor legislation in its humane and its practical aspects has, I believe, no superior anywhere in this country.

I am more strongly convinced today than ever before that wise, sound and workable social legislation is in the interest of all the people of a community. Thinking people must realize that the interests of all groups—worker and management, farmer and city dweller, the rich and the poor, the strong and the weak, are today interdependent. If the chain of our social and economic life is to be strong, we cannot afford to have any weak links. . . .

Throughout my public service, my philosophy of government has been simple and clear. I believe with all my heart that government is for the people. It must be clean and honest and efficient, but it must be more than merely an administrative machine. It must ever concern itself with the solution of human as well as material problems. It must satisfy the needs and aspirations of its people, and in order to satisfy those needs and aspirations it must be flexible enough to meet the changing conditions of the world today.

[4] Lieutenant Governor Charles Poletti served as acting governor for the remainder of Lehman's term, which ended on December 31, 1942.

Republican Rule in War and Peace

The barriers are breaking down. . . . We are on our way, leading the Nation toward a recognition of the great funda- mental that all men are, in truth, created equal. Most impor- tant of all, we are achieving an acceptance of genuine equality of opportunity in all walks of life, and the war against preju- dice and discrimination is being won.
—THOMAS E. DEWEY, *June 15, 1950*

IN THE election of 1942 the Republicans elected a governor for the first time since 1920. During the next twelve years Thomas E. Dewey and successive Republican legislatures dominated the state government. Al- though Dewey carried to completion many of the programs inaugurated by Lehman, he gave an unmistakably Republican stamp to the govern- ment. Aggressive, efficient, and imaginative, he both revived his party and provided New York with an administration that maintained the gen- eral standards of performance set by his immediate predecessors. Despite different party affiliations, he agreed with Smith, Roosevelt, and Lehman that the governor should lead the state and that the state should lead the nation.

Dewey's industry, ambition, and perfectionism were all revealed long before he became governor. Born in 1902 in Owosso, Michigan, he grew up in a politically oriented family, for his father was Republican county chairman, local postmaster, and publisher of the Owosso *Times*. A choir- boy and Boy Scout, he set some sort of local record by never being late or absent during his entire school career. After graduating from the University of Michigan in 1923, he went to New York City to study music and law. Although he had to earn his living by singing in churches and synagogues, he was able to complete the regular three-year law course at Columbia Law School in two years. In 1931, after six years of private prac-

432

tice, he became chief assistant to George Z. Medalie, United States attorney for the Southern District of New York. He also joined the local Republican organization and spent many evenings working for the party in his Manhattan district.

Dewey's rapid rise in politics was the direct result of his success as a public prosecutor. He first demonstrated his remarkable ability in this field when, following Medalie's resignation, he was in sole charge for five weeks of the prosecution of Waxey Gordon, a notorious gangster who was subsequently sentenced to ten years in prison for tax evasion. After an eighteen-month interlude in private practice, Dewey returned to public life. In July 1935 Lehman was requested by a "runaway" grand jury to institute an investigation of racketeering in New York City. Lehman responded by agreeing to appoint any one of three well-known Republican lawyers as a special prosecutor. But at Medalie's suggestion, all three proposed that Dewey be named. Although the governor thought Dewey too young and inexperienced for the post, he offered him the job, and Dewey accepted.

Surrounding himself with a group of young and extremely able attorneys, Dewey began a series of prosecutions that were to make him a figure of national prominence. Of the many cases he conducted, none attracted more attention than that of Lucky Luciano, an Italian immigrant who ran the business of prostitution like a grocery-store chain. Luciano and eight others were found guilty, but in the protracted trial it was impossible to tell whether newspaper readers were more interested in the exploits of the "King of Vice," the lurid and detailed testimony of a succession of prostitutes, or the triumphs of the relentless special prosecutor. Hostile critics asserted (but did not substantiate the charge) that the trial cost the taxpayers $111,000. But regardless of cost, the press and its readers agreed that they had received their money's worth. Dewey's subsequent investigations of racketeering in the trucking, restaurant, poultry, and baking businesses, while in some respects more significant than the Luciano case, seemed almost anticlimactic, but one observer thought that they were "a sort of front-page Arabian Nights series about New York, with the same hero for each installment."

As special prosecutor Dewey instituted a number of innovations that proved highly effective. Through the care with which he picked his staff and the firmness with which he ruled its members, he prevented all leaks to the press and underworld. He assured witnesses of protection, and once they realized that he would safeguard their lives, they willingly testified. He obtained from the legislature special conspiracy laws which made it possible to convict a group through evidence that linked members of the group individually to parts of the crime. Finally, he relied heavily on "blue ribbon" juries whose members were usually well-to-do and more intelligent and better educated than run-of-the-mill jurors. Some critics complained occasionally of the methods employed by Dewey to secure convictions, but the people thought differently. To them he was a "gang-buster," and radio serials that were thinly disguised rehashes of his ex-ploits were never quite as convincing as the original.

It was Dewey's repeated triumphs over the racketeers that set him on the road to Albany and led him up to—but not through—the doors of the White House. In 1937, when the anti-Tammany coalition was looking for a candidate for district attorney of New York County on the La Guardia ticket, Dewey was the logical and obvious choice. Campaigning on his record as a conqueror of the underworld, he was elected by more than 100,000 votes. He was such a popular candidate that on election day Brooklyn officials posted signs on polling booths reading, "Dewey is not running in this county," so that the borough's voters would not feel cheated when they did not see his name on the ballot. A year later he was the Republican candidate for governor and missed defeating Lehman by a narrow margin. As district attorney, he broke up a ring of thieving subway employees, sent dishonest landlords to jail, secured convictions of lawyers for ambulance chasing, and bagged such assorted big fish as Richard Whitney, a prominent Wall Street broker; Fritz Kuhn, head of the German-American Bund; James J. (Jimmy) Hines, a Tammany big-wig; and Louis (Lepke) Buchalter, a leading member of the underworld's upper classes. Although he was still only a district attorney in one county of one state, the press had made his record known to almost every news-paper reader in the nation, and in 1940 he was the leading preconvention candidate for the Republican presidential nomination. He received 360 votes on the first ballot, but he was soon outdistanced by Robert A. Taft and Wendell Willkie, and the latter was eventually nominated. In 1942, he was elected governor by more than 600,000 votes.

Dewey's victory in 1942 was due at least in part to the political bank-ruptcy of the Democratic party in New York. When Lehman announced that he would not run again, the Democrats had no other candidate of comparable stature. Although James Farley had broken with Roosevelt, he remained Democratic state chairman and was easily the most popular figure in state politics among organization Democrats in New York. Mov-ing into the void created by Lehman's withdrawal, Farley decided to make John J. Bennett, Jr., the state attorney general, the Democratic candidate for governor. Bennett had been an able attorney general, but he had little vote-getting appeal and was considered too conservative by New Dealers in general and organized labor in particular. With Roosevelt's support the New Dealers tried to block Bennett, but Farley had the votes, and his choice was nominated. The party was, however, hopelessly split. The break-up of the coalition that had repeatedly elected Lehman was still further emphasized when the American Labor party nominated Dean Alfange for governor instead of supporting the Democratic candidate, as it had done in the past. These developments all but ensured the Democrats' defeat, and on election day Dewey polled more votes than the total cast for both his opponents. He ran particularly well upstate, but there is also reason to believe that many New York City Democrats sought to punish their party by voting for Dewey.

The election of 1942 proved to be only the first of many Republican victories in New York. In a 1943 by-election to fill the vacancy caused by the death of the lieutenant governor, the Republican candidate, Joseph R. Hanley, defeated his Democratic opponent by 350,000 votes. Although Dewey lost the state and the nation in the 1944 presidential election, two years later he inflicted a crushing defeat on James M. Mead in the campaign for governor. In the same year, Irving M. Ives beat Lehman for the United States Senate. Once more, in 1948, Dewey lost the presidency— this time to Harry S. Truman—but in 1950 he was re-elected governor by more than 572,000 votes. In 1952 Ives was returned to the United States Senate with the largest plurality ever accorded a candidate in a state-wide election. Although Lehman was elected to the Senate in 1948 to fill an unexpired term and was re-elected in 1950, this was evidence of his own, rather than his party's, popularity. For two decades the Democrats had been led by a trio of remarkable vote-getters; in the 1940's no one appeared on the scene to take their place, and a decrepit organization virtually let the elections go by default.

The decline of the Democrats in New York State politics was due as much to Dewey's skill as a party leader as to their own failure of nerve. As governor, he was his party's leader in fact as well as in theory. Dewey's original political sponsor had been Kenneth F. Simpson, the Republican leader in New York County in the late 1930's, but in 1940 Dewey became his own and his party's boss. He was unopposed for the gubernatorial nomination in 1942, and soon after assuming office he built up one of the most effective state-wide political organizations in the history of New York. The basis of the newly revived Republican party in New York under Dewey's leadership was the support of the county chairmen. By skillful—his opponents called it "ruthless"—use of the patronage he held the county leaders in line. Those who were not amenable to this type of control were replaced by others who were. The local bosses, in turn, got out the voters in record-breaking numbers and put their influence behind the governor's program between election days. As was to be expected, this technique was particularly effective upstate, where the Republicans had always been strong, but Dewey also revitalized the party in metropolitan New York. The Republican vote downstate increased markedly, and in 1952 Ives actually carried the city.

Throughout Dewey's three terms, his all but absolute control of the party made it relatively easy for him to dominate successive Republican legislatures. During the 1930's the Republicans had built up a progressive and enlightened legislative leadership that presented a genuinely constructive opposition to Lehman. The most prominent of the new leaders, all of whom were in the Assembly, were Speaker Oswald D. Heck, Majority Leader Irving M. Ives, and Ways and Means Chairman Abbott Low Moffat. Young, forward-looking, and opposed to the Old Guard, they became the party's policy makers. But when Dewey became governor, he assumed this task, and the former legislative leaders either accepted the new dispensation or moved on to other fields. Dewey's power over the legislature was so complete that he was able to institute a so-called "pre-veto" system, by which he informed Senate and Assembly leaders in advance of measures to which he was opposed. These bills were then killed in committee, and he was spared the necessity of publicly going on record against acts passed by his own party. Only on rare occasions did some legislators reveal their opposition to this system, and those who did were usually disciplined.

Dewey's power over both his party and the legislature was in the last analysis the product of his popularity with the electorate. He was obeyed because he was a vote-getter. He could, in short, deliver. Many of his political opponents complained that he had an excessively cold personality and that he subordinated all other considerations to his political ambitions. But if these criticisms were correct, they had little appreciable effect on a majority of New York's voters. In the northern and western portions of the state he repeatedly piled up huge majorities. In part, his strength upstate was the result of the organization that he had developed, but it was also due to his undoubted appeal to the bias of the region. Suspicious of the city and all its ways, upstate voters viewed him as a small-town boy who had invaded the metropolis and beaten it on its own terms. To them his career was a succession of battles in which rural virtue had invariably triumphed over urban sin.

The other major source of Dewey's voting strength was in the suburbs, which had expanded rapidly at the expense of the city during the war and postwar years. As land in New York City was increasingly pre-empted by slums and office buildings and by such public structures as bus terminals, bridge approaches, and arterial highways, those who could afford it often fled to the suburbs and became commuters. Many of them were young couples who wished to raise their children in what they liked to call "the country." Many, moreover, were urban Democrats who became suburban Republicans. This shift in party allegiance can be explained in part by the fact that the environment into which they were moving was predominantly Republican, and it was both easy and natural to vote the way their neighbors voted. The rise in income which had made possible their escape from the city also inclined them toward Republicanism. Finally, it should not be overlooked that Dewey was their kind of candidate. He, too, was a young man who had made good, and he believed in a type of middle-of-the-road Republicanism that former Democrats found far more palatable than Old Guardism. In the Depression of the 1930's, most young voters were Democrats; in the 1940's the simultaneous rise of Dewey and the suburbs substantially undermined what had once been an important bloc of New Deal voters in New York.

Dewey imparted to the state administration a more partisan tone than had prevailed under Lehman. The major appointive posts went to Republicans, most of whom, while admittedly able, were not averse to promoting their party's welfare. In addition, by selecting Republicans rather than members of the opposition to serve as special prosecutors, he broke a precedent that had been followed by his three Democratic predecessors and that had been partially responsible for his own spectacular rise in politics. To spread before the people his own and his party's accomplishments, he established what one veteran Albany correspondent called "the most elaborate public-relations set-up the capital had ever seen." Numerous newspapermen, press agents, and speech writers were given state jobs, and the position of press secretary was created. Although Dewey generally received a good press, he was not overly popular with the reporters, many of whom complained that he often withheld material from them and that he attempted to prevent them from using other sources to obtain information about the state government.

Dewey's enthusiasm over the accomplishments of his administration and party often led him to a degree of partisanship that his opponents considered extreme. Moreover, in praising the Republicans, he was not always altogether just to his Democratic predecessors. He once, for example, stated that the Democrats had talked for years about reapportionment but that it had remained for the Republicans to act on the proposal. What he failed to add was that the Republican reapportionment bill of 1944 made it a virtual certainty that the Democrats would never again control the legislature. In his campaign speeches on his fiscal achievements he never mentioned that he had inherited a surplus from Lehman, and he repeatedly created the erroneous impression that the Democrats had starved the schools. Although students of state government have found much to praise in the administrations of Smith, Roosevelt, and Lehman, Dewey complained that his Democratic predecessors had bequeathed him a "mess" and "twenty years of cobwebs and dry rot." His record as governor was in many respects outstanding, but invidious comparisons—and at times, misleading comparisons—were not needed to prove this point.

Dewey entered office with a reputation as an efficient, hard-working, absolutely honest public servant. His record as a war governor demonstrated that this reputation was deserved. Although he retained the administrative framework that he had inherited from Lehman, he expanded the state's war efforts in many areas and shifted the emphasis of the government from the protection of civilians to an expansion of military production. The War Council, with Dewey serving as its chairman, was at various times concerned with such diverse matters as housing for war workers, shortage of farm labor, gasoline rationing, civilian defense, military production, salvage campaigns, lack of cattle feed, care of the children of working mothers, vocational training, the Civil Air Patrol, repair of farm machinery, and conservation of food.

Under Dewey's direction the state government did all within its power to assist New York firms in obtaining government contracts for military production. In his campaign speeches he had held the Democrats responsible for a labor surplus in New York City. Soon after entering office, he appointed a committee to study employment and business conditions in the city. As a result of the committee's findings and recommendations, more government contracts were awarded to manufacturing concerns in the city by the War Production Board, and within a year the labor surplus had disappeared. At the same time, the state Division of Commerce, which had been established in 1940, opened a Washington office to assist those New York firms which wished to secure work from the federal government. The Division of Commerce also provided legal and technical advice to companies with problems created by the war, aided industrial areas in their over-all adjustment to changes produced by the war, sought to anticipate and relieve labor shortages, and maintained a number of research projects for the development and expansion of New York business enterprise. In 1944 these tasks were assumed by the Department of Commerce, which was authorized by a constitutional amendment and legislative enactment. The work of the division and department undoubtedly contributed to the fact that, while the state's industrial plant did not expand as rapidly as that of the rest of the country during the war, New York's contribution to war production exceeded that of any other state.

Organized labor also had an outstanding record during the war. When the United States entered the war, New York's workers relinquished many rights formerly guaranteed by the state, and, as the war progressed, individual plants and industries were allowed through a system of dispensations to ignore specific provisions of the labor laws. But full employment, high wages, and extra pay for overtime more than compensated for the temporary relaxation of the state's high labor standards. New York's workers, who were perhaps more aware of their rights than those of any other state, showed a commendable reluctance to use the strike weapon during the war. Of the eleven leading industrial states in the nation, New York was the only one in which time lost from strikes declined each year from 1941 to 1945. The evidence is clear, moreover, that New York's unions on the whole preferred to work out their differences with employers through established government channels than to rely on work stoppages. From 1940 to 1945 the United States Conciliation Service disposed of 6,305 New York industrial disputes without work stoppages, while from 1942 to 1945 the State Board of Mediation handled 1,958 cases and prevented strikes in most of them. Unlike workers in many other parts of the country, most of those in New York had a well enough established tradition of trade unionism and government protection so that they did not feel impelled to view the war as an opportunity to place their own welfare above that of the nation. The Dewey government provided them with machinery for settling industrial disputes and with assurances that the rights which they had won or been granted would be preserved. A labor force distinguished by its political and economic maturity and an enlightened government combined to spare New York from strikes that seriously affected the war effort in other parts of the nation.

To achieve maximum farm production during the war, an Emergency Food Commission was established and made responsible to the War Council. The principal problems facing the farmer and the commission were a shortage of labor, inadequate machinery, and a scarcity of feed for the state's dairy cattle. None of these problems could be fully solved, but it is likely that without the numerous expedients adopted by the commission the state's entire agrarian economy would have collapsed. To relieve the labor shortage, the commission arranged for the transportation and housing of migrant labor, worked closely with Selective Service officials on the deferment policy for farm workers, set up a program by which high-school students did farm work during vacations, and prevailed on the Army to permit both prisoners of war and soldiers stationed in the state to be released for farm work during the harvest season.

Because relatively no new farm machinery was manufactured during the war, the commission immediately realized the necessity for conserving the available supply. Under a program inaugurated in 1941, mobile repair units were formed throughout the state, and by the end of the war the mechanics in these units had repaired more than seventeen thousand farm machines. The commission also assumed responsibility for allocating among the state's farmers the small number of new machines that were made available for purchase. The perennial shortage of feed for poultry and cattle was perhaps the most difficult problem with which the commission had to deal. In 1943, a severe wheat shortage, low ceiling prices on corn which induced midwestern corngrowers to feed their crop to hogs rather than ship it to the Northeast, and the failure of the New York oat crop all combined to produce the worst feed shortage in the state's history. Total ruin was avoided by day-to-day improvising until the shortage was relieved by imports from Canada and the federal government's increase in the ceiling price of corn. In addition to its many other responsibilities, the commission administered the programs for victory gardens, food conservation, and the transportation of farm crops to market.

While devoting their major efforts to increasing industrial and agricultural production, New York officials also sought to use the state government to help individuals adjust their lives to the changed conditions produced by the war. With the aid of the federal government, the state established child care centers at which working mothers could leave their children during the day. A commission was created to combat juvenile delinquency, which had increased rapidly because of the large number of families disrupted by the war. The Emergency Maternity and Infant Care Program provided for the state distribution of federal funds for maternity care for the wives and medical care for the babies of servicemen in the "four lowest pay grades in the armed services." Finally, because of the large number of draftees rejected for physical reasons, the state instituted a comprehensive physical fitness program for both adults and school children.

Soon after the United States entered the war, New York State began to prepare for a subsequent orderly transition to peace. By 1945, when Japan surrendered, various divisions of the state government had drawn up plans for assisting the veteran to return to civilian life, reconverting the state's industrial facilities, providing adequate housing for a peacetime population, and developing a series of public works to reduce the unemployment that was expected to develop in the postwar years. To finance these plans there was a large surplus in the state treasury. During the war there was relatively little on which the government could spend its money. At the same time the war boom resulted in a marked increase in the revenue the state received from taxes on business and personal incomes. Despite considerable pressure, Dewey rejected all proposals either to cut taxes or to earmark future expenditures from the surplus during the war. Instead, he recommended the establishment of a special fund for postwar reconstruction, which would consist of any present and future cash balances in the state's general fund. Under a law adopted by the legislature in 1944, a Postwar Reconstruction Fund was created. When the fund was established, it totaled $140,000,000. By 1946, when the state first began to make substantial withdrawals from the fund, it contained approximately $450,000,000. As opportunity arose, additional sums were placed in the fund, and in 1949 its name was changed to the Capital Construction Fund.

Although most Americans thought that the war would be followed by a severe recession, actually the transition to a peacetime economy occurred with relatively little hardship. In the five months following V-J Day, employment in New York declined only 7.7 per cent, or approximately half the decline for the nation as a whole. Within a short time both the state and the nation had achieved full employment. The relative ease with which New York shifted from war to peace was due in part to the fact that few new plants had been built in the state during the war. Instead, existing facilities had been converted to military production, and at the end of the war it was a comparatively simple matter to reconvert them. Reconversion was also facilitated by the state government. A State Reconversion Agency assisted industrial firms in obtaining machinery and supplies for civilian production; a State Plan for Small Business Expansion was inaugurated to help fill the void that had been created by the failure of almost 100,000 of the state's small concerns during the war; and the Department of Commerce launched a publicity campaign to attract new business to New York. These programs indicated that Dewey was not only far more interested than his Democratic predecessors had been in the welfare of business, but also that the return of prosperity had shifted the government's emphasis from public relief to the expansion of private enterprise.

New York's veterans' program equaled or surpassed that of any other state. In 1945, following the recommendations of a Temporary Veterans Commission established during the war, the state created a Veterans Service Agency as a co-ordinating unit for a state-wide network of local advisory committees for veterans and a Division of Veterans Affairs to serve as a central planning agency. While counselors, appointed and trained by the division, furnished the veteran with advice and information concerning his rights, privileges, and benefits under state and federal statutes, the local committees attempted to help him solve his immediate economic problems. The state also operated a rest camp for veterans at Mount McGregor, helped the federal government administer an on-the-job training program for veterans, and paid out veterans' bonuses ranging in individual amounts from $50 to $250.

Of all the problems facing New York's 1,700,000 veterans, none was more vexing than those arising from the housing shortage. First the depression and then the war had produced what in effect was a fifteen-year moratorium on residential building. New York had a long-run postwar housing program, but the veterans' needs were immediate. Because the state authorities were reluctant to divert funds and labor from permanent to temporary housing projects, every effort was made to use existing facilities. Dewey urged communities to convert vacant buildings into apartments for veterans, offered to provide hard-pressed localities with trailers, and requested the federal government to turn over surplus military housing to the state. On December 5, 1945, the Federal Surplus Property Administration made available several Army and Navy installations throughout the nation to state and local governments. The following March the first veterans' families moved into housing projects located on former military bases at Fox Hills on Staten Island and at Manhattan Beach, Brooklyn. Meanwhile, the state made funds available for temporary housing, gave veterans an eligibility preference in state-aided public housing projects, and provided emergency housing for veterans at colleges and universities. By 1947 the state had housed some thirty thousand veterans and their dependents in 214 projects.

In contrast to the numerous emergency programs for veterans were many long-term projects for the expansion of the state's physical assets. Such projects included the Thruway, parks, parkways, schools, prisons, hospitals, public office buildings, and the elimination of grade crossings. In addition, the state's slum-clearance and public housing program that had been initiated by Lehman was greatly expanded by the Dewey administration.

New York's war effort was directly or indirectly responsible for numerous innovations in administration and policy that remained permanent features of the state government after the war. Of these, none was more important than the Ives-Quinn Law forbidding discrimination in employment. Although this measure was in some respects a product of the same forces that led to the creation of the Federal Fair Employment Practices Commission, it should also be viewed as the culmination of earlier attempts by the government of New York to eliminate discriminatory hiring policies. In March 1941 Lehman had appointed a Committee on Discrimination in Employment to foster the use of members of the state's minority groups in defense work. Lacking the right to coerce, the committee had to rely on publicity and moral suasion to achieve its objectives. In 1942 it established a field force—the first in the nation—to visit employers and to urge them to hire workers without reference to their race, color, religion, or national background. At the same time the committee investigated the extent and nature of discrimination in labor unions, employment agencies, training schools for warworkers, and housing.

As the war progressed, minority groups, numerous liberal organizations, and several prominent Democrats demanded that the state force employers to end job discrimination. Soon after assuming office, Dewey reorganized the Committee on Discrimination in Employment and directed it to "undertake intensive and continuous work in the elimination of economic and social discrimination in the development of ever greater unity in the war effort." In 1944 the committee proposed the creation of a permanent commission "for the declaration and enforcement of the right of employment regardless of race, creed, color, national origin or ancestry, and for investigation of the various problems of discrimination." When Dewey objected to a bill embodying these proposals on the ground that the question required further study, the legislature rejected it for a measure establishing a Temporary State Commission against Discrimination. In 1945 the commission, with Irving M. Ives, the Assembly's majority leader, serving as its chairman, submitted recommendations that met with the approval of both the governor and legislature. When Dewey on March 12, 1945, signed the Ives-Quinn Anti-Discrimination bill, New York became the first state in the nation to place on the statute books a law forbidding discrimination in employment.

Among the most notable features of the Ives-Quinn Law was its lack of equivocation, for it proclaimed that "the opportunity to obtain employment without discrimination because of race, creed, color or national origin is hereby recognized as and declared to be a civil right." Provision was made for a five-man commission which would seek to end discriminatory hiring practices through consultations with employers. If in a specific instance this method failed, the commission had the authority to issue cease and desist orders which were enforceable in the courts. The penalty for a violation of a commission order was a fine of not more than five hundred dollars or imprisonment up to one year, or both. Soon after it was established, the commission set up conciliation councils in the state's largest cities to hear complaints, proceeded to eliminate discriminatory clauses in job-application forms and want ads, investigated firms suspected of discriminatory practices, and held a series of conferences on discrimination in education. From the outset the commission emphasized that it wished to reform rather than punish, and during the first year of its existence it considered almost five hundred complaints without once going to the courts. Because the commission was remarkably successful in avoiding both publicity and judicial proceedings, it is difficult to measure its accomplishments by any absolute standards. Most qualified observers, however, agree that it compelled many firms to abandon discrimination, and that in doing so it did not stir up any of the bitterness that had been predicted by its opponents. If the Dewey administration had done nothing else, the people of New York would still be immeasurably in its debt for its pioneering work in the field of anti-discrimination.

The creation of a state university ranks with the antidiscrimination law as one of the major accomplishments of Dewey's administration. Many of those who first favored an antidiscrimination law also helped to arouse interest in proposals for a state university. Members of minority groups, protesting that they were discriminated against in existing institutions of higher education, urged the establishment of a state university that would be open to all on an equal basis, and the Democrats took up this demand. Many New Yorkers also thought that a state university would provide the most equitable and efficient solution to the problems posed by the large number of veterans wishing to attend college. Dewey, while admitting the validity of the points raised by the proponents of a state university, refused to support plans for what he called a "jerry-built institution," and at his request the legislature in 1946 authorized the establishment of a temporary commission "to examine into the need for and to make recommendations relative to the creation of a state university."

The commission, which was appointed in the summer of 1946 with Owen D. Young, industrialist and former member of the Board of Regents, as its chairman, faced a formidable task, for it had to contend with conflicting opinions and prejudices. In addition to the clear-cut division between those who favored a state university and those who did not, there was widespread disagreement over the purposes of the proposed institution. The cleavage was along sectional lines. Those from the rural regions of the state favored a university for upstate residents to balance the free colleges of New York City, while spokesmen for the metropolitan area, where the minority groups were most numerous, wanted a university that above all would be open to those who had been discriminated against by private institutions. Nor was there any agreement on the university's form or organization. Some thought that the state should take over and operate existing colleges; others urged a single large university comparable to those in the midwestern states; and still others advocated the establishment of a series of colleges and professional schools throughout the state.

Following two years of hearings and research, the commission issued a report recommending the creation of a university which would have as its nucleus the existing institutions operated by the state. The idea of a single huge university was rejected, but provision was made for the future expansion of the present state system of higher education. The state was to furnish financial support for community colleges and to give assistance to certain professional schools which might need additional funds to maintain their standards of instruction and research. The commission also proposed that racial and religious considerations be forbidden by statute as criteria for admission to any nondenominational college or university in New York.

The commission's recommendations were adopted by the legislature of 1948 in five bills. Four of these provided for the creation of a state university, while the fifth measure outlawed "discrimination in the admission of applicants" to educational institutions in New York. Critics of the

new program, most of whom favored one large university, complained
that the state had created a paper organization and that the commission
had been more interested in saving the taxpayers' money than in meeting
the needs of the people. Such charges, however, do not take into account
the unusual features of the system. In the first place, it differed from most
other state universities in its emphasis on decentralization. For example,
if a community wished to establish a two-year college and had adequate
funds for such an undertaking, the state would pay for one-half of the
college's capital costs and one-third of its operating expenses. Although
the two-year community college would be a part of the state system, it
would be administered by its own board of trustees. In the second place,
the new program made it possible for the government to enter the field
of medical education, an area in which the shortage of doctors and repeated complaints of discrimination made immediate expansion imperative. Finally, the system was distinguished by its flexibility, for it embraced a variety of educational institutions and it could be readily adapted
to any foreseeable demands of the future.

Dewey demonstrated his interest in education in many ways other
than by his support of the State University. During his administration
veterans' scholarships were created; the value of the regular state scholarships was increased; and medical scholarships were established for the
first time in the state's history. At the same time New York's public
schools were expanded and improved with the state's assistance. Although state aid to education was generally lower during the war than in
the Depression years, this trend was sharply reversed in the postwar
period. Thus, state aid to education, which had totaled $111,814,000 in
1943–1944, had risen to $242,616,000 in 1950–1951. On the other hand,
during most of the Dewey administration the ratio of state aid to total
expenditures for elementary and secondary education was lower than
had been the case when Lehman was governor. This, however, does not
obviate the fact that under Dewey the government carried out substantial reforms in the state's public schools. Among the most important of
these were the establishment of new facilities for the education of handicapped children, a library program to which the state contributed
$1,000,000 annually, and a state-aided teachers training program in the
New York City colleges.

The labor and welfare legislation enacted during the Dewey administration was in large part restricted to the reorganization and expansion
of programs that had been inaugurated by his Democratic predecessors.
The benefits paid under both the workmen's compensation and unemployment insurance laws were repeatedly increased. The workmen's
compensation law was amended to provide for the payment "of benefits
for disabilities resulting from non-occupational injury and sickness."

Women were guaranteed equal pay for equal work. The coverage of the workmen's compensation, unemployment insurance, and minimum-wage laws was extended to include many new job categories. Comparable changes were made in New York's health and welfare programs. The state's share of the cost of home relief and its monthly grants for the care of dependent children were increased; the wartime commission to check juvenile delinquency was continued into the postwar years; special schools were built for retarded children; and large sums of money were expended to aid the victims of cerebral palsy, cancer, and tuberculosis.

Dewey's welfare and labor policies provide a key to his entire administration. Although his reforms never went as far as the Democrats wanted, they usually went much further than most Republicans in other states and in Washington were willing to go. In at least two respects he was not a typical Republican. He did not hold to the general Republican view that the executive should at best be no more than equal in power to the legislature, and he believed that his party should capitalize on, rather than resist, Democratic agitation for reform. On repeated occasions (but notably in the case of the controversies over the antidiscrimination law and a state university), he permitted the Democrats to arouse the public's interest in a particular proposal; but just when the opposition thought that it had hold of an appealing issue, he endorsed the proposal, tailored it to fit his party's needs, and secured its adoption by the legislature as a Republican measure. This was a technique that had been perfected long ago by Britain's Tories, but it was perennially new to New York's Democrats, and they never learned to cope with it while Dewey was governor.

Throughout its recent history New York's government has been administered by a succession of executives who surpassed in ability those of any other state in the nation. Theodore Roosevelt, Hughes, Smith, Franklin Roosevelt, Lehman, and Dewey were more than outstanding governors, for each in his own way possessed a genius for leadership and each became a national as well as a state figure. Five of them were presidential candidates, two were vice-presidential candidates, two became presidents of the United States, one became chief justice of the United States, and one became a United States senator. In a very real sense they were the makers of modern New York, and they were, without exception, progressive, imaginative statesmen. All were strong leaders, and all derived their strength from the people they served.

PART FIVE

Economic Development of the Empire State

✸✸✸✸✸✸✸✸✸✸✸✸✸

Our Changing Population

We must face the inevitable. The new civilization is certain to be urban; and the problem of the twentieth century will be the city. Many English sovereigns attempted to arrest the growth of London by proclamation. Equally idle will be all attempts to turn back from the modern city the tide of population flowing up to it. One who thinks to circumvent or to successfully resist economic and social laws is fighting against the stars in their courses.—Josiah Strong

WHEN one sees, hears, or uses the word "population," he is likely to think immediately of the number of people living in a particular area. In this chapter the term population is used in a broader sense. Here we are concerned not only with the number of the state's inhabitants at any particular time but with their heterogeneity, their sources, including immigration, their mobility and distribution, their vital statistics, their urbanization, their housing and its relation to crime and delinquency, and their corrective institutions, especially prisons and institutions for the mentally ill.

The state of New York had an estimated population of over 16,000,000 on July 1, 1955. Although the federal census returns indicated that many states, notably California, showed a higher rate of growth in population during the decade 1940–1950, New York has since 1820 been the most populous state in the Union. Between 1790 and 1830 the state's population increased at a faster rate than that of the entire nation, and between 1830 and 1890 at a lesser rate. The state again went ahead of the nation in the interval between 1890 and 1930, but during 1930 and 1940 its increase of 7.1 per cent was about the same as that of the United States. During the decade of the 1940's the state's rate of increase rose to 9.4 per cent, a rate again higher than that of the country as a whole. In this century New York's rate of increase in population has risen from 9.6 per cent in 1900 to over 11 per cent in 1950.

There were fewer large families as the nineteenth century drew to a close. The birth rate continued to decline steadily from 29.6 per thousand population in 1900 to 13.8 in 1936, the lowest in the history of the state. Thereafter it rose sharply, reaching 22.6 per thousand in 1947, the highest rate in twenty-nine years. This phenomenal spurt in birth rate can be attributed to the many postponed marriages and delays in starting families during the Depression of the 1930's, followed by the wartime period

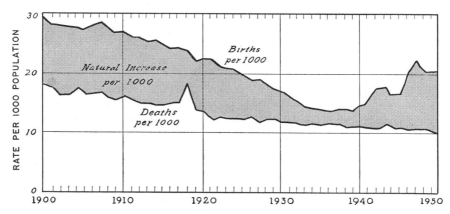

Chart 1. The rate of population growth in New York State, 1900–1950. This chart excludes deaths of armed forces overseas during World War II. (Adapted from *New York State Commerce Review*, March 1950.)

which provided the economic basis for earlier marriages and more children. Since 1947 New York State's birth rate has fallen off somewhat, but the rate of more than 20 per thousand is still high in comparison with the low rates of the 1930's. Incidentally, the birth rate for New York State has followed the same general trend as that for the United States but has continued to fall short of the national rate. The higher average age as well as the greater urbanization of the state's population is largely responsible for this disparity.

No state in the Union has a more cosmopolitan population than New York. People from every part of the world are to be found residing within its boundaries. Immigration from foreign countries was, until the federal restriction of the 1920's, one of the most important forces in New York's population growth. Even before 1865 thousands upon thousands of persons from northwest and central Europe migrated westward to improve their economic lot—Englishmen, Welshmen, Scotch-Irish from Ulster, Germans from the Palatinate and the Rhineland, Catholics from Ireland. In the 1870's and 1880's more English, Germans, and Scandinavians sought economic opportunity here, dazzled by the promises of railroad and steamship companies. Then in 1890's, 1900's, and 1910's came tidal wave after tidal wave from southern and eastern Europe—Croats, Ruthenians, Italians, Poles, Russians, Jews, Greeks, Turks. After World War I there was an influx of Puerto Ricans, Cubans, Filipinos, Mexicans, French Canadians. Between 1861 and 1900, fourteen million entered; between 1901 and 1914, another thirteen million came. It is not without significance that in the one-hundred-year period between 1820 and 1920 approximately 70 per cent of the immigrants to this country entered the port of New York. As a consequence, many of them, attracted by the varied employment opportunities and the amenities of the metropolitan area, as well as by the opportunity of contact with others of their national groups, who were already established in the city or elsewhere in the state, remained. In the larger cities of the state, notably New York, the immigrants of a particular nationality frequently settled in a particular area or region. Thus within the boundaries of the city there were neighborhoods or communities where almost the entire population would be composed of persons of one national extraction. New York, for example, had its "Chinatown," "Little Italy," Deutschland or German West Side, and a dozen other nationalistic neighborhoods where not only the language but the customs of the homeland were retained. In a real sense they were culturally nationalistic colonies within the limits of the city. Their presence helped to give vitality and diversity to the state's labor force. Some industries were built almost entirely on the specialized skills of workers and proprietors belonging to certain national groups. New York City's strong position in the garment trades, for example, stems in large measure from the contribution of settlers from the other side of the Atlantic.

Restrictions on immigration during recent decades are reflected in the figures for foreign-born residents in this state and in the country as a whole. There were fewer natives of other countries in New York in 1950 than in any of the previous census years back to 1910; the proportion of foreign-born persons in the state's total population fell from 30.2 per cent in 1910 to 17.4 per cent in 1950. During the same period the comparable percentage for the United States dropped from 14.7 to 6.9.

Despite the barriers to immigration, the state had 2,577,000 inhabitants of foreign birth in 1950, or twice as many foreign born as California, the second-ranking state in this respect. Illinois, Pennsylvania, and Massachusetts followed with between seven and eight hundred thousand each. Since 1920 New York has also had a higher percentage of foreign-born residents than any other state; in earlier years this proportion was higher in Massachusetts and, on occasion, in Rhode Island. States other than New York in which at least one in every ten residents was foreign born include New Jersey, California, and the New England states except Maine and Vermont. In some of the southern states the ratio of foreign born was less than one in one hundred.

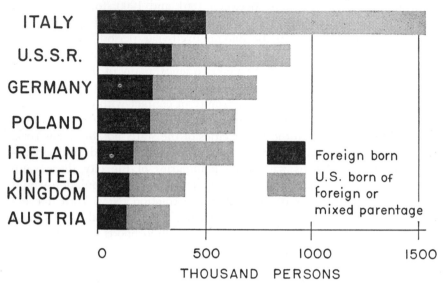

Chart 2. Country of origin of largest foreign-born and second-generation groups in New York State, 1950. This chart shows white residents only. (Adapted from *New York State Commerce Review*, October 1954.)

Of the 2,500,000 white foreign-born residents of the state at the mid-twentieth century, seven out of every ten were migrants from Italy, U.S.S.R., Germany, Poland, Ireland, United Kingdom (England, Wales, and Northern Ireland), and Austria. The same seven countries also accounted for over 80 per cent of the state's 4,300,000 American foreign-born residents of foreign or mixed parentage. New York ranked first among the states in 1950 in the number of the inhabitants from each of the following countries: England and Wales, Scotland, Northern Ireland, Ireland, France, Germany, Poland, Austria, Hungary, U.S.S.R., Lithuania, Rumania, Greece, Italy, and Spain. It ranked second in number of natives of Norway, Denmark, Netherlands, Switzerland, and Czechoslovakia.

Within the state there was a pronounced concentration of the foreign element in New York City. In 1890 about 42 per cent of the city's population were immigrants, and in 1950 about 56 per cent of the city's residents were foreign born or of foreign or mixed parentage. Whereas some 50 per cent of the total population of the state lived in New York City in 1950, it was the place of residence of more than 70 per cent of the state's foreign-born white inhabitants. In the case of natives of certain countries the city's share of the state total was even greater: Rumania and U.S.S.R., 90 per cent; Austria, Greece, Spain, Ireland, Norway, and Mexico, 80–83 per cent.

The only other cities in the state for which similar data are available are Buffalo, Rochester, Syracuse, and Yonkers. Combined, these four urban centers contained more than half a million residents of foreign birth or of foreign and mixed parentage. Yonkers had 53 per cent of its total population in this group. The upstate cities had lower components of foreign born and second generation: 45 per cent for Rochester, 44 per cent for Buffalo and 38 per cent for Syracuse. Only 32 per cent of the persons of foreign birth or of foreign and mixed parentage lived outside of these five cities. As the accompanying table shows, Italy was the principal country of origin for the foreign born and for the second generation, or American born of foreign or mixed parentage in each of the five cities except Buffalo, where Poland held first place and Italy second. Other countries which ranked high as contributors were Germany in each of the five cities; Ireland and Poland, each in four cities; United Kingdom and Canada, in three of the cities; U.S.S.R. in New York City only.

Table 6. Leading foreign-born and second-generation groups, five largest cities, New York State, 1950.

New York (4,444,000)				Buffalo (253,000)	
Per cent		Per cent			Per cent
Italy	23.2	United Kingdom	4.5	Poland	26.1
U.S.S.R.	18.2	Hungary	2.6	Italy	20.3
Ireland	10.1	Canada	1.8	Germany	16.8
Germany	9.6	Rumania	1.6	Canada	10.0
Poland	9.1	Czechoslovakia	1.5	United Kingdom	6.3
Austria	6.6	Other	11.4	Other	20.7

Rochester (149,000)		Syracuse (83,000)		Yonkers (80,000)	
	Per cent		Per cent		Per cent
Italy	35.0	Italy	27.1	Italy	23.3
Germany	15.2	Germany	13.1	Ireland	13.7
Canada	10.4	Poland	12.0	United Kingdom	9.9
United Kingdom	8.2	Canada	10.5	Poland	9.3
Ireland	6.6	Ireland	10.4	Germany	8.7
Other	24.6	Other	27.0	Other	35.1

Note: White residents only. Figures in parentheses show the combined total of both the foreign-born white and the native white of foreign or mixed parentage. Percentages may not add to 100.0 because of rounding.

Source: United States Bureau of the Census.

Mobility of population has been one of the hallmarks of American life from pioneer days to the present. Of the many ways in which New York has justified its title of "Empire State," unquestionably one has been its ability to attract natives of all other states to settle within its boundaries as well as to send its sons and daughters to all parts of the United States. The effect of America's great interstate mobility upon the population of New York or any other state is not easy to measure and, as yet, has not been ascertained with exactitude. We do know that prior to 1890 the net flow of internal migration was away from the eastern states. Thereafter the current was reversed because settlement advantages declined in the West, industrial expansion still continued to be largely concentrated in the Northeast, and the trend toward urbanization favored states like New York. New York City itself with its colleges, museums, libraries, churches, theaters, and art centers, on the one hand, and its varied array of light and heavy industries and vast mercantile establishments, on the other, made it a veritable magnet. Careful estimates indicate that from 16 to 18 per cent of the total population gain in New York from 1900 to 1950 was due to immigration from other states. New York has been fortunate, however, in avoiding the extreme of very heavy in- and out-migration which tends to make for instability of economic and political life. At the same time, it has not been endangered by the opposite situation, where a relatively static and ingrown population may become too complacent and lose the spirit of initiative and responsiveness to new ideas and methods.

Further analysis of interstate population mobility upon New York is most interesting and informative. Sixty-six per cent of the residents in New York State in 1950 were born here. About 17 per cent were born in foreign countries, 13 per cent in other sections of the United States, and the rest in territories or possessions of the United States or to American parents abroad.

Two out of every three New York State residents who had migrated from south of the Mason and Dixon Line were nonwhite. This northward movement gained impetus after 1900 partly because of the growing mechanization of southern agriculture and partly because of the more varied job opportunities in the Northeast, especially in New York City. The southern Negro was becoming increasingly dissatisfied with his status as a "second-class citizen." As late as 1930 only three southern states—North Carolina, Louisiana, and Florida—had repealed the poll tax. County boards of education tended to allot to white institutions a disproportionate share of public school funds and insisted upon segregation. To an ever-increasing number, New York seemed one of the most promising areas where positive action against discrimination was likely.

Almost without exception the Negroes migrating to New York settled in the larger urban centers, particularly in New York City. The first

Negro community of any considerable size in New York City was centered in lower Manhattan and in the area around the Pennsylvania Railroad Station. In the San Juan Hill region large numbers were wedged in among the whites of Irish extraction. The more respectable and exclusive families preferred Brooklyn, where they were able to buy or lease scattered homes rather than live in tenements. Among those who lived in Brooklyn were Negro butlers of old Knickerbocker families, bank messengers, caterers, and head waiters of downtown clubs and hotels.

During World War I great waves of southern Negroes flowed into the metropolitan area. The old Negro centers were unable to accommodate the newcomers, who overflowed into Harlem, which quickly became the Negro capital of the world. By 1920 the solid Black Belt extended from 125th to 145th Streets between Fifth and Eighth Avenues. Three decades later it had expanded southward to 110th Street and Central Park North and northward to 164th Street. The Harlem River virtually constituted its eastern boundary, and Morningside Avenue from 110th to 123rd Street and Amsterdam Avenue from 123rd to 164th Street its western boundary. Great peninsulas of Negro residents extended north and westward over Washington Heights to Riverside Drive. In this area reside approximately two-thirds of New York City's 730,000 Negroes. In the New York metropolitan area exclusive of New Jersey there were in 1950, according to the Bureau of the Census of that year, 371,580 male Negroes and 448,687 females, or a total of 820,267 Negroes.

Negroes constitute a portion of the population in every urban community in the state, be it large or small. Although the status of the Negro in New York is far superior to what it is in some other parts of the nation, there is yet much to be done before he will have attained the actual and psychological goal of first-class citizenship. In housing, education, political participation, and in the continuing disappearance of discriminatory treatment there is evidence that progress is being made.

Neighboring states were the most popular locations for native New Yorkers who had left the state, although no state was without its share, ranging from 462,600 in New Jersey to 1,300 in South Dakota. Inasmuch as parts of New Jersey and Connecticut belong in the Greater New York metropolitan area, it is not surprising that three out of every ten native New Yorkers living elsewhere in the United States were in these two nearby states. Many of them were still actively participating in the industrial and commercial life of New York State as commuting workers, shoppers, and vacationists. Daily commuters to Manhattan from New Jersey and Connecticut are estimated to number approximately 200,000.

Other states with more than 100,000 New York–born residents in 1950 were Pennsylvania, Massachusetts, Florida, and California. A fairly even balance existed between the movement of New Yorkers to the rest of the middle Atlantic region and to New England. The same is true of the west south central area. Regions from which New York State had a sizable net inflow of residents were the east south central and south Atlantic, where the northward migration of those (especially Negroes) seeking wider economic opportunities more than offset the flow of retired persons and others to Florida. Technological changes and economic returns in the grain-growing sections of the west north central region also resulted in a net influx to New York from those states. Regions gaining more population from New York State than they supplied to it are the rapidly developing Pacific, the east north central with its expanded industries, and the sparsely peopled Rocky Mountain states.

Although the federal Bureau of the Census fails to give complete data on the migration to the state of persons from United States territories and possessions, no account of the state's population should ignore the influx of Puerto Ricans, especially during the period since 1940. New York City has been the center of the migratory movement. At the end of the year 1953, the first- and second-generation Puerto Rican population of New York City was estimated to be 469,000, an 89-per-cent increase over the 1950 figure of 246,306. By 1955, the number had dropped to 380,000; many Puerto Ricans had returned to Puerto Rico, while others had left New York for neighboring states. No less than 72,000 came in the single year 1953. About four immigrants in ten were men between the ages of fifteen and forty-five. Between three and four of every ten were children under fourteen, of both sexes. Between two and three of every ten were women between the ages of fifteen and forty-four, together with persons of both sexes over forty-five. Few immigrants are forty-five years of age or over.

Puerto Ricans are filling tens of thousands of jobs opened up by residents who have moved up the social-economic scale and many of whom have taken up residence outside the city. Thus the Puerto Rican migrants have enabled many of the city's businesses and industries—hotels, restaurants, garment trades, department stores, machine operations, maintenance—to carry on.

Like most newcomers, the Puerto Ricans tend to cluster together. Comparatively few have gone beyond the metropolitan area. Even within this area they tend to concentrate. In the early 1900's the small number who came were cigar makers living on the Lower East Side or waterfront workers who live in the Red Hook and Williamsburg areas of Brooklyn. During the prosperous 1920's small numbers went to the outskirts of Harlem. With the big migrations after World War II, Harlem and southeastern Bronx were concentration areas. Today, however, Puerto Ricans have spread into virtually every section of the city as the accompanying table indicates:

Table 7. Number of Puerto Ricans in the boroughs of New York City.

	1930	1940	1950	1953
Manhattan	41,700	54,000	138,507	211,000
Bronx	1,500	10,100	61,924	94,000
Brooklyn	9,600	11,200	40,299	62,000
Queens	900	1,300	4,836	8,000
Richmond	200	200	740	1,000

Their presence has created serious but not insurmountable housing and educational problems.

New York's relatively high standards of health are reflected in death rates lower than those of the United States for every age group up to forty-five. This is the more remarkable when we take into account the upward trend of the proportion of older persons in the state's population. Over the last half century, the death rate has declined from 18.1 deaths per thousand in 1900 to 10.5 per thousand in 1950. These gains in longevity can be attributed primarily to advances made in the prevention and control of communicable disease, particularly among children, and to the sharp reduction of infant mortality and maternal deaths. Other factors contributing to the decline in the mortality rate include the rising standard of living, better knowledge of diet, and generally improved working conditions—elimination of sweatshop and child labor, and reduction of the workweek. The above-average death rates for older people are apparently attributable to concentration of the state's foreign born in the upper age brackets. The increase in traffic accidents in recent years also should be mentioned as an added factor in the state's death rate.

The death rate in the state has followed closely that of the country as a whole. The average length of life of the American people has increased from about forty-nine years in 1900 to approximately sixty-seven years in 1950. The period 1865–1910 compared with that of 1920–1950 reveals two highly significant facts: first, birth rates per family for the earlier period were much higher than for the later years; and, secondly, that for more recent decades the population is older than for the first period. Since 1945 the average age has remained fairly even due to the increase in the birth rate, emigration of older people to other states, and immigration of young people from Puerto Rico and other states.

We should observe that the proportion of the state's residents aged sixty-five and over almost doubled from 1920 to 1950. It was 8.7 per cent in 1950 and 4.8 per cent thirty years earlier. The relative increase in importance of this older group is emphasized by the fact that in 1920 there were four children under ten for every oldster, whereas in 1950 there were fewer than two. As the number sixty-five or over increases and the retirement age is reduced, the problem becomes more significant.

The New York State Joint Legislative Committee on Problems of Aging, after an intensive study of the economic status and employment opportunities of older persons, has already addressed itself to this knotty question. The committee was impressed by the opinion held by many authorities that there is no chronological age which should determine retirement and that older workers should retire only when they "can afford to, have to, or want to."

For most of the period since the close of the Civil War, women have outnumbered men in New York State. During the last half century and especially during the last fifteen years, the disparity has become more pronounced. In 1950, only for the group under ten years was there an excess of males. In all probability the presence of New York City within the boundaries of the state explains this disparity. The metropolitan cen-

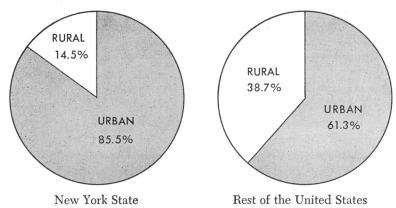

New York State   Rest of the United States

Chart 3. Distribution of urban and rural population in 1950. (Adapted from *New York State Commerce Review,* June 1951.)

ter has for a century or more and particularly since World War I annually attracted thousands of young people from other parts of the country in search of careers in business or in the professions. Nowhere in the world, perhaps, do women find such varied employment opportunities. In 1950, of the 2,300,000 residents who had migrated from other states, 1,300,000 were women. New York State, with 12 per cent of the nation's total manufacturing employment, accounted for 15 per cent of the female employees in manufacturing.

The marriage rate in the state has long tended to follow the business cycle. Thus the depression of the 1930's tended to reduce the number of marriages. In recent years, and partly because of World War II, the marriage rate has been much higher. In 1950, for example, the state could report that 65 per cent of its adult population consisted of married persons, as against 58 per cent in 1940. In this connection it is worth noting that today the state has 675,000 fewer single adults than it had in 1940.

With the growth of cities, birth control and divorce—both largely urban occurrences—have greatly increased.

From colonial times to the present, and especially since 1880, the urban-rural proportions of the state have just about reversed themselves. In 1790 over 80 per cent of the people lived on farms, and in 1950 roughly 80 per cent lived in urban communities (places of 2,500 inhabitants or more); this is about 20 per cent more than in the nation as a whole. In 1950 all of the rural dwellers were not necessarily farmers, for all persons living in places with populations of less than 2,500 were counted as rural dwellers.

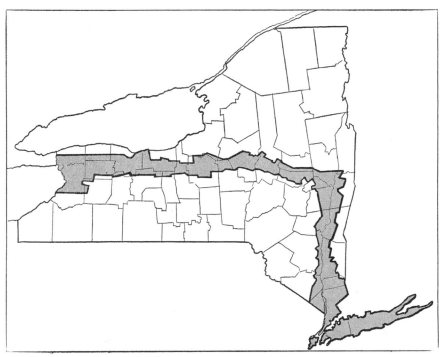

Map 10. Concentration of population in valley belt of New York State, 1950. (Adapted from *New York State Commerce Review,* June 1951.)

Rural population and farm acreage grew until the 1880's, when it began to feel the impact of industrialism. Thereafter, farming became more mechanized and employed fewer hands, and farmers in ever-larger numbers moved into urban neighborhoods or sought better farmlands outside the state. This movement, which gathered great momentum in the 1880's, was noticeable as early as the 1840's not only in New York but in New England as well.

Within the state itself there has been a growing tendency for population to concentrate in the New York City metropolitan area and in the right-angled industrial belt extending up the Hudson Valley and thence westward from the Troy-Albany area to the Great Lakes. According to the census of 1950 no less than 85 per cent of the state's residents lived in this belt. The density of population in the New York metropolitan area is 4,474 per square mile; in New York City it is 26,000 persons per square mile. In the upstate part of the belt it is 500 per square mile, or almost as great as in such states as Connecticut and Massachusetts. There is also a rising island of population density in the southern-tier counties where a growing industrial area has emerged.

One reason for the tremendous growth in the state's urban population is, of course, the phenomenal growth of New York City and the suburban areas tributary to it. Probably no city in the world in any period of the world's history has had such an amazing numerical growth. After the Revolution its population was only 12,000, not much more than half what it had been in the 1770's. By 1800, however, it had increased threefold. A quarter of a century later it boasted 162,000 inhabitants. In 1840 the figure stood at approximately 325,000—practically double what it had been fifteen years earlier. By the eve of the Civil War it had doubled again. The losses sustained as a result of the war were quickly recovered, and by the 1870's the million mark was reached. Thereafter, the population curve mounted upward still more rapidly. Industrial expansion and migration, both internal and foreign, were responsible for another half million during the 1890's. Between 1900 and 1940 the percentage increase in population for New York City was 117 and for its suburban counties—Westchester, Rockland, Nassau and Suffolk—252 per cent. During the same period upstate New York percentage increase was 37, that of the state as a whole was 85 and the United States 73. The growth of New York City by decades from 1870 to 1950 is indicated in Table 8.

Table 8. Population of New York City, 1870–1950.

	Population	Per cent of increase over preceding decade
1870	942,292	15.8
1880	1,206,299	28.0
1890	1,515,301	25.6
1900	3,437,202	126.8
1910	3,766,883	38.7
1920	5,620,446	17.9
1930	6,930,446	23.3
1940	7,454,995	7.6
1950	7,891,957	5.9

A glance at Table 8 indicates that the city's percentage curve upward tended to flatten after 1930, reflecting the city dweller's desire to escape the congested areas, to enjoy better recreation facilities, and better

schools, to garden, to participate in community affairs, and, in the event
of war, to live in a place less exposed to bombing.

The city's suburbs grew rapidly. The rise of the suburb and the motor
vehicle and rapid transit were closely related developments. It is difficult
to exaggerate the changes in American living occasioned by the increased
use of the automobile and rapid transit facilities. After 1920 the population of New York's four suburban counties—Westchester, Rockland,
Nassau, and Suffolk—expanded at a very much more rapid rate than
during the first two decades of the century. The latter two each gained
a quarter of a million people between 1940 and 1950. Equally significant,
perhaps, is the fact that car registrations in the same four counties more
than tripled between 1921 and 1930, whereas they only doubled in the
state as a whole. In 1947 car registrations in the same counties were 41
per cent above those of 1930, compared with a state increase of 27 per
cent. These suburban counties account for more than a quarter of the
station wagons registered in the state.

In matters of population, manufacture, trade, building construction,
and other economic considerations, it has long been customary to think
of the state in the dual terms of metropolitan New York and upstate.

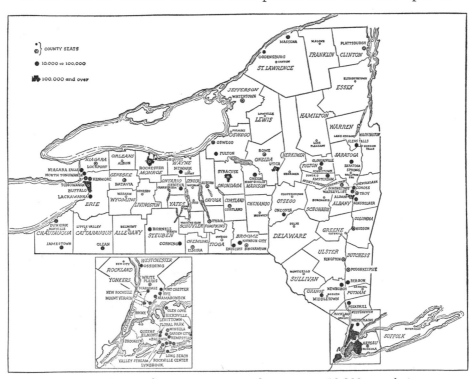

Map 11. New York State counties and cities over 10,000 population.

Table 9. Principal cities and towns arranged according to population, 1955.

100,000 and over

New York	7,892,000	Yonkers	153,000
Buffalo	580,000	Albany	135,000
Rochester	332,000	Utica	102,000
Syracuse	221,000		

25,000 to 100,000

Schenectady	92,000	Watertown	34,000
Niagara Falls	91,000	Amsterdam	32,000
Binghamton	81,000	Newburgh	32,000
Mt. Vernon	72,000	Ithaca	29,000
Levittown	60,000	Hempstead	29,000
Elmira	50,000	Kingston	29,000
White Plains	43,000	Lackawanna	28,000
Jamestown	43,000	Valley Stream	27,000
Rome	42,000	Lockport	25,000
Poughkeepsie	41,000	North Tonawanda	25,000
Auburn	37,000	Freeport	25,000
Irondequoit	34,000		

13,000 to 25,000

Port Chester	24,000	Ogdensburg	16,000
Gloversville	24,000	Ossining	16,000
Baldwin	24,000	Bellmore	16,000
Olean	23,000	Long Beach	16,000
Oswego	23,000	Saratoga Springs	15,000
Middletown	23,000	Watervliet	15,000
Rockville Center	22,000	Glen Cove	15,000
Elmont	22,000	Hornell	15,000
Cohoes	21,000	Mamaroneck	15,000
Wantagh	21,000	Oceanside	15,000
Kenmore	20,000	Mineola	15,000
Endicott	20,000	Tonawanda	15,000
Glens Falls	20,000	Floral Park	15,000
Johnson City	19,000	Garden City	14,000
Cortland	18,000	Beacon	14,000
Dunkirk	18,000	Hicksville	14,000
Batavia	18,000	Fulton	14,000
Plattsburgh	18,000	Harrison	14,000
Peekskill	18,000	Oneonta	14,000
Corning	18,000	Scarsdale	13,000
Lynbrook	17,000	Massena	13,000
Geneva	17,000	Franklin Square	13,000

Source: Rand McNally and Company, *Commercial Atlas and Marketing Guide* (New York, 1956).

In recent years, however, with the increasing concentration of the state's population in the comparatively narrow belt stretching from Long Island and the mouth of the Hudson to the Great Lakes, it becomes more and more evident that several metropolitan areas are developing upstate. While no one of them may ever reach the dimensions of the New York City metropolitan area, each, nevertheless, is a central city with tributary suburban communities and closely resembles the New York City metropolitan district. The principal upstate metropolitan areas are Buffalo–Niagara Falls, Rochester, Syracuse, Utica-Rome, Binghamton, and Albany-Schenectady-Troy. All of these upstate metropolitan areas are products of favorable location and twentieth-century developments. From 1900 to 1940 their combined population rose 66 per cent, while that of the rest of upstate New York rose only 1.8 per cent.

Between 1940 and 1950 the entire upstate area gained 480,000 persons, bringing the total to 5,252,000. Upstate, counties with already populous industrial centers had the greatest absolute increases, as for example, Madison, Niagara, Broome, Schenectady, and Onondaga. Even in the longer period, 1850 to 1950, most upstate counties which have not developed industrially show only slight increases or actual declines in population.

Agriculture and forestry, which had their greatest development relatively early, did not greatly expand their employment requirements. Growth in employment and in population has taken place, therefore, where manufacturing, trade, and service industries have developed. Declines in population can be attributed principally to the abandonment of marginal land by farmers or to the lack of economic opportunity sometimes occasioned by the shift of industrial enterprise.

The population of the state, both rural and urban, and especially the latter, has long been concerned with the problem of inadequate housing. New York City has been conscious of bad housing for more than a century. In 1834 Gerritt Forbes, city sanitary inspector, called attention to the connection between bad housing and high death rates. In 1842 his successor, Dr. John H. Griscom, issued a carefully prepared report showing how the then-frequent epidemics of smallpox, typhus, yellow fever, and cholera got their start in crowded and unsanitary slums. Subsequent surveys, notably that made by the Association for Improving the Condition of the Poor in 1853 and the Report of the Council of Hygiene and Public Health—a citizens organization—in 1865 so aroused the public that a city department of health was created in 1866. The next year saw the enactment of the first tenement house law. This act as amended in 1879 required fire escapes and better facilities for ventilation and sanitation.

Table 10. Population of principal cities of the state for fifty years.

City	1900	1920	1940	1950	Rank in U.S. population 1950
Albany	94,151	113,344	130,577	134,995	68
Amsterdam	20,929	33,524	33,329	32,240	374
Auburn	30,395	36,192	35,753	36,722	329
Binghamton	39,647	66,800	78,309	80,674	139
Buffalo	352,387	506,775	575,901	580,132	15
Elmira	35,672	45,393	45,106	49,716	234
Hempstead Village	3,582	7,350	20,856	29,135	420
Ithaca	13,136	17,004	19,730	29,275	417
Jamestown	22,892	38,917	42,638	43,354	274
Kingston	24,535	26,688	28,589	28,817	426
Lackawanna *	14,549	17,918	24,058	27,658	445
Lockport	16,581	21,308	24,379	25,133	479
Mount Vernon	21,228	42,726	67,362	71,899	162
Newburgh	24,943	30,366	31,883	31,956	378
New Rochelle	14,720	36,213	58,408	57,725	196
New York City	3,347,202	5,620,048	7,454,995	7,891,957	1
Bronx	200,507	732,016	1,394,711	1,451,277	
Brooklyn	1,166,582	2,018,356	2,698,285	2,738,175	
Manhattan	1,850,093	2,284,103	1,889,924	1,960,101	
Queens	152,199	469,042	1,297,634	1,550,849	
Richmond	67,021	116,531	174,441	191,555	
Niagara Falls	19,457	50,760	78,029	90,872	125
Poughkeepsie	24,029	35,000	40,478	41,023	293
Rochester	162,608	295,750	324,975	332,488	32
Rome	15,343	26,341	34,214	41,682	286
Schenectady	31,682	88,723	87,549	91,785	123
Syracuse	108,374	171,717	209,326	220,583	47
Troy	60,651	71,996	70,304	72,311	160
Utica	56,383	94,156	100,518	101,531	106
Valley Stream Village			16,679	26,854	456
Watertown	21,696	31,285	33,385	34,350	354
White Plains	7,869	21,031	40,327	43,466	272
Yonkers	47,931	79,803	100,176	152,798	64

* U.S. Census of 1910.

Sources: U.S. Department of Commerce, *Statistical Abstract of U.S. 1954* (Washington, D.C.: U.S. Government Printing Office, 1954); U.S. Department of Commerce, *County and City Data Book, 1952, A Statistical Abstract Supplement* (Washington, D.C.: U.S. Government Printing Office, 1953).

As the ever-increasing stream of immigrants poured into the city from the Old World, population mounted rapidly. The 312,000 residents in 1840 had become 3,437,000 by 1900. Existing on small income by unskilled labor and with little money for rent, the newcomers were without freedom of choice as to where they would live. The first-comers occupied the former homes of those who had moved to more desirable residential quarters. Much of New York, therefore, rapidly became a community of overcrowded racial neighborhoods. In the wards below Fourteenth Street the foreign born and children of foreign born equaled about seven-eighths of the population. In 1894 Carroll D. Wright, United States Commissioner of Labor, in a lengthy special report on slums, indicated that 360,000 of the people of New York City were living in slums. The disclosures in the Wright report were partly responsible for the appointment of the Tenement House Committee by Governor Roswell P. Flower. The findings of this committee confirmed what was already widely known by those who were familiar with the housing situation in the city. The cellar population, which had numbered 20,000 in 1860, still existed, though it had declined in number. Sheds and shanties hurriedly and flimsily built in back yards of once-substantial houses but now located in slum areas were still in use as human habitations. The system of subleasing had become highly developed and enormous profits were being made by heartless exploitation of tenants. Tenement houses built for speculative profits were often little more than unsanitary fire traps with privies in the cellars or under sidewalks; even in the so-called modern or up-to-date structures there was want of provision for air, light, water, cleanliness and the flats were small and overcrowded. The streets and alleys were buried with garbage and even human excrement thrown from the windows; the sidewalks were frequently strewn with decaying refuse of greengrocers and in winter piled high with heaps of ashes which in summer intermingled with the foul filth. Everywhere in the slum there was unescapable filth.

As a result of the widespread complaints coming from residents of the city representing all walks of life, a Tenement House Commission was appointed by Governor Theodore Roosevelt in 1900 to study and report on the tenement situation in the cities of New York and Buffalo. Under the guidance of Robert de Forest and Lawrence Veiller, the commission made an exhaustive study, which pointed up even more sharply the findings of the 1894 report.

The commission's recommendations for correcting these shortcomings were incorporated in the Tenement House Act of 1901, which was to serve as the chief working model for most of the tenement house legislation in America since that date. Indeed, the standards adopted for new tenements in the Act of 1901 were so much higher than what had been obtained before that the tenements of New York have been officially classified ever since as old-law (built before 1901) or new-law (built since 1901). The old-law tenements fall into two main classes, those built prior to 1879, when an amendment to the tenement law first required a window to the outer air in every room, and those built between 1879 and 1901.

The former, sometimes called railroad tenements, have a minimum of windows. The toilets, originally in yard or cellar, and sometimes still there, have usually been installed in the apartments. Water originally carried from the yard to the cellar is now supplied in almost all cases to a sink in the kitchen. Electric lights have generally been introduced. Bath tubs, hot water, and steam heat are decidedly rare.

When the tenement house department of New York City completed its first survey in 1909, it found that there were 641,344 apartments or family units in the old-law tenements of New York. Twenty-three years later there were still 425,894 and by the middle of the twentieth century the number was over 200,000.

As long as immigration was unrestricted, concentration in slum areas remained very high. The seriousness of the situation led to the appointment in 1911 of the New York City Commission on Congestion of Population. The commission found that, at the eve of World War I, 18.45 per cent of the city's total population was living in 1.15 per cent of the city's total residential area. In Manhattan there were 122 blocks with density of 750 persons to the acre and 30 blocks with a density of 1,000 or over to the acre. The causes of congestion were given as poverty, concentration of factories and offices, intensive use and high price of land, cost of transit, lack of city planning, methods of administering public and private charity, and failure of the city to adopt measures to attract people to outlying boroughs, notably Queens and Richmond. During the decade of the 1920's the population of Manhattan declined by 416,791 persons. The development of transportation—including subways, bridges, arterial highways, motorcars, and buses—and suburban attractions account in large measure for the lessened numbers. Even with this substantial loss, Manhattan had an average density of 85,000 persons per square mile in 1930.

After World War I the state became increasingly interested in the housing problem. In 1919 the legislature, following the recommendations of a commission headed by Charles C. Lockwood, adopted a series of bills to prevent rent gouging and wholesale evictions during the postwar housing shortage. These measures were at best expedients to meet an emergency, for the problem of slums—particularly those in New York City—remained unsolved. Both Governor Smith and the Reconstruction Commission recommended the establishment of a bureau of housing in the state architect's office, but it was not until 1923 that the legislature adopted this proposal. As a result of inquiries and investigations conducted by the bureau, a plan for low-rent, urban housing was drawn up by the bureau and submitted to the legislature by Smith in 1926. This plan called for the creation of limited-dividend corporations to construct apartments at rentals not to exceed a figure fixed by the state. Corporations willing to undertake such projects would be given power of condemnation, reduced real estate taxes, and exemption of their securities from taxation by the state. To aid in financing the projects, a state housing bank similar to the Federal Farm Loan Bank was to be established with authority to borrow large sums at low interest rates and to lend these funds to the limited-dividend corporations. The entire program was to be supervised by a newly created New York Board of Housing.

Although Smith's housing program was attacked by the Republican leadership, it was popular with the voters, and the opposition was forced to compromise. As a result, the legislature in 1926 adopted all of Smith's proposals except that for a housing bank. Smith, disappointed by the rejection of his bank plan, maintained that without it the law was largely ineffectual. Some progress, nevertheless, was made under the 1926 statute. The Amalgamated Clothing Workers Union established a pioneering project in the Bronx; another group of low-cost apartments was built in Brooklyn; and Lieutenant Governor Herbert H. Lehman and Aaron Rabinowitz, a member of the State Housing Board, formed a limited-dividend corporation for the construction of low-rent housing on Grand Street in Manhattan's Lower East Side. But although the board gave considerable attention to the non-New York and Buffalo areas, little real progress was made until a number of upstate cities set up housing authorities in the 1930's.

The emphasis in housing since 1932, both in the state and in larger cities, notably New York, has been on new forward-looking policies rather than restrictive legislation. Sometimes the police power has been used to regulate zoning and building codes and the like in the interest of safety, health, and general welfare. Moreover, there has been a growing tendency since the 1930's for the national, state, and local governments to co-operate in helping to solve the housing problem. In 1934, the legislature, at Governor Lehman's suggestion, made possible the creation of municipal housing authorities. No state funds were involved, for these authorities merely made the cities concerned eligible to receive subsidies and loans under the United States Housing Act. In 1938, however, the voters approved a constitutional amendment permitting the state to grant loans and subsidies for municipal housing projects. In the following year, the legislature adopted four bills implementing the constitution's low-rent housing amendment. The state was empowered to lend $150,000,000 to municipalities for the construction of public housing. The state's part in the housing program was administered by a state housing administrator, and discrimination on the basis of race, creed, or color in the selection of tenants was prohibited. Construction on the first state-aided housing project in New York and the nation began at Fort Greene, Brooklyn, in May 1941. A year and a half later, when the first units of the Fort Greene Houses were dedicated, the war had intervened, and the project was used to house warworkers rather than slum dwellers. Public housing, like so many other reforms, had to be postponed until the return of peace.

When Dewey became governor, $150,000,000 had already been earmarked for public housing and one project had been partially completed. By 1950 the public housing fund had been increased to $735,000,000, and New York State was building nearly 35,000 apartments to house 136,000 people. Of the 55 housing projects in 1950 under the state-aid program, 22 were completed, 17 were under construction, and 16 were under contract or in the planning stage. New York's slum-clearing and housing program was vaster than that of any other state, and perhaps surpassed the combined efforts of all other states.

Although the state housing administrator declared in 1940 that the public housing law of 1939 was not enacted for the sole benefit of large cities and that his division was currently making an intensive study of the means of adapting the program to the needs of communities of population of less than ten thousand, the larger communities seem to have fared better. Bad housing affected adversely health, morals, safety, and general welfare. Slum tenements became breeding places for poverty, ignorance, ill health—both physical and mental—delinquency, and crime. Studies of the tenement population of New York City show that three out of four babies living in places without sunlight have rickets. Overcrowding and lack of fresh air account for the high percentage of many diseases. Infant mortality in congested homes is still about twice as high as in homes where there is sufficient space. Within the crowded tenement there is no play space. Restless and cramped at home, the tenement child finds his way to the street, where he associates with bad companions. There are gangs of all types, and the youngster, usually an imitator, soon joins one. Crime and juvenile delinquency are closely linked, as several studies in the state indicate. In New York and Buffalo and even in smaller cities the highest rates of crime are in the slum areas. Homicides, houses of prostitution, and low-grade amusement places are also concentrated in the same areas.

Bad housing also is a fire hazard. The fire record in New York City, for example, indicates that during the last half century the largest loss of life from fire has been in the old-law tenements. In 1934 no less than eighty-one persons were burned to death in New York tenements.

Bad housing is partly responsible for the existence of the state's prisons, reformatories, penitentiaries, and hospitals for the insane and feeble-minded. The state had long had a Department of Correction, an outgrowth of the Board of State Commissioners of Public Charities established in 1867. In 1925, when by constitutional amendment the government of the state was reorganized and the State Commission of Correction was established and made a part of the Department of Correction, there were 15,819 persons—14,610 males and 1,209 females—detained in the prisons, reformatories, penitentiaries, and county jails of the state. At that time there were outside of New York City four state prisons Auburn, Clinton, Great Meadow, Sing Sing—one state reformatory for men and two for women, one Institution for Defective Delinquents, five county penitentiaries, and approximately sixty county jails. New York City penal and correctional institutions held a little under one-third of the total 15,819 noted above.

Twenty-five years later the total number of persons had increased to 21,630; of these, 4,802 were in New York City institutions, and the number of females in the entire state was 1,186. In other words, in this quarter of a century, the number of males showed a marked increase. By 1950 four new state prisons had been added to the four older institutions. These were Attica in Wyoming County, Greenhaven in Dutchess, Wallkill in Ulster, and Westfield State Farm for Women at Bedford Hills, Westchester.

The treatment of female miscreants prior to 1925 left much to be desired. The movement for a woman's reformatory in the state, though begun in the first decades of the nineteenth century, made slow headway. Prior to 1837, females convicted of a felony in the western part of the state were all herded into one suffocating room in the attic of Auburn prison. Those convicted in the eastern part were nominally sentenced to Sing Sing. Because there were no accommodations for them at this institution, they were kept at Bellevue Penitentiary in New York City under the jurisdiction of the almshouse department. There was no segregation on the basis of age or sex or degree of offense. The only attempt at classification was the separation of black and white convicts. In 1837 a separate building for women was built within the walls of Sing Sing to which all women felons from all parts of the state were to be sent.

This arrangement was far from satisfactory. With passing years champions of reform, especially Josephine Shaw Lowell, for years a member of the Board of Charities, increasingly called attention to the disgraceful situation. To this end during the 1870's and 1880's Mrs. Lowell conducted a series of investigations into the conditions of women in the state's correctional and charitable institutions. Her campaign, which was given impetus by the opening of the Elmira Reformatory for men in 1876, finally resulted in the passage of a state act establishing a House of Refuge for women in Hudson in 1887. In 1894 the Western House of Refuge at Albion (now Albion State Training School) was completed, and female offenders from the western part of the state were sent there. The Westfield State Farm at Bedford was established ten years later. In 1933 female felons from the official woman's prison established at Auburn in 1894 were transferred to Bedford and the Auburn plant was dismantled.

All of the prisons except Sing Sing operate farms, and all except Wallkill are engaged in industrial production. Attica has extensive textile and sheet metal industries, Auburn, the state's oldest prison, manufactures wooden office furniture and sheet metal products. The state's automobile license plates are produced there. Great Meadow at Comstock in Washington County is the smallest of the state's prisons. Its industries are comparatively small and include a chair shop, stone quarry, and tobacco processing plant. Sing Sing, whose population turnover is far greater than that of the other prisons, has a large printing department and extensive shops for the manufacture of sheet metal products, knit goods, shoes, mattresses, brushes, and brooms. Wallkill, in Ulster County, specializes in academic and vocational training. It has no industries. At Westfield State Farm, the only prison for women, the one industry is the manufacture of sleeping attire, dresses, sheets, and pillowcases.

The Department of Correction operates two institutions exclusively for mental defective delinquents. The Institution for Male Defective Delinquents is located at Napanoch, Ulster County; the Albion State Training School at Albion, Orleans County, houses women. The Woodburne Institution for Mental Delinquents at Woodburne, Sullivan County, houses both mental defective delinquents and dull normals of borderline intelligence. There are also a number of private institutions for the mentally defective and subnormal.

New York City operates approximately one hundred institutions and places of detention subject to inspection by the State Commission of Correction. Largest of these is the penitentiary on Riker's Island. This is the reception and classification center of the Department of Correction for all male prisoners sentenced to the penitentiary and workhouse and for all reformatory parole violators. Here the department's medical center receives practically all the medical and mental cases and self-committed drug addicts. An extensive academic and vocational program is also provided. The fifty police station jails of the city are under the jurisdiction of the Police Department.

Although the causes of mental disease are usually multiple, bad housing is frequently an indirect cause. Moreover, mental disease is more characteristic of urban than of rural areas. This helps to account for the location in or near the state's large cities of the majority of the public and private hospitals for the mentally ill.

Prior to 1858 there was considerable uncertainty in New York as to the status of the criminal insane. Criminal and noncriminal insane were permitted to mingle indiscriminately in the poorhouses and prisons of the state. In 1858, however, the legislature provided for a state asylum for the criminal insane within the grounds of Auburn Prison. Opened in 1859, the first of its kind in the United States, it received all the criminal insane of the state until 1892, when a similar institution was opened at Matteawan.

In 1843 a state lunatic asylum was opened at Utica. This historic asylum was authorized to receive acute cases of insanity from county poorhouses. Here the inmates were subjected to more humane treatment than they had ever known at the poorhouses. A few years earlier (1839) the first county hospital for the insane in the state was erected by New York County on Blackwell's Island. This institution received insane paupers formerly cared for at Bellevue Hospital in New York City.

No provision for state care of chronic cases of insanity was made until 1865. Following the exposure of the intolerable evils of such diseases by the great reformer, Dorothea L. Dix, the legislature somewhat tardily authorized a sweeping investigation under the direction of Dr. Sylvester D. Willard in 1864. Acting upon the recommendations contained in the report submitted by Dr. Willard, the legislature in 1865 provided for "the establishment of a state hospital for the chronic insane, and for the better care of the insane poor to be known as the Willard Asylum for the Insane." All chronic insane in poorhouses and pauper cases pronounced incurable at the Utica asylum were to be transferred to the new institution. With the passage of the State Care Act in 1890 the confinement of any insane person in poorhouses was forbidden. Henceforth all the insane in New York, with specified exceptions, were wards of the state.

Meanwhile (1875), thanks largely to the efforts of the Children's Aid Society founded in New York City in 1853, the legislature passed the Child Care Act forbidding the retention of children between the ages of two and sixteen in almshouses. The passage of this measure was another historic landmark in the history of the care of needy and sick of the state.

With the growth in population, state attention for the care and treatment of the mentally ill, mental defectives, and epileptics has mounted. By 1954 the state maintained twenty-seven institutions, including eighteen hospitals, six schools for the mental defectives, a colony of epileptics, the New York State Psychiatric Institute for research and teaching, and the Syracuse Psychopathic Hospital for observation and temporary treatment of mental patients. The state also operated three aftercare clinics for patients following release from hospitals.

Agriculture in the

Empire State

*The greatest business in the world is agriculture. It gives us
everything we eat except salt and sea food and everything we
wear except watches and jewelry. Everybody in America,
then,—country men and city men alike—must be interested in
agriculture, for we can never have a full measure of prosperity
in America until the greatest business in America is itself
prosperous.*—E. PARMELEE PRENTICE, 1935

IN THE minds of many people, New York State means bustling cities,
the hum of a seemingly limitless number of factories, giant mercantile
establishments, and a state gridironed with power lines, superhighways,
and air lanes. The state is also a checkerboard of farms. In this chapter
we shall be concerned primarily with the transformation of the agricultural enterprise of the state resulting from the application of machinery, agricultural education, and specialization. The dairy industry,
farm labor, credit, and markets will also be emphasized. Finally, brief
attention will be given to the effects of the revolution in methods upon
farm life and outlook.

The land area of New York is 30,675,000 acres, and more than seventeen million acres of this is in farms. About one-half of this farmland,
less than in 1865, is devoted to crops; the rest is used for pasture.

In the period between 1870 and 1950 many factors lowered the state's
agricultural rating in comparison with the other states of the Union.
In 1870 New York led all other states in the number of farms and value
of farm property and was second only to Illinois in improved acreage,
and its farm population of over one million constituted the largest single
occupational group and nearly one-fourth of the total population of
the state. By 1950 its farm population had decreased to less than 15
per cent of the total population. Nevertheless, in 1954 New York ranked

thirteenth among the states in value of its farm products, which sold for $816,854,000 as against $874,702,000 in 1953, when it ranked tenth. It led all others in the cash value of its ducks, cabbage, fluid milk, and onions; was second in value of its snap beans, apples, cauliflower, brussels sprouts, maple products, hay, buckwheat, grapes, cherries, and beets; third in value of its eggs, carrots, potatoes, and lettuce; and fourth in pears and celery. Its buckwheat crop of some two million bushels was about one-third of the total national product. It had virtually a monopoly of the production of buckwheat honey. Though its leadership as an agricultural state has declined, its place in the nation's agriculture is still a most important one.

During the ninety years between the end of the Civil War and the 1950's, New York State agriculture has been transformed by a series of developments that revolutionized not only the methods of farm production and the position of the farmer in the economy of state and nation but the whole of rural life as well. Improved transportation, the opening up of new agricultural areas outside the state, the over-all growth in population, the expansion of industrial enterprise and the growth of urbanization, the increasing use of machinery and dependence on scientific experimentation in such matters as insect control and plant diseases, and the changing character of the farmers' market have virtually destroyed the farmer as an economic individualist. The New York State farmer has increasingly become a specialist who is compelled to operate within the framework of a complex modern economy over which he has little control.

Like those of the other northeastern states, the farmers of New York State were keenly aware from early times of the competition arising from new agricultural areas both at home and abroad. Prior to World War I this competition was occasioned for the most part by improved transportation and the expansion of population westward. From 1860 to 1910 the number of farms in the United States increased from approximately 2,000,000 to more than 6,000,000; the area of land under cultivation rose from 160,000,000 acres to 347,000,000 acres; and the number of farm families rose by more than 1,500,000 to a total of 6,123,610. Although every section of the country contributed to the expansion of American agriculture during these years, it was in the new lands of the Middle and Far West that the more significant advances occurred and from which New York State farmers experienced greatest competition. Especially was this true of those self-sustaining general farmers who annually marketed their surplus wheat and livestock as a means of acquiring ready funds for taxes and other necessary cash outlays. Because of this competition and in order to make ends meet, they were virtually compelled to abandon general farming and to become agricultural specialists either on a large or small scale. Even as a specialist the New York farmer, though he might possess a fertile Genesee Valley farm admirably adapted for the production of wheat, could not compete with the prairie wheatgrower of the upper Mississippi Valley, where conditions are almost ideal for wheat farming. That the competition of the West early became important is evident when we observe that among the ten leading wheat-producing states in 1860 New York ranked seventh and that it thereafter fell below the first ten. By the end of the century New York, though growing rapidly in population, was producing a diminishing amount of wheat and other cereal breadstuffs.

Most of the more important types of farm machinery after 1865 were manufactured in prairie-state factories—although most of the harvesting machinery used by New York State farmers prior to 1900 was manufactured by New York State firms; Adriance-Platt (Poughkeepsie), Walter A. Wood (Hoosick Falls), Osborne (Auburn), and Massey-Harris (Batavia).

After 1910 the New York farmer, though a specialist—dairy, fruit, truck, or poultry—continued to face regional competition. The New York milk producer had to compete with producers in New England, Pennsylvania, and Wisconsin; the Bullard Orchards of Saratoga County with Washington, Virginia, and Michigan applegrowers; and the potato farmer of Long Island and central New York with the potatogrower of Maine and Idaho. Some New York farmers also faced increasing foreign competition; in this respect, however, they were far more fortunate than those American farmers who specialized in cotton, grains, wool, and meat products and, therefore, faced competition from Canada, Australia, New Zealand, Egypt, Argentina and other parts of the world.

Depending upon soil, climate, topography, consumer demand, and the farmer's own interest, background, and inclination, there is considerable agricultural regionalism within the state. If any one agricultural enterprise may be thought of as being statewide it is the production of fluid milk and cream. With the exception of the Suffolk-Nassau and the New York metropolitan areas, almost every part of the state is engaged to a greater or lesser degree in the production of dairy products. Counties especially notable for milk production are Chautauqua, Cattaraugus, Chenango, Delaware, Dutchess, Herkimer, Jefferson, Madison, Oneida, Onondaga, Otsego, Schoharie, St. Lawrence, and Washington. Good grazing lands, proximity of a huge consumer market, and adequate transportation facilities are the principal factors which make dairying the state's leading agricultural activity in terms of capital investment, number of persons employed, and total value of products sold.

Ranking next to dairy commodities in value of products sold are poultry and eggs. Although most farmers keep sufficient hens to provide eggs for the household and an occasional chicken dinner, the poultry industry is concentrated within Cayuga, Chautauqua, Chenango, Columbia, Cortland (turkeys), Delaware, Dutchess, Niagara, Onondaga, Orange, Oswego, Otsego, Suffolk (a large producer of ducks), Sullivan, Ulster, and Wayne counties. Nearly all of these counties have sizable cities within their boundaries or are near large urban centers. A number are in the vicinity of vacation and recreation areas, such as the Catskills.

Table 11. The top five dairy states in milk production (billion pounds).

	1945–49	1951	1952	1953	1954	1955	Dairy income as % of total farm cash income
Wisconsin	14.8	15.0	15.3	15.9	16.3	16.5	50%
New York	8.1	8.8	8.9	9.3	9.5	9.8	45.6
Minnesota	8.4	7.9	8.1	8.6	8.6	8.8	18.5
California	5.8	6.0	6.1	6.6	7.0	7.2	12.0
Pennsylvania	5.3	5.6	5.7	5.9	6.1	6.4	34.2

Source: U.S. Department of Agriculture.

Similarly, the majority of the vegetable and truck farms are concentrated in areas close to populous centers, although soil and climate are also responsible for the location of farms in particular areas. The mucklands of the central part of the state make it especially suitable for onions and celery. The sandy loam of Long Island accounts in some measure for the fact that Suffolk ranks third among the counties of the nation in potato yield and that it devotes extensive acreage to truck farming, with cauliflower, fresh beans, sweet corn, and cabbage as leading products. The soils and climatic conditions of parts of Saratoga and Washington counties help explain the heavy annual production of melons. Soil and climate enable Chautauqua County to rank among the seven leading grapegrowing counties in the nation. The Chautauqua grape belt, the Finger Lake region, and Ulster County give the state a high place on the list of grape-producing states of the nation.

As a commercial producer of apples New York has long been in the forefront. Here again soil and nearness to large bodies of water are determining factors; the thriving orchards of the state are located along the shores of Lake Ontario, Lake Erie, the Finger Lakes, Lake Champlain, and the slopes of the Hudson Valley. Wayne and Ulster counties rank first and second among the apple producers of the state. Orleans, Monroe, Columbia, and Dutchess counties have sizable orchards.

Several of these same counties, especially Ulster, have long been well known for their production of pears, peaches, plums, cherries, currants, and berries. In recent years a few counties have experimented with new crops. Greene, Ulster, and Columbia, for example, have developed a thriving mushroom industry. Areas with large dairy herds to feed have emphasized forage crops. Onondaga, Madison, and Cayuga counties rank high nationally in the production of alfalfa.

One of the most interesting farm enterprises in the state is the maple-sugar and syrup industry, producing in an average season about 1,000,000 gallons of syrup and 500,000 pounds of sugar. St. Lawrence County in the north, Cattaraugus, Allegany, and Broome counties in the southern tier, Cortland and Chenango counties in the central part of the state, and Wyoming in the west, are the principal producers. A large proportion of the New York products are exported to Vermont, where they are resold as "Vermont" maple syrup or sugar.

Table 12. Principal crops of New York.

Crop	1955	1954	Average 1944–53
Corn (bu.)	30,573,000	29,568,000	26,326,000
Wheat "	10,048,000	10,065,000	10,352,000
Oats "	30,299,000	26,888,000	25,692,000
Barley "	3,162,000	2,560,000	2,535,000
All hay (tons)	5,078,000	5,512,000	5,735,000
Dry beans (100 lbs.)	1,314,000	1,396,000	1,452,000
Soy beans (bu. bags)	84,000	88,000	102,000
Potatoes "	29,760,000	31,560,000	33,341,000
Apples "	17,100,000	16,900,000	14,046,000
Peaches "	1,300,000	1,010,000	1,337,000
Pears "	495,000	285,000	548,000
Grapes (tons)	75,400	94,000	58,920
Cherries "	38,200	30,100	22,100
Maple sugar (lbs.)	37,000	24,000	51,000
Maple syrup (gals.)	461,000	378,000	448,000

Source: U.S. Department of Agriculture. This table does not include the yields of the numerous truck farms or farm gardens, nor does it indicate a number of other items of farm income. In 1954, for example, cattle sold for meat were valued at $53,175,000 and the sale of milk and other dairy products amounted to $369,998,000. In addition, federal government payment to farmers of the state in 1954 were $3,753,-000, compared with $4,949,000 in 1953.

The value of livestock and poultry on farms of the state as of January 1, 1955, was $337,214,000. This included 2,356,000 cattle, 14,887,000 chickens, 73,000 horses, 1,000 mules, 160,000 hogs and 153,000 sheep. Turkeys raised in 1954 totaled 942,000.

The state is also known for its horticulture, which has long been fostered by the State Horticultural Society. Numerous nurseries produce an abundance of ornamental trees, shrubs, and flowering plants. Newark in Wayne County is the center of one of the best-known nursery areas in the state. Rhinebeck in northern Dutchess County, nationally famous for its production of violets, is the exclusive grower east of the Mississippi. The finest anemones in the United States are also grown in this area.

In New York, as elsewhere in the nation, no one factor has contributed more significantly to the revolutionizing of farm methods and farm life than the introduction of improved machines and new techniques. As a consequence, agriculture has been transformed during the last one hundred years from a simple pioneer and largely self-sufficient occupation into a modern business organized on a scientific, commercial basis.

Roughly, four phases of this development are discernible: (1) beginnings, prior to 1860; (2) the general displacement of men by horses for motive power which occurred between 1860 and 1910; (3) the substitution of mechanical power for horsepower following World War I; and (4) continuing mechanization and application of science to every phase of agriculture.

Before 1840 the New York State farmer used simple inexpensive tools, many of which were manufactured at home. His land was turned with heavy and clumsy plows drawn by horses and oxen raised on the farm. The seed was sown by hand and harrowed into the ground by home-built drags or bundles of bushes. The grain was cut by a sickle or a cradle, bound by hand, and threshed with wooden flails. The grain was separated from the chaff by a manually operated fanning mill. The corn crop was planted, hoed, cut, and husked by hand. If the farmer happened to be a producer of dairy products all the work was by hand; the cows were milked by hand, the milk was strained by hand into pans, the cream was skimmed by hand and churned and worked into butter, which, in turn, was packed into jars or wooden containers by hand. The cows were fed and their stables cleaned by hand. The tasks were endless, the hours of labor long, and the opportunity for profit limited.

After 1860, with the invention of improved plows, harrows, and cultivators and of harvesting machinery, especially the mower, reaper, and thresher, the situation improved markedly. But the hours of toil were still long and the tasks that still had to be performed by hand were numerous. On the dairy farms the old methods still prevailed at the close of the century. During the 1880's and 1890's New York farm boys arose at four A.M. to help with the milking. To the end of their lives they never forgot the cold winter mornings when, half awake, they shivered into their clothes in an unheated house and made their way to the cow stable, where they warmed their hands on the cow's udders before beginning to milk. Before the coming of the hay loader, all of the hay, though cut and raked with machines, was harvested by hand. It was pitched on the hayrack and off the rack into the haymows and mowed back by hand. The corn was still cut and husked by hand. During the years 1860 to 1910 there was, at best, a gradual and partial transition from the tool to the machine.

Farm mechanization in the state came into its heyday during the first half of the twentieth century when mechanical power displaced the horse and new machines and gadgets were substituted for the older ways. Space forbids more than brief mention of a few of the machines which have so profoundly changed agricultural production in all parts of the state. Any list would include the tractor, milking machine, cream separator, refrigerator, grain combine, hay baler, cornhusker, side delivery rake, silo-filling machinery, the high-power sprayer, mechanical washing machine, manure loader and spreader, and the numerous electrically operated gadgets which have replaced hand tools.

Despite the extent to which agricultural mechanization has advanced, there are as yet several farm operations in the state which require human hands. Among these are the picking of beans and berries, apples and other tree fruits, melons, and tomatoes. Moreover, the efficiency of farm machines depends upon constant inspection and attention.

The mechanization of the farm has had vast social consequences. The backbreaking and spirit-deadening toil of the New York farm men and women has been reduced. One has only to compare the status of the farmer's wife and daughters in the 1880's with that of the mid-twentieth century to appreciate this change. At the earlier date the farm women of the state, with few exceptions, were busy from early morning to late evening. Without the conveniences of the modern farm home, and devoted to the principle of self-sufficiency, they not only reared children but prepared the meals, did all the baking and laundry work, tended the garden and sometimes the poultry, and on occasion helped with the milking and the harvest. Mechanization of the farm home has, within limits, urbanized the farm women of today. Even though many of them may still do their own laundry, for example, the washing machine is a vast improvement over the wash tub and the ribbed washboard over which our grandmothers perspired.

Mechanization was a powerful factor in bringing the independent, self-sufficient farmer into the orbit of capitalistic agriculture. In earlier days when agricultural implements were few and often homemade, it was relatively easy to become a farmer. All one needed was plenty of brawn, a yoke of oxen or a team of horses, a farm wagon, a plow, a homemade harrow, a horse cultivator, a horse-drawn mower and hay-rake, and a few tools. A few hundred dollars would suffice for equipment. Farms were available for rent or could be worked "on shares." With the increase in mechanization, however, more funds were imperative to purchase the additional machinery and to acquire land, which, despite periodic depressions, rose steadily in value from the close of the Civil War to the end of World War I. To obtain the necessary funds, the farmer turned increasingly to specialization and "cash" crops. Although general farming did not succumb entirely, each passing year witnessed the growth of agrarian capitalism. Despite the change, not all farmers of the state were prosperous. Much depended on the competence and business acumen of the individual farmer, the location of his farm, the quality of its soil, and his speciality. Every farmer was also subject to factors beyond his control, such as frosts, droughts, excessive rainfall, wind and hail storms, unseasonable temperatures and the like. Many, if not all, were affected by fluctuation of the business cycle, credit facilities, government policies, labor supply, the international situation, the price system, and the demand for their speciality. Although accurate statistics portraying the exact economic status of the farmers of the state from 1865 to the end of the nineteenth century are lacking, reliable material for this period indicates that most of the farmers of the state like most of those of the rest of the nation, the South excepted, shared in the general prosperity which prevailed for a few years after the Civil War. "The reports from our Societies," said the New York State Agricultural Society in 1865, "show that improvement is the order of the day, and never in the history of our Society, during 24 years past, have the prospects of the agricultural interest of our state been equal to the present." The golden age of New York agriculture of forty cents a pound for butter and two dollars per bushel for wheat came to an end with the depression of the mid-1870's, which severely curtailed the demand for the state's agricultural products. Prices declined sharply and did not recover during the upswing of the business cycle which immediately followed the depression.

The extension and improvement of transportation facilities, especially with lands west of the Mississippi Valley after 1865, contributed adversely to the situation. The New York farmers, especially the grain-growers, could not compete successfully with the western producer. Too much of the land of the state being farmed was marginal to begin with, or was depleted by continued faulty husbandry. Moreover, the western farmer could employ the fruits of technological change to better advantage than could the New York farmer. Railroad rates also favored the Westerner. Diversification of farm products on the farms of the state did much to cushion the financial strain but not enough to prevent widespread economic hardship. Prices of farm products declined sharply, and land values momentarily nosed downward.

Farsighted persons expressed the need for better farming. Some advocated co-operative buying and selling. Sharp economic cleavages also occurred within the state. The attitude of friendliness and support of an earlier generation toward the railroads changed to one of bitterness and demands for government ownership or at least control. Many joined the Patrons of Husbandry and supported the Greenback movement. Greenback candidates for Congress received some eighty thousand votes in 1878.

Crop failures in Europe temporarily eased conditions, but with the coming of the depression of the 1890's the situation again worsened. Many dairy farmers wholesaled their milk for two and one-half cents a quart. Potatoes sold for from fifty cents to a dollar a barrel. Fruit was so cheap that it did not pay to pick it. Many farmers found it extremely difficult to realize enough from their farm operations to pay their taxes and provide for their families. It was during this discouraging decade of the 1890's that a considerable number of the state's rural people began to ponder the advisability of abandoning farming and seeking urban employment. Others, wedded to farming not only as an occupation but a way of life, hung on grimly. Some began to experiment with other crops as sources of income. With the growth of the state's urban population, the poultry and dairy industries flourished, and new attention was given to fruit and vegetables. Fortunately, by the end of the century, the business cycle was again on the upswing and the farmers of the state and nation entered upon a period of prosperity which lasted until the close of World War I.

The gradual mechanization of the state's farms, though lessening the need for workers, did not to any great degree minimize the need for manual labor during the decades after the Civil War. The labor of the farmer and members of his family was often supplemented by that of at least one or two "hired men." If the farm speciality was fruit, vegetables, or dairy products, the operator had need for "extra hands," especially in harvest time. Many of the well-to-do farmers of the state also employed household help. To them the "hired girl" was as indispensable as the "hired man." Most of this hired help was recruited from the local community. During the 1870's, 1880's, and 1890's many a farm-reared youth hired out to a neighboring farmer for several years in the hope of accumulating sufficient savings with which to buy stock and equipment to rent his own farm. Many of the hired farm workers, however, had no such incentive and were individuals lacking in occupational skills, education, or mobility. Some were ne'er-do-wells, "rolling stones," or persons who had winter jobs but turned to the farm for summer employment.

The traditional hired man who had steady employment, if single, usually lived in the farmer's house and was treated as a member of the family. If married, he might live in the "tenant" house provided by the farmer. Many of these houses are still to be found on the farms of the state. Most farmers did not need or could not afford a year-round hired man and hired their helpers from April 1 to December 1. Wages were miserable, ranging from fifteen to twenty-five dollars a month and "keep," which meant food, lodging, and laundry. Though some farmers' sons thought of the role of hired man as a rung up the agricultural ladder, the low wages was a major deterring factor. Certainly few young people of the state deliberately chose the occupation of hired farm laborer as a life's vocation. For them, the glamour of the urban community with its economically more attractive opportunities was always a mecca. Though in terms of wages the farm labor situation in the state is more favorable today than it was in the last decades of the nineteenth century, the modern farm laborer, unless employed by the large scale commercial farms, is still at a disadvantage in comparison with industrial workers, both as to wages and hours.

One final observation should be made: During the whole period since the Civil War, farm wages in the state as in the nation rose and fell in accordance with successive changes in the selling price of farm products. The farm laborers of the state have felt every turn in the economic fortunes of agriculture. In periods of either inflation or deflation farm wage rates have been the first to move. During the deflationary period following World War I, for example, as soon as farm prices started to decline farm wage rates also declined. Farm wage rates have also been influenced by variations in the supply of farm laborers. The supply, in turn, has largely been determined by birth rate, the number of immigrants, the slight amount of experience or training required to do farm work, and above all by cyclical economic change. It is obvious and perhaps ironical that the farm labor supply of the state has been greatest during periods of depression.

Of the approximately 125,000 farms in the state in the 1950's, a number somewhat less than fifty years ago, almost 94 per cent are owner-occupied. Nearly all are regarded as family-size farms. Comparatively few farms of the state remained in the hands of the same family for a long period of time; many old-line farming families of native extraction who, a half century ago, were regarded as the mainstay of their respective communities abandoned the soil. In their declining years many of these farmers, left alone by their children, decided to sell out. Others quit the farm because of the economic attractive-

ness of some other occupation. Still others came to the conclusion that
after years of work and worry they were entitled to spend their last
years in more leisurely fashion in a nearby village or a more distant
urban community. Some became absentee landlords, either renting their
farm for a cash stipend or on a share basis. Whatever the cause for
their retirement, they were replaced by the sons of a neighboring
farmers, by the owners of poor farms who desired to continue farming
on better land, or by an immigrant of peasant background. In 1920
the foreign-born farm population of the state numbered 71,276, and of
these 25,776 were farm operators. Irish, Italians, and Poles predominated,
but there were also some Germans, Scandinavians, and Canadians.
Available data seems to indicate that the foreign born have stuck to
farming more tenaciously than others. Hard workers, quick to learn,
they readily adapted themselves to American farm methods and practices.

Though most of the farms of the state are family farms, there has
been a growing tendency in recent years toward big-scale farming.
The Bullard Orchards at Schuylerville, Saratoga County, is a good
example. Beginning with one speciality, apples, this enterprise expanded
from an area of approximately one hundred acres to two thousand
acres, all cultivated on a highly scientific basis. In 1955 the apple yield
was over a third of a million bushels. In addition, large acreages are
annually planted to vegetables—string beans, sweet corn, cabbage,
potatoes, carrots, melons, tomatoes, and squash. A large part of the
enormous yields of beans, carrots, and squash go to the canneries. A
dairy is the most recent development planned for this already large
farming venture which annually employs about 150 migratory workers.
Similar ventures in other parts of the state are perhaps indicative of the
future pattern of New York State agriculture. Unquestionably they
reflect a trend in American business enterprise.

Another growing trend in the agricultural history of the state has
been the rapid increase in recent years of the part-time farmer. With
the rapid expansion of manufacturing and other industrial enterprises,
many farmers have sought to improve their economic status by obtaining employment in nearby industrial plants, often commuting by
means of car-pools. Their farm operations are either curtailed or carried
on by other members of the family, the operator himself helping out
on Sundays, holidays, and after his return to the farm at the end of
each day. A surprising number of these part-time farmers not only
produce sufficient commodities, such as poultry products, milk, vegetables, and fruit, for their own household but a surplus for sale. Many,
but not all, of these part-time farmers occupy farms of limited acreage

or poor quality. All belong in that half of the state's farmers who produce less than 10 per cent of the state's farm products.

As one reviews the history of New York State farming during the last hundred years, he is impressed with the contribution which education has made to this particular activity. Despite considerable agitation, little was accomplished prior to 1865 in the way of private or state educational aid to agriculture. It was not until the close of the Civil War that a real beginning was made when the state established the Cornell College of Agriculture, destined to be famous the world over. In 1881 the legislature authorized the establishment of the Geneva Agricultural Experiment Station, which in 1923 became a part of Cornell University. Subsequently three other state-supported institutions of great aid to farmers came into being. These were the New York State Veterinary College (1894), the New York State College of Forestry (1911), and the State College of Home Economics (1927). State school or technical institutes of agriculture were also established at Canton (St. Lawrence University; 1906), Alfred University (1908), Morrisville (1908), Cobleskill (1911), Farmingdale (1912), and Delhi (1913).

It is difficult to exaggerate the beneficial effects of these institutions upon the state's farming industry. Almost every aspect of New York agriculture and rural life reflects their influence. From them has come the latest technical information on improving crop and livestock production and marketing and on farm operation by the most profitable methods. They have not waited for the farmer to come to them for advice. In this connection, the pattern was set when, in 1886, the Farmers Institute program came into being. Organized largely through the efforts of Professor Isaac Phillips Roberts of Cornell University and J. S. Woodward of the *Rural New Yorker,* the first Institute was held at Cornell the same year. Attendance was large, and the addresses, each followed by a spirited discussion, convinced everyone that this was an admirable way of helping the farmers of the state with their problems. The program was broadened and Institutes continued to be held in various parts of the state until 1911, when they were superseded by the county extension work. During the twenty-five-year period of their existence, the staff of the State College of Agriculture and the Geneva Experiment Station participated as Institute lecturers and demonstrators. Those who attended the Institutes had opportunity, moreover, to discuss their problems with practically every important agricultural leader in the state.

The agricultural extension service supported in part by county, state, and federal governments made it possible for every farming county to have the services of at least one extension agent trained in agricultural science and practice. The agricultural agent and his staff bring the latest developments in methods and materials to all of the farmers of the county. Through demonstrations, meetings, field and farm visits, and conferences, he made available to farmers, individually and in groups, information on all phases of farming. Closely in touch at all times with the State College of Agriculture at Cornell University through its extension service, the county agricultural agent is kept informed of all the latest results of research. He also has at his service specialists in each of the many subjects related to farming: crops and livestock, insect pests, diseases of plants and animals, new machines and gadgets, and economic information such as costs, prices, and farm management. Assisting the county agents in the distribution of this information are the almost two million bulletins sent free each year by the State College of Agriculture and the Geneva Experiment Station. The daily and weekly press of the state, the agricultural magazines, the county farm bureau newsletter (the first farm bureau was organized in Broome County in 1911), and the State Department of Agriculture and Markets broadcasts and reports are also important agencies of dissemination of agricultural information.

County home demonstration agents aid homemakers in obtaining the latest information on instruction, food preparation, home decoration, child care, and home management. County 4H (Health, Head, Heart, and Hand) Clubs for youth are shown the best and latest agricultural methods, and they practice them in crop and livestock projects of their own suitable to their age.

The farmer has also had the benefit of two other helpful agencies. These are the state fair and the State Department of Agriculture and Markets. Although the proposal for a state fair was urged by several of the members of the New York State Agricultural Society soon after it organized in 1832, it was not until 1841 that interest seemed to warrant undertaking the project. The first state fair—of two days' duration— was in that year held in Syracuse. Departments were few and prizes small, but attendance and interest were excellent. Thereafter the fair was held annually at different places: Albany, Rochester, Poughkeepsie, Utica, Saratoga, Buffalo, New York City (where it was poorly attended and was financially a failure), Elmira, and Watertown. By the late 1880's it became apparent that the fair would benefit greatly if it could be held every year in the same place. Syracuse was chosen, and since 1890 it has been the fair's permanent home. From its beginning it has served agriculture of the state well. Fortunately it has escaped the major defects of the commercialization which has all but ruined the county fairs of the state.

The origins of the New York State Department of Agriculture and Markets date back to 1884, when a Dairy Commission was organized by the state. This organization continued to function until 1893, when, in response to the demand that all branches of the state's agriculture should be included, the name was changed to Department of Agriculture. Approximately a quarter of a century later—in 1917—this department, largely for political reasons, was supplanted by a Council of Farms and Markets which elected a commissioner, or administrator. Under this arrangement matters went from bad to worse until in 1921 the legislature placed responsibility in the hand of a single commissioner. In 1926 the Department of Farms and Markets became the Department of Agriculture and Markets. It has increasingly concerned itself with the enforcement of laws and regulations relating to agriculture. With passing years, as the state has assumed control over such problems as plant and animal diseases, insect pests, the grading of fruit and vegetables, feeds, fertilizers, seeds, adulteration and misrepresentation of product, weights and measures, conservation—to mention the more important—the work of this department has greatly expanded.

Most of the state's farmers during the post-Civil War decades had an apparent disregard for the problems of soil conservation and of better returns on farm investments. Many of these farmers were traditionalists —they employed the same methods and procedures that had prevailed in their grandfathers' time. Many feared change and had no use for "new-fangled ways." "Soil mining" by the use of faulty rotation or no rotation at all was a common practice. The land was cropped to death. Manure, if it left the barnyard at all, reached only the nearest fields; those at a distance went unfed. Land that craved lime to counteract the acidity remained sour and was labeled by the farmer as "no good" or "worn out" when it refused to grow corn, wheat, or hay. Hillsides were washed and gullied because of improper methods of plowing and cultivation. There is still evidence in almost every county of these bad practices.

While some wastage still prevails, progress in the direction of better farming and soil conservation during the last half century has been a source of great satisfaction to all those who work for the wise development of the state's natural resources. The period 1900 to 1930 was devoted primarily to the gathering and dissemination of information. This educational work was carried on primarily by colleges and schools of agriculture, the New York State College of Forestry, and farm journals, especially the *Rural New Yorker* and the *American Agriculturalist*. It was not easy to convince the citizenry of the state and especially farmers and lumbermen that the state's resources were not inexhaustible and that more intelligent methods had to be employed if farm and forest lands were not to be damaged beyond repair. Among those who have failed to heed the pleas of those who preach the gospel of conservation are the tenant farmers. The percentage of such farmers in the state is much smaller than in many other states of the Union (it has varied from 10 to 25 per cent for many years), but their numbers threaten the state conservation effort. The tenant farmer is interested in extracting everything he can while he is on any particular farm. Short tenures, about three years on an average, do not make a conservation program profitable. He is not interested in soil improvement nor in keeping fences and buildings in repair. The heavily mortgaged farmer, as well, is under terrific pressure to keep on mining his soil.

The state does not restrict its conservation activities to the preservation and wise use of farmlands. It has long been interested in game, fisheries, protection of streams, state forests, parks, and recreation grounds. More than ever it appreciates the need of urban people to get away from factories and offices and to go where they can hike, swim, boat, fish, ski, hunt, picnic, and relax.

During the last hundred years the farmers' most pressing problem has been an economic one—markets, prices, and credit. The farmers of the state have been fortunate in that they have had as a market the most populous industrialized commonwealth in the Union. At the present time, of the state's population of approximately fifteen million people, more than half live in the area of metropolitan New York City and the greater part of the remainder in the six upstate urban centers: Buffalo, Rochester, Albany-Schenectady-Troy, Syracuse, Utica-Rome, and Binghamton. The real pinch in the matter of markets, therefore, has never been the lack of a large consuming population. Nor has it been want of transportation facilities, which have improved enormously since the coming of the motor truck and better highways. Rather, the problem arose and has persisted because of competition and the farmer's inability to exert in any considerable degree control over marketing conditions and the price he obtains for his products. Historically the farmer has been a producer and not a marketer.

The majority of the commercial farmers of the state have never been retailers. They market their product through dealers or middlemen who are either direct buyers for processors like the canning companies or are agents for wholesalers. In either case the farmer, who receives only about 40 per cent of the price the consumer pays for his product, rightly or wrongly feels that the middleman profits at his expense. This situation has led to efforts to improve marketing through the establishment of public markets in urban centers, auction sale of farmer produce, and the formation of co-operative associations for both purchasing supplies and marketing produce.

If the farmer is a wholesaler in the marketing of farm commodities, he is a retailer in what he has to buy. As such, he feels that he is victimized by the prices he has to pay for supplies and equipment. When he purchases a milking machine or spraying equipment, for example, he does not determine the price. Prices are fixed by forces over which he has little or no control. The average New York State farm is so small that it does not make sufficiently large purchases of supplies to obtain quantity discounts. In fact, it has often and rightly been said that farmers are the only economic group which buys at retail and sells at wholesale.

Of the co-operatives serving the farmers of the state, the Patrons of Husbandry, organized in 1867, has been most successful. Its local units were called "granges" and its members "grangers." Farm co-operatives during the last century have had a checkered career. Without question their influence for farmer betterment has been healthy. Among other things, they have directed their activities to providing larger and more efficient local plant facilities for handling produce, the lowering of dealers margins, better grading and packaging of farm products, and the education of their members as to how agricultural products are actually marketed and prices determined. In 1953–1954 co-operatives in the state numbered 396, with a total membership of 160,367. The dollar volume of their net business—covering marketing of farm products for their patrons, furnishing patrons with farm machinery and equipment, feed, fertilizer, petroleum products, seed, and other supplies (including building materials, containers and packaging supplies, sprays, dusts and other farm chemicals, meats and groceries, and miscellaneous supplies), and services such as storage, feed grinding, trucking, machinery repair and credit facilities—was approximately $450,000,000.[1]

The third pressing economic problem confronting the farmers of the state and nation is the matter of agricultural credit. They have long felt that they were exploited by bankers and other moneylenders. Credit requirements for farmers necessarily differ from those of many kinds of business. Many farming operations are seasonal, and the time element in credit needs is subject to various conditions. Thus a ninety-day note would fail to fit the needs of a farmer whose crops, planted in the spring, yield no returns until harvest, which may be as much as four or five months later. An apple orchard represents an investment for several years before it begins to bear fruit. Similarly, the dairy farmer must house, feed, and otherwise care for his young stock for a period of two and a half years until they become milk-producing cows.

[1] See Anne L. Gessner, *Statistics of Farmer Cooperatives, 1953–54: Marketing, Farm Supply and Service* (U.S. Department of Agriculture, *General Report 23*, June 1956), App. 1. This seventy-one page report is indispensable for anyone interested in farm co-operatives.

Prior to World War I, short-time credit was frequently extended by the country merchant from whom the farmer bought his supplies and sometimes his equipment. There was no signed contract, but merely a verbal stipulation that when the farmer harvested his rye or potato crop he would settle for his spring purchases. If interest was charged, it was included in the purchase price. The principal drawback to this arrangement was that it compelled the farmer to sell his produce as soon as harvested, even though the price might be low. The farmer was the loser and the dealer the gainer.

Farm credit arrangements in the state today are far better. Banking institutions, especially in rural areas, are increasingly taking greater concern in farm credit problems. The president of the bank or some other officer make farm loans his speciality. When a prospective farm borrower comes to the bank for a loan, the bank is in a position to pass sound judgment as to the borrower and the project for which he desires the loan.

The farmers of the state may, of course, obtain loans from private individuals, such as well-to-do neighboring farmers. Farmers have another source of credit in the local credit associations set up and directed by leading farmers and affiliated with governmentally assisted regional and national farm credit associations.

Perhaps the most striking change one observes when one compares the agriculture of the state in 1865 with that of the 1950's is the extent to which New York has become primarily a dairy land. In 1950 no less than 50 per cent of farm income was produced by the dairy industry, principally from the production of fluid milk.

Prior to the Civil War the cheese and butter industry had become important in New York agriculture. The fluid milk industry did not begin to grow until after the war, although in the middle 1840's farmers within convenient distance of New York City established milk wagon routes. Up to this time the city had been consuming chiefly unsanitary distillery milk, which was not completely eliminated until the turn of the century. About the same time a group of farmers known as the Orange County Milk Association began shipping milk by rail to grocers in New York City. In 1853 the city milk supply was the target of a blast in the interest of public health in a volume entitled *The Milk Trade in New York County*, which denounced the widespread adulteration practices employed by both producers and distributors. A statute of 1864 permitted the adding of ice but not water! Despite this act the Board of Health in 1869, alarmed about the extent of adulteration, estimated on the basis of tests that New Yorkers drank 40,000,000 quarts of water with its 120,000,000 quarts of milk consumed annually. In 1875 it was shown pretty conclusively that adulteration was netting milk dealers

$4,000,000 a year. When a customer of one upstate dealer found a minnow in her milk container, the dealer freely admitted that the spring in which he cooled his milk was the most profitable cow he ever owned. The question of adulteration was one of the problems which confronted the State Dairy Association created in 1884.

The first organization for the purpose of negotiating milk prices was made in 1882, when the Milk Exchange League was formed in New York City. Organized under the laws of New York State, it was supposed to represent both producers and consumers; in reality it was a powerful combine of dealers designed to keep prices to producers low. Its activities led to the state's first milk strike, in 1883. The strike lasted eight days and was settled by a price compromise and a promise on the part of the Exchange of better prices to the producers. The ultimate result was higher prices for consumers but not to producers.

With the growth in population and increasing demands for more milk, the producing area was expanded and shipping plants were established in Ulster, Sullivan, Delaware, and Chenango counties. Dealers soon discovered that they could play one section against another and thereby not only keep prices low but forestall the threat of farmer combinations.

Dealers continued to keep prices so low that many dairy men felt justified in adulterating their shipments. They also formed a Milk Producers Union for the purpose of controlling production and securing fair prices. The farmers efforts in these directions were thwarted by means of dealer (exchange) spies and emissaries who kept dealers forewarned. By 1891 the practices of the Milk Exchange League had become so ruinous to both producer and consumer that, following action by the attorney general of the state, the Exchange was dissolved. Within six months the same officers, directors, and stockholders formed the same kind of an organization under the laws of New Jersey. Only the name was changed—it was then the Consolidated Milk Exchange. It rented the same offices and followed the same practices as before.

Meanwhile several large distributing companies were coming into the New York area. Most important were the Borden Condensed Milk Company, second largest milk and dairy products company in the United States, and the Sheffield Farms–Slawson Decker Company, a subsidiary of the National Dairy Products Corporation. The prices paid by these newcomers were virtually identical with those of dealers belonging to the Exchange. In other words, the dealers had a monopoly. To combat the dealers, the producers organized a Five States Union, including producers in New York, New Jersey, Connecticut, Massachusetts, and Pennsylvania. Its objectives were to sell milk directly to the consumer and to take care of surplus milk in its own creameries. It attempted too much and, faced with conditions growing out of the depression of the

1890's, failed in 1898. It was soon succeeded by the Five States Milk Producers Association. Almost constant warfare went on between this organization and the dealers, culminating in a five-day strike in 1902, which collapsed because the producers did not stick together. The association never recovered and went out of existence in 1907.

Though their pioneer efforts had failed, dairy farmers had gained much valuable information and experience. The need for some kind of milkshed-wide association became ever clearer to thousands of farmers as the resistance of the dealers became more solidified and their practices more offensive. To meet this need, the Dairymen's League, Inc., was born in 1907. Sponsored by the Pomona Grange of Orange County, it had at the outset a membership of 691 dairymen. During its first ten years the new organization marked time. It desired to avoid the mistakes of its predecessors of moving too fast and of trying to accomplish too much too quickly. By 1916 it had a membership of sixteen thousand. Milk prices at the time were unjustifiably low, and in June of that year the league asked for a minimum price effective October 1. The dealers refused, and an eleven-day strike ensued which resulted in a victory for the league. Dairymen now flocked to the organization by the thousands. In January 1919 another milk strike occurred. This lasted eighteen days and resulted in a second victory for the league. Its membership by this time had soared to ninety thousand.

During the interval between these two major strikes, the mayor of New York City appointed a commission to investigate the milk situation. Shortly after it issued its report, which was very critical of the league, the officers of the league were indicted by a New York County grand jury on the charge of conspiracy in trying to raise the price of milk in New York City. Immediate pressure on the legislature by the dairy farmers of the state associated with the league resulted in statutory changes making it lawful for farmers to co-operate in a marketing organization to secure better prices for their products. On May 21, 1921, the Dairymen's League was superseded by the Dairymen's League Cooperative Association, Inc. Its predecessor had been a price-negotiating agency; the new league was a full-fledged selling agency.

The decade of the 1920's was not an encouraging one for the farmers of the state. It was a period of almost constant warfare between the new league and the New York City milk dealers. With the downward swing of the business cycle and the coming of the Depression milk prices tumbled. The Class I price dropped from $2.90 to $1.79 per hundred pounds. By 1933 producers were averaging less than one dollar. In August of that year a general strike ensued, as producers blockaded highways, dumped milk, and threatened to blow up milk plants and to derail milk trains. In the "Battle of Boonville" north of Utica, forty state troopers with tear gas and riot sticks dispersed a crowd of about three hundred striking dairymen and bystanders, injuring seventeen.

It was obvious that the existing situation in the milk industry could not be permitted to continue and that government control was necessary. As a first step in this direction the state legislature a year before the strike of 1933 had appointed a committee headed by Senator Perley Pitcher of Watertown to inquire into the causes of the spread in prices between producers and consumers of milk. The committee, after holding hearings in many parts of the state, recommended the establishment of a state Milk Control Board with authority to investigate the production and distribution of milk in all its phases, to license milk dealers, and, as an emergency measure, to fix the price to be paid farmers for milk for a year. The big distributors opposed the proposal openly and strenuously. The dairy farmers fought for it. One of their spokesmen said:

We are now in desperate straights. Our taxes and interest on the mortgages are due. Our feed bills are unpaid. Our credit is exhausted. We have no money to buy seed or other essential supplies and the Spring season's near. Every can of milk we sell leaves us further in debt than we were before we produced it. This robbery must stop soon or reform will be too late to help us.

Debate on the Pitcher bill was stormy. As finally passed, it provided for minimum prices to producers on a classified basis and also set wholesale and retail prices in the market. It also made provision for a Milk Control Board. Many dairymen felt that the producers had been tricked, and a hearing before the board almost immediately after its organization proved to be one of the most stormy farm meetings on record at Albany.

Almost from its inception the Pitcher Law was doomed to failure. In the first place the law was challenged by the dealers on the ground that the legislature of New York could not regulate interstate commerce, and in the famous Seelig case the court explicitly stated that the New York Milk Control Board had no control over prices paid to producers for milk moving in interstate commerce. Under this ruling New York metropolitan dealers were quick to desert plants in New York State and establish additional facilities in other milkshed states, as, for example, Vermont and Pennsylvania. (To guard against outside competition, the dairy interests of the state had repeatedly resisted the attempts of the milk producers of the north central states to widen the boundaries of the New York metropolitan "milkshed," which is largely confined to the state.) Some rerouted New York–produced milk so that it became interstate milk. Secondly, the law lacked provision for the producers to share markets and proceeds.

The Pitcher Law was superseded in 1937 by the Rogers-Allen Law.

Its chief feature was the provision that all bona fide co-operatives regardless of size or type be legally permitted to function together in establishing and enforcing prices and marketing programs. Meanwhile, the Federal Trade Commission, after a study of the New York Metropolitan milk situation, submitted a report in 1936 indicating that monopoly conditions virtually prevailed on the distributive side. A year later the Metropolitan Cooperative Milk Producers Bargaining Agency was established. Charges were now made by many dairy farmers and others that the league had now become a subsidiary of Bordens. On September 1, 1938, after approval of the dairy farmers of the New York City metropolitan milkshed representing seven states, a new federal-state milk-marketing program went into effect. Under it farmers were promised a fair and stable price for milk, unfair competition among dealers was to be prevented, and consumers were assured an adequate supply of milk at a reasonable cost. Though challenged on the ground of constitutionality, the state-federal marketing agreement administered by a market administrator was upheld by the United States Supreme Court. Although the dairy farmers of the state continued to have their ups and downs occasioned by weather conditions, inflation, and fluctuations of the business cycle, their economic status during the last fifteen years was vastly better than during the period of the 1920's and 1930's.

Although agrarian discontent emerged at times in the state, especially during the last three decades of the nineteenth century, it was never as widespread or as deep-seated as it was in the South and Middle West and other parts of the nation. Even so, there was general rural agreement that the farmers' ills, like those of the dairymen, stemmed primarily from monopolistic avarice.

If, in the course of the last hundred years, the technical side of New York State agriculture has undergone revolutionary change, so also has New York rural life. Those of Jared van Wagenen's generation or those who have read his highly informative and delightfully written volume, *The Golden Age of Homespun,* can fully appreciate this change.

During the decades following the Civil War and, indeed, up to the close of World War I, farm life in New York was very different from what it is today. As already observed, the hours of work were from before daylight to dark. Farmhouses were heated only by stoves and an occasional fireplace. Only the more affluent could afford coal for fuel. The wood fires, not replenished at night, might mean frigid homes until the fires were rekindled in the morning. Bathrooms were a rarity in most farm homes, and bathing facilities were limited to the wash basin or wash tub. Outside toilets prevailed. Water for house and barns, unless the farm was so situated that it might be piped by gravity from a mountain or hillside spring, was pumped from wells—by hand unless the farmer could afford a windmill. Kerosene lamps and lanterns, which required frequent filling and wick-trimming, afforded the only artificial light. The one-room country school, which for many farmers' children was at a considerable distance from their homes, furnished the beginnings of educational opportunity. Aside from the local weekly newspaper and a copy of the Bible, *Pilgrim's Progress* and one or two other books, there was no reading matter in most farmers' homes. These were the horse and buggy days, and not many farm families journeyed far from home. Roads were poor—clouds of dust in summer, sloughs of mud in the spring, and snow-blocked in the winter.

Not all of course was on the dark side. In summer there was the "old swimming hole," picnics, the circus, and the county fair. Many of the farm families went to church, where they saw friends and neighbors and gossiped, as well as listened to the sermon. In fall and winter, when there was less rush, neighbors gathered for a game of dominoes, "authors," or cards. And despite all the hard work there was time, energy, and enthusiasm for the country dance, the corn-huskings, the school entertainments, and the skating and sleighing parties where friendship ripened into courtship and ultimately into marriage for youth and where many members of the older generation relived their younger days.

Then came the age of electricity and the motor. Not only has the farmhouse undergone transformation, but every aspect of rural life has changed as well. Electricity is now available to practically all farms of the state and up-to-date facilities and appliances are rapidly being installed. Every farm home will soon have a telephone, a radio, and a television set. This, with the automobile and good roads, means that rural isolation is a thing of the past. Rural life in New York State has not only become mechanized and specialized but urbanized.

A Century of

Industrial Enterprise

*Our capacity to go beyond the machine rests upon our power
to assimilate the machine. Until we have absorbed the lessons
of objectivity, impersonality, neutrality, the lessons of the
mechanical realm, we cannot go further in our development
toward the more richly organic, the more profoundly human.*—LEWIS MUMFORD

FOR more than a century, New York has been the most important industrial and commercial state in the nation. Its manufacturing industries
outrank those of every other state in number of establishments, volume
of employment, size of manufacturing payrolls, and value added to raw
material by manufacture.

Although in 1952 New York was the leading manufacturing state—
employing 1,942,000, or 300,000 more than Pennsylvania, the second-
ranking state—its economy is less dependent upon manufacturing than
that of any of the other leading industrial states. In 1950 there were
117 manufacturing wage earners in New York State for every one thousand population as compared with 95 per thousand in the United States
as a whole and 182 per thousand in Connecticut, the most highly industrialized state in the nation. In 1953 the state's manufacturing firms
added $14,410,234,000 in value to the raw and semifinished material they
purchased for processing, compared with $3,313,649,000 in 1939.

There are many factors which over the years have been responsible
for New York's industrialism: (1) proximity to raw materials, (2) proximity to the world's most important industrial and consumer market,
(3) availability of labor supply, (4) "Yankee" ingenuity and organiza-
tional ability, (5) abundance of capital, (6) comparatively low transportation costs, (7) abundant water power, (8) geographical location of the

state with its great port of New York, and (9) the stimulation of war. The Civil War marked a great turning point in the history of American industry, and although, contrary to popular belief, it did not cause what is popularly known as the American Industrial Revolution, it did speed up a process that had been evolving at a relatively slow rate during the antebellum period. Before the Civil War almost all of the features of a modern industrial nation existed in isolated and embryonic form within the United States. The war stimulated northern industry through its demands for war materials and, more fundamentally, it transformed the American productive processes. As a result of the war, merchant capitalism gave way to industrial capitalism. Henceforth, manufactures in New York, as elsewhere in the nation, moved steadily in the direction of big-scale establishments, having many of the features of present-day enterprise: mechanization, mass production, concentration of capital, corporate enterprise, divorce of ownership from control, and ultimately the increasing combination of finance capitalism. Similarly, both world wars of the twentieth century were stimulating and powerful agencies in affecting changes in methods and processes, if not in control.

From the Civil War to the present New York's pattern of manufacturing activity has differed markedly from that of the rest of the nation. Nondurable goods, for example, have always been in the lead. In 1950 the nondurable-goods industries employed 64 per cent of all the state's manufacturing workers, compared with 48 per cent in the rest of the nation. The most striking divergence is found in the proportion devoted to clothing manufacture. Apparel trades account for 21 per cent of all manufacturing employees in New York State in contrast with only 6 per cent for the rest of the nation. About a third of the clothing workers of the country are employed in the needle-trade shops of the state. Another peculiar character of New York industry is that in most of the state apparel manufacture is organized on a small scale and not on a corporate basis. The New York industry is not dependent upon finance capital and is free from banker control. This is the more interesting when we remember that the apparel industry is primarily concentrated on Manhattan Island in the shadow of the banking and financial capital of America.

New York has long been famous for its variety and diversity of manufactures. Consequently the state enjoys a degree of economic stability notably lacking in those states which are largely dependent upon one or two industries, and particularly on the heavy industries. On the other hand, emphasis on nondurables subjects the state and especially New York City to seasonal variations. Despite the fact that the manufacture of nondurable goods has long overshadowed durable goods, the latter is making steady headway, as Table 13 indicates:

Table 13. Ten leading manufactures in New York State in order of importance of value.

1860	1880	1930	1950
Flour and meal	Men's clothing	Women's clothing	Apparel
Men's clothing	Women's clothing	Printed and pub-	Printed and pub-
Refined sugar	Flour	lished materials	lished materials
Leather	Foundry and	Men's clothing	Food
Liquors	machine-shop	Foundry and	Machinery
Lumber	products	machine-shop	Chemicals
Printed materials	Textiles	products	Fabricated metals
Boots and shoes	Printed and pub-	Bread and other	Electrical machin-
Machinery	lished materials	bakery prod-	ery
Oil	Boots and shoes	ucts	Textiles
	Tobacco products	Electrical machin-	Instruments
	Primary metals	ery	Transportation
	(iron and steel)	Meat products	equipment
	Lumber products	Motor vehicles	
		Fur goods	
		Boots and shoes	

During the decade of the 1940's the trend toward the manufacture of durables was very pronounced. Between 1940 and 1951 the proportion of the production workers in the state employed in the durable industries rose from 28 to 40 per cent. The demand for durables following World War II and requirements for military equipment during the early 1950's account in large measure for this increase. Moreover, it should be noted that the industries with the greatest increase in the state's production workers are producers of heavy goods—the metals, machinery, transportation equipment, and precision instruments. The largest relative decline in recent years in any of the state's manufacturing industries occurred in the leather, textile, and apparel groups. Pulp and paper production in the state are declining but at a lesser rate.

Heading the list of the state's manufactures as measured by value of product in 1860 was flour milling. With a product valued at over $34,-000,000, the state led all other states in the Union. It retained this leadership until 1890, when it yielded first place to Minnesota. By 1920 Kansas had also outstripped New York, but subsequently yielded second place to the Empire State. Even so, the flour-milling industry in comparison with the state's other industries failed to retain its importance. By 1880 it had slipped to third place within the state, and by 1900 to twelfth place.

Though New York City was itself an important milling center during the pre–Civil War era, the state's leader in the flour-milling business was Rochester, long known as the "Flour City." After 1870 Albany and Buffalo were not only milling but marketing centers. By 1900 the flour-milling business was rapidly shifting to the Northwest, with Minneapolis virtually succeeding Rochester as the flour-milling capital of the United States. With this shift also came greater economic concentration of the industry. Three concerns—C. A. Pillsbury and Company, Washburn-Crosby Company, and the Northwest Consolidated Milling Company—were among the leaders in this movement. By 1921 five firms operating forty-nine mills produced approximately one-fourth of the national output.

Because of its strategic position for receiving Canadian wheat and cheap water transportation on the Great Lakes, Buffalo has in the last half century become one of the leading flour-milling cities of the western world. For this phenomenal growth, Buffalo is indebted to the Minneapolis millers, who, realizing Buffalo's advantages, shifted part of their business to New York's second most populous city. For many years the greater part of the Buffalo flour output has been from mills owned and operated by Minneapolis millers.

Of all of New York State's industries, none, perhaps, has been of more continuing importance from Civil War days to the present than the manufacture of apparel—men's and women's clothing, furs, millinery, footgear, and fashion accessories. Since 1860 the men's clothing industry has been one of the leading industries of the state. Even before the Civil War, New York City merchants had begun to produce ready-made clothing.

The invention of the sewing machine in 1846 was revolutionary in its effect, coming as it did at a time when there was great demand for cheap, ready-made clothing, or "hand-me-downs," as they were then called, for sailors, especially in the ports of New England, for Negro slaves on Southern plantations, and adventurers prospecting for gold in California and other parts of the West. The sewing machine demanded a speed-up in other processes, especially cutting. Hence it is not surprising that the old-fashioned shears were soon replaced by the short knife. During the 1880's the sword knife and the circular disc made it possible to cut greater thicknesses of cloth. Production was further speeded and labor lightened with the introduction of power-driven equipment such as the band saw and reciprocating electric knife. Ultimately cutting machines were developed which could slice through forty or fifty piles of woolen cloth at one time. Technological improvements were also made in pressing apparatus. The Civil War brought large orders for uniforms, helping to transform the industry from homework to mass production in factories. With the extension of the western frontier and the rapid growth of cities came vast new markets for ready-made clothes. In 1860 about 80 per cent of men's clothing was still made to measure by custom tailors. By 1880 the proportion had shrunk to 50 per cent. The development of half sizes and odd sizes in 1900 practically eliminated the necessity for made-to-measure suits for the hard-to-fit.

With the ever-increasing flow of immigrants into New York the apparel industry has been blessed with an abundance of labor. In the early period the English, Irish, and Germans predominated. By the 1880's the Germans had crowded out the English and Irish and were in complete control of the technical processes of the industry with the exception of the cutting, which was still monopolized by the Irish. Then came the Jews and Italians, who have since been the backbone of the industry. In the mid-twentieth century Puerto Ricans have added to the labor reservoir.

By 1900 the state was producing no less than 45.7 per cent of the men's clothing in the United States. New York City produced 37 per cent, and Rochester, ranking sixth among the clothing manufacturing centers of the nation, produced about 4 per cent. By the mid-twentieth century the proportions were not markedly different from what they were fifty years earlier—42 per cent of the nation's total for the state and 37 and 6 per cent for New York City and Rochester, respectively.

Though it developed later, the history of the women's apparel industry is, in many respects, very similar to that of men's clothing. By 1900 the state produced two-thirds of the women's clothing manufactured in the United States. New York City made 96 per cent of the product of the state and 64 per cent of the entire country. In terms of the number of workers engaged and value of product, this segment of the apparel industry has surpassed all others.

New York State has long been important as a producer of millinery and since 1930 has been responsible for more than half of the total value of the product in the United States. The manufacture of fur goods in the state goes back to an early date. Since the mid-1920's, however, the industry has declined.

A rapidly growing segment of the apparel industry is what is familiarly known as fashion accessories, manufactured from leather and other materials. Here again New York leads all other states. Today approximately thirty-five thousand workers in the state are engaged in manufacturing handbags, dress gloves, luggage, apparel belts, wallets, watch straps, and related personal leather and fabric goods. These workers constitute more than one-half of the total employed in such manufacture in the nation.

There are a number of reasons why the women's accessories industry should be concentrated in New York State, and largely in New York City:

1. The metropolitan area affords an unparalleled retail market.

2. New York City has long been the established fashion center of America. No other place in America—not even Hollywood—has an at-

mosphere as favorable to fashion creation as the great metropolis. Besides providing designers with a social group interested in new styles, New York City offers these designers the world's largest and most easily accessible array of art relating specifically to costume design: the distinguished fashion library of Cooper Union; the magnificent textile and costume collections of the Brooklyn Museum, the Museum of Costume Art, with over seven thousand items of dress representing three centuries of fashion, which recently became a part of the Metropolitan Museum of Art; and, of course, the incomparable collections of the famous Metropolitan Museum itself.

3. Workers skilled in leather working and related techniques, such as cutting, sewing, and binding, are nowhere more plentiful than in New York City, to which has come a long stream of artisans.

4. Large quantities of imported hides and skins, necessary to this segment of the apparel industry, enter the port of New York. The tanning industry which converts raw hides to finished leather for accessories is located in the Northeast, in and around New York. Tanners settled in this region because of the raw material imports and a ready supply of hemlock, chestnut, and oak bark, and, later, of foreign tanning chemicals, the calf-skin supplies from the expanding dairy regions, the existence of skilled labor necessary to tanning, and the excellent water resources.

5. New York City is the wholesale center for the apparel and leather accessories industries. Buyers from all parts of the nation make certain not to miss New York City showings famed for completeness in all ready-to-wear lines. Large stores throughout the country maintain New York City buying offices, while more distant stores are represented by resident buying agents.

These factors have resulted in the location of 90 per cent of the state's handbag and personal leather goods establishments within New York City. These concerns manufacture more than four-fifths of the state's production of such items. No less than 95 per cent of the state's luggage manufacturers, producing six-sevenths of the state's output, are located in New York City. Virtually all of the apparel belts and miscellaneous leather articles are made in New York City.

The dress glove industry, one of the oldest in the nation, was founded in Fulton County two hundred years ago by the British agent Sir William Johnson, who brought from Scotland a community of expert tanners and glovemakers. These veteran crafts-people—men and women—passed on their skills from generation to generation. To this day the production of fine leather gloves continues, mainly in the cities of Gloversville and Johnstown in Fulton County. This county is also an important source of knit gloves and, to a lesser extent, fabric gloves. New York City firms manufacture almost one-tenth of the leather dress gloves of the state and a substantially larger portion of the knit and fabric dress-glove output.

The firms engaged in the manufacture of fashion accessories are generally small in size and highly specialized and competitive. Of the 1,767 establishments in the state in 1947, 72 per cent had fewer than twenty employees. Another 24 per cent had from twenty to ninety-nine employees and only 4 per cent had as many as one hundred employees. Another source of competition in the leather accessories business are products made of plastics and fabrics.

Another New York State industry closely related to the apparel industry, and in a sense a part of it, is the manufacture of boots and shoes. This was a handicraft industry until after the Civil War, when it moved to factories and became mechanized. Although the state ranked second to Massachusetts in the nation it was, during the closing decades of the nineteenth century, a poor second. In 1890, for example, the state's production was only one-fifth that of Massachusetts. By 1914, however, New York's output was mounting rapidly, though the leadership of Massachusetts was not seriously threatened. In 1914 New York City and Rochester were the chief centers of the industry within the state. They ranked fourth and seventh, respectively, in the United States.

Leather raw materials for the industry come from both home and abroad. Cattle, sheep, hogs, and goats are the source for most hides. Imported hides supplement the domestic supply. Footwear ordinarily takes four-fifths of the total leather supply and furnishes the principal demand for leathers made from the hides of cattle, calves, and goats. Little finished leather is imported into the United States. Almost 10 per cent of goat hides domestically tanned are imported. These come principally from India. Sheep and lamb hide imports comprise about one-half our domestic needs. They come chiefly from Australia and New Zealand. Foreign hides make up about 15 to 20 per cent of cattle hides used for the manufacture of leather. These come principally from South America—Argentina and Brazil especially furnishing large quantities. Because the hide of domestic hogs does not make good leather, pigskin used for leather is nearly all imported, mostly from Mexico and South America. Quality horsehides are imported from France, Argentina, Canada, the United Kingdom, Belgium, and the Netherlands. Reptile skins are imported from Mexico, India, and South America, and alligator skins from Cuba, Mexico, and Central America.

In the manufacture of textiles—knit goods, carpets, and silks—the state also had an early start and soon gained prominence. Particularly was this true of carpets. In 1841 E. S. Higgins and Company opened a carpet-manufacturing establishment in New York City, but by 1900 their largest plants were located outside the state. Approximately thirty years later (1872) Alexander Smith and Sons opened their famous carpet plant in Yonkers. Until its removal in the 1950's this was the largest such establishment in the metropolitan area. Montgomery County boasts two large carpet firms.

Silk manufacture in the state gained foothold shortly after the Civil War, and for many years New York virtually monopolized the industry. By 1900, however, many operators motivated by the desire to find cheaper land, power, and labor were already locating elsewhere, many in New Jersey and Pennsylvania. As a consequence New York slipped from first to third place among the states as a producer of manufactured silk.

Twentieth-century surveys of New York's manufacturing enterprise indicate not only its magnitude but its diversity. Out of a possible 453 different types of manufacturing listed by the federal Bureau of the Census no less than 430 are carried on today in New York State. Out of this large number, 273 industries each employ at least one thousand persons. Some industries are represented in many parts of the state, while others are concentrated in limited areas, as the following discussion of the eleven industrial areas of the state will show. Variations in natural resources, geographical features, nonmanufacturing activities of the population, and other factors assist in explaining the industrial make-up of each region.

While manufacturing in the New York metropolitan area is preponderately devoted to nondurables, in the upstate area, with its somewhat greater emphasis on the production of durable goods, the industrial pattern is more similar to the over-all national output. New York City and upstate manufactures contrast in another way. Upstate firms more often have mass-production factories with many hundreds of workers, while those in New York City generally have smaller plants with fewer employees and turn out less standardized products.

Let us now look briefly at the character of manufactures in the economic areas of the state:

I. *Niagara Frontier:* Counties—Erie and Niagara

This is one of the great industrial areas of the state. In 1950 its manufacturing workers exceeded in number those of any other upstate region. No other area of the state, except New York City, has a more advantageous location. Situated at the eastern terminus of the Great Lakes shipping lanes and at the western end of the low-level water route from the East this area has long been a stopping-off place for immigrants, travelers, and cargoes of raw and finished goods. The completion of the Erie Canal in 1825 enhanced its commercial and industrial growth. In 1826 a foundry was built in Buffalo to make plow irons and castings; by 1832 there were forty factories of various kinds in the city.

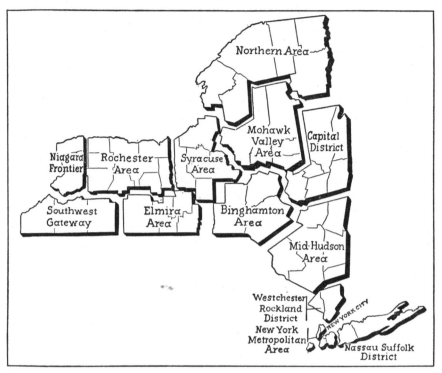

Map 12. Economic areas of New York State.

In the 1950's more than 35 per cent of the labor force of the region is engaged in manufacturing. Two out of every three are employed in durable-goods plants: primary metals, transportation equipment, and rubber products. It ranks first among the upstate areas in these industries: chemicals, food, electrical machinery, fabricated metals, printing, stone, clay and glass products, and petroleum, and coal products.

No less than one-half of all workers in the state engaged in the production of primary metals are to be found in this area. Buffalo has long been one of the nation's notable iron and steel centers. It has the necessary iron ore coming via the Great Lakes, coal from nearby Pennsylvania, the mighty power resources of the Niagara River, and excellent railway facilities.

Second-ranking in the area is transportation equipment. Approximately 15 per cent of the area's manufacturing workers are employed in this industry, which was established at the beginning of the twentieth century as a primary eastern assembly and distribution center for automobiles. Today this industry also produces automobile parts, buses, airplanes, and railroad equipment.

The chemical industry employs almost one-tenth of all manufacturing workers in the area. Employment in this industry is about evenly distributed between the two counties comprising the area. Low-cost power and ample water resources are important considerations in attracting and retaining this particular industry, whose range of products is wide.

The manufacture of foods and of electrical machinery each engages about 8 per cent of the factory workers of the area, and both are situated mainly in Buffalo. Printing specialities include business forms as well as sales and account books. The paper firms in this area manufacture boxes, cartons, and other paper products.

Military goods production in this area during World War II amounted to over $5,000,000,000. The building of new plant capacity worth upwards of $200,000,000 were initiated between the close of World War II and 1953. Over half of this was for the expansion of iron and steel capacity, chiefly at Lackawanna but also at Buffalo, Lockport, and Niagara Falls.

II. *Rochester Area:* Counties—Genesee, Livingston, Monroe, Ontario, Orleans, Seneca, Wayne, Wyoming, Yates

At first Rochester was principally a marketplace and shipping point for wheat and other farm products of the fertile Genesee River Valley and the shores of Lake Ontario. Its real start as an industrial center came when, in the 1850's, the foundations were laid for what was to become the world-famous Bausch and Lomb Company, manufacturer of optical goods, organized in 1880. Before the end of the nineteenth century the city of Rochester was one of the most thriving industrial centers in the state. The leading industries in the 1950's of the Rochester area are precision instruments, apparel, machinery, food, and electrical equipment. Approximately 125,000 workers, or 36 per cent of the labor force, were employed in the area's manufacturing activities in 1950. Three out of every five manufacturing workers are employed in durable-goods plants.

With the exception of one important optical-instrument plant, virtually all the state's firms which produce photographic, optical, and scientific instruments are located in Rochester. More than half of all the workers in these fields in the state are employed in this area. Firms in this group employ 30 per cent of the area's manufacturing workers. In addition, some 7,600 persons are employed in auxiliary establishments, offices, and laboratories.

Eastman Kodak, which produces photographic equipment and supplies, leads the world in the manufacture of cameras and camera equipment. Its origin dates back to 1878, when George Eastman, a young bank clerk in Rochester, became interested in photography as an amateur. At this time photographers used the "wet plate" process, which involved a bulky view camera, heavy tripod, glass plates, dark tent, nitrate bath, and water carrier. "Dry" plates, however, had just been introduced, and Eastman became interested in their manufacture and sale. By 1880 he had succeeded in making dry plates of high quality which sold readily. His first factory was a small room over a downtown store. In 1881 he induced Henry A. Strong to become a partner in the business. An entire floor of another building was fitted up as a factory, and there, under the name of Eastman Dry Plate Company, the business flourished. In 1882 a new and larger factory was built on the site of the present office building of the company on State Street. Meanwhile, Eastman had perfected a machine for coating glass plates, but he soon discovered that the coating deteriorated. Moreover, the glass was heavy and cumbersome. His next step was to find a material which was light, flexible, and unbreakable and which would hold an emulsion of bromide of silver and gelatin. Eastman's first attempt was a coated roll film to which the sensitized emulsion was applied. A device called a roll holder was developed. This solved the mechanical end of the problem, but the paper film had its drawbacks. In 1889 the discovery of a nitro-cellulose film base came about almost entirely by accident, after four hundred experiments had been made. Meanwhile the company was reorganized as the Eastman Dry Plate and Film Company. By 1888 Eastman had evolved his great invention, the Kodak camera. It was a simple box camera combining the role-film idea and the plate camera in a compact, portable, and easily manipulated form. It included an instantaneous shutter which could be wound up for a number of exposures by simply pulling a string. It took round pictures two and one-half inches in diameter and was loaded for one hundred exposures. When the roll was exposed, the Kodak—the name was coined by Eastman as a trade-mark—and the roll holder were returned to the factory for unloading, reloading, and developing. The first Kodak was priced at twenty-five dollars. In 1889 the name of the company was changed to Eastman Company, and in 1892 it became the Eastman Kodak Company. The company continued to make improvements: daylight loading was patented in 1891; production of the pocket Kodak began in 1895; and by the following year a new and cheap camera priced as low as five dollars was developed. This was a long stride toward Eastman's goal of reaching the man on the street. In 1923 the first amateur motion-picture camera, the Ciné-Kodak, was put on the market. With the development of the moving picture and the coming of Kodacolor, the business increased enormously. In the late 1920's the Eastman

Teaching Films, Inc., was established to produce an extensive program of classroom motion pictures; the material was directed to many educational groups—from primary to medical schools.

The Kodak Research Laboratories established in 1912 are among the most famous in the world. Here every conceivable kind of investigation relating to photography is carried on. In addition to its special department devoted to photography itself, it covers the whole field of chemistry and physics as applied to photography. In both World War I and II the Eastman laboratories were of inestimable value to the federal government. Research results unless confidential were almost always published in leading scientific journals of the day. A library containing the most complete collection of photographic literature in the world is maintained by the laboratories with a trained librarian in charge. The Kodak Research Laboratories have become the great center and clearinghouse for scientific problems connected with all phases of the photographic industry.

From the company's inception, Eastman was interested in improving the working conditions of his employees. In 1911 an employee benefit fund of $500,000 was created. In 1912 the first wage-dividend—a bonus of 2 per cent on wages received during the previous five years—was declared. Safety appliances, a medical department, shorter hours, and social as well as lunch-room facilities were introduced as Eastman sought to decrease turnover, discourage strikes, and head off minimum-wage legislation. The sale of Eastman stock at par to older employees climaxed his efforts to cement the relationships of company and employees, who by 1920 exceeded fifteen hundred.

The company was enormously prosperous, and George Eastman became one of America's wealthiest men. His greatest joy in life, however, was giving his money to good causes—not some of it but all of it. During the first quarter of the twentieth century he was one of America's five leading philanthropists. His total benefactions were approximately $100,-000,000.

Other firms in the Rochester area specialize in measuring, scientific, and engineering instruments. They produce a great variety of devices which record and control temperature, pressure, humidity, flow liquid level, and sensitive industrial processes. The group also includes those firms which produce medical, surgical, and dental equipment.

The second-ranking industry in the Rochester area is the manufacture of apparel. Aside from New York City, it is the leading apparel center in the state. The manufacture of apparel, like that of instruments, antedates the Civil War. About 1840 a small shop operated by a Rochester couple made and sold boy's trousers; in the 1950's the area is the home of some of the top producers of men's clothing. With only nineteen men's apparel manufacturers—1 per cent of the national total—the Rochester area accounted for over 6 per cent of the nation's suit output in 1947. The bulk of the output is centered in Rochester, although facilities have been set up outside the city to tap the supply of skilled needleworkers in surrounding communities.

The making of machinery (other than electrical) furnishes employment for about 10 per cent of the area's manufacturing workers. Rochester itself is noted for the production of gear-cutting machinery, food-processing equipment, pumps, carburetors, and check-protecting devices. In Batavia the Massey-Harris Company produces combines, corn pickers, mowers, manure spreaders, and other farm implements. In Seneca Falls one of the nation's largest pump plants makes pumps not only for moving water but for use in processing such products as wood pulp, molten lead, bread dough, and printer's ink.

Linked closely with the abundant crops of the fertile farmlands of the Genesee Valley, the Finger Lakes region, and the farms along Lake Ontario is the thriving food-products industry. While most of the food establishments are in Rochester, some are located in Medina, Newark, Geneva, Canandaigua, Batavia, and Penn Yan. The food-products industry includes wine manufacture, canning of fruits and vegetables, milling of cereals, and production of candy, baby foods, flavorings, and spices.

Other large industries in the Rochester area are those which produce electrical machinery, printed matter, and fabricated metals. Also important is the production of porcelain goods, pianos, chemicals, paper products, textiles, leather goods, and automotive equipment.

III. *The Capital District:* Counties—Albany, Rensselaer, Saratoga, Schenectady, Schoharie, Warren, and Washington

For many decades this area devoted its energies primarily to agriculture and trade. During the nineteenth century, however, and especially after the opening of the state's canal system, it increasingly turned to varied types of industrial enterprise. After the 1880's, when the Industrial Revolution gained momentum, many of these early ventures expanded rapidly and others were added. By 1950 the area employed almost 100,000 persons, or about 30 per cent of the area's labor population, in its manufacturing plants. Slightly more than half of the manufacturing workers are in plants turning out durable goods. The leading industries of the area are electrical machinery, foundry and machine-shop products, apparel, transportation equipment, and paper.

The largest employer in the area is the General Electric Company at Schenectady. The early history of this company, one of the three largest manufacturers of electrical apparatus in America, is like that of many other present-day New York manufacturing enterprises and admirably illustrates the rapid trend toward expansion and consolidation of business enterprise in America during the half century after 1870. Following the establishment of the Edison Electric Company in 1878, the electric industry expanded rapidly. In 1880 the Edison Lamp Company, a subsidiary of the Edison Electric Light Company, was formed and in 1882 located at Harrison, New Jersey. Other Edison subsidiaries came into being about the same time. Bergmann and Company in New York City, headed by a former Edison employee, began the manufacture of light sockets, switches, and other such items in 1880. Later in the same year the Edison Machine Works began operations in New York City. Cramped for space, it transferred its plant to Schenectady in 1886. In 1881 the Electric Tube Company began functioning as a part of the expanding Edison enterprise. For the direct installation of equipment on customers' premises, the Edison Company for Isolated Lighting was formed in 1882. Rounding out the list of subsidiaries was the Canadian Edison Manufacturing Company. In 1889 all the Edison lighting companies, with the exception of those operating central stations, consolidated into the Edison General Electric Company.

Meanwhile, dozens of competing concerns had sprung up in many parts of the nation. Among the more important of these were United States Electric Lighting Company (organized in 1878), the Consolidated Electric Light Company (organized in 1882), the Brush Electric Company (founded in 1880), the United Switch and Signal Company (organized in 1882 by George Westinghouse and becoming the Westinghouse Electric Company in 1886 and the Westinghouse Electric and Manufacturing Company in 1889), the Thomson-Houston Company (organized in 1883), and the Swan Lamp Manufacturing Company (organized in 1885). Alleged infringement of patents by the Edison interests led to an expensive warfare during the 1880's and 1890's. The net effects of this warfare was to reduce the number of manufactures of electric equipment, especially lamps, and to hasten the process of consolidation. In 1890, for example, the Edison General Electric Company absorbed the Sprague Electric Railway and Motor Company. The Thomson-Houston Company of Lynn, Massachusetts, absorbed the Brush Electric Company in 1889, and the Schuyler Electric Company in 1890. But the biggest consolidation of all occurred in 1892 when under the guiding hand of J. P. Morgan and Company, the Edison General Electric Company and the Thomson-Houston Company were merged to form the General Electric Company. Its board of eleven directors included three Boston financiers and five New York bankers, J. P. Morgan being one of them.

A number of distinguished citizens of the state have contributed to the scientific growth and business stature of this ever-expanding industrial giant. Among these were the scientists Charles P. Steinmetz, German-born immigrant who landed in New York in 1889, Willis R. Whitney, and Irving Langmuir, whose research in the laboratories of the Schenectady plant of the company won world renown. Their scientific contribution was matched on the executive side by the outstanding leadership of Gerard Swope, Owen D. Young, Philip Reed, and C. E. Wilson.

In addition to the great plant at Schenectady covering approximately six hundred acres (which alone employs about forty thousand persons, including scientists and technicians engaged in the tremendous laboratories established there for studies in engineering physics, chemistry, metallurgy, and atomic power), the company also has auxiliary plants at Waterford and Fort Edward. The bulk of the machinery, other than electrical, produced in the area consists of steam turbines produced by General Electric. Lesser machinery firms employ about 12 per cent of the area's total manufacturing workers.

Eleven of every one hundred manufacturing employees in the area are apparel workers. The invention of the detachable collar by a Troy housewife in the early part of the nineteenth century gave the men's collar, cuff, and shirt industry its start. Today Cluett, Peabody Company and Ide's, not to mention lesser manufacturers, make Troy and its environs an important center for the manufacture of men's shirts, pajamas, underwear, and suits and women's blouses and undergarments.

A Schenectady firm, the American Locomotive Company, forms the backbone of the area's transportation-equipment industry. This industry, founded at Schenectady in 1848 and known throughout the world for its manufacture of steam locomotives, today produces Diesel electric locomotives and automotive parts.

Forest and water resources of this district, notably in Saratoga, Warren, and Washington counties, have made it one of the state's important woodpulp and paper producers. The chemical industry produces pharmaceuticals and dyes. The stone and clay group make cement, bricks, slate and abrasives. The primary metals industry, especially in Troy and Albany, produce stainless steel and bells that top churches, schools, city halls, and office buildings. The federal arsenal at Watervliet, with five thousand employees, produces guns, cannon, and other military equipment. And at West Milton in Saratoga County, on a four-thousand-acre site owned by the Atomic Energy Commission, an atomic power plant for submarines has been constructed.

Textile firms are widely distributed in the district. Their principal products include papermakers' felts, woven cotton and rayon underwear products, knitted gloves, and knitted cotton and wool hose. Cotton-spinning centers, such as Victory Mills and Cohoes, have declined under the pressure of regional competition. The former cotton-mill plant at Victory Mills now manufactures paperboard cartons.

In this district as in other economic areas of the state the needs for national defense have stimulated industrial expansion. Following the termination of World War II, $6,000,000 was expended at Watervliet for additional steel ingot and stainless steel production capacity, $1,000,000 at Rotterdam for radio equipment, $4,000,000 at Mechanicville for papermaking, and $5,000,000 at Waterford to enlarge a silicone plant.

IV. *The Elmira Area:* Counties—Chemung, Schuyler, Steuben, Tioga, and Tompkins

For many years this region was primarily agricultural. Hornell and Elmira, both situated on the Chemung River, utilized their waterway locations for trading, sawmills, and gristmills. Their products were floated down the Chemung and its tributaries and then by way of the Susquehanna to Baltimore. Lack of adequate transportation facilities handicapped the region as far as New York markets were concerned. Not until 1832 did a canal open the northerly markets to the Elmira area. In 1849 the Erie Railroad opened the area to the markets of New York City; with wider outlets for their products, local plants were able to expand. During the century following 1850 the industrial growth of the Elmira area, while not phenomenal, indicated future promise.

Manufacturing employees at the mid-twentieth century totaled over 30,000, composing 28 per cent of the labor force of the area, a proportion somewhat less than for the upstate region as a whole. At the close of the Korean War three out of every four workers employed in manufacturing were in durable-goods plants—a higher concentration than that prevailing in any other area of the state.

The Elmira area's leading industry is the production of nonelectrical machinery, which employs about 34 per cent of its manufacturing workers. More than one-third of these are employed in Chemung County, another one-third in Tompkins, and one-quarter in Steuben. There is considerable diversification of product. The city of Elmira manufactures typewriters, adding machines, machine tools, milling machines, carburetors, and valves for power plants, oil refineries, and other industrial plants. Groton makes typewriters; Ithaca adding machines, clutches, flexible couplings, roller chain drives, and guns; Montour Falls large cranes and hoists; and Painted Post air and gas compressors, engines, and building machinery.

The second-ranking industry of the area and the one which has made Corning famous is the glass industry, established in 1868. Low-cost coal and an abundance of Pennsylvania glass-sand rock close at hand were primary reasons for the local development of this industry. Ready rail connections to eastern markets was another compelling reason. In the mid-twentieth century glass objects for home, factory, laboratory, and office are produced in almost endless variety. The Corning Glass Center, opened in 1951, houses the world's largest library devoted to glass, a large museum tracing the use of glass from man's earliest days, a crystal glass factory where visitors may watch the hand-blown glass operations, and greatly expanded research facilities. Corning is noted for the manufacture of precision scientific glassware, of which the two-hundred-inch mirror of the Mount Palomar Observatory is an outstanding example. Other important products of the Corning glassware industry include light bulbs, radio tubes, glass cooking utensils, technical and colored glasses, cut and engraved tableware, glass tubing, insulators, glass bricks, and many speciality glass products. Elmira produces glass containers for milk, beverages, and food.

Four other industrial groups in the Elmira area deserve brief mention: printing, transportation equipment, food, and electrical machinery. All are centered in Chemung County except the food industry, which is mostly in Steuben. Printing specialities are greeting cards, business forms, commercial photoengraving, and labels. The transportation-equipment industry includes the nation's largest manufacturer of fire-fighting apparatus. Food products include canned and frozen peas and spinach; and the area is famous for its champagne. The principal electrical items are starter drives, ignition parts, and electric heating units. The area has two large electronics centers—one at Bath and the other at Horseheads.

A number of lesser industries are also found in this area. Of these, the manufacture of textiles—synthetic yarns and fabrics, cotton knit cloth, underwear, knit shirts, and hosiery—is largely concentrated in Steuben County.

V. *The Mohawk Valley Area:* Counties—Fulton, Hamilton, Herkimer, Montgomery, and Oneida

Although much of the area is mountainous and lake-studded, ideal for recreation, and a good part of the rest is best suited for farming, the Mohawk Valley area, measured by the proportion of the working population engaged in manufacturing, is the most heavily industrialized of all the state's economic divisions, including that of New York City. In 1950 approximately 67,000 persons, or about 47 per cent of the area's labor force, were employed in manufacturing plants. Most of its factories are concentrated in a belt of cities along the Mohawk River from Rome to Amsterdam. Inasmuch as most of these cities lie along the natural east-west channel of immigration and commerce, many of them had their beginning in the eighteenth century. They profited economically from the completion of the Erie Canal in 1825 and later the New York Central Railroad, which followed the water route.

The trading and processing of furs and skins was the area's first major industry. Because of its strategic location, the availability of industrial water and power, and an abundant labor supply including a large corps of skilled technicians, manufacturing enterprise was increasingly attracted to the area. Today its leading industries are textiles, leather goods, sterling and silverplated tableware, primary metals, machinery, food products, and apparel. It is evident from this list that the Mohawk Valley area devotes more of its industrial production to nondurable goods than do most of the other upstate areas. Two out of every three manufacturing workers in this district are employed in plants making nondurable goods.

Although in recent decades successful efforts have been made to increase the area's production of durables, textiles still ranked first in 1950. Nevertheless, the textile industry has for many years been declining because of southern competition. Most of the textile industry is divided about equally between Utica and Amsterdam. Utica, which opened its first woolen mill in 1847, specializes in cotton and woolen fabrics, underwear and other knit goods, and yarns. Amsterdam, foremost city in the nation for the manufacture of rugs and carpets, established its first carpet mill in 1838.

The manufacture of textiles is also important in many other communities of this area: Little Falls produces sweaters, men's sport and work socks, and knit underwear; Waterville and Mohawk make underwear and knit goods; Oriskany manufactures papermakers' felts, and Oriskany Falls gauze and cheesecloth. St. Johnsville, Johnstown, and Chadwicks dye and finish rayon and other synthetic fabrics.

The leather-goods group constitutes the second major industry of the Mohawk Valley area. The industry was founded over two hundred years ago when hides acquired through trade with the Indians were dressed and sewn into mittens. This industry is today largely concentrated in the two Fulton County cities of Gloversville and Johnstown. Women's footwear, house slippers, and play shoes are manufactured at Dolgeville, Little Falls, and St. Johnsville.

Oneida County has long been famous for the production of sterling and silverplated tableware. This enterprise was the outgrowth of an experiment in communal living begun in 1848 by a group that had migrated to Sherrill from New England. In addition to silverware, Oneida County has several basic metal establishments—the products of Rome's copper and brass works, for example, are nationally known. Rome also produces iron castings, steel strips, and steel tubing. Iron castings are also manufactured at Oriskany, Clayville, and Utica. About 7 per cent of all manufacturing employees of the area are engaged in making a wide assortment of metal tools and nonelectrical machinery. Little Falls has the largest bicycle factory in upstate New York. On French Road, Utica, General Electric has recently opened its Light Military Electronic Equipment Department. Here work in research, development, and manufacture of complex electronic systems and devices is carried on.

Food products and the manufacture of apparel are also important in this area. Beechnut at Canajoharie, to cite one firm, processes a wide range of foods. Local apparel plants make men's and boy's suits and coats and women's dresses. Other important industries of this area include electrical machinery, furniture, office and library equipment, and firearms and ammunition.

VI. *Northern Area:* Counties—Clinton, Essex, Franklin, Jefferson, Lewis, St. Lawrence

Pioneers more than two hundred years ago established what was to be the area's first industry, the production of lumber. The magnificent stands of timber and their accessibility to the numerous rivers made it relatively easy to transport the logs from mountainside forest to sawmill. Although no longer first-ranking in the area, this industry is still high on the list. In 1950 over 11 per cent of all those employed in manufacturing were in the lumber industry. Wood and wood products are turned out in every county of the area and include flooring, veneers, wooden tableware, sashes, doors, and other millwork materials.

The forest lands of the area, however, have long contributed to what at present is its top-ranking industry, the pulp and paper business. Prior to the latter part of the nineteenth century, papermakers had depended largely upon rags for raw material. With the discovery that wood pulp could be used came a shift not only in raw material but in the location of the papermills. The area had plentiful stands of spruce and balsam and abundant water resources. While the pulp and paper plants of the area today are obliged to import much of the wood used from Canada and other countries, pulp and paper manufacture still comprises the northern area's principal industry, and mills are found in every county except Franklin. This area is the key supplier to New York City's giant printing and publishing enterprises. Paper firms of the northern area also produce annually an enormous output of packaging materials in the form of boxes, cartons, bags, paperboard, and wrapping paper. Manufacture of paper cups, napkins, writing paper, index cards, paper plates, wallpaper, and paper towels has increased greatly during the last two decades.

Ranking second to pulp and paper is the manufacture of primary metals, mostly aluminum and its products, at Massena in a big establishment built in 1902 by the Aluminum Company of America. An abundance of water for electric power made available by diverting water from the higher level St. Lawrence River into the Grass River explains in large measure the location of this Massena plant.

Other large industries of the area include transportation equipment, nonelectrical machinery, and processed foods, especially powdered milk and cheese.

Another industry closely related to manufacture is the area's mining industry. The economy of Essex, Clinton, and St. Lawrence counties rests heavily on the mineral industries, particularly iron ore, titanium, zinc, and lead mining. Even before the Revolutionary War, ores from the colony of New York provided a large share of the metal used through-out the colonies. Steel made in Troy from iron mined on the shores of Lake Champlain was used in building the famed *Monitor,* whose historic encounter with the *Merrimac* in 1862 revolutionized naval construction. New York City's stately George Washington Bridge is supported by metal cables made from the famous Chateaugay ores of the northern Adirondacks. In 1880 New York was credited with 15.8 per cent of the national production of iron ore; but with the development of the great ore deposits of the Lake Superior region New York's proportionate con-tribution to national production declined. In the period from 1920 to 1940 the state accounted for only about 1 per cent of the national total. In 1938 several of the large iron and steel corporations began to acquire and develop the mining properties of New York. Most of the ore from the northern area now goes to the Republic Steel Company's furnaces at Troy, Buffalo, and Cleveland. Some ore also goes to the furnaces of the Jones Laughlin Steel Company in Pittsburgh.

The iron ores of the northern area are rich in titanium compounds now in great demand for the manufacture of white and light-tinted paints and paint products. In 1941 the National Lead Company, an important titanium pigment producer, took title to eleven thousand acres of mineral-rich lands in the Sanford Lake region of Essex County. In 1950 the National Lead Company and the Allegheny Ludlum Steel Corpora-tion formed a new company, Titanium Metals Corporation, for the pur-pose of producing metallic titanium.

St. Lawrence County has profitable deposits of lead and zinc as well as graphite. The mineral wollastonite, important as a filler in the manu-facture of certain kinds of papers and in welding processes, is mined near Willsboro, Essex County. It is the only deposit of commercial pro-portions known to exist east of California.

With the development of the St. Lawrence River as a source of hydro-electric power the northern area is likely to become more important industrially. At present the region has a lower proportion of workers employed in manufacturing than in any other upstate area.

Table 14. Mineral production of New York in 1953
(in short tons except as noted).

Mineral	Quantity	Value
Cement (bbl.)	14,965,000	$ 39,388,000
Clays	961,000	1,303,000
Coke *	4,590,000	69,907,000
Gypsum	987,000	3,507,000
Ferro alloys *	268,000	71,735,000
Iron ore	3,825,000	36,346,000
Iron, pig *	4,698,000	237,030,000
Lead	1,000	376,000
Natural gas		
(thousand cu. ft.)	2,347,000	742,000
Petroleum (bbl.)	3,800,000	16,260,000
Salt	3,323,000	17,351,000
Sand and gravel	22,531,000	23,494,000
Slate	114,000	1,733,000
Stone	15,962,000	25,251,000
Talc	156,000	941,000
Zinc	52,000	11,852,000
Other minerals		8,324,000
Totals		$186,868,000

* Values for processed materials not included in the totals.
Source: U.S. Department of Commerce. In 1953 New York was first among the states in the output of ilmenite and talc; second in salt; third in slate and zinc; fifth in cement, gypsum, iron, sand and gravel; and nineteenth in the value of its mineral output.

VII. *The Southwest Gateway:* Counties—Allegany, Cattaraugus, Chautauqua

It was not until 1811 that Jamestown, now the area's largest city, was founded and its first dam and sawmill were built. Olean, in Cattaraugus County, became important early because of its location at the navigable headwaters of the Allegheny River, down which thousands of immigrants journeyed on their way to the Ohio Valley and points farther west. Dunkirk, on Lake Erie, was founded in 1805. Although the area was active in agriculture and trade, it did not become industrially significant until it was opened up by the building of the Erie Railroad. Another helpful influence in the industrial growth of the area were the supplies of natural gas and petroleum found within its boundaries. After 1865 a number of industries grew in size. Among these were furniture, machinery, fabricated metals, and processed food. The manufacture of durable goods has long preponderated and in the 1950's employs three-quarters of the manufacturing workers. With two of the principal production centers of the area, Jamestown and Dunkirk, Chautauqua County has nearly two-thirds of all the manufacturing employees of the Southwest Gateway.

Almost from its founding, Jamestown began to produce wooden cabinets and other household articles of high quality. The fame of its workmanship brought this industry nation-wide markets, and Jamestown became the furniture-making capital of the East. As timber became more scarce, the manufacturers shifted largely to metal. Falconer, Mayville, Brocton, and Frewsburg—all in Chautauqua County—have furniture-manufacturing establishments.

Machinery, the second-ranking industry in the area, is, like furniture, concentrated in Chautauqua County, and the major center is Dunkirk. From 1851 to 1930 the building of locomotives was the top industry. Since the latter date there has been a shift from locomotives to industrial equipment. Jamestown, Olean, and Wellsville also turn out some machinery. Almost all of the prefabricated metal manufacture is to be found in Chautauqua County, as also are the primary metal products.

Inasmuch as Chautauqua County is one of the nation's leading grape-producing areas, it is not surprising that grape juice, preserves, and jelly should rate high in the food-processing industry. Fruit and vegetable canning is also important. The area also manufactures some textiles, and the oil refineries at Olean and Wellsville produce some of the finest lubricating oils. The first New York oil well of importance was completed at Wellsville in 1879. This led to the rapid development of the Allegany field, and by 1882 the annual production was almost 6,500,000 barrels. Thereafter production declined until shortly after World War I, when water flooding, a new technique of extracting petroleum, was introduced. In 1950 there were more than 20,000 producing wells in the state from which over 4,000,000 barrels of oil were produced. About three-quarters of this production comes from Allegany County; most of the rest from Cattaraugus County, and minor amounts from Chautauqua and Steuben counties. A miscellany of other products are manufactured in the area.

VIII. *The Binghamton Area:* Counties—Broome, Chenango, Delaware, and Otsego

Although rich in fertile farmlands, the Binghamton area is one of the most industrialized regions of the state. Thirty-seven out of every one hundred persons in the labor force are employed in manufacture. The center of industrial activity, from the time the area was settled, has been located in its southwestern corner, in and around the "triple" cities of Broome County—Binghamton, Endicott, and Johnson City. Four-fifths of the area's manufacturing employees are in Broome County.

Binghamton, the oldest of the "triple" cities, was, during its first half century, an agricultural-trading center. Although prosperous from the beginning, it gained momentum economically when the Chenango Canal, connecting Binghamton with the Erie Canal at Utica, was completed in 1837. An even greater lift was given to the area when, in 1848, Binghamton was first linked to New York City by the Erie Railroad. Later, rail service was extended to Buffalo, Albany, Pennsylvania, and other industrial sections. Not only did Binghamton flourish as a trading center, but it became the processing center for regional produce.

An important factor in Binghamton's development was its nearness to Pennsylvania's coal deposits. The coal supply led to the establishment in the mid-nineteenth century of the city's first iron foundry. At about the same time, the first shoe factory came into being, using leather made of hides from the local dairy herds. The lumber resources of the locality were the basis for a wood-working industry. Thereafter, not only Binghamton but the entire four-county area developed rapidly. In the 1950's approximately fifty thousand workers are employed by manufacturing enterprises.

No less than 30 per cent of these are employed by leather firms, either tanners or the manufacturers of shoes. Although Binghamton is still the leading producer of leather footwear, the industry has overflowed to adjoining communities—Johnson City (since 1890) and Endicott (since 1901). Norwich in Chenango County also has a shoe factory. Tanneries are operated locally by the shoe industry, and at Endicott there is a leather-welting plant.

Largely because the main plant of International Business Machines is located at Endicott, the machine industry is the area's second-ranking manufacture. Beginning at Endicott as a small tabulating machine enterprise, IBM was consolidated in 1911 with several concerns in related fields and, under the guidance of Thomas J. Watson, became one of the nation's giant corporations.

The manufacture of photographic equipment, books (Binghamton), and electrical equipment (Sidney), and the production of processed milk products such as cheese, ice cream mix, butter, and condensed milk are other important industries. Rubber firms, closely associated with shoe manufacturing, make rubbers, shower caps, baby pants, and rubber bags. Lumber plants turn out wooden heels for women's shoes.

IX. *The Syracuse Area:* Counties—Cayuga, Cortland, Madison, Onondaga, Oswego

Geographically in the center of the state, this area has been bolstered by the constant improvements in transportation. The leading manufacturing centers of the area today—Syracuse, Oswego, Fulton, Auburn, and

Cortland—had their beginnings during the last two decades of the eighteenth century.

The production of salt was the region's first important industry, but it did not reach full stature until after the building of the Erie Canal. Before that time the marketing of salt—a bulky, weighty commodity— was costly, almost prohibitive for long distances. Other early manufactures suffered somewhat from the same handicap. With the building of the Erie Canal and the railroads, manufacturing strode rapidly forward. By 1865 it was evident that the area would center its attention primarily on the production of durable goods—machinery of various kinds, agricultural implements, office equipment, chemicals, and the like.

Today more than a third of the area's labor force are employed in manufacturing establishments. Onondaga County, in which Syracuse is located, accounts for two out of every three manufacturing workers in the area. The five leading industries of the area—machinery, electrical equipment, primary metals, food, and transportation equipment—are concentrated in this county. Papermaking machinery and paper products, especially food containers, are centered in Oswego County, principally at Fulton and Oswego where raw material and waterpower are available.

The Syracuse area leads all upstate regions in the production of non-electrical machinery. Numerous products from Syracuse are known the world over, such as typewriters, household washing machines and ironers, and air-conditioning equipment. Other Syracuse manufactures include industrial heating and vacuum-cleaning equipment, can-making machinery, package conveyers and pneumatic tubes, industrial furnaces, and commercial laundry and dry-cleaning equipment.

Other cities of the Syracuse area also turn out machinery products. Auburn makes stationary marine and locomotive Deisel engines; Fayetteville, dies and jigs; and Cortland, typewriters and adding and duplicating machines.

The electrical-goods industry ranks second in the Syracuse area. Here is located a huge General Electric plant which specializes in radio and electronics, producing transmitters, radio and television sets, and industrial electronics apparatus.

The largest plant in the primary metals group—third-ranking industry in the area—is at the Syracuse suburb of Geddes. It is famous for its production of stainless, tool, and speciality steels. Another notable factory in this locality makes its own steel, rolling and drawing it to turn out wire, wire cloth, wire netting, nails, and related products. Forgings are produced at Syracuse and Cortland.

The food-processing industry obtains its materials from the area's farmlands. Fulton is famous for its chocolate bars and chocolate candy coatings, and frozen foods. Syracuse produces cheese, ice cream, carbonated beverages, and beer. Cortland has a long-established reputation for its meat products.

The transportation equipment industry produces aircraft engines and gears as well as a number of automotive items, buses, trucks, truck cabs, and accessories. Chlorine, manufactured by the Allied Chemical and Dye Corporation, pharmaceuticals, textiles, chinaware, and cutlery are among the other important manufacturing enterprises of the area.

X. *The Mid-Hudson Area:* Counties—Columbia, Dutchess, Greene, Orange, Putnam, Sullivan, Ulster

Prior to 1850 the products of the mid-Hudson area found a ready market in New York City, but as the metropolis expanded in population and economic activity, the industrial products of the area, especially its textiles, were less in demand. During the twentieth century the area has not kept pace industrially; it is today the least industrialized area of the state. Farming and the resort business, on the other hand, have increasingly flourished. Apparel production is the area's leading industry. Orange, Ulster, and Dutchess counties, in that order, are the principal producers. Within each there is considerable specialization of product. Newburgh, Middletown, Port Jervis, Walden, Kingston, Hudson, and Catskill are the chief manufacturing centers.

The area's machinery plants constitute its second-largest industry. With the recent opening of new branches of the International Business Machines Corporation in Kingston and Poughkeepsie, this area has become increasingly important in the production of machinery. For a long time the city of Poughkeepsie has manufactured typewriters, dairy equipment, commercial refrigerators, and elevators. It was also for many years the home of Adriance-Platt farm equipment until that concern was swallowed up by the International Harvester Company.

Other industries, some of them long established, are: textiles, which employ 16 per cent of the area's workers engaged in manufacturing; leather, concentrated for the most part in Newburgh; stone-clay-glass, with the major cement plants (Lehigh and Atlas) in Columbia and Greene counties, brick firms in Columbia and Ulster, and a large glass company in Orange; printing, chiefly in Dutchess; food processors found principally in Orange, Dutchess, Ulster, and Columbia counties, are noted for their wines, canned fruits and vegetables, prepared meats, canned mushrooms, and fruit flavors. Paper production, which includes paperboard products, tissues, towels, and other items, is also important.

XI. *The New York Metropolitan Area:* Counties—Those comprising New York City plus the four suburban counties, Nassau, Rockland, Suffolk, and Westchester

New York City, with its four suburban counties, is the nation's foremost manufacturing center, and it leads the rest of the state in well over half of the manufactures listed in Table 13. For more than a century manufacturers have been attracted to this area by its huge, concentrated markets, its ample pool of labor, its superb location for the export trade, its fine wholesaling facilities, and the variety of its business services.

The New York area manufacturing is characterized by its diversity and its emphasis on nondurables. No other area in the state has such an array of manufactures. The manufacture of apparel is the area's leading industry. Printing and publishing, one of the area's oldest industries, ranks second. Nowhere in the nation are there to be found so many great printing houses, so many daily newspapers, so many business, trade, and professional journals and periodicals. A seemingly unending stream of books and technical materials are turned out annually by the city's presses. In 1900 no less than 81.5 per cent of the newspaper and periodical manufacturing business and 77.9 per cent of the book and job products of the state were located in New York City.

A wide range of industries labeled "miscellaneous" employed almost 8 per cent of the area's manufacturing employees in 1950. The variety of products is only suggested by the following list: artificial flowers, buttons, musical instruments, athletic equipment, smoking pipes, hairpins, buckles, brushes, life preservers, mannikins, dolls, and fire extinguishers. Of every five persons employed in the miscellaneous category, three work in Manhattan and one in Brooklyn. The manufacture of precious jewelry and silverware, of toys and sporting goods, and of pencils and other office supplies is also large.

Food processing was the earliest of New York City's major industries. Sugar refining is largely concentrated here. Bakery products, beverages, confectionary, meat products, and canned goods are also important food-processing industries. A wide array of fabricated metals are produced, chiefly in Brooklyn. Leather, textiles, chemicals, and machinery also rank high on the list of New York City's manufactures. In the manufacture of all of these products the borough of Brooklyn has especially been prominent. In 1880, for example, it was the nation's second-ranking city in the production of chemicals. Even today it remains the location of E. R. Squibb and Sons, McKesson and Robbins, Charles Pfizer and Company, the New York Quinine and Chemical Works, and other important pharmaceutical concerns. Paints and varnishes and other chemicals are produced in this borough on a large scale.

Of the area's suburban counties, Nassau and Suffolk have witnessed during the last half century the coming of a giant aircraft industry, the world's largest book-publishing plant, and large electrical-machinery and scientific-instrument manufacturing concerns.

Table 15. Manufacturing establishments in New York State by county and size, March 1950.

County	No. of establishments	No. of employees	Employees							
			0–3	4–7	8–19	20–49	50–99	100–249	250–499	500 or more
Albany	347	20,426	82	54	75	52	37	27	14	6
Allegany	61	2,954	23	14	4	10	5	1	2	2
Broome	214	35,962	54	33	42	22	22	16	11	14
Cattaraugus	132	8,697	30	20	29	22	13	11	4	3
Cayuga	105	9,320	28	15	26	12	8	6	3	7
Chautauqua	273	20,507	59	46	49	39	26	36	8	10
Chemung	95	13,400	22	12	20	15	8	7	4	7
Chenango	71	3,079	18	18	12	4	8	7	1	1
Clinton	46	2,858	11	7	10	9	10	3	2	2
Columbia	76	4,258	13	9	16	17	2	8	5	0
Cortland	84	4,804	25	12	10	14	8	8	4	1
Delaware	58	3,421	16	12	11	11	10	3	0	2
Dutchess	194	14,303	54	24	27	36	24	16	8	5
Erie	1,436	127,185	374	223	309	214	117	107	40	52
Essex	64	1,822	21	20	6	11	1	4	0	1
Franklin	67	1,688	26	16	8	9	3	3	2	0
Fulton	277	8,416	75	54	53	41	32	19	3	0
Genesee	75	5,522	18	12	15	9	7	8	3	3
Greene	46	1,473	14	12	3	9	3	4	1	0
Hamilton	10	147	4	2	1	2	1	0	0	0
Herkimer	96	10,811	19	11	14	19	14	12	2	5
Jefferson	114	6,024	37	16	26	7	8	17	1	2
Lewis	48	1,719	16	9	7	4	7	4	1	0
Livingston	47	2,547	8	10	12	7	2	5	2	1
Madison	51	1,491	20	8	6	10	3	4	0	0
Monroe	871	94,936	225	113	205	152	62	49	27	38
Montgomery	106	14,365	23	17	23	14	15	7	3	4
Nassau	605	39,749	206	111	130	93	26	27	5	7

County										
Niagara	273	41,884	59	31	48	39	32	31	15	18
Oneida	326	30,457	93	53	59	40	27	27	12	15
Onondaga	513	51,093	122	83	103	90	41	35	19	20
Ontario	93	4,456	26	10	17	21	5	10	3	1
Orange	276	14,685	59	42	36	50	47	34	6	2
Orleans	41	1,778	8	7	10	8	4	2	2	0
Oswego	109	8,735	32	12	21	15	10	12	3	4
Otsego	65	1,473	26	10	11	9	5	4	0	0
Putnam	14	279	4	3	2	4	1	0	0	0
Rensselaer	193	14,997	61	23	33	25	17	20	9	5
Rockland	127	8,916	39	8	22	28	14	8	5	3
St. Lawrence	93	7,929	27	16	20	7	15	9	6	4
Saratoga	105	7,814	33	15	16	7	15	9	6	4
Schenectady	124	37,097	33	18	26	8	3	13	11	12
Schoharie	23	648	10	4	3	3	0	3	0	0
Schuyler	20	972	8	2	4	2	0	3	1	0
Seneca	39	2,667	13	9	3	6	2	3	1	2
Steuben	100	12,062	25	15	27	10	9	10	2	2
Suffolk	307	7,102	102	63	63	52	15	8	2	2
Sullivan	68	504	38	15	5	9	1	0	0	0
Tioga	41	1,587	4	12	10	7	3	4	1	0
Tompkins	58	4,416	19	8	14	7	4	2	1	3
Ulster	205	7,547	54	26	36	51	21	13	3	1
Warren	88	4,259	24	17	17	14	5	5	5	1
Washington	80	3,825	25	16	12	5	11	6	5	0
Wayne	86	3,554	27	15	17	13	6	6	1	1
Westchester	990	45,145	244	164	222	200	85	50	14	11
Wyoming	44	2,866	7	9	7	4	8	7	1	1
Yates	28	863	8	3	8	5	3	0	1	0
New York City	39,886	993,855	11,147	7,027	10,043	7,574	2,579	1,121	247	148
New York State	50,130	1,788,912	13,916	8,657	12,068	9,184	3,458	1,874	540	433

521

The two other suburban counties—Westchester and Rockland—were primarily devoted to agriculture during the greater part of the nineteenth century. With improved transportation these counties became highly residential—an area of wealthy families, suburban estates, and gentlemen farmers. It was not until World War I that industry in either county made any appreciable advance. Even in 1950 the Westchester-Rockland district was one of the least industrialized of the state's regions, with but one worker in manufacturing out of every five persons employed in the district. One out of every three manufacturing employees of the two counties works in either the needle trades or the textile field. The apparel makers are employed in small shops which sprang up during the closing years of the nineteenth century. Approximately two-thirds of the textile workers were employed in the Alexander Smith carpet factory in Yonkers prior to its removal in the early 1950's.

Rockland County is important for manufacture of chemicals, Pearl River being the home of the largest plant in the world for the production of penicillin, aureomycin, and several hundred other biologicals and pharmaceuticals. Other products of the chemical industry manufactured in the district include cosmetics, paints, pigments, and dyestuffs. Machinery, including electrical equipment, is manufactured in a number of Westchester cities. One of the largest plants of the Otis Elevator Company, world's foremost producer of elevators, is located in Yonkers. Food processing and printing are also growing industries, especially in Westchester.

Irrespective of economic area two developments affecting the state's manufactures during the last three-quarters of a century deserve brief mention: (1) shift in location and (2) concentration. Some industries have moved out of the state entirely. Thus, the Victory Mills Manufacturing Company, a cotton textile concern, moved to Alabama to benefit from nearness of raw material and lower labor costs. Similarly the Union Bag and Paper Company shifted from New York to the South. Shifts have also occurred as a result of industrial combination and concentration. In the process, small plants have been abandoned or have moved to more favorable locations within the state. For example, seventy years ago each of the half-dozen villages along the banks of the Kayderross, a small river which empties into Saratoga Lake, boasted at least one manufacturing plant, in addition to gristmills and sawmills. Middle Grove had two papermills, Rock City Falls had two paper and one pulp and papermill, Milton Center a tannery, West Milton a papermill, Bloodville an ax and scythe factory, and Ballston Spa a tannery and two papermills. Of all these, only the two papermills at Rock City Falls remain. Moreover, shifts are being made from highly congested urban centers to suburbs or to rural locations. A number of reasons (including fear of bombing in the event of war) motivate this third type of shift.

Industrial concentration has deeply affected manufacturing enterprise in both state and nation. The rapid expansion of American industry after the Civil War produced a corresponding increase in competition. Price wars resulted, and sometimes industry was compelled to operate at a loss. Consequently, a growing number of business leaders not only condemned competition as inefficient and wasteful but sought means to control it. There was a steady trend toward combination and concentration until, by 1914, the control of a large segment of American industry was in the hands of a relatively few individuals and corporations. Indeed, by the first decade of the twentieth century there were few branches of American industry that had not been affected by the consolidation movement.

With the exception of a few manufacturing enterprises, notably the apparel industry, the industries of New York did not escape the concentration process. Sugar refining and other parts of the food industry, the production of electrical equipment, chemicals, transportation equipment, pulp and paper, agricultural machinery, the manufacture of aircraft, as well as many other leading New York industries as they operate today are the product of combination and concentration.

Despite this move toward concentration there are still many hundreds of small independent manufacturing establishments in New York State as Table 15 indicates.

New York is the manufacturing leader of the Union. It can boast rich natural resources, an outstanding production plant, and a highly skilled working population. Since the Civil War a productive mechanism has been developed capable of turning out goods and services in abundance. The state as well as the nation has yet to discover how to bridge the gap between our productive capacity and the consumptive ability of our people. In other words, the means of distributing the products of our farms and factories is still ineffective.

Changing Status of Labor

For after all, economic radicalism arises neither from a merely stupid desire for more material goods, nor from an intellectual adherence to a particular formula of industrial organization. It arises from the desire to be free, to achieve dignity and independence. Poverty is distressful not so much because of its physical hardships as because of its spiritual bondage.—George Soule, 1921

THE growth of manufacturing and service industries and the expansion of commerce in New York State between 1865 and the mid-twentieth century was accompanied by a fundamental change in the social and economic status of its labor force. The nature of this change and of the forces responsible for bringing it about are considered in this chapter. Specifically to be covered are: the size and changing composition of the working population; the status of labor prior to the Industrial Revolution; labor's quest for economic security and social well-being through unionization and collective bargaining and protective legislation; government control and inspection; and machinery for adjusting disputes between management and labor.

Since the close of the Civil War, New York has been blessed with a constantly increasing and competent labor supply. In addition to the native-born element, New York City was the port of entry of those armies of immigrants who poured into America prior to the restriction of immigration in the 1920's. A large percentage of these newcomers did not go beyond the boundaries of New York City and its immediate environs. And of those who did, many settled in upstate urban communities. Even as late as 1940 in the economic areas heavily engaged in manufacturing as, for example, the Niagara Frontier, the Rochester and Syracuse areas, and the capital district, the percentage of the foreign born in the labor force varied from 10 to almost 20 per cent. Earlier the percentage would have been much higher. Another increasingly important factor was a shift of many agricultural workers to urban communities. Availability of jobs was also a magnet attracting workers into the state from other parts of the country. Finally, and very important, has been increased employment of women and children (though employment of the latter has been sharply restricted during the last half century). In 1950 women workers represented 31 per cent of all employed persons in the state. Although this percentage is somewhat lower than at the peak production years of World War II, as the accompanying table indicates, it is much higher than for 1900. The percentage for New York State has usually been a little higher than that for the country as a whole.

Table 16. Number of women employed in New York State, 1900–1950.

Year	Women employed	Percentage women of total employed
1900	667,373	22.4
1910	982,434	24.6
1920	1,134,561	25.2
1930	1,414,736	25.6
1940	1,453,355	29.4
1944	1,988,800	33.1
1950	1,741,766	31.0

Source: U.S. Department of Commerce, 1950.

During World War II women played an essential and dramatic part in war production. In 1944 one out of every three workers in the major war industries in the state was a woman; then there were 350,000 women employed in plants producing war materials. The efficiency of women was notable not only in the war industries but also in all other manufacturing and civilian industries. Of the approximately two million women working in New York State in 1944, close to 800,000, or two in every five, were employed in manufacturing plants. Following manufacture as the largest woman-employing industry was the wholesale and retail trade, with 294,000 women. Next in importance were professional services, with 241,000, and domestic service with 178,000 (the latter a drop of 20 per cent in comparison with 1940).

A further examination of the above table indicates that the war effort alone was not responsible for the heavy employment of women. Rather, it is a growing and longtime trend. Women are increasingly reluctant to go into low-paying occupations. It is for this reason, in part, that there has been a decided shift of women from domestic service and from the comparatively low-paying professions of teaching and nursing into better-paying activities.

Irrespective of source, the ever-increasing labor supply of the state since 1865 has kept pace with the employment demands of its rapidly expanding industrial needs. During the ten-year period 1940–1950, the state's employed labor force increased 16 per cent, bringing the total number to 5,762,000 persons. During the last sixty years jobs of all kinds have multiplied much faster in New York City than in the state or nation. The city's large population and diversity of economic activities and cultural opportunities are the principal explanatory factors. They also help to explain why, in the largest center of manufacturing America, considerably more than half of its working population are clerical workers, salesmen, professionals, or employees in other nonmanufacturing occupations.

The state's labor supply underwent revolutionary change in the hundred years 1850–1950. In fact, not until one compares the status of the worker prior to the Industrial Revolution with his status in the age of machine production can he fully appreciate the transformation which occurred in the worker's way of life and outlook.

Before the widespread application of machinery to the manufacturing process, the worker was often a skilled craftsman. He usually owned his own tools which, along with his skills, enabled him to approach the status of the creative artist. Frequently he performed all the operations in the manufacture of a single product. Often he worked in his own home or was employed in the home of a neighbor. In either case he was an individualist and, as such, had certain freedoms which the workers of the machine age were not privileged to enjoy. For example, when the growth of the factory system compelled the craftsman to become a machine tender, he lost some of his most precious possessions. In place of his tools which had been his servants was a machine that he did not own and that left him little or no scope for individual initiative. As a machine tender he was forced to subordinate his creative instincts to the relentless motions of the machine. Even the product which the machine produced was not of his design.

The machine also robbed many workers of their sense of security. Before the coming of the machine, the worker as craftsman had possessed an undeniable asset when he bargained with an employer. He knew, as did the employer, that he and other workers with similar skills alone could perform certain operations in the manufacturing process. But as a mere machine tender he had comparatively little bargaining power as an individual. Almost any person of average intelligence could tend a machine, and if he complained about his wage or sought shorter hours or in any other way expressed dissatisfaction with his job he could be discharged and another man easily found to take his place.

Especially was this true at a time of frequent depressions and when a never-ending stream of immigrants poured into the state.

When a craftsman was virtually compelled to exchange his own tools for a machine that belonged to his employer, he relinquished whatever control he, as a craftsman, had once had over his working conditions. Wage, hours, and the physical environment of the factory were all determined by the employer. If the worker lost his job, he knew that the possibility of finding another position depended more upon luck than any ability he might possess. Moreover, there was always the possibility that he might become unfit for any type of manual labor through accident or sickness. If he lost a foot or a hand in the machine he was tending, he not only lost his job but often was unable to obtain another. If he became too old to keep up with the pace of the machine he was "fired." If he lost his job through no fault of his own but was discharged or "laid off" because of a business recession or some other reason, he received no financial aid or unemployment insurance.

With the rapid mechanization and concentration of some of the state's industries following the Civil War, the worker's situation became even worse. Before the coming of the machine and the corporation, manufacturing establishments were small. Often the owner worked alongside his employees. He knew them personally and frequently helped them with their more pressing home problems such as family illness, mortgage indebtedness, and other hardships. Employer and employee greeted each other by their first names. As business became mechanized and corporate, this close personal relationship between employer and employee disappeared. Labor became a mere bookkeeping item in an enterprise whose principal goal was the realization of financial profit to management and stockholders. The consequences to the worker during the closing decades of the nineteenth century were little short of disastrous: the hours of labor were long; economic warfare between employer and employee frequently prevailed; cyclical and seasonal unemployment constantly threatened; physical conditions of employment, particularly in some industries and especially in the City of New York, were intolerable; the health of many workers was seriously impaired; the percentage of accidents was high; and, above all, the morale of the majority of the workers was low. The sense of belonging or being appreciated for one's contribution as a human being to the enterprise which his labor, in part, made possible was almost entirely lacking.

If the individual worker sought to improve the conditions of employment brought into being by the Industrial Revolution, he quickly learned that he was powerless to do so. He was in competition with other wage earners whose necessity for a job was as great as his own.

Moreover, if he agitated for change, his employer was glad to get rid of him and to replace him with one more docile. This was one reason why many of the state's employers welcomed the coming of the immigrant, who frequently arrived with only a few cents in his pocket and the clothes on his back and was virtually impelled to take whatever kind of work was offered without raising questions about wages and conditions of employment. It was for this reason that the native-born worker opposed the coming of the immigrant. This attitude on the part of the American-born worker plus the lack of training for the better and higher-paid jobs also account for the fact that everywhere in the state the more menial and often most hazardous and poorly paid jobs were assigned to the immigrant or Negro. But whether native born or a new-comer from a foreign land, the worker could not, singlehanded, better the conditions of his employment. This could be done only by means of unionization and the passage of protective legislation. Recourse was had to both of these devices with gratifying results, especially after 1900.

New York has long been the greatest center of organized labor in the United States. Indeed, organization of workers for the purpose of improving their economic status was not unknown in New York City in the late 1820's and early 1830's. The budding labor movement, however, was too weak to withstand the impact of the Panic of 1837 and was completely crushed. In the 1850's trade unionism reappeared only to be checked again by the depression of 1857. Nevertheless, a few unions, notably the printers, stonecutters, machinists, and hatworkers, managed to survive. During the Civil War and the years immediately following, the labor movement gathered strength. New trade unions composed of skilled workers were founded, but the mass of unskilled workers remained unorganized.

During this period the trade unions were primarily concerned with preventing their members from being reduced to a proletarian status. They were far more interested in restoring economic individualism than in developing class consciousness. Most of the demands of organized New York labor during the 1870's were not unlike what they had been prior to the Civil War. Heading the list was the demand for a shorter working day. Many, inspired by the argument of Ira Steward of Boston, a member of the Machinists and Blacksmiths Union, advocated an eight-hour day for all workers, but insisted that this reform be achieved by legislation rather than by use of the strike. Organized labor also struggled to prevent wage cuts and in many cases to increase the workers' daily or weekly pay. Some labor spokesmen, in the hopes of discovering some way to escape the growing hardships of the machine age, advocated the establishment of co-operative stores in which workers could purchase goods and co-operative factories owned and managed by the workers, who would share in any profits which might accrue. The co-operative ventures launched during these years were, for the most part, dismal failures, either because of mismanagement or the superior power exercised by private enterprise in the same industry.

During the 1880's, at the very time when the Knights of Labor movement—a national movement for one big labor union—was at its peak and when the common man felt that he was the victim of corporate greed and monopoly, New York City suffered from an epidemic of strikes. Of these none did more to center attention on the status of labor than the 1882 strike of the freight handlers at the city's railway terminals in New York and Jersey City. The strikers sought a three-cent increase in their then seventeen-cents-an-hour wage (for a fourteen- to sixteen-hour day). The average weekly wage was from $7.50 to $9.00, which was barely enough to provide food. Many of the merchants, who also suffered at the hands of the railroads, supported the workers. Otherwise, their pleas for assistance did not meet with favorable response. Of the press, only *Justice,* an antimonopoly newspaper, rallied to the strikers' support. Despite the fairness of their demands, the strikers failed to win. Meanwhile, under the leadership of two New York officials of the cigarmakers union, Samuel Gompers and Adolph Strasser, the American Federation of Labor was in process of formation, an organization which by the 1890's was the most important labor body in the United States.

A loose alliance of national trade unions, the American Federation of Labor was essentially a conservative organization that was committed to few changes in the status quo. It shunned political and economic reforms and centered its attention almost exclusively upon attempts to raise wages and shorten the work week. To it the strike was a class-conscious weapon to be used only when employers refused to co-operate with labor in signing collective-bargaining contracts. By restricting its membership to highly skilled workers, the A.F. of L. did little for the masses of unskilled workingmen.

From 1886, when Gompers was elected to the presidency of the Federation, to the present, labor within the state and particularly in New York City has experienced numerous changes of fortune which need not be detailed here. Nevertheless, certain summary observations should be noted: (1) prior to 1930, with some exceptions, unionism was most successful in industries dominated by the small employer as, for example, in the apparel industries; (2) during the period 1865–1900 little headway was made in organizing labor in the larger industries in upstate New York; (3) since the founding of the American Federation of Labor, New York City labor leaders have played an important role in the American labor movement; (4) in economic, political, and ideological matters New York labor has exhibited a variety of views, running all the way from the communism of the furriers union to the conservatism of the craft unions in the building industry; (5) labor legislation within the state, and to a considerable degree within the nation, has been the result of powerful labor pressure; (6) several of the unions active within the state have been increasingly interested in labor education both for union officers and rank and file (with the International Ladies' Garment Workers' Union leading the way); (7) in the older unions of the state and especially those blessed with wise leadership, there has been in recent decades increasing evidence of growing maturity and responsibility on the part of organized labor (here again with the needle-trades unions and Local No. 3 of the International Brotherhood of Electrical Workers in the forefront); (8) and, finally, one is impressed by the great strides made during the last quarter of a century in the membership growth of organized labor in the state.

Anyone who examines the history of labor in New York State during the last hundred years, and especially during the decades between Appomattox and the beginning of World War I when the workingmen of the state were fighting an uphill battle to improve their social and economic status, is impressed by the fact that with a few exceptions the wage earners of the state were not attracted by the preachments of left-wing theorists and agitators. The reasons for their lack of interest are not difficult to explain. Those who espoused the gospel of Karl Marx and sought to induce the American workingman to undertake a revolution that would overthrow American capitalism were mainly immigrants. It was difficult for immigrants of one nationality to win over other foreign groups to their ideas, and it was virtually impossible to interest native-born Americans. They failed utterly to appreciate that they were directing their appeal to workers who, living in an essentially fluid social order, had little or no sense of class consciousness so prevalent in the rigidly class-structured Old World. The American workingman, whether native or foreign born, had no desire to overthrow the American economic system; all he wanted was what he believed to be his rights and his just share of the fruits of capitalistic enterprise.

Of the leading critics of American capitalism during these decades none was more outspoken and vitriolic than Daniel De Leon. Born on the island of Curaçao and educated in Germany and Holland, De Leon migrated to New York City in the mid 1870's. He studied law at Columbia University and taught for a short time. Having become interested in various labor movements, he abandoned both the law and teaching, joined the Knights of Labor in 1888, and thereafter devoted the remaining years of his life (he died in 1914) to propagating his version of socialism. An out-and-out Marxist, he took a militant stand against traditional trade unions, whose leaders, including Gompers, he termed "labor fakers," and urged all workingmen to join in an independent political movement which would win control of the government and establish a "socialist or cooperative commonwealth whereby the instruments of production shall be made the property of the whole people." In 1892 De Leon joined the Socialist Labor party and the following year became its candidate for governor of New York. Meanwhile, as a member of the Knights of Labor, he made an unsuccessful attempt to capture control of that organization. In 1895 he withdrew from the Knights to form the Socialist Trade and Labor Alliance, which devoted its principal efforts to attacking the conservative leadership of the American Federation of Labor and the wing of the Socialist party that lent its support to the existing structure of trade unionism in America. De Leon was both autocratic and doctrinaire, and he soon alienated all but a small coterie of his most devoted followers. Unable to destroy Gomperism, he joined the Independent Workers of the World in 1905. Even this anarchistic organization ousted him. A rival workers' International Industrial Union, which he then founded, did not flourish. Wholly apart from the character of his leadership, De Leon's ideology did not fit America. Were it to have found acceptance anywhere in the United States it would have been in the City of New York, but even here it failed to make headway.

The greatest gains achieved by New York labor in its quest to improve its status have been won in legislative halls—both state and federal—rather than on the picket lines. Labor laws enacted by the federal government during the half century after the termination of the Civil War affected only a small percentage of the workers of the state. The creation of the Bureau of Labor Statistics in 1884 and the Department of Labor in 1913 were possible exceptions. The other federal measures enacted during this period, however, were limited in application either to government workers or to those employed by firms engaged in interstate trade. In sharp contrast to the labor legislation in Washington was that accomplished at Albany, particularly after 1883. Several factors account for this growth in state regulatory legislation.

Labor itself, increasingly conscious of its strength when organized, exerted tremendous pressure from time to time upon both the public and the legislature. Of the spokesmen for labor in this respect none was more influential than the New York State Federation of Labor. This organization, which antedated the formation of the American Federation of Labor by two decades, was organized in 1865 under the name of the New York State Trades Assembly. It had its inception when, in 1864, antilabor representatives in the legislature attempted to strengthen existing legislation prohibiting combinations of workers for the purpose of conducting a strike. The trade unions protested vigorously, holding mass meetings in Albany and New York. In 1898 the Trades Assembly changed its name to the New York Workingmen's Federation of the State of New York and again in 1910 to the New York State Federation of Labor. The "political branch" of the organization, formed in 1882, existed until 1888, when a regular legislative committee with an active chairman as sole legislative agent was created.

Although the organization has changed its name, its purpose remains the same:

To agitate such questions as may be for the benefit of the working classes in order that we may obtain the enactment of such measures by the State Legislature as will be beneficial to all of us and the repeal of all repressive laws which now exist; to use all means consistent with honor and integrity to so correct the abuses under which the laboring classes are laboring as to insure to them their just rights and privileges; to use our utmost endeavors to impress upon the various divisions of workingmen the necessity of a close and thorough organization and of forming themselves into local unions wherever practicable.

The history of the State Federation of Labor roughly parallels the great legislative efforts at industrial reform. As far back as 1870, the federation was principally responsible for the enactment of legislation circumventing the common-law ruling that a labor union was an unlawful conspiracy which could be punished criminally.

But the New York State Federation of Labor should not alone be credited for the imposing body of labor legislation enacted during these years. Among the other contributing factors has been the weight of public opinion. Many forces are responsible for shaping people's minds. Among these are incidents which arouse public indignation and spur the demand for reform. For example, probably the most far-reaching single reform in the field of labor legislation ever enacted in New York State was the outcome of a disastrous fire in the Triangle Shirt Waist factory on Washington Square, New York City, in 1910 in which 143 workers (mostly girls) were killed. The immediate result of this tragedy was a mass meeting held in the Metropolitan Opera House. This in turn resulted in the formation of a Citizens Committee on Safety to make investigations and to promote public policies for the prevention of industrial accidents and fires. On the basis of data furnished by this committee, the State Factory Investigating Commission, headed by Robert F. Wagner with Alfred E. Smith as vice-chairman, was appointed in Albany in June 1911. The purpose of the investigation, as Smith later wrote, was "the conservation of human life," and the three volumes of its report contain an appalling record of the destruction of human life. Men, women, and children worked at night as well as during the day in inadequately ventilated and poorly lighted factories and tenement houses. Many workers suffered from occupational diseases, and there were few safeguards against accidents or fire. In the state's canneries, where conditions were particularly bad, women and small children worked as much as sixteen hours a day. Few factories contained the necessary sanitary facilities. In several industries wages were so low that every member of a family was forced to seek employment. Finally, the existing state's labor laws were almost never enforced, and factory inspection was a farce. The outgrowth of the extended investigation by this commission was not only a new set of labor laws, as we shall see, but the creation of the State Industrial Commission with broad powers.

The vote of the worker is another factor which accounts for the large body of industrial legislation affecting labor enacted during this period. Also, severe cyclical changes, like that which produced the Depression of 1929, often affect adversely not only the workers but the majority of the state's population as well. Out of these conditions come demands for reform and the passage of social-economic legislation. To illustrate: Late in 1933 the state legislature enacted a "baby" N.R.A. (National Recovery Act), which was declared unconstitutional by the New York Court of Appeals in 1935. In the same year, out of Albany came a "baby" Norris–La Guardia Act in the form of Section 876-a of the Civil Practice Act. In many respects, too, the New York State Labor Relations Act was a "baby" Wagner Act. These and other legislative measures were the direct results of a long period of industrial depression and of the efforts of the state administration to raise wages and afford the worker greater economic security.

The main body of labor legislation enacted during the last hundred years has been concerned with: (1) the regulation of woman and child labor, (2) safety and sanitation, (3) prevention and insurance of industrial accidents, (4) insurance for old age and unemployment, (5) laws pertaining to trade unions, and (6) the administration of labor law. Distinct from the slow development of legal measures to deal with these problems was the comparatively rapid enactment of the Ives-Quinn Law forbidding racial and religious discrimination in employment (1945). This is discussed at length in Chapter 33.

Prior to 1880, when the number of gainfully occupied in the state numbered 360,000, protective labor legislation was rudimentary and badly administered. Enforcement was practically nonexistent. The work of women in stores and factories was wholly unregulated until 1881, when a law was passed requiring employers of women in stores and factories to provide seats for their use. Legislation concerning the employment of women has centered on such problems as reducing hours of labor, prohibiting night work, limiting the occupations in which women are permitted to work, and providing special working conditions for female labor. At first, this legislation applied only to women employed in manufacturing, but later it was extended to apply to women who worked in stores. Before public indignation was aroused by the Triangle Shirt Waist factory fire in 1910, the preliminary report of the Factory Investigating Commission in 1911, and its final voluminous report in 1915, all legislative measures affecting the employment of women and especially those proposing to prohibit night work were vigorously opposed by employers and others on economic and constitutional grounds. The first law, enacted in 1899, providing for prohibition of night work for women was, in fact, declared unconstitutional by the New York Court of Appeals in 1907. In 1913 the state legislature, in response to the strong urging of the Factory Investigating Commission, again enacted a measure prohibiting night employment for women in factories between the hours of 10 P.M. and 6 A.M. The constitutionality of this law also was tested in the courts, and in 1924, almost ten years after its passage, it was upheld by the United States Supreme Court in the case of *Radice* v. *New York*.

What was true of women workers was substantially true of child labor. A general eight-hour law and prohibition of child labor had been agitated by organized labor since 1850. Beginning in 1869 and for six successive years a child-labor bill was unsuccessfully introduced in the legislature. The compulsory education legislation enacted in the 1870's provided that

all children between eight and fourteen years of age shall attend school at least fourteen weeks of each year, eight of these weeks at least to be consecutive; the employment of a child under fourteen in any business during school hours is forbidden unless the child has attended school at least fourteen weeks out of the fifty-two weeks next preceding the year of employment and presents a certificate so stating to the employer.

The state's penal code provided that any person might be held guilty of a misdemeanor

who having the care or custody of a minor either (1) wilfully causes or permits a minor's life to be endangered, or its health to be injured, or its morals to become depraved; or (2) wilfully causes or permits the minor to be placed in such a situation or to engage in such an occupation that its life is endangered, or its health is likely to be injured, or its morals likely to be impaired.

Neither of these laws were enforced.

Perhaps the first clear-cut bill to regulate child labor was framed by the Society for the Prevention of Cruelty to Children in 1882. It failed, however, to become law. It was not until 1886 that an act providing for the regulation of the employment of women and children in manufacturing establishments, and for the appointment of inspectors to enforce the law, was passed. By the provisions of this act no boy under eighteen years of age and no woman under twenty-one were to be employed in a factory for more than sixty hours a week, unless for the purpose of making necessary repairs. Moreover, the employment of children under thirteen years of age was forbidden. The employer was to keep a register of all children under sixteen and have on file certificates stating their age and birthplace, verified by parent or guardian or by the child himself. This legislation also ran into enforcement difficulties, largely because of self-interest on the part of both parents and employers.

During the 1890's the legislation affecting the employment and working conditions of children was stiffened. Among other things, the hours of labor were reduced to nine a day, employment of children in street trades was regulated, and both the compulsory education law and the factory law were amended to the end that educational requirements were broadened and made more effective. Since World War I child labor legislation has been primarily concerned with advancing the age of entry into employment, raising educational requirements, extending the list of prohibited employments, and strengthening methods of enforcement.

Legislative efforts to put an end to the sweatshop type of homework have not been too successful. The law of 1883 prohibiting the manufacture of cigars in tenement houses was declared unconstitutional. The principal form of regulation has been licensing. The licensing power rests in the hands of the industrial commissioner of the state, who is empowered to determine within what industries conditions may permit of industrial homework. Organized labor, especially in those industries susceptible to sweatshop production, has done much to curtail if not to eliminate such labor.

In the field of labor legislation, the state has made great strides since the beginning of the twentieth century. In fact, legislation which in the 1880's and 1890's would have had no chance of being enacted is now on the statute books. In this respect three pieces of legislation, each designed to afford the worker greater economic security, deserve brief consideration. These are the minimum-wage law and laws providing for compulsory insurance against industrial accident—familiarly known as "workmen's compensation"—and for compulsory insurance against unemployment.

Agitation in the state for fixing minimum wages for women and minors goes back to the beginning of this century. Enthusiasm for such legislation was dampened when, in 1923, the United States Supreme Court in the case of *Adkins* v. *Children's Hospital* declared the minimum-wage law of the District of Columbia to be unconstitutional. Hopes were revived, however, by the impetus labor legislation received from the distressing conditions resulting from the Depression. Furthermore, those who championed governmental control of wages believed that it might be possible to draft an act which would be found to be constitutional. Governor Lehman shared this opinion and, in a special message to the state legislature in 1933, stated, "I am . . . advised by competent constitutional authority that present-day conditions are so changed from those prevailing when the original statute was before the Court, that a mandatory, minimum wage law based on the minimum value of the services rendered might well be upheld by the Supreme Court of the United States."

Accordingly, a minimum-wage law effective April 20, 1933, was enacted, only to be declared unconstitutional by the highest court in 1936 in the case of *Moorehead* v. *New York ex rel. Tipaldo*. In a dissenting opinion Justice Harlan F. Stone (later chief justice) protested against the majority's basing their decision and opinion on their own "economic predilections."

The action of the court in this case precipitated a storm of disapproval and criticism. The issue of the power of a state to enact protective legislation was injected into the presidential campaign of 1936. Proposals to restrict the power of the Supreme Court by constitutional amendment were revived and widely debated. As a consequence, on May 5, 1937, the court overruled its earlier decision, this time holding that the more or less illusory freedom of an individual to bargain with a corporation should be supplemented or even replaced by the protection of the weaker members of society.

New York was the first state in the Union to enact compulsory accident insurance. Passed in 1910 as a result of the report of a legislative investigation (the Wainwright Commission) instituted to inquire into the nature, cause, and consequences of industrial accidents, the Workmen's Compensation Act provided for elective compensation for most industries but compulsory coverage for an enumerated list of hazardous employments. The compulsory feature of the act was promptly declared unconstitutional in 1911 in the now-famous Ives case (*Ives* v. *South Buffalo Ry. Co.*) on the grounds that it conflicted with both the Fourteenth Amendment and the state constitution.

This decree proved to be only a passing rebuff, for in 1913 a special enabling amendment to the state constitution made it possible to enact a new compensation law which became effective January 1, 1914. As with its predecessor, the constitutionality of the act was soon challenged (*Rhemwald* v. *Builders Brick and Supply Co.*). This time, however, the court upheld the legislation. In doing so it explained that injuries sustained by those who perform the manual and mechanical tasks of an industry must be deemed to have been intended by this statute to be made a social risk, a liability of the industry, a charge upon the production cost of the article manufactured or the service rendered.

The compensation law adopted in 1913 had provided that the state supervise the settlement for the injured worker, but under Governor Whitman provision was made for direct settlements between employers and employees. It soon became apparent that the latter was no match for the former in these proceedings, and an investigation instituted by Governor Smith in 1919 revealed that under the revised law underpayments totaled $50,000 for 114 cases. As a result of this investigation, the legislature in the same year restored the original plan for the state's supervision of all settlements for compensation cases. In the ensuing years the types of claims recognized under the law were considerably expanded and the weekly benefits were increased from fifteen to twenty-five dollars.

Since its inception the system of accident insurance has been periodically improved by the increase in standards of compensation, drastic reforms in administration, the development of the State Insurance Fund, and the gradual extension of the list of hazardous occupations to include industries giving rise to occupational diseases.

With the growth in population, increased mechanization, and more efficient management, there was growing evidence even as early as the 1920's, the golden age of American business, of unemployment problems. Efforts in the state to solve or at least alleviate this problem by the passage of unemployment-insurance legislation met with little success at first. In fact, it was not until the impact of the Depression of 1929 made itself felt that the climate of opinion within the state changed sufficiently to enable the proponents of unemployment insurance to make headway. In April 1931 the legislature appointed the Marcy committee, which, after careful study of the whole subject, recommended legislation in the form of individual employer reserves. Taking the view that no additional costs should be imposed on employers until business had substantially improved, the committee held that the time was not ripe for mandatory legislation.

At the same time, Franklin D. Roosevelt, then governor of the state, invited the governors of Massachusetts, Ohio, Pennsylvania, Rhode Island, and New Jersey to confer with him on the common problems of unemployment, relief, and public works. One result of this conference was the creation of an interstate committee on unemployment insurance, composed of representatives of the six governors. In its report this committee advocated compulsory unemployment insurance modeled after the Wisconsin plan.

This recommendation lent strength to the growing demand for legislation. So also did the change in policy of the American Federation of Labor, traditionally opposed to this type of legislation. Further support came when Roosevelt, having moved on from Albany to Washington, appointed a cabinet committee, under the chairmanship of Secretary of Labor Frances Perkins, to draft a federal law. Meanwhile, the New York State Federation of Labor left no stone unturned in its efforts to secure the passage of the desired legislation. Under the impact of this combination of forces, the opposition crumbled, and in April 1935 a compulsory unemployment insurance law was signed by Governor Lehman. Under the provisions of this measure, employers contributed a fixed percentage of their payrolls to a fund from which benefits up to a maximum of fifteen dollars a week were paid to each unemployed worker for a maximum of sixteen weeks in any one year.

In 1930 the state had adopted a state-wide mandatory system of old-age pensions. Although Governor Lehman had on numerous occasions requested the legislature to liberalize the provisions of this system, no action was taken until the Social Security Act made it advantageous for the state to conform to the standards set by the national government. Accordingly, in 1936 the legislature amended the 1930 measure to reduce the minimum age from seventy to sixty-five and to cut the residence requirement from ten years to five out of the nine years preceding the application for assistance. Because these provisions conformed to those of the Social Security Act, the state payments to needy persons over sixty-five were matched by grants from the federal government. Disability insurance, strengthening of the machinery for settling labor-management disputes, and a State Labor Relations Act were also enacted.

During 1954 the state certified unemployment insurance claims totaling over $290,000,000. At the end of the year 1954 the New York State Unemployment Insurance Trust Fund had a balance of $1,267,384,177.

At its session of 1955 the legislature also broadened labor benefits from thirty to thirty-six dollars a week. Coverage of unemployment insurance was extended to employers of three instead of four or more persons, except domestics, and, after December 1, 1956, to firms of two or more employees. Workhours of children under sixteen were reduced from forty-four to forty hours per week in factories and in mercantile and other establishments.

With passing years New York State, like its sister commonwealths, has learned that the efficacy of social legislation depends largely on the quality of its administration. Many of the early labor laws were barren of results because of lack of proper machinery of enforcement. With the growth of population, the increase of the working class, and more favorable public support for labor-industrial legislation came notable advances in the field of administration.

A beginning in this direction was made during the late 1880's, but progress was slow. A real step forward was made in 1890 when eight women deputies were added to the inspection force, and the number periodically increased thereafter. The next major step toward improvement was taken in 1901, when the State Department of Labor was organized through the consolidation of the Bureau of Labor Statistics, the office of the Factory Inspector, and the Board of Mediation and Arbitration.

Another decade elapsed before another landmark was erected. This came as a result of the investigations and recommendations of the State Factory Investigating Commission of 1911 and is known as the Reorganization Act of 1913. By the terms of this act an industrial board was created as a "special legislative agency whose duty was to be the formulation and passage of an industrial code of rules and regulations which should have the force and effect of law." After two years of experience with two coordinate bodies, the Department of Labor and the Industrial Board, the Factory Investigating Commission recommended their consolidation. Consequently, the Industrial Commission assumed charge of the Department of Labor in 1915. Further reorganization occurred during the administration of Governor Miller when, in 1921, the Industrial Commission was replaced with a single commissioner, who was head of the Labor Department. To the department was added an Industrial Board empowered to hear "appeals from orders of the Commissioner issued by him to employers or factory owners directing compliance with various provisions of the Labor Law, and also applications for variations from the provisions of the Labor Law or of the Industrial Code." The volume of these administrative orders has multiplied and they have become as important as the provisions of the legislation. During the last quarter of a century the Department of Labor has grown enormously in size, responsibility, and accomplishment.

One phase of the history of labor development in the state which over the years has attracted more and more attention is the machinery for the settlement of disputes arising between management and labor. This machinery had its beginning when the first Board of Arbitration was set up in 1886. At that time there were few collective bargaining contracts and even fewer provisions in these contracts for arbitration of disputes which might arise. Now almost all of the thousands of agreements provide for arbitration as the final step in grievance procedure.

The New York State Board of Mediation constitutes the present machinery for adjusting disputes between management and labor. It was created "to promote permanent industrial peace and the health, welfare, comfort and safety of the people of the State." It has the duty not only to mediate disputes between unions and employers but also, with the consent of the parties involved in a dispute, to arbitrate their grievances.

The board has seven members, appointed by the governor, who serve on a per diem basis. The board determines general policy, and, on occasion, its members serve individually as mediators and arbitrators. Four district offices are maintained in the state: in New York City, Albany, Buffalo, and Syracuse. Heading each office is a district director; attached to each of these offices is a staff of full-time mediators who regularly act as arbitrators. Each district office maintains a panel of citizens which it may draw upon in the selection of arbitrators. Unquestionably, the work of this board has reduced to a minimum the number of strikes or near-strikes which the state would otherwise have experienced.

Only when one compares the status of labor in the state in 1865 with that of today can he fully appreciate the great strides which have been made in bettering the conditions of employment and elevating the social and economic standards of the worker. Wages in terms of purchasing power have increased, hours have been shortened, greater security has been provided, and the battle for the right of the worker to unionize and bargain collectively has been won. Because of this changed condition, class consciousness is conspicuously absent. Instead of being proletarian, labor in the state is middle class in way of life and, above all, psychologically. Within the state, as elsewhere within the nation, the unity of organized labor was long disrupted by the A.F. of L.–C.I.O. controversy. The mending of this schism in the ranks of organized labor has now been accomplished. It was hastened by the fact that, in last analysis, both sought the same objectives—more money, shorter hours, and greater security for their members. Differences in theory between the two organizations disappeared as the A.F. of L increasingly recognized the need for broad trade—i.e., industry—unionism. Irrespective of A.F. of L. or C.I.O. affiliation, unions in the state, as elsewhere, have openly expressed their opposition to either state or federal legislation which in their opinion sought to weaken them. This accounts for their unanimous criticism of the Taft-Hartley Act. At the same time, no one acquainted with the labor situation in the state could truthfully deny that many unions are today demonstrating a greater sense of responsibility not only to their membership but also to the public welfare than they were a few decades ago.

As evidence of the growing tendency in this direction the results accomplished by Local No. 3 of the International Brotherhood of Electrical Workers should be noted. During the early 1930's this New York City local had the reputation of being one of the most irresponsible in America. Under new and enlightened leadership the union began in 1933 to change its tactics. Labor management warfare was replaced by labor-management teamwork. A Joint Industry Board of the Electrical Industry was set up with twenty-four directors—twelve from the union and twelve from the employing contractors—with an employer as chairman.

Established in 1939, the Joint Board, or "the team" as it is known, has accomplished results that are many and widespread; strikes have ceased, wages have been increased, working conditions are vastly improved, an unhappy and inefficient working force has been transformed into one whose efficiency and production are second to none, a twenty-million dollar housing development has been sponsored by a pension fund, a rest home for members of the union has been established at Southampton, Long Island, dental and medical clinics have been set up, and a generous scholarship program for the sons and daughters of the members of the union has been created. Meanwhile the union has expanded its membership from six to thirty thousand in the state.

Similarly, the International Ladies' Garment Workers' Union has made enormous strides in demonstrating what a labor union can accomplish, not only for the benefit of its membership but for the promotion of the public welfare. Its educational program, dating back to the early 1920's, its interest in political liberalism, manifested in its support of the Liberal party in the State, and its most recent ventures into the field of slum clearance and better housing are evidence of its sense of public responsibility.

Labor's future in New York State will depend in large measure upon this growing evidence of trade-union maturity and responsibility and upon the economic prosperity of those within the state who employ labor.

From Towpath to Airway

It is hard for us today to realize how very widely communities were separated from one another when they depended for transportation wholly on the railroad and the horse and wagon—and when telephones were still scarce, and radios non-existent. A town which was not situated on a railroad was really remote. . . . No wonder that each region, each town, each farm was far more dependent upon its own resources—its own produce, social contacts, amusements—than in later years.—FREDERICK LEWIS ALLEN

FEW of those who participated in the ceremonies marking the formal opening of the Erie Canal foresaw that within a half century its primacy as a carrier would be challenged by the railroad and, later, by the motor carrier.

The railroad industry of New York reached maturity as well as supremacy in the field of transportation in the period between 1865 and 1900. By the latter date approximately 90 per cent of the mileage of all railway construction within the state had been completed and the great railway systems had come into being. Long before the end of the century most of the short lines constructed in the 1860's and early 1870's in response to the enthusiastic demand on the part of localities in every part of the state had been absorbed by the New York Central, the Erie, the Lehigh Valley, the Delaware, Lackawanna, and Western, and the Delaware and Hudson. The New York Central, expanding rapidly within as well as outside the borders of New York, was, by 1900, running trains to Manhattan Island, Montreal, St. Louis, and Chicago. During this period the railroad corporations were the most important aggregations of capital in the state, exerting strong influence upon both state and local governments. By the end of the century the flamboyant freebooters and construction giants of the age of promotion were already giving way to technically trained managers and persuasive spokesmen for Wall Street.

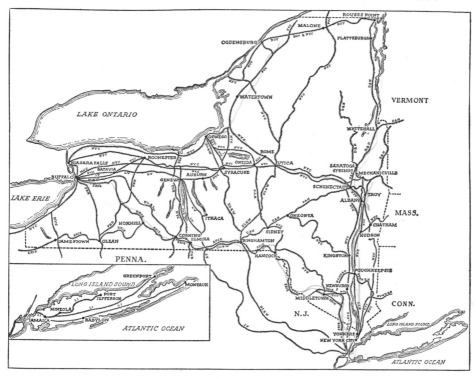

Map 13. Main railroad lines of New York State today.
D & H—Delaware and Hudson; DL & W—Delaware, Lackawanna and Western; ERIE—Erie; LI—Long Island; LV—Lehigh Valley; NYC—New York Central; NYNH & H—New York, New Haven and Hartford; NYO—New York, Ontario and Western; PRR—Pennsylvania; RUT—Rutland

Two companies—the New York Central and the Erie—were well established by 1860, but there remained the task of constructing the network of capillary lines needed to nourish the main arteries, to stimulate industry and trade in small and more remote towns, and to encourage commercial agriculture in the isolated counties of the state. By 1900 over 5,400 miles of new track were added to the 2,682 miles constructed by 1860.

Most communities were willing to take drastic, indeed desperate, measures to attract a railroad. When private capitalists proved reluctant to finance the lateral lines threading through the north-south valleys, citizens along the route rushed to bond their townships. No less than 310 cities, towns, and villages in fifty-five counties granted $36,888,190 in cash or municipal bonds to eighty-five railroad companies. Throughout the state, farmers were eager for rail service. Businessmen, fearing isolation and consequent economic loss, were equally enthusiastic. Many of them hoped that the lateral lines would enable their communities to secure cheap coal from Pennsylvania. Rochester, for example, subscribed over $1,000,000 to two railroad lines leading to the coal fields.

The Panic of 1873 bankrupted many companies and brought construction to a halt. In many instances bondholders brought foreclosure action. With some exceptions, towns and villages lost their holdings in the process of reorganization, inasmuch as their capital stock had inferior standing to the bonds representing the funded debt of the roads. Several towns attempted to repudiate their debts on the ground that the promoters had defrauded the stockholders. Their search for legal technicalities that would enable them to wiggle out of the debt were unavailing. With few exceptions, the courts, and especially the federal courts, upheld the rights of the bona fide bondholders.

So loud was the outcry against the misuse of local aid that the Constitutional Commission of 1872–1873 recommended the prohibition of such aid in the future. After the ratification of the amendment in 1874, railroad promoters had to rely upon private sources for capital. Economic recovery was so rapid in the late 1870's, however, that plenty of capital became available for railroad construction.

Several trunk-line railroads connecting metropolitan New York with Buffalo were completed after 1860. Two of the anthracite coal roads— the Delaware, Lackawanna, and Western and the Lehigh Valley—realized their ambitions of expanding from small local roads into trunk lines competing for the through freight between New York and the Great Lakes. The D.L. and W., swollen with Civil War profits, acquired terminal facilities in Newark and Hoboken as well as thousands of acres of rich coal lands. By leasing several short lines, it reached the port of Oswego in 1869. It then freed itself from dependence upon the Erie by completing its own line from Binghamton to Buffalo in 1882.

The Lehigh Valley struck eastward to the terminals of Jersey City and northward to Lake Ontario, which it reached by taking over several bankrupt companies, including the Geneva and Ithaca and the Ithaca and Athens. For a time the Lehigh assigned its freight to and from the West to the Erie Railroad at Waverly. This arrangement, however, proved unsatisfactory because the Erie went out of its way to keep for itself most of the through traffic. In 1892 the Lehigh extended its line westward from Geneva to Buffalo, thus affording this lake port another through connection with the port of New York.

The collapse of the Oswego Midland in 1873 brought despair to the thousands of individuals and scores of townships along its route. Perhaps no other major road in New York had less chance for success. Portions of its route from Oswego to Oneida to Norwich and thence to Jersey City ran through a sparsely populated countryside. After reorganization, the road took the name of New York, Ontario, and Western, but the change of name did not bring the road prosperity.

The West Shore, extending up the west bank of the Hudson and paralleling the New York Central across the state, was the result of speculative daring. Although promoters had planned it for many years, it was not until 1880 that the banker Edward Winslow succeeded in enlisting the support of George Pullman and other wealthy capitalists including (probably) Jay Gould. Once the project was under way, the interests behind the Pennsylvania Railroad, principal rival of the New York Central, offered their aid.

Furious at what he deemed to be a plot against the Central, William H. Vanderbilt—who had succeeded his father, the famous Commodore, as president of the Central—declared war on his enemies by slashing rates. In 1884, the unfinished West Shore went bankrupt. Its receivers tried to force Vanderbilt to buy the bankrupt property, threatening another rate war. Vanderbilt, still smarting from the stiff price he had just paid for the New York, Chicago, and St. Louis which paralleled that part of the New York Central system south of Lake Erie—so stiff that he is said to have thought the rails must be made of nickel plate—refused. In the rate war which ensued, Vanderbilt not only matched every reduction made by his rival but carried the war into the enemy camp by investing heavily in the South Pennsylvania Company, a rival of the Pennsylvania. In this move he was joined by Andrew Carnegie, the Rockefellers, and other capitalists, who were anxious to break the tight monopoly of the Pennsylvania Railroad.

This bitter conflict, which threatened to ruin both the Central and the Pennsylvania and to demoralize all railroad securities, was terminated only when J. P. Morgan, Sr., hurried home from England and succeeded in inducing the warring parties to make peace. As a consequence, the Pennsylvania took over the South Pennsylvania, and Chauncey M. Depew, attorney for the Central, leased the West Shore. Shortly thereafter the latter road was sold at foreclosure to parties acting for the Central; the bondholders received fifty cents on the dollar for their claims. The Central promptly leased the road for 475 years. Vanderbilt thus acquired, at the bargain price of $2,000,000 in annual interest charges, another route to Buffalo which has proven useful in freight carriage.

The Delaware and Hudson, originally a canal company, became the third most important railroad system in New York. Scarcely had the Albany and Susquehanna Company completed its road from Albany to Binghamton in 1869 when the Delaware and Hudson Canal Navigation Company and the Erie sought control of this important link. Rival boards of directors armed with conflicting decrees from pliant judges sent out armed bands to seize control of the track. After much bickering, the Delaware and Hudson faction made good its claims. The company also acquired many small lines north of Albany and extended the road up the western shore of Lake Champlain to Plattsburgh, from whence a line was constructed to Montreal.

The Rome, Watertown, and Ogdensburg was the most important railroad in the north country in 1861. Its managers pushed a line westward to Oswego and acquired a short line from that lake port to Syracuse. When the Lake Ontario Shore Railroad was sold at auction in 1875, the directors of the Rome, Watertown, and Ogdensburg could not resist the temptation to acquire this line, which certain Oswego enthusiasts had pushed toward Rochester along the southern rim of Lake Ontario. Far from increasing the prosperity of the Watertown road, the new property dragged it into bankruptcy.

In 1882 Charles Parsons, a capitalist interested in the north country, captured control of the Watertown road, and in 1886 he absorbed his only rival in that region, the Utica and Black River, which had thrust northward to Ogdensburg in 1878 and had also made direct connection with Watertown. Parsons' system boasted half the mileage of the New York Central within the state. Fearing that Parsons would build a line from Rome eastward to Mechanicville and there make connections with the Fitchburg line of Massachusetts, the managers of the New York Central in 1891 leased the 643-mile Parsons system. About this same time Dr. W. Seward Webb, a son-in-law of William H. Vanderbilt, bought control of the Herkimer, Newport, and Poland, a tiny narrow-gauge line running northward from Herkimer. Webb pushed his line through the Adirondacks to Malone, where another company thrust a prong through to Montreal. Late in 1892 parlor and sleeping cars were running from New York to Buffalo to Montreal over this route. These satellites of the New York Central eventually lost their corporate form and became absorbed into the mother system.

The Long Island Railroad was originally laid out to facilitate the through passenger traffic between New York and Boston via Greenport and ferry to Stonington, Connecticut. It failed to serve most of the communities on the island and missed some of the more fertile agricultural regions. Oliver Charlick, president of the company between 1863 and 1874, seemed intent only on money-making, to the disgust of many communities. Citizens along the south shore backed a new South Side Railroad in 1866 and communities along the north shore promoted several short lines. Rate wars brought ruin to most of the companies, including the Long Island. During the 1880's the system got back on its feet, especially as the summer recreation industry developed, and the management built several branches to serve new communities. The Long Island needed an entrance into Manhattan Island and secured it from the legislature in 1899. The next year the Long Island Railroad became part of the Pennsylvania system.

Cornelius Vanderbilt rapidly became the outstanding figure in New York railroads in the period after 1860. A half century of experience in the rough school of shipping had sharpened his native shrewdness and had brought him one of the largest fortunes of the time. As his steamship lines expanded, the Commodore took more interest in the railroads serving the various ports. In the 1850's Vanderbilt acquired a large interest in the New York and Harlem Railroad. By 1863 he also owned a large block of shares in the Hudson River Railroad. Skillfully, he fought off raids by "bears" who tried to depress the value of Harlem Railroad shares by abrogating its franchises.

Relations between the New York Central and the Hudson River Railroad were not cordial. The Central, guided by the politically powerful Erastus Corning, held a whip hand over the Hudson River company. It could and did throw much eastbound business to the steamboats at Albany during the season of navigation. When ice choked the river, the Central would send its freight and passengers to the Vanderbilt line, forcing it to keep additional locomotives and freight cars on hand.

Corning and his close associate and successor, Dean Richmond, appealed to Vanderbilt in 1864 to help them prevent another faction from getting control of the Central. In exchange, Richmond granted to the Vanderbilt road a pro rata share of through freight rates and also an annual bonus of $100,000. A new faction headed by William Fargo and Henry Keep got control of the Central soon after the death of Richmond. These gentlemen canceled the agreement, whereupon the Commodore struck back hard. Vanderbilt announced on January 14, 1867, that his railroad would not accept through tickets on freight or passengers from the New York Central. As a result eastbound freight piled up at the Albany warehouse and passengers were forced to clamber across the river ice carrying their baggage. Indignation ran high, but the old Commodore pressed his advantage. Finally the Central agreed to furnish as much freight to the Hudson River Railroad as it received and to prorate the tariffs.

Vanderbilt in late 1867 won over a majority of the board of directors of the New York Central and two years later he combined his two railroads. Vanderbilt also secured control of the Lake Shore, which ran westward from Buffalo toward Chicago, but his attempts to gain control of the Erie (described in Chapter 27) were not successful.

Vanderbilt and his able son, William, took a keen interest in improving the operations of his railroads. He constructed the huge Grand Central Terminal at Forty-second Street in Manhattan and, under civic pressure, began the tedious and costly job of lowering the tracks on Park Avenue, north to Ninety-sixth Street. In 1873 he borrowed enough money to lay another set of double tracks across the state west from Albany. In general, Vanderbilt paid little attention to the manipulation of securities, which activity occupied the energies of so many railroad magnates of his day. To be sure, Vanderbilt did not hesitate to declare a stock dividend of 80 per cent, and on occasion he operated pools in Wall Street. His blunt speech and rough and piratical tactics did not endear him to the public, which envied his wealth and feared his power. As the largest corporation in the state, the New York Central had to take a hand in politics not only to secure privileges but also to fend off attacks, such as proposals for regulatory commissions.

By the middle 1870's the era of lavish public assistance to the railroads was over. The enthusiasm for railroads so evident in pre-Civil War years gave way to indifference and in many instances to open hostility. Labor leaders, antimonopolists, land reformers, and shippers of all kinds began to be increasingly critical of railroad rates and other aspects of management. The activities of Drew, Fisk, and Gould, in connection with the Erie (see Chapter 27) and the large number of railroad bankruptcies and reorganizations which usually benefited insiders at the expense of farmers, merchants, and other taxpayers, were influential factors in the change. Exorbitant charges plus rate discriminations were prime factors in rousing hostility. The climax came, as already noted, in 1872, when the United States Supreme Court ruled that counties, townships, cities, and villages were fully liable for all debts contracted to foster railroad building.

Wherever there was competition between two or more railroads within the state there were rate wars. Especially was this true in the 1870's, when the various trunk lines began to carry grain from Buffalo, Chicago, and other western points. Each railroad did its utmost to secure as large a proportion of the grain-carrying business as possible. After several disastrous rate wars, followed by poorly kept agreements to maintain rates, the presidents of four trunk lines—the New York Central, the Erie, the Pennsylvania, and the Baltimore and Ohio—affixed their signatures to the famous agreement of April 5, 1877, which has survived with minor modifications, temporary suspensions, frequent evasions, and intermittent attacks. The heart of this agreement provided that export rates from Chicago to Philadelphia and Baltimore should be two cents and three cents per one hundred pounds, respectively, below the rate for New York. Equally important was the decision by these four railroads to set up machinery for enforcement of the compact. All traffic westward was to be pooled.

A storm of criticism greeted this agreement, which undoubtedly gave impetus to the establishment of a state commission in 1882 to investigate railroad practices and to the creation of the Federal Interstate Commerce Commission in 1887. To both of the commissions the railroads made token compliance, but despite the continuance of popular protest high rates and secret agreements continued. Indeed, not until the passage of the Hepburn Act in 1906, giving the Interstate Commerce Commission more effective control over railroad rates, was the door opened to the solving of this most vexing of railroad abuses.

During the last half century the railroads of the state have spent millions of dollars on improvements. Roadbeds have been widened and better ballasted; curves eliminated; greater care has been exercised in the selection and preservation of the wooden ties to which the rails are anchored. "Tie plates" of iron or steel have been placed between the rail and the tie to lengthen the life of the tie and to prevent shearing of the spikes which fasten the rail to the tie. Heavier steel rails have been substituted for the lighter and much less durable rails. Gigantic bridges of steel and concrete have replaced lighter structures.

Better roadbeds and improved trackage have made possible larger and heavier rolling stock. The passenger car of the mid-twentieth century, for example, is vastly different from the long wooden car of the 1880's with its raised roof, its crude wood- or coal-burning stoves, and its kerosene or gas lights.

Facilities for the handling of freight have also been greatly improved. Indeed, the crudely constructed open cars and boxcars, mounted and with a capacity of three to five tons, were playthings in comparison with the fifty-ton-capacity freight cars of today. Today all of our coal cars and an increasing percentage of our boxcars are made of pressed steel. With the increase in industrial specialization, carriers have varied their equipment. There are now cars for special kinds of freight ranging from containers for gases under high pressure to specially designed refrigerator cars.

Heavier trains, both freight and passenger, made heavier demands on motive power. As a consequence, heavier and heavier steam locomotives were built. In 1914 the Baldwin Locomotive Works delivered to the Erie a Triplex Articulated locomotive with twenty-four drivers. This engine weighed 853,050 pounds. In recent years electric and Diesel engines have displaced the steam locomotive.

Shifts in both industry and population within the state have led to the abandonment of some feeder lines. On the other hand, the rejuvenation of mining in certain Adirondack areas has occasioned some new construction. Even so, the railway mileage within the state was less in 1955 than in 1900. The bankruptcy of the New York, Ontario, and Western and its recent abandonment of operations are the latest evidence that railway mileage in the state is decreasing.

During the last seventy-five years the railroads of the state have been threatened by other means of transportation: the electric railway, the automobile, aircraft, and water transport.

The application of electricity to transportation dates back to the late 1880's, when Lieutenant Frank J. Sprague successfully operated electrically propelled cars by means of an overhead trolley, over the street railway tracks of Richmond, Virginia. No sooner had the success of this new method of transportation been demonstrated than a veritable craze for "trolley lines" within the state ensued. Not only were they cheap to construct and maintain, but they were faster, cleaner, and more remunerative. By the end of the century most of the cities of the state had installed the new system, and the tempo of urban transit was revolutionized.

Although the managers of the Erie, the New York Central, the Delaware and Hudson and the other steam railroads of the state were greatly interested in this new means of transportation and regarded it as a most useful substitute for the old-fashioned and slow moving city horsecar, few of them foresaw it as a competitor of their own lines. By the turn of the century, however, it was rapidly extending into the suburbs and even linking interurban communities. By 1910 most of the towns in the more thickly settled regions of the state were connected with newly constructed electric railways, as Map 14 indicates. Over four thousand miles were built by the one hundred companies that were organized.

The effect of the electric railway upon the railroads is difficult of meas-

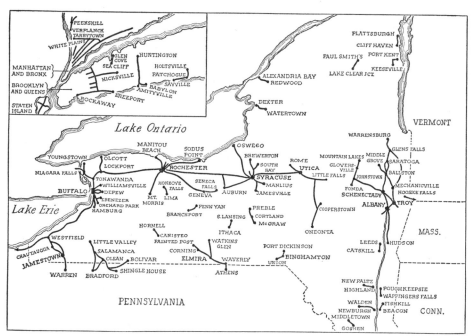

Map 14. Electric railways in New York, 1910. (Adapted from Stephen A. McGuire, *Empire State Trackage*, New York, 1938.)

urement. Some of the area served by the electric lines had not been tapped by the steam roads, and the traffic, therefore, was noncompetitive. Where the electric lines paralleled the steam roads, however, and especially where the electric lines attempted to equal or excel their steam rivals in frequency, comfort, and convenience of service, their adverse effect was felt in passenger, express, and light freight business. To meet this competition, the older roads had recourse to fare reductions, elimination of unused cars, fewer passenger trains, improved service, agreements with their competitors, or outright purchase of the electric lines.

But the competitive threat of the electric railway to the railroads proved to be only temporary, for, like the horsecar which it replaced, it was only a stage in the evolution of American transportation. By the beginning of World War I it reached its zenith and was on the decline. Spokesmen for the electric railways maintained that the extravagant demands of labor, the high cost of raw materials, inability to secure capital at reasonable rates, the evils of government regulation, and, above all, motor vehicle competition, were responsible for the decline. This did not tell the full story. The electric railways were suffering just as the steam railroads had long suffered from overexpansion, overcapitalization, and gross manipulation. Especially was this true in New York City, where financial buccaneers of the type of William C. Whitney and Thomas Fortune Ryan, and lesser promoters, using methods strikingly similar to those employed by Jay Gould, literally plundered many of the electric railway properties. Unquestionably the methods employed by Whitney and Ryan were largely responsible for the development of the movement which ultimately led to the public ownership and operation of the city's elevated and subway lines in the twentieth century.

Had there been no jobbery and mismanagement of the electric lines, the coming of the motorcar, bus, and truck would have brought their doom anyway. Like so many other products of the machine age, the motor vehicle passed through an embryonic experimental stage. The motor industry was not sufficiently important in 1899 to be listed in the federal census under a separate heading. Everywhere doubt was expressed as to its real worth. Some thought it might be useful for military purposes; others were of the opinion that at best it was an expensive toy —a "plaything of the rich." The few who dared prophesy that the day was not far distant when thousands of motor vehicles per year would be produced were held up to scorn and ridicule. But doubts as to the practicability of the automobile did not discourage its makers, and during the two decades following 1900 enormous strides were made. Handicraft methods gave way to standardization and mass production. Mechanical improvements by the thousands were made: in materials and construction, spring suspension, chassis design, tire construction, steering devices, starting apparatus, and electrical equipment. The breakdowns and uncertainties so characteristic of earlier years were greatly minimized. The vestiges of bicycle and buggy design were eliminated. Continued competition, skilled manufacturing technique, consideration for the pocketbook of persons of different economic levels, high-pressure salesmanship, and the use of the installment-purchase plan were the principal factors which made people, irrespective of their social status, motor-conscious.

Mechanical imperfections and resultant breakdowns were not the only difficulties that confronted the pioneer motorist. The roads over which he had to drive were frequently abominable. With the exception of isolated stretches, the highways of the state were little better in 1890 than at the close of the Civil War. After the craze for plank roads which swept the state in the 1850's almost nothing was done in the way of highway improvement. Construction and maintenance rested almost entirely in the hands of local, town, or road-district commissioners and roadmasters who had neither the money nor the competence to build all-weather roads. Farmers usually paid their road taxes by personal and team labor on the highways. During the winter roads were usually clogged with snow, and in summer were either clouds of dust or seas of mud. At all times they were rutted, uneven, and dangerous for the motorist. With the coming of the bicycle and more particularly, the motor vehicle, the demand for better highways gathered momentum.

One of the first steps in the interest of better roads was taken by the League of American Wheelmen, a group of bicyclists. Organized in 1880, it carried on an incessant campaign for improved roads through its magazine, *Good Roads*, which had a wide circulation. In 1887 the legislature enacted the "Liberty Bill" granting Wheelmen the right to use the highways. Bicycle paths were also authorized by local units of government.

During the 1890's the demand for better roads increased in volume and enlisted the support of many political spokesmen. The state government, however, took no important action prior to 1900. Only the counties adjacent to the larger cities, notably in the New York metropolitan area, actually constructed some hard-surfaced roads before the beginning of the twentieth century. Water-bound macadam and gravel were first used but soon gave way to bituminous macadam. Little or no effort was made in these early days to eliminate curves, to widen the roadways, or to cut down hills and knolls. The "improved roads" in the state in 1890 were merely the traditional roads with a hard surface.

But the increasing use of the motor vehicle made better roads imperative. The table below, giving the number of motor registrations between 1915 and 1955, indicates the phenomenal rise in the use of automobiles.

Table 17. Motor vehicle registrations, 1915–1955, for passenger cars, buses, trucks.*

Year	New York	United States
1915	255,000	2,491,000
1920	676,000	9,239,000
1925	1,626,000	19,491,000
1930	2,308,000	26,532,000
1935	2,331,000	26,230,000
1940	2,743,000	32,025,000
1945	2,330,000	30,638,000
1950	3,693,000	48,567,000
1955	4,787,087	61,334,000

* These registrations include all types of motor vehicles other than motorcycles.

Source: *Statistical Abstract of the United States, 1951;* State of New York, Department of Taxation and Finance, Bureau of Motor Vehicles. *Motor Vehicle and Motorcycle Registrations . . . for the Year 1955; Britannica Book of the Year, 1956.*

In 1956 approximately 5,000,000 licenses were issued by the state. To accommodate this huge number of vehicles, the state has a complex road system of 103,000 miles ranging in quality from the Thruway, the landscaped parkways, and modern urban arterial routes to the dirt roads still untouched, at this writing, by the state's town-road improvement program, launched in 1950. When broken down into categories the state's highway mileage in the mid-1950's is roughly as follows:

	Miles
State hard surfaced highways	14,000
Urban arterial roads	601
County roads	18,000
Town roads	54,000
Parkways	279
City streets	11,300
Village streets	3,800

Because of the scarcity of funds during the Depression of the 1930's, the scarcity of materials and manpower during World War II, and the phenomenal increase in automobile ownership since the war, many of the highways of the state are unequal to the present demands of traffic, which is now growing at the rate of 11 per cent annually. Moreover, many of the older state highways are in bad repair and must be rebuilt. In 1954 the State Temporary Commission on Highway Finance Planning proposed the expenditure of $2,886,200,000 for the next ten years. The greater part of this sum will be used for the improvement of 5,600 miles of state highways, 7,500 miles of county roads, 14,000 miles of town roads, 192 miles of parkways, and the elimination of 56 grade crossings. New

York's share of the $33,480,000,000 appropriated by Congress in the mid-1950's for highway building totals $451,300,000.

To ease the situation, after several false starts a 427-mile toll pike known as the Thruway, between New York City and Buffalo, was built by the Thruway Authority. Most of the route was open to motorists by 1955. Spurs projected to New England and Massachusetts turnpikes, to Niagara Falls and the Pennsylvania state line from Buffalo, and to New Jersey's Turnpike and Garden State Parkway, will bring the total length of the Thruway to 564 miles. Paralleling the Hudson River to Albany and the route of the Erie Canal across the state, the Thruway and its connections,

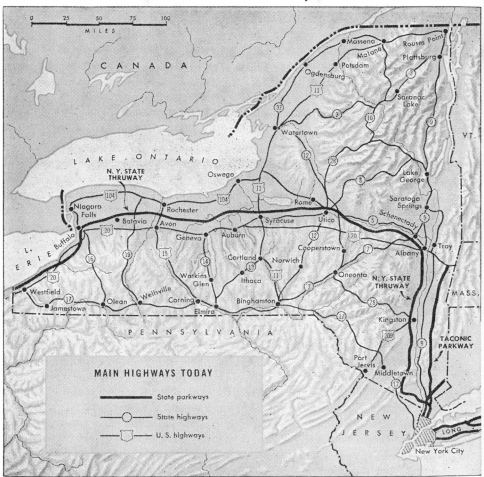

Map 15. Main highways of New York State today. (By Harold K. Faye from *Exploring New York* by Wainger, Furman and Oagley, © 1956 by Harcourt, Brace and Company, Inc.)

when completed, will serve the most densely populated and the richest agricultural and industrial area of the state. Its long-range effects for business, industry, agriculture, and recreation may be even more revolutionary than were those of the canal and the railroad which preceded it.

Wholly apart from its social and economic aspects the Thruway represents one of the most gigantic engineering feats in the history of the state. The Tappan Zee Bridge across the Hudson between Tarrytown and South Nyack is a great engineering undertaking in itself. Four other major bridges and hundreds of small spans had to be built. Across Onondaga Lake Outlet, northwest of Syracuse, a three-span girder bridge of 450 feet was constructed; southwest of Rochester a 304-foot cantilever bridge spans the historic Genesee River. In the Herkimer area of the Mohawk Valley there are two more big bridges—one spans the New York Central Railroad tracks and U.S. Highway 5, and the second is over the Barge Canal and the Mohawk River. These bridges are, from the point of view of engineering, companion pieces to the beautiful George Washington Bridge, the vehicular tubes under the Hudson connecting New York and New Jersey, and the Triborough Bridge and the other remarkable engineering accomplishments which have done so much to transform the New York City metropolitan area.

In addition to the Thruway, Governors Lehman and Dewey proposed the construction of four superhighways to be integrated with the Thruway and built to Thruway standards. These expressways, if built, will parallel existing routes for a distance of approximately eight hundred miles. Two of these will follow north-south routes. One will extend from the Thruway at Albany to the Canadian border at Rouses Point, paralleling Route 9 and serving Saratoga Springs, Glens Falls, Plattsburgh, and the Adirondack region. A second would extend from Binghamton and Elmira on the south to Syracuse. A third expressway would replace or parallel

Route 17 between Harriman and Binghamton and thence westward to Dunkirk. The fourth would extend from the New York City line sixty miles eastward to Riverhead, Long Island.

Access to Greater New York was made easier after World War I by a series of outstanding engineering feats. These included the stately George Washington Bridge over the Hudson from 180th Street to New Jersey. Designed by the architect Cass Gilbert and completed in 1931, it is one of the longest suspension bridges in the world. The Triborough Bridge Authority, established as an independent self-supporting corporation in 1933, completed the four-span Triborough Bridge connecting the Bronx, Manhattan, and Queens in 1937 and the beautiful Bronx Whitestone Bridge farther up Long Island Sound in 1939. At the mid-twentieth century plans were under way to bridge the Narrows, thus connecting Brooklyn with Staten Island.

Robert Moses, one of the state's most distinguished public servants, as head of the Hendrick Hudson Parkway Authority completed the Henry Hudson Bridge at the northern tip of Manhattan in the 1930's. Also, under his direction, four-lane superhighways were built along the east and west sides of Manhattan and through the other boroughs to connect with parkways of Long Island and those extending northward and eastward through Westchester. The entrance of the Thruway into New York City also opened up a new and much-needed artery with the rest of the state.

To further increase the city's accessibility, three great vehicular tunnels were built. The Holland Tunnel, commenced by the states of New York and New Jersey at the end of World War I and completed in 1927, connects lower Manhattan with Jersey City. The first of the three tubes of Lincoln Tunnel from New Jersey to midtown Manhattan was opened in 1937, the Queens-Midtown Tunnel to Long Island City in 1940, and the Brooklyn-Battery Tunnel in 1949. Most of these tunnels and bridges are financed by tolls.

Flanked to the west and north by two of the Great Lakes and the St. Lawrence River, bisected by the Barge Canal and the Hudson River, and terminating in the south with America's greatest harbor, New York State has an abundance of waterways which are among its richest commercial assets.

Between 1865 and 1914 the American merchant marine flourished on the Great Lakes and in the protected coasting trade but slumped badly on the high seas, where by 1914, the percentage of imports and exports carried under the American flag, on the basis of value of the world's cargo, had fallen to only 9.7. The reasons for this remarkable drop from approximately 75 per cent in the 1850's are to be attributed in part to a lag in American technological progress in shipbuilding and partly to the higher cost of building and operating ships under the American flag.

The coastal and intercoastal shipping of New York City grew tremendously during the last half of the nineteenth century.[1] From Maine came spruce for piling, lime for industry, brownstone for new residences, granite for government buildings, ice for slaughterhouses. From the southern ports came shiploads of cotton, which New York City merchants distributed in every direction. Anthracite coal came overland to the Jersey shore by rail, but most bituminous coal came by barge or collier from the

[1] Coastal trade includes traffic movement between the state's ports (primarily the port of New York) and other Atlantic ports. Intercoastal shipments cover trade with Gulf and Pacific ports and with territories and possessions of the United States.

coal ports of Virginia. Coastwise schooners and steamboats carried from the piers of Manhattan a wide assortment of merchandise to other coastal points along the Atlantic and the Gulf. The development of north-south rail lines attracted passengers and high-priced goods, but prior to 1900 the bulky products were mainly waterborne.

Steamships on Long Island Sound remained formidable competitors of the railroads throughout the nineteenth century. Businessmen going between New York and Boston preferred to patronize the overnight steamships since they could spend a full day in either city and reach their destination the next morning without experiencing the discomforts of poorly ventilated sleeping cars. Competition between the various lines kept rates low for both freight and passengers. In 1881 the major contestants came to an agreement and fixed rates. Furthermore, the New York, New Haven, and Hartford system in the 1890's absorbed many of the railroads leading to the sound and set the rate policies for their steamship affiliates.

During the first half of the twentieth century coastal and intercoastal trade through New York State ports fluctuated greatly. In 1948 it reached an all-time high of 60,000,000 tons, but it fell off the following year to 56,095,000 tons. The major items of coastal and intercoastal trade are bulk commodities, such as petroleum and petroleum products, coal, phosphates, sulphur, sand, and gravel. These materials account in recent years for 70 to 80 per cent of all coastal and intercoastal traffic. The balance is general cargo and includes such commodities as lumber, raw and refined sugar, iron and steel and their products, canned foods, citrus fruits, and paper products. General cargo makes up a larger proportion of intercoastal than of coastal trade.

Ordinarily inbound movements far exceed outbound cargoes in the state's coastwise shipping. Since the state serves a large industrial and consumer market, inbound cargoes consist of heavy bulk commodities for manufacturing processes and foodstuffs for consumption. Outbound freight is less bulky, consisting primarily of manufactured goods.

Although business among coastwise carriers is markedly influenced by the general swing of the business cycle, particularly for goods in the general cargo category, the Depression years had less effect upon the volume of waterborne trade than on freight carried by the railroads. Thus, average tonnage carried by the nation's Class I railroads declined by 29 per cent during the Depression period as compared with a 6 per cent drop in waterborne commerce. During this period of shrinking profit margins, the marine carriers, with comparatively lower rates, were able to retain a larger share of their tonnage. In some instances they attracted a portion of the freight normally carried by the railroads.

Prior to World War II the coastal and intercoastal business of the state, particularly of the port of New York, was sporadic. In 1927 it reached a pre-Depression high of 46,025,000 tons. During the decade of the 1930's it fell to an annual average of 36,171,000 tons, but improvement was evident from 1932 on. In 1941 no less than 70 per cent of the United States merchant marine was operating in coastal services. General cargo carriers at the port of New York maintained an average of 188 monthly sailings, with 239 registered vessels. Sixty ports were served by eleven coastal and nine intercoastal shipping companies.

Despite substantial recovery from the low tonnages handled during the early stages of the Depression, the earnings trend continued to be unfavorable. During the 1930's the steamship companies were caught between the intense rivalry of the railroads and steadily rising terminal costs. According to a survey made by the Port of New York Authority, an administrative control agency, nine steamship lines engaged in general cargo service between the port of New York and other Atlantic and Gulf ports lost over $4,000,000 during the period 1931–1940. When World War II broke out, a large part of the coastal and intercoastal fleet was approaching obsolescence and most shipping companies were in a doubtful financial condition.

During the war, coastal and intercoastal trade was sharply curtailed. Enemy submarine action claimed many ships, and an additional large number was requisitioned by the War Shipping Administration for military use. By 1944 coastal commerce of the port of New York had declined to less than two-fifths of the 1939–1941 average of 42,415,000 tons. Most of the traffic during the war consisted of inbound bulk commodities. General cargo trade on intercoastal lanes was all but suspended. With the cessation of hostilities, two years of transition and adjustment were required for the coastwise shipping companies to regain their prewar level of business, despite continued high production and trade. During and immediately after the war, wages and other voyage expenses, terminal charges, and fuel prices all advanced rapidly. In addition, the railroads were in many instances able to hold on to business acquired during the war by successfully competing on routes paralleling those of water carriers.

Coastwise traffic in 1947 exceeded the prewar tonnage. General cargo vessels in use were larger and faster than prewar models but fewer in number. The decline in the port of New York's coastwise tonnage in 1949 was occasioned by a trade recession and proved to be only temporary. By the close of the year 1950 the tonnage trend was again upward.

In the course of the last one hundred years important changes have taken place in the Lake marine of the state. Many of these occurred during the last half of the nineteenth century. Among these were the shift from sail to steam, the trend from wooden to steel ships, the growth of the "long trade" from Lake Superior to Lake Erie ports, and the relative decline in short coastal trips.

During the 1850's steam-propelled vessels drove most of the sailing vessels out of the passenger and high-class freight business. After 1860 operators swung over to the propeller-driven ships, which were more economical than the sidewheelers. During the 1870's the railroads slashed rates so drastically that most of the passenger traffic and a good share of the grain freight deserted the Lake vessels. The shipping interests fought back by building larger steam barges, capable of carrying one thousand tons and towing a sailing vessel as well. By 1890 the shipyards were beginning to shift from wood to steel. Gradually steel ships and barges became predominant.

Several factors were responsible for the growth of the Lake traffic. These include the rapid expansion of the winter wheat belt, the construction and enlargement of the Sault Ste. Marie Canal, and the rise of the iron-ore traffic from the Mesabi range in Minnesota. New York State enjoys only a portion of the Great Lakes trade, but as early as 1907 Buffalo was first among all the Lake ports in actual tonnage received. The seaborne traffic of Buffalo and other state ports located on Lakes Erie and Ontario will, in all probability, be greatly increased by the St. Lawrence Seaway project.

During the last half century the volume of the Lake traffic, both foreign and domestic, has depended in large measure on the volume of steel production and the size of the grain harvest. In 1932, for example, when the nation's steel production was only at 20 per cent of capacity, domestic lakewise traffic at the port of Buffalo dwindled to 5,957,000 tons. With a 70-per-cent increase in steel production the following year, the port's Lake traffic increased by 55 per cent. Shippers operating out of the major Lake ports in New York State in 1949 carried approximately 12 per cent of all the waterborne trade in the state. Buffalo, one of the five largest lake ports in the United States, handled 78 per cent of the state's Lake tonnage. Buffalo's favorable location at the eastern extremity of Lake Erie and the western terminus of the New York State Barge Canal makes it an important point of transshipment. Other New York State ports handling a significant volume of lakewise commerce include Oswego, Rochester, and Great Sodus Bay—all on Lake Ontario.

At mid-century Lake trade with Canada amounted to approximately 14 per cent of total Lake traffic. This water trade, however, constitutes only a small proportion of the total trade between New York State and Canada. In terms of value, about 97 per cent of the foreign trade passing through the Buffalo customs district in 1948 was transported by rail and by means other than water. Canadian Lake traffic consists largely of incoming grains, iron ore, and stone products and outgoing bituminous coal and coke. Foreign commerce on the Lakes in 1949 was below prewar levels, due in part to changes in the destination of grain consignments. In recent years Canadian lower Lake ports have been receiving more Dominion grain than ports on the American side. Consequently, Buffalo, which for three-quarters of a century was prominent as the gateway through which Canadian grains flowed to the seaboard, has been receiving less than its former share.

About four-fifths of the Lake commerce consists of cargo shipments between United States Lake ports; in 1949 this domestic freight totaled 19,590,000 tons. Buffalo handled 88 per cent of this tonnage. Almost 40 per cent of the port of Buffalo's freight receipts in 1948 consisted of iron ore and 17 per cent of bituminous coal. Grains, largely wheat and some corn, oats, barley, and rye, represented 16 per cent of incoming cargoes and limestone 13 per cent. Lakewise shipments from Buffalo to other United States ports are also concentrated among a handful of bulk items —iron and coal represented 45 per cent of outgoing cargoes, anthracite coal 35 per cent, and petroleum and its products 10 per cent. Buffalo, however, is primarily a receiving port, its receipts being ten times as large as its shipments in 1948.

Exclusive of the Great Lakes traffic the state has considerable internal and local traffic on its major rivers and canals. During 1949 eight of the larger ports of the state handled a million tons of local traffic.

The length of New York's entire canal system including canalized lakes and rivers exceeds eight hundred miles. In addition to Lake Champlain and the Hudson River, the system consists of four principal divisions: (1) the Champlain Canal from Troy on the Hudson River to Whitehall on Lake Champlain; (2) the Erie Canal from Waterford on the Hudson to Buffalo on Lake Erie; (3) the Oswego Canal, from the Erie Canal at Three Rivers, northwest of Syracuse, to Oswego on Lake Ontario; (4) the Cayuga and Seneca Canal from the Erie Canal at Montezuma to Ithaca on Cayuga Lake and to Montour Falls and Watkins Glen on Seneca Lake.

Transportation on the canals of the state has had its ups and downs. Prior to the coming of the railroad the importance of the canals to the growth of the state is difficult to exaggerate. The Erie Canal in particular became the leading route over which much of the nation's inland commerce was transported. It was the canal, too, that gave great impetus to the growth of Albany, Buffalo, Rochester, Syracuse, and Utica.

By the close of the Civil War, however, canals were in growing disfavor. The Panic of 1873 not only reduced the normal amount of traffic, but it also forced the overextended and financially harassed railroads to compete savagely with the canals as well as with each other. The Erie Canal, hampered by mismanagement, technological obsolescence, the

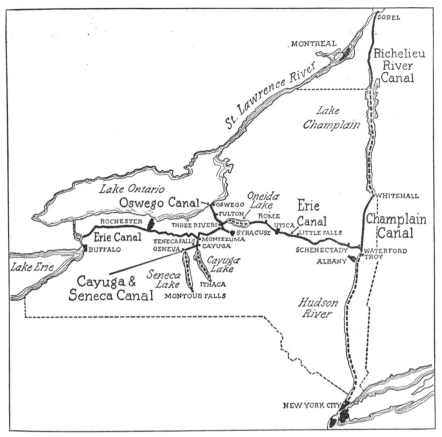

Map 16. The New York State Barge Canal system. (Adapted from *New York State Commerce Review*, February 1953.)

high costs of transshipment at Buffalo, and the inability of the canal men to match the financial resources of the railroad princes, fell on evil days.

A constitutional committee in 1872 proposed that the clause in the Constitution of 1846 prohibiting the sale of the canals should be amended to include only the Erie and Black River, Oswego, Cayuga and Seneca, and Champlain canals. In 1874 the proposed amendment was approved by an overwhelming majority of the voters. As a result state operation of the Chenango and Genesee Valley canals ceased.

Criticism of canal administration mounted during the 1870's. Governor Samuel J. Tilden brought to light flagrant frauds in contracts for canal repairs. The boodlers in the Canal Ring had performed their repair work so carelessly that breaks in the walls and accumulation of unremoved silt in the channel caused serious delays in navigation. Keepers of the locks and boat inspectors required "beering up" before they would allow boats to pass. Constitutional amendments were enacted forbidding extra compensation for contractors and providing for the appointment by the governor of a superintendent of public works with more powers than the former canal commissioners had been permitted to exercise.

Despite its short-comings, the canal system still had many champions, the most notable being former Governor Horatio Seymour. Boat operators and the commercial interests of Buffalo, who gained more from water traffic breaking cargoes in their city than from unbroken passage rail freight, also rallied to the defense of the canals. But the most influential supporters of all were the New York City merchants and their powerful organizations—the New York Chamber of Commerce and the New York Produce Exchange who profited from the cheap cost of transportation afforded by the canals and their influence on railroad rates. These organizations dispatched delegations to canal conferences and were represented at legislative hearings. The activities of these groups combined with the antirailroad sentiment of the time persuaded the voters of the state in 1882 to eliminate canal tolls and persuaded the legislature to set up a railroad commission to study railroad transportation charges.

The "free canal" amendment did little, however, to prevent the decline of the canals. Shipments continued to fall off until only 5 per cent of the total tonnage reaching New York from the interior in 1900 came by way of canal and river. Nevertheless, canal partisans argued that the mere presence of the canals helped to keep down railroad rates, which neither state nor federal commissions could regulate effectively. Undoubtedly, the water rate was the controlling factor in transportation between Chicago and New York. Late in 1887 the new-born Interstate Commerce Commission noted the importance of the Erie Canal in influencing the railroad rates to New York City, but by 1900 the New York Produce Exchange sadly noted that the canal had almost ceased to be a factor in regulating rates.

Nation-wide revival of interest in waterways during the closing decade of the nineteenth century coupled with continued antirailroad sentiment led to agitation for an improved canal system in the state. Accordingly, the constitutional convention of 1894 paved the way by submitting an amendment whereby the legislature might improve the canal system without regard to limits on the borrowing power of the state. The amendment carried, and the following year another amendment—submitted this time by the legislature—calling for a $9,000,000 appropriation, also carried by a large majority. This appropriation was largely wasted.

Meanwhile, New York City businessmen, increasingly alarmed that the city might lose its commercial supremacy, put on a vigorous campaign for the improvement of the Erie Canal system, and in 1903 the voters of the state approved an appropriation of $101,000,000 for the Barge Canal, as the remodeled system was called. Here and there a voice was raised for the building of an even larger ship canal across the state. Unfortunately, the judgment of this small minority went unheeded.

From 1918, when the modernized Barge Canal began operations, to 1951, the volume of cargo moved over the canal system of the state per year rose from 1,159,000 tons to a record 5,211,500. This upward trend was interrupted during World War II, when tanker sinkings along the Atlantic seaboard cut sharply into petroleum shipments intended for the canals. Oil shipped through the canals during this period was principally eastbound. The canals played important roles during World War II in transporting military landing craft from shipyards on the Great Lakes to ports of embarkation on the Atlantic Coast, in carrying essential sulphur from the Middle West to eastern defense industries, and in shipping South American bauxite to aluminum plants at Massena and in the province of Quebec.

The principal commodities transported on the New York State Barge Canal system are bulk items—in 1952 petroleum, chiefly in the form of gasoline, heating oil, and kerosene, constituted over 75 per cent of the canal tonnage, while grains comprised the second most important group of products handled. The total tonnage of petroleum and grain rose from 55 per cent of the canal trade in the early 1930's to almost 90 per cent, in 1952. Oil is shipped from depots in the port of New York to tank farms and other petroleum distribution points along the Hudson River and the canal system. While some grain is forwarded from Buffalo, the greater part of this traffic comes by Lake steamer to Oswego on Lake Ontario. There it is transferred to canal vessels and taken to Albany, where there are grain elevators equipped with every facility for large-scale handling of grains. The movement of oil is mainly westward, while that of grain is primarily eastward.

With the exception of the periods of World War II and the Korean conflict, both the federal and state governments since 1935 have cooperated in improving the canals, rivers, locks, and bridges of the system. From the inception of this joint project until the beginning of 1951, more than sixty contracts for canal improvements were awarded. These included deepening of channels; construction of bridge clearances, new lighthouses, buoys, bridge markings, and range towers; and straightening of curves. Plans are also under way to improve the approaches to the canal system. The deepening of the Hudson River channel from twenty-seven to thirty-two feet between the port of New York and Albany would allow large ocean-going vessels to reach the year-round port facilities at Albany. It is also anticipated that in time the Canadian program of deepening the Richelieu River canal system will be completed. This system connects the Barge Canal system with the St. Lawrence River and Montreal. When completed it will permit some 2,500 barges to operate between New York City and Montreal.

The New York Barge Canal system has numerous connected reservoirs, dams, and other controls in lakes and natural watercourses designed not only to meet the needs of shipping but also to control floods, particularly in the Mohawk and Hudson valleys. The impounding reservoirs and feeder canals which help maintain adequate depth in the Barge Canal system tend to minimize fluctuations in the levels of the Mohawk and Hudson rivers. The dams and spillways of the canalized sections of the Mohawk also provide controls on the rivers' flow.

The canals serve as a drainage system for central New York. To conduct water to the central portions of the Erie and Oswego canals, a series of feeder canals were dug through the Montezuma Swamp between Rome and Lyons. These feeder canals drew off much of the surface water and transformed the swamp into thousands of acres of fertile farmland.

The canal system of the state is also a source of water power. Two state hydroelectric plants at Crescent and Vischer Ferry, between Waterford and Schenectady, use surplus canal water and sell power to utility companies. Along the canal routes, surplus water is made available for farm and domestic purposes, and permits are granted for occupancy of unused canal lands.

Finally, the canal system of the state is used by those in search of recreation and relaxation. During the summer months the waters of the canal system are used by thousands of boating enthusiasts, fishermen, and vacationists. In 1952 registrations of privately owned pleasure boats on the canals numbered 2,308, and 2,068 lock permits were issued to boatmen. Along the banks of the canals are picnic grounds and camps, mostly private, on lands leased from the state. New York residents and visitors are permitted to use the canals for fishing, canoeing, and boating, except at locks and dams. It should be noted, on the other side of the picture, that the state canal system, for all its advantages, costs the taxpayers a large sum of money, since it produces little revenue.

Air transport, of minor significance during the first quarter of this century, became increasingly important for passengers and freight. The domestic commercial air traffic originating in the state in 1951 totaled 2,000,000 passengers, 10,000 tons of air mail, and 34,000 tons of air cargo. The New York State Department of Commerce estimates that by 1960 the demand for air service will have grown to 7,000,000 passengers, 25,000 tons of air mail, and 75,000 tons of air cargo.

Recent studies indicate that the demand for air express and air freight service is largely for such items as machinery, automotive parts and equipment, printed matter (including news publications), photographic and projection goods, textiles, and apparel, perishable items, and medical and pharmaceutical preparations. The Auburn plant of the American Locomotive Company has used air service to rush parts weighing several tons to disabled ships thousands of miles away, and the International Business Machines Corporation sends heavy units by air freight to all parts of the United States from its Endicott and Poughkeepsie plants. Lobstermen of Long Island have greatly widened their market by shipping by air. Increasing quantities of perishables, such as flowers, fruits, and vegetables, are going by air.

Greater New York became a terminal for the leading airlines of the world. At first, air traffic was served by Newark Airport, which was easily reached by the Lincoln Tunnel, but pressure on Newark was relieved when La Guardia opened in 1939. So rapidly did air transport grow, however, that the combined facilities of Newark and La Guardia were inadequate. As a consequence New York's largest field, at Idlewild on Jamaica Bay, was opened in 1948. Since its opening, imports and exports by air have more than doubled, and this international port has had to expand its facilities almost constantly. Air terminals within the city maintain a transportation service with all three airports. The larger cities of the state have direct service to New York City and interconnections linking them with each other and with the Middle West, the South, and New England. Service for smaller communities of the state is rapidly increasing. In 1950 the state had 291 airports, including commercial, military, municipal, and seaplane bases; twenty-one of these were served by scheduled airlines.

Any account of transportation in the state would be incomplete which failed to mention the revolution in the means of urban travel and communication. Prior to the Civil War, horse-drawn vehicles were the only means of conveyance in the cities of the state. Horse-drawn stages or omnibuses were put on tracks in the 1850's, and for half a century they furnished the principal means of city passenger traffic. But the horse-cars were small, slow in their movement, and wholly inadequate to the needs of rapidly expanding centers of population.

In the 1870's New York City pioneered with "elevated" or railroad lines built above the streets. The cars, more commodious than the horsecars, were drawn by small steam locomotives. In the 1890's the shift from steam to electricity was made, and the city did not bid farewell to this means of transportation until 1956, when the seventy-seven-year-old landmark, the Third Avenue El, was demolished. With the successful application of electric power to railway cars came the first really great revolution in city transportation. The transition from horse to electric power began in 1890 and was almost complete by 1902. The need for better transportation was so great that there was no lack of entrepreneurial interest or available funds. Soon cities and even towns and villages throughout the state, convinced that their hopes of future growth and power depended upon a "trolley line," became enthusiastic boosters of the electric street railway. In New York City the entrepreneurs Thomas Fortune Ryan and August Belmont struggled for control of the rapidly expanding transit lines. Their activities in this respect were reminiscent of the practices employed by Jay Gould and Cornelius Vanderbilt in their fight for the control of the Erie Railroad: financial manipulation, overcapitalization, political bribery, and corruption.

Although the elevated and surface lines were a vast improvement over horsedrawn transport, they were wholly inadequate to the needs of the rapidly growing metropolitan area. New York, therefore, followed the example of London, Paris, and Boston in providing underground transportation. Its first subway of what is today by far the largest underground transportation system in the world was opened in 1904. In 1940 the city purchased the privately owned Interborough Rapid Transit (IRT) and the Brooklyn-Manhattan Transit (BMT) system, combining them with the city-built and operated Independent Subway System. In the mid 1950's the system comprised approximately 250 miles of lines. Trains operate day and night on a schedule of one and a half to fifteen minutes. The lines use twelve bridges and eleven underwater tunnels and carry as many as 100,000 people at peak hours of operation. In general the subway is considered as the quickest as well as the safest means of transportation in the metropolitan area.

In recent years the automobile and the motorbus have supplemented the subways and practically supplanted the surface lines. As early as 1905 the Fifth Avenue Coach Company had imported a single twenty-four-passenger double-decked motorbus. In a few cities electrically powered buses made use of overhead trolley wires.

Taxis operate in almost every city and village of the state. In the larger cities large company-operated taxi fleets compete with each other and with the other means of transportation. The presence of the motorbus and the ever-growing number of taxis have greatly increased traffic and parking problems. In 1955 New York City's subway and bus system was put under the professional management of a Transit Authority, a three-man salaried team with expert knowledge of labor management, banking, and transportation. Traffic direction and parking is also one of the chief concerns of the police department. The erection of bus terminals and public garages in recent years, together with provision for one-way traffic on designated streets, has eased somewhat the congestion in the crowded and what at times seems to be a hopelessly entangled metropolis.

Every region of the state has almost instantaneous communication with every other region as well as with the outside world. As a result of a series of inventions: first, the telegraph, then the telephone, then the radio, and finally television, space and time are no longer barriers; the range of intercourse has been widened; contacts are more numerous. Isolation and parochialism have tended to disappear.

Market Place of the World

It appeared to be part of the commercial destiny of New York from a very early period that, in addition to being an important agricultural and manufacturing state, it should become conspicuously a center for wholesaling, retailing and general merchandising of goods. . . .

Nearly every important primary or staple product now has a definite exchange located in the city of New York, and designed for the facilitation of trading operations in that particular kind of product.—H. PARKER WILLIS

NEW YORK'S world leadership in trade and commerce can be attributed to its geographical location, its large population, its excellent transportation facilities, the diversity of its industries, the high average income of its people, its large aggregation of firms in varied financial fields—banking, insurance, corporate security underwriting, security and commodity brokerage—and the concentration of highly specialized business and professional services available in many fields. In this chapter both domestic trade and commerce with foreign lands will be considered.

The internal trade of the state is determined, in large measure, by the size and buying power of its population. New York has long been the most populous state in the Union, and it tops all the leading industrial states of the nation in per capita income. In 1950, for example, the average money income for each man, woman, and child was $1,864, or $428 above the national average. The total of almost $30,000,000,000 in income to individuals led all other states and exceeded that of California, the second-ranking state, by almost $9,000,000,000.

Income payments in the state are derived from the sources listed in Table 18. New York led every state in each of the five income segments except agriculture, but even its income from farming was greater than that of all the New England states combined.

Table 18. Sources of income to individuals in New York in 1952.

Source	Total	% of state income	% of total in N.Y.C.
Trade and service industries	$9,694,500,000	42.4	76
Manufacturing payrolls	7,513,900,000	33.2	48.4
Construction payrolls	968,300,000	4.2	52.7
Government	4,080,700,000	17.9	61
Agriculture	341,200,000	1.5	.14

Trade and service industries have provided a greater share of total income for almost a half century. New York City, because of its many shops and department stores, wholesale establishments, hotels, theaters, museums, and specialized business services, derived more than a third of its income from these sources and thus served to raise the state's proportion from the upstate average of approximately 25 per cent. In the resort counties, notably Sullivan, 40 per cent of all income came from these sources.

While the proportion in New York from manufacturing payrolls was very close to the national percentage of 23.9 in 1952, it was by no means representative of all parts of the state. Although New York City's manufacturing payrolls accounted for more than half the total for the state, the city was dependent upon manufacturing wages and salaries only to the extent of 19 per cent of total income, whereas in the remainder of the state manufacturing payrolls supplied 33.2 per cent of all income. According to the state Department of Commerce, manufacturing income and that from service and trade tend to complement each other. In other words, in those parts of the state where one is high the other is low. In the mid-Hudson and northern areas, where attention is centered chiefly on farming and where there are many resort areas, the proportion of income from manufacturing is slightly under that of the state as a whole. In the other areas the dependence upon manufacturing as a source of income is greater, ranging from just under 30 per cent of the total in the Elmira area to about 40 per cent in the Mohawk Valley. The Niagara Frontier and the Rochester area run a close second and third, respectively, to the Mohawk Valley in industrial concentration.

Payments from government included salaries and wages to civilian and military personnel, pensions, benefits of various kinds, bonuses, and the like. On a county basis the range varied from 10 to 35 per cent of total income. In almost every instance in which a high percentage is derived from this source, one finds a state institution of some kind. Thus in Albany County, where the state capital is situated, about 26 per cent of the income came from this source in 1952.

Income by counties varies greatly. In 1952 Westchester County led all

others with an average income of $2,701 per capita. Nassau was second
with $2,386, and Schenectady was third with $2,351. Two other counties
in addition to New York City bettered the state's per capita figure of
$2,062—Monroe and Niagara. Of the counties outside the New York
metropolitan area, eight were above the upstate average of $1,682 and
forty-five were below. The counties in which industrial centers are located
almost without exception have higher incomes. Counties whose residents depend to a great extent on farming for a livelihood have the lowest per capita incomes.

New York City accounted for over 60 per cent of all income received
by individuals in the state. It is also significant that in 1954 no less than
53 per cent of the state's retail sales were made in New York City. The
city and its suburban counties are less dependent upon salaries and wages
than the upstate counties. They derive 16 per cent of their income from
investments in securities, real estate, patents, and copyrights. The corresponding figure for the rest of the state in 1951 was 9 per cent.

Not only has there been a great increase in the amount of money per
capita which the people of the state have had at their disposal during the
last hundred years, but there have been new conditions under which domestic trade has been conducted—new methods of distribution, changes
in transportation, emphasis on design and packaging of merchandise, and
the stimulation of buying through advertising and other activities. The
growth and urbanization of population has also had a large effect on the
character of domestic trade.

Distribution of goods, in the two decades after the 1860's, was largely
carried on by commission merchants—who usually handled staple goods
—wholesalers, country general stores, and peddlers. Most manufacturers
at this time sold their goods directly to wholesalers, who in turn sold to
the specialized shops in their own city and to general stores in the outlying towns and villages. Many of the wholesale houses began as general
stores. The wholesaler saved the manufacturer the expense of salesmen,
relieved him of the burden of delivering small quantities and of the bookkeeping and credit expense of handling a multitude of small accounts,
warehoused his products, and often helped to finance his operations. The
manufacturer was thus free to devote himself entirely to production.
Dependence upon the wholesaler, however, placed the manufacturer at
his mercy when disputes arose over prices, quality of product, and other
matters. As a consequence, large manufacturers increasingly sold directly
to the consumer.

Some trade was carried on by peddlers, who either on foot, on horseback, or by wagon journeyed about the state selling to housewives a miscellany of articles from tinware to textiles. By 1870, however, the heyday

of the itinerant peddler was at an end, although a constantly decreasing number continued their activities to the end of the century.

Some general stores carried on both wholesale and retail operations. The country merchant was both a buyer, or assembler, as well as a retailer who might sell sugar, molasses, salt, kerosene, and other manufactured articles and imported luxuries for cash or in exchange or "trade" for the farmer's surplus, butter, cheese, potatoes, and other products. Before the federal government authorized the establishment of the Rural Free Delivery, the general store also housed the local post office. Almost down to the present, the general store also served as a social club—a gathering place for the menfolk of the neighborhood who, seated on cracker barrels or nail kegs around a barrel or box stove, told tall tales of individual prowess or carried on heated political debates. Not until the coming of radio and television did the country general store cease to function as a social center. The proprietor of the small store, irrespective of location, had very elementary ideas of merchandising and accounting. He had little or no knowledge of the business cycle and consequently sometimes overstocked his store at high prices. As late as 1890 some stores had on their shelves bolts of calico which were acquired in 1865 at sixty cents a yard. Sales methods at these stores were also costly and time consuming.

Before the end of the nineteenth century small general stores, especially in the urban centers of the state, began to face competition from large-scale retailers of three kinds: department stores, mail-order houses, and the chain store.

The department store, of which A. T. Stewart's was a forerunner, was, and still is, really a collection of specialized stores housed under one roof. Few of the early department stores were developed from general stores, although some of the later ones came into being in this way. The department store had distinct advantages over the old-fashioned store. Among these were acquisition of products at lower costs, one sale price for everybody, lower retail prices, elaborate display facilities, and larger volume of business. Today, New York City alone has more than a dozen of these tremendous department stores, of which Macy's, Gimbel's, Lord & Taylor, Bloomingdale's, Altman, Abraham & Straus, Stern's, and Saks are among the better known. Almost every upstate city of any considerable size has at least one department store.

If the small, old-fashioned store had reason to regard the department store as a dangerous competitor, it had even more reason to fear the appearance of the mail-order house. The first of these, established in the Midwest in 1872 by Montgomery Ward, was soon doing a flourishing business by mail, especially with farmers. A second mail-order house, Sears, Roebuck, came into being when a young station agent in 1884 began selling watches by mail. Both companies incorporated and moved to Chicago, where within a short time the volume of business of each far outstripped that of any department store in the nation. Other mail-order houses were subsequently established and built up substantial businesses. In New York the effect of the mail-order house was at first most heavily felt by the country store. In due time merchants in all parts of the state were to experience mail-order house competition. Even in the city of New York the mail-order houses affected adversely the volume of department-store trade.

Historically the chain store, the third competitor of the small retail store, antedated all other competitors. The oldest retail chain store, and still one of the largest in America, is the Great Atlantic and Pacific Tea Company, established in the 1850's. Its early policy was to eliminate wholesalers, brokers, and other middlemen and to sell tea at lower prices than its competitors. This was accomplished through a chain of stores and by mail orders to clubs of consumers. In the 1880's spices and other groceries were added to the tea and coffee line. Peddlers with horses and wagons were sent out to do door-to-door selling. Premiums and trading stamps were used to stimulate store sales. But the fundamental principle upon which the prosperity of the business was predicated has always been that of buying in quantity and selling at the lowest possible prices.

In 1879 F. W. Woolworth established his first five-and-ten-cent store in Utica. When this failed, he opened another in Pennsylvania. Many older retail merchants scoffed at this undertaking but changed their minds when the "five and ten" business netted its founder a fortune. The Woolworth Building near City Hall in New York City, at the time of its erection the tallest building in the world, is a monument to Woolworth's vision and enterprise. Many other chains, such as Gristede in New York City, have been organized during the last three-quarters of a century. As a result, the old small independent stores have either been forced out of business or have been compelled to organize into groups to preserve individual ownership and operation while benefiting from the economies of chain organization. In recent years manufacturers' retail chains have appeared in increasing number. Oil and automobile and ready-made-clothing manufacturers and others have also established their own retail agencies as, for example, Bond's, the makers of men's suits.

It is difficult to exaggerate the influence of the automobile on retail trade. The automobile now makes it possible for rural dwellers to shop in larger communities where they usually have the advantages of both low prices and variety. On the other hand, the movement of people into the suburbs has led to a decentralization of business. Today several of the great New York City department stores have branches in suburban areas.

The supermarket now found in all sections of the state is entirely possible because of the automobile. Usually located in the outskirts of towns and cities where land is available at a rental or purchase price much less than within the more populous areas, these markets afford an abundance of parking space and more spacious quarters for the display of goods. In the state in 1952 there were 1,413 food supermarkets which did a gross business of $1,300,000,000. The larger supermarkets of the state not only offer a complete line of grocery items, but also in recent years have extended their operations into such nonfood lines as drugs, toys, books, clothing, florist stocks, and hardware. They are fast becoming twentieth-century "general" stores. Many of these stores, unlike their early counterparts, are air conditioned and have lunch counters, rest rooms, music, parcel checking, and counter-to-car delivery. They have also initiated the merchandizing technique of self-service, which has had a profound effect upon store arrangement and equipment, packaging, advertising, display of goods, store personnel, and the marketing habits of customers.

Commercial advertising, perhaps the most important device used to stimulate buying, is largely a post-Civil War development. Prior to 1865 most newspaper advertising was confined to patent medicines. Large advertisements were rare. P. T. Barnum, the showman, was one of the first to have recourse to spectacular newspaper advertising. Prior to 1880 few general, or "literary," magazines, with the exception of the *Galaxy* and *Scribner's Monthly*, would accept advertising matter. In the early 1870's *Harper's Monthly* was reported to have refused an offer by the Howe Sewing Machine Company of $18,000 for its back cover for a year. By 1890, however, both newspapers and magazines were carrying an increasing amount of commercial advertisements. Religious periodicals, many of which had a considerable circulation within the state, depended financially upon advertising, welcomed advertisements of all kinds, and were not overscrupulous as to their character. Unlike several of the general magazines, they accepted liquor and patent medicine advertisements. On the whole, the standards of advertising in the magazines was higher than those in the state's newspapers.

At first the newspapers of the state were reluctant to accept large-space advertisements, but this policy changed during the last decades of the nineteenth century. Today the newspapers of the state, particularly those published in large urban centers, carry an enormous amount of commercial advertising.

New York State has also witnessed the development of a considerable amount of outdoor advertising during the last few decades. At first this type of advertising was unorganized and unregulated. Bills were posted in any prominent place. Signs were painted on fences, rocks, and even buildings, often defacing scenery and private property and violating public rights. Beginning in 1891 outdoor advertising was systemized and subjected increasingly to public control. The radio and television are the most recent media of the commercial advertiser.

Prize contests, premiums, and installment buying have also been used to stimulate consumer buying. No one of these is limited to New York. The first two gained popularity during the early years of the Depression. Prizes of ocean trips, merchandise, or cash were offered to contestants who solved puzzles, wrote letters, essays, or verses or coined names or slogans. The label or boxtop of the concern's package had to accompany the entry. Studies of this method of stimulating sales show that the response is large but often temporary. Similar stimulants are so-called premiums, offered from coupons inside the packages.

Installment selling is not new. It was widely used during the 1920's and was in part responsible for the Depression of 1929. People are encouraged to purchase goods—automobiles, furniture, household appliances, clothing, and other articles—even though at the time of purchase they do not have the funds with which to pay for them. Consequently they pay "something" down at the time of purchase and the remainder in installments at future specified times. For those whose income is derived from wages or salaries or even from a business of their own, installment buying is risky. Unemployment insurance helps to alleviate the dangers of this practice.

New York in recent years has witnessed increased attention on the part of manufacturers, farmers, and merchants to the designing, packaging, and display of their products. As the income of the state's population increased, people became more concerned with the brands, styles, and designs of what they purchased. Advertising, shifts in population, and changes in the consumer's buying habits were also contributing factors. Families who migrated from the country to a city apartment with limited storage space tended to buy more canned goods and packaged foods. Similarly, with the decline in home manufactures people bought more ready-to-wear clothing. With the decline in the number of domestic servants came an increasing interest in labor-saving household appliances. Change in styles, whether in wearing apparel or in automobiles, is still another factor which has caused producers and distributors of goods and commodities to be design conscious.

Packaging and display of food products have become increasingly important. In 1890 the grocery store customer waited while the storekeeper scooped oatmeal, sugar, or tea from a barrel or box into paper bags, which then had to be weighed and tied. Today the same commodities are packaged in attractive cans, boxes, and transparent containers before they ever reach the grocer's place of business. They are no longer handled in bulk. As a result the products are likely to be cleaner and easier to identify and to handle.

Total consumer spending for food has climbed steadily in both state and nation since 1932. Increase in population and income, the spread of education relating to nutrition and health, the increased consumption of prepared foods both at home and at restaurants, and the shift from farm to nonfarm living are factors which largely account for this increase.

While the average New Yorker eats somewhat more food, by weight, than he did two decades ago, the more striking changes in his eating habits have taken place in the kinds of food he consumes. In New York in 1910 the per capita consumption of grain was close to 300 pounds; in 1952 it was about 165 pounds. Fruit and vegetable consumption, on the other hand, rose from approximately 330 pounds to 450 pounds, thereby increasing the intake of vitamins, iron, and calcium by about one-third. Fresh farm products are now available the year round in all parts of the United States. Modern transportation, refrigeration, packaging, and large-scale purchasing by chain stores and supermarkets have stimulated the development of extensive truck farms and fruit orchards far removed from retail markets. Today no less than 50 per cent of the fruit crops and 60 per cent of the truck crops of the nation are marketed in fresh form. Quick freezing, one of the outstanding recent developments in food processing, has further transformed the typical diet. Strawberries and peas were the leaders in the frozen foods until the advent of frozen orange juice.

Consumers in various parts of the state, but especially in New York City, have, from time to time, been outspoken in their condemnation of the high cost of living. At these times they have been prone to place responsibility upon the middleman. Numerous legislative investigations and private inquiries have been made. Typical of these public investigations was the New York State Food Investigating Commission of 1912. A sub-committee of this commission, charged with the task of investigating markets, prices, and costs, reached the conclusion that high costs to the consumer were occasioned by outgrown facilities, especially in urban centers, and by a haphazard system of distribution which enabled commission men, wholesalers, speculators, jobbers, and retailers to take from 40 to 70 per cent of the amount paid by the consumer. Despite their analysis, made almost a half century ago, the gap between what the producer receives and the consumer pays is a wide one.

If the state of New York is a great center of domestic trade, what of its foreign trade? For over a hundred years New York has been famous for its large export and import trade. The state's manufacturers are favorably located for selling in international markets and for obtaining imported raw and semiprocessed materials from all parts of the world. Today, the state handles more than one-half of the nation's imports and more than one-third of its exports; these percentages are somewhat lower than they were a century ago. This trade passes through the four customs districts of the state: New York (which includes Albany and the New Jersey ports of Newark and Perth Amboy), Buffalo, Rochester, and St. Lawrence (Ogdensburg). In 1950 the New York district alone accounted for one-half of the national waterborne shipments to foreign countries.

By far the larger proportion of imports funnels through the port of New York. Especially is this true of imports coming from areas other than North America. The imports coming through the customs districts of Buffalo, Rochester, and St. Lawrence (Ogdensburg) come chiefly from Canada and in recent years are of growing significance in the state's total trade. The port of New York has long been and still is a mecca for importers of both finished and semifinished goods and raw material of foreign origin. Since the Civil War and more especially during the last half century the port has developed a series of specialized areas. Newark, for example, has become a great lumber entrepôt; Elizabeth port is a center for spices, pepper, cocoa, beans, cotton; the port of Tompkinsville handles and stores tea and rubber; Brooklyn receives the raw products of the tropics in great volume; Constable Hook, Bayonne, to which comes crude oil by tanker and pipeline, is the scene of perhaps the largest concentration of oil refineries in the East. Raw rubber and raw silk, coffee, tin bars, vegetable oils, undressed furs, copper ore and semimanufactures, diamonds, cane sugar, fruits, nuts, and alcoholic beverages, in terms of dollar value, have been leaders in the import trade of the New York customs district during the last quarter century.

Leading exports of New York State products have varied somewhat since the Civil War. The biggest change has been the growing precedence both in volume and dollar value of manufactured goods over raw materials. At the top of the list in monetary value during the period since 1920 have been copper manufactures, petroleum products, electrical machinery, automobiles and trucks, chemicals, furs, photographic and projection goods, coal, wheat and grain mill products, and dairy products.

That the New York customs district should overshadow the other three customs districts, which together account for only about 15 per

IMPORTS

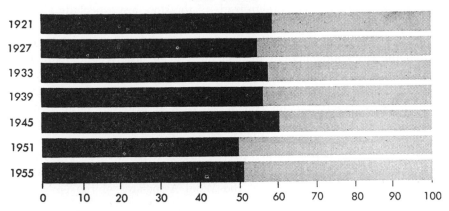

EXPORTS

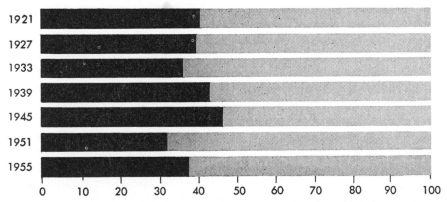

Chart 4. Percentage of the nation's imports and exports passing through New York, 1921–1955. Solid areas indicate per cent of nation's imports and exports (excluding re-exports) by New York State. Shaded areas indicate per cent of nation's imports and exports (excluding re-exports) by areas other than New York State. (Adapted from *Statistical Abstract of the United States,* 1956, pp. 822 ff.; Department of Commerce, Bureau of Foreign Commerce, *Monthly Summary of Foreign Commerce,* 1950–1954; U.S. Bureau of the Census, *Foreign Commerce and Navigation of the United States* [Washington, D.C., 1950].)

cent of the state's foreign trade by volume, is not surprising. The excellent physical facilities of the port of New York, with its 650 miles of water front, and the variety of services provided by the foreign departments of the metropolitan area's banks, its commodity exchanges staffed by specialists in foreign trade are to be found nowhere else in America.

Both the domestic and foreign trade of the state are especially affected by the six commodity exchanges whose home is New York City. The oldest of these, the New York Produce Exchange, was formed in 1862, when the city's independent dealers needed an orderly and more convenient method of buying and selling flour and provisions. Today the New York Produce Exchange is still one of the principal markets for wheat to be exported from North America. It also has large markets for other grains and lesser markets for cottonseed oil, lard, tallow, and other commodities. The New York Cotton Exchange was organized in 1870. During the period July 1945–June 1951, it handled 64 per cent of the cotton trade of the nation. Wool is also traded on the floor of this exchange under the auspices of the Wool Associates of the New York Cotton Exchange, Inc.

The New York Coffee and Sugar Exchange, Inc., organized in 1882 by a group of coffee brokers who desired to create stable conditions in the coffee market, is the largest of the world's exchanges for both coffee and raw sugar. The existence of this exchange has contributed to making New York City the principal warehouse center and leading import point for coffee in the United States. About half of all coffee imported into this country comes through the port of New York, and over one-fifth of all wholesale coffee sales are made by New York wholesalers. Trading in raw sugar futures did not become important on this exchange until World War I. The Commodity Exchange, Inc., was formed in 1933, when, in an effort to reduce expenses, the New York Hide Exchange, the National Metal Exchange, the National Raw Silk Exchange, and the Rubber Exchange of New York were consolidated. The formation of the New York Cocoa Exchange, organized in 1925, was prompted by marketing difficulties. Today approximately one-half of the world's production of cocoa beans is consumed by the American chocolate industry. The New York Mercantile Exchange is one of the oldest organized commodity exchanges in New York City, having been established in 1872 for the purpose of dealing in butter and eggs. This exchange also operates a futures market for potatoes, rice, onions, turkeys, and dry beans.

Of the several functions performed by the commodity exchanges, two are of outstanding significance. First, the exchanges make hedging, or the practice on the part of merchants and processors of attempting to avoid the risk of unforeseen major price movements, possible by buying or selling future contracts on a commodity exchange. A second function is control of price direction by employing the supply and demand formula. The passage of the Federal Commodity Exchange Act has assisted the exchanges in preventing manipulation, fraud, and dissemination of false information—practices long frowned upon by the exchanges.

Table 19. Commodity exchanges in New York City, 1951.

Exchange	Commodity
New York Cotton Exchange	Cotton
Wool Associates of the New York Cotton Exchange, Inc.	Wool and wool tops
New York Coffee and Sugar Exchange, Inc.	Coffee beans, raw sugar, molasses
Commodity Exchange, Inc.	Hides, crude rubber, copper, lead, zinc, tin
New York Produce Exchange	Cottonseed oil, soybean oil, black pepper
New York Cocoa Exchange	Cocoa beans
New York Mercantile Exchange	Potatoes, butter, processed eggs, onions, turkeys, rice, dry beans

Trade with Canada, Mexico, Central and South America, and Africa has grown in relative importance and is now over one-half of the United States total. Trade with Europe and Asia has fallen off sharply, while trade with Canada is expanding, and almost one-third of United States–Canadian trade comes through the upstate customs districts. Since the end of World War II, New York has faced keener competition from the Gulf Coast ports. The rapid industrial development in the South and the Southwest and the mounting Latin-American trade has been very favorable for these ports. Certain Atlantic Coast ports, notably Baltimore, Philadelphia, and Hampton Roads have also succeeded in attracting somewhat larger shares of foreign trade than formerly.

The prospects for foreign trade through the ports of the state will depend not only on national foreign-trade policies—extension of the Reciprocal Trade Act, liberalization of tariffs, simplification of customs procedures, the volume and nature of foreign aid—but also upon the action taken by the ports in the state to combat growing competition from other ports. To this end both the New York and New Jersey portions of the port of New York are spending millions of dollars for rehabilitation and modernization. The opening of the Thruway by providing better trucking facilities, will also help. The greatest competition of all is likely to come from the development of the St. Lawrence Seaway which will enable ocean freighters to dock at inland cities on the Great Lakes. These cities, together with Montreal, may challenge New York's supremacy.

Foreign trade by air is still very small but is growing in importance (see Chapter 38).

World War II and the disruptive years immediately following brought changes in both the countries with which the state traded and in the volume of the trade. The war itself was a retarding factor. Many commodities in demand by countries before the war were no longer needed or, if needed, could not be delivered. Trade also shifted from European and Asiatic areas to Caribbean and South American countries. During the postwar years many countries were too impoverished to purchase American goods. To retain and also expand the state's foreign commerce, the legislature in March 1946 provided for a World Trade Corporation "to establish and develop a world trade center to be located within the state of New York for exhibiting and promoting the purchase and sale of products in international trade." The corporation has been organized and is surveying the possibilities of establishing such a center.

The people of the state are increasingly aware of the fact that their economy cannot be maintained without foreign trade. They depend almost entirely upon foreign sources for a number of materials vital to their industries—tin, cobalt, copra, shellac, industrial diamonds, manganese, nickel, and quartz. Moreover, their living standards would be reduced without the importation of such commodities as coffee, sugar, cocoa, furs, and tropical fruits. Nor can they maintain some of their present industries without foreign markets. The economy of the state and, indeed, of the nation would be severely dislocated by any sudden interruption of foreign trade.

New York not only became a great import-export center but ultimately the world's leading market for the exchange of stocks and bonds and other types of securities. Business on the New York Stock Exchange grew in volume especially after the discovery of gold in California and the expansion of industry and transportation. It was during the Civil War, however, that the exchange experienced its first big wave of speculative business. Securities, gold, and commodities were subject to unheard-of activity. Merchants, brokers, lawyers, politicians, and even clergymen and women prominent in society were infected with the fever of speculation. So great was the activity that brokers dealing in securities not listed on the New York Stock Exchange had recourse to trading on the sidewalk. This was the beginning of the New York Curb Exchange, which took more tangible form in 1873, when it moved from its narrow confines in William Street to Broad Street almost adjacent to the banking firm of J. P. Morgan and Company. Eventually, in 1921, the Curb Exchange moved indoors. In comparison with the rules of the New York Stock Exchange, the rules for listing stocks on the Curb Exchange are less rigid and exacting, permit younger and less strongly established companies to list, and are less expensive. The Curb Exchange is often regarded as a testing ground for the securities of younger corporations. Most of these usually graduate to the New York Stock Exchange.

Speculative booms have characterized the New York exchanges from time to time. The most historic of these developed with increasing intensity in the years after 1927. As more investors put their money into securities in the hope of making a quick profit on a speculative rise in stocks, the character of the New York Stock Exchange was fundamentally altered. Instead of serving primarily as a device for the accumulation of capital for industrial enterprises, the exchange became a betting ring where people gambled on stocks in much the same fashion that gamblers wagered on roulette or horseraces. Security prices were forced up by competitive bidding rather than by any fundamental improvement in corporate enterprise, and there was little correlation between actual conditions in industry and stock-market quotations.

Part of the capital that flowed to the New York Stock Exchange in the last two years of the 1920's was supplied from corporations with unexpended cash reserves who could think of no other way of employing their surplus funds than of placing them at the disposal of the investment market. The traditional function of the exchange was thus reversed. Instead of being used as a device for gathering funds for corporate expansion it was transformed into a receptacle for the profits of corporations. These corporate profits deposited in New York banks in turn helped swell the funds available for stock speculation. By buying on margin, the investor had to pay only a fraction of the quoted price of any particular security. The additional money needed to cover the purchase was supplied by the broker, who obtained these funds from a bank using his customers' stock as collateral.

If the shares of stock so purchased advanced, the owner could sell at a profit. If, however, they declined, the owner would have to pay the broker additional money to cover the corresponding decrease. If he were unable to do so, the broker would be compelled to sell the stock to protect himself at the bank. It was these three factors—availability of money at low rates of interest, buying on low margins, and the craze for speculative profits which contributed in no small measure to the economic collapse of 1929.

Over the years, as the volume of business on the two New York exchanges increased, sharp practices tended to develop which roused the ire of the public. Because the stock market was as yet unregulated, unscrupulous operators like Daniel Drew, Jim Fisk, and Jay Gould took advantage of the ignorance and naïveté of investors. To them, stock watering and stock manipulation were fine arts. If they wanted additional funds, they merely printed more Erie Railroad stock and sold it to gullible investors. Their expenses stopped with the cost of printing, for the new stock issues were not accompanied by an addition to the railroad's physical assets. Furthermore, these stock jugglers could change the price of Erie stock whenever they wished. By dumping high quantities on the market they forced down its value. When it had reached a suitable low point they would buy it back, trade in it furiously among themselves to force up the price, sell it profitably when it could be pushed no higher, and then repeat the process. Railroad companies whose stocks were listed often failed to divulge all the facts concerning earnings, expenses, and indebtedness.

An act compelling business corporations to make regular reports was defeated in Albany in 1900. Nine years later, however, a special committee appointed by Governor Hughes in 1907 made a number of detailed recommendations covering the whole range of stock-exchange activities including internal reforms by the exchange itself. In 1912 the Pujo committee of the House of Representatives went far beyond the recommendations of the Hughes committee both in its denunciation of certain practices of the New York Stock Exchange and in its proposals for reform. As a result, the legislature enacted a number of reform measures. A bill to compel the exchange to incorporate passed the Assembly but was defeated on the floor of the Senate. Elimination of some of the more flagrant shortcomings of both the New York exchanges had to await the passage of the Federal Securities Exchange Act of 1934.

The importance of the two New York exchanges in the securities business is shown by the table below.

Table 20. Comparative volume of stocks sold on national security exchanges in 1950.

Exchanges	% of market value of all stocks sold on national securities exchanges	% of number of all shares sold on national securities exchanges
New York Stock	85.99	76.49
New York Curb	6.80	13.39
Fourteen other stock exchanges in the United States	7.21	10.12

Source: *Seventeenth Report, Securities and Exchange Commission* (Washington, D.C., 1951).

The state's domestic and foreign markets as well as its trade in securities have been continuously affected since 1865 by the status of the currency, credit facilities, and cyclical change. During the Civil War, when the nation was faced with extraordinary expenses, Congress authorized the issue of $450,000,000 of paper notes, or greenbacks, as they were called from the color of the ink used in printing them. Meanwhile the federal government suspended specie payments, so that gold and silver passed from circulation, and the greenbacks depreciated in value. In the summer of 1864 they reached a low of thirty-nine cents per gold dollar. As a consequence, prices rose sharply. When the war ended, however, the demand for foodstuffs and other war commodities declined. At the same time a movement for contraction of the paper currency and a return to the gold standard was launched. Farmers feared that contraction would depress prices for what they had to sell and make it increasingly difficult for them to pay debts incurred for the purchase of stock and equipment. In other words, a return to the gold standard would have meant paying debts contracted in fifty-cent dollars with one hundred-cent dollars. One of the most important aspects of the state's economic and political history from the close of the Civil War to the end of the century was the effort of the farmers and other debtor groups to maintain prices at somewhere near war levels.

With the passage of the Resumption bill in 1875 by the national government, which called for the restoration of specie payments on January 1, 1879, those in favor of cheap money and inflation joined the Independent or Greenback party. When they failed to accomplish their goal by this means, the inflationists sought another expedient, bimetallism, believing that if enough silver could be injected into the monetary system, at an inflated ratio of sixteen to one, the value of currency would be forced down. The Bland-Allison Act of 1878 and the Sherman Silver Purchase Act of 1890 temporarily established bimetallism, but the Currency Act of 1900 reinstated the gold dollar—a victory for those in favor of "hard" money and deflation.

New York City, with its varied array of financial institutions of all kinds, ranging from a home loan company to the House of Morgan, is the financial capital of the world. Since 1865 New York businessmen have been increasingly dependent upon banking institutions for credit needs. No state in the Union is more amply supplied with commercial banks, savings banks, saving and loan associations, licensed lenders, investment concerns, and insurance companies. Together they constitute a network providing services to business and individuals at approximately three thousand offices throughout the state.

About half of these are commercial banking offices whose resources constitute over one-fourth of the assets of all such banks in the United States. Ranging in size from small institutions like the National Bank of Schuylerville to the giant Chase Manhattan Bank of New York City, the commercial banks, in addition to their main function of extending credit, render many services related to sound business management. These include acting as fiduciaries in handling the security transactions of corporations, establishing and managing pension trusts and profit-sharing trust funds, serving as transfer agents in the purchase and sale of stock certificates, and administrating wills and trusts.

A catalogue of the New York banking houses which were organized during the last three-quarters of a century is an impressive one. Nowhere else in the world at the present time are there to be found so many powerful financial agencies. If the number of banks is slightly less in 1956 than in 1926, amalgamation is the explanation. Recent mergers resulted in the formation of the Chemical and Corn Exchange, the Chase Manhattan Bank, and the First National City Bank. Bankers Trust, Guaranty Trust, Hanover, Irving Trust, Manufacturers Trust, Lehman Brothers, and the House of Morgan are among the internationally known New York citadels of finance capitalism.

Of these, the House of Morgan is one of the most influential. Its founder, J. Pierpont Morgan, spent a lifetime in the banking business. Son of Junius Spencer Morgan, an international banker with headquarters in London, young Morgan after finishing his schooling served an apprenticeship in his father's firm. In 1857 he entered the banking house of Duncan, Sherman and Company of New York. Three years later he became the New York agent for the London financial firm of George Peabody. In 1864 he became the junior partner of Dabney, Morgan and Company, and in 1871 he became associated with the Drexels of Philadelphia and founded the firm of Drexel, Morgan and Company of New York. When, in 1895, Anthony J. Drexel died, the firm became J. P. Morgan and Company. It soon became associated with Drexel and Company of Philadelphia, Morgan Harjes Company of Paris, and J. S. Morgan and Company of London (after 1910 Morgan, Grenfell and Company). Before the end of the century the House of Morgan in New York had become one of the most powerful financial concerns in the world.

The House of Morgan has specialized primarily in financing reorganizations and mergers. Railroad reorganizations enabled Morgan to get control of a railroad empire. This dates back to his successful contest with Jay Gould for control of the Albany and Susquehanna Railroad, now a part of the Delaware and Hudson, in the 1860's. In the field of industrial finance, Morgan formed the United States Steel Corporation, the International Harvester Company, General Electric Company, and the American Telephone and Telegraph Company. By 1910 the House of Morgan not only had a powerful voice in banks, trust companies, insurance concerns, a score of railroads, several streetcar systems, the International Mercantile Marine, and many lesser concerns. In alliance with the First National Bank of New York and the National City Bank, it constituted a kind of banking monopoly or money trust. Eleven Morgan partners held seventy-two directorships in forty-seven of the largest corporations in America. Morgan also made handsome profits when, on occasion, he came to the financial assistance of the federal government.

The savings banks of the state, which now number over 130, are primarily concerned with financing small residential properties, modernizing or constructing of commercial projects, and aiding small savers in developing regular habits of thrift. School savings plans and Christmas Clubs are well-known parts of the thrift program. The type of investment in which a savings bank may invest is carefully limited by law. The amount of funds which may be deposited by any one depositor is also restricted.

Savings and loan associations exist primarily to help their members finance home construction co-operatively. Most of the investments of these institutions continue to be made in mortgages. Credit unions serve the purpose of making small personal loans and providing facilities for saving to their members. Participation in these organizations is usually restricted along trade-union or fraternal lines or to those who work for a common employer. Licensed lenders are another source of personal loans. For many years, many needy borrowers who were not sufficiently good credit risks could not obtain funds from banking organizations and fell prey to loan sharks. When other methods of combatting this evil failed, the state adopted in 1932 a Small Loan Law based on the principle of allowing licensed and carefully supervised lenders to charge rates of interest substantially above those permitted to banks. Approximately three hundred of these licensed lending offices now operate within the state.

The Equitable, the New York Life, and the Metropolitan Life insurance companies, cleansed by the Hughes investigation and legislation resulting from the report of the Armstrong committee, have continued to prosper. In 1950 the combined assets of twenty-two companies with home offices in the state totaled about $23,000,000,000. All but three operate from New York City. Four of these home offices are the control centers for almost two-fifths of total assets held by all United States life insurance companies, thus helping to establish New York City as the management and financial capital of the nation. In 1950 life insurance companies domiciled in this state had issued one-third of the total life insurance in force in the United States.

The three major investment outlets of life insurance companies have been corporate stocks and bonds, government securities (federal, state, and local), and real-estate mortgages and real estate. The state has drawn an especially large portion of these investments.

Cyclical changes during the period have been many. Most notable of these have been downward turns of the cycle, resulting in the panics of

1873, 1893, 1907, and 1929. While all of the downward turns of the cycle were not of equal severity, in most instances business was hard hit. The crash of 1873, for example, was followed by the closing of the New York Stock Exchange for a ten-week period "to save the entire Street from utter ruin." Prices of commodities tumbled, commercial failures mounted in number, many of the state's mills and factories closed, and unemployment became widespread. It was not until 1880 that full recovery was achieved. The depression of the 1890's was of shorter duration. The bottom fell out of prices, and farmers of the state as well as laboring people were squeezed hard. Severest of all in every way was the Panic of 1929 and the Depression which immediately followed. The pattern, however, was much the same as for earlier panics. As customers began to limit their purchases, business leaders began to retrench. Orders were canceled, wages reduced, hours of work shortened, and workers laid off. Increasing unemployment and a falling wage-scale were accompanied by a corresponding decrease in purchasing power. The bottom fell out of the stock market. Foreign trade declined sharply. Private debts contracted in boom days became an almost intolerable burden. As individuals and business firms defaulted on their obligations, foreclosures and bankruptcies mounted in number. New York, like the rest of the nation, experienced a depression during the 1930's the like of which it had never known.

Even in times of nondepression, the market for certain industries has been affected adversely by seasonal demands, changes in tariff schedules, and the competition of newly invented products.

PART SIX

Culture in an Industrial Age

✸✸✸✸✸✸✸✸✸✸✸✸✸✸✸✸

The Expanding Classroom

The responsibility of education is for the emancipation of intelligence from the anachronistic beliefs we cherish and, on the positive side, for the teaching of those meanings, significances, and processes which our science has experimentally verified. When anything whatever is to be accomplished, processes have to be invoked that can be depended upon. To put into operation processes that will generate specific results is the method of intelligence.—LAWRENCE K. FRANK

EDUCATIONAL facilities in the state have greatly expanded in the past one hundred years, as the state has reorganized its educational system and increased its financial support to elementary and secondary schools. In higher education, too, the state has founded colleges and vocational schools and created scholarship programs, while private philanthropy has established new colleges and universities, proving particularly active in higher education for women.

In the period following the Civil War, educational developments in both the city and the state differed only in detail from educational developments in the rest of the nation. In every section of the United States, there were a rapid expansion of elementary school facilities, an increase in the number of high schools, a broadening of curricula, and the establishment of new colleges and universities. Each of these generalizations can accurately be applied to New York during the postwar years, but neither the state nor the city deserved credit for originating the movement for the enlargement of educational opportunities.

The history of education in New York is complicated by the rivalry between the Board of Regents of the University of the State of New York and the State Department of Public Instruction. While the Board of Regents was a policy-making body in charge of higher education and the superintendent of the State Department of Public Instruction was concerned with the work of the primary schools, the functions of the two agencies were not always clearly delimited, and there were many jurisdictional disputes. At times educational progress occurred in spite of, rather than because of, the dual control within the state government.

It was not until the twentieth century that an attempt was made to reorganize the administration of the state's educational system. Under the terms of the Unification Act of 1904, the Regents retained authority over colleges and universities, while a newly established commissioner of education was granted "all the powers and duties in relation to the supervision of elementary and secondary education." In addition, the commissioner of education, as the executive officer of the Board of Regents, had the authority "to create such departments as in his judgment shall be necessary and to appoint deputies and heads of such departments, subject to the approval of the Board of Regents." In 1910 the law was amended to make the University of the State of New York a division of a State Education Department, in which the commissioner would serve as an executive and the Regents as a legislative body. After approximately a century of divided control, the management of the state's entire educational system was placed under the authority of a single, responsible agency.

Despite the disadvantages of dual control, New York's elementary and secondary educational system expanded rapidly during the half century following the Civil War. In 1867, with the abolition of the rate bills (under which parents who were not paupers paid public-school tuitions on the basis of the number of school days), the opportunity for an elementary school education was made available to all children on the same basis. In the ensuing years the old academies declined in numbers and influence, and the state's public school system entered a period of unprecedented growth. From 1869 to 1917 public school enrollment increased from 998,664 to 1,626,051, the number of public school teachers from 17,140 to 51,036, and annual expenditures for public schools from $11,312,325 to $76,408,430. Although high schools did not appear until the Civil War era, they grew rapidly. By 1895 there were 373 high schools in New York, and twenty years later the number had reached 740. At the same time the public school curricula was broadened considerably. Kindergartens became increasingly popular, and many school systems offered courses in art, music, physical training, commercial subjects, and manual training as well as in the usual academic subjects.

An inventory of elementary and secondary education in the state since World War I reveals three important changes: centralization or the consolidation of the state school districts, curriculum expansion, and new teaching methods.

New York was one of the first states to lay out its whole area in self-governing school districts. This action was taken in 1812. Frontier conditions prevailed, and naturally the districts were made very small; even cities were divided into small districts. By the end of the nineteenth century the small district with its one-room schoolhouse, its one teacher, and fewer than ten pupils was outmoded. In 1911 steps in the direction of consolidation were taken when twelve hundred small districts were abolished within the boundaries of cities. In 1925, on the recommendation of Governor Alfred E. Smith, another act of the legislature provided that districts electing to form one central district would be entitled to additional state aid. The state also agreed to pay 50 per cent of the cost of transporting students to these central schools and 25 per cent of the cost of construction of the central school. These financial inducements, together with the growth of sentiment for better schooling in rural areas, had the desired effect. By the summer of 1938 more than 250 central rural districts had been established. There remained, however, 7,756 small rural districts. So great was the momentum of the centralization movement that by 1956 less than 10 per cent of the original number of small districts remained, and it was merely a question of a short time when these would become part of a central system.

As significant as the development of centralization and better facilities was the expansion of the average school's curriculum. The elementary schools, which at one time had taught little beyond the "three R's," enlarged their curricula to such an extent that by 1930 some of them included as many as thirty different subjects. There was a corresponding multiplication of courses in the high schools. Since large numbers of pupils were drawn from every background and represented different degrees of intelligence, considerable emphasis was placed on "practical" subjects "for living and making a living." Boys were taught machine-shop practices and woodworking; girls attended classes in sewing and cooking; all could study typewriting, stenography, and bookkeeping. By 1950 there were forty-two vocational high schools in the state—twenty-six in New York City, seven in Buffalo, two in Rochester, and one each in Syracuse, Schenectady, Utica, Yonkers, Elmira, Niagara Falls, and Ogdensburg. In forty other communities trade and technical courses were offered as departments of local high schools. Trade courses for boys include: electrical trades, auto mechanics, carpentry, printing trades, sheet-metal trades, commercial art, plumbing, building maintenance and construction, photography, baking, tailoring, pattern-making, welding, and refrigeration service. For girls: dressmaking, beauty culture, garment-machine operating, millinery, cafeteria and tea room service, commercial art, clothing trades, and vocational dramatics. Technical courses open to girls are electrical techniques, mechanical design, architecture, drawing, industrial chemistry, aviation, and structural drafting. Traditionalists complained that the schools were teaching young people how to earn a living rather than how to think and that no amount of vocational training was an adequate substitute for a thorough grounding in the accepted academic subjects.

In some of the state's schools, curriculum changes were accompanied by new teaching methods sponsored by the advocates of progressive education. Learning by rote and complete reliance on textbooks gave way to an emphasis upon individual differences among pupils and an attempt to make learning an exciting experience rather than a series of dreary tasks. Severe classroom discipline was abandoned for a more informal attitude based on the assumption that interested pupils seldom present behavior problems. Efforts were also made to integrate subjects, and frequent use was made of available library resources. Tests were used to determine individual capacities and interests; slow learners were given special assistance; and children of unusual ability were permitted to progress at a much more rapid rate than others. Traditional schools were characterized by their rigidity; progressive schools were distinguished by their willingness to experiment and their flexibility.

With the increase in population, the cost of maintaining the public school system mounted. Early in its history the state accepted the principle implanted by the Dutch in New Amsterdam in 1638 that the responsibility for the support of common schools should be shared jointly by the state and the school district. By 1900 the total amount provided by the state was approximately $3,700,000, or about 11 per cent of the total cost of education. Shortly after the turn of the century (1902) the amount of state funds to be distributed was based upon the assessed valuation of the taxable property within the district, recognizing the difference in ability of school districts to support education. Under this arrangement each district with an assessed valuation of $40,000 or less was entitled to $150, and each of the wealthier districts to $125.

During the first quarter of the present century many methods were adopted for increasing the amount of state support by means of special quotas. As a consequence, by 1924 no fewer than twenty-five various bases were in use for the distribution of $41,402,497 of state aid. Fortunately, in 1925 the legislature enacted the historic Cole-Rice Law, effectively establishing the principle of equalization. Every district received $1,200 (later $1,500) for every "teacher unit" in the elementary grades and $1,600 (later $1,900) for high school work—less $1.50 (later reduced to $.60) on each $1,000 of the true value of the property in the district. Two years later a special commission headed by Michael Friedsam recommended that the amount of state aid be increased to $89,-000,000 by 1930. By acting favorably upon this recommendation, the legislature not only adhered to the principle of equalization but shifted part of the tax burden from property owners by distributing state funds derived from other than property taxes to the localities that did not have recourse to such forms of tax. By 1943–1944 the amount of state aid had risen to $111,814,000.

With the inflation following World War II, further revisions of the equalization formula were imperative. During the years 1945–1951 a series of changes were made. The pupil was substituted as the unit of measure for state aid instead of the teacher. Most important of all, the amount of aid from the state was increased from $100 for each elementary and secondary pupil to $220 and $274 respectively. More recently the Temporary Commission on Educational Finances, appointed in 1954 and headed by Dr. Henry T. Heald, then chancellor of New York University, recommended that the amount of state aid be further increased by $56,000,000, and this received legislative approval. Thus the total amount of state contribution beginning with the school year 1957 was $457,000,000, or 25 per cent over the $366,000,000 for the school year 1955–1956. A substantial part of this increase went to raise teachers' salaries.

After World War I enrollments continued to increase as they had after the Civil War. The number of individuals enrolled in elementary schools during the thirty years 1920–1950 was approximately 96 per cent of all persons in the state between the ages of six and thirteen years; the number in secondary schools was 78 per cent of all persons between fourteen and seventeen; and the number enrolled in advanced and professional schools was nearly 25 per cent. In the decade 1940–1950 population growth turned sharply upward, with the consequence that it soon became apparent that there were not enough elementary school buildings and teachers and that the same would soon be true of the secondary schools. The educational statistics for the school year 1953–1954 were testimony of this fact when approximately 3,275,000 students were registered in New York educational institutions. Of these, 2,300,000 were enrolled in public schools—1,453,706 children in grade six and below and 849,109 in grades seven through twelve. There were approximately 560,000 pupils in elementary grades and 95,000 in secondary grades of the private and parochial schools. About half of those in attendance at parochial schools were in New York City.

New York's facilities for higher education were enlarged after the Civil War. Cornell, which opened in 1868 with the aid of a 960,000-acre grant under the Morrill Act and a $500,000 gift from Ezra Cornell, offered programs in engineering and agriculture as well as in the traditional liberal arts subjects. Equally notable were the increased opportunities for women desiring a college education. In addition to Cornell, which was coeducational, there were a number of new women's colleges.

Table 21. Fifty years of progress in education in New York State.

	1903–1904	1951–1952
Total number of school districts	10,696	3,175
Public school houses and sites	11,936	5,785
Public secondary schools	655 *	978 *
Private and parochial secondary schools reporting	145	299
Universities, colleges, and professional schools	74	111
Net value of property		
Public schools	$107,553,134	$1,789,617,268
Private and parochial schools reporting	13,010,823	328,594,583
Universities, colleges, and professional schools	99,758,763	468,358,652
Volumes in public school libraries	2,009,820	8,017,430
Total expenditures		
Public schools	43,750,277	686,883,519 †
Private and parochial schools reporting	2,096,029	39,537,260
Universities, colleges, and professional schools	13,398,425	262,532,145
Number of children between 5 and 18 years of age	1,760,986	2,629,812
Registration at schools		
Public elementary schools	1,211,390	1,540,162
Public secondary schools	88,675	518,864
Part-time and continuation schools	15,864	3,766
Indian schools	791	1,754
Institutions for defectives (deaf and blind)	1,995	1,619
Private and parochial elementary and secondary schools	213,105	578,087
Universities, colleges, and professional schools		
Liberal arts	7,707	176,301
Professional and other schools	38,663	276,688
Total	46,370 ‡	443,989 ‡
Number of teachers		
Public elementary schools	32,189	54,980
Public secondary schools	3,363	28,983
Private and parochial elementary and secondary schools	10,945	19,038
Universities, colleges, and professional schools	4,220	21,950
Graduates		
Public secondary schools	6,756	94,351
Private and parochial schools reporting	943	18,098
Universities, colleges, and professional schools		
Without degree	3,227	2,254
Bachelor's degree	3,403	39,942
Master's degree	259	11,395
Doctor's degree	793	2,573

Source: Harlan H. Horner, ed., *Education in New York State, 1784–1954* (Albany, N.Y., 1954).

* Includes senior, middle, and junior high schools.

† Less moneys received from bonds, bond anticipation notes, and capital notes.

‡ Including summer school and, in 1952, extension schools.

Vassar held its first classes in 1865; the Normal College, which was re-named Hunter in 1914, was established in New York City in 1870 as the first free college for women; and Barnard College, which was af-filiated with Columbia, was founded in 1889. To these should be added

Elmira, which was chartered as a women's college before the Civil War. The Elmira Female College (in 1890 it became Elmira College) held its first classes in 1856.

During the same years substantial progress was made in graduate education. As early as 1857 Samuel B. Ruggles, a Columbia College trustee, had worked out a program for transforming the college into a university. Columbia established a law school in 1858, the School of Mines in 1864, Teachers College in 1888, and the School of Engineering in 1896. Meanwhile German standards of graduate training were introduced at Columbia with the creation of the School (later Faculty) of Political Science in 1880 and the faculties of Philosophy (1890) and Pure Science (1892). Under the direction of Nicholas Murray Butler, who became president of the university in 1902, Columbia built up one of the world's outstanding communities of scholars.

Although New York, unlike many other states, did not establish a state university, the government took an active part in higher education. Under a program approved by the legislature, the state awarded four-year tuition scholarships for Cornell to one student from each of the state's assembly districts.[1] It was with Cornell, moreover, that the state first developed its plan for farming out various fields of public instruction to private institutions. Thus, the College of Agriculture, established by Cornell in 1878, was taken over by the state in 1904. Students attending the College of Agriculture paid no tuition, and the Regents approved and supervised the college's budget. Similar arrangements were made for the Veterinary College and the College of Home Economics at Cornell, the College of Forestry at Syracuse University, and the College of Ceramics at Alfred University. By 1914 the state also operated the State Nautical School (founded in 1875 and renamed the State Merchant Marine Academy in 1929) in New York City; schools of agriculture at Canton (1906), Alfred (1908), Cobleskill (1911), Farmingdale (1912), Delhi (1913); and eleven normal schools and teachers colleges.

After World War I the institutions of higher learning in the state expanded even more rapidly than the elementary and secondary schools. During the prosperous 1920's when a college degree was often viewed as a badge of social distinction and a passport to business success, large numbers of boys and girls, who in earlier years would have been satisfied with a high school diploma, decided that their formal education would not be complete without a bachelor's degree. At the time of the Depression, when it was often impossible to obtain a job, many young people preferred four years of college to the harsh realities of the busi-

[1] After 1913 this plan was expanded, and provision was made for 750 four-year scholarships of one hundred dollars each for study in any New York college or university approved by the Regents.

ness world. Because of these considerations college enrollments steadily increased.

To accommodate the ever-increasing number of students seeking education beyond the secondary level, both private and public institutions expanded their facilities and enrollments. In New York City, for example, two new free colleges—Brooklyn College (1930) and Queens College (1937)—were established to help City College and Hunter College take care of the steadily mounting number of students. By 1956 these four tuition-free colleges were handling seventy-eight thousand students. Nineteen private colleges and universities located within the metropolitan area also offered broad programs of higher education. Elsewhere in the state, large institutions such as Syracuse, Cornell, Buffalo, Vassar, and Rochester felt the pressure of added numbers. Even the smaller private colleges like Hamilton, Colgate, Hobart, Union, and St. Lawrence felt the pressure. In 1941–1942 no less than 31,600 New York youth went out of the state for their college education. True, 17,453 students migrated to New York colleges, coming principally from Connecticut, Massachusetts, New Jersey, and Pennsylvania.

The veterans of World War II also imposed a severe strain on the state's institutions of higher learning. Although the Department of Education had as early as 1943 begun to prepare for the influx of college students at the end of the war, few authorities realized just how many veterans would take advantage of the educational provisions in the federal government's G.I. Bill of Rights. By 1946 it was evident that existing educational facilities were inadequate, and in the spring of that year Governor Dewey called together eighty-six college and university presidents to consider the problem. Following the conference's recommendation that the state sponsor a junior-college program, the legislature appropriated funds for the establishment of three two-year colleges. In the fall of 1946 Dewey formally opened Sampson College at the Sampson Naval Training Center, Champlain College at Plattsburgh, and Mohawk College in Utica. In their first year, the three institutions had a total enrollment of 5,000, and in 1948 they were attended by 8,500 students. Later, when the state system expanded, these three colleges were abandoned.

It was in part the increasing pressure for higher educational facilities which led to the establishment of the State University of New York in 1948. This organization converted the various state colleges and schools into a single system, which included eleven state teachers colleges, six agricultural and technical institutes, five experimental institutes of applied arts and sciences, the New York State Maritime Academy (became a college in 1949), the College of Forestry, and the five contract colleges—the Colleges of Agriculture, Home Economics, and Ceramics, the Veterinary College, and the School of Industrial and Labor Relations. In 1950 two health and medical centers were added: the Downstate Medical Center became a reality when the State University took over the facilities of the Long Island College of Medicine; the Syracuse University College of Medicine was acquired by the state and became the State University Upstate Medical Center. In 1950, also, an extension center, previously operated at Endicott in Broome County by Syracuse University, was taken over by the State University and transformed into a new four-year liberal arts institution named Harpur College.

To meet the ever-pressing needs of those seeking education beyond the high school level, the Young commission, influenced in part by the action of California, gave special attention to the desirability of creating a system of publicly supported community colleges limited to two-year programs offering a combination of technical training and general education. This recommendation—together with others which would eliminate discrimination in admissions to colleges and universities of the state on the basis of race, color, creed, or national origin, enlarge the state scholarship plan, and make better financial support available for teacher education in the municipally supported colleges of New York City—also received legislative approval.

Jamestown Community College was the first institution of its kind to become a part of the State University. It accepted its first students in 1950. Since that date five similar institutions were established in Middletown, Auburn, New York City, White Plains, and Staten Island. In 1953 the State University organization comprised thirty-seven units of which ten were community colleges. Special state schools include 133 schools of nursing, three institutes for the blind, and six for the deaf.

At the beginning of 1956 the State Education Department reported that 325,370 students were enrolled in the colleges of New York. Of these 112,526 were women. The total was an advance of 7,000 over the enrollment of the previous year. First-semester freshmen showed an increase of 15 per cent over the corresponding semester of 1954–1955 and again emphasized the need for securing more good teachers. Expenditures for higher education in the state during the last fifty years increased in round numbers $83,000,000 to $270,000,000. The full-time instructional staff has increased from approximately 4,000 to 23,000.

One of the most outstanding sources of encouragement to young people to continue their formal education beyond the secondary level has been the state's scholarship program. Established in 1913, it first provided for 750 scholarships each year, carrying an annual stipend of $100 for four years of undergraduate study. In 1946 the annual stipend was increased from $100 to $350, and the following year the number of awards was increased from 750 to 827. In 1949 the number was doubled to 1,654.

This was far short of the Regents' 1944 recommendation of 12,000 yearly scholarships of $350. Prior to 1944 these awards were based on the average marks in the Regents' examination; since 1944 the awards have been made on the basis of the scores achieved in a comprehensive examination prepared under the auspices of the State Examinations Board. In 1946 the state began to award medical scholarships of $750 a year, and, also under the Dewey administration, 4,800 scholarships, each worth $350, were created for veterans.

One of the most significant and encouraging developments in the long history of the state has been the growth of adult education under both public and private auspices. No survey of education in either the state or the nation would be complete without some mention of the Chautauqua Institution. Organized at Lake Chautauqua in 1874 as a summer study group for Sunday-school teachers, Chautauqua soon became the most notable force in adult education in the United States. Although the major emphasis was placed on the lectures and concerts given in the annual summer sessions, the Chautauqua University offered a full and varied program of continuous study through extension work and both reading and correspondence courses. The Chautauqua Literary and Scientific Circle directed a four-year reading program for local groups of interested adults; the Chautauqua Book-a-Month Club supplied such books as John Richard Green's *Short History of the English People* to an estimated half-million readers; and during the summer Chautauqua audiences were addressed by outstanding authorities on a wide variety of subjects. The Chautauqua summer sessions proved so popular that within a short time similar meetings were being held in many other parts of the state and nation. In addition, city dwellers were provided with numerous opportunities for adult education on a year-round basis. In New York City evening lecture series were conducted by The Cooper Union for the Advancement of Science and Art, the People's Institute (founded in 1897 by Charles Sprague Smith), and the Board of Education. Extensive adult education programs were also offered by the Brooklyn Institute of Arts and Sciences, the Buffalo Society of Natural Sciences, and similar institutions in other cities throughout the state.

Adult education at this time was carried on chiefly by private philanthropy and special interest groups. Public adult education dates back to the beginning of the twentieth century and was occasioned in part by the great new wave of immigrants flooding into the state. By 1912 continuation, home, factory, and evening schools were serving 200,000 adults. Fifteen years later the number had increased to over 300,000. Free night schools were opened, supervisors appointed, and teachers trained for special work with the foreign born. Though immigration was severely restricted by the federal acts of the 1920's, the continued presence of large numbers of foreign-born adults, the steady influx of displaced persons of two world wars, and the recent arrival of hundreds of thousands of Puerto Ricans have kept the Americanization phase of the adult education program constantly expanding.

But adult education was not limited to the foreign born. The Depression, World War II, and increased leisure occasioned by mechanization stimulated the movement. During the Depression years much emphasis was given to consumer education and occupational retraining. No less than 400,000 adults were enrolled in the enormous W.P.A. project for upstate relief. Large numbers of adults studied cultural subjects in their enforced leisure time.

World War II gave not only adult education but all education a tremendous push in the direction of vocationalism. Following the war it became more and more evident that education was a continuous process that should go on from birth to the end of life. The State Education Law was amended to provide financial assistance to the local public schools to enable each community to meet its own adult education needs. The response exceeded expectation. In the seven-year period 1946–1953, the number of community programs for adults increased from 65 to 569 and the enrollment from 51,000 to 58,700. Opportunities for public adult education are now available in 98 per cent of the state's cities and in 91 per cent of the centralized district schools.

Meanwhile the colleges and universities of the state, both public and private, have established night schools and hundreds of extension courses for adults. The New York Adult Education Council, the New York State Citizens' Council, and other organizations have rendered outstanding service of various kinds and types in the cause of adult education. Several of the leading foundations have contributed to adult education projects within the state. Nor should the contributions of radio and television be overlooked in this respect.

The schools and colleges of the state and radio and television and other agencies which contribute to the education of adults have revealed the inability of most of us to resolve the problems posed by two contrasting—and often conflicting—patterns of culture. On the one hand, there is the machine civilization with its relentless pressure toward conformity and standardization. On the other hand, there are those who protest that mechanization, standardization, and conformity do not mean progress but "robotism," stagnation, and spiritual and intellectual decay. Unquestionably the machine can provide us with many more social and material advantages than have ever been available to man in the past; unquestionably, too, it is capable of destroying man's individualism and making him its slave.

New York's educational facilities were immeasurably improved by the development of the state's libraries. In 1865 the few public libraries in New York had small collections and elaborate rules that seemed designed above all else to prevent readers from obtaining books. Although a state library law was enacted in 1872, it was not until the mid 1880's that any substantial progress was made. The individual most responsible for the growth of libraries in New York was Melvil Dewey, who founded the first library school (at Columbia College) in the United States and served as state librarian from 1888 to 1905. At his instigation the books in the district school libraries were used as a nucleus for new public libraries, traveling libraries were established, extension courses and lecture series were offered, and the State Library at Albany was made a clearinghouse for all public libraries in the state. At the same time, several wealthy individuals supplied libraries with books, money, and buildings. In 1895 the Astor, Lenox, and Tilden libraries—each of which was the product of private philanthropy—were merged to form the magnificent New York Public Library. Andrew Carnegie gave approximately $6,500,000 to cities and villages in New York for the erection of more than one hundred library buildings. By 1920 New York had more than 660 libraries.

In the last twenty-five years many of the libraries of the state have been compelled to expand. The Depression, in particular, boomed public library circulation. In small and large urban areas, the public library became a poor man's club. Circulation of books in larger communities such as Buffalo, Rochester, Syracuse, Albany, and New York City increased almost 50 per cent in the single year 1933. New York City, housing approximately half of the state's population, has three public libraries. Smallest of these is the Queens Borough Library. Brooklyn Public Library has an annual circulation of over five million volumes. The New York Public Library serving Manhattan, Bronx, and Richmond (Staten Island) is the largest and most important. The Circulating Division with almost seventy branches has a daily circulation of enough books to make a stack two and one half times as high as the Empire State Building. More than three million people come each year to its Reference Library, which is second only to the famous Library of Congress. The Reference Library at the state capital is also one of the best of its kind in the nation.

In retrospect, anyone who reviews the history of educational endeavor in the state of New York will be impressed with the over-all record of progress. On occasion, voices have been raised in opposition to the changing character of the educational pattern or the increasing demand for financial outlay in support of education. But these have not long delayed the great progress that has been made. With passing years more of the state's inhabitants have realized that education is a liberating process—liberating in the sense that it frees us from ignorance, superstition, fear, and unnecessary physical handicaps. They have come to realize, too, that education at all levels should help us to discover ourselves—our strengths, weaknesses, aptitudes, latent talents, and potentialities. They have come to see that education teaches us how to plan, to work, to play together, and to have respect for facts, excellence of performance, the aesthetically beautiful, and moral and ethical values. They have come to understand that education is the most potent weapon that free men have for the defense of freedom. Finally, they have come to appreciate that, in the last analysis, the greatest power on earth stems from educated, unregimented, highly committed men and women dedicated to human betterment.

The Cultural Ascendency

of the Metropolis

We have been two months in New York. . . . . It's immensely interesting. . . . There are lots of interesting young painting and writing fellows, and the place is lordly free, with foreign touches of all kinds all thro' its abounding Americanism: Boston seems of another planet.
—WILLIAM DEAN HOWELLS, *April 14, 1888*

IN THE years following the Civil War, New York City supplanted Boston as the leading center of intellectual activity in the United States. Manhattan not only provided writers, artists, and educators with a cosmopolitan and stimulating atmosphere, but it was also the single largest source of the wealth that was used to finance their endeavors. Most of the major publishing houses were located in New York City; the city's newspapers and magazines were among the most famous in the nation; it served as the home office for several national religious organizations; more authors and painters lived there than in any other city in the United States; it possessed excellent library and museum facilities; and it was the home of most of the country's richest art patrons. As American culture was increasingly organized along business lines, it was both fitting and understandable that New York City should become the intellectual as well as the business capital of the United States.

It is easy, however, to exaggerate the importance of the city's pre-eminence in intellectual affairs. It set styles, but it also reflected trends that were nation-wide. The city dominated the state in many respects, but the state was also a part of the nation, and as such it was not immune to developments beyond its borders. As a consequence, the course of the state's intellectual and social history was determined not only by the somewhat unique features of New York City's relationship to the rest of the country, but also by certain national forces that affected all

Americans to some degree. In general, New York's religious history was not unlike that of many other states, while in literature, the arts, and drama New York City enjoyed a position of undisputed leadership.

In religion New York tended to conform to a larger pattern of thought and development that was a product of forces that transcended state lines. In both the state and nation, religious views and church organization were altered to meet new intellectual theories, the rise of big business, urbanization, and the increase in immigration. New York's wealth, size, and diversity gave it a certain pre-eminence in religious affairs; but pre-eminence, at least in this instance, should not be confused with leadership. Nor was New York's religious history necessarily unique, for deviations from what might be termed the national norm were in large part differences in degree rather than in kind.

The most obvious if not the most significant fact of New York's religious history was the rapid growth of the various church groups within the state. In 1855 the Protestant churches of New York had 457,971 members. The single largest denomination was the Methodist, followed by the Presbyterian, Baptist, and Episcopal. Some seventy years later (1926) Protestant church membership totaled 1,712,898. This represented a 274-per-cent increase over the earlier figure and stands in contrast to a 222-per-cent increase in the state's population for the same period. By the 1920's the four largest denominations were the Episcopal, Methodist, Presbyterian, and Lutheran. With the exception of the Lutherans, most New York Protestants were native-born Americans, and their churches exerted a more powerful influence in the state's rural areas than in its cities.

Roman Catholic and Jewish religious organizations were the principal beneficiaries of the increase in immigration and urbanization. During the postwar years a large percentage of immigrants were either Catholics from southern and eastern Europe or Jews from Russia and from the European states that bordered it. New York City was the principal port of debarkation for most immigrants, and large numbers of them made the city their home. As a consequence, New York City became a major center of Catholic and Jewish population. The number of Catholics in New York State increased from 242,225 in 1855 to 3,115,424 in 1926, a majority of whom lived in New York City. By the time of the Civil War there was still only a negligible number of Jews in New York. But from 1880 to 1914 more than a million Jews migrated to the United States, and a large proportion of them settled in New York. In 1880 there were 60,000 Jews in the state; in 1914 more than 1,500,000; and in 1927 almost 2,000,000. The state's Jews were heavily concentrated in New York City, where they comprised approximately 30 per cent of the total population.

Religion was one of the few possessions that immigrants were able to bring with them to America, and they clung to their old faiths in their new homes. The neighborhood synagogue or Catholic church was a cohesive force that helped to create social as well as spiritual communities among poverty-stricken foreigners living in the slums of a strange land. The Protestant churches, on the other hand, held relatively little appeal for most immigrants. Moreover, as various Protestant churches increased in wealth, many poor people in the cities came to view them as exclusive institutions to which only the well-to-do could belong. Some indication of the impact of new conditions on American Protestantism is revealed by the fact that from 1868 to 1888 seventeen Protestant churches moved from an area in lower Manhattan into which some 200,000 new residents had moved in the same period.

In several cities Protestant clergymen sought to meet the problems growing out of industrialization and immigration by making their churches agents of humanitarian reform and social centers for their parishioners. William A. Muhlenberg, an Episcopal minister in New York City, is generally credited with being the originator of what has come to be known as the institutional church. While serving as pastor of the Church of the Holy Communion from 1846 to 1858, he allied his church with such charitable enterprises as the Sisterhood of the Holy Communion and St. Luke's Hospital. A somewhat similar program was adopted in 1868 by Grace Episcopal Church in New York City. In 1872 Thomas K. Beecher, rector of the First Congregational Church of Elmira, opened a new church building that included lecture rooms, a library, and a gymnasium. The role of the institutional church in urban religious life is indicated in part by the experience of St. George's Episcopal Church in New York City. In its first fifteen years as an institutional church its membership increased from seventy-five to more than four thousand.

New York's religious leaders, like those in other states, were compelled to deal with new ideas as well as with new social and economic problems. Darwinian thought, the conflict between modernism and fundamentalism, and the controversy arising over the higher criticism (or the analysis of the historical validity of the Bible) in varying degrees occupied and often divided most of the Protestant groups within the state. With significant exceptions, churches in the rural regions generally adhered to the established views, while those in the cities proved relatively receptive to new ideas. Modernism, for example, won many more adherents in the city than in the country, and Darwinian evolutionary theory was treated with far more tolerance in urban than in rural pulpits. It was, moreover, the preachers in the state's larger cities who took the lead in the movement to reconcile evolution and traditional Christianity. Among such preachers were Henry Ward Beecher and Lyman Abbott, successive pastors of Plymouth Church in Brooklyn, both of whom maintained that the evolutionary process was created by God and revealed His omniscience and all-pervading wisdom. Finally, the higher criticism never aroused the opposition in the cities that it did in the country, and it is perhaps significant that in the mid 1880's a revised version of the New Testament sold 200,000 copies in New York City within a week of its publication.

If religious developments in New York conformed to a national pattern, the literature and art of New York City often set the pattern for the rest of the nation. The concentration of what might be termed the business of the intellect in Manhattan enabled the city—and indirectly the state—to impose many of its values on the rest of the nation. Men in downtown offices in New York City decided what books should and should not be published. Newspaper owners in the metropolis established standards that were accepted by many country editors in every section of the United States. The city's theatrical producers selected the plays that would be sent on the road to other cities and towns. Millionaires in Fifth Avenue mansions became arbiters on matters of taste in painting, sculpture, and architecture. New York City was the nation's wealthiest metropolis, and money talked in the world of books and art almost as much as it did in the countinghouse.

New York City, however, had attractions other than money, for it provided writers and artists with an environment that many of them found irresistible. Novelists, poets, playwrights, painters, and sculptors often were—or at least they liked to think that they were—unconventional people, and the city's relative indifference to convention permitted them to pursue their careers without the restrictions imposed by the mores of the village or small town. New York City, moreover, was one of the few places in the United States where they could associate with others who spoke their language and shared their interests. Finally, it was the most cosmopolitan city in the nation, and its close ties with Europe gave its inhabitants a chance to know—if not to participate in— the Old World's intellectual and artistic life. New York may not have been Paris, but it was the next best thing.

After 1900 Greenwich Village in downtown Manhattan became a major center of intellectual life in America. In the Village rents were low, inhibitions were considered poor taste, and the neighbors did not pry. Almost every resident took pride in being a nonconformist. *Avant garde* writers, artists in revolt against the academy, anarchists, playboys, revolutionists, pacifists, editors of *The Masses*, and composers of the new poetry conducted a never-ending, multifronted, joyous offensive against middle-class America and its values. To outsiders the Village was where people stayed up all night, drank too much, and practiced free love. But it was also where a number of dedicated individuals did a great deal of work that was to shape the future of intellectual America. Eugene O'Neill's early plays were produced in the Village before they appeared on Broadway; modern art was brought from Europe to the United States by Villagers; and many of the prominent authors of the 1920's and 1930's served their apprenticeships in the Village during the years that preceded World War I.

Although, after the Civil War, New York State may not have produced any writers comparable to Cooper, Melville, and Whitman, New York City attracted most of the prominent literary figures of the age. If they did not live in New York City, they visited it frequently. Writers came to Manhattan to talk with other writers; to arrange for the publication of their books by such firms as Harper and Brothers, Henry Holt, Scribner, Macmillan, and Putnam; to sell stories or articles to the editors of the city's magazines; to take jobs on its newspapers; to escape an environment that they found stultifying; to embark for Europe; to have a good time. Boston was no longer the hub of the literary universe, and William Dean Howells' move from there to New York City in 1889 was belated recognition by America's dean of letters of Massachusetts' decline and New York's ascendency.

Although writers were attracted to New York City, they did not comprise a New York school of literature. During the postwar years there was a marked decline in intellectual parochialism. Authors often used regional material, but they were seldom provincial, and they wrote for a national audience. Under the circumstances, New Yorkers were not in a position to assume a possessive attitude toward those poets, novelists, dramatists, and journalists who happened to have been born or to have lived in New York. Such diverse writers as Paul Leicester Ford, Frank Stockton, Richard Harding Davis, Jacob Riis, John Burroughs, Theodore Roosevelt, and H. C. Bunner were all New Yorkers; but they had little else in common, and the reading public correctly viewed them as Americans rather than as American regionalists. In a similar vein, Henry James, although born and brought up in New York City, was rightfully considered an international literary figure rather than a product of the locality in which he had spent his early life.

The diversity and complexity of life in New York City provided many novelists and short-story writers with material and themes. Although James became an expatriate whose subject matter was derived in large part from Europe, his native city was not entirely excluded from his work. In *Washington Square* he used a setting that he had known intimately as a boy. The locale of *Washington Square*, however, has little to do with the novel's plot, and of far greater interest to the local historian is *The American Scene*'s beautiful and highly impressionistic sketch of a Jewish community on the lower East Side. But if James's interest in

New York was at best incidental, Edith Wharton found it an ideal setting for her fictional studies of the upper reaches of society. A member of the local aristocracy by birth and background, she knew her material at first hand, and she approached it with the subtlety of an artist and the objectivity of a sociologist. Above all, she was a craftsman, and in such novels as *The House of Mirth* (1905) and *The Age of Innocence* (1920) she wrote with perception and precision of the emotional conflicts and conventions in the tight little world of New York's upper classes.

In contrast to Edith Wharton, most writers preferred to emphasize the more colorful and distinctive features of the city and its people. Thus, Ernest Poole in *The Harbor* (1915) used his personal experiences as the basis for what is undoubtedly the outstanding novel about the city's water front; Paul Leicester Ford's *The Honorable Peter Stirling* (1894) was, in effect, a case study of ward politics in New York; and Theodore Dreiser incorporated in *Sister Carrie* (1900) a description of a strike which had occurred in the neighboring city of Brooklyn.

The city's poor also proved an invaluable source of material for many authors. In addition to Jacob Riis's factual reports on the slums in *How the Other Half Lives* (1890) and *A Ten Years' War* (1900) were H. C. Bunner's stories in *Short Sixes* (1890) on life in the tenements; and William Sidney Porter (O. Henry) wrote ironic tales with unexpected endings about shopgirls, policemen, clerks, and other members of the city's lower middle class. Although Bunner and Porter did not ignore the sordid features of urban existence, they infused enough sentimentality into their stories to leave the impression that most city dwellers—even the poorest ones—lived in the midst of excitement and adventure.

Some writers, however, preferred to treat urban life realistically, and of these Howells and Stephen Crane were easily pre-eminent. *A Hazard of New Fortunes* (1890), which is the most rewarding of Howells' New York novels from both a literary and historical viewpoint, deals with the city's principal classes and emphasizes the conflicts among them. Representatives of the new and old rich, the very poor, and the middle classes are presented with accuracy and understanding in a framework of social unrest and struggle. Howells' sympathy with the underprivileged seldom interfered with his objectivity, and *A Hazard of New Fortunes* is realistic without being propagandistic. Stephen Crane's *Maggie: A Girl of the Streets* (1892) lacks the scope of *A Hazard of New Fortunes*, but surpasses it in both intensity and depth of feeling. The author depicted life in the slums as brutal and ugly, and his characters never emerge from the degradation and misery that have engulfed them. Harsh, merciless, and authentic, *Maggie* was a landmark in American fiction that set standards to which many subsequent realists have aspired.

The rural regions of the state produced no literature comparable to that written in and about the city. Perhaps the outstanding novel with an upstate locale written during the period under consideration is *Seth's Brother's Wife* by Harold Frederic, published in 1877. It is distinguished by its realistic treatment of rural society. Although Hamlin Garland is often credited with being the first American author in the postwar years to depict life in the country in all its drabness and harshness, *Seth's Brother's Wife* appeared four years before Garland's *Main-Travelled Roads* and deserves to rank with it. Many other novels about the New York countryside, however, were folksy, anecdotal accounts of shrewd local characters. The most famous example in both the state and the nation of the so-called "B'Gosh School" of literature was *David Harum* (1898) by Edward Westcott of Syracuse. The central character was an upstate banker and horse trader, who entranced readers with his hard-headed philosophy and homespun wit. The book's enormous popularity can be attributed at least in part to the nostalgia of an increasingly urbanized America for a vanishing way of life. As such, it tells us more about the reading public than it does about upstate New York at the turn of the century.

American journalism, unlike the book-publishing business, was not concentrated in the hands of a relatively small number of firms, but in this field, as in so many others, the city's supremacy was undeniable. There were, of course, outstanding papers in other states and in other cities and towns in New York State. The Albany *Argus* and *Evening Journal*, the Brooklyn *Eagle* and *Union*, the Schenectady *Union*, the Ithaca *Journal*, the Rochester *Express*, the Utica *Observer*, and the Buffalo *Express* were all papers of unusual distinction at various times in their careers, and each had some feature or policy that set it off from other journals. They were, however, papers whose influence was confined to a comparatively limited area, while those in New York City were often national as well as local institutions. For many years before the Civil War, the *Herald, Times, Tribune*, and *Post* had been known, if not read, throughout the country, and their editors were as famous as many of the nation's business and political leaders. Country editors either quoted or paraphrased the editorials and news stories of the metropolitan papers, and the tone of the press throughout the land more often than not was set by those who controlled the principal journals of New York City.

For approximately a decade and a half after the Civil War, the *Sun* and the *Post* were the city's foremost newspapers. Believing that other papers were stuffy and overwritten, Charles A. Dana made the *Sun* witty, entertaining, and incisive. Filled with human-interest stories, the *Sun* was invariably amusing, but it was seldom profound, and it often seemed more concerned with trivia than with the news. The *Post*, under the editorship of E. L. Godkin, was all that the *Sun* was not. Its editorials were scholarly analyses of current problems, and no attempt was made to write down to the paper's readers. Godkin was a nineteenth-century liberal, and both he and his paper stood for low tariffs, civil service reform, the abolition of war, and an economy unhampered by government interference or regulation. Although the *Post's* circulation seldom exceeded twenty thousand, it was read by many other newspapermen, public officials, and members of the professions throughout the United States.

Joseph Pulitzer's acquisition of the New York *World* in 1883 marked the advent of yellow journalism in the United States and the beginning of a new era in the American newspaper business. Written for the poorly educated and underprivileged urban masses, the *World* appealed to its readers with spectacular stories of crime and sex, blaring headlines, cartoons or pictures on almost every page, and comic strips. But Pulitzer was not content with mere sensationalism. For many years the *World's* international news was unsurpassed; at one time or another most of the country's ablest reporters were on its payroll; and it sponsored more reforms than did any other major paper in the United States. At any given time its editorial page provided what in effect was a check list of current reforms, and its news columns were filled with exposés that substantiated its editorial crusades. The mixture of reform and sensationalism proved to be good business, for within a short time after Pulitzer purchased it the *World* had the largest circulation in the United States.

The *World's* supremacy was soon challenged by William Randolph Hearst's *Journal*. After acquiring the *Journal* in 1895, Hearst hired some of the *World's* leading reporters, copied all of Pulitzer's sensational techniques, and devised some new ones of his own. The two papers were soon engaged in a furious fight for circulation, and during the Spanish American War their own battle for readers often overshadowed the conflict in Cuba. But although Hearst learned about sensationalism from Pulitzer, he did not adopt the *World's* other features. The *Journal's* editorial policy was both superficial and erratic; the paper was frequently used to advance its owner's political ambitions; and at times its news reports were slanted to make them conform to Hearst's prejudices. The *Journal* attracted readers, but it did not always enlighten them.

A year after Hearst took over the *Journal*, Adolph Ochs purchased the *Times*. Since Henry J. Raymond's death in 1869, the *Times* had declined in prestige and influence, and by 1896 its circulation was down to nine thousand. Shunning sensationalism and all other forms of journalistic pyrotechnics, Ochs transformed the *Times* into a vehicle for well-written, comprehensive, and detailed accounts of "all the news that's fit to print."

His concept of the news, moreover, was broad enough to include literature, music, the arts, and drama, and he hired authorities to report on each. The *Times's* coverage rivaled that of the giant press associations, while no other paper approached the objectivity of its news columns. In addition, its format and typography served as models for many other papers throughout the United States. No other paper printed more news and no other paper printed the news with less bias.

Despite the influence and prestige of the *Times,* it was yellow journalism rather than the conservative press that prepared the way for New York's modern mass-circulation magazines. For several years *Harper's,* the *Atlantic Monthly,* the *Century, Scribner's, Putnam's,* and the *Galaxy* were the nation's leading periodicals. With the exception of the *Atlantic Monthly,* they were all published in New York, and they all had certain features in common. They ran serials by leading English and American novelists, contained few advertisements, sponsored good-government reforms rather than changes in the economic system, were relatively expensive, and appealed to the most educated—and, therefore, a very small part—of the population. It was only a matter of time, however, before the forces of industrialization and urbanization that had produced the mass-circulation newspaper would effect similar changes on New York's periodicals. *McClure's Magazine,* founded in New York City in 1893, was among the first magazines to reach a mass audience. Priced at fifteen cents (later reduced to ten), profusely illustrated, filled with articles and stories of general interest, and crammed with advertisements, *McClure's* established a pattern that was copied by the *Cosmopolitan Magazine, Munsey's Magazine,* and many others. By 1900, when *Harper's* and *Scribner's* each had a circulation of only 150,000, *Munsey's* was selling 650,000, and both *McClure's* and *Cosmopolitan* exceeded 350,000.

In painting and sculpture, as in literature and journalism, New York achieved a pre-eminence that was in considerable measure due to the presence of the nation's largest and richest city within its borders. Representatives of all the leading art movements were attracted to the city, and it was there that the academicians and insurgents waged their never-ending war. With considerably more insight and technical proficiency than had been displayed by their predecessors in the Hudson River School, Alexander H. Wynant, George Inness, and Homer Martin painted landscapes of the Catskills, Adirondacks, and Mohawk Valley. Albert P. Ryder, by far the most imaginative of the *post-bellum* painters, went beyond reality into the realm of his own mind to produce a series of haunting, symbolic pictures in which individuals became ghostlike figures and shadowy masses supplanted details. August Saint-Gaudens, the son of an Irish mother and French father and a product of the streets of New

York City, became the nation's foremost sculptor. His statues of Admiral David Farragut at Madison Square and General William T. Sherman on the plaza at Fifth Avenue and Fifty-ninth Street are masterpieces that remain as evidence of his pre-eminence in his field. All these men were in some degree innovators. Their acknowledged leader was John La Farge. An eclectic, he painted landscapes and figures, did drawings and water colors, and earned his most lasting fame for his murals and pioneer work in the design of stained-glass windows. A champion of the new styles and new artists that emerged in the postwar decades, he led the revolt against the standards imposed by the highly respected and equally conservative National Academy of Design. With his assistance a group of rebels in 1877 organized the Society of American Artists and set up the Art Students' League as the Society's school. The Society flourished from the outset, and within a short time its membership included most of the country's outstanding artists.

During the first decade of the twentieth century a group of young painters in Greenwich Village attracted considerable attention with their realistic studies of commonplace scenes in New York City. The leading exponents of the new school of urban realism were eight rebels (among whom were Arthur B. Davies, Robert Henri, John Sloan, and George Luks) who were collectively known as "the Eight" and whose work was derisively labeled "the Ash Can School" by the critics. Painting scenes of tenements, elevated railroads, bars, and city streets, the Eight peopled their pictures with salesgirls, pugs, drunks, push-cart peddlers, prostitutes, bums, and almost every other type of New Yorker who neither lived on Fifth Avenue nor worked in Wall Street. Their war cry was: "Don't imitate; be yourself!" They shocked the traditionalists, and they reveled in their own iconoclasm. In subject matter—and to some extent in technique—they represented a break with the past and provided undeniable evidence that America was capable of an indigenous art.

The battle between the modernists and traditionalists erupted into a full-scale war with the opening of the International Exhibition of Modern Art in the early winter of 1913 at the armory of the Sixty-ninth Regiment on Park Avenue and Thirty-fourth Street in New York City. Sponsored by some of the Eight and by such other representatives of the Ash Can School as George Bellows, the so-called "Armory Show" contained sixteen hundred exhibits of American and European painting and sculpture. The work of foreign artists, many of whom were representatives of advanced schools of European art, attracted the greatest attention and aroused the most indignation. While conservatives protested that modern art was obscene and fraudulent, the critics—with a few exceptions—could neither understand nor appreciate the distortions and unusual color combinations used by Marcel Duchamp, Pablo

Picasso, Francis Picabia, and others. Meanwhile, the press treated the exhibition as news as well as art, and the armory was jammed with the curious. The Armory Show may have made few converts among the Philistines, but it was more responsible than any other single event for stimulating popular interest in modern art in America.

New York City was not only the center of new art movements, but it was also the home of some of the most valuable collections of painting and sculpture in the world. Steel, coal, and oil barons, searching for some way to spend their money and display their wealth, bought up European art treasures in much the same fashion that they purchased their daughters' husbands from among the European nobility. A contemporary wrote that "private galleries in New York" were "almost as common as private stables," and many of the new acquisitions undoubtedly belonged in stables. But as millionaire connoisseurs gained in experience and learned to rely on the advice of experts, both their taste and their galleries improved. Because they were buying prestige as well as art, they generally neglected American artists. Native art was not, however, completely ignored, and by World War I there were several well-to-do New Yorkers who were collecting American painting and sculpture.

Most of the private collections eventually were either opened to the public or given to one of the city's museums. Of the museums, the largest was the Metropolitan Museum of Art, which was opened in 1872 and moved to its present location on Fifth Avenue in 1880. Other important galleries opened in Greater New York before World War I included the Museum of the Brooklyn Institute of Arts and Sciences (1897), Cooper Union's Museum for the Arts of Decoration (1896), the Pratt Institute Free Library's Art Gallery (1896), and the Museum of the Hispanic Society of America (1908). In addition, public buildings such as the City Hall contained portraits of prominent Americans, while collections of paintings of considerable merit were owned by the New-York Historical Society, the New York Public Library, and several other institutions. Outside of New York City the principal museums were the Albright Art Gallery–Buffalo Fine Arts Academy (1901) in Buffalo and the Memorial Art Gallery of the University of Rochester (1914).

Millionaires collected homes as well as paintings, and their baronial residences made New York City's architecture distinctive, if not distinguished. For some years after the Civil War the rich, like the middle class, lived in brownstones, but by the 1880's home-grown millionaires and those who had migrated from the hinterland were building palaces and chateaus of marble and granite on upper Fifth Avenue. Every new mansion was larger, more sumptuous, and more expensive than those already built, and almost all were modeled on famous European structures. Richard Morris Hunt and other architects for the plutocracy were willing to employ any style that happened to suit the fancy of their patrons. As a consequence, the "millionaires' colony" stretching along Fifth Avenue was a bewildering array of baroque, rococo, classical, renaissance, and romanesque buildings. But the "battle of the styles" was not confined to Manhattan, for in cities, towns, and villages throughout the state were examples of every variety of home architecture from the bungalow in the suburbs to the factory-owner's Victorian house on the hill.

Public buildings, like private residences, were usually built along the lines of European models that had been designed centuries before the advent of industrial America. For many years the city's leading architectural firm was McKim, Mead, and White, and its buildings—among which in New York City were Columbia University's Low Memorial Library, the University Club, and the Pennsylvania Railroad Station— were usually done in a classical style of which the firm's members were acknowledged masters. But classicism, however excellent, bore little relation to the needs of a highly urbanized, business civilization. The skyscraper rather than the Greek temple was to become the hallmark of the twentieth-century city. Although Chicago architects were the first to use the steel framework for multistoried commercial buildings, it was Manhattan that became the home of the skyscraper. The first example of the school of vertical architecture in New York City was the Flatiron Building, designed by Daniel Burnham of Chicago and completed in 1902. Within a decade, however, its twenty stories had been dwarfed by the Woolworth and Singer buildings and the Metropolitan Tower. McKim, Mead, and White, succumbing to the demand for height and to the pressure of urban real estate values, designed the skyscraping Municipal Building in 1907.

By the turn of the century the theater, like other forms of creative endeavor, had become a major business enterprise, with its headquarters in New York City. Repertory, which had once flourished in almost every city, was in large measure supplanted by touring companies from Broadway. Plays were increasingly built around star performers who were under contract to New York producers. In 1893 Charles Frohman took over the city's Empire Theatre and made it "the greatest of all American star factories." Three years later he joined forces with Al Hayman, Marc Klaw, and Abraham Erlanger of New York and Sam Nixon and Fred Zimmerman of Philadelphia to form what came to be known as the "Theatrical Trust." Controlling many of the nation's leading performers and theaters in several cities, the trust's system of production and distribution was not unlike that of the industrial trusts. After 1900 the Schubert brothers—Sam, Lee, and Jacob—were able to break the trust's near-monopoly and establish a rival syndicate of stars and theaters.

But competition did not change the basic features of the system, for both combines operated from New York City and used it as the manufacturing and distributing center for their wares. By World War I most other cities in the United States had become "road towns" for plays that originated in New York, were financed by New York capital, and were under New York management.

Regardless of who controlled the theater, the fact remained that from the Civil War to World War I the popular stage in New York was distinguished by a kind of uninhibited flamboyance that was altogether pleasing to the customers. And the customers responded by making folk heroes of many of the leading actors of the day. The result may have not been great art, but all agreed that it was great fun. *East Lynne,* which opened in 1863 with Lucille Western in the lead and which the critics decided was "trash," ran for ten years to set a record that was never surpassed. But *East Lynne* and its successive stars had no monopoly of the affection and support of the city's theater goers. By the 1880's Lily Langtry (the "Jersey Lily") and Sarah Bernhardt had arrived from Europe to captivate audiences as much by their well-publicized private lives as by their acknowledged beauty and ability. There were also more than enough American stars to suit every taste. Lillian Russell was acclaimed for her voice and beauty, and no other actress in the history of the New York stage ever so completely captivated male audiences over a long period of time. Among the male performers, John Drew and Otis Skinner, who starred with Ada Rehan in *The Merry Wives of Windsor* and *The Taming of the Shrew,* were particular favorites. There was, moreover, no dearth of comedians in the city, and variety acts usually drew large audiences; but the Harrigan and Hart shows were generally acclaimed the funniest in town. Written by Ned Harrigan who also starred in them, such Harrigan and Hart comedies as *The Mulligan Guards* and *Cordelia's Aspirations* were hilarious farces about the topics of the day and the rivalries of the city's various immigrant groups. As popular as the plays were their songs, and there were few New Yorkers who did not know the words and tunes of such Harrigan and Hart favorites as "McNally's Row of Flats," "The Salvation Army," and "The Charlestown Blues."

By the 1890's the enthusiasm for Harrigan and Hart had begun to subside, and Joe Weber and Lew Fields had become the city's favorite comedy team. Holding forth at the Music Hall in a series of variety acts and aided by stars of the caliber of Lillian Russell, Weber and Fields convulsed their audiences with outlandish parodies of New York's most successful plays. The Music Hall also had the prettiest chorus girls on Broadway. But in 1900 with the appearance of the *Floradora* sextet, all the chorus lines of the past were forgotten. *Floradora* ran for more than five hundred nights, and on every one of them the six pretty girls wearing frilly dresses and carrying parasols stopped the show. Each of the original sextet married a wealthy admirer, and before the show closed seventy-nine other girls had at one time or another comprised the sextet. It remained for Florenz Ziegfeld, a young producer who had scored his first success with a show starring Anna Held, to make beautiful chorus girls a standard fixture of the Broadway musical comedy. His first *Follies* opened in 1907, and for the next twenty years he employed famous comics and strikingly handsome chorus girls in a series of *Ziegfeld Follies* that became lavish institutions of the New York theater.

In the two decades preceding the outbreak of World War I, Clyde Fitch's plays were among the most notable features of the New York stage. Fitch, the only American playwright of the period with an international reputation, began his career in 1890. *Beau Brummell* was produced in New York. Written by Fitch especially for Richard Mansfield, *Beau Brummell* was a social comedy that was both a critical and financial success. By the turn of the century, Fitch's reputation was secure, and in 1901 four of his plays (*Captain Jinks of the Horse Marines, The Climbers, Lovers' Lane* and *Barbara Frietchie*) were running simultaneously in New York, while a fifth (*The Way of the World*) was produced there in the same year. Among his subsequent plays, the most distinguished were perhaps *The Truth* (1906) and *The City* (1909). Although Fitch was a versatile dramatist, he was most at home with the comedy of manners, and he gained his major successes in this field. The author of thirty-three plays in two decades, he was without any doubt America's most distinguished playwright in the prewar years.

New York City's location, wealth, and size eventually made it the musical as well as the theatrical capital of the United States. Although Boston held this position for some years after the Civil War and no New York music school ranked with Boston's New England Conservatory, by the turn of the century New York's supremacy was, nevertheless, uncontested. As late as World War I, the United States had virtually no serious music of its own. But if Americans found it difficult to produce a native music, they found it relatively easy to fill the void with European imports. And this fact was in part responsible for New York City's preeminence in musical affairs, for it served as the principal port of entry for Europe's outstanding musical performers and masterpieces. It was, moreover, one of the few cities in the nation that could meet the costs involved in the production of serious music by professionals. For approximately a decade and a half after the Civil War the musical life of the city centered on the concerts of the Philharmonic Orchestra, the activities of various choral and orchestral societies, and the performances of European concert stars and opera companies. Whether the performers were natives or foreigners, amateurs or professionals, the music was invariably European.

A landmark in the city's music history was the founding of the Metropolitan Opera Company in 1883 by a group of wealthy New Yorkers who could not obtain boxes at the Academy of Music. Although the first season was a financial disaster and Leopold Damrosch, the company's director, died in the middle of the 1884–1885 season, within fifteen years of its founding the Metropolitan was a firmly established New York institution and the only American opera company to rival those of Europe. In 1903 Enrico Caruso made his debut at the Metropolitan; five years later Giulio Gatti-Casazza became its director, and Alfred Hertz, Gustav Mahler, and Arturo Toscanini became conductors.

While New York City had ample facilities for the production of music, it produced few notable musicians and composers. It had several music schools, but none approached either the New England Conservatory or the better institutions in Europe. Most performers appearing in New York were Europeans offering European works. This was not so much a manifestation of cultural snobbism as it was an indication of the paucity of native talent. Edward Alexander MacDowell, who was born in New York City and taught at Columbia from 1896 to 1904, was a composer who was acclaimed on both sides of the Atlantic, but his position was unusual enough to be unique. It is significant that *From the New World,* which is generally recognized as the outstanding symphony with an American theme composed before World War I, was the work of Anton Dvořák, a Czech, whose only firsthand knowledge of the United States was acquired during the four years he served as the director of the National Conservatory in New York City. Popular music, on the other hand, was both made and consumed in America. Although jazz as late as 1910 was played by only a small number of musicians in New Orleans, ragtime was a national craze and almost all of its composers worked in New York City's Tin Pan Alley.

Other cities in the state, lacking New York City's resources, had to rely almost exclusively on touring professionals and amateur organizations for musical entertainment. Most cities had an academy of music (Brooklyn's, for example, was founded in 1859 and Rochester's in 1864), where local choral societies and orchestras as well as touring stars performed. Adelina Patti, Ignace Paderewski, and Theodore Thomas were among the musicians known and admired in such cities as Syracuse, Rochester, and Buffalo, while visits from opera companies and Gilbert and Sullivan troupes were annual occurrences. Immigrant groups often took the lead in forming musical organizations. There was at least one German singing society in every city, and Buffalo had two musical societies founded by and for the city's Poles. A further indication of the widespread interest in music throughout the state were the annual music festivals sponsored by numerous New York communities.

If wealth made New York City the nation's principal cultural center, wealth also made it the home and focal point of what is generally termed "society." Before the Civil War the city's aristocracy had been composed of old families whose members for generations had lived off the income derived from real estate holdings and mercantile enterprises. Following the war, the old aristocracy's supremacy was challenged by men—or perhaps, more accurately, by the wives of men—who had made their own fortunes as industrial capitalists. The situation became so alarming that in the 1880's Mrs. William Astor, with the assistance and tutelage of Ward McAllister, set herself up as the queen and dictator of the highest echelons of American society. To gain entree into this self-proclaimed aristocracy required an invitation from Mrs. Astor, and this, in turn, could be obtained only by those who had secured McAllister's approval. Society, as organized by Mrs. Astor and McAllister, required that its members follow a strict and expensive routine. Attendance at the opera was virtually compulsory. Everyone had to make a point of spending outrageous amounts of money on balls and other parties to which were invited only those on whom Mrs. Astor had smiled. An interest in horses was almost mandatory, and every male member was expected to belong to at least one exclusive club. A mansion on Fifth Avenue was not absolutely essential, but it certainly did no harm. In the summer, Newport, Rhode Island, was considered the most desirable of all resorts, although several well-to-do New Yorkers had country homes at Tuxedo Park.

Mrs. Astor's reign ended with her death in 1908, but long before this the barriers had been let down. Despite all efforts, money had its way, and it seldom required more than a generation for the new rich to become old aristocrats. Moreover, throughout her reign New York never lacked men who had money and were willing to spend it on their own entertainment regardless of the dictates of Mrs. Astor. Vulgar, uninhibited, and raucous, such men gravitated to the one city in which they could purchase the pleasures they desired with fortunes obtained from speculation, jobbery, and corruption. Jim Fisk, who was murdered by the lover of his mistress, was an example of this type before Mrs. Astor had mounted her throne, and "Diamond Jim" Brady with his matching sets of jewels ("Them as has 'em, wears 'em," he liked to tell admirers) and his spectacularly beautiful women was a worthy successor to Fisk during Mrs. Astor's declining years. These big spenders and gay livers, along with their gaudy companions, never would have been admitted to Newport or Tuxedo Park, but this presented no problem, for they preferred Saratoga (or Saratoga Springs, to call it by its actual name). New York's oldest spa drew many visitors who wished to benefit from the curative effects of its renowned mineral springs, and several of Mrs. Astor's followers were there during the racing season, but its reputation rested on its attraction for the flashier residents of New York City. Famed for its race track, its rich men and beautiful women, the invention of the potato chip and the Saratoga trunk, and its two enormous hotels, Saratoga was the gaudiest of America's nineteenth-century summer resorts.

Neither Fisk nor Brady ever attempted to storm the citadels of high society; but like Mrs. Astor and her followers, they helped to make New York City as pre-eminent in conspicuous consumption as it was in every other field of endeavor. And conspicuous consumption was not altogether unrelated to the city's leadership in the arts. Sponsoring the opera or endowing museums and libraries was one of the accepted ways of converting the owner of a mere fortune into an aristocrat, while even those plutocrats of the Fisk and Brady stripe were enthusiastic supporters of the popular stage. This system of subsidizing the arts through patrons who had more money than taste may have been wasteful, but it was the only system that was known at the time, and it deserves to be judged by its results.

New York City's leadership in arts and letters did not always endear it to the rest of the United States. Those living west of the Hudson and north of the Bronx often considered the city more European than American, and they accused its citizens of lacking all the pioneer virtues that had made the nation great. But critics could not help being influenced by what they professed to despise. The countryside could cherish its past, but the present and future of intellectual America had been monopolized by the metropolis. Culture had become a commodity, and New Yorkers were its largest producers. Most other Americans had to be content with being consumers.

Changing Cultural Horizons

A wise people, like a wise individual, takes counsel of things
in the making as well as those already entered on the books.
Indeed, it may always hope to devise or revise the future
whereas the past lies beyond recall.

—Arthur M. Schlesinger

THE first half of the twentieth century wrought changes in the cultural atmosphere of New York State almost as radical as those which occurred in its technical and industrial structure. Essentially, these changes served to make the state more homogeneous, to bind its different areas more intimately together. A few years before World War I a good deal of the state still lived, culturally, in what has been well called "the golden age of homespun." Despite heavy concentrations of industry in major cities, a man could still live in the traditional complex of separate communities, plying a handicraft industry, or acting the role of a sturdy, independent proprietor who was his own master economically, socially, and culturally. After World War II this pattern was a rarity—for most New Yorkers nothing more than a nostalgic memory cherished by a dwindling group of old-timers. Bombarded by new inventions and applications of the communications industries, the twentieth-century New Yorker was magnificently and continuously in touch with everyone and everything. Sometimes he may have felt too much in touch, but the fact of change was not to be denied. By telephone, radio, newspaper, television, airplane, railroad, and motorcar, by magazines, newspapers, billboards, and by the immense, intricate, yet almost intangible impulses of mass production, the inhabitants of the state were enabled, encouraged, and impelled to communicate with one another. Pessimists sometimes proclaimed that the process led to standardized human beings, and perhaps it did. But it led in other directions, too—as will perhaps appear, if we look at the process itself in more detail.

If the prompt and widespread dissemination of basic information is

619

an essential of democracy, New York State became infinitely more democratic during the first fifty years of the twentieth century. The newspapers of the state had, in 1950, a combined daily circulation of about
nine million copies. That is an enormous number of daily newspapers,
and from this many newspapers a great deal of information can be
gleaned. To be sure, on any given day most of the headlines might blare
forth information about the latest sex crime, love nest, gang murder, or
confidence swindle. But if one wanted to, one could gain some general
information from even the yellowest of the yellow journals. And, over
the years, New York built up a tradition of publishing, not only a few
loud yellow scandal sheets, but also the nation's most intelligent and
free-ranging journalism.

The New York *Times,* for example, is a metropolitan daily; it reprints
the wire-service stories, keeps the public informed of local developments,
and covers the police news. One can even find accounts of sex crimes
and love nests in the *Times,* though they will be hidden under small,
quiet captions at the bottom of page 46. But in addition, the *Times* gives
unexampled coverage to national and international news stories. Its team
of correspondents is carefully selected, highly trained, and widely dispersed; and it keeps the *Times* reader up to the minute on developments
in Kuala Lumpur and Marrakesh—as well as in Washington, D.C. The
importance of such day-to-day coverage in the conduct of democratic
government is indicated by the fact that most congressmen and senators
subscribe to the *Times* as well as to their own local papers. What the
Times says often influences national legislation; and to question the
accuracy of a *Times* story is to question, almost, the public record itself.

Not only does the *Times* offer an unequaled opportunity for the interested reader to keep up with current events as they happen; through
constant surveys, reviews, and feature articles, it provides guidance
through the confusing masses of contemporary detail. Its surveys of
educational developments are models of their kind; its reporting of scientific discoveries is lucid, detailed, and exact; its political analyses, though
in the nature of things they can never please everyone, are usually
thorough and painstaking. The *Times* reader must have at least one
mark of a mature mind, a long attention-span; for the writing is often
prolix by journalistic standards. Still, the *Times* is a great newspaper, and
a worthy American counterpart to its famous London namesake. Its hun-
dredth anniversary, celebrated in 1951, brought world-wide tributes.
Other fine newspapers in New York are the *Herald Tribune* (like the
Times, a morning paper), and the *World-Telegram and Sun,* which appears in the afternoon. The *Daily News* and *Daily Mirror* (established
1924) are tabloids as was the now extinct *Graphic;* these papers are
small of size and sensational in coverage, with short stories and big

pictures. The *News* has now more than two million daily circulation—which is a commentary of sorts on the American reading public. There are, of course, other millions who don't read anything. The *Journal American* is the New York link in the Hearst chain. Many of these newspapers sponsor some sort of charitable enterprise as a sideline; for example, the *Times* is famous for its annual promotion of a drive to aid the Hundred Neediest Cases; while the *Herald Tribune* has operated, for nearly seventy-five years, a Fresh Air Fund, aimed at providing summer vacations for needy city children.

Despite their vast circulations and the increasingly high esteem in which they are held, the metropolitan dailies have not, over the past fifty years, exerted great political influence, at least on the local scene. During the 1890's, and earlier, many newspapers embarked boldly on crusades—either political, economic, or social. They fought great battles against Entrenched Evil and won (sometimes) great victories. Of recent years, they have been more peaceful, embarking on fewer crusades for specific changes and encountering less success in those which they undertook. With the exception of the La Guardia and Wagner administrations, hardly a word could be found in a metropolitan newspaper expressing approval of the municipal government; but nobody seemed to feel a need to change this government or even to throw out the rascals of the moment. The existence of racketeering along the water front was a matter of public knowledge for years before various scandals made it advisable recently to get rid of certain overfamiliar figureheads. But the newspapers of the city have attempted little in the way of exposure or reform, and their few efforts have usually gone astray. Perhaps the papers themselves are less responsible for this change than their increasingly apathetic readers; at all events, the change has rendered New York journalism definitely less exciting than it used to be.

Naturally enough, the metropolitan newspapers have the largest circulation in the state; in addition, several of them are widely read throughout the nation. Upstate, the Gannett enterprises, headed by Frank E. Gannett, operate a highly successful and notably independent chain of newspapers in such cities as Elmira, Binghamton, Rochester, Albany, Utica, Newburgh, and Ithaca. There are also dozens of independent local hometown newspapers, such as, for example, the weekly Rhinebeck *Gazette*, the Watertown *Times*, the Greenwich *Journal*, the Schuylerville *Standard*, and the daily Canandaigua *Messenger*, which keep thousands of readers informed and entertained. As for fortnightlies and monthlies, their name is legion. Of the 719 publications classified as newspapers in New York State in 1950, no less than 561 were published either once a week or less frequently than that.

Because so many of its citizens are of foreign ancestry, the state has twenty-eight foreign-language dailies, almost a third of the nation's total. In all, approximately 190 foreign-language newspapers and periodicals are published in New York State, making it the foreign-language center of the United States. No less than thirty languages other than English are used to print these periodicals. A Czech, a Finn, a Greek, a Chinese, or an Arab may find a New York periodical in his native tongue. Hungarian, Portuguese, Polish, Ukrainian, Albanian, and Carpatho-Russian are other languages used. One may even read New York publications in Welsh and Latin!

Because it is a major financial center and the home of the New York Stock Exchange, the metropolis is also a major center for the publication of business and financial journals. Pre-eminent among these is the *Wall Street Journal,* first published in 1889, and ever since then required reading for budding and blooming capitalists. A special branch of this industry is that devoted to newsletters and other forms of advice for investors: these have become more numerous lately, as ownership of American industry has steadily been dispersed among thousands of small investors. And of course many specialized trade journals are published in New York, calling attention to developments in such fields as finance, law, clothing and textiles, metals, commerce, motion pictures, house furnishings, and agriculture.

Practically all daily newspapers, and many weeklies, subscribe to one or more of the wire services, such as the Associated Press, International News Service, and United Press, which have branches in all the major news centers of the world. Other syndicated services disseminate special feature stories, photographs, cartoons, fiction, advertising (known irreverently around the newspaper office as "boilerplate"), and articles on fashions, sports, religion, homemaking, and science. By making use of these syndicated services, small-town newspapers can compete qualitatively with the big-city publications. Almost half of the 219 newspaper feature, picture, and news syndicates in the United States are located in New York.

Periodical publications, whether newspapers or magazines, tend to pass through something like a life cycle. They are born, flourish, are successful, and then, unless carefully watched, tend to wither and fade or to be absorbed in some more successful enterprise. The outstanding leader of newspaper consolidation in the state was Frank A. Munsey, an old newspaperman who had long cherished the idea of establishing a newspaper chain. His first effort in this direction ended in failure, but in 1916 he consolidated the New York *Press* with the New York *Sun* and *Evening Sun.* He then acquired the New York *Herald* and its satellite the New York *Evening Telegram;* when he tried and failed to buy the New York *Tribune,* he sold the *Herald* to the *Tribune*'s owners, Mr. and

Mrs. Ogden Reid. Thus emerged the *Herald Tribune* in 1924. Meantime Munsey acquired the *Evening Globe* which he merged with the *Sun*. Just before his death he purchased the *Evening Mail* and merged it with his *Evening Telegram*. And now in recent years the *Sun* has been merged into the offspring of a merger between the old *World* and the *Evening Telegram*, so that we have a triple product, the *World-Telegram and Sun*.

Very much the same process of merging and emerging projects goes on in magazine publishing, but here the hopeful signs of birth are more in evidence. True, the magazines which made such a tremendous reputation during the old muck-raking era generally failed to survive that era. And the old *Literary Digest* ran into such difficulties, when it predicted the overwhelming election of Alfred Landon over Franklin Roosevelt in 1936, that it folded soon thereafter. But in New York, at least, the sprouting of new magazines seemed like almost a continuous process. The *Reader's Digest* sprang into prominence during the 1920's by shrinking long articles into short ones and presenting a monthly selection. Americans, who appreciate being reminded of how busy they are, responded enthusiastically; and soon the *Reader's Digest* was an established and influential journalette. But the most sensational successes in magazine publishing during the 1920's were those wrought by Henry R. Luce. In 1923 he created *Time*, the first weekly news magazine, a compressed, clever, brightly written and strongly edited magazine of news and news interpretation. Its point of view was that of the business community; its prose style was often so mannered that, in the words of a famous parody, "Backward ran sentences till reeled the mind." But it was brisk, crisp, sententious, and opinionated writing, often illuminated by a high order of intelligence. Inopportunely titled, *Fortune* appeared on the scene just as the Great Depression was setting in (1930). It was, and remains, an expensive and beautiful publication for the business and technical community. These were such successful ventures that in 1936 Mr. Luce climaxed his career by revitalizing the old and moribund joke-and-cartoon magazine, *Life*. He turned it into a magazine of news photographs, the pictures beautifully selected and completely timely, the surrounding captions and predigested text ruthlessly simple. The success of *Life* as measured by the pitiless barometer of newsstand sales was phenomenal beyond precedent; indeed, the magazine was soon so securely entrenched that it could afford occasional ventures into the unsensational field of public education. Here its lucid, simple texts and brilliant illustrations performed a major function in making Americans aware of the world about them, of the facts of their own history, and of the first grand principles of scientific thought. *Life* is now an American institution, a barbershop fixture. With these three major blocks in place, the Luce empire was essentially complete; and to this day it stands as the most massive and influential of New York's magazine-publishing structures.

Look and *Pic* are broadly similar to *Life; Newsweek* is similar to *Time*. There are imitations of the imitations, there are mortalities, rehabilitations, and brave new ventures. And behind all the shifting façades of periodical publication lies the omnivorous and sleepless "angle-worm" —the periodical feature-writer on the lookout for a fresh approach to old material, the editor who wants the old story told with a new gimmick. He is out to hook the reader's curiosity in order to build up national newsstand sales as a bait to attract advertisers, who pay the freight that makes the difference between profit and loss.

In the years after World War I, a magnificent new medium of dramatic entertainment burst upon New York State, as upon the nation. Many of the early movies were made by Broadway stars in New York City studios; others were made by the woods, gorges, lakes, and falls of upstate Ithaca. Executive offices, cutting studios, and some rather specialized production operations still remain in New York; but by and large the production phase of the industry has been inveigled westward to Southern California. New York money remains powerful in the industry and serves to lure New York talent to the golden fleshpots of the West. But for the average New York citizen, movies have become strictly a consumption item. They are consumed in quantity and with gusto. The Saturday-night movie date became a staple item in America's entertainment diet. The star system and the mass audience combined to encourage the creation of a standardized product; and a mysterious, businesslike arrangement known as "block booking" created something close to absolute uniformity of distribution. Sooner or later everyone, whether he lived in a hamlet or a metropolis, saw the same movie. This had both good and bad aspects. While it standardized experience, it widened many people's range of experience, and it provided, on occasion, intellectual stimulation of a fairly high order. People could be found discussing the merits of a movie who would have had the greatest difficulty discussing the merits of a book—even supposing they had all read the same book.

Of course there are always problems for a medium which depends, like the movies, on a mass audience. Timid producers with their eyes riveted on the box office tended to produce only scripts guaranteed not to offend, irritate, or arouse disagreement. Innocuous banality heavily flavored with sex appeal has been a successful formula for years; and the unrelenting pursuit of it has thwarted, in some measure, the full development of the movie industry's enormous potential. Yet a few fine movies do break through the barrier; and when current production is thin and banal, fine old films are often brought back to the neighborhood houses. Moreover, several small companies and more or less informal organizations in the city are devoted to the appreciation or production of experimental movies. Perhaps the best known of these is Cinema 16.

Because of its vast resources of wealth, population, technical skills, and technical facilities, New York State has pioneered in the radio broadcasting industry. Radio broadcasting had its beginning in the state, as in the nation, during the early 1920's. In 1922 there were about 400,000 radio receivers in the entire nation; twenty-five years later there were more than ten times that many receivers in New York State alone. By the middle of the twentieth century, 98 per cent of all the families of the state had at least one receiver. New York was not only the birthplace of the great radio networks but also of commercial broadcasting. In 1923 Station WEAF had twenty-five sponsors, including the R. H. Macy Department Store, the Metropolitan Life Insurance Company, the Colgate Company, and I. Miller Shoes. In a very real sense, this was the beginning of commercial radio, not only for New York but for the world.

Most early radio stations were owned by radio-equipment manufacturers who broadcast programs in order to sell their equipment. The high cost of adequate programing, however, soon convinced manufacturers that profits from the sale of radio sets were insufficient to finance the radio stations. Hence, the sale of air time to advertisers. This proved to be a lucrative business. Since half the state's fifteen million population live in the five boroughs of New York City, this is a tremendous, compact market. It is supplemented by other millions in the metropolitan area outside New York City boundaries, who easily hear broadcasts emanating from the city. Consequently, it is not surprising that more than thirty radio stations are concentrated in the New York City area.

It was New York City, too, which acted as the first center for the major networks which spread across the entire country. In 1926 the Radio Corporation of America formed the National Broadcasting Company in New York City; the following year, it built its second, or "Blue" network, which, in 1943, became the American Broadcasting Company. The third major network to be established was the Columbia Broadcasting System, organized in 1927 in New York City on the basis of a sixteen-station hookup. The Mutual Broadcasting System started operations in 1934 with four stations; today this system has a larger number of stations than any other. In the field of regional broadcasting, New York can boast of the Rural Radio Network centered at Ithaca. Through a combination of AM and FM facilities and a unique system of remote-control broadcasting, this network covers the state.

The leadership in the radio industry which New York City early attained has been buttressed over the years. The city has increasingly become the entertainment capital of the nation, continually attracting great numbers of talented people: musicians, singers, actors, dancers, directors, writers, producers, and stage artists of every description. Particularly since the advent of television after World War II, New York has assumed leadership in the business of entertaining the nation. With its insatiable appetite for new faces and fresh material, television has vastly enlarged the field of the entertainment industry. It has made possible audiences of millions for performers who previously played only to hundreds. And it has brought headline performers into hamlets which had never seen entertainment more exalted than a traveling medicine show. As with radio and with motion pictures, the mass audience has imposed a certain leveling and simplification of taste. But wonderful programs may now and then be seen on television; the happy viewer may visit Greenland or the castle of Hamlet at Elsinore, as well as take a participant's seat at the historic events of the day, from boxing bouts to political campaigns.

Not usually considered a cultural so much as a technical phenomenon, the automobile changed the folkways of New Yorkers and of Americans generally. Over the last three or four decades, it has transformed America from a nation of homebodies to one of gadabouts. Gone are the days when a York-Stater might live and die within the bounds of his native village; gone, indeed, is the old distinction between the country bumpkin and the city slicker. Nothing has done more than the automobile to obliterate the distinction between town and country. Indeed, of a weekend, when long lines of cars stand bumper-to-bumper along the parkways, it is often a question whether there are more city people leaving town for the weekend or more country people escaping from the birds, flowers, and trees for a weekend in the city.

With the possession of vast quantities of automobiles (more than four million in 1953), New Yorkers have become surpassingly mobile. Huge belt parkways enable the motorist to travel, without the interruption of a single traffic light, from Manhattan Island to the border of Indiana; the great New York Thruway permits one to drive clear across the heart of the state without so much as the impediment of a grade crossing. A great public park like Jones Beach on the south shore of Long Island is as much a creation of the automobile as is the drive-in theater. The home has lost some of its importance, the neighborhood has lost some of its distinctness, now that one may be forty miles away in less than an hour. Automobiles are, of course, marks of social prestige; they are art-objects, perhaps the most exciting aesthetic experience that the American ever undergoes; they have gone a long way toward replacing the bus, the train, and the vacation resort. With trailers attached, they become moving vans or complete traveling homes; at drive-in theaters, they turn into mobile movie seats. Versatile and enormously glamorous, automobiles have radically transformed New York's economy and the cultural life of her people.

The very popularity of the automobile has led, of course, to tremendous problems. In less than fifty years, more Americans have been killed by the automobile than by all the wars in which our country has engaged since the days of George Washington. The big cities of the state are being gradually choked by their own traffic and parking is a perpetual problem.

One advantage of the automobile is almost completely unchallenged. It has opened up to the citizens of the state the real beauty and variety of their natural heritage. Nothing has done more than the combination of fine cars and good roads to bring Americans out of doors and into the country. Within a few hours' time, any inhabitant of New York State can be in the depths of the Catskills or the Adirondacks, climbing a mountain, riding a horse, hooking a trout, or paddling a canoe. For those who crave the rugged and isolated wilderness, the forests and mountains of the Adirondack and Catskill State parks are ideal. In the fall, hunters swarm through all the wild areas of the state, in pursuit of game ranging from squirrels and rabbits to bears (and, alas! too often, other hunters); during the winter months skaters and skiers visit by the thousands the great resort areas like Lake Placid. And all year round there are visitors who come to the natural scenic areas of the state simply to look at the scenery, sniff the fresh air, and smooth out the wrinkles in their faces and their souls.

Particularly popular in these days of high-priced hotels are the state-operated camping areas which are maintained in strategic locations throughout the state. Along the Finger Lakes, by the shores of Lake Ontario, and in the depths of the Adirondacks, there are camping grounds in the public parks where for a few dollars a day one can rent a tent or a cabin and enjoy the outdoor life as energetically or as lazily as one chooses. At the juncture of Lake Ontario and the St. Lawrence River are the famous Thousand Islands, which annually attract hordes of vacationists. With the completion of the St. Lawrence Power and Seaway Projects, the St. Lawrence below the Thousand Islands will be an added attraction for tourists and visitors. The creation of a new thirty-mile lake, from Massena to Point Rockaway in the town of Lisbon will transform once-turbulent rapids into broad, placid waters for fishing, boating, swimming, and the enjoyment of the region's scenic beauties. The state has also provided public picnic grounds along main highways, lean-tos or open camps along principal trails in the forest preserves of the Catskills and Adirondacks, and places for tents on the islands of Lake George and in many other locations.

Other outstanding scenic attractions in the state include the world-renowned Niagara Falls, famous in song and story as the habitat of honeymooners; the Genesee Gorge in Letchworth State Park near Rochester; the Howe Caverns near Cobleskill; Watkins Glen near Ithaca; Ausable Chasm near Lake Champlain; and the petrified forest near Saratoga Springs. And, of course, for sheer scenic magnificence, there are very few regions anywhere in the world which can rival the splendid stretch of the lordly Hudson River Valley.

New York State has at least fifteen hundred summer camps for boys and girls. Many of these are run by groups such as the Boy Scouts, religious and fraternal organizations, and educational and community centers. All camps must be registered with the state Department of Health.

Although it flourishes there, sport is not by any means confined to bucolic surroundings. The metropolis nurtures its own natural breed of athletic contest, stickball, hopscotch and other sidewalk games, touch football, and the infinite varieties of handball. And of course the city is the home par excellence of professional sports. Since the turn of the century, New York City has been represented in the major leagues by three professional baseball teams; and many of the truly great figures of the game have performed for the home team within the hallowed precincts of Ebbets Field, the Polo Grounds, and Yankee Stadium. The Stadium is often known in the special parlance of the sportswriter as The House That Ruth Built, for it was conceived as a showcase for the home-run hitting of the mighty Babe. If the Polo Grounds were to be assigned a similar title, it might be called the House That McGraw Inhabited, for the Giants have not been a supreme power in their league since the legendary days of John J. McGraw and the peerless Christy Matthewson. As for the Dodgers (once the Robins), those long lean years during which the players won from their fans the affectionate, contemptuous nickname of "Bums" came to an end with the 1940's. In the modern era, the team has won pennants—even, in 1955, a World Series! Few things render the national pastime more endearing than its ability to achieve the unexpected and improbable. In addition to its major-league representation, New York State has entries in the International League, the Eastern League, the Pony League, and numerous semiprofessional and industrial circuits. The Little League movement, started in Williamsport, Pennsylvania, just after World War II, spread quickly throughout New York State and has been highly influential in making the pastime available, in an organized and supervised way, to the youngsters of the state.

In 1925 Madison Square Garden was opened as a sports arena and convention hall; and since then, almost every form of professional sport has been housed in the great Eighth Avenue arena. Boxing bouts and wrestling displays are regularly scheduled in the Garden. Six-day bike races, ice hockey contests, basketball games, tennis matches, horse shows, dog shows, and political rallies fill out the Garden's program. And every spring, early in April, the circus comes to town and settles down in Madison Square Garden for a long stand before going on tour. On a smaller scale, upstate cities, notably Buffalo, Rochester, and Syracuse, are centers of commercialized sport.

Growing interest in promoting health and in dealing constructively with juvenile delinquency put a premium on the providing of recreational facilities, particularly in urban centers, where adequate space for parks, playing fields, golf courses, tennis courts, and skating rinks was not always easy to obtain. Fortunately the state of New York and its largest city have had the devoted services of Robert Moses as head of their park systems for several decades. He has made great strides, often in face of what seemed insuperable difficulties, in providing for recreational needs.

For those who are interested in history, the state abounds in landmarks and relics of early American life and Indian culture. Seven Indian reservations are still maintained, for example; and while the ancient rites are no longer a matter of everyday practice, customs and traditions are carefully preserved. The New York State Historical Association operates an interesting museum of antiquities at Cooperstown, not far from the equally memorable Baseball Hall of Fame. At Hyde Park the beautiful country estate of former President Franklin D. Roosevelt is maintained as a public memorial, while Washington Irving mementos crowd the area around Tarrytown and Sleepy Hollow. On the west bank of the Hudson, forty miles north of Albany, is the state's only national park, the Saratoga Battlefield National Park, marking the scene of the Battle of Saratoga and of the surrender of General Burgoyne.

Following World War I, interest in the conserving of things artistic grew apace. The Metropolitan Museum of Art now extends for four blocks along Fifth Avenue and welcomes some two million visitors a year. Its Egyptian collection, begun in 1906, is the largest and most representative of its kind in the United States. It also displays extensive Greek and Roman, Near Eastern, and Far Eastern collections. It has a section of decorative arts, of arms and armor, and an American Wing —all this in addition to its main attraction, the superb picture galleries.

The 1940's witnessed a series of collaborative movements, under the leadership of the Metropolitan, of more than passing importance. In 1943 the Whitney Museum of American Art, established in 1931, entered into an agreement with the Metropolitan providing for the eventual housing of the Whitney in the Metropolitan and the enlargement of its modern American collections. This means that the whole history of art in America will be represented in one place. In 1947 the Metropolitan entered into an agreement with the Museum of Modern Art, founded in 1929, by which paintings owned by the latter will be sold to the Metropolitan. Finally, in 1947, the Costume Institute moved into the Metropolitan, the latter having acquired it for the purpose of making available to students, designers, and manufacturers their combined resources.

Perhaps best known of New York City's newer museums is the Cloisters in Upper Manhattan. Made possible through the generosity of John D. Rockefeller, Jr., it houses the medieval collection of George Grey Barnard, the sculptor. Some of the city's historic dwellings are also preserved as museums or shrines. Among these are the Lefferts homestead in Prospect Park, Brooklyn, the Edwin Markham home on Staten Island, the Van Cortlandt House in the Bronx, and the Edgar Allan Poe cottage in Fordham. The Jewish Museum, first of its kind in the United States, is located in the former home of Felix Warburg. Opened in 1947, it shows representative works of Jewish life and culture, past and present, illustrating the history and continuity of the Jewish tradition.

One of the most fascinating museums in New York City is the Museum of the City of New York. Here miniature groups depict scenes in the city's history. Art collections of considerable value are owned by the New-York Historical Society, founded in 1804 and enlarged in the late 1930's, by the National Academy of Design, the New York Public Library, and the American Academy of Arts and Letters. Portraits of prominent American citizens are assembled in the City Hall of New York, the Borough Hall of Brooklyn, the New-York Historical Society, the Museum of the City of New York, the Chamber of Commerce of the State of New York, and the Long Island Historical Society.

There are also important museums and galleries in other parts of the state. Unique among these is the Farmers' Museum at Cooperstown, one of the few genuine folk museums in the western world, one which seeks to re-create the culture, labors, and way of life of the pioneers and their children in upstate New York. Others are the Syracuse Museum of Fine Arts, the first in this country to organize educational work between the museum and the city's schools; the New York State Historical Association's Fenimore House at Cooperstown; the Albany Institute of History and Art; Binghamton Society of Fine Arts; Arnot Art Gallery of Elmira; the Art Gallery of the James Prendergast Free Library of Jamestown; Fine Arts Building, Heckscher Park, Huntington; Parrish Memorial Art Museum, Southampton; Thomas Moran Memorial Gallery, Guild Hall, East Hampton; Taylor Hart Art Gallery at Vassar College; and Remington Art Memorial, Ogdensburg.

Like those interested in the preservation of art, those concerned with science and its accomplishments formed societies and established museums and other institutions for the promotion of their interest. In New York City the Botanical Gardens in Bronx Park and in Brooklyn's Prospect Park are not only places of beauty but centers for scientific study. Similarly, the Zoological Gardens in the Bronx, Brooklyn, and Staten Island afford pleasure and instruction for thousands annually. Oldest, largest, and most important of all the state's scientific institutions is the American Museum of Natural History (1867) facing Central Park West in New York City. Covering twenty-three acres, it is at once a museum, a laboratory, a school, a publishing house, and headquarters for exploring expeditions to every part of the world. The museum is the energizing center of the New York Academy of Sciences, a federation of scientific societies. Scientists plan the expeditions, conduct them, bring back their findings, analyze, classify, and relate their discoveries to other knowledge; publish and disseminate the results of their investigations; and prepare exhibits for display. The miniature wax groups picturing animal life in its appropriate environment—a technique developed by the late Dr. Roy W. Miner—has been extremely useful educationally and has been copied elsewhere. Its collection of dinosaurs and birds are the finest in the world. Close at hand is the museum's Hayden Planetarium opened in 1935. Ultimately, the museum will have a hall of comparative anatomy, a hall of physiological foundations of human and animal behavior, a hall showing the origins and spread of material culture, and other halls which will depict the nature and development of civilization in specific areas. In other words, the museum aims to give man a "conception of the Cosmos and his place in it."

The American Indian collection at this great museum has long been famous but for many years has been rivaled by the Museum of the American Indian at Broadway and 155th Street.

Science museums outside New York City continued to grow and to serve their respective communities. Among the more important of these are the State Museum at Albany, the Buffalo Museum of the Natural Sciences, and the Rochester Museum of Arts and Sciences. Not only in the last half century but also over a longer span, scientific interest and accomplishment within the state have enormously affected our material life and our culture. The hold of science upon our imagination has not lessened; if anything, it has increased.

In the last half century many Americans believed that natural science provided mankind with the possibility of unlimited material progress. The scientist was an inventor who discovered new products and devised new machines that made life easier for all; and everywhere they looked, New Yorkers could see the beneficent results of the scientists' labors, such as plastics, improved means of communication and transportation, "wonder drugs," and energy-giving vitamins. Although many New Yorkers, particularly in the Depression years, attributed unemployment to the increasing application of science to industry, and with the spread of automation in the 1950's many are again haunted by the fear of unemployment, few were or are prepared to reject science's practical achievements. The popular view of the role of science was re-enforced by newspapers and magazines that publicized applied rather than pure science, by industrial firms that spent millions annually on research programs, and by universities that spent larger sums on scientific research than on other forms of scholarly activity.

In subsidizing industrial research, New York concerns were in the forefront: the American Telephone and Telegraph Company, the Eastman Kodak Company, the Bausch and Lomb Company, the Corning Glass Works, and the General Electric Company among them. The laboratories of the last-named, for example—developed under Charles P. Steinmetz, carried forward under the direction of Dr. Willis R. Whitney, and supporting the work of Dr. Irving Langmuir and scores of others—became one of the world's significant centers of physical research.

The almost universal respect accorded science and scientists by the people of the state had little apparent effect on church membership, which between the world wars increased at practically the same rate as the population. Although the Depression seriously impaired church finances and cut down on the rate of growth in membership, there was a marked revival of church strength and influence during the war years. The statistics of church membership in Table 22 are taken from the United States religions censuses of 1926 and 1936.

Despite the growth in church membership, the influence of organized religion declined precipitously in the years that followed World War I. Many Protestants were no longer concerned with the strict observance of the Sabbath; Sunday movies, despite the opposition of some church groups, had become commonplace; and ministers repeatedly complained from their pulpits that the automobile and the golf course provided Sunday diversions more attractive to many parishioners than church. Since the battle between religion and science had been settled to the satisfaction of the vast majority, religious controversies occurred less frequently and were conducted with less vehemence than in former years. Agnosticism was common enough, especially in the larger centers of population, to go unnoticed, while even those who attended church regularly seemed to lack much of the enthusiasm and intensity that had once been considered an essential ingredient of religious experience.

In an effort to check the declining influence of the churches, many

Table 22. Church memberships in 1926 and 1936.

Denomination	1926		1936	
	Churches	Members	Churches	Members
Adventists, Seventh Day	81	5,271	76	5,620
Baptist	857	161,142	694	181,918
Baptist, Negro	111	46,823	165	86,187
Baptist, Seventh-Day	21	2,076	18	1,524
Roman Catholic	1,783	3,115,424	1,757	3,075,428
Christian	62	4,577	59	3,656
Congregational	280	69,187	302	70,164
Disciples	59	12,479	52	10,583
Evangelical	62	7,762	54	7,555
Evangelical Synod	66	23,592	90	34,333
Friends	47	4,868	99	4,999
Lutherans (all bodies)	567	240,672	569	326,393
Methodist Episcopal	1,930	345,307	1,505	301,458
Methodist Protestant	62	3,804	48	3,213
Methodist Wesleyan	81	2,360	58	2,201
Methodist Free	108	3,227	88	3,315
Methodist Negro	142	31,975	147	40,945
Presbyterian	813	243,845	766	233,961
United Presbyterian	63	11,498	70	13,819
Protestant Episcopal	882	354,700	875	349,528
Reformed (Dutch)	294	62,855	277	66,812
Reformed (German)	25	7,105	31	7,644
Unitarian	26	5,144	21	5,788
Universalists	68	8,099	45	6,994
Jewish	1,228	1,899,597	1,560	2,197,418
Church of Christ, Scientist	141	1,530	157	15,875
TOTAL		6,799,146		7,150,501

religious leaders in the state made special efforts to appeal to the more mundane tastes of church members. Practically all urban as well as many rural churches had ambitious social and recreational programs that covered almost every range of activity. Some churches provided their members with psychiatric assistance, others conducted classes in subjects that ranged from dancing to manual training, still others conducted extensive athletic programs. Some established settlement houses, orphanages, clinics, and schools. An exhaustive study of the church and society carried on from 1920 to 1934 by the Institute of Social and Religious Research repeatedly stressed the trend away from orthodoxy toward a ministry of human welfare. Similarly, American Catholics paid less attention to expounding a gospel of hell-fire and damnation and made new efforts in response to the principles of social justice emphasized by Pope Pius XI in his encyclical *Quadrigesimo Anno* (1931). The following year the Central Conference of American Rabbis drafted its Program of Social Justice, and the Federal Council of Churches reaffirmed its stand on collective bargaining and social security.

The liberalizing tendency in religion during the last half century was clearly evident in the work of some of the state's great religious leaders. S. Parkes Cadman made the Central Congregational Church of Brooklyn famous through his dynamic radio sermons and his work as a founder and president of the Federal Council of Churches of Christ in America. Riverside Church on Morningside Heights in Manhattan, opened in 1929, won immediate repute, through the leadership of Dr. Harry Emerson Fosdick, for its community and interdenominational activities. As pastor of Corpus Christi Church, also in the Morningside area, Father George B. Ford demonstrated the abundant benefits for both the individual and the community which result from putting into practice the principles of social justice expounded by Pope Pius XI. Rabbi Stephen S. Wise's Free Synagogue was the center of many thousands who believed in child labor reform, international peace, improvement of labor laws, and other forms of social legislation. Indeed, throughout the state, social and economic themes became increasingly popular as sermon topics. Prayer meetings often took the form of groups for the discussion of "problems of human relationships."

Outside the old denominations there was also evidence of the growth of the social gospel. The Society of Ethical Culture founded in 1876 by Felix Adler, the Salvation Army, and, more recently, Georgia-born George Baker, who was called Father Divine, won numerous adherents in New York's Harlem and in Negro sections of other cities on a gospel combining religion, morality, and low-cost food and housing.

Although the church seemed less important to New Yorkers than it once had, there was still widespread interest in religious matters. Throughout the 1920's, books on religious subjects enjoyed considerable popularity. Lewis Browne's *This Believing World* and Bruce Barton's *The Man Nobody Knows* and *The Book Nobody Knows* were bestsellers, while in the next decade Lloyd Douglas' *Magnificent Obsession* and *Green Light* and Henry S. Link's *The Return to Religion* attracted numbers of readers. The theologian Reinhold Niebuhr's first volume of *The Nature and Destiny of Man* (1941) also emphasized the necessity for religious faith.

As they grew more cosmopolitan and worldly, New Yorkers began to give up some of their more earnest and self-conscious efforts at self-improvement. Starting about the year 1874, culture-conscious New Yorkers used to congregate during the summer months along the shores of Chautauqua Lake in western New York, where they sipped orange phosphates and were harangued by distinguished ladies and gentlemen on various moral issues. The Chautauqua soon became an institution quite independent of any particular locality; Chautauquas dotted the countryside, and Chautauqua speakers trained for the "circuit" as rigorously as six-day bicycle racers. Ever since the first New England meetinghouse played host to its first visiting preacher, Americans have had a passion for being "edified." The direct ancestor of the Chautauqua was the village Lyceum, where such men as Emerson and Thoreau did not scorn to be heard; and the Chautauqua itself flourished mightily in the days of gaslight and the bustle.

Its place has not really been filled today. The New York World's Fair of 1939–1940 had some Chautauqua aspects, but it was in essence a bigger, noisier, gaudier project, set up to celebrate "A Century of Progress" and drawing on the different cultures of the entire world as well as the marvels of science and of the future. It attracted astronomical numbers of visitors to the site of Flushing Meadows; and it stimulated violently the already-excited imaginations of industrial designers and technological dreamcasters. But it did not have that earnest atmosphere of moral and cultural uplift which is the hallmark of the Chautauqua lecture.

If the New York World's Fair was inspired, in a thoroughly modern way, by nostalgia for the future, a less elaborate gathering, which takes place twice a year, is inspired by nostalgia for the past. The New York Folklore Society not only publishes a quarterly magazine, but foregathers in not-too-solemn conclave, to swap tall tales, sing Revolutionary War ballads, and re-enact Indian legends. For all that it is a highly industrialized state, New York has an immense stock of popular folk materials surviving from the distant past. In the remote corners of the Adirondacks or along the Erie Canal, rich popular legends are cherished. The Folklore Society, in conjunction with the New York State Historical Association, preserves for New Yorkers on records, in museums, and on the printed page, the memory of a cruder and lustier day—the day of Clinton's Big Ditch, of Deerslayer and Joseph Brant and even of Peter Stuyvesant and Henrik Hudson. The books of Walter D. Edmonds (*Drums along the Mohawk*), Carl Carmer (*Listen for a Lonesome Drum, Dark Trees to the Wind*), Harold W. Thompson (*Body, Boots and Britches*), and Samuel Hopkins Adams (*Grandfather Tales*) have also done much to recreate the flavor of New York's early days.

The WPA's Historical Records Survey, instituted in 1936, enabled relief workers in many counties and local communities of the state to take inventories of public records stored in city-hall cellars, courthouse garrets, and library lofts, to index old newspaper files, and to examine business archives and church records. As a consequence, historical material of inestimable value was preserved. In recent years, growing interest in local history has led to the beginning of a movement for the preparation of up-to-date county histories. No account of historical activity in the state during the last half century should omit the accomplishments of the New York State Historical Association. Founded in 1899 by a group primarily interested in preserving the military history of the Champlain Valley, the Association in 1939 shifted its headquarters from Ticonderoga to Cooperstown on beautiful Otsego Lake. Here it has increasingly broadened its program by emphasizing social, economic, and cultural aspects of the state's history as well as the military and political. Not only does it operate three museums but also it carries on a vigorous publications program. This includes publishing the well-known quarterly, *New York History,* sponsoring numerous volumes relating to the history of the state, and publishing *The Yorker,* a lively journal for the association's growing number of secondary-school members. The association's library is rich with material pertaining to the social and cultural history of the state.

The preservation of the past has seemed particularly urgent, because, like many other sections of the nation, New York State seems sometimes on the verge of being suburbanized completely. Both world wars have had as an aftermath building booms; and in both eras, a tawdry, inefficient, ugly, and thoughtless manner of building has predominated. Suburban architecture, whether it takes the form of the Tudor cottage with flying buttresses, or the ranch-type, split-level, picture-window box with expansion attic and attached breeze-way, is rarely cheerful to contemplate. And even in the splendid office structures of New York City, one might feel that the architects, though technically dexterous, had allowed themselves to atrophy imaginatively and humanistically. The basic structure of a New York City building remained a framework of structural steel, on which were hung geometrical fabrics of brick, glass, and aluminum, which served to divide space. For sheer height, the Empire State Building, erected in 1931, stood unchallenged; but vertical masses of this sort proved uneconomical for most purposes. Newer buildings, like the main United Nations structure on East Forty-second Street or Lever House on Park Avenue, were more modest in size and more casual about proclaiming their defiance of the law of gravity. Dissolving the solidity of external walls, and relying more and more on the glittering insubstantialities of glass, they tended at their best to look at once cold and angular and brilliantly audacious. Much dreary, unambitious box work of course continued to be produced, in the city as well as outside of it; perhaps the old brownstone, with its dark interiors, gloomy front, and dank courtyard, was scarcely more melancholy than the huge square hives huddled together under the name of "Stuyvesant Town." And the new Coliseum at Columbus Circle seems to make no bones about being flatly, unashamedly ugly. New York State was once the scene of some splendidly imaginative building. But styles as distinctive as Hudson River Bracketed and experiments as courageous as the octagonal stone house have been allowed to languish.

For the fact is that, culturally, neither America nor New York State represented, during the first half of the twentieth century, any one trend or direction or set of values. If American architecture was banal and eclectic as a rule, one reason was that American taste as a whole was undecided among several possibilities. Should one be sternly efficient and ruthlessly functional, or nostalgic and traditional? When one described a style as "traditional," what tradition was one referring to? The cultural atmosphere of New York and America grew steadily more complex and diffuse, but it had more and more the characteristics of a museum culture, it was less and less lightened by the spark of imagination and feeling. By the middle of the century, one could build a house, write a book, paint a picture, or compose a piece of music, in about any style one wanted, without fear of public disapproval. Tolerance was enormous, all but universal; discrimination and direction were other matters entirely.

Elsewhere, the relativism was less absolute. A Parisian public, for example, could still on rare occasions be shocked. By a display of provocative taste, it was not impossible to provoke riots and the throwing of elderly vegetables among the excitable Gauls. One had the sense that Americans, especially New Yorkers, would yield a polite patter of applause to anything which took itself seriously, but that they loved nothing and hated nothing. Overwhelmingly, the culture gave one an impression of uniformity and conservatism. Perhaps it was simply that by mid-century the big revolts and revolutions had blown themselves out; there was nothing more to revolt against. At all events, one could scarcely help contrasting the stormy, tempestuous 1920's with the conservative, almost effete 1950's.

In literature, for example, the difference made itself felt at once. During the 1920's, New York City especially harbored, off and on, a remarkably promising group of young literary radicals. They were radical, not only politically but artistically. Novelists like Ernest Hemingway, Sinclair Lewis, and F. Scott Fitzgerald conveyed a tremendous, exciting impression of having seen through something. Whatever they had discovered behind outworn conventions (and it was something fresh and unique in each case), they saw it with excitement and a sense of blinding immediacy. It was in this spirit of fresh discovery that Lewis fell upon mid-western Babbittry and Hemingway opened up a vein of heroic, stoical manhood. Ring Lardner and H. L. Mencken discovered American speech and rejoiced in its flat, repetitious rhythms; Fitzgerald discovered the fascinating society of the very rich and Mike Gold the equally fascinating society of the very poor. Edna St. Vincent Millay, fresh out of Vassar College and inspired with a lyric vein as rich if not quite as disciplined as that of Keats, sang mockingly and ironically of the trials and complexities of love. Hart Crane, unhappy in Ohio, came to New York and as he walked across Brooklyn Bridge saw in the strength and delicacy of its soaring lines a symbol of the American dream, a poignant and tantalizing vision. Huge and unhappy, Thomas Wolfe wandered the East-Side streets, remembering his home in Asheville, North Carolina, and composing long, tumultuous, rhapsodic novels out of his lonely, poetic memories. At different times and to very different effects, literary radicals like Max Eastman, John Reed (*Ten Days That Shook the World*), Lincoln Steffens (*The Autobiography of Lincoln Steffens*), and John Dos Passos (*U.S.A.*) carried on a thriving trade in ideas both literary and political. After being ejected from more tender-minded schools around the country, tough old Thorstein Veblen (*The Theory of the Leisure Class*) was giving his sardonic, analytic lectures at the New School for Social Research. Altogether, it was an age of ferment and direction-seeking. The authors mentioned were not all or exclusively New York writers, but there was not one of them who did not have intimate and congenial contacts with New York; and they contributed to the enormous sense of turmoil and search which typified the 1920's.

During the 1930's and 1940's a great deal of this ferment was channeled in the direction of social protest. The so-called "proletarian novel" became a popular art-form; *The Underground Stream* by Albert Maltz and *Union Square* by Albert Halper were interesting samples of this literary genre. Poets such as Genevieve Taggard and critics such as Granville Hicks joined in what was often envisaged as a great crusade to purify society, to redeem the injustices of the underprivileged, and to create a new moral atmosphere in which art, truth, and brotherhood would flourish. There is no need to recount the melancholy disillusion which overtook this movement, or to list the causes for its general abandonment. Suffice it to say that the generation after World War II was, often avowedly, a generation dedicated to conformity, conservatism, and orthodoxy. "The new conservatism" was a phrase in many mouths; Burke, Plato, Joseph de Maistre, and Alexander Hamilton were names to conjure with. Indeed, the new conservatism was often so conservative that it insisted upon conserving all the liberal virtues and attitudes; in point of fact it was less conservative than neutralist.

The need for disciplined understanding of world issues led to a fear, often irrational and uncontrolled, of nonconformity at any level. Political pressures and tensions generated a suspicion which verged, sometimes, on the pathological, and men sometimes hesitated to speak their minds freely. And finally, apart from intimidation and conformity for its own sake, mid-century America seemed to have run out of its big ideas—at least for the moment. In the background lay Freud, Marx, Einstein, and Darwin—gigantic minds, formed in the heroic mold by the nineteenth century and now the subject of violent, contending criticisms. But new theories, new impulses, new social attitudes were rarely being put forward; the values of thinking conservatively were being explored to the point where they verged on the values of not thinking at all. The cultural climate of New York at mid-century, as of America in general, was tentative and hesitant; our age was often described as an "age of anxiety."

But while the intellectuals hesitated and drew back before the opportunities and responsibilities of the twentieth century, the twentieth century rolled irresistibly onward. America must have a culture, whether made by intellectuals or not; and in the absence of clear ideas about what the public ought to have, men of enterprise were not lacking to furnish what it wanted. New York City furnished, to a very surprising degree, material for a judgment of what was good and what bad in the mass conformist culture with built-in areas of individual variation.

Least pleasing to contemplate, among all the mid-century developments, was the growing standardization of culture imposed by the immense expansion of those "mass media," which had just become really massive between the two world wars. Big commercial radio programs sought to find a simple formula and stick to it indefinitely; magazine stories were tailored to appeal to the most primitive fantasies of the twelve-year-old mind; book clubs put a premium on nationally merchandised mediocrity; plays, articles, and programs of public entertainment were all too often pruned of everything "controversial" before being considered fit for public consumption. In the larger sense, these facts were evidence of national and perhaps international trends; New York State took part in these developments, along with the rest of the nation, and New York City, as a major hub of communications and center of the nation's entertainment business, typified them. The phrase "Madison Avenue huckster" in one or another of its many variants came to describe a man, often of great intelligence and discrimination himself, who in the interests of the big advertisers ruthlessly imposed infantile entertainment and hypnotic slogans on the apathetic appetites of the great American public. Standards of taste declined precipitously; on the one hand, anything sensational or sentimental, on the other hand the merest empty trivialities of give-away programs and the glib patter of comedians, came to fill the lives of the mass audience. Even the act of reading often became too much for an audience which had less demanding diversions at hand in television and radio.

If we look only at the mass media, the period after World War II presents a depressing picture indeed. Fortunately, the significant culture of any nation is rarely dependent upon the vehicles of the mass media. Alongside the business of purveying clichés in volume, New York City developed, in the course of the first half of the twentieth century, one of the richest and most eclectic cultures in the world.

Periodic complaints were heard of the decadence and debility of the commercial theater, menaced by the competition of radio, the movies, and television, squeezed by high rents, and hamstrung by labor regulations. These complaints were not altogether without foundation. The number of plays and musicals produced each season declined from an aggregate of 186 in 1923–1924 to an aggregate of sixty in 1953–1954. Compared with London or Paris, New York had relatively few plays before the lights, and those few were in good measure ripe old chestnuts of well-tested appeal. A revival of Shakespeare or Shaw might be expected to hold the boards; a "leg show" was usually a good bet; but even with the best of reviews an intelligent and challenging new play sometimes faded for lack of public support.

Still, no theater could be described as "decadent" which continued to produce the powerful family dramas of Arthur Miller (*Death of a Salesman*), the tortured symbolic visions of Tennessee Williams (*A Streetcar Named Desire*), and the religiously colored social comedy of T. S. Eliot (*The Cocktail Party*), not to mention musical comedies like *Oklahoma!, South Pacific, Guys and Dolls,* and *My Fair Lady.*

Around the time of World War I native American drama received a great stimulus with the development of little theaters, especially the Provincetown Players, and with the emergence of a particularly creative group of New York playwrights. Previous American playwrights had tended to avoid contemporary problems and had attempted to amuse their audiences with stereotyped characters and melodramatic or sentimental plots. But during and immediately after World War I there appeared a number of workmen in the theater who were interested in social satire, dramatic realism, and psychological expressionism, who put meat into their dramas and vitality into their writing.

Foremost among these authors, by common consent, was Eugene

O'Neill. Catholic in his tastes as in his background and receptive to new ideas and dramatic techniques, O'Neill at various stages in his career could be described as a Freudian, a mystic, a nihilist, a radical, a romanticist, and a realist. His writing was often turgid and bombastic and his thinking sometimes muddled, but his instinct for the theater was powerful and sure. He wrote neither to instruct, to entertain, nor to reform, but to explore man's tragic relation to the universe without —the cosmos—and the universe within—his own psyche. *Beyond the Horizon* (1919) won a Pulitzer Prize, as did *Anna Christie* and *Strange Interlude* in the 1920's. The height of his achievement was probably his Civil War trilogy on classical themes, *Mourning Becomes Electra.* O'Neill's talent earned for him the Nobel Prize for literature in 1935, and it has caused him to be genuinely revered by later writers for the serious American stage. For example, Elmer Rice's *The Adding Machine* makes use of many symbolic devices akin to those used by O'Neill; Clifford Odets' *Awake and Sing!,* in addition to its Chekhovian overtones, analyzes the flawed American dream in a way made familiar by O'Neill; and Arthur Miller has written tragedies about humble and half-articulate characters which are in the very spirit of *The Hairy Ape* or *The Emperor Jones.*

Other fine plays which have graced the New York stage are *Winterset* (1935) by Maxwell Anderson; *Abe Lincoln in Illinois* (1938) by Robert Sherwood; *The Little Foxes* (1939) by Lillian Hellman; *Our Town* (1938) by Thornton Wilder. Tennessee Williams, in the 1940's and 1950's, was contributing many excellent plays. George S. Kaufman, Marc Connelly, S. N. Behrman, Rachel Crothers, and Philip Barry wrote popular comedies. On another level were those great successes, *Abie's Irish Rose* and *Tobacco Road.*

During the 1920's the musical comedy stage was largely, though not entirely, devoted to the production of lush extravaganzas, featuring splendidly undressed showgirls and loud and vulgar jokes—such for the most part were the *Ziegfeld Follies* and George White's *Scandals.* But at the same time Sigmund Romberg was writing his sentimental, well-loved musicals; Cole Porter was beginning his long and successful career as a composer of musical comedies (later to include such hits as *Anything Goes,* the *Gay Divorcee,* and *Kiss Me Kate*); the sophisticated review *Three's a Crowd* and the Negro review *Blackbirds of 1929* won wide acclaim; and Jerome Kern was writing *Sunny, Sally,* and the immortal *Show Boat.*

In the 1930's more comedy and satire were brought into musical comedy. In 1931 *Of Thee I Sing* appeared, a side-splitting travesty on politics, the vice-presidency, and life in the White House which won the first Pulitzer Prize ever bestowed for a musical play. This frothy satire combined the comic talents of George S. Kaufman, Morrie Ryskind, and Ira Gershwin with the music of George Gershwin, who was later to write the score for the classic folk opera *Porgy and Bess*. Meanwhile, Richard Rodgers was rapidly coming to the fore as a composer of popular scores. He teamed at first with the lyricist Lorenz Hart, and then with Oscar Hammerstein II, and in both combinations his output was little short of prodigious. When he and Hart dissolved partnership in 1942 they had collaborated on twenty-three musical shows, including *Garrick Gaieties, A Connecticut Yankee,* and *Pal Joey.* Nine of their shows had been made into motion pictures, and together they wrote nearly four hundred songs.

The new musical-comedy team of Rodgers and Hammerstein has already produced such hits as *Oklahoma!* (1943), *Carousel* (1945), *South Pacific* (1949), and *The King and I* (1951). Frank Loesser's *Guys and Dolls,* based on the short stories of Damon Runyon, was another tremendous success; and so was a musical version of Bernard Shaw's *Pygmalion,* titled *My Fair Lady* (1956). Indeed, so far as the musical stage was concerned, it might fairly be argued that the New York stage had become more adult and sophisticated during the 1950's than it ever was before.

As an economic enterprise, to be sure, the commercial theater in any form is clearly the very next thing to suicide and insanity. From 1948 to 1953, members of Actors' Equity averaged only $790 a year from their theatrical work; and they worked, on the average, only ten weeks out of the fifty-two. Before it ever opened on Broadway, a show might cost anywhere from $30,000 to $375,000; and its chances for survival in the Big Town were desperate indeed. If it survived at all, a musical might have to attract packed houses for as much as a year (selling its seats at up to ten dollars each), before it recovered the cost of production. An accepted break-even figure for a one-set dramatic play with no orchestra and few characters was $20,000 a week. Yet the professional theater continued to exist and in its own febrile, half-commercial, half-artistic way, to flourish.

The theatrical climate was immensely enriched, too, by the mushroom growth of an off-Broadway theater. Playing in converted warehouses and lofts, the amateurs and semiprofessionals making up these companies were able to produce plays of relatively limited appeal. They had their problems with copyright and fire regulations, with inexperienced or unreliable performers, with ramshackle organizations and an appalling lack of capital. Yet they survived and flourished, producing many young actors who graduated to Broadway or Hollywood and many memorable shows in their own right.

A federal, municipal, or state subsidized theater was often discussed as a means of providing training for young actors, a place for production of standard items of the repertoire, and an economic cushion for a desperately uncushioned industry. But, except for a brief and promising venture into federal theater made by the Works Progress Administration during the 1930's, the idea of a subsidized theater has remained an idea. Actors and actresses, meanwhile, solve the problem of making a living by working as bellhops and elevator operators. During the summers they sometimes venture forth to act in converted barns or on the resort circuit. This depressing and familiar story provides evidence of the theater's irresistible attraction for young people of undaunted and resilient optimism.

One branch of show business, indeed, succumbed as early as the 1930's, under the impact of competition from the movies. Vaudeville died when the famous old Palace closed in 1932; and periodic attempts to revive it only emphasized its total demise. In one sense, it was the purest of the performing arts; for a great vaudevillian like Frank Fay had no prepared act, no special tricks or routines. He commanded each audience he faced by sheer power of personality, and to see him work a Sunday night audience at the Palace (an audience itself composed almost entirely of theatrical people) was a tremendous experience. Other famous vaudevillians were Tony Pastor, Sophie Tucker, W. C. Fields, Ed Wynn, Will Rogers, and Nora Bayes. Something of the old-time vaudevillian's sharp and rakish attitude may still be seen in the pages of *Variety*, a newspaper put out by, for, and about the boys and girls in show-biz. *Variety*, like most of its readers, has a fondness for New York City which borders on the chauvinistic; and the city responds with a special affection for its brightest, noisiest, and most flamboyant children.

To the music lover, New York City offers probably the richest diet of any city of the world—a perpetual festival of musical art. In the field of opera, New York is still the only city in America where one can see and hear the full standard repertoire, spread out over a five-month season; where the great voices and the great performers regularly and inevitably appear. The Metropolitan Opera House is of course the center of operatic production. Undeniably conservative in its selection of operas for production, the management offsets this quality by lavishness in the acquisition of singers. Caruso, Chaliapin, Flagstad, Baccaloni, Pinza, and Erna Berger—the list is all but endless. One goes a long time at the "Met" between productions of Berg's *Wozzeck* and Stravinsky's *Rake's Progress;* yet where else in America can one hear them at all? If the standard repertoire is performed and overperformed, it is only by European standards that one can complain of lack of variety. And in opera, as in the theater, the big commercial enterprise is augmented by more or less informal groups—no less than fifty-three of them in New York City. The New York City Opera, the Amato Opera Company, Community Opera, Inc., the L. Petri Opera Co., the San Carlo Opera Co., the Juilliard School of Music, and the Little Orchestra Society are only a few of the groups sponsoring operatic performances.

Only in the melancholy sense that their devotion was meagerly rewarded could one call the practitioners of modern dance "amateurs," for their training was always arduous and their standards exacting. The great period of vital experiment in this medium was the 1930's; many groups and soloists sprang into prominence at this time, and recitals were numerous and enthusiastic. But the talent which gained public notice through dance recitals was quickly drained off into more lucrative lines of endeavor. Jerome Robbins, Michael Kidd, and Agnes de Mille, for example, concerned themselves more and more with work for the movies or the musical-comedy stage; and only a few established companies, such as those of Martha Graham, Pearl Lang, and José Limon, continued into the 1950's the old, unrelenting experiment of expressive modern dancing. To some extent this void was filled, after World War II, by a revived interest in ballet. The most talented and glamorous companies of Europe—the Sadlers Wells Company of England, for example, and the Ballet Russe de Monte Carlo—established New York seasons, and were received with éclat. Fine ballet is a very fine spectacle indeed, and one would not wish New York to be without it. Yet the modern dance had, at its best, a creative spark, a flair for the distinctively modern idiom, which one hopes the vogue for ballet will not permanently extinguish.

After the great days of Arturo Toscanini in the 1930's and 1940's, the New York Philharmonic was not quite as distinctive a force in the musical world as, say, the Boston Philharmonic under Koussevitsky or the Cleveland Symphony under Rodjinski. A succession of guest conductors gave the New York organization no chance to develop an individual character of its own. Still, it was a fine symphony orchestra, more widely heard (owing to the Sunday afternoon broadcasts) than any other orchestra in the nation. And around it there flourished an amazing proliferation of more or less specialized musical organizations. "Little symphonies" were numerous; chamber-music groups were beyond computation; vocal ensembles and composers' forums flourished. Throughout the city organizations might be found for the performance of baroque music, medieval music, music for wood-winds, Finnish music, children's music, music for ancient instruments. There was no limit to the amount and variety of music that New Yorkers made and heard. Recitals, of course, continued to be the order of the day—recitals so many and so various as practically to defy description. There are also fine musical organizations outside the metropolis. One thinks at once of the Rochester and Buffalo symphonies and the fine orchestra associated with the Eastman School of Music at Rochester—but for sheer richness of musical life, New York City stands alone.

Above all, the musical climate of the city was enriched by a variety of radio programs available over small stations, and appealing to an audience of specialized interests. On the big networks, a lover of classical music had to content himself with two hours of Sunday-afternoon symphony; in New York City, one had available, via long-playing records, frequency modulation radio, and high-fidelity sound reproduction, twenty-four hours a day of string quartets, operas, cantatas, concerts, and symphonies. Composers clustered together in New York in sufficient numbers to create at least the illusion of a community; and in the circles they frequented, the twelve-tone scale, the prepared piano, and the intricacies of atonality were discussed with passion and understanding. Here at least "the world of music" was not a mere metaphor; a person of musical interests and abilities might actually live in New York amid a society where the language of music was constantly spoken and where the value of fine music was accepted without question. Aaron Copland, William Schuman, Paul Creston, Norman Dello Joio, Randall Thompson, Virgil Thompson, David Diamond, Ulysses Kay, and Douglas Moore are all well-known New York composers.

On a somewhat different plane, New York City also became the great jazz center of the nation. The Original Dixieland Five had played New York, of course, as early as 1919; but this venture represented an excursion into the hinterland from the great central headquarters of jazz in New Orleans and Chicago. It was not till the middle 1930's that jazz really became domesticated in New York, and not till after World War II that New York became a central headquarters of the art. Originally, the best music in this genre was to be heard either uptown in Harlem, or downtown in Greenwich Village. But after a while, Benny Goodman and others brought jazz into Carnegie Hall, and then the art acquired practitioners in the bistros of the East Fifties. Nowadays, one may hear good jazz at Nick's, Eddie Condon's, or Café Society in the Village; at the Savoy Ballroom or the Apollo Theater in Harlem; and at The Embers or Birdland, in midtown. "Cool" styles have had their vogue, and for a while the cry of the bopster was loud in the land; but the backbone of jazz remains good old polyphonic Dixieland with a solid beat.

New York City in its relation to literature offers us a wide and wonderful topic, too bewildering in its multiplicity for easy analysis. As the center of the American book-publishing business, New York provided writers with a marketplace and a germinal source of ideas. Perhaps these two functions did not always harmonize perfectly. A marketplace is not always the best place to carry out projects of high imaginative quality, especially when it is dominated (as is the New York literary marketplace) by mass-distribution organizations like the Book of the Month Club and its several imitators. Some writers were distracted by professional operations involving paperbacks, reprint houses, movie rights, and anthologies; others were drawn into commercial projects like quiz shows, blurbwriting, and gossip mongering; still others succumbed to the general pursuit of fashionable and merely flashy ideas. As a rule, authors tended to find the intellectual atmosphere of New York too thick, the pace of ideas, projects, and personalities too distracting to encourage their best work. Typically, they dipped into the turbid stream of literary ferment and discussion for a while, and then withdrew to a retreat in Westport, Connecticut, the south of France, or Oxford, Mississippi, where life was more leisurely and rents more reasonable. In their seclusion they evolved manuscripts, which were sent to New York, to be produced as books, which produced more ferment, into which they dipped again. And thus the cycle proceeded.

Of "New York City novelists" in the strict definition, there were not, perhaps, very many. Miss Betty Smith recorded her childhood in the borough across the river (*A Tree Grows in Brooklyn*); Mr. Thomas Gallagher etched some memorable pictures of the neurotic lace-curtain Irishry around Columbia University (*The Gathering Darkness*); and Mr. Jerome Weidman did an incisive study of the manners and mores of the garment district titled *I Can Get It for You Wholesale*. But in general the New York novel at the midpoint of the century did not seem to be concerned, as it once was, with the analysis of a neighborhood. After a splurge during the 1930's, when the so-called "proletarian" novelists tried to make their novels out of their neighborhoods (usually the Lower East Side), a change took place. Perhaps the chief practitioner today of the older genre is Mr. Budd Schulberg; *What Makes Sammy Run?* had a tenderness and *Waterfront* a toughness which seem to be derivative from the novels of social protest which dominated the 1930's. But on the whole, the neighborhood novel has now moved to the suburbs, where the fate of the pretentious intellectual snob is investigated by Mr. Edmund Wilson and that of the man in the gray flannel suit by Mr. Sloan Wilson.

By and large, then, New York City became a backdrop for novelists, rather than a subject matter. John O'Hara did a fine mordant study of a doomed young wanton and an advertising man at the dangerous age, in *Butterfield 8*; Frederic Wakeman, in *The Hucksters*, explored the gilded slave-marts of Madison Avenue; and Herman Wouk, in

Marjorie Morningstar, reported at length on the difficulties of being a nice young lady on West End Avenue. Ludwig Bemelmans created around the Plaza Hotel (in his terms, the "Splendide") an entire world of imagination, not so much New York in its coloring, or even American, as cosmopolitan. And Greenwich-Village novels continued to chronicle the grubby events of that grubby little Bohemia, though not (on the whole) with great zest.

If one can generalize abruptly on a slippery subject, the relation of the novelist to New York City seems to have become more flexible; he is not dependent on it for his materials, at least not exclusively dependent; rather, he uses as he needs them its literary facilities, its colorful properties and social materials, its editors and advisers, its perpetual interest in style, its reservoir of literary ideas—and occasionally its magnificent gift of absolute privacy. William Faulkner could only have written *The Sound and the Fury* out of a lifetime of frustration and angry torment in Mississippi: but the breakthrough just happened to come during the solitude and concentrated travail of a two-month sojourn in the apartment of his Manhattan editor. Mr. John Steinbeck is known as a California novelist; but his imagination dwells most lovingly on the rancheros of the San Fernando Valley from the security of a brownstone in the East '90's.

That a number of the big news, picture, and feature magazines make their headquarters in New York adds a certain flavor to the town. *Time, Life, Fortune, Newsweek, Look, Pic,* and many of their cousins are staffed, for the most part, with bright and agile people, skilled at their trade and intelligent far beyond the level of intellectual appetite which it is their business to satisfy. These big enterprises are part of New York City as the great midtown advertising agencies or broadcasting companies are part of the metropolis. Though they exist in the city, they are not really integrally connected with it; they are nuclei in a worldwide apparatus for collecting information, simplifying it, making it palatable, and disseminating it. In a word, they are commercial enterprises, as pure and as simple as such enterprises usually are.

Much more intimately related to the cultural atmosphere of New York City, and much more distinctly a New York contribution to the American scene, is the publication appropriately titled *The New Yorker.* Started as a weekly magazine just after World War I, it has steadily published short stories of distinction and comment of a dry, casual, understated character, framed in meticulous prose. The sense of economy and easy, urbane intelligence which characterize this magazine render it unique among American periodicals. In a sense, *The New Yorker* is a local publication, for and about inhabitants of the metropolis;

but it is also circulated nationally, and it exerts a national influence. If there is an occasional smart-aleck tone to be detected in its pages, the dry astringency of its wit and the humanity of its sentiment have certainly been forces for the betterment of American writing.

Three publications which take as their audience the more or less professional literary public testify to New York's pre-eminence as a literary center. The *Saturday Review* acts in considerable measure as a clearinghouse for information about the book business. Its interest in the best books is sometimes rather diluted by a competing interest in the best-sellers; its taste is, in the cant phrase, middlebrow. *Publishers' Weekly* and *Printers' Ink,* on the other hand, are publications for the entire trade, including the retail bookseller, the production man, the printer, and the paper salesman. All these publications serve to keep publishers, authors, and bookmakers aware of one another and of the larger trends in the book business. As in every trade, there is a great deal of gossip in the book *geschaft;* one sometimes gets the impression, around New York, of a large and busy family, spread out over the entire city, which foregathers constantly at publishers' parties, and exchanges chit-chat through the columns of the *Saturday Review, Publishers' Weekly,* and the two Sunday book supplements of the *Times* and the *Herald Tribune.* The atmosphere is surprisingly amicable, and very congenial to those literary artists who are tolerant or appreciative of gossip and professional small-talk.

Higher of brow and smaller of circulation than the *Saturday Review,* are various literary publications which aim at reaching, or constituting, the *avant garde.* The names of these publications change from time to time, but their contents do not vary much. Lots of criticism, either literary or social or both, a few short stories, an occasional poem— this was the fare offered by *The Dial* or *Hound and Horn* thirty years ago; it is the diet provided by *Partisan Review* and *Hudson Review* today. Like the big news magazines, these little reviews and quarterlies are in New York only by accident. Probably they could not very well help being in a metropolis, but they might well exist in another metropolis, as *Poetry* exists in Chicago, *The Criterion* existed in London, and *Little Review* in Paris. Surviving as they do from hand to mouth, or angel to angel, they provide an unusual measure of intellectual stimulation and independent thinking, which frequently reverberates far beyond the limited circle of their subscription lists.

Among the poets who inhabit New York without making it the primary subject of their work, space allows us to distinguish only a few of the most eminent and most firmly-rooted. Mr. E. E. Cummings has been writing spry and cryptic verses, for more than thirty years now, from his home on Patchen Place in the Village. Mr. Langston Hughes, the unofficial poet laureate of Harlem, is another old-time resident who continues to publish. W. H. Auden, a bird of passage from Europe, described permanently one nostalgic aspect of the city when he stage-set his baroque eclogue, *The Age of Anxiety,* in a Third Avenue bar. And Miss Marianne Moore continues to produce exquisite ironic arrangements of words from her headquarters in Brooklyn. During the winter, these poets as well as their visiting confrères may be regularly heard by devotees of the art, reading their verses at the Ninety-second Street Young Men's Hebrew Association. Out of a differing environment and dealing with differing themes is the poetic work of Mark Van Doren.

Even more cheerful to consider was the situation of the decorative arts. The galleries and museums of New York have long held unquestioned pre-eminence in the nation; the only peril which they present is that of swamping New Yorkers under an embarrassment of riches. In this respect, the Museum of Modern Art plays a central role in the city's cultural life. Since 1939 it has been a major force for clean, uncluttered, and functional design. As in any cosmopolitan metropolis, taste in New York has a tendency to indulge the dramatic, the showy and unrestrainedly eclectic; but the museum, by force of its example as well as of its precepts, has spearheaded a movement in the direction of restraint, simplicity, and artistic chastity. A single show may have repercussions in many different directions; for instance, the Japanese house and allied exhibits, which were on display in 1954–1956, provided ideas not only to architects but to designers of furniture and furnishings, to painters, fashion experts, and commercial artists of all sorts. And in the area of industrial design, as well as in the appreciation of good moving pictures and in the encouragement of experimental work in sculpture and painting, the museum has performed yeoman service.

Naturally, a steady trade in antiques and old masters continues to occupy the big commercial galleries; but painters in the modern manner flourish throughout the city, wherever they can find a good north light at a reasonable rental. Some years ago, all the apartments answering this description seemed to be located in Greenwich Village; nowadays, they are likely to be more widely dispersed throughout the five boroughs and the suburbs, even though the major display galleries continue to cluster around Washington Square and Fifty-seventh Street.

During the 1930's and early 1940's much art, like fiction, focused on social themes, and three artists who were trained in and have lived in the city were outstanding in this movement—Philip Evergood, Ben Shahn, and William Gropper. Gropper's cartoons have frequently appeared in the press, and Shahn has done murals for several public buildings.

The most interesting recent developments in modern art seem to lead the painters further and further from surface realism, in the direction of free expression. Picasso, Braque, and their American counterpart John Marin made familiar enough the reduction of external reality to a set of interrelated planes and angles; but the newer schools (none of them sufficiently established as yet to be symbolized by a name) seem intent on transcribing mental states directly on canvas without the mediation of a "natural" form. The results are often disturbingly powerful and immediate; but how far this trend can go without producing radical limitations on the communication between artist and audience, remains to be seen. Sculptors such as Julio Gonzalez who weld their statues in steel, and painters such as the late Jackson Pollock who pour enamel from the can over the canvas, have at least established one sort of direct pathway for the expression of their feelings. And feelings which are freely and fully expressed do not often fail of being, at least partially, communicated. Outside the metropolitan area, no painter has attracted more attention than "Grandma" Moses, lifelong resident of Eagle Bridge, Rensselaer County. Beginning late in life, she has depicted, in brilliant color, scenes with which she has long been familiar.

As a center of the publishing and advertising businesses, New York City is particularly hospitable to what might be called the applied graphic arts. And the generally high standards set by American books, both in beauty and legibility, may someday be recognized as a significant index of cultural achievement. Book designers and illustrators flourish here in profusion; many of the nation's finest typographers, calligraphers, photographers, layout men, and color-reproduction people are found in the city or within a short radius of it. One particularly notable exception is upstater Rockwell Kent, whose well-known woodcuts and lithographs have complemented many books.

A particular influence on the cultural life of the metropolis is that exerted by the immense and growing fashion industry. New York has been a garment-manufacturing center for many years; but only after the outbreak of World War II, when it was cut off from the Paris designers, did the city develop in any major way as an independent originator of fashions. Nowadays New York designers create more models than Paris itself, set more styles, and influence more women in the all-important matter of dress. Most of the nation's fashion magazines—*Vogue, Harper's Bazaar,* and *Mademoiselle,* for example—are published in or near the city; and designers Mainbocher, Claire McCardle, Anne Fogarty, and Jo Copeland hold their shows, release their designs, and sell their dresses from headquarters in New York.

What is more, New York is a city of beautiful women, beautifully dressed. There is no such heartwarming sight in all America as can be seen by strolling down midtown Fifth Avenue on a fine spring afternoon.

Showgirls and shopgirls, models and housewives and actresses and secretaries—they dress up to the city, and like so many glowing flowers, illumine the dank canyons of New York's asphalt and concrete streets. Visitors from the great capitals of the world all pay tribute to the freshness and sophistication of the New York woman.

Finally, no discussion of New York's cultural atmosphere would be complete which did not make mention of the magnificent array of eating and drinking places which make New York the gourmet's particular oyster. Of course there have always been fine restaurants in town; one hears tales of Luchow's which suggest Lucullan luxury at the turn of the century. And there are still restaurants like the Chambord where, for a mere twenty-five dollars or so per plate, one may eat a very good dinner indeed. But the real enchantment for the New York diner-out is the magnificent variety of good food available at everyday prices for his selection. One night he may eat pork sweet and sour, prepared as only a skilled Chinese chef can do it; the next night it may be *arroz con pollo*, a lavish smorgasbord, bouillabaisse, or shish-kebab topped off with delicious paklava and clotted cream—or a broiled lobster—or a succulent oyster stew—or something as simple as a three-inch charcoal-broiled steak. Many years ago New York committed a deadly gastronomical sin when it introduced the tomato into clam chowder; but the town has long since atoned for this atrocious crime, and there is now no city in the world which does such gracious reverence to seafood—even though it still puts tomatoes in its clam chowder.

Aside from formal restaurants, a word must also be said on the immense subject of the New York delicatessen. This home of the delicate bagel and the rosy lox, purveyor of the preroasted turkey, the smoked kipper, the creamy cheesecake, the infinite varieties of Danish pastry, and that mysterious, intricate, exalted structure known usually as "Max's Submarine Sandwich"—if this is not a cultural phenomenon, where shall we find one? The best foods from many lands are found here. Is it not true that the beer is always cold, the pickles always tart, and the hot pastrami always juicy between its slabs of crunchy rye bread? These happy thoughts are apt to press upon the nostalgic exile from Manhattan to the point of making him forget that one can also eat badly in the city. But if he has the mature discretion and the well-lined pocketbook which are essential, the wise New Yorker can make a fine art of dining-out.

In describing the social atmosphere prevalent in New York, one must draw upon reports so diverse as to be contradictory in every particular and from every angle. The man who came to town for a big time, stayed in a tourist hotel off Times Square, and frequented the night clubs set up for the out-of-town trade went home with an understandable view of the city. It was a cold, hard, brassy place, where everyone tried to cheat him. By frequenting the museums, libraries, and concert halls one could get an image of New Yorkers as dreamy, soft-spoken, slightly neurasthenic folk, rich in culture and indifferent to pelf. A nocturnal adventure in the lower Bronx or East Harlem might leave one with the impression that New Yorkers were ravening beasts, delighting in viciousness for its own sake. An evening of casual conversation with a circle of cultured acquaintances might equally well convince a visitor that New Yorkers were the warmest, most gracious and affable people in the world. What you saw in New York seemed to depend in large measure on the personality and interests you brought to it.

Still, certain characteristics can and should be described. New York society is surpassingly mobile. There are not many social circles into which an assured manner, a minimum concern with respectability, and an immense lot of money cannot carry one. Formerly the "Four Hundred" were a distinct, self-defined, and strictly limited body; in modern times, real society shades rather indistinctly into "café society," and café society does not always distinguish itself meticulously from "saloon society"—which is the next thing to no society at all. The woman who lives on Park Avenue cannot be distinguished by a casual eye from the woman who only works there; the pseudo-Oxonian who sells one shoes sometimes looks more like the genuine article than any real Oxonian would ever dare to do. New York taxi drivers are known to spend their vacations in Europe; the man who works in the sewer is as likely as not to correct your misquotation of La Rochefoucauld, and subway conductors can sometimes be inveigled, during the slack hours of early morning, into delivering a recitative and tenor aria from the third act of *La Bohème*. And when they parade into the psychoanalyst's office (as by mid-century practically every New Yorker seems to be doing) all social classes stand in humble equality before the immense tribal deities labeled Id, Ego, and Superego.

Because the New Yorker sees so many people every day, perhaps as an act of defiance against the masses of which he makes so small a part, he often cultivates rich veins of eccentricity and individuality. Where else in America are there so many waiters who will argue you out of ordering the soup you thought you wanted, give you a red-hot tip on the third race at Jamaica, and serve up their personal philosophies of life with the Nesselrode cream pie? Where else would the owner of a stationery store tell you that the delicatessen on the south corner of the street made better roast-beef sandwiches, but advise you to go to the one on the north corner because the proprietor there had a dry sense of humor? The New York taxi driver has been famous for many years as a source of universal wisdom and practical counsel in the deepest affairs of life. One would not dispute this judgment; but something of the same humane and cynical wisdom seems to be spreading throughout the whole metropolis. The cop on the beat, the girl at the hosiery counter, the newsboy, and the boot-black have become the repository of a wisdom which is more than individual. It is the wisdom of the city itself, flavoring the perception of the individual with a smoky and hard-bitten sentiment, for which the convinced New Yorker, whether he be native or adopted, can find no substitute throughout the world.

Bibliographical Essay

THE literature on New York and its history is voluminous and is constantly growing. The following bibliographical essay can necessarily refer to only a fraction of the books, articles, and manuscripts dealing with the Empire State. Our basic aim has been to include the most significant works and to give essential information about them. To assist the scholar and the general reader, the New York State Historical Association is making plans to compile and to publish an exhaustive bibliography of New York.

We have excluded whole categories of material in order to keep the bibliography within bounds. Specifically we have not included (1) works of fiction, poetry, or drama, (2) most local histories such as those dealing with counties, villages, churches, and the like, (3) articles in historical journals except for a few of the most significant, (4) general histories of the United States all of which pay some attention to New York, (5) books for children, (6) the manuscript papers of individuals except for a few that have been published. In exceptional cases we have trespassed over these lines.

The bibliography is divided into three parts: the Introduction deals with general questions and discusses comprehensive histories, historical periodicals, and atlases. Part I covers the period from 1609 to 1865. Part II covers the period from 1865 to 1956. This part is divided into three sections organized around the topics of (1) politics and government, (2) population and economic changes, (3) social and intellectual history.

Many books are useful for several topics and periods. In order to save space we have shortened titles and dropped the date of publication after the first reference.

INTRODUCTION

Bibliographical Guides

The history of New York is so inextricably tied to that of the nation that readers will find useful almost any bibliography for the United States. The most convenient way to find such bibliographies is through H. P. Beers, *Bibliographies in American History: Guide to Materials for Research* (1942). Every student will find indispensable the *Harvard Guide to American History* (1954). Annual volumes of bibliography prepared by G. G. Griffin *et al.*, *Writings on American History*, covering the years 1906–1940 and 1948–1950, list articles as well as books. Prior to 1906, articles are listed in A. P. C. Griffin, *Bibliography of American Historical Societies, The United States and the Dominion of Canada* (2nd ed., 1907), or as Volume II of the *Annual Report of the American Historical Association* (1905).

A useful list of books is given in C. E. Van Norman, ed., *The Empire State Yesterday and Today* (1944). There are also valuable references at the end of most chapters in A. C. Flick, ed., *History of the State of New York* (10 vols., 1933–1937). A valuable guide to economic history is A. R. Hasse, *Index to Economic Material in Documents of the States of the United States: New York, 1789–1904* (1907). Advanced students will find a great deal of excellent material in dissertations at scores of colleges and universities. J. T. Dunn has compiled two useful lists in his articles "Masters' Theses and Doctoral Dissertations on New York History," *New York History* (Oct. 1952; April 1955).

Two indispensable guides to manuscript sources were published by the Historical Records Survey of the Works Progress Administration in 1941: *Guide to Depositories of Manuscript Collections in New York State* and *Guide to Manuscript Depositories in New York City*. See also *A Guide to the Principal Sources for Early American History (1600–1800) in the City of New York*, ed. by E. B. Greene and R. B. Morris (1929; rev. 1953).

Atlases, Guidebooks, Manuals, and Maps

The most satisfactory atlas is J. R. Bien, *Atlas of the State of New York* (1895). W. P. Munger, *Historical Atlas of New York* (1941), was revised by Wallace Lamb and H. R. Shipherd in 1957. It includes much new material such as separate histories of eleven regions of the state. Old but still useful is J. H. French, comp., *Gazetteer of the State of New York: Embracing a Comprehensive View of the Geography, Geology, and General History of the State* (1860). A convenient place to find miscellaneous information is the annual volume put out by the secretary of state, *Manual for the Use of the Legislature of the State of New York*. The W.P.A. sponsored two valuable guidebooks in the American Guide Series which also contain descriptions of historical developments in many fields such as music, religion, immigration, and the like. These are *New York: A Guide to the Empire State* (1940) and *New York Panorama* (1938). A good source for information on elections, governors, and agencies is E. A. Werner, comp., *Civil List and Constitutional History of New York* (1889).

Maps are the source of much valuable information, especially in regard to transportation and the rise of urban areas, and they are found in many places. The state government and its agencies have published many maps. See appropriate departments, such as the Canal Board, the Railroad Commission, and the Department of Commerce. Large libraries have excellent collections. Famous individual maps useful for New York include Lewis Evans, *General*

Map of the Middle British Colonies in America (1755); Claude J. Sauthier, *A Chorographical Map of the Province of New-York in North America* (1779); Simeon De Witt, *A Map of the State of New York* (1802). David H. Burr published several maps of New York State between 1829 and 1834. Amos Lay was another early mapmaker of New York.

The student will find the more important maps included in various collections of source materials. See especially the collections, cited below, which were edited by I. N. P. Stokes and E. B. O'Callaghan. The various regional histories sometimes include important maps of different sections of New York State. For example, see Harold Hochschild, *Township 34: A History, with Digressions, of an Adirondack Township in Hamilton County in the State of New York* (1952), which contains reproductions of many maps of northern New York from colonial times to the present.

Natural Setting, Description, and Interpretation

A competent work is W. J. Miller, *The Geological History of New York State* (1914), and a parallel volume, D. H. Newland, *The Mineral Resources of the State of New York* (1921), each published by the University of the State of New York. R. S. Tarr, *The Physical Geography of New York State* (1902) is an early text. Elmer Fippin, *Rural New York* (1921), has several chapters dealing with soil, forests, plant life. U. P. Hedrick wrote several monographs on the fruits of New York as well as a broadly conceived *History of Agriculture in the State of New York* (1933).

The list of writers who have described New York City or the upstate region is almost endless. Alexander Klein, ed., *The Empire City: A Treasury of New York* (1955), is an anthology of short selections by many authors, American and foreign. This collection tends to stress the unusual and colorful aspects of metropolitan life. Better balanced and more scholarly is Bayrd Still, *Mirror for Gotham* (1956). It contains a long list of writers and visitors who have described the metropolis. The best guide to travel accounts and novels dealing with New York is C. E. Van Norman, comp., *The Empire State Yesterday and Today* (1944).

Twentieth-century observers have kept the stream of interpretive books about New York flowing from the press. Carl Carmer and S. H. Adams have probably done the most to interpret modern New York folkways by the light of the past. Carmer's books include *Listen for a Lonesome Drum* (1936), *Dark Trees to the Wind* (1949), *The Hudson* (1939), *The Susquehanna* (1953). S. H. Adams, *Grandfather Stories* (1955), is a delightful collection of tales of western New York life during the early part of the nineteenth century. The best volume on folklore remains Harold Thompson, *Body, Boots, and Britches* (1940). Edward Hungerford in *Pathway to Empire* (1935) has written a pleasant book of impressions of the various parts of the Empire State. The reader should supplement this book with Wallace Nutting, *New York Beautiful* (1927), which contains many fine photographs of scenery and famous buildings of New York.

No one should miss the magnificent collection of pictures and maps of New York City in J. A. Kouwenhoven, *The Columbia Historical Portrait of New*

York (1953). Another notable book of photographs of the metropolis is K. H. Dunshee, *As You Pass By* (1952).

A good introduction to the life of modern New Yorkers is Meyer Berger, *The Eight Million: Journal of a New York Correspondent* (1942). Interesting and informative is Simeon Strunsky, *No Mean City* (1944). E. B. White's delightfully written sketch of the metropolis, *Here Is New York,* appeared in 1949. It is included in Klein's anthology cited above.

Historical Periodicals, Publications of Societies, and Libraries

The New-York Historical Society, founded in 1804, has an excellent library and has published much source material in its *Collections: First Series* (I–V, 1809–1830); *Second Series* (I–IV, 1841–1859); *Proceedings* (I–VI, 1843– 1849); and *Publication Fund Series* (1868–). It has also published a quarterly since 1917. The New York State Historical Association, with its headquarters in Cooperstown, was founded in 1899 and began its *Proceedings* in 1901. In 1919 the *Proceedings* became *New York History,* a quarterly which contains articles, documents, reviews, and notes on the activities of the local societies. Another journal with a wealth of fascinating material is the *New York Folk-lore Quarterly* (1945–). Readers interested in periodicals devoted to New York should consult J. T. Dunn, "Checklist of Current York State History Magazines (Revised)," *New York History,* XXXII (April 1951), 236–242.

There are scores of local and county historical societies in New York. Two are outstanding for their publication programs: the Buffalo Historical Society, whose *Publications* date from 1879; and the Rochester Historical Society, which issued its *Publications* from 1892 to 1898 and began its *Publication Fund Series* in 1922.

The research student will find rich collections in New York City at the New-York Historical Society, Columbia University Library, and the New York Public Library. The best collections upstate are found in the New York State Library at Albany, the Grosvenor Library in Buffalo, and the Cornell University Library, with its Collection of Regional History. Syracuse University and the library of the New York State Historical Association also have useful collections.

New York State has had a state historian since 1895. His office maintains some twenty historic sites, publishes manuscripts, and offers aid to the local historians. Approximately 1,600 towns, counties, and villages are required by law to appoint local historians.

Source Materials

Collections of source materials are abundant but scattered. Most confine themselves to certain periods and will be noted in connection with those periods. Listed at this point are a few outstanding collections and those covering more than one period. The research student of New York City will find indispensable I. N. P. Stokes, *The Iconography of Manhattan Island, 1498– 1909, Compiled from Original Sources and Illustrated by Photo-Intaglio Reproductions of Important Maps, Plans, Views and Documents* (6 vols.,

1915–1928). This invaluable account contains a detailed chronology collected from the sources, and many original maps and plates. Interesting social and economic material is brought together in Clayton Mau, *The Development of Central and Western New York from the Arrival of the White Man to the Eve of the Civil War as Portrayed Chronologically in Contemporary Events* (1944). The student of agriculture will find useful information in the *Proceedings of the New York State Agricultural Society, 1841–1920*. Vols. 1–34 (1841–1886) were known as *Transactions*.

The state documents are indispensable even for fields beyond the political story. The activities of the executive branch are recorded in: C. Z. Lincoln, ed., *Messages from the Governors, Comprising Executive Communications to the Legislature and Other Papers . . . 1683–1906* (11 vols., 1909). The state has also published the public papers of most of the governors from George Clinton to Thomas Dewey. The legislative branch has left its record in the *Journals* of the Assembly and the Senate and in the *Documents* of the two houses. The legislature has also made special studies and investigations of national significance. For example, the Hepburn investigation into railroad practices in 1879; the Armstrong investigation in insurance matters in 1907; the *Report on Retrenchment and Reorganization in the State Government*, Oct. 10, 1919, on proposals for reform which Governor Smith carried out during the 1920's.

Students of constitutional change will find valuable the records of the constitutional conventions of 1821, 1846, 1867–1868, 1877, 1894, 1915, and 1938. The decisions of the N.Y. State Court of Appeals and the Supreme Court of Judicature throw light on many issues.

Statistical material may be found in the guidebooks and manuals noted above and in the federal and state censuses. Useful summaries of the various provincial, state, and federal censuses from 1628 to 1855 are given in the *Introduction to the Census of the State of New-York for 1855* (1857).

Comprehensive Histories of New York

No individual work covers the history of New York from its beginning to the present. The most successful history was the co-operative undertaking edited by Flick, *History of the State of New York*. The most recently written one-volume history is the textbook for junior high schools by B. M. Wainger, Dorothy Furman, and Edith Oagley, *Exploring New York State* (3rd ed., 1956). The lengthy work by C. Z. Lincoln, *The Constitutional History of New York* (5 vols., 1906), should be compared with the one-volume summary by J. H. Dougherty, *Constitutional History of the State of New York* (1915). Still important, although unsatisfactory for many periods, is De A. S. Alexander, *Political History of the State of New York* (4 vols., 1906–1923). R. B. Smith, ed., *Political and Governmental History of the State of New York* (4 vols., 1922), is a rather pedestrian summary of political changes. D. M. Schneider, *The History of Public Welfare in New York State, 1609–1866* (1938), has continued the story into the latter period. See Schneider's book with Albert Deutsch, *The History of Public Welfare in New York State, 1867–1940* (1941). Hedrick's, *History of Agriculture* is also a valuable work.

Three works on New York City should be mentioned here. Old fashioned but standard is J. G. Wilson, ed., *Memorial History of the City of New York from Its Earliest Settlement to the Year 1892* (4 vols., 1892–1893). Cleveland Rodger and Rebecca Rankin, *New York: The World's Capital City* (1948), is well written and topically organized. *New York Panorama* has a series of articles on all aspects of city life.

I

COLONIAL PERIOD 1609–1763

General Works (not previously cited)

No one has written a comprehensive history of colonial New York, although the early histories devoted most of their attention to this period. The classic history written by a participant is William Smith, *The History of the Late Province of New York from Its Discovery to 1762,* which appeared in *New York Historical Society Collections* (2 vols., 1829–1830). The standard account for the seventeenth century remains the old work by J. R. Brodhead, *History of the State of New York* (2 vols., 1853–1871). The student can find excellent chapters on the political and administrative history of New York scattered through the volumes of H. L. Osgood; see his *American Colonies in the Seventeenth Century* (3 vols., 1904–1907) and *American Colonies in the Eighteenth Century* (4 vols., 1924). C. L. Becker, *The History of Political Parties in the Province of New York, 1760–1776* (1909), remains the best account of those troubled years. Brief, popular, but superficial is Maud Goodwin, *Dutch and English on the Hudson* (1919).

The developments in New York City can be traced in Mrs. Schuyler Van Rensselaer, *History of the City of New York in the Seventeenth Century* (2 vols., 1909), and A. E. Peterson and G. W. Edwards, *New York as an Eighteenth Century Municipality* (1917). Brilliant studies by Carl Bridenbaugh on cities in colonial America include several excellent chapters on New York City. See his *Cities in the Wilderness* (1938) and *Cities in Revolt* (1955). The long struggle between New York and New England over borders is charmingly described in D. R. Fox, *Yankees and Yorkers* (1940). Customs and everyday life are pleasantly described in A. M. Earle, *Colonial Days in Old New York* (1896).

Source Materials

An indispensable collection is E. B. O'Callaghan, ed., *Documents Relative to the Colonial History of the State of New York* (10 vols. and *Index,* 1853–1861, Berthold Fernow, ed., vols. XII, XIII, and XIV, 1877–1883). This tremendous work contains papers from Holland, London, and Paris and documents relating to the early settlements in the Mohawk region and on Long Island. The writings of royal officials are generously represented in these volumes though their one-sided reports must be used with care. O'Callaghan was also editor of *The Documentary History of the State of New York* (4 vols., 1849–1851), which contains many miscellaneous documents and is particularly valuable for the Leisler revolt of 1689. The student will find considerable information about Indians and the French missions in central and western New York in R. G. Thwaites, ed., *The Jesuit Relations and Allied Documents* (73 vols., 1896–1903). Iroquois negotiations with the English colonies from 1666 to 1723 are described in Lawrence H. Leder, ed., *The Livingston Indian Records* (1956).

Cadwallader Colden, who was active in politics for over fifty years, was a keen but biased observer. See *The Letters and Papers of Cadwallader Colden, 1711–1775* (9 vols., 1917–1937); *The Colden Letter Books* (2 vols., 1876–1877); *The Colden Letters on Smith's History: New-York Historical Society Collections* (1868). A heroic achievement in collecting and editing are the *Papers of Sir William Johnson* (11 vols., 1921–1953). These documents are basic for any study of the fur trade, the land system, and the English relations with the Indians and the French during the third quarter of the eighteenth century. Religious and denominational history is treated in Hugh Hastings, ed., *The Ecclesiastical Records of New York State* (7 vols., 1901–1916).

In addition to Stokes' *Iconography*, the student interested in New York City will find valuable H. L. Osgood, ed., *Common Council Minutes of New York City, 1675–1776* (1905). Records and information of Albany are given in Joel Munsell, ed., *Annals of Albany* (10 vols., 1850–1859).

Much history is codified in the *Colonial Laws of New York from the Year 1664 to the Revolution* (5 vols., 1894). The significant land history must be searched for in *Calendar of New York Colonial Manuscripts, Endorsed Land Papers, 1643–1803* (1864).

Algonkians and Iroquois

The leading authority on the Iroquois, A. C. Parker, has written several studies, many of which have appeared in the New York State Museum *Bulletin*. He has an excellent brief summary in the Flick history, vol. I. W. N. Fenton is the author of "Problems Arising from the Historic Northeastern Position of the Iroquois," in *Essays in Historical Anthropology of North America, Smithsonian Miscellaneous Collections*, I (1940). The earliest French contact is beautifully told in Morris Bishop, *Champlain, The Life of Fortitude* (1948). An old but useful account of the Indians of eastern New York is E. M. Ruttenber, *History of the Indian Tribes of Hudson's River* (1872). P. A. W. Wallace, *The White Roots of Peace* (1949), tells the legend of the founding of the Five Nations Confederacy. T. R. Henry, *Wilderness Messiah: The Story of Hiawatha and the Iroquois* (1955), is a lively biography which may exaggerate the significance of the Iroquois Confederacy. A provocative interpretation of the rise of the Iroquois to supremacy in the seventeenth century is presented in G. T. Hunt, *The Wars of the Iroquois: A Study in Intertribal Trade Relations* (1940). For the following century, the best account of Iroquois relations with the English remains the introduction by C. H. McIlwain to his edition of *Wraxall's Abridgement of the Indian Affairs Transacted in New York* (1915). No student should miss L. H. Morgan, *League of the Ho-de-*

no-sau-nee or Iroquois (1851), the monumental study by the father of American anthropology. Less valuable but still interesting is Cadwallader Colden, *The History of the Five Indian Nations* (1747), which has appeared in many editions since 1902. An account of New York's relations with the Iroquois is contained in J. W. Lydekker, *The Faithful Mohawks* (1938).

The Dutch in New York, 1609–1664

Valuable are the Flick, Brodhead, and Osgood volumes cited above. A recent account stressing religious, literary, and social aspects is E. L. Raesly, *Portrait of New Netherland* (1945). Students interested in architecture and the Americanization of the Dutch Reformed church will find stimulating comments in T. J. Wertenbaker, *The Founding of American Civilization: The Middle Colonies* (1938). A popular account is J. H. Innes, *New Amsterdam and Its People* (1902). The best collection of source materials is J. F. Jameson, *Narratives of New Netherland, 1609–1664* (1909). A. J. F. Van Laer, ed., *Van Rensselaer Bowier Manuscripts* (1908), has many documents relating to the colony of Rensselaerswyck.

Revolt against Autocracy and the Rise of the Assembly

Competent surveys of political changes are given by Osgood and the contributors to the Flick history, vol. II. Provocative and thorough, but not easily accessible, is the thesis of Beverly McAnear, "Politics in Provincial New York" (Stanford University, 1932). J. R. Reich, *Leisler's Rebellion: A Study of Democracy in New York, 1664–1720* (1953), analyzes the career of this controversial figure. A recent monograph tracing the influence of prominent lawyers associated with the Livingston party from 1750 to the Revolution is D. R. Dillon, *The New York Triumvirate: A Study of the Legal and Political Careers of William Livingston, John Morin Scott, William Smith, Jr.* (1949). Useful despite its poor organization is A. M. Keys, *Cadwallader Colden: A Representative Eighteenth Century Official* (1906), the biography of an important eighteenth century official. Most of the sources listed at the beginning of the colonial section of this bibliography are useful. See especially the two massive collections edited by O'Callaghan.

Outpost of Empire

There are dozens of general histories of the United States which have a good account of the Anglo-French wars of the eighteenth century. Francis Parkman, *Montcalm and Wolfe* (2 vols., 1884), should be read for its literary charm as well as for its solid worth as history. The role of New York is well treated in the monumental work by L. H. Gipson, *The British Empire before the American Revolution* (vols. IV–VII, 1940–1949). F. H. Severance, *An Old Frontier of France, the Niagara Region and Adjacent Lakes under French Control* (2 vols., 1917), describes French activities in New York. T. W. Clarke, *The Bloody Mohawk* (1940), follows the struggle in the Mohawk Valley and includes several excellent maps. F. P. Van de Water, *Lake Champlain and Lake George* (1946), and Arthur Pound, *Lake Ontario* (1945), are popular accounts of warfare on those historic water routes. No first rate life of William Johnson is yet available, although Arthur Pound, *Johnson of the Mohawks* (1930), has much interesting material on his personal life. The student must turn to the *Papers of Sir William Johnson*. M. Hamilton, editor of the Johnson Papers, has written a brilliant exposé of some of the so-called biographers of Johnson. See his "Myths and Legends of Sir William Johnson," *New York History*, XXXIV (Jan. 1953), 3–26. Fortunately there are two excellent biographies of important Indian agents and land speculators: A. T. Volwiler, *George Croghan and the Westward Movement, 1741–1782* (1926); P. A. W. Wallace, *Conrad Weiser, 1696–1760* (1945).

Society and Culture

Population estimates are assembled in *American Population before the Federal Census of 1790* (1932), compiled by E. B. Greene and V. D. Harrington. The most thorough analysis of immigrant elements is the "Report" of the Committee on Linguistic and National Stocks in the Population of the United States, printed in American Historical Association, *Annual Report for 1931*, 1. An outstanding monograph is W. A. Knittle, *The Early Eighteenth Century Palatine Emigration: A British Government Redemptioner Project to Manufacture Naval Stores* (1936). The best account of the Negro population is included in Samuel McKee, *Labor in Colonial New York 1664–1776* (1935).

Problems facing the Dutch Reformed church are touched upon by Wertenbaker, *Founding of American Civilization*. The most helpful guides to Anglicanism in New York are D. R. Fox, *Caleb Heathcote, Gentleman Colonist: The Story of a Career in the Province of New York, 1692–1721* (1926), and F. J. Klingberg, *Anglican Humanitarianism in Colonial New York* (1940). Information on the Anglican church is also given in the *Papers of Sir William Johnson*, and Herbert and Carol Schneider, eds., *Samuel Johnson, President of King's College: His Career and Writings* (4 vols., 1929). C. H. Maxson, *Great Awakening in Middle Colonies* (1920), has little information about New York.

Readers interested in comparing New York City's development of cultural institutions with those of Boston, Philadelphia, Newport, and Charleston should consult Bridenbaugh, *Cities in the Wilderness* and *Cities in Revolt*, and Michael Kraus, *Intercolonial Aspects of American Culture on the Eve of the Revolution* (1928). For Anglican schools, see William Kemp, *The Support of Schools in Colonial New York by the Society for the Propagation of the Gospel in Foreign Parts* (1913). Two accounts with choice material on social life in New York have been left by the Swede, Peter Kalm, *Travels into North America* (1770, translation; and later editions), and the Scot, Dr. Hamilton. See Carl Bridenbaugh, ed., *Gentleman's Progress: The Intinerarium of Dr. Alexander Hamilton 1744* (1948).

Landlords and Farmers

A scholarly and well-organized analysis of the land system and tenant unrest is Irving Mark, *Agrarian Conflicts in Colonial New York 1711–1775*

(1940). Older accounts containing information on land are E. W. Spaulding, *New York in the Critical Period, 1783–1789* (1932), and R. L. Higgins, *Expansion in New York with Especial Reference to the Eighteenth Century* (1931). Readers interested in a detailed and exhaustive study of the land activities of a royal official should see E. M. Fox, *Land Speculation in the Mohawk Country* (1949). S. G. Nissenson, *The Patroon's Domain* (1937), is a microscopic study of Van Rensselaer Manor. The Vermont difficulties are covered in many books. Perhaps the best balanced short account is found in Fox, *Yankees and Yorkers.*

The important source collections on the colonial period listed above are full of material on land questions. The recollections of Mrs. Anne Grant, *Memoirs of an American Lady* (2 vols., 1808), are an idyllic picture of manorial life. No one should miss the inimitable observations of M. G. J. de Crèvecoeur, *Letters from an American Farmer* (1783). The best source on agriculture is *American Husbandry*, published anonymously in London (1775) but recently edited by H. J. Carman (1939).

Traders and Artisans

The best general account of the economic pattern is the sketch by Samuel McKee, Jr., in Flick, *History,* vol. II. McKee, *Labor in Colonial New York,* is an exhaustive study and contains information on slave as well as free labor. Carl Bridenbaugh, *The Colonial Craftsman* (1950), is thorough. An account of mercantile activities is given by Virginia Harrington, *The New York Merchant on the Eve of the Revolution* (1935). A scholarly analysis of trade between North American colonies and the West Indies is Richard Pares, *Yankees and Creoles* (1956). Two articles deal with both the fur trade and imperial rivalries: A. H. Buffinton, "The Policy of Albany and English Westward Expansion," *Mississippi Valley Historical Review,* VIII (March 1922), and Helen Broshar, "The First Push Westward of the Albany Traders," *ibid.,* VII (Dec. 1920).

RISE OF THE EMPIRE STATE, 1763–1825

General Works (not previously cited)

Perhaps the best introduction to this period is J. A. Krout and D. R. Fox, *The Completion of Independence 1790–1830* (1944). The writings of E. W. Spaulding provide a good survey of the period from the Revolution to 1800. See his important studies: *New York in the Critical Period* and *His Excellency, George Clinton, Critic of the Constitution* (1938). An outstanding study is D. R. Fox, *The Decline of Aristocracy in the Politics of New York* (1919). A well-rounded survey covering social, economic, and political events in the "metropolis" is S. I. Pomerantz, *New York—An American City, 1783–1803* (1938). Merrill Jensen, *The New Nation: A History of the United States during the Confederation, 1781–1789* (1950), refutes the earlier stress on intercolonial bickerings. T. C. Cochran, *New York in the Confederation* (1932), examines changes in land, trade, and the like.

Source Materials

Source materials dealing with specific topics are listed under topical headings. Interesting and often very helpful are the accounts of travelers. Timothy Dwight, president of Yale College, left some excellent descriptions as did Crèvecoeur, already mentioned. One of the keenest observers was Elkanah Watson, whose writings are very useful. See *Men and Times of the Revolution; or, Memoirs of Elkanah Watson . . . 1777–1842* (1856); *Rise, Progress, and Existing State of Modern Agricultural Societies on the Berkshire System* (1820); *History of the Rise, Progress, and Existing Condition of the Western Canals in the State of New York* (1820). The reader can find lists of travelers in such books as J. L. Mesick, *The English Traveller in America, 1785–1835* (1922); Frank Monaghan, *French Travellers in the United States, 1765–1932* (1933); H. T. Tuckerman, *America and Her Commentators* (1864).

New York in the Revolutionary War, 1763–1783

Brief but authoritative is the account in A. C. Flick, *The American Revolution in New York* (1926). General histories are satisfactory for the causes and events of the Revolution. For the events leading to the break with England in the province of New York, see Becker, *History of Political Parties;* Dillon, *New York Triumvirate;* the first chapters of T. J. Wertenbaker, *Father Knickerbocker Rebels* (1948); and Keys, *Cadwallader Colden*. An excellent life of a significant figure is E. P. Alexander, *A Revolutionary Conservative: James Duane of New York* (1938).

The opening of the Edmund Burke papers in 1949 has led to many scholarly publications. R. J. S. Hoffman has described Burke's work as a colonial agent and included many letters in his *Edmund Burke, New York Agent, with His Letters to the New York Assembly and Intimate Correspondence with Charles O'Hara, 1761–1776* (1956). An interesting account by a Loyalist who is often critical of British policy is Thomas Jones, *History of New York during the Revolution* (E. F. DeLancey, ed., 1879). A. C. Flick, *Loyalism in New York during the Revolution* (1901), is penetrating and exhaustive. The confiscation of Tory holdings is told in H. B. Yoshpe, *The Disposition of Loyalist Estates in Southern New York* (1939). The role of New York City is ably presented by Wertenbaker, *Father Knickerbocker Rebels;* W. C. Abbott, *New York in the American Revolution* (1929); O. T. Barck, Jr., *New York City during the War for Independence* (1931).

The campaigns in New York are described in all general accounts of the Revolution. One of the most recent is J. R. Alden, *The American Revolution, 1775–1783* (1954). Howard Thomas, *Marinus Willett: Soldier Patriot, 1740–1830* (1954), gives a lively account of an almost-forgotten but important figure. A well-balanced account of Benedict Arnold's treason is given in Willard Wallace, *Traitorous Hero: The Life and Fortunes of Benedict Arnold* (1954). For the war on the frontier, see Howard Swiggett, *War out of Niagara* (1933); A. C. Flick (chairman), *The Sullivan-Clinton Campaign in 1779* (1929); Francis W. Halsey, *The Old New York Frontier* (1901); and Hoffman Nickerson, *The Turning Point of the Revolution* (1928). The latter deals authoritatively with the Burgoyne campaign.

Valuable source materials can be found in the two multivolume works edited by O'Callaghan and in the following materials published by the state of New York: *Journal of the Legislative Council of the Colony of New York: 1691–1775* (2 vols., 1861), *Journal of the Votes and Proceedings of the Colony of New York from 1766–1776* (1820); *Journals of the Provincial Congress, Provincial Convention, Committee of Safety and Council of Safety of the State of New York, 1775–1777* (2 vols., 1842); and *Minutes of the Commissioners for Detecting and Defeating Conspiracies in the State of New York: Albany County Sessions 1778–1781* (3 vols., 1910). Useful for both military and civilian affairs are the papers of the first governor, *Public Papers of George Clinton* (10 vols., 1899). W. Smith, one of the Whig triumvirate who also adhered to the Crown in 1776, has left a fascinating memoir of political intrigue. One must use with caution the highly partisan *Historical Memoirs from 16 March 1763 to 9 July 1776 of William Smith . . .* (ed. with an Introduction, Biography, and Notes by W. W. H. Sabine (1956).

Political Change, 1783–1825

General works dealing with politics in this period are listed under comprehensive histories of New York in Part I. For an over-all view Fox, *Decline of Aristocracy,* is extremely valuable. J. D. Hammond, *The History of Political Parties in the State of New York* (2 vols., 1842), is excellent and is a primary source for many aspects of politics. The period of the Confederacy and the ratification of the federal Constitution are best covered by Spaulding, *New York in the Critical Period; The Federalist,* written by Alexander Hamilton, James Madison, and John Jay, edited by P. L. Ford (1898); and *Journal of the Convention of the State of New York . . . 1788,* published by New York State. J. M. Smith, *Freedom's Fetters: The Alien and Sedition Laws and American Civil Liberties* (1956), is the standard work on this subject. Smith has several chapters on Jedediah Peck and other victims of the Sedition Law. The early history of New York City after independence is best treated in Pomerantz, *New York—An American City.* The War of 1812 is covered in general histories of the period. A good monograph on the subject is L. L. Babcock, *The War of 1812 on the Niagara Frontier* (1927).

The constitutional convention of 1821 lacks definitive treatment. Good summaries can be found in Fox, *op. cit.,* and in John Horton, *James Kent* (1939). The student will find the full story in N. H. Carter, W. L. Stone, and M. T. C. Gould, eds., *Report of the Proceedings of the Convention of 1821* (1821).

The *Autobiography of Martin Van Buren,* ed. by J. C. Fitzpatrick (1920) has some material on New York politics. Of the biographies the most useful are: Dorothie Bobbé, *De Witt Clinton* (1933); D. T. Lynch, *An Epoch and a Man: Martin Van Buren and His Times* (1929); and Spaulding, *His Excellency George Clinton.*

Heyday of the Land Speculator

Higgins, *Expansion in New York,* provides a good introduction. An excellent analysis of the role of the land agent is found in N. A. McNall, *An Agricultural History of the Genesee Valley, 1790–1860* (1952). For information on the land system and antirent troubles of eastern New York, see D. M. Ellis, *Landlords and Farmers in the Hudson-Mohawk Region 1790–1850* (1946). Henry Christman, *Tin Horns and Calico* (1945), has a colorful defense of the antirenters. Scholarly studies of foreign investments in New York lands are H. I. Cowan, *Charles Williamson: Genesee Promoter* (1941), and P. D. Evans, *The Holland Land Company* (1924). For informative articles on land proprietors, see Raymond Walters, Jr., and P. G. Walters, "David Parish: New York Land Promoter," *New York History*, XXVI (April 1945), 146–161; and J. G. Van Deusen, "Robert Troup: Agent of the Pulteney Estates," *New York History*, XXIII (April 1942), 166–180. K. B. Porter, *John Jacob Astor, Business Man* (2 vols., 1931) describes the leading speculator in urban real estate.

Orsamus Turner's classic histories of western New York contain much source material: *History of the Pioneer Settlement of the Phelps and Gorham Purchase and Morris Reserve* (1851) and *Pioneer History of the Holland Purchase of Western New York* (1849). A significant booklet by a large promoter is William Cooper, *A Guide in the Wilderness* (1810). The problems of land development are revealed in R. W. Bingham, ed., *Holland Land Company Paper Reports of Joseph Ellicott*, Buffalo Historical Society *Publications* (2 vols., 1937–1941).

Farm and Forest

A good general account with excellent material on social aspects of rural life as well as agricultural developments is Hedrick, *A History of Agriculture*. Monographs dealing with the pioneer experience in important regions of the state are Ellis, *Landlords and Farmers*; J. A. Frost, *Life on the Upper Susquehanna, 1783–1860* (1951); and McNall, *Agricultural History*. An admirable discussion of the tools used in the household manufacture is found in Jared Van Wagenen, Jr., *The Golden Age of Homespun* (1927; rev. 1953).

For source material, many excellent memoirs and travel accounts are available. No student should miss Crèvecoeur's charming essays, *Letters from an American Farmer*. For Long Island agriculture, see William Cobbett, *A Year's Residence, in the United States of America* (1828). Conditions in eastern and central New York are described in Levi Beardsley, *Reminiscences* (1852), and Dwight, *Travels in New-England and New-York*. The anonymous author of *American Husbandry* made penetrating observations on New York agriculture.

Founding the Business Empire

Albion's admirable study, *The Rise of New York Port*, analyzes the role of the Manhatten merchant. Informative lives of two merchants are Porter, *John Jacob Astor*, and H. B. Howe, *Jedidiah Barber, 1787–1876* (1939). Information on transportation is abundant although not readily summarized. J. A. Durrenberger, *Turnpikes: A Study of the Toll Road Movement in the Middle Atlantic States and Maryland* (1931), is thorough, but it should be supplemented by O. W. Holmes's chapter in Flick, *History*, vol. V, and Hedrick, *History of Agriculture*. Bobbé, *De Witt Clinton*, describes the founder of the Erie Canal. McNall, *Agricultural History*, has information on roads and river travel in western New York. The best account of labor is

McKee, *Labor in Colonial New York*. The rise of capitalistic enterprise in one upstate region is contained in Frost, *Life on the Upper Susquehanna*.

The Yankee Invasion of New York

The most interesting analysis of the transit of Yankee institutions to New York is found in the delightful essays *Yankees and Yorkers* by Fox. L. K. Mathews, *The Expansion of New England* (1909), is outmoded. An excellent study on New England migration is Lewis Stilwell, "Migration from Vermont (1776–1860)," *Proceedings of the Vermont Historical Society*, V (1927). The Yankee impact on commercial life can be traced in R. G. Albion, *The Rise of New York Port, 1815–1860* (1939), and in Blake McKelvey, *Rochester, the Water-Power City: 1812–1854* (1945). R. H. Gabriel, *The Evolution of Long Island* (1921), has information on Connecticut influence on that region. A convenient summary is given in D. M. Ellis, "The Yankee Invasion of New York, 1783–1850," *New York History*, XXXII (Jan. 1951). Robert Ernst, *Immigrant Life in New York City 1825–1863* (1949), is informative.

For source material, see travel accounts and memoirs. A fine account by a pereeptive observer is Timothy Dwight, *Travels in New-England and New-York* (4 vols., 1821–1822). The two works by Orsamus Turner cited previously contain much source material on migration to western New York. County histories are uneven. One of the best is Pomroy Jones, *Annals and Recollections of Oneida County* (1851). For a fictional description of a Yankee squatter, see James Fenimore Cooper's *The Chainbearer* (1846).

Social and Cultural Life, 1775–1825

An excellent introduction to social life in the countryside is Hedrick, *History of Agriculture*. Urban problems are well handled in Pomerantz, *New York;* Ralph Weld, *Brooklyn Village, 1816–1836* (1938); McKelvey, *Rochester*. The role of the upstate printer has received exhaustive treatment by Milton Hamilton, *The Country Printer New York State, 1785–1830* (1936). Orsamus Turner's volumes on western New York, cited above, contain much social history. Whitney Cross, *The Burned-Over District: The Social and Intellectual History of Enthusiastic Religion in Western New York, 1800–1850* (1950), has a good section on the early religious pattern of upstate New York.

Perhaps the most interesting autobiography of this period is the *Autobiography of Thurlow Weed*, which was edited by his daughter, Harriet Weed (1884). For education, see T. E. Finegan, *Free Schools, A Documentary History of the Free School Movement in New York State*. This study appears in the *Fifteenth Annual Report*, I (1919), of the New York State Education Department. The novels of James Fenimore Cooper and the *Diedrick Knickerbocker History* by Washington Irving must be read if one is to appreciate the authors' treatment of New York themes. The literature on Cooper is quite extensive. The most recent estimate of his place in history is a special issue of *New York History* (1954) in which several authorities comment on Cooper's works and career. This issue also appeared as a separate title: *James Fenimore Cooper: A Re-Appraisal* (1954).

NEW YORK IN THE NATIONAL PERIOD, 1825–1865

General Works (not previously cited as such)

Histories dealing with various regions and cities are helpful for this period. Among those previously cited are books by McKelvey, Ellis, Frost, McNall, and Albion. Political affairs can be traced in the works of Flick, Alexander, and Lincoln.

Source Materials

Political and social events in New York City are candidly revealed in *The Diary of Philip Hone*, ed. by Allan Nevins (2 vols., 1927), and the *Diary of George Templeton Strong* (4 vols., 1952). The state has published the papers and messages of the various governors. Source materials which deal with specific aspects are listed under topical headings.

Politics, 1825–1861

Hammond, *History of Political Parties*, gives an informed account. Hammond in a third volume (1852) brought the history down to 1847. H. D. A. Donovan, *The Barnburners* (1925), is scholarly and readable. For the nativist movement see L. D. Scisco's excellent study *Political Nativism in New York State* (1901). The autobiographies of Van Buren and Thurlow Weed previously cited are useful. Horace Greeley, *Recollections of a Busy Life* (1868), is well done. Beardsley, *Reminiscences,* is the interesting account of a man active in state politics. Valuable material is contained in the published works of Daniel S. Dickinson, William H. Seward, Horatio Seymour, and Samuel J. Tilden. John Bigelow, *Life of Samuel J. Tilden* (2 vols., 1895), is outdated and should be supplemented by A. C. Flick, *Samuel J. Tilden* (1939). G. G. Van Deusen has written two penetrating lives of notable New York politicians: *Thurlow Weed: Wizard of the Lobby* (1947) and *Horace Greeley: Nineteenth-Century Crusader* (1953). A modern life of William H. Seward is badly needed. The student must use two outdated biographies: F. W. Seward, *William H. Seward* (3 vols., 1891), and Frederic Bancroft, *Life of William H. Seward* (2 vols., 1900). The following biographies give excellent insight to pre-Civil War politics: Stewart Mitchell, *Horatio Seymour of New York* (1938); R. V. Harlow, *Gerrit Smith* (1939); Arthur Garraty, *Silas Wright* (1949); Lynch, *An Epoch and a Man,* which is a biography of Van Buren.

Building the Transportation Network

The books of Hedrick, McNall, Ellis, Frost, and Gabriel should be consulted for information on waterways, turnpikes, and railroads. The Erie Canal deserves a history which can match its significance. Meanwhile readers must rely on N. E. Whitford, *History of the Canal System of the State of New York* (2 vols., 1905), which is excellent on engineering and construction but weak on economic and political history. The major railroads have their chroniclers. For the New York Central, see F. W. Stevens, *The Beginnings of the New*

York Central, 1826–1853 (1926), and the most recent account by Alvin Harlow, *The Road of the Century* (1948). Much valuable information on New York steamboats and railroads is included in Edward Kirkland's monumental work, *Men, Cities, and Transportation* (2 vols., 1948).

The Businessman

The best recent survey of economic activity in this period is G. R. Taylor, *The Transportation Revolution, 1815–1860* (1951). Admirable treatments of the merchant marine are found in J. G. B. Hutchins, *The American Maritime Industries and Public Policy, 1789–1914* (1941), and R. G. Albion, *Square-Riggers on Schedule* (1938). Albion's *Rise of New York Port* is a valuable analysis of the foreign trade by New York City. The career of New York's greatest shipowner is well handled in W. J. Lane, *Commodore Vanderbilt* (1942). The literature on domestic commerce is less plentiful and less reliable. F. M. Jones, *Middlemen in the Domestic Trade of the United States, 1800–1860* (Univ. of Illinois studies in the social sciences, vol. XXI, no. 3, 1937), pays much attention to New York and the auction system in particular. Porter's *John Jacob Astor* is a model study of one of Manhattan's greatest businessmen and landowners.

The chapter "The Rise of the Factory System" by H. J. Carman and A. B. Gold in Flick's *History*, VI, 191–245, is the best account of manufacturing. Students will find statistics on manufacturing in the volume on *Manufactures* in the *Eighth Census of the United States, 1860,* and in Hough, *Census.*

A specialized study of banking policy is R. E. Chaddock, *The Safety Fund Banking System in New York, 1829–1866,* found in *Senate Document,* no. 581, 61 Cong., 2 Sess., IV, no. 2. M. G. Myers, *The New York Money Market* (4 vols., 1931), has a detailed description on the development of the stock exchange.

The Diary of Philip Hone is a splendid source for the social and political life of a prominent businessman. J. A. Scoville (Walter Barrett, pseud.), *The Old Merchants of New York* (5 vols. in 3, 1863–1866), is a garrulous but indispensable source for the early merchants of Manhattan.

Rise of the Dairy State

The various regional studies by Ellis, McNall, Frost, and Gabriel are the most informative and useful. The general description by Hedrick, *History of Agriculture,* should be consulted. H. J. Carman, *Jesse Buel, Agricultural Reformer* (1947), throws much light on the movement for agricultural improvement. John Burroughs, *My Boyhood* (1922), is a charming account of life on a Delaware County farm. Van Wagenen, *The Golden Age of Homespun,* includes excellent sketches of farm tools and machinery as well as accurate descriptions of farming practices.

Immigration and Labor

Population statistics are conveniently presented in F. B. Hough, ed., *Census of the State of New York for 1855* (1857). An admirable treatment of the

European background of immigration is given in M. L. Hansen, *Atlantic Migration 1607–1860: A History of the Continuing Settlement of the United States* (1940). Ernst, *Immigrant Life*, describes the housing, economic, and cultural activities of workingmen in New York City. Two recent studies on the Irish are objective and thorough: Florence Gipson, *The Attitudes of the New York Irish toward State and National Affairs, 1848–1892* (1951), and Carl Wittke, *The Irish in America* (1956). The political reaction of Americans to the foreign-born is covered by L. C. Scisco, *Political Nativism.*

An old but valuable history of labor is J. R. Commons, et al., *History of Labour in the United States* (4 vols., 1918–1935). Philip Foner, *History of the Labor Movement in the United States* (1947), has much detail on the Working Men's party, the rise of unions, and the Utopian movement, but his interpretation has a Marxist slant. Norman Ware, *The Industrial Worker, 1840–1860* (1924), concentrates on New England. The most systematic analysis of a municipality's attempt to meet the problems of fire and police protection and water supply is found in McKelvey, *Rochester.* New York City's quest for water is well described in Nelson Blake, *Water for the Cities: A History of the Urban Water Supply Problem in the United States* (1956). Students should consult Horton's excellent study on Buffalo which is found in *History of Northwestern New York* (3 vols., 1947), vol. I: J. T. Horton, *Old Erie— The Growth of an American Community.* R. E. Riegel, *Young America 1830– 1840* (1949), is the best general introduction to the social conditions of the period.

Source material: J. R. Commons et al., *Documentary History of American Industrial Society* (10 vols., 1910–1911), vols. III–VI, has a good deal of material on the early unions and parties of New York. For the comments of the upper-class business and political leader on immigration and urban problems, see the diaries of Philip Hone and George Templeton Strong. Greeley, *Recollections*, has much pertinent information on labor and urban problems.

Religion and Reform

The best introduction to Protestant, Catholic, and Jewish activities is in Flick, *History*, IX, 127–229. The life of Archbishop Hughes is well covered in J. G. Hassard, *Life of the Most Rev. John Hughes, D.D., First Archbishop of New York* (1866). J. H. Hotchin, *History of the Purchase and Settlement of Western New York, and of the . . . Presbyterian Church in That Section* (1848), has much contemporary material about the Calvinist churches in western New York. C. G. Finney, *Memoirs Written by Himself* (1876), is an account by a leading revivalist and reformer.

The literature on religious extremism in New York is large and constantly growing. The basic study is by Cross, *The Burned-Over District.* Perhaps the most interesting account is Carmer, *Listen for a Lonesome Drum.* A first-rate study of the Shakers is E. D. Andrew, *The People Called Shakers: A Search for the Perfect Society* (1953). P. B. Noyes, *My Father's House* (1937), is a memoir of Oneida Community by one brought up there.

An excellent recent study of the reformers of this period is C. C. Cole, Jr., *The Social Ideas of the Northern Evangelists, 1826–1860* (1954). Harlow's life of Gerrit Smith is solidly based on the reformer's papers. The introductory chapters in G. H. Barnes, *The Antislavery Impulse, 1830–1844* (1933), contain much information on New York State reformers. The best account of the temperance movement is J. A. Krout, *The Origins of Prohibition* (1925). S. L. Knapp, ed., *Life of Thomas Eddy* (1836), contains some of the correspondence of an important but little-known reformer.

A thorough study of hospitals, asylums, and relief problems is given in Schneider, *History of Public Welfare.* A summary of this study can be found in Flick, *History,* vol. VIII. The famous Yates report on poor laws is indispensable for students. It was originally published in New York *Senate Journal,* 47 Sess. (1824), pp. 95–108. It is more easily found in New York State Board of Charities, *Annual Report for the Year 1900* (1901), I, 937–1145. Prisons are covered in Philip Klein, *Prison Methods in New York State* (1920). D. L. Dix, *Remarks on Prisons and Prison Developments in the United States* (1845), is a contemporary account by a famous reformer. The movement for the social, economic, and political emancipation of women is treated by E. C. Stanton, S. B. Anthony, *et al., History of Woman Suffrage* (6 vols., 1881–1922).

School and Society

An old but detailed account of elementary education is S. S. Randall, *History of the Common School System of the State of New York* (1871). See also Charles Fitch, *The Public School: History of Common School Education in New York* (1904), and D. E. W. Hodge and L. F. Hodge, *A Century of Service to Public Education* (1945). The best description of the academy is G. F. Miller, *The Academy System of the State of New York,* which appears in the *Fifteenth Annual Report of the New York State Education Department,* II (1919). Short histories of the various colleges can be found in F. B. Hough, *Historical and Statistical Record of the University of the State of New York* (1885), and Sidney Sherwood, *The University of the State of New York* in the United States Bureau of Education's *Contributions to American Educational History* (1900).

Van Deusen's brilliant lives of Thurlow Weed and Horace Greeley are the best studies of editors. Allan Nevins has a good survey of the press in Flick, *History,* vol. IX.

Literary figures are best approached through the appropriate chapters in R. E. Spiller *et al., Literary History of the United States* (3 vols., 1948). The third volume has an extensive bibliography of the writings of New York authors. The advanced student of literature will find a detailed analysis of the literary background in Perry Miller, *The Raven and the Whale: The War of Words and Wits in the Era of Poe and Melville* (1956).

The most penetrating description of the creative arts in this period is Oliver Larkin, *Art and Life in America* (1949). Short but adequate accounts of architecture, art, music, and sculpture are included in the American Guide Series on New York State and New York City. See also the chapters in Flick, *History.* A prominent artist has received a balanced treatment in Theodore Bolton and I. F. Cortelyou, *Ezra Ames of Albany: Portrait Painter, Craftsman, Royal Arch Mason, Banker, 1768–1836* (1955).

New York and the Civil War

The most detailed history of political events is S. D. Brummer, *Political History of New York State during the Period of the Civil War* (1911). Biographies of two prominent Democratic politicians give us an idea of the position of the peace Democrats: Mitchell, *Horatio Seymour*, and S. A. Pleasants, *Fernando Wood of New York* (1948). The many ties between New York City businessmen and the South are well handled in P. S. Foner, *Business and Slavery* (1941). J. A. Rawley, *Edwin D. Morgan, 1811–1883: Merchant in Politics* (1955), gives a good account of the Republican governor during the first part of the Civil War.

The impact of the Civil War upon urban life is examined in three studies: Basil Lee, *Discontent in New York City 1861–1865* (1944); McKelvey, *Rochester;* Horton, *Old Erie.* An excellent description of life in upper-class circles in New York City can be found in *The Diary of George Templeton Strong,* vol. III.

Much military information about New Yorkers in the Civil War is available in Frederick Phisterer, *New York in the War of the Rebellion, 1861–1865* (5 vols., 1912), and H. G. Pearson, *James S. Wadsworth of Geneseo* (1913). The financial developments are explained in Don Sowers, *The Financial History of New York State from 1789 to 1912* (1914). A. D. White, *Autobiography of Andrew D. White* (2 vols., 1922), has acute observations on intellectual and political trends.

II

1865–1956

The history of New York State became increasingly intermingled with that of the nation after the Civil War. The number of books dealing with purely state history is rather limited. On the other hand, many books which on the surface describe national developments devote a large part of their pages to developments within New York. For example, books dealing with music, painting, architecture, the theater, and other arts naturally devote much space to events in New York State. It is for this reason, therefore, that this part of the bibliography includes more books describing national developments.

POLITICS, 1865–1956

General Works

There is no single history covering New York politics and government from the Civil War to the present. The multivolumed works edited or written by Alexander, Flick, and Smith (all of which have been cited earlier) deal in part with this period, but none is adequate. Matthew Josephson, *The Politicos* (1938), although a history of national politics, throws considerable light on developments in New York. Interesting and frequently revealing anecdotes by contemporary observers of the state's politics in the period after the Civil War can be found in W. C. Hudson, *Random Recollections of an Old Political Reporter* (1911), and M. P. Breen, *Thirty Years of New York Politics Up-to-Date* (1899). Special mention should also be made of Lee Benson, *Merchants, Farmers & Railroads: Railroad Regulation and New York Politics, 1850–1887* (1955), a monograph that is distinguished by the excellence of the author's scholarship and the originality of his interpretations. There is also a large amount of important governmental history in Schneider and Deutsch, *History of Public Welfare.*

Although there is no adequate study of New York City politics in this period, useful summaries of the ups and downs of Manhattan's Democratic organization are available in M. R. Werner, *Tammany Hall* (1928), and Gustavus Myers, *History of Tammany Hall* (1917). A careful description of one aspect of New York City's government is given in Frederick Shaw, *The History of the New York City Legislature* (1954). Metropolitan politics are briefly summarized in Allan Nevins and J. A. Krout, eds., *The Greater City: New York, 1898–1948* (1948). For studies of two municipal problems that concerned reformers as well as politicians, see Gordon Atkins, *Health, Housing and Poverty in New York City, 1865–1898* (1947) and H. J. Carman, *The Street Surface Railway Franchises of New York City* (1919).

Several recent books have examined the governmental machinery of New York. Students will find an especially rewarding treatment in Warren Moscow, *Politics in the Empire State* (1948). Moscow, a former Albany correspondent for the New York *Times,* provides both an inside story of the workings of state government and a stimulating mixture of colorful anecdotes and perceptive analyses. His book should be supplemented by David Beetle, *The New York Citizen* (1955), a sprightly written but accurate account of the various state departments. A thorough but somewhat heavy-handed account is L. K. Caldwell, *The Government and Administration of New York* (1954). A concise and clear analysis of state and local government put out by the New York State Education Department is Robert Rienow, *Our State and Local Government* (1954).

Source Materials

The *Public Papers* of successive governors, the *Journals* of the Assembly and the Senate, and the reports of the various legislative committees are invaluable sources. For constitutional changes, see *Journal of the Constitutional Commission of the State of New York, . . . 1872–73* (1873); *Journal of the Constitutional Convention of the State of New York, . . . 1894* (1894); *Revised Record of the Constitutional Convention of the State of New York, . . . 1894* (1900); *Journal of the New York Constitutional Convention, 1915* (1915) and *Record of the Constitutional Convention of the State of New York, 1915, . . .* (1915). The constitutional histories of the state by Dougherty and Lincoln (both have been cited earlier) are helpful.

The Democrats in the Postwar Years, 1865–1876

J. K. McGuire, ed., *The Democratic Party of the State of New York* (1905), covers this subject, but this book is not always reliable, and biographies of the party's leading figures are generally more rewarding. Mitchell, *Horatio Seymour*, is as indispensable for the immediate postwar years as for the war years. Flick, *Samuel Jones Tilden*, is a scholarly and authoritative study, but those interested in Tilden's career should also consult John Bigelow, ed., *Letters and Literary Memorials of Samuel J. Tilden* (2 vols., 1908) as well as Bigelow's *Life of Samuel J. Tilden* (2 vols., 1895).

The story of Tweed's rise and fall has been told by countless authors. The essential facts concerning Tweed's influence in state politics are furnished in Werner, *Tammany Hall;* Myers, *History of Tammany Hall;* Flick, *Tilden;* and D. T. Lynch, *"Boss" Tweed: The Story of a Grim Generation* (1927). For a contemporary account by one of Tweed's opponents, see S. J. Tilden, *The New York City "Ring"* . . . (1873). There is also a great deal of pertinent information concerning Tweed and his machinations in *Report of the Special Committee of the Board of Aldermen Appointed to Investigate the "Ring" Frauds, Together with the Testimony Elicited during the Investigation* (Board of Aldermen, Jan. 4, 1878, Doc. no. 8, 1878).

Conkling and the Republican Organization, 1865–1883

The most rewarding volume on Conkling is D. B. Chidsey, *The Gentleman from New York: A Life of Roscoe Conkling* (1935). A. R. Conkling, *The Life and Letters of Roscoe Conkling* (1889), is far too laudatory, but it does contain many interesting and significant Conkling letters. For Conkling's struggle with Hayes over civil service reform, see V. L. Shores, *The Hayes-Conkling Controversy, 1877–1879* (*Smith College Studies in History*, vol. IV, no. 4, 1919); H. J. Eckenrode, *Rutherford B. Hayes, Statesman of Reunion* (1930); C. R. Williams, *Life of Rutherford Birchard Hayes* (2 vols., 1914); and Josephson, *Politicos*. Chester A. Arthur's role as a Conkling lieutenant is discussed in detail in F. G. Howe, *Chester A. Arthur: A Quarter-Century of Machine Politics* (1934). For the life of a leading opponent of Conkling within the Republican party, see Edward Cary, *George William Curtis* (1894).

Cleveland and Hill, 1884–1890

There have been many articles and books about Cleveland, but Allan Nevins, *Grover Cleveland: A Study in Courage* (1932), is clearly superior to all other works on the man. Nevins has also edited the *Letters of Grover Cleveland, 1850–1908* (1933). Every student of this period should also consult the scholarly and exhaustive M. D. Hirsch, *William C. Whitney, Modern Warwick* (1948).

One of the most distressing gaps in the historiography of New York's politics and government occurs for the years in which David B. Hill dominated the state's government and Democratic party. There is no biography of Hill, and to date no intensive study has been made of the state's government and politics while he was governor. Although Hill's administration was perhaps the most important in New York's history from the Civil War to the turn of the century, it is treated only in cursory and perfunctory fashion in the standard multivolumed histories of the state. Under the circumstances, the student wishing to examine in detail Hill's methods and policies must consult the *Public Papers of David B. Hill, Governor* (1886–1892), the Assembly and Senate *Journals,* and contemporary newspaper accounts.

Tammany Hall's history following the downfall of Tweed can be followed in the accounts by Myers and Werner as well as in T. L. Stoddard, *Master of Manhattan: The Life of Richard Croker* (1931), and A. H. Lewis, *Richard Croker* (1901). For developments in three of the state's other cities, see McKelvey, *Rochester;* Horton, *Erie;* and H. C. Syrett, *The City of Brooklyn, 1865–1898* (1944).

Platt and the Republican Machine, 1890–1900

The multivolumed works on the state's political history and many of the books cited in the preceding section cover New York's government and politics in the decade of the nineties. The standard work on Platt, although in some ways outdated, is H. F. Gosnell, *Boss Platt and His New York Machine: A Study of the Political Leadership of Thomas C. Platt, Theodore Roosevelt and Others* (1924). This, however, should be supplemented by T. C. Platt, *The Autobiography of Thomas Collier Platt* (comp. and ed. by L. J. Lang, 1910). In addition, the works on Theodore Roosevelt cited below in the section on the Progressive movement throw considerable light on Platt's machine and his methods.

The Progressive Movement, 1900–1918

The standard works on the Progressive movement in the nation provide an essential background and contain much useful material on New York. Among such works are John Chamberlain, *Farewell to Reform* (1928); C. C. Regier, *The Era of the Muckrakers* (1932); B. P. DeWitt, *The Progressive Movement* (1915); Louis Filler, *Crusaders for American Liberalism* (1950); H. U. Faulkner, *The Quest for Social Justice, 1898–1914* (1931); and Lincoln Steffens, *Autobiography* (1931).

In some ways the most valuable sources on the operation of the state government during the Progressive era are *Journal of the New York Constitutional Convention, 1915* and *Record of the Constitutional Convention of the State of New York, 1915.* Among the secondary materials, biographies are not only useful, but in most instances they furnish the only accounts of important developments available to students who cannot go to the primary sources. H. F. Pringle, *Theodore Roosevelt, A Biography* (1931), is an outstanding, if not definitive, study of Roosevelt's entire career. It should be supplemented by Theodore Roosevelt, *Autobiography* (1913); H. L. Hurwitz, *Theodore Roosevelt and Labor in New York State, 1880–1900* (1943); and G. F. Mowry,

Theodore Roosevelt and the Progressive Movement (1946). M. J. Pusey, *Charles Evans Hughes* (2 vols., 1951), in addition to being a biography of unusual merit, contains a great deal of pertinent information on Hughes's utility and insurance investigations and the best summary available of Hughes's gubernatorial administration. H. L. Stimson, *On Active Service in Peace and War* (1948), deals in passing with the Progressive movement in New York politics, while Frank Freidel, *Franklin D. Roosevelt* (1952–1954), treats the same subject from an entirely different point of view.

Tammany Hall's role in state politics immediately preceding and during the impeachment of Governor Sulzer is examined in detail in J. A. Friedman, *The Impeachment of Governor William Sulzer* (1939); S. B. Thomas, *Boss or Governor* (1914); J. W. Forrest and James Malcolm, *Tammany's Treason* (1913); and *Proceedings of the Court for the Trial of Impeachments, The People of the State of New York by the Assembly Thereof against William Sulzer, as Governor* (1913). For New York City politics in the Progressive era, see H. C. Syrett, ed., *The Gentleman and the Tiger: The Autobiography of George B. McClellan, Jr.* (1956); L. H. Pink, *Gaynor* (1931); Mortimer Smith, *William Jay Gaynor* (1950); and Lenora Arent, *Electric Franchise in New York City* (1919). Lincoln Steffens, *The Shame of the Cities* (1904), contains a chapter on New York City's government.

From Smith to Dewey, 1918–1952

No one has yet written a definitive biography of Alfred E. Smith or a detailed analysis of his work as a legislator and governor. In many respects the best book on his career is his autobiography, which is entitled, *Up to Now: An Autobiography* (1929). Although the autobiography is obviously biased, it is no more so than books on him written by others. When Smith emerged as a presidential candidate, several popular studies were made of his career. These books, which should be used with some caution, include T. H. Dickinson, *The Portrait of a Man as Governor* (1928); Norman Hapgood and Henry Moskowitz, *Up from the City Streets: Alfred E. Smith . . .* (1928); and H. F. Pringle, *Alfred E. Smith: A Critical Study* (1927). Freidel, *Roosevelt*, is somewhat critical of Smith's administration as governor, while Frances Perkins in *The Roosevelt I Knew* (1946) writes as a friend and former associate of Smith.

Bernard Bellush, *Franklin D. Roosevelt as Governor of New York* (1955), is a model study of its kind and emphasizes the need for similar histories of the administrations of some of the state's other leading governors. E. K. Lindley, *Franklin D. Roosevelt* (1931), tells part of the story of Roosevelt's years in Albany in considerable detail, but it tends to be laudatory rather than analytical. E. J. Flynn, *You're the Boss* (1947), is indispensable, although it is in some respects disappointing for students whose primary interest is Roosevelt's governorship. Perkins, *The Roosevelt I Knew*, is engaging and informative, but it deals only incidentally with Roosevelt's accomplishments as governor. The first volume of S. I. Rosenman, ed., *The Public Papers and Addresses of Franklin D. Roosevelt* (1938), furnishes a useful, but not complete, set of documents on Roosevelt's four years as governor. For a more comprehensive and detailed record, consult the four volumes entitled *Public Papers of Franklin D. Roosevelt, Governor* (1930–1933).

There is no satisfactory account of the administrations of Herbert Lehman and Thomas E. Dewey, and it seems unlikely that this period will be examined by scholars in the near future. Much of Moscow, *Politics in the Empire State*, is devoted to the 1930's and 1940's. In general, Moscow is critical of Dewey and favorably disposed toward Lehman. The official version of the state's role in World War II, as well as a discussion of other phases of the state government during the war, can be found in K. D. Hartzell, *The Empire State at War: World War II* (1949). For the rest, the student interested in the Lehman and Dewey administrations in peace and war must consult the newspapers and the various printed materials published by the state.

ECONOMIC DEVELOPMENT OF THE EMPIRE STATE

Our Changing Population

Most of the data for this chapter is from the U.S. Bureau of the Census publications. Two Cornell University Experiment Station bulletins are very informative: B. L. Melvin, *Rural Population of New York, 1855–1925* (no. 116, 1928); and W. A. Anderson, *Population Trends in New York State 1900–1940* (no. 786, 1942). Publications of the N.Y. State Department of Health and those of the Welfare and Health Council of New York City supply vital statistics. Valuable for its summaries and charts are the publications of the New York State Department of Commerce.

Immigration is best approached through books dealing with immigration to the United States. See M. L. Hansen, *The Immigrant in American History* (1940); M. R. Davie, *World Immigration* (1936); Oscar Handlin, *The Uprooted* (1952). *New York Panorama* has a good chapter on the various nationality groups in the metropolis. R. F. Weld, *Brooklyn Is America* (1950), is appreciative of the diverse groups making up the population of that borough.

On the Negro in New York City see Claude McKay's lively account, *Harlem: Negro Metropolis* (1940). The literature on the immigration from Puerto Rico is growing rapidly. The latest and most valuable study is Bureau of Applied and Social Research of Columbia University, *Puerto Rican Population of New York City* (1954). See also New York County Lawyers Association, "The Rising Puerto Rican Problem," *Bar Bulletin*, IX (March 1952); Catholic Youth Organization, Archdiocese of New York, *Leisure-Time Problems of Puerto Rican Youth in New York City* (1953); C. W. Mills, C. Senior, and R. K. Golden, *The Puerto Rican Journey* (1950); Puerto Rico Department of Labor, Employment and Migration Bureau, *The Puerto Ricans of New York City* (1953); U.S. Bureau of the Census, *Puerto Ricans* in Continental U.S., Special Report P-E No. 30, 1950. Migration from New York to other states is covered by C. J. Galpin and T. B. Manny in *Interstate Migration among the Native White Population as Indicated by Differences between the State of Birth and State of Residence* (1934).

The problem of housing, especially that in New York City, has aroused much comment and investigation. Jacob Riis was one of the first to stir up widespread interest. See his *The Battle with the Slums* (1902) and *A Ten Years War* (1900). Another early commentator was C. D. Wright, *The Slums of Baltimore, Chicago, New York and Philadelphia* (1894). Various investigations by both state and city were carried on in almost every decade. For examples, see *Report of the New York City Tenement House Commission in 1884* and again in 1900. In the 1930's public attention to housing was renewed. See H. M. Shulman, *Slums of New York* (1938); New York State, *Report of the State Board of Housing for 1933* and *1934*. M. L. Walker, *Urban Blight and Slums* (1938); E. E. Wood, *Slums and Blighted Areas in the United States* (1936); James Ford *et al.*, *Slums and Housing, with Special Reference to New York City* (2 vols., 1936).

For a description of recent accomplishments in the New York State public housing program see the *Ten Year Look in State Housing—Past and Future* (1949). Useful are Dorothy Shaffter, *State Housing Agencies* (1942); Twentieth Century Fund, *American Housing, Problems and Prospects* (1947); Catherine Bauer, *Modern Housing* (1934); Henry Bruère, *Slum Clearance and Urban Development in the City of New York* (1956).

A pioneer and highly significant study of regional planning appeared in 1926 in the *Report of the Commission of Housing and Regional Planning*. Another important regional survey was the *Regional Survey of New York and Its Environs* (8 vols., 1927–1929).

The *Annual Reports* of the Departments of Public Welfare and Correction contain excellent summaries. Schneider and Deutsch, *History of Public Welfare*, is the best introduction. Good chapters appear in Caldwell, *Government and Administration of New York*.

Agriculture in the Empire State

The bibliography covering New York agriculture in its various phases is very extensive, running into thousands of titles. Here are listed only a few of the more useful and accessible books and reports.

The impact of the transportation revolution upon farmers in the last half of the nineteenth century is best described in Benson, *Merchants, Farmers & Railroads* (1955). A helpful article is Eric Brunger, "A Chapter in the Growth of the New York State Dairy Industry, 1850–1900," *New York History*, XXXVI (April 1955), 136–145. The autobiography of the first Dean of the College of Agriculture at Cornell University tells much about farm life and about the difficulties of setting up a progressive agricultural college. See I. P. Roberts, *Autobiography of a Farm Boy* (1916). Liberty Hyde Bailey, one of the leading agricultural thinkers at the turn of the century, has left us his analysis of New York agriculture in *York State Rural Problems* (2 vols., 1913–1915) and in the *Cyclopediae of American Agriculture* (4th ed., 1912), IV, 547–628. One of the first to make a sociological study of a rural town was J. M. Williams. His *An American Town* (1906) is a thinly disguised account of Waterville, New York. He also wrote *Our Rural Heritage—The Social Psychology of Rural Development* (1925). A similar study is F. F. Hill, *et al.*, *Erin—*

The Economic Characteristics of a Rural Town in Southern New York (1943). Opposing views on the role of the Dairymen's League emerge from J. J. Dillon, *Seven Decades of Milk* (1941), and D. J. Carter, ed., *The Fifty Year Battle for a Living Price for Milk: A History of the Dairymen's League* (1939). Useful information, some of which applies to New York, can be found in W. C. Neely, *The Agricultural Fair* (1935), and C. B. Smith and M. C. Wilson, *The Agricultural Extension System of the United States* (1930). Christopher Rand, in "A Reporter at Large: County Fair," *New Yorker*, Oct. 6, 1956, pp. 96–119, gives an excellent account of the modern Dutchess County Fair.

There is a wealth of solid information in the hundreds of *Bulletins* issued by Cornell University Agricultural Experiment Station. Among the more valuable items are: R. S. Beck, *Types of Farming, New York* (1935); Charles Blanford, *The Milk Supply for the New York Market* (1938); F. B. Howe, *Classification and Agricultural Value of New York Soils* (1935); S. E. Ronk, *Prices of Farm Products in New York State, 1841–1935* (1936); H. S. Tyler, *Factors Affecting Labor Incomes on New York Farms* (1939); S. W. Warren, *Results of Farm Mortgage Financing in Eleven Counties in New York State* (1939); T. E. LaMont, *Agricultural Production in New York, 1866–1940* (1940).

A great amount of source material is available in publications of the federal and state governments. The U.S. Department of Agriculture issues an annual volume on *Agricultural Statistics,* which gives comprehensive statistics by states. *Agricultural Situation* is a monthly survey. The N.Y. State Department of Agriculture and Markets has some useful publications: *Agricultural Manual of New York State Arranged by Counties* (Bulletin 133); *Annual Reports.* See also *The Agriculture of New York State* (Bulletin 259); *Statistics Relative to the Dairy Industry in New York State 1938–1941* (Bulletin 339). The legislature has made numerous investigations of agricultural conditions. One of the most important recent investigations was the *Report of New York State Temporary Commission on Agriculture 1945–46 and 1946–47.* The N.Y. State Department of Commerce includes useful information in its many publications. See the article by G. B. Robinson, "Agriculture in New York State," *Commerce Review,* I (Nov. 1947). An important federal investigation was that by the Federal Trade Commission, *Report on the Sale and Distribution of Milk and Milk Products through Certain Farmers Cooperatives and Distributors in the New York Metropolitan Area and the Effect of Distribution by Nation-Wide Distributors* (1936).

Much valuable information dealing with the dairy industry is available in the files of the Dairymen's League *News.* For farm co-operatives consult A. L. Gessner, *Statistics of Farm Cooperatives, 1953–54,* U.S. Department of Agriculture, General Report 23, Washington, 1956.

A Century of Industrial Enterprise

The New York State Department of Commerce publishes a great many pamphlets and studies. Perhaps the best introduction to the recent business life of the state is *Business Facts New York State* (1952). For each of thirteen areas, the Commerce Department has published a separate booklet in the *New York State Business Facts* series. The *Commerce Review* contains much up-to-date detail about the economic life of the state. Another useful state publication is the *Industrial Directory of the State of New York: Directory of Manufacturing and Mining Firms in New York State* (1953). It gives pertinent descriptive details for about 50,000 establishments. Firms are listed alphabetically by industry and by county in which they are located. One can also find a good deal of information about manufacturing in New York State in the various U.S. *Census Reports*.

The clothing industry, the largest in the state, has attracted several commentators: J. E. Pope, *The Clothing Industry in New York* (1905); M. E. Popkin, *Organization, Management and Technology in the Manufacture of Men's Clothing* (1929); M. Van Kleeck, *A Seasonal Industry: A Study of the Millinery Trade in New York* (1917); Joel Seidman, *The Needles Trade* (1942). Donald Sheehan, *This Was Publishing: A Chronicle of the Book Trade in the Gilded Age* (1952), is an excellent study. See also O. H. Cheney, *Economic Survey of the Book Industry, 1930–31* (1931).

E. D. Fite, *Social and Economic Conditions in the North during the Civil War* (1910), has some information on New York. Flick, *History*, has the best over-all summary of developments since 1865. Manufacturing in upstate centers can be traced in the history of Buffalo by Horton and the excellent history of Rochester by McKelvey completed to 1925. For the story of Eastman Kodak, see C. W. Ackerman, *George Eastman* (1930); Eastman Kodak Company, *The Home of Kodak* (1935); F. W. Lovejoy, *The Story of a Practical Idealist* (1947). A good summary of the various industries in New York City is available in the *Regional Plan of New York and Its Environs*, which has reports on leading industries.

The electrical industry is important for the state. See J. W. Hammond, *Men and Volts* (1941); H. G. Prout, *Life of George Westinghouse* (1922); J. T. Broderick, *Forty Years with General Electric* (1929); P. W. Keating, *Lamps for a Brighter America: A History of the General Electric Lamp Business* (1954); T. C. Martin and S. L. Coles, eds., *The Story of Electricity* (1919). Food processing is one of the top five industries in the state. See J. P. Arnold, *History of the Brewing Industry and Brewing Science in America* (1933); C. B. Kuhlmann, *The Development of the Flour-Milling Industry in the United States* (1929); H. Kyrk and J. S. Davis, *The American Baking Industry, 1849–1923* (1925); C. L. Alsberg, *Combination in the American Bread-baking Industry* (1926).

A Century of New York State Labor

The best account is by Leo Wolman in Flick, *History*, vol. X. The scope of the State Department of Labor is described in Caldwell, *Government and Administration of New York*, and Beetle, *New York Citizen*. Much information is available in the *Annual Reports* of the State Department of Labor and in the publications of the New York State School of Industrial and Labor Relations at Cornell University.

A graphic picture of labor conditions emerges from the *Report and Testimony Taken before the Special Committee of the Assembly to Investigate the Condition of Female Labor in the City of New York, Assembly Document*

no. 97 (1896). Hurwitz, *Theodore Roosevelt and Labor,* is also helpful for
the period around the turn of the century. After the Triangle fire there were
several investigations. Some of the findings are given in *Reports of the
Factory Investigating Commission (1912–1915).* An early study is F. R. Fair-
child, *The Factory Legislation of the State of New York* (1905).

The U.S. Bureau of the Census has issued many studies concerned with
labor. Representative among them are: *Immigrants and Their Children,* Monograph VII (1920); decennial reports on *Occupations* and *Population.*

Conditions in the clothing industry are described in Seidman, *Needles
Trade.* E. F. Baker, *Protective Labor Legislation, with Special Reference to
Women in the State of New York* (1925), has much information. There are
various editions of the *Labor Law* of the state. A recent article by Lester
Velie, "The Union That Gives More to the Boss," *Reader's Digest* (Jan. 1956),
is typical of the better relationships between capital and labor.

From Towpath to Airway

There is no adequate history of transportation in New York State. The
most convenient introduction is found in Flick, *History.* H. H. Pierce, *Railroads of New York: A Study of Government Aid, 1826–1875* (1953), is a
model of scholarship. The previously cited works by Frank Stevens and Edward
Hungerford tell the story of the New York Central. The D. and H. Railroad
Company published in 1925 *A Century of Progress: History of the Delaware
and Hudson Company* (1925). The lurid history of the Erie Railroad has
attracted much comment. The classic account is C. F. and Henry Adams,
Chapters of Erie (1871), which can be supplemented by F. C. Hicks, ed.,
High Finance in the Sixties (1929). Lane, *Commodore Vanderbilt,* is a
balanced account of the leading railroad figure. E. H. Mott, *Between the
Ocean and the Lakes: The Story of Erie* (1899), describes the construction
and traffic of the railroad. For street railways, the standard monograph is
H. J. Carman, *Street Surface Railway Franchises of New York City* (1919).
See also J. B. Walker, *Fifty Years of Rapid Transit* (1918) and D. F. Wilcox,
*Analysis of the Electric Railway Problem: Report to the Federal Electric
Railways Commission* (1921). Mark Hirsch's life of William Whitney has a
good deal of information about the street railway system of New York City.

Inland waterways continued to play an important role in New York trade.
J. C. Mills, *Our Inland Seas, Their Shipping and Commerce for Three Centuries*
(1910), and R. G. Plumb, *History of Navigation on the Great Lakes* (1911)
are the best accounts so far. Noble Whitford, *History of the Barge Canal of
New York State* (1922), is primarily the story of construction. It can be supplemented by Henry Hill, *Waterways and Canal Construction in New York
State* (1908), which contains much information on the movement for canal
enlargement. H. G. Moulton, *Waterways versus Railroads* (1926), gives the
arguments by proponents for each form of transport.

The *Dictionary of American Biography* should be consulted for accounts
of Jay Gould, Daniel Drew, Cornelius Vanderbilt, and other prominent people
associated with the history of transportation and communication. A good introductory account is John Moody, *The Railroad Builders* (1919).

There is no adequate history of the development of highways in New York. The extensive activities of the Port of New York Authority is described in E. W. Bard, *The Port of New York Authority* (1939); F. L. Bird, *A Study of the Port of New York Authority* (1949).

The N.Y. State Department of Commerce has issued many publications including its *Commerce Review* which contain valuable summaries of water, air, and highway transport.

Market Place of the World

The several publications of the N.Y. State Department of Commerce, especially the *Commerce Review*, are excellent for statistical information. The Port of New York Authority has also issued many important documents about its activities and the business trends in the great seaport. A. E. Elbrecht, *About Foods and Markets* (1932), is a valuable teacher's handbook and consumer's guide. Its bibliographical materials are most helpful.

The material on foreign trade is extensive. For representative studies, see E. R. Johnson *et al.*, *History of Domestic and Foreign Commerce of the United States* (2 vols., 1915); Hutchins, *op. cit.*, Stuart Chase, *Tomorrow's Trade, Problems of Our Foreign Commerce* (1945). The monthly summaries of the foreign commerce of the U.S. compiled by the U.S. Bureau of the Census are also useful to the student of New York trade.

Retail trade has attracted many students and observers. Among the better books are: G. B. Hotchkiss, *Milestones of Marketing* (1938); P. H. Nystrom, *Chain Stores* (1930) and *Fashion Merchandising* (1932); E. B. Weiss, *Selling to and through the New Department Store* (1948); A. B. Young, *Recurring Cycles of Fashion* (1937). The distribution of food can be studied in W. P. Hedden, *How Great Cities Are Fed* (1929); H. E. Erdman, *American Produce Markets* (1928); E. R. French, *Pushcart Markets in New York City* (1925); W. A. Sherman, *Merchandising Fruits and Vegetables* (1928); L. D. H. Weld, *The Marketing of Farm Products* (1916).

L. D. Brandeis, *Other People's Money* (1913), summarized much of the material which the Pujo committee unearthed about finance capitalism. F. L. Allen, *The Great Pierpont Morgan* (1949), and Lewis Corey, *House of Morgan* (1930), contain much interesting material about the great financier. A. D. Noyes, *Forty Years of American Finance* (1909), is a fascinating memoir by a participant. Marquis James, *The Metropolitan Life: A Study in Business Control* (1947), describes the corporation with the largest assets in the world. More penetrating is S. B. Clough, *A Century of Life Insurance* (1946).

CULTURE IN AN INDUSTRIAL AGE

General

Most books dealing with this subject are concerned primarily with the nation rather than the state. An important exception to this rule, however, is Flick, *History*, vol. IX, which consists of a series of topical essays by acknowledged authorities. Although the essays are not of equal merit, this book re-

mains the starting point for anyone interested in New York social and intellectual history.

Although the volumes in A History of American Life series describe national rather than local developments, each contains a great deal of pertinent information on New York. The volumes in this series covering the period under consideration are Allan Nevins, *The Emergence of Modern America, 1865–1878* (1927); A. M. Schlesinger, *The Rise of the City, 1878–1898* (1933); H. Faulkner, *Quest for Social Justice;* Dixon Wecter, *The Age of the Great Depression, 1929–1941* (1948). Every student of this period should consult Mark Sullivan, *Our Times* (6 vols., 1926–1935), which covers roughly the first twenty-five years of this century and comprises an indescribably rich source of information on the habits and mores of the American people.

A convenient and lively account of New York City's cultural and social history from 1850 to 1950 is furnished in L. R. Morris, *Incredible New York; High Life and Low Life of the Last Hundred Years* (1951). Although Morris is not interested in historical analysis or interpretation, his book is filled with colorful and amusing details that he uncovered through diligent research. See also Morris, *Postscript to Yesterday; America: The Last Fifty Years* (1947). *The Diary of George Templeton Strong* covers only a small part of the period after the Civil War, but it is a constant delight and required reading for any student of New York City's history. Klein's anthology *The Empire City* concentrates on the picturesque, if not lurid, aspects of the metropolis.

1865–1914

Education and Libraries

The problems of education in the state have produced an immense literature. An adequate history of public school education in New York since the Civil War remains to be written, but there is a great deal of valuable material in Fitch, *The Public School,* and in the *Annual Reports of the New York State Department of Education.* Some attention is given to developments in New York in E. P. Cubberley, *Public Education in the United States* (1934). Somewhat specialized contributions to the growth of secondary education are discussed in C. W. Blessing, *Albany Schools and Colleges, Yesterday and Today* (1936), and D. E. W. Hodge and L. F. Hodge, *A Century of Service to Public Education* (1945). Kindergartens are discussed in N. C. Vanderwalker, *Kindergarten* (1908), and C. D. Aborn et al., *Pioneers of Kindergarten* (1924). The Regents of the State of New York authorized the inquiry, *Education for American Life* (1938).

Adult education has received attention in C. A. Whipple, *Adult Education, University of the State of New York* (1931), and Lester Dix, *Higher Education Services to Adult Education in New York State* (1948). For the history and unique contributions of the Chautauqua movement, see J. L. Hurlburt, *Chautauqua* (1921), and R. L. Richmond, *Chautauqua* (1943). Although settlement houses are not usually considered educational institutions, their contributions in this field have been considerable. The history of one of New

York City's most important settlement houses is recounted in L. D. Wald, *The House on Henry Street* (1915).

Surveys of higher education can be found in C. F. Thwing, *A History of Higher Education in America* (1906); Abraham Flexner, *The American College* (1908); and Thomas Woody, *A History of Woman's Higher Education in the United States* (2 vols., 1929). Developments in higher education in New York before the twentieth century are summarized in Sherwood, *The University of the State of New York*. For trends in higher education, see C. M. Armstrong, *The Need for Higher Education in New York State* (1948); O. C. Carmichael, *New York Establishes a State University* (1955); R. F. Butts, *The College Charts Its Course* (1939). The most recent history of education is H. H. Horner, ed., *Education in New York State, 1784–1954* (1954). Although there have been several histories of Columbia University, they have been supplanted by a series of volumes which are now in the process of publication under the general editorship of D. C. Miner. For Cornell University, see C. L. Becker, *Cornell University: Founders and Founding* (1943), and the autobiography of Andrew D. White. Brief histories of individual institutions can be found in E. E. Slosson, *Great American Universities* (1910), and Flexner, *The American College*. The financial problems of the schools and the need for more state aid is well examined in the report of the Heald Commission of 1956.

There are several books on the public library movement which deal in part with the situation in New York. Among those that are most helpful are S. H. Ditzion, *Arsenals of a Democratic Culture: A Social History of the American Public Library Movement in New England and the Middle States, 1850–1900* (1947); S. S. Green, *The Public Library Movement in the United States, 1853–1893* (1913); A. E. Bostwick, *The American Public Library* (rev. ed., 1929); R. D. Leigh, *The Public Library in the United States* (1950); W. I. Fletcher, *Public Libraries in the United States* (1894); and U.S. Bureau of Education, *Public Libraries in the United States of America: Their History, Condition, and Management* (1904). The influence of Melvil Dewey on the libraries of New York is fully treated in G. G. Dawe, *Melvil Dewey: Seer, Inspirer, Doer, 1851–1931* (1933), and Fremont Rider, *Melvil Dewey* (1944). For developments in an upstate center see Blake McKelvey, ed., *The History of the Libraries in Rochester and Monroe County* (Rochester Historical Society Publications, XVI).

Religion

There is a vast literature on the history of religion in America, and almost all the books on this subject devote considerable attention to developments in the most populous state in the Union. Two of the best general surveys are W. W. Sweet, *The Story of Religion in America* (rev. ed., 1939) and A. P. Stokes, *Church and State in America* (3 vols., 1950). The histories of the various denominations are treated in separate volumes in Philip Schaff, H. C. Potter, S. M. Jackson, eds., *The American Church History Series* (13 vols., 1893–1898). More recent studies of religious groups in the United States (and New York) include Joseph Leiser, *American Judaism: A Historical Survey* (1925); C. E.

Corwin, *A Manual of the Reformed Church in America, 1628–1922* (1922);
Theodore Maynard, *The Story of American Catholicism* (1941); and W. W.
Manross, *A History of the American Episcopal Church* (1950). For the history
of two leading New York City churches, see Morgan Dix, *A History of the
Parish of Trinity Church in the City of New York* (4 vols., 1898) and Shepard
Knapp, *A History of the Brick Presbyterian Church in the City of New York*
(1909). R. F. Weld, *A Tower on the Heights: The Story of the First Presbyterian Church of Brooklyn* (1946), is especially valuable, for it contains far
more social history than is usually found in studies of this type.

In the years after the Civil War the churches were confronted with a
variety of new problems that demanded new solutions. Some of these problems and solutions are dealt with in C. H. Hopkins, *The Rise of the Social
Gospel in American Protestantism, 1865–1915* (1940); A. D. White, *Warfare
of Science with Theology* (1896); Edward Judson, *Institutional Church* (1899);
John O'Grady, *Catholic Charities* (1931); A. I. Abell, *Urban Impact on American Protestantism, 1865–1900* (1943); and H. F. May, *Protestant Churches
and Industrial America* (1949). For two special branches of religious endeavor,
see C. H. Hopkins, *History of the Y.M.C.A. in North America* (1951), and
E. W. Rice, *The Sunday School Movement, 1878–1917* (1917). There are
too few biographies of New York's many religious leaders between the Civil
War and World War I, but R. R. Sharpe, *Rauschenbusch* (1942), is one that
should not be missed by anyone interested in the growth of Social Christianity
in both the state and the nation. Walter Rauschenbusch's numerous books are
indispensable for an understanding of his ideas and the movement of which
he was a leader.

Literature

The most recent and in every way the most valuable general survey of
American literature is Spiller *et al.*, *Literary History*. This work can be sup-
plemented with Oscar Cargill, *Intellectual America: Ideas on the March* (1941);
W. P. Trent *et al.*, *The Cambridge History of American Literature* (4 vols.,
1917–1923); Alfred Kazin, *On Native Grounds* (1942); Horace Gregory and
Marya Zaturenska, *History of American Poetry* (1946). There is no history of
New York's literature as such, but books by or about the leading literary figures
who lived in the state are often remarkably helpful. In addition, Sheehan,
This Was Publishing, should be consulted by those interested in what might
be called the business of literature in New York City.

Newspapers and Magazines

Among the general histories of newspapers and press associations that can
be consulted with profit are W. G. Bleyer, *Main Currents in the History of
American Journalism* (1927); W. A. Dill, *Growth of Newspapers in the United
States, 1704–1925* (1928); Oliver Gramling, *AP, the Story of News* (1940);
R. W. Jones, *Journalism in the United States* (1947); A. McL. Lee, *The Daily
Newspaper in America* (1937); F. L. Mott, *American Journalism: A History
of Newspapers in the United States through 260 Years, 1690–1950* (rev. ed.,

1950); G. H. Payne, *History of Journalism in the United States* (1920); and Victor Rosewater, *History of Cooperative News-Gathering in the United States* (1930).

For the history of individual newspapers within the state, see Frederick Follett, *History of the Press in Western New York* (1920); H. W. Baehr, Jr., *The New York Tribune since the Civil War* (1936); Royal Cortissoz, *The New York Tribune* (1923); Meyer Berger, *The Story of the New York Times* (1951); Elmer Davis, *History of the New York Times* (1921); J. L. Heaton, *The Story of a Page: Thirty Years of Public Discussion in the Editorial Columns of the New York World* (1913); Allan Nevins, *The Evening Post: A Century of Journalism* (1922); F. M. O'Brien, *The Story of the Sun* (1928); D. C. Seitz, *The James Gordon Bennetts, Father and Son, Proprietors of the New York Herald* (1928) and *Joseph Pulitzer: His Life & Letters* (1924).

The standard work on the history of magazines is F. L. Mott, *A History of American Magazines* (3 vols., 1930–1938). Volume III covers the period since the Civil War. The stories of two of the nation's (and the state's) leading magazine publishers can be found in George Britt, *Forty Years—Forty Millions: The Career of Frank A. Munsey* (1935), and S. S. McClure, *My Autobiography* (1914). Rollo Ogden, *Life and Letters of Edwin Lawrence Godkin* (2 vols., 1907), discusses the career and policies of the editor of the *Nation* and *Evening Post*.

Painting, Sculpture, Music

The two best general surveys of the development of the fine arts in America are H. Cahill and A. H. Barr, *Art in America: A Complete Survey* (1935), and Larkin, *Art and Life in America*. Homer St. Gaudens, *The American Artist and His Times* (1941), contains much information that is difficult to find elsewhere and is distinguished by its illustrations.

The standard works on the history of American painting include C. H. Caffin, *The Story of American Painting* (1907); Alan Burroughs, *Limners and Likenesses: Three Centuries of American Painting* (1936); Samuel Isham, *The History of American Painting* (rev. ed., 1927); and J. C. Van Dyke, *American Painting and Its Tradition* (1919). Special or allied fields of the pictorial arts are covered in Frank Weitenkampf, *American Graphic Art* (rev. ed., 1924); William Murrell, *A History of American Graphic Humor* (2 vols., 1933–1938); A. B. Maurice and F. T. Cooper, *The History of the Nineteenth Century in Caricature* (1904); and E. H. Blashfield, *Mural Painting in America* (1913).

For sculpture, the following books can be consulted with profit: Joseph Hudnot, *Modern Sculpture* (1929); Lorado Taft, *The History of American Sculpture* (rev. ed., 1924); Adeline Adams, *The Spirit of American Sculpture* (rev. ed., 1929); and J. W. McSpadden, *Famous Sculptors of America* (1924). The work of an outstanding sculptor is discussed in Royal Cortissoz, *Augustus St. Gaudens* (1907), and Homer St. Gaudens, ed., *The Reminiscences of Augustus Saint Gaudens* (2 vols., 1913).

The history of American music is recounted in J. T. Howard, *Our American Music: Three Hundred Years of It* (1939); L. C. Elson, *The History of Amer-*

ican Music (rev. ed., 1925); W. L. Hubbard, ed., *The American History and Encyclopedia of Music* (12 vols., 1910); Arthur Farwell and W. D. Darby, eds., *Music in America*, vol. IV of *The Art of Music* (14 vols., 1915–1917). For opera, see E. E. Hipsher, *American Opera and Its Composers* (1934), and H. E. Krehbiel, *More Chapters of Opera* (1919). Among books on popular music are C. K. Harris, *After the Ball: Forty Years of Melody* (1926); Sigmund Spaeth, *Read 'Em and Weep* (1926); Wilder Hobson, *American Jazz* (1939); Winthrop Sargeant, *Jazz* (1946).

Architecture

There are several competent histories of American architecture, including S. F. Kimball, *American Architecture* (1929); T. E. Tallmadge, *The Story of Architecture in America* (1927); T. F. Hamlin, *The American Spirit in Architecture* (1926); and G. H. Edgell, *The American Architecture of Today* (1928). W. A. Starrett, *Skyscrapers and the Men Who Build Them* (1928), is a useful summary. For the student interested in interpretative studies of architecture there is an abundance of stimulating material, much of it applying to New York, in Wayne Andrews, *Architecture, Ambition and Americans: A History of American Architecture* (1955), and in Lewis Mumford, *Sticks and Stones: A Study of American Architecture and Civilization* (1924) and *The Brown Decades: A Study of the Arts in America, 1865–1895* (1931). For biographies of two leading New York architects, see Charles Moore, *The Life and Times of Charles Follen McKim* (1929), and C. C. Baldwin, *Stanford White* (1931).

Drama

Among the numerous histories of the American theater, the following should be mentioned: W. L. Phelps, *Twentieth Century Theatre* (1918); Archibald Henderson, *Changing Drama* (1914); O. M. Sayler, *Our American Theatre* (1913); C. D'A. Mackay, *Little Theatre* (1917); M. J. Moses, *American Dramatist* (1925); Douglas Gilbert, *American Vaudeville* (1940); and Lloyd Morris, *Curtain Time: The Story of the American Theatre* (1953). For countless details concerning every variety of theatrical performance in New York City before the turn of the century, see G. C. D. Odell, *Annals of the New York Stage* (15 vols., 1927–1949).

1914–1956

Mechanization: Communication and Standardization

There is much colorful information on the spread of the automobile in Lloyd Morris, *Not So Long Ago* (1949), and D. L. Cohn, *Combustion on Wheels: An Informal History of the Automobile Age* (1944). Llewellyn White, *The American Radio* (1947), is a general history. For facts about radio in the Empire State, see "Radio Broadcasting in New York State," *New York State Commerce Review*, VIII (Sept. 1954). The interrelationships between radio and reading is brought out in P. F. Lazarsfeld, *Radio and the Printed Page* (1940). *Not So Long Ago* by Morris has interesting material on motion pictures.

Margaret Thorp, *America at the Movies* (1939), is a well-balanced history. See also Edgar Dale, *The Content of Motion Pictures* (1935). Mott's *American Journalism* and *A History of American Magazines*, vol. III, are authoritative on journalism. Jones, *Journalism in the United States*, is useful. The comic sheet has played an important role in New York City publishing. The standard account is Coulton Waugh, *The Comics* (1947).

Leisure and Recreation

The standard work on sports is F. R. Dulles, *America Learns to Play* (1940). Valuable also are J. F. Steiner, *Americans at Play* (1933) and Gove Hambidge, *Time to Live* (1933), on the use of leisure time. G. D. Butler, *Introduction to Community Recreation* (1940), is helpful. Few New Yorkers have done as much to stimulate public interest in parks as Robert Moses. For a typical statement by Moses, see his article "The Moses Recipe for Better Parks," New York *Times Magazine* (Jan. 8, 1956).

Literary Output in a Technological Revolution

The literature on "literature" is enormous. The following titles are representative: J. W. Krutch, *The American Drama since 1918* (1939); Malcolm Cowley, *Exile's Return* (rev. ed., 1951); Oscar Cargill, *Intellectual America;* H. E. Luccock, *American Mirror: Social, Ethical and Religious Aspects of American Literature, 1930–1940* (1940); Maxwell Geismar, *Writers in Crisis* (1942).

The Creative Arts

Larkin, *Art and Life in America*, is the best introduction and also has a good bibliography. Good for background is F. P. Keppel and R. L. Duffus, *The Arts in American Life* (1933). See also Martha Cheney, *Modern Art in America* (1939).

On the theater the monumental work by Odell has a wealth of detail. For a shorter account of the modern stage, see Krutch, *American Drama*. During the 1930's the New York stage received government support which stirred up much controversy. For the W.P.A. venture into the theater, see Hallie Flanagan, *Arena* (1940), and Willson Whitman, *Bread and Circuses* (1937). Cecil Smith, *Musical Comedy in America* (1950), is satisfactory.

On painting and sculpture, begin with Peyton Boswell, *Modern American Painting* (1940), an excellent text, or Sheldon Cheyney, *The Story of Modern Art* (1941). Frederick Wight, *Milestones of American Painting of Our Century* (1949), is stimulating. The Museum of Modern Art Catalogue, *New Horizons in American Art* (1936), shows the best work done under the W.P.A.

On architecture, see John McAndrew, *Guide to Modern Architecture, Northeast States* (1940). F. L. Wright, *Modern Architecture* (1931), is a provocative statement by the master of modern architecture. An able statement by a well-known historian of architecture is Talbot Hamlin, *Architecture: An Art for All Men* (1947). Huson Jackson, *New York Architecture, 1650–1952* (1952), is a detailed list of outstanding buildings in Greater New York. For contrast, see the small but beautifully illustrated booklet by L. C. Jones, *Cooperstown* (1953).

On music, see J. T. Howard's detailed and authoritative *Our American Music* (3d ed., 1946). The latter chapters of Gilbert Chase, *America's Music from the Pilgrims to the Present* (1955), are suggestive. Useful are: Aaron Copeland, *Our New Music* (1941); C. Reis, *Composers in America* (1938); Herbert Graf, *The Opera and Its Future in America* (1941); S. W. Finklestein, *Jazz: A People's Music* (1948).

Science and Religion

For general introductions to physical science in the machine age, read S. M. and L. F. Rosen, *Technology and Society* (1941) and Lewis Mumford, *Technics and Civilization* (1934). A more recent account is James Stokley, *Science Remakes Our World* (1946).

For religion, see items cited for period 1865–1914. The religious situation is discussed in H. S. Commager, *The American Mind* (1950) and William Sperry, *Religion in America* (1946). A liberal Catholic analyzes the religious situation in the depression years: J. A. Ryan, *Seven Troubled Years, 1930–1936* (1937). For the Protestant churches in the same period, see H. P. Douglass and E. de S. Brunner, *The Protestant Church as a Social Institution* (1935). The story of the cults is told in Marcus Bach, *They Have Found a Faith* (1946). H. W. Schneider, *Religion in Twentieth Century America* (1952), is the best recent survey.

Index

Page numbers for maps are given in italics. The illustrations found between pages 338 and 339 are listed as page *338*.

Boards, commissions, and departments are listed under the principal descriptive word of their titles. They are state bodies unless described differently. Buildings, streets, and other landmarks are in New York City unless stated otherwise.

For the location of cities, see map on page 550, also pages 107, 110, and 461.